Harvard Historical Studies

Published under the direction of
the Department of History
from the income of the
Henry Warren Torrey Fund

Volume LXXXVI

The Mediterranean Naval Situation
1908-1914

by Paul G. Halpern

Harvard University Press
Cambridge, Massachusetts
1971

Distributed in Great Britain by Oxford University Press, London

Library of Congress Catalog Card Number 79–131469

SBN 674-56462-6

Printed in the United States of America

To the memory of my father

Preface

In discussions of naval affairs in the period from the turn of the century to the outbreak of the First World War, there has been a natural tendency for historians to concentrate their attention on the naval race between Great Britain and Germany in the North Sea. This is hardly surprising in light of its momentous effects on relations between the two countries and on the diplomatic position of Britain. The situation in the Mediterranean, on the other hand, has been greatly neglected. The official and semiofficial naval histories of the war obviously can devote relatively little space to the prewar period, perhaps a chapter or two at best. A notable exception to this is the official Italian naval history, *La Marina italiana nella Grande Guerra*, whose first volume covers the period from the end of the Tripolitan War to Italy's intervention in the World War. It was Italy's decision in August 1914 not to join her Triple Alliance allies that automatically rendered the Mediterranean a secondary theater from the naval point of view. Despite the submarine threat that developed during the war, Austria-Hungary alone never possessed the naval power seriously to challenge British and French control of the seas. Perhaps this accounts at least partially for the tendency to forget what a delicate balance of power actually existed in the Mediterranean before August 1914, when Italy's position was still uncertain. Then the combined Austrian and Italian fleets were strong enough to challenge with some chance of success the French navy and whatever forces Great Britain could spare from the North Sea. The ambivalent relations between Austria-Hungary and Italy, officially allied but traditionally rivals, raised the question whether the two would really cooperate. Could the British or especially the French safely assume they would not? To complicate the picture still more, Greece, Turkey, Spain, and Russia (in the Black Sea) were all to

vii

varying degrees renewing their fleets, and by the end of 1912 a small but powerful German force had also appeared in the Mediterranean. The naval challenge of the Triple Alliance to Britain and France was a serious one, for in 1910 the Italians and Austrians had begun construction of dreadnoughts. The transformation of the Austro-Hungarian navy from a mere coastal defense force into a powerful modern war machine was a new and particularly disturbing factor to all concerned.

It is this prewar period, when all the Mediterranean powers were expanding their naval armaments in a highly unstable situation, that I shall study here. Because several different powers and navies are involved, it seemed best to approach the problem in a topical rather than strictly chronological manner. British and French naval activity in the Mediterranean is examined first. This is followed by a study of Austrian and Italian naval development and the formation of the Triple Alliance naval convention. The renascent navies of Spain and Russia merit a chapter because of their potential for the Mediterranean situation. The Balkan naval race between Greece and Turkey is also the subject of a special chapter.

In the course of this study I have visited four countries and have naturally benefited from the advice and patient assistance of a large number of individuals. I should like to thank Baron Rennell of Rodd for allowing me to use his father's papers; Mr. Mark Bonham Carter for permission to see the Asquith Papers; Mr. David McKenna for permission to use the McKenna Papers; Count Georg Nostitz for permission to consult the Nachlass Erzherzog Franz Ferdinand; and the Librarian of the Foreign Office for allowing me to use certain of the Grey Papers. I am also indebted to Vice Admiral R. D. Oliver, R.N., for his hospitality and helpful recollections, as well as permission to consult his journal. For their invaluable assistance I am most grateful to: Mr. D. S. Porter of the Department of Western Manuscripts at the Bodleian Library; Messrs. M. Roper and L. G. Seed, Miss Gifford, and the staff of the Public Record Office; the Historical Manuscripts Commission; Lieutenant Commander P. K. Kemp, R.N., former Admiralty Librarian and former Head of the Naval Historical Branch, Ministry of Defence, who took great pains to find some misplaced records; Mr. H. Langley and Mr. J. D. Lawson of the Naval Historical Branch, Ministry of Defence; Mr. A. H. W. Pearsall, Custodian of Manuscripts at the National Maritime Museum; Mr. J. J. Ritchie, Assistant Keeper, Department of Manuscripts, National Library of Scotland; Mr. M. A. F. Borrie, Assistant Keeper, Department of Manuscripts, British Museum; Mr. Joël Audouy, Chef du Service des Archives, Mlle. Morel, and the staff of the Archives Centrales de la Marine; Mr. Busson, Conservateur,

Bibliothèque Historique de la Marine; Mme. Odette Helleu of the Service des Archives, Ministère des Affaires Etrangères; Mr. Georges Dethan, Conservateur, Archives du Ministère des Affaires Etrangères for permission to consult the unbound remnants of the Spanish and Italian files which disappeared from the Quai d'Orsay during the last war; the staff of the Service Historique de l'Armée at the Château de Vincennes; the staff of the Library of the Institut de France; Ammiraglio di Squadra Giuseppe Fioravanzo, Contrammiraglio Vittorio Tognelli, and the staff of the Ufficio Storico della Marina Militare; the staff of the Archivio Centrale dello Stato; the late Professor Mario Toscano, director of the Servizio Studi, and Professor Renato Mori, superintendent of the Archivio Storico, Ministero degli Affari Esteri; Dr. Walter Wagner, Dr. Maria Woinovich, Dr. Egger, Dr. K. Peball, and the staff of the Kriegsarchiv, Vienna; and Dr. Anna Coreth and the staff of the Haus-, Hof- und Staatsarchiv.

This study grew out of a dissertation whose topic was originally suggested by Professor William L. Langer of Harvard University, who also gave much valuable advice. For suggestions, criticism, and assistance in many ways, I would particularly like to thank my dissertation adviser, Professor Ernest R. May of Harvard, as well as Professor Arthur J. Marder of the University of California, Irvine; Professor Theodore Ropp of Duke University; Captain Stephen W. Roskill, R.N., Fellow of Churchill College, Cambridge; Professor Pierre Renouvin of the University of Paris; Professor Oron J. Hale of the University of Virginia; and Professor H. Stuart Hughes of Harvard.

Those who graciously answered my queries include: the late Admiral of the Fleet, The Earl of Cork and Orrery; Admiral of the Fleet, Earl Mountbatten of Burma; the second Earl Beatty; Rear Admiral W. S. Chalmers, R.N.; Captain D. S. Sutton, R.N.; Lieutenant Commander Peter Troubridge, R.N.; Dr. Howard M. Smyth of the United States State Department; Messrs. Philip P. Brower and Robert Wolfe of the National Archives and Records Service; and Mr. Henry I. Shaw, Jr., of the Historical Branch, U.S. Marine Corps. Valuable criticism and advice based on his own study of the Anglo-French staff conversations before 1914 was generously given by Dr. Samuel R. Williamson, and helpful suggestions, especially on archival sources, were received from Dr. Samuel F. Wells, Dr. Ronald Coons, and Mr. Brian Villa. My former colleague Professor J. N. Westwood critiqued those sections dealing with the Russian navy, and Henri Le Masson was good enough to provide invaluable data on French warships in 1914. Mr. H. Whitehead is the cartographer. I am also grateful to Harvard University for a travel grant and fellowships while my dissertation was in progress; and to both the Research Council and the Department of History of the Florida State University for financial assistance and relief from teaching duties in order to complete this book.

For permission to quote unpublished material, I should like to thank the following individuals: Admiral of the Fleet Earl Mountbatten of Burma (Papers of Prince Louis of Battenberg); 2nd Baron Rennell of Rodd (Papers of the 1st Baron Rennell of Rodd); Mr. Martin Gilbert and Fladgate and Company (Papers of Sir Winston Churchill); Sir Robin Edward Dysart Grey, Bt. (Papers of 1st Viscount Grey of Fallodon); the late Sir Victor Mallet (Papers of Sir Louis Mallet); Mr. Nigel Nicolson (Papers of 1st Baron Carnock); the Trustees of the National Library of Scotland (Papers of 1st Viscount Haldane); and the Trustees of the National Maritime Museum (Papers of Admiral Sir Herbert Richmond and Admiral Sir W. A. H. Kelly). Excerpts from Crown copyright records appear by permission of the Controller of Her Majesty's Stationery Office.

I am grateful to the following for permission to quote from published works: Charles Scribner's Sons, Winston S. Churchill, *The World Crisis;* Houghton Mifflin Co., Randolph S. Churchill, *Winston S. Churchill;* and the Controller of Her Majesty's Stationery Office, G. P. Gooch and H. V. Temperley (ed.), *British Documents on the Origins of the War, 1898–1914.*

PAUL G. HALPERN

Tallahassee, Florida
April 1970

Contents

Maps

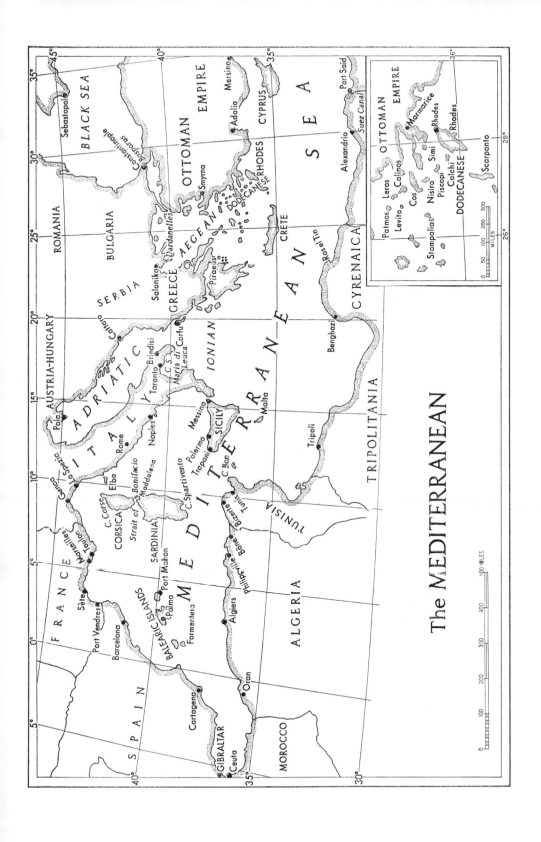

The MEDITERRANEAN

Abbreviations Used in Citations

ACS   Archivo Centrale dello Stato, Rome (EUR)

Adm   Admiralty Archives, PRO

AMF   Archives Centrales de la Marine, Paris

BD   *British Documents on the Origins of the War, 1898–1914*

Cab   Cabinet and Committee of Imperial Defence Archives, PRO

DDF3   *Documents diplomatiques français, 3rd series*

DDI   *I Documenti diplomatici italiani*

EMA   Etat-major de l'armée, Service Historique, Vincennes

FO   Foreign Office Archives, PRO

GFM   German naval documents microfilmed at the Admiralty for Cambridge University and the University of Michigan

GP   *Die grosse Politik der Europäischen Kabinette, 1871–1914*

GSTB   Archives of the Generalstab, Kriegsarchiv, Vienna

HHSA   Haus-, Hof- und Staatsarchiv, Vienna

Int. Bez.   *Die internationalen Beziehungen im Zeitalter des Imperialismus*

MAE   Archives du Ministère des Affaires Etrangères, Paris

MKFF   Militärkanzlei Erzherzog Franz Ferdinand, Kriegsarchiv, Vienna

MKSM   Militärkanzlei Seiner Majestät des Kaisers und Königs, Kriegsarchiv, Vienna

OeU   *Österreich-Ungarns Aussenpolitik*

OK/MS   Operationskanzlei, Marinesektion, Kriegsarchiv, Vienna

PK/MS   Präsidialkanzlei, Marinesektion, Kriegsarchiv, Vienna

PRO   Public Record Office, London

USM   Ufficio Storico della Marina Militare, Rome

I

The Royal Navy and
the Mediterranean, 1885–1912

The blue waters of the Mediterranean seem always to have fascinated
the people of Great Britain. The colorful lands bordering the Mediterranean invoke many historical memories from antiquity and more recent
times. During the Napoleonic Wars this was the scene of Nelson's triumph
in the Battle of the Nile, at a time when all other British schemes seemed
to end in nothing but disaster. The numerous Eastern crises involving the
Ottoman Empire which erupted at varying intervals throughout the nineteenth century did not permit attention to stray from the area for long,
and the opening of the Suez Canal in 1869 enhanced its strategic and
economic importance. With Gibraltar guarding the western end and Malta
the center, the Mediterranean was the shortest and fastest route to India
and the Far East—the "lifeline of Empire." The acquisition of control over
Cyprus in 1879 and Egypt in 1882 reinforced this situation. But the
importance of the Mediterranean to Great Britain was not limited to
the Suez route. A substantial portion of food imports, including nearly five
sixths of her barley and one half of her oats, came from southern Russia
through the Black Sea and the Straits.[1] By 1911 the Black Sea accounted
for one third of Britain's annual food imports and, when the traffic from
the Suez Canal was included, nearly half of all her food supply passed
through the Mediterranean.[2] With these economic and political interests,
and with the ever present possibility of a collapse of the Ottoman Empire
and the certain scramble that would follow, Britain's strength in the

[1] Memorandum by the Board of Trade, May 1912, p. 3, Bodleian Library, Asquith
MSS, box 107. Totals are from the year 1910.
[2] "Strategy and Food Supplies: The Mediterranean Route," *The Times* (London),
4 June 1912. Asquith had a clipping of this article sent to the Board of Trade with a
query as to how typical 1911 was. The reply was that, as regards the importation of
cereals, it was "fairly typical." Note from Board of Trade, 25 June 1912, Asquith MSS,
box 13.

Mediterranean—which almost by definition had to be naval strength—was of vital importance.

The Mediterranean naval problem was not something that presented itself suddenly to Great Britain in 1912, although some who spoke in Parliament gave this impression. In the diplomatic situation of the last quarter of the nineteenth century, France and Russia had loomed up as the most likely enemies. France, by her geographical position and interests in Algeria and Tunisia, was obviously a Mediterranean power. Russia, through pressure on the weakly defended Straits, was a potential one. The ratio of strength between the Royal Navy's Mediterranean Fleet and the naval power of France and Russia was a frequent source of alarm. There were naval scares in 1888, 1893, and after 1894, when the Franco-Russian Military Convention became a reality; a possible combination of the French and Russian fleets might have jeopardized England's use during war of the Mediterranean route for commerce and transport. There were influential voices, including the well-known *Times* correspondent and naval writer W. Laird Clowes, who even went so far as to advocate complete evacuation of the Mediterranean in the event of war.[3]

The Mediterranean deployment of British naval and military strength reflected this situation. The period from 1885 to 1901 was one in which the relations between Britain on one side and France and Russia on the other tended to grow more and more strained. The strength of the British Mediterranean Fleet was almost constantly increasing in terms of first-class battleships, although not necessarily in total numbers.[4] There were six first-class battleships in 1885, the year of the Penjdeh incident. This was the usual strength until 1890, when the new Russian Black Sea fleet began to cause apprehension. The Mediterranean Fleet was then increased to ten first-class battleships, and this was its average strength through 1901.

The forces that held the British possessions in the Mediterranean were comparatively small by continental standards, an example of how their real security depended on Britain's sea power. The garrison at Malta was steadily increased, however. From 1885 until 1912 it generally varied di-

[3] Arthur J. Marder, *The Anatomy of British Sea Power* (New York, 1940; Hamden, Conn., 1964), pp. 209–211.

[4] Table Showing the Naval and Military Provision of Great Britain in the Mediterranean from 1886–1912 Inclusive, Together with the Principal Foreign Navies in the Same Sphere and the Principal Circumstances Affecting the Strength Maintained. Public Record Office, London, Cabinet Office, Committee of Imperial Defence, Correspondence and Miscellaneous Papers (hereafter cited Cab. 17)/3. This table was prepared by the Secretary of the Committee of Imperial Defence for the personal use of the Prime Minister. Together with the accompanying explanatory letter (Hankey to Asquith, 8 July 1912), it forms the basis of this paragraph. It is compiled from official Admiralty figures and uses first-class battleships as the standard.

rectly with the navy's strength, being greatest when the fleet was greatest and vice versa. From approximately 5300 men in 1885, it rose steadily to over 9600 in 1898, the year of the Fashoda incident. The Egyptian garrison was maintained solely for the purposes of internal order and not to contend with any foreign attack. It usually varied between 3500 and 5500.[5]

The period 1902–1905 was one in which British naval and military strength was at its peak. Fourteen first-class battleships cruised the Mediterranean waters in 1902. Although this was the largest number for the years under consideration, the British total was still less than the combined French and Russian strength, which the Admiralty estimated at nineteen first-class battleships (fourteen French and five Russian) the same year. The Mediterranean Fleet was almost always numerically inferior to a possible French-Russian combination. This fact caused much controversy between the Admiralty and the Mediterranean Commander-in-Chief (1899–1902), Admiral Sir John Fisher.[6] As is so often true, the paper strengths were actually quite misleading. The Russian fleet was still in the Black Sea, a fact that was not completely inconsequential even though the Turkish defenses of the Straits were recognized as weak. Moreover, and this was of even greater importance, both the French and the Russians maintained a considerable portion of their ships in reserve.[7] They could not make their influence felt until days and perhaps even weeks after mobilization. As a result, the British force was usually clearly superior to the French active fleet. According to plan reinforcements would arrive from England before any mobilization of the French reserve ships or a merging of the French and Russian Black Sea fleets could be effected. The location of the Mediterranean Fleet while awaiting these reinforcements—Gibraltar or Malta—was one of the variables of Mediterranean strategy that was always under discussion.

The April 1904 entente with France did not immediately influence the Mediterranean naval situation because of the tension between Britain and Russia arising out of the Russo-Japanese War. The incident in which the Hull fishing trawlers were fired on in error by the Russian Baltic fleet

---

[5] The Boer War caused a temporary reduction of the Malta garrison to 7441 in 1900, which was largely made good the following year by the raising of militia. The small Cyprus garrison averaged around 500 until 1896, when it was reduced to about 120. *Ibid.*

[6] *Ibid.* See also Marder, *Anatomy of British Sea Power*, pp. 398f. Hankey's figures do not always coincide exactly with those cited by Marder, probably because of the difficulty of defining first-class battleships, among other technical reasons.

[7] Hankey to Asquith, 8 July 1912, Cab. 17/3. In 1902 the Admiralty considered only six French battleships to be in commission permanently; the remainder of the French-Russian force was considered in reserve.

on its way to the Far East, and the danger that the Russian Black Sea fleet might try to pass through the Straits, caused a strained atmosphere throughout the year.[8] However, the expansion of the German navy began to exert a growing influence on the size of the Mediterranean Fleet, resulting in its steady reduction. It was cut to eight battleships by Admiral Fisher in his sweeping reorganization of the Royal Navy at the end of 1904, after he became First Sea Lord of the Admiralty. The Home Fleet was renamed the Channel Fleet, and the former Channel Fleet was renamed the Atlantic Fleet and assigned to Gibraltar as its permanent base. Its eight battleships were to reinforce either the Mediterranean or the Channel Fleet.[9] Therefore, in theory, sixteen battleships were available for the Mediterranean if necessary. Significantly, the newest and best warships were now to be concentrated in home waters. Combined maneuvers by the Atlantic and Mediterranean fleets were to be held twice a year. The Atlantic and Channel fleets were to maneuver together once a year.[10] In late 1906 Fisher withdrew two battleships from the Mediterranean, Atlantic, and Channel fleets to form a fully manned division (the Nore Division) of a reorganized Home Fleet, whose remaining two divisions were to consist of ships in reserve. [11] From 1907 until 1912 the strength of the Mediterranean and Atlantic fleets remained at six battleships each.

The realization that Germany and not France or Russia was the most probable enemy was also reflected in the varying strength of the Malta garrison. In 1905 it was reduced from over 11,000 to 8700. This was partially offset by the establishment of a small, and admittedly not very effective, naval defense force. A further reduction occurred after the ninetieth meeting of the Committee of Imperial Defence in July 1906. The Admiralty promised in case of emergency to send out the naval force required to assure the safety of Gibraltar and Malta.[12] By 1912 the garrison numbered around 7800 men.

Britain's Mediterranean situation was to a certain extent simplified by the evolution of France, and later Russia, from potential enemy to potential ally. But it was complicated again by new factors: the growth of the Italian and Austro-Hungarian navies, particularly the latter, in terms of effective naval strength. Prior to 1905, and even for some time afterwards,

[8] *Ibid.* See also A. J. Marder, *From the Dreadnought to Scapa Flow*, I: *The Road to War, 1904–1914* (London, 1961), 110–111.

[9] Marder, *Anatomy of British Sea Power*, pp. 491–492.

[10] Marder, *Dreadnought to Scapa Flow*, I, 40–43. The complete text of the memorandum outlining the reorganization scheme (dated 6 Dec. 1904) is in P. K. Kemp, ed., *The Papers of Admiral Sir John Fisher*, I (Publications of the Navy Records Society, CII; London, 1960), 189–196.

[11] Marder, *Dreadnought to Scapa Flow*, I, 71–72.

[12] Hankey to Asquith, 8 July 1912, Cab. 17/3.

they did not enter into British calculations.[13] Since both were allies of Germany, though, they could not be ignored indefinitely. By early 1912 the *Dante Alighieri*, Italy's first dreadnought, was completing her trials; three others had been launched, and two more were under construction. Of even greater importance was the Austro-Hungarian fleet, for in the event of war it was considered more likely to be an active ally of Germany. The *Viribus Unitis*, first of a projected division of four dreadnoughts, was rapidly approaching completion; another had been launched, and the remaining two were still on the slips. The Austrian navy also had three battleships of the "Radetzky" class (completed 1910–11) which were powerful enough to be considered semi-dreadnoughts.[14] Clearly Austria-Hungary could no longer be treated as an insignificant factor at sea.

During the summer of 1905 the possibility was discussed of recalling at least part of the Mediterranean Fleet in the event of a war with Germany in which France and Britain were allies.[15] The elaborate collection of war plans drafted by the Admiralty in 1907 and 1908 reveal a growing readiness to draw on the Mediterranean Fleet in wartime to meet the German danger. The commander of the Channel Fleet was told that in the event of war with Germany alone, the Atlantic Fleet would be placed under his orders. If, however, France and England were both at war with Germany, his forces might eventually include all or part of the Mediterranean Fleet.[16]

The word "might" should be emphasized, for in an undated memorandum bound in with the war plans there is a discussion of the contingency of a war involving the Triple Entente against the Triple Alliance. In this case, those responsible for the memorandum held that the aim of Anglo-French naval action was to bring pressure to bear on all three countries by a complete stoppage of their maritime trade, best achieved through the destruction of their naval forces. Although geography indicated the general spheres of naval action (Britain in the North Sea, France in the Mediterranean), England would not evacuate the Mediterranean since France, by herself, did not have a great superiority over the combined Austro-Italian force; and England's position in Egypt, plus the necessity of keeping the Suez Canal open and of preventing any Austrian action in the Aegean, would compel England to keep a force in the Mediterranean. Moreover, under the existing ratio of strength between the British and German navies, the six Mediterranean battleships were not really

[13] *Ibid.*

[14] Viscount Hythe, ed., *The Naval Annual, 1912* (Portsmouth, 1912), pp. 48–49, 51–53, 73–74.

[15] Marder, *Anatomy of British Sea Power*, pp. 503, 512 n. 51.

[16] Public Record Office, London, Admiralty, Secretary's Department (hereafter cited Adm. 116), case 1037, War Orders A.L. no. M.0636, 14 June 1907.

needed in home waters. Should this British superiority be threatened, evacuation of the Mediterranean would naturally have to be considered.[17] Obviously there was a division of opinion within the Admiralty on this question: in a scheme labeled "A-1" included in the printed 1907 war plans, there is a reference to the French fleet as being "more than a match" for the combined Austro-Italian force. As a result, Britain would be able to withdraw from the Mediterranean and provide an "overwhelming force" in the northern theater of war, leaving France to safeguard her interests in the Mediterranean area.[18] This view was not shared by Admiral A. K. Wilson, commander of the Home Fleet until March 1907. In a separate minute, he observed that the great drawback of having France as an ally would be that Germany might win compensation on land for the slaughter of her commerce at sea. Consequently Wilson expressed himself in favor of "splendid isolation." [19]

The 1907–1908 collection of war plans bears the notation that none should be considered as definitely adopted. Their highly theoretical character is illustrated by a discussion of the seizure of Pola and Trieste to prevent them and the Austrian fleet from falling into German hands in the event of absorption of Austria by Germany following the death of Emperor Franz Joseph.[20] The war plans formulated in 1908 were somewhat less fanciful. Among the various contingencies studied, one principle appears consistently: if England alone were engaged in a war against Germany alone, the Atlantic Fleet would join the Channel Fleet, but the Mediterranean Fleet apparently would remain on station.[21] If, however, it appeared likely that Austria would join Germany, the Mediterranean would be reinforced by the Atlantic Fleet.[22] Should England have France as an ally in a war against Germany alone, the British Mediterranean Fleet was to join the Atlantic Fleet in home waters while the French force in the Mediterranean was to guard against the intervention of Italy and Austria.[23]

[17] Unsigned memorandum, n.d., Adm 116/1043B, pt. 1.

[18] War Plans, 1907, p. 76, *ibid.*

[19] Remarks on War Plans by Admiral of the Fleet Sir A. K. Wilson, p. 9, *ibid.* The memorandum is dated May 1907.

[20] War Plans, 1907, pp. 12–15, *ibid.* Commander Kemp has included a judicious note of caution on these war plans, and the considerable distinction between war plans and war orders. See P. K. Kemp, ed., *The Papers of Admiral Sir John Fisher,* II (Publications of the Navy Records Society, CVI; London, 1964), xii, 316–317.

[21] War Plan, Germany W.1, June 1908, Adm 116/1043B, pt. 1.

[22] War Plan, Germany W.2, June 1908, *ibid.*

[23] War Plan, England and France v. Germany W.3, *ibid.* Various parts and revisions of this plan were printed from June to December 1908. Recall of the Atlantic and Mediterranean fleets was also foreseen in the extremely unlikely event of a war against Germany and the United States: War Plan England v. Germany and U.S.A. W.4, Dec. 1908, *ibid.*

The least favorable set of circumstances from England's point of view, a war alone against the entire Triple Alliance, did not unduly trouble the Admiralty. Projecting the situation in the autumn of 1909, they considered the preponderance of British naval strength over the combined forces of their foes large enough to give Britain numerical superiority in both the northern and Mediterranean theaters of war. The Atlantic Fleet was to join the Mediterranean Fleet and seek to prevent a junction of the Austrian and Italian fleets, bringing each or both into action if the opportunity presented itself. The objective was to sever Italy, regarded as the weakest link because of her long coastline and widespread irredentist feeling, from the Triple Alliance. The inducement for Italy to conclude a separate peace would be provided by a British capture of Sardinia and, if the inhabitants showed signs of revolt against the Rome government, Sicily as well. With Italy out of the war, pressure could be brought to bear against Austria, the second weakest link. Vague mention was made of possible operations against Cattaro and joint action with Serbia or Montenegro.[24] Operations against Germany in the north were to be limited to retaining command of the sea and complete stoppage of German overseas trade. The offensive limitations of Britain's small army were recognized. The plan is an interesting example of the use of maritime supremacy to strike at the weak points of continental foes who have far greater strength on land. In this it is strongly reminiscent of the Napoleonic wars.

The scheme of withdrawing the six Mediterranean battleships to home waters even if France was not an active ally became increasingly attractive. In two different plans for war with Germany alone, one dated 1909 and the other April 1911, the displacement of the Mediterranean Fleet at least as far north as the Channel is advocated.[25] Acceptance of these ideas was not unanimous. Captain Herbert Richmond, foreshadowing his subsequent career as a well-known writer and teacher of naval history, wrote a paper on the naval war plans of 1909 in which he criticized the policy of including the Mediterranean ships in calculations of strength in home waters. Richmond argued that the possibility of French assistance should not be considered and that it appeared "only ordinary wisdom to count Germany and Austria as one state in the case of war." Even without entering the war, Austria could affect British strategy by mobilizing troops and transports at Trieste, an obvious threat to Malta that would require an appropriate countermove. Richmond used examples from the eighteenth century wars against France and Spain to support his arguments and

[24] England v. the Triple Alliance W.6, n.d., Adm 116/1043B, pt. 2.
[25] Sketch of the Action Necessary for War with Germany Alone, 1909, and Alternate Sketch Plan for War with Germany, April 1911, *ibid.*

pointed especially to the loss of Minorca as a warning for the future of Malta. He considered the abandonment of the Mediterranean before Austria had declared herself as "most dangerous," for with her entry into the war "a force of battleships and cruisers will be absolutely necessary in the Mediterranean or Malta will be lost and our trade will suffer severely."[26]

There is a certain ambiguity in all the British plans dealing with the Mediterranean at this time. It concerns the position of France. But the question of a formal alliance was naturally one of general policy, far beyond the competence of naval planners. Until the outbreak of the war in 1914, all references to the neighbor across the Channel had to be prefaced by a big "if," although after the events of 1912 one might consider the size of the "if" to have been considerably reduced. In December 1905, a small group of naval and military advisers began to meet informally to discuss possible action if Britain became involved with France in a war against Germany. The results of the talks were not conclusive, possibily because Fisher opposed sending the small British army to the Continent and so withdrew the naval representative.[27] The notes of these conferences reveal that the neutrality of Italy and Austria was considered "most probable," and there was even some talk of withdrawing the French naval force from the Mediterranean to blockade Germany's North Sea coastline.[28] Unofficial conversations between the French and British general staffs began at this time (December 1905–January 1906), but little of significance resulted, perhaps because Fisher did not rate the French navy very highly and considered its help unimportant.[29]

The First Sea Lord was capable of changing his mind, however, and at the end of 1908, probably under the stimulus of the Bosnian crisis, he told Captain Mercier de Lostende, the French naval attaché, that in the event of combined action England would be disposed to give France the responsibility for the Mediterranean operations against Italy and Austria.

26 "Remarks on War Plans, 1909," n.d., National Maritime Museum, Greenwich, Richmond MSS. Richmond repeated his criticism that the Admiralty war plans did not take into account Austria's appearance as Germany's ally in his diary entry of 25 March 1911; quoted in A. J. Marder, *Portrait of an Admiral: The Life and Papers of Sir Herbert Richmond* (Cambridge, Mass., 1952), p. 78.

27 Maurice P. A. Hankey, *The Supreme Command,* I (London, 1961), 62–63.

28 Notes of Conferences held at 2, Whitehall Gardens (6 Jan. 1906), p. 5. Public Record Office, London, Cabinet Office, Committee of Imperial Defence, Miscellaneous Volumes (hereafter cited Cab. 18)/24.

29 Marder, *Dreadnought to Scapa Flow,* I, 117–118. See also Samuel R. Williamson, *The Politics of Grand Strategy: Britain and France Prepare for War, 1904–1914* (Cambridge, Mass., 1969), chap. III. Unfortunately Williamson's book appeared too late to be fully cited. It is indispensable to any discussion of the problem.

This would include the defense of Malta and the Suez Canal. All British ships in the Mediterranean (except for some left in reserve at Gibraltar) would be brought north, where England would take charge of operations in the North Sea and the Baltic. Guarding the Strait of Dover would also be left to French torpedo craft and submarines, which would have free use of the port of Dover. The attaché immediately returned to Paris, reported to the Minister of Marine, and the scheme was presented to the Premier, Georges Clemenceau, and his Foreign Minister, Stephen Pichon. The French naval General Staff after careful study of the project was forced to admit that they did not feel strong enough to undertake so large a task, especially since they had to safeguard their own communications with Algeria. Consequently, French action was to be restricted to the western basin of the Mediterranean. To maintain complete secrecy, and at the request of the British, the agreement was not put in writing.[30]

Fisher resigned as First Sea Lord in December 1909 and was replaced by Admiral of the Fleet Sir A. K. Wilson, who in his comments on the 1907 war plans had revealed himself to be far from enthusiastic about cooperation with France. Neither the Admiralty records nor the French naval records reveals any further naval conversations until July 1911; at this moment the Agadir crisis was in full blossom. It is interesting to note how successive international crises—Morocco in 1905, Bosnia in 1908, and Agadir in 1911—prodded both sides into further conversations. On July 12 Lostende's successor, Captain René Pumperneel, discussed the possibility of a joint naval code with Wilson; but Pumperneel died suddenly on August 19. Captain Lostende returned to London for his funeral and Paul Cambon, the French ambassador, judged the moment propitious to resume talks with the Admiralty and to ascertain Wilson's views. He arranged a meeting between Wilson and Lostende on August 24. Wilson accepted the general line of Fisher's agreement except for the part about France's defense of the Strait of Dover. Because of the frequent movements of British warships along that coast, he requested that spheres of action be assigned to both forces there, and that the French not approach too closely. He proposed that the French sphere in the Mediterranean be extended eastward to include the Gulf of Taranto. The Admiralty was to have general direction of the maritime war. It was stressed that each fleet would be completely independent within its sphere. There was absolutely

---

[30] Memorandum by Minister of Marine, 17 Dec. 1908, France, Archives Centrales de la Marine Française, Paris (hereafter cited as AMF), carton Es-10. See also the memorandum "Conventions verbales avec l'amirauté Anglaise pour les operations . . . contre l'Allemagne," 29 Aug. 1911.

no question of fighting together in tactical formations. The French fleet, concentrated in the Mediterranean, would seek to destroy the Austrian and Italian naval forces should those countries enter the war on Germany's side. The French would not enter the Adriatic but would attack the Austrian fleet if the latter came out to join the Italians. The entrance of the Adriatic would be watched by the British, who would also assume protection of commerce in the Mediterranean and guard the northern entrance of the Suez Canal.[31]

A French wireless expert, Lieutenant Charles Gignon, was sent to London early in September with two new propositions for the Admiralty. Cambon briefed him on the impossibility of giving diplomatic sanction to the agreement on fleet operations, or even of obtaining a written convention between the naval authorities. The ambassador added that the Admiralty knew it was surrounded by a net of spies in the pay of Germany and had on many occasions proof of important leaks on the most secret questions. Therefore it was opposed in principle to any written agreement. Moreover, a secret accord between the governments was incompatible with the English constitution.[32] Duly warned, Gignon presented Wilson with a project for a secret code to be used for communication between the two powers in time of war. In addition, the French proposed to take charge of operations throughout the Mediterranean, for they now felt assured of their superiority at sea against the Italians and Austrians. They would also guarantee the security of navigation in this region insofar as it could be guaranteed by any fleet. Wilson readily agreed to this proposition, as well as to the signal code. However, he added the reservation that England would maintain cruisers in the Mediterranean for commerce protection, since France would be unable to divide her forces between the Adriatic and west coast of Italy, and thus unable to prevent raids against commerce by enemy cruisers at the beginning of hostilities. As Cambon had previously warned, Wilson termed diplomatic sanction of the agreements an impossibility.[33]

The Admiralty's passion for secrecy led to some amusing results. It is easy to appreciate the discomfort felt by Wilson in dealing with a foreign power, especially since he himself had misgivings about an alliance with France and realized that the recent conversations were a secret to most

---

[31] *Ibid.* See also Williamson, *Politics of Grand Strategy,* pp. 245–246.

[32] Lt. Gignon, "Compte-rendu d'une Mission à Londres," 11 Sept. 1911, AMF, carton Es-10. One wonders where Cambon obtained this story (Fisher?) and to what extent it was a device to evade a firm commitment.

[33] *Ibid.* Wilson added, "Nous ne pouvons pas mettre de politicians dans les choses d'action." The fragmentary British records of the Wilson-Gignon interview (5 Sept. 1911) are in Admiralty Archives, case 0091.

of the Cabinet, let alone Parliament and the nation. The only British record of the September 1911 conversations appears to be a handwritten note, almost in outline form, on Admiralty embossed stationery. In contrast, the French officers wrote detailed reports, which were carefully filed. Commander Howard Kelly, British naval attaché in Paris, was completely ignorant of these vague understandings with the French although he was well versed in French affairs, having been head of the French section of the Naval Intelligence Department (NID) for two years prior to his appointment as attaché in February 1911.[34] He learned of them only when Théophile Delcassé, French Minister of Marine (March 1911–January 1913), referred to the agreements during a conversation, assuming that Kelly was au courant. It was, needless to say, rather embarrassing for Kelly, who had to stumble through as if he knew all about them before finally managing to extricate himself. That same afternoon he left for London, "seething with indignation," and considered resigning his appointment on the grounds that his position would be untenable without the full confidence of the Admiralty. The information the Admiralty provided Kelly seems to have been something less than precise, for on his return to Paris he asked Delcassé to see the French records of the agreements and suggested that a copy might be taken to London to eliminate any discrepancy with the Admiralty copy (which was, of course, practically nonexistent).[35] Vice-Admiral Paul Auvert, chief of the French naval General Staff, permitted Kelly to copy the Lostende and Gignon reports, and the attaché admitted to him that Admiral Bridgeman wanted more precise particulars than those available to him.[36] The result, not without its irony, is that the most detailed Admiralty record of the 1908 and 1911 conversations is apparently based on Kelly's translation of the French reports.[37]

The incident illustrates the vague and somewhat haphazard manner in which the Admiralty tended to deal with the French. It was similar to the casual way in which the naval forces of Austria and Italy, Germany's allies, had been dismissed. But the situation was changing. The Austrian and Italian fleets were becoming more potent. On September 29, 1911, the Tripolitan War broke out. Italian forces quickly occupied Tripoli and

[34] H. Kelly, "Journal as Naval Attaché" (16 Feb. 1911–16 Mar. 1914), p. 1, National Maritime Museum, Greenwich, Kelly MSS. Kelly wrote this journal, apparently after the war, with an eye to possible publication. Because of the time lapse he is, unfortunately, sometimes vague on exact details.

[35] *Ibid.*, pp. 23–24. Kelly refers to this as taking place in the autumn of 1911. It probably occurred shortly before November 28, when Admiral Sir Francis Bridgeman replaced A. K. Wilson as First Sea Lord.

[36] Note by Admiral Auvert, 12 Dec. 1911, AMF, carton Es-10.

[37] Admiralty Archives, case 0091.

other coastal towns in Tripolitania and Cyrenaica, and on November 5 the annexation of Tripoli was proclaimed. Another European power, and an ally of Germany at that, now controlled the territory adjacent to Tunisia and Egypt, with a long coastline flanking the Suez Canal route. Moreover, the Tripolitan War dragged on and threatened to spread to other portions of the eastern Mediterranean. Even more ominous from the British point of view were signs that Germany, in the wake of the Agadir crisis, would push through a supplementary law to increase its naval strength. Rising German pressure in the North Sea could be expected.

On October 25 the young Winston Churchill became First Lord of the Admiralty, and by the end of November Admiral Sir Francis Bridgeman replaced A. K. Wilson as First Sea Lord. A new team was in charge, and, with Churchill as its leader, it was not apt to pursue a passive policy. Bridgeman did not share his predecessors' reticence about cooperation with the French. When the new French naval attaché, Commander (Capitaine de frégate) Christian-Marie Le Gouz de Saint-Seine, paid his first visit, the First Sea Lord told him that he completely approved of the present French naval dispositions, with high-seas squadrons in the Mediterranean and flotillas and submarines in the Channel. He added, most significantly, that the Admiralty would gladly study a project for the division of the Channel into zones of action for the flotillas of the two nations.[38]

Since 1905 the Admiralty had been moving hesitantly toward recall of the Mediterranean Fleet in time of war, first under some and then under most contingencies. There had also developed a movement toward actively planning for cooperation with France in time of war. In 1912, under the vigorous and imaginative direction of Churchill, both projects were to receive fresh impetus.

[38] St.-Seine to Minister of Marine, 11 Dec. 1911, AMF, carton Es-10. See also private letter, St.-Seine to [?], 16 Dec. 1911, *ibid.*

II

The 1912 Reorganization
of the Royal Navy

In early 1912, changing diplomatic, military, and naval circumstances forced the Admiralty into some hard thinking about the Mediterranean situation. The result of this was the new reorganization of the fleet announced by Churchill in the House of Commons on March 18. The underlying causes of the reorganization were the growth of the German, Austro-Hungarian, and Italian navies in the preceding few years. It was, however, the failure of the Haldane mission to achieve a détente in the naval race with Germany that finally forced Churchill and the Admiralty to act.

Throughout the autumn of 1911, rumors of an increase in the German building program had been rife. Sir Ernest Cassel, noted banker and friend of the late King Edward VII, had expressed to his friend Albert Ballin, head of the Hamburg-Amerika Line, his alarm over the deterioration of relations between Germany, the land of his birth, and England, his adopted country.[1] Through the efforts of both men, extremely influential in their respective countries, conversations between the two nations were initiated with a view to easing tensions. At first Cassel served as intermediary, traveling to Berlin at the end of January, 1912. He was followed in early February by a prominent member of the Cabinet, Lord Haldane, Secretary of State for War, who had been educated in Germany and was fluent in the language. Haldane met with the Kaiser, Chancellor Theobald von Bethmann Hollweg, and Admiral Alfred von Tirpitz. The talks fell

---

[1] The relevant documents are published in G. P. Gooch and Harold Temperley, eds., *British Documents on the Origins of the War, 1898–1914* (11 vols. in 13, London, 1927–1938; hereafter cited *BD*), VI, 666–761; Johannes Lepsius, Albrecht Mendelssohn-Bartholdy, and Friedrich Thimme, eds., *Die Grosse Politik der Europäischen Kabinette, 1871–1914* (40 vols. in 54, Berlin, 1922–1927; hereafter cited *GP*), XXXI, 95–251. For a recent account see Marder, *Dreadnought to Scapa Flow*, I, 272–287.

into three categories: political, naval, and colonial. The colonial agreement may have presented the least difficulty. The political agreement and the naval agreement became linked, and it was over which should precede the other that the talks deadlocked in March, after Haldane's return to England. The British were unable to give the Germans the desired guarantee of absolute neutrality if Germany became involved in war, since they feared being unable to come to the assistance of France if she were attacked. Consequently the British government would not go beyond a promise not to make any unprovoked attack on Germany. The Germans made delay of their planned *Novelle*—the supplementary naval law—contingent on reaching a satisfactory political formula. The British linked any colonial agreement to the naval issue. Caught in what amounted to a vicious circle, the talks reached a stalemate and collapsed. The Novelle was published on March 22 and introduced in the Reichstag in April. It was against the background of these futile negotiations that Churchill formulated his plans concerning the Mediterranean.

Bethmann Hollweg gave Cassel a sketch of the impending Novelle while Cassel was in Berlin. Its most serious provision was the creation of a permanent third battle squadron of the active fleet.[2] It would number eight battleships, formed from five pre-dreadnoughts drawn from the reserve fleet and three new dreadnoughts to be laid down in addition to the existing program in 1912, 1914, and 1916.

Churchill, after the Admiralty had scrutinized Cassel's report, wrote Sir Edward Grey, the Foreign Secretary, on January 31 that the German proposal would require a new and vigorous British response. To match the old German six-year program of 2-2-2-2-2-2, Britain had to build 4-3-4-3-4-3. The Novelle would mean a German building program of 3-2-3-2-3-2; this would require a British program of 5-4-5-4-5-4 to maintain a 60 percent superiority in dreadnoughts and dreadnought cruisers. During the six winter months, the first and second squadrons of the German High Seas Fleet were full of new recruits, thus easing some of the strain on the Royal Navy. The creation of a permanent third squadron would maintain the pressure throughout the year. The German strength would be twenty-five battleships—all dreadnoughts within a few years' time—permanently in commission. After the widening of the Kiel Canal was completed, this force would be able to concentrate rapidly in either the North Sea or the Baltic without having to make the long detour around Denmark.[3]

[2] A translation of the Novelle may be found in A. H. Burgoyne, ed., *The Navy League Annual, 1912–1913* (London, 1913), pp. 115–123.

[3] Churchill to Grey, 31 Jan. 1912, quoted in Winston S. Churchill, *The World Crisis,* I: *1911–1914* (London, 1923), 96.

According to a memorandum prepared by the Admiralty for the Prime Minister and Cabinet, this would mean: "The British fleet must be prepared to meet, at any moment not chosen by them, an attack by the above [German] force at its most favourable moment. The Admiralty consider that 41 Battleships (5 battle squadrons and a fleet flagship) is the least force available in 24 hours that they could maintain." [4] Churchill told Grey the consequences of this were that "to meet the new German Squadron, we are contemplating bringing home the Mediterranean battleships." This would mean relying on France in the Mediterranean, and no change of the entente system would be possible, even if desired.[5]

In Berlin the Kaiser gave Haldane a copy of the actual text of the Novelle. After it was studied by the Admiralty, Churchill's concern increased, for, as he reported to the Cabinet on February 14, "The main feature in the new law is the extraordinary increase in the striking force of ships of all classes immediately available throughout the year." [6] The Admiralty formerly had to contend with only seventeen battleships, four battle cruisers, and twelve small cruisers in the active German fleet. This force was partially demobilized during the winter season. In the future, the German fleet must be assessed at twenty-five battleships, twelve battle cruisers, and eighteen small cruisers; this force would also be at a higher degree of readiness during the winter than before. Corresponding increases in personnel, degree of readiness, and material strength were also to be provided for the destroyer and submarine forces. To illustrate the seriousness of the proposed German measures, it was noted that the Admiralty maintained only twenty-two battleships in full commission at that moment; and this total included the six battleships of the Atlantic Fleet at Gibraltar.[7]

A report by Captain Hugh Watson, British naval attaché in Berlin, could not have been very encouraging. Watson, whose dispatch was circulated to the Cabinet, came to the reluctant conclusion after three years as attaché that there was no way of stopping the naval expansion of Germany

[4] Admiralty memorandum, n.d. [probably early Feb. 1912], Asquith MSS, box 24.

[5] Churchill to Grey, 31 Jan. 1912, quoted in Churchill, *The World Crisis*, I, 97. The Admiralty memorandum put it somewhat euphemistically. The probable withdrawal of the Mediterranean battleships would "make it desirable from a naval point of view . . . to seek for other support in those waters." Admiralty memorandum, n.d., Asquith MSS, box 24. This measure had been strongly supported by Prince Louis of Battenberg before he became Second Sea Lord. Battenberg to Churchill, 20 Nov. 1911, quoted in Mark Kerr, *Prince Louis of Battenberg* (London, 1934), pp. 233–234.

[6] Churchill, *The World Crisis*, I, 102.

[7] Report to the Cabinet, 9 Mar. 1912, *ibid.*, p. 103. On February 15 Churchill circulated a memorandum to the Sea Lords requesting proposals for implementation of his policy of concentration. Randolph S. Churchill, *Winston S. Churchill*, vol II: *Young Statesman, 1901–1914* (Boston, 1967), 547.

unless answering naval increases by England drove home to the German people the impossibility of continuing. The Foreign Office recognized that Watson in his early days as attaché had tried very hard to keep an open mind, and this added weight to his disillusioned warning that German naval policy was manipulated by the naval authorities so that it would always appear that England did the provoking while Germany did the responding.[8] In a minute to this report, Sir Eyre Crowe, Assistant Undersecretary of State for Foreign Affairs, remarked that if the Germans were really anxious for friendly relations, they would have to give some tangible proof.[9] He was obviously referring to the Haldane mission.

Rumors of an impending shift in the Mediterranean were afoot by early March. Haldane frankly told the Germans that the Mediterranean ships might be brought home if the third squadron were established.[10] The *Army and Navy Gazette* took up this notion and deplored it, pointing out that, far from warranting the withdrawal of any ships, the situation required modern reinforcements for those ships already there. The same issue carried an article on the effects of the extension of the Baghdad Railway to a point where it could transport Turkish troops to within striking distance of the Suez Canal. The writer stressed the desirability of at least selecting, if not fortifying, positions covering the canal to enable the Egyptian forces to hold out for three weeks, until reinforcements could arrive from England or India.[11]

Great Britain's new naval policy in the Mediterranean was outlined by Churchill on March 18 in his speech during the debate on the naval estimates. Not wishing to violate the Kaiser's confidence, he did not reveal that he knew the text of the Novelle. The principles of future British naval construction were put on a hypothetical basis. The standard was to be a 60 percent superiority over Germany in dreadnoughts, so long as the Germans kept to their present program, and two keels to one for every additional ship they laid down, exclusive of any ships provided by the Dominions. The two "Lord Nelsons," designed before the *Dreadnought* but completed afterwards, were to be counted as dreadnoughts, since in armor and subdivision they were actually stronger than the original *Dreadnought*. Without any increase in the German program, the British

[8] Watson to Goschen, British ambassador at Berlin, 8 Feb. 1912, Public Record Office, London, Foreign Office, Political Correspondence (hereafter cited as FO 371), vol. 1372, Germany, file 6060.

[9] Minute by Sir Eyre Crowe, 12 Feb. 1912, *ibid.*

[10] Churchill, *The World Crisis*, I, 101–102.

[11] *Army and Navy Gazette*, 9 Mar. 1912, pp. 218, 226.

cided that in the existing circumstances—the Italians were in the process of occupying Rhodes and other islands in the Dodecanese—a meeting of the CID at Malta probably would "give rise to misunderstandings and perturbations both at home and abroad." [23] The military representatives were to be told that their presence was no longer required, and the CID meeting would be postponed until the Prime Minister's return to London. Asquith still expected to meet Kitchener and requested that the Malta meeting be treated as confidential.[24] If the Prime Minister hoped to dampen public speculation about the Malta trip, he was to be sadly disappointed: his very presence along with Churchill, the Board of Admiralty, and Lord Kitchener was bound to cause comment, despite the technical distinction that it was not a formal meeting of the CID.

The Admiralty's reorganization plans were naturally based exclusively on naval considerations. In this they were logical and easily defended. But their weakness lay exactly in this narrowness. There were other British interests besides the naval defense of the British Isles. And there was reason to believe that these interests might be harmed by the Admiralty's proposals. The Foreign Office became a center of opposition to the scheme. Sir Arthur Nicolson, Permanent Undersecretary of State for Foreign Affairs, considered it a "most risky and unfortunate proceeding"; he did not think that, when the European situation was in such a state of chaos and the status of the Mediterranean about to undergo considerable change, it was at all wise to withdraw the naval forces.[25] He doubted that the French would safeguard British interests in the Mediterranean without a guarantee of assistance from Britain in regard to France's eastern frontier. If the navy insisted on evacuating the Mediterranean, only two courses were possible. One would be an expensive addition to the naval budget, which Nicolson doubted the government would accept after the large sums voted in March. The other alternative would be to come to an understanding with France which would be very much in the nature of a defensive alliance. It was doubtful that the members of the Cabinet inclined to accept this would be able to convince the rest of their colleagues. Nicolson repeated this line of argument when he transmitted to Grey a copy of the memorandum prepared for the CID by the Foreign Office. He also mentioned another alternative: an alliance with Germany. This he ruled out for a

[23] Asquith to Hankey, 11 May 1912, Cab. 17/99; Asquith to King George, 13 May 1912, Asquith MSS, box 6.
[24] *Ibid.* Presumably Asquith was referring to the suggested CID meeting; the news that he would meet Kitchener had already been published.
[25] Sir A. Nicolson to Sir F. Bertie, British ambassador at Paris, 6 May 1912, *BD*, X (pt. 2), no. 384, p. 584.

building program would be, starting in 1912–13: 4-3-4-3-4-3.[12] As the relative fighting value of the British pre-dreadnought battleships declined, the ratio of the new construction would have to rise above the 60 percent standard. Churchill emphasized the flexibility of the British program, saying that if Germany chose to reduce any portion of her program, this would be followed by a reduction of the corresponding British quota. If, for example, Germany took a naval-construction holiday in 1913 and did not lay down three ships, the five potential British super-dreadnoughts would be canceled. With a touch of humor, Churchill added that this was more than "they could hope to do in a brilliant naval action." [13] His speech is noteworthy for the public disappearance from Admiralty calculations of the old two-power building standard and the substitution, and actual naming, of Germany as the object of the 60 percent standard.

The proposed reorganization of the fleet was of particular interest for the Mediterranean. The First, Second, and Third fleets, comprising eight battle squadrons of eight battleships each plus supporting cruiser squadrons, flotillas, and auxiliaries, were each to represent a different administrative status and standard of commission. The First Fleet was to consist of four battle squadrons of ships in "full commission"—that is, always ready—plus a flagship. It was to be formed as follows: The first and second divisions of the Home Fleet became the First and Second Battle Squadrons; the Atlantic Fleet became the Third Battle Squadron and was to be based in home ports instead of Gibraltar; and the Mediterranean Fleet became the Fourth Battle Squadron and was to be based on Gibraltar instead of Malta. The Second Fleet, composed of two battle squadrons, consisted of ships in "active commission" but with about 40 percent of their crews—all active service ratings—in special schools, such as gunnery and torpedo. The Third Fleet, consisting of two battle squadrons and five cruiser squadrons, included the oldest ships in "reserve" status.[14] The Fourth Battle Squadron (former Mediterranean Fleet) would be raised ultimately, and if necessary, from six to eight battleships. Furthermore, it would "from

[12] Churchill, *The World Crisis*, I, 107–108. The Germans postponed laying down one of the three extra ships originally planned in the Novelle, thus setting their program at 2-3-2-2-3-2. Therefore the British program was fixed at 4-5-4-4-4-4. In the summer of 1912 the Federated Malay States presented the battleship *Malaya*, a "splendid gift" which raised the British first year total to 5. *Ibid.*, p. 108.
[13] *The Naval Annual, 1912*, pp. 418, 420. The editors reproduce the complete text of Churchill's speech. By 1912 dreadnoughts had greatly increased in size, speed, and gun power over the original *Dreadnought*, hence the term "super-dreadnought." Instead of the original 12-inch guns, the latest British battleships carried 13.5-inch guns and those to be laid down would have 15-inch guns.
[14] Churchill, *The World Crisis*, I, 116–117.

its strategic position at Gibraltar, be able to give either immediate assistance in home waters or to operate in the Mediterranean, should naval combinations in that sea render its presence necessary or useful. Its movements will be regulated by the main situation." [15] This last provision was apt to be purely academic in the event of war with Germany, for, with the creation of the new German squadron in permanent commission, it is extremely unlikely that the Fourth Battle Squadron would have been sent into the Mediterranean. The challenge represented by the German *Novelle* had been met by the Admiralty with its redeployment of the fleet and building program.

The 1912 reorganization was another step, and a large one, in the shifting of British naval strength toward home waters to meet the German menace. As such it is the logical continuation of the policy begun by Fisher at the end of 1904. The practical details of Churchill's scheme were set out in a circular letter of March 29, to take effect on May 1. Of the six Mediterranean battleships, the four "Duncans" (*Exmouth, Russell, Cornwallis,* and *Duncan*) were to form the Fourth Battle Squadron at Gibraltar. *Triumph* and *Swiftsure* went into reserve in the Third Fleet. A cruiser squadron would be kept at Malta.[16] This deployment ties in with the secret, unofficial, and generally vague agreements with the French of the preceding summer, whereby Great Britain was to maintain a cruiser squadron in the Mediterranean for the purpose of commerce protection.

Obviously such an important reshuffling was bound to raise a whole spectrum of military problems. The Board of Admiralty was to inspect the Mediterranean station at the end of May, making use of the Admiralty yacht *Enchantress.* On April 25 Churchill informed Captain Maurice Hankey, secretary of the Committee of Imperial Defence (CID), that the Prime Minister would make the trip with the board. Although the trip was to be something of a holiday, Asquith thought it convenient and useful to take advantage of his presence at Malta to hold a meeting of the CID at which Lord Kitchener, then serving as Consul-General and de facto Viceroy in Egypt, could be present. Hankey was to arrange for the necessary position papers to be formulated by the War Office and the Chief of the Naval War Staff.[17]

The Admiralty's war plans were of course highly secret and known only to a relatively small number of people. The general public, and even many highly placed officials, could not have known the extent to which the

pressure of changing circumstances had brought the Admiralty aro[und] to the idea of partially evacuating the Mediterranean. Churchill's sche[me] once announced, gave a strong hint of what was astir, and the new[s] Asquith's trip to Malta aroused considerable comment.[18] The presenc[e] Kitchener also increased speculation, and by the time of the Malta [con]ference a flood of articles had appeared touching off the great pu[blic] debate over Mediterranean policy which was to fill the columns of [the] press, occupy much time in Parliament, and continue on into Aug[ust] But while Hankey was diligently arranging for papers from the vari[ous] government departments interested in the upcoming meeting, a new [con]troversy was taking shape within the government. Its crucial mome[nts] were to take place at the Malta conference in late May and at the C[ID] meetings in July.

On April 29 an informal meeting was held between Hankey, Rear Adm[iral] ral E. C. T. Troubridge, Chief of the War Staff, Brigadier General H. [Geme]ral Wilson, Director of Military Operations, General Staff, and Sir Eyre Cro[we] of the Foreign Office. Both Wilson and Troubridge expressed the opini[on] that it was extremely difficult to formulate views unless the Forei[gn] Office could offer some guidance about the strongest combination[s of] powers which might reasonably be called hostile to Great Britain.[19] Cro[we] said that he would prepare the necessary paper.[20] Similar requests for [a] statement of position went out to the India Office, the Colonial Office, a[nd] the Board of Trade. The Malta conference was to be considered a pr[e]liminary meeting of the CID, the results of which would be discussed [in] subsequent CID meetings in London.[21]

When the Cabinet met on May 10, objections were raised to a meeti[ng] of the CID at Malta. Lord Morley, then Lord President, who learned of [it] while aboard the *Enchantress,* seems to have led the opposition. Haldan[e] feared the navy would have too much influence in the absence of adequat[e] War Office representation, and Grey supported him.[22] The Cabinet de[cided]

[15] *Parliamentary Debates* (Commons), 5th ser., XXXV, 1564.
[16] Cited by Marder, *Dreadnought to Scapa Flow,* I, 287.
[17] Churchill to Hankey, 25 Apr. 1912, Cab. 17/99.

[18] *The Times,* 10 May 1912, p. 8. The innocuous headline was "The Prime Minister['s] Holiday."
[19] Hankey to Grey, 30 Apr. 1912, *BD,* X (pt. 2), no. 381, p. 580; C. E. Callwell[,] *Field-Marshal Sir Henry Wilson: His Life and Diaries* (London, 1927), I, 113.
[20] Minute by Sir E. Crowe, 30 Apr. 1912, *BD,* X (pt. 2), no. 382, pp. 581–582.
[21] Topics to be discussed were: the scale of overseas or land attack to be anticipated at Malta and Egypt with regard to the new naval dispositions in the Mediterranean, and the degree of reliance to be placed on the French fleet; the defenses and garrisons necessary to meet these attacks; the possible use of Alexandria as an additional Mediterranean base; arrangements for the protection and diversion of trade in the Mediterranean; and the effect of the new naval dispositions on India and the dominions and colonies east of the Mediterranean. Agenda, 29 Apr. 1912, Cab. 17/99.
[22] Sir Almeric Fitzroy, *Memoirs* (5th ed., London, n.d.), II, 485–486.

number of reasons: Scandinavia and the Low Countries would be forced into the German camp; relations with Russia and France would probably become cold and unfriendly, thus threatening Great Britain's position in the Middle East and on the Indian frontier; and Germany would increase pressure on France with the subsequent risk of a European war. Nicolson concluded that an understanding with France for the safeguarding of British interests in the Mediterranean at the price of some reciprocal commitment by Britain "offers the cheapest, simplest and safest solution." [26]

In his memorandum prepared for the CID Sir Eyre Crowe examined the effects on foreign policy of withdrawal from the Mediterranean. The "somewhat indeterminate" position of Italy would be altered, for the presence of a powerful British battle fleet was a restraint on the Italian government's support of the Triple Alliance. With a large portion of her army tied down in the Tripolitan War, Italy was at the mercy of Austria on her northeastern frontier. Consequently, without the pressure of the Royal Navy, there was the danger that the Italians would throw themselves "unreservedly into the arms of Germany for better or for worse." [27] Italy, having now become a potential enemy, might view Malta as part of *Italia irredenta*. The French navy's ability to check Austria and Italy would be dependent on its being able to concentrate forces in the Mediterranean without fear of a German attack on France's Atlantic coasts. This, in turn, would be dependent on some definite naval understanding between England and France involving mutual assistance in case of attack by the Triple Alliance. Spain, which feared France, undoubtedly considered England a check on any anti-Spanish activities by the French in the current agreements among major powers for cooperation in Morocco. The presence of the Royal Navy near its coasts and islands undoubtedly would keep Spain out of the Triple Alliance. As long as the British maintained sea supremacy, it was unlikely that Spain would bind herself to join in a war against Great Britain, but she might be persuaded to join in a scheme of common operations against France.

In the eastern Mediterranean the withdrawal of the fleet would lead to a loss of influence in Constantinople; alter the diplomatic situation to the advantage of Germany; and might induce Turkey to join the Triple Alliance as a means of securing effective assistance against Russia and possibly reconquering Egypt. Without any definite agreement with the Royal Navy,

[26] Nicolson to Grey, 6 May 1912, *ibid.*, no. 385, p. 585.
[27] CID. Paper no. 147-B, "The Situation in the Mediterranean, 1912," 9 May 1912, p. 3, Public Record Office, London, Cabinet Office, Committee of Imperial Defence, Memoranda, Miscellaneous (hereafter cited as Cab. 4)/33.

the French fleet must necessarily be concentrated in the Channel, and this would afford the Turks the opportunity for a descent on Egypt.[28] The mere possibility of this, in addition to the loss of prestige which would accompany the withdrawal of the fleet, would create a state of dangerous unrest in Egypt and gravely embarrass the administration of that country. Efforts to maintain the status quo, particularly in respect to Crete and possibly Cyprus, would be nullified. Most of these consequences might be averted if a powerful French fleet took the place of the British Mediterranean fleet, although the hold over Egypt might still have to be materially strengthened and the position in Turkey would still be questionable. The Foreign Office memorandum clearly implied that an assurance of British-French cooperation if either country went to war with the Triple Alliance would put the French fleet in a good position to win command of the Mediterranean.

Sir Edward Grey feared that England could not hold Egypt if command of the Mediterranean was lost, and he questioned Kitchener on the subject, emphasizing the importance of his being at Malta to speak his views to the Prime Minister.[29] Kitchener did not look on a withdrawal of the Mediterranean Fleet with very great anxiety, if it were a question of war with Germany alone. Presumably the navy would be able to leave enough small ships to deter a Turkish attack by sea, and an attack by land would have to be made from the desert east of the Suez Canal. It would be very difficult for the Turks to effect a large enough concentration to force passage across the canal if the defenders were supported by gunboats. From the military point of view, the withdrawal would make Egypt dependent on India instead of Malta and England for future support and reinforcements. In the event of war with the Triple Alliance, Kitchener felt he could not hope to hold the Mediterranean coast of Egypt. The British would have to defend the country internally and with reinforcements from India, as the Turks were doing in Tripoli. It was of the greatest importance that the government of India be in a position to send to Egypt three or four divisions of troops whenever they might be required.[30]

Churchill sought support from the Secretary of State for War, Lord Haldane. In his own unmistakable style, he summed up his and the Admiralty's position:

[28] The Foreign Office was completely wrong in this. See below, pp. 60f.

[29] Grey to Kitchener, 8 May 1912, *BD*, X (pt. 2), no. 387, p. 590.

[30] Kitchener to Grey, 19 May 1912, *ibid.*, no. 390, p. 592. Major Fitzgerald, Kitchener's aide and friend, considered the naval moves as putting them all in a difficult position and recalled that the withdrawal of the British fleet from the Mediterranean led to Bonaparte's invasion. Fitzgerald to Sir G. Arthur, 19 May 1912, Public Record Office, London, Kitchener MSS, PRO 30/57/42.

The Malta Conference can settle nothing . . . The actual point has been settled long ago by the brute force of facts. We cannot possibly hold the Mediterranean or guarantee any of our interests there until we have obtained a decision in the North Sea.

The war-plans for the last 5 years have provided for the evacuation of the Mediter' as the first step consequent on a war with Germany & all we are doing is to make the peace dispositions wh approximate to war necessities. It wd be vy foolish to lose England in safeguarding Egypt.

Of course if the Cabinet & the House of Commons like to build another fleet of Dreadnoughts for the Meditern. the attitude of the Adm'l wde be that of a cat to a nice fresh dish of cream. But I do not look upon this as practical politics . . . But if we win the big battle in the decisive theatre, we can put everything else straight afterwards. If we lose it, there will not be any afterwards. London is the key of Egypt. Don't lose that.

Considering you propose to send the whole Br Army abroad, you ought to help me keep the whole Br navy at home.

Whatever the French do, my counsel is the same, & is the first of all the laws of war—overpowering strength at the decisive point.[31]

Churchill was not successful in securing Haldane's support. In a memorandum on the effect of the loss of sea power in the Mediterranean, the Secretary of State for War maintained that all strategic plans had been based on superiority at sea, and if, as now implied, the enemy were to have command of the sea for a least two months, the fundamental basis of the existing plans was completely altered. Malta, for example, had been considered liable to attack for a maximum of fourteen days before the navy could arrive in force, but without command of the sea there could be no question of reinforcing the island after the outbreak of hostilities. Egypt might be reinforced by India, but this would take five or six weeks. At the moment there was not a single infantry unit available in the United Kingdom for any unforeseen emergency, despite the fact that, even under existing arrangements guaranteeing British naval supremacy, there was a case for reinforcing Gibraltar, Malta, and Egypt by a battalion each. Haldane concluded:

It will therefore be seen that we have barely sufficient battalions to make good the want of strength at home and in the Mediterranean under the existing conditions . . . the strategical requirements governing our existing military distribution are based on a supposition that we hold sea command in the Mediterranean. If, however, such is not to be the case, and it is considered desirable to garrison our possessions in the Mediterranean and Egypt in time of war independent of seapower, the steps necessary to give effect to this will put a strain upon our military resources which, at their present strength and under their existing organisation, they are quite unable to bear.[32]

In preparation for the Malta meeting, the General Staff prepared a series of papers dealing with Mediterranean and Egyptian defenses. The broad assumption was made that, in a war between England and the Triple Alliance, the command of the Mediterranean would be lost for at least two months.[33] Considering the geographical position of Malta and the scanty garrison of the fortress, and assuming the French fleet to be employed for ten to fourteen days with the transport of Algerian troops back to France, a possible attack on the island by Italy was a "practical operation" given the steady weather of the summer season. However, considering the small number of suitable landing places, an adequate mobile sea defense might prove "an absolute deterrent to any landing at all and the safety of the island can be guaranteed more economically by increased sea defence than by increasing the garrison." [34] The garrison strength had been calculated on the assumption of friendly relations with the Mediterranean powers, and the assumption that the garrison would have to resist attack only for a fortnight before reinforcements arrived.[35] If command of the Mediterranean were lost, Austria could also land a force large enough to capture Cyprus within fifteen days without disturbing any of her plans on the Continent.[36]

The situation in Egypt was equally serious. Hardly a man could be

[32] "Memorandum by the Secretary of State for War on the effect of the loss of seapower in the Mediterranean on British military strategy," 9 May 1912, Asquith MSS, box 107. Haldane's personal preference was to provide the navy with the money for more ships. The army leaders, General Sir John French, Chief of the Imperial General Staff and Brigadier General H. Wilson, Director of Military Operations, advocated an alliance with France. Callwell, *Sir Henry Wilson*, I, 113.

[33] CID. Paper no. 148-B, "Note by C.I.G.S. Covering . . . papers . . . 92-C; 93-C; and 149-B," 9 May 1912, Cab. 4/4/33.

[34] CID. Paper no. 92-C, "1. The Attack on Malta by Italy; 2. Defence of Malta against deliberate invasion," 9 May 1912, Asquith MSS, box 107.

[35] CID. Paper no. 91-C, "Considerations on which the existing defences of Malta are based," May 1912, Public Record Office, London, Committee of Imperial Defence, Memoranda, Colonial Defence (hereafter cited as Cab. 5)/3/1.

[36] CID. Paper no. 93-C. "1. The Attack on Cyprus by Austria; 2, The Defence of Cyprus," 9 May 1912, Asquith MSS, box 107.

spared from the existing garrison to resist external aggression and, once the Mediterranean was closed to the transport of reinforcements from England, it would take four to six weeks for reinforcements of two to three divisions to arrive from India. By then it was estimated that Turkey could have landed 10,000 men at Alexandria; have 23,000 men coming overland from Syria within four days' march of the Suez Canal; and have another 10,000 landing at Tinch Tay, to the east of Port Said. The General Staff considered a peacetime garrison of 30,000 necessary to ensure the safety of Egypt until the arrival of reinforcements from India.[37]

There was a more hopeful memorandum by the Board of Trade, on the effects of the cessation for a period of two months of all trade in British bottoms in the Mediterranean and Black Sea and a diversion of the Far Eastern and Australian trade in British bottoms from the Mediterranean route to the Cape. Aside from inconveniences, some delay at the outset, and an increase in freight charges, there was no reason to anticipate any very serious effects from the diversion to the Cape route of those foodstuffs and raw materials drawn from countries beyond the Mediterranean; nor would the temporary cessation of such trade with the Mediterranean itself cause a serious disturbance in British trade, although there would doubtless be appreciable immediate difficulties.[38]

Early in May, Cambon hinted to the Foreign Office that the French naval attaché was ready to resume conversations.[39] When Saint-Seine saw Churchill he was told that, in view of the new dispositions to be discussed, the subject would have to wait until after the Whitsuntide recess. Grey considered this enough for the present.[40] The question was discussed in the Cabinet and, after it became apparent that the whole Mediterranean situation had to be resurveyed, postponed until after the Prime Minister's trip.[41] The departure of Asquith and Churchill for Genoa, where they were to join the *Enchantress*, was the signal for a new wave of speculation in the press. The *Times* in its Empire Day edition carried a lengthy article by its military correspondent implying that the Mediterranean garrisons were inadequate.[42] Criticisms of the naval concentration had also ap-

[37] CID. Paper no. 149-B, "1. The Attack on Egypt by Turkey; 2. The Defence of Egypt against External Aggression," 9 May 1912, *ibid.*; CID. Paper no. 146-B, "Considerations on which the Existing Arrangements for the Defence of Egypt are Based," 6 May 1912, Cab. 4/4/33.

[38] CID. Paper no. 150-B, "British Trade in the Mediterranean Sea," May 1912, *ibid.*

[39] Nicolson to Grey, 4 May 1912, *BD*, X (pt. 2), no. 383, pp. 582–583.

[40] Memorandum by Churchill, 14 May 1912, *ibid.*, no. 398, pp. 591–592.

[41] Asquith to King George, 17 May 1912, Asquith MSS, box 6.

[42] "The Mediterranean—Ministers and Lord Kitchener at Malta," *The Times*, 24 May 1912.

peared in the service periodicals. It was argued that Churchill's estimates had taken into account only Germany and not the Triple Alliance. One writer criticized the concentration in home waters as not sufficiently appreciating the needs of Empire, using the analogy, "The heart is undoubtedly the most important, but if the limbs are atrophied it must react upon the heart." [43]

The information that the *Enchantress* would call at Bizerte on her way home caused a new flurry of speculation over a possible alliance with France.[44] The Liberal press in general was opposed to the idea of an alliance. The Conservative press was more favorable, but also more inclined to stress the obligations of Empire, and sharpest in its criticism of any "abandonment" of the Mediterranean.[45] The debate in the British press was naturally picked up and commented upon in the French press, and these remarks in turn were discussed in the British press. *Figaro* (May 26) considered the British naval dispositions an indication that the defense of the Mediterranean was henceforth delegated to France's squadrons.[46] *Le Temps* (May 27) expressed the opinion that the introduction of compulsory military service in England was the necessary corollary of an alliance with France.[47] The question of whether or not England was willing to reorganize her military strength to provide an army on the level with those of the continental powers was also raised in the *Aurore*. Several of the French correspondents in London informed their papers that while a certain section of British public opinion, particularly Conservative circles, might be favorable to alliance proposals, this was not true of the majority of the people—an opinion also held by some officials in the Foreign Office.[48] The question of a British obligation on land in return for France's Mediterranean services was a touchy one. Sir Francis Bertie, British ambassador to France, warned that one could expect the French to make use of England's desertion of the Mediterranean to extract some tangible concession.[49] A scathing comment on the press discussions in England and especially France was given by George Grahame, secretary at the Paris embassy,

[43] Admiral Sir E. R. Fremantle, "The Navy Estimates," *United Service Magazine*, no. 1002 (May 1912), p. 117. A warning that by the summer of 1914 the Triple Alliance might have a large superiority over France in completed dreadnoughts was given by Percival A. Hislam, "The Navy Estimates and Naval Policy," *ibid.*, p. 129.

[44] "Great Britain and France—Present and Future Relations—Conditions of Cooperation," *The Times*, 27 May 1912, p. 7.

[45] Marder, *Dreadnought to Scapa Flow*, I, 289–290.

[46] Carnegie to Grey, 26 May 1912, FO 371, vol. 1367, France, no. 22488.

[47] Carnegie to Grey, 27 May 1912, *ibid.*, no. 22490.

[48] Carnegie to Grey, 28 May 1912, and minute by G. H. Villiers, 29 May, *ibid.*, no. 22822.

[49] Bertie to Nicolson, 9 May 1912, *BD*, X (pt. 2), no. 388, p. 591.

in a private letter to William Tyrrell, Grey's private secretary. Grahame indignantly refuted the idea that the French should be "paid" for guarding the Mediterranean with British land support on their eastern frontier. As for guarding the Mediterranean, Grahame declared the French would like nothing better and were already talking of the "Empire de la Méditerranée." The security of France's northern coasts, brought about by the British naval concentration in the North Sea, was sufficient "payment." [50]

While the press of both countries occupied itself in diverse conjectures, Asquith, Churchill, and Prince Louis of Battenberg, the Second Sea Lord, cruised the sunny waters of the Mediterranean. The trip had some of the aspects of a holiday for the *Enchantress* called at Elba, Naples, Agropoli, and Syracuse before reaching Malta. Asquith was reported to have spent his time "immersed in a Baedeker Guide"; Churchill spoke of nothing but the sea and the navy.[51] The two-day visit of the *Enchantress* to Naples was arranged to give the First Lord an opportunity to see Fisher. Churchill had used Fisher as an unofficial adviser but was reluctant to call him back as First Sea Lord for fear of reviving the feuds that had arisen during Fisher's term of office; also, the admiral was now over seventy. Fisher preferred to live abroad and help Churchill through correspondence in order to avoid delicate personality questions and other embarrassments that might have resulted had he remained in England. A frequent exchange of letters took place between the two.[52] Fisher, having himself started the movement of the fleet toward home waters, naturally approved of Churchill's reorganization scheme. He had long been an advocate of Alexandria instead of Malta as the Mediterranean base and thought that the development of the submarine would make heavy warships unnecessary in that sea: "Let the French take care of the Mediterranean, and a hot time they'll have of it with submarines poking about in that lake! We are well out of it." [53] Fisher came on board as soon as the *Enchantress* docked and was immediately closeted with Churchill.[54] The talk obviously ranged far beyond the Mediterranean problem, for the First Lord wanted Fisher to be chair-

[50] Grahame to Tyrrell, 27 May 1912, Grey MSS, Public Record Office, London, FO 800, vol. 52.

[51] Rear Adm. W. S. Chalmers, *The Life and Letters of David, Earl Beatty* (London, 1951), p. 211. For the delightful memoirs of another passenger aboard the *Enchantress* see Violet Bonham Carter, *Winston Churchill: An Intimate Portrait* (New York, 1965), pp. 202, 209f.

[52] A. J. Marder, *Fear God and Dread Nought: The Correspondence of Admiral of the Fleet Lord Fisher of Kilverstone*, II: *The Years of Power, 1904–1914* (London, 1956), 401–402.

[53] Fisher to Churchill, 5 Mar. 1912, *ibid.*, p. 437.

[54] Beatty to his wife, 24 May 1912, Chalmers, *Life and Letters of Beatty*, p. 114.

man of a proposed royal commission that was to examine the problems involved in a conversion from coal to oil as fuel in the Royal Navy.[55]

Unfortunately, since the Malta talks (May 29–June 1) were not a formal meeting of the CID, there is no record of them in the regular CID minutes. Kitchener was delighted at the opportunity for "some fresh air" and a cruise on a warship.[56] He surprised Churchill and the admirals by his grasp of the naval detail that he used to support his demands for what he considered to be necessary naval strength in the Mediterranean.[57] The Sea Lords were anxious to reduce this to the lowest possible figures, but Kitchener received some support from Asquith.[58] It was considered essential to reach a definite agreement with France whereby England would defend the French northern coast so that France could concentrate her fleet in the Mediterranean together with a sufficient number of British warships to ensure victory over Italy and Austria in a war with the Triple Alliance. The Admiralty agreed to maintain permanently in the Mediterranean two and preferably three battle cruisers in addition to an armored cruiser squadron, two ships of which were to be of the large "Devonshire" class (10,850 tons). The remaining pair were also to be of this class as soon as circumstances permitted. The battle squadron based on Gibraltar, then four "Duncans," was to be increased to eight ships by the end of 1913. It was to cruise in the Mediterranean but would be available in home waters in case of war with Germany.[59] All smaller ships then in the Mediterranean were to be retained for "diplomatic purposes," and the Malta submarine flotilla—and if necessary the destroyer flotilla—would be increased to provide a system of local defense. A flotilla of long-range submarines was to be established at Alexandria, with an old battleship manned by a nucleus crew to serve as parent ship. A wireless station would be established there, together with a fort to protect it

[55] Marder, *Fear God and Dread Nought*, II, 404–405; Fisher to Fiennes, 28 May 1912, *ibid.*, II, 465.

[56] Beatty to his wife, 29 May 1912, Chalmers, *Life and Letters of Beatty*, p. 115. With tragic irony the cruiser placed at Lord Kitchener's disposal was the *Hampshire,* the same ship on which Kitchener was lost after she struck a mine in 1916.

[57] Haldane to Grey, 10 June 1912, Haldane MSS, vol. 5909; Sir George Arthur, *Life of Lord Kitchener* (London, 1920), II, 336–337; Chalmers, *Life and Letters of Beatty,* p. 115.

[58] Kitchener to Grey, 2 June 1912, *BD*, X (pt. 2), no. 392, p. 594.

[59] *Ibid.*, pp. 594–595. This had been foreseen by Churchill in his March statement. The two "Lord Nelsons" were to join the squadron around January or February 1913 as crews became available. This would make a rather hybrid squadron of one dreadnought; two semi-dreadnoughts; and five old "Duncans." See Churchill's memorandum, "Naval Situation in the Mediterranean," 15 June 1912, Asquith MSS, box 107. Kitchener had understood that eventually the whole squadron would be of the dreadnought type. See *BD*, X (pt. 2), no. 392, p. 595.

and the harbor. Its armament, together with complete mountings, would be provided by the Admiralty. The Malta dockyard was to be maintained at its present complement, and the Admiralty agreed to provide four gunboats for the Suez Canal when necessary.

Kitchener considered that under the circumstances these were the best arrangements that the Sea Lords would agree to. All British defense schemes, after all, had stipulated that the Mediterranean Fleet was to be removed in time of war. But Kitchener asked Grey to push for certain points he had been unable to obtain even with Asquith's support. Grey was to insist on three instead of two battle cruisers, and the armored cruiser squadron was to be a homogeneous one composed of the larger "Devonshires." Furthermore, he wanted the battle squadron based on Gibraltar not to be removed from the Mediterranean in peacetime without the concurrence of the Foreign Office. Kitchener had also stressed to Asquith the importance of an entente with Turkey once the Tripolitan War was ended.[60] Haldane, who received an account of the meeting from General Ian Hamilton, Inspector General of Overseas Forces, thought that "we must now back up K's [Kitchener's] *maximum* for all we are worth." [61]

On her way back to England the *Enchantress* visited Bizerte and Tunis, adding fuel to the press speculations about an alliance with France. Since this was officially an inspection trip, a day-long visit was also made to Gibraltar, where the Board of Admiralty inspected the dockyard, and the Prime Minister and Churchill took the opportunity to confer with the Governor and Sir Maurice de Bunsen, British ambassador to Spain, who had been summoned for the occasion. Bunsen stressed the importance of keeping Spain in the right camp and encouraging her to resist the perennial temptation to seek refuge from France in Germany. As an enemy she could create, with the aid of foreign artillery, an unpleasant situation at Gibraltar. By massing her army on her northern frontier, she could immobilize a French army corps; and to have the Canary Islands in hostile hands would obviously be dangerous. Fortunately, as long as she was assured fair play, Spain preferred to stay on the British side.[62]

The *Enchantress* docked at Portsmouth on June 10. The Prime Minister's three-week "holiday" was over and he again faced the daily cares of government business. At Malta Kitchener had reached a compromise agree-

---

[60] Kitchener to Grey, 2 June 1912, *BD*, X (pt. 2), no. 392, p. 594.

[61] Haldane to Grey, 10 June 1912, Haldane MSS, vol. 5909.

[62] De Bunsen to Nicolson, 8 June 1912, *BD* X (pt. 2), no. 393, p. 595. The ambassador also favored facing the necessary expenditure to make the Mediterranean secure, rather than relying on positive alliances with anyone. See also E.T.S. Dugdale, *Maurice de Bunsen: Diplomat and Friend* (London, 1934), p. 268.

ment with the Admiralty. Churchill was now faced with the problem of making it acceptable to the Cabinet, and to a Parliament and a country quite agitated by all the public discussion of the Mediterranean problem.

Churchill's ability with the pen was a great asset to the Admiralty, for the young First Lord was able to prepare persuasive papers that could be printed and circulated to the Cabinet. In a memorandum, "Naval Situation in the Mediterranean," dated June 15 the Admiralty's policy was clearly, cogently, and candidly explained.[63] The German fleet was the crux of the matter. The minimum number of fully commissioned ships to be maintained by Great Britain was to be thirty-three vis-à-vis the twenty-five provided by the new German naval law. The Admiralty could not afford to keep the six Mediterranean battleships in full commission. It was not so much the ships but the men that were wanted. Much stronger ships were being laid up at home with only skeleton crews in order to man the Mediterranean battleships. The Third Battle Squadron, comprising the eight "King Edwards," had been created for the First Fleet and was to be kept in full commission. If the Atlantic Fleet had not been brought home, and the Mediterranean battleships moved to Gibraltar in its place, it would have been necessary to lay up the "King Edwards" ship by ship in order to man the five new vessels that would be ready to join the fleet within the next twelve months.[64] The four Mediterranean "Duncans" (14,000 tons) were completed in 1903–04, with a primary armament of four 12-inch guns, and the two other ex-Mediterranean battleships, the *Triumph* and the *Swiftsure* (11,800 tons), were completed in June 1904, with a primary armament of four 10-inch guns. In contrast, the "King Edward VII" class (16,350 tons), completed in 1905–07, had a primary armament of four 12-inch and four 9.2-inch guns. Newer and more powerful than the "Duncans" or "Swiftsures," their maintenance in full commission and concentration in the decisive theater was obviously a clear gain for the Royal Navy.

In addition, Churchill wrote, the utility of the Mediterranean Fleet's battleships was almost exhausted. Within a few months the first Italian dreadnought would be ready, and by January 1915 there would be ten

[63] Asquith MSS, box 107.

[64] The old battleships of the former Atlantic Fleet of the "Formidable" and "London" classes (completed 1901–1904) were reduced to skeleton crews. Technically, the real saving in personnel occurred here rather than with the Mediterranean ships. Oscar Parkes, *British Battleships* (London, 1956), pp. 407, 410–411.

Austrian and Italian dreadnoughts in service.[65] A comparison of the ships supports Churchill's argument. The first of the Italian dreadnoughts, the *Dante Alighieri* (18,300 tons), had a speed of twenty-three knots and a primary armament of twelve 12-inch guns, and the three ships of the "Conte de Cavour" class (21,500 tons), already afloat, were to have thirteen 12-inch guns. The four Austrian dreadnoughts—the first of which, the *Viribus Unitis* (20,000 tons), was close to completion—were also to have twelve 12-inch guns; the three older "Radetzkys" (14,226 tons), though not dreadnoughts, had the relatively powerful armament of four 12-inch and eight 9.4-inch guns.[66] Against this sort of competition, the old "Duncans" and "Swiftsures" were clearly outclassed. When just two of the Austrian dreadnoughts were completed, the Austrian fleet alone would be stronger than the British Mediterranean Fleet, at least on paper. The British faced the danger of being overwhelmed in a subsidiary theater when their crews might have manned better ships in the decisive theater. In Churchill's words:

> It would be both wrong and futile to leave the present battle squadron at Malta *to keep up appearances*. It would be a bluff which would deceive nobody. The influence and authority of the Mediterranean Fleet is going to cease, not because of the withdrawal of the Malta battleships, but because of the completion of the Austrian and Italian Dreadnoughts. It will cease certainly and soon whether the Malta battleships are withdrawn or not, only in the latter case we shall have more to lose in a subsidiary theatre and less to win with in the decisive theatre . . . This fact is perfectly appreciated by every General Staff in Europe. The power will have passed automatically to others, and only the empty but expensive symbols will remain. The Malta battleships left in the Mediterranean will in time of peace be only a pretence of strength which everyone would see through; and in time of war, a loss serious in themselves—still more serious by their subtraction from the decisive sphere.[67]

To maintain a purely British supremacy in the Mediterranean as well as adequate margins in the North Sea would require construction of a

[65] Actually this was an excessive estimate. As a result of construction delays in Italy, and to a lesser extent in Austria, the total by January 1915 was only six, a matter which was far less critical following the Italian declaration of neutrality at the outbreak of the war.

[66] Data from *The Naval Annual, 1912.*

[67] Memorandum by Churchill, 15 June 1912. See also Memorandum by Rear Admiral E. C. T. Troubridge, Chief of the War Staff, "Conditional Mediterranean Requirements, 1915, 1914, 1913," 28 June 1912, Asquith MSS, box 107.

new squadron of modern battleships. Churchill considered this extravagant and not necessary for the fundamental safety of the British Empire or its ultimate victory and supremacy at sea. But the alternative did not really exist. Even if Parliament voted funds for the construction of a special Mediterranean dreadnought squadron, it could not be completed in time and trained officers and seamen could not be provided for it. The fact had to be faced that "the naval control of the Mediterranean is swiftly passing from our hands whatever we do, while we remain single-handed." The Royal Navy must therefore adopt the role of a weaker naval power in the Mediterranean, falling back on the torpedo instead of the gun as the primary weapon. It was hoped that the strong destroyer and submarine flotillas to be established at Malta would give that base the reputation of a hornet's nest, so that Austria and Italy would not care to pay the possibly disproportionate cost in heavy ships and transports that capture of the island would entail. A submarine flotilla to be established at Alexandria would serve the same deterrent purpose for an invasion of Egypt by sea. The submarines were to have a sufficient radius of action to enable them to threaten the Dardanelles as well as cover the approaches to the Suez Canal. Alexandria must, however, be provided with a defended harbor in order to resist an attack by armored vessels. It was hoped that these flotillas, along with the cruiser squadron to be left in the Mediterranean for diplomatic purposes, would suffice to influence the Turks in other, less important, matters.

The entire situation changed when France was taken into account. The French fleet, if supported by an adequate British naval force and enjoying the use of British bases as well as its own, would be superior to any Austro-Italian combination. Full control of the Mediterranean would be maintained and the necessary protection given to British and French territorial and commercial interests without impairing British margins in the North Sea. For these reasons, Churchill recommended that a definite naval arrangement, to come into force only if the two powers were allies in war, should be made with France.[68]

The naval War Staff was less enthusiastic than Churchill about a permanent arrangement with France; enlargement of the Royal Navy to the extent necessary to maintain its position in the face of the Triple Alliance would be "more satisfactory from every point of view except that of expense," since it "would provide the Imperial interests involved with a much more stable foundation." It was recognized that though submarine and destroyer flotillas might provide local defense, they could not protect the

[68] Churchill's memorandum, 15 June 1912.

eastern trade route if it was exposed to attack by heavy warships. Yet diversion of traffic to the Cape route, according to the War Staff, would involve "immense financial losses." In dreadnoughts built or building, the Triple Alliance had the slight advantage of 30:27 over Britain. But Britain could partially offset this by the advantage of a single fleet working on interior lines over fleets not used to working with one another and having widely scattered bases. As for the future, the War Staff thought the position could be made secure from 1915 onward without "extraneous assistance" (from France) if the necessary extra ships were laid down in the current financial year and the necessary extra men enlisted. For a superiority of 25 percent in home waters and a reasonable equality in the Mediterranean in 1915, it would be necessary to begin ten additional battleships at once, or buy the six battleships building or projected in British yards for foreign powers and lay down four more. The extra personnel required would number around six thousand. In the interim, of course, the French fleet would be reinforced by whatever battle cruisers that could be spared.[69]

Churchill did not advocate building ships to match the entire Triple Alliance force, possibly because he realized that the argument advanced by the naval War Staff became completely untenable if either Austria or Italy increased their building programs. As an increase by one would almost be sure to provoke retaliatory building by the other, Great Britain could be drawn into almost unlimited naval construction should she try to keep up. He must also have realized that a Liberal government would hardly accept this. Instead Churchill concentrated on the practical question of what addition of strength to the French fleet would be necessary to assure its superiority over an Austro-Italian combination. At the moment the French fleet alone was slightly superior to this combination, but during 1913 and 1914 it would fall to the same level as the total of the two powers in terms of modern units and would not be restored to superiority until October 1915, assuming no increase in the present Austro-Italian programs.[70] To assure the French of at least equality in dreadnoughts, the Admiralty proposed to send two battle cruisers to the Mediterranean. It was felt they were the ships that could best be spared from home waters. There were no ships like them in the Mediterranean, nor were any of the

[69] "War Staff Memorandum on the Mediterranean Situation," 21 June 1912, Admiralty Archives, case 0091. Also "Conditional Mediterranean Requirements," 28 June 1912, Asquith MSS, box 107.

[70] Churchill's memorandum, 15 June 1912. The question of what ships to consider "modern units" would naturally be subject to different interpretations. Here it reflects Admiralty thinking.

Mediterranean powers projecting battle cruisers. The two to be sent were "Invincibles" (17,250 tons), which had been completed in 1908. They were fast (25 knots) and carried the heavy armament of eight 12-inch guns and sixteen 4-inchers. As battle cruisers, however, they had relatively thin armor protection, a fact that was to have disastrous results at the battle of Jutland.[71] At the time it was thought that their speed and power would enable them to look after themselves in all eventualities, and to concentrate at home in a minimum of time if necessary. Their large and powerful appearance, plus the fact that the battle cruiser class had caught the public imagination, made them valuable for reasons of prestige as well as for purely naval purposes. After proposing the cruisers, Churchill was careful to add that some new construction would be required to compensate for sending them out to the Mediterranean.

Of the various possible contingencies, the Admiralty considered that the proposed deployment would "secure" the Mediterranean in case of war between Britain and France against Germany and Austria. It would be "adequate" if Britain and France—and possibly Russia—were opposed to the entire Triple Alliance. In the less probable situation of Britain alone at war against Germany and Austria, it was thought that by good management Britain could maintain herself simultaneously in both theaters—the North Sea and the Mediterranean—once mobilization was complete; but until a decision was reached in the North Sea many risks would have to be taken in the Mediterranean. In the improbable contingency of Britain alone against the entire Triple Alliance, the situation "would then be grave" with certain heavy losses in the Mediterranean, although a meeting between the hostile Mediterranean fleets (Austria and Italy) and the German fleet could probably be prevented, and each could be attacked separately with superior strength.[72] This was a far cry from the casual acceptance of the same possibility in the 1908 war plans and reflects how far the situation had altered to Great Britain's disadvantage in only four years.

After Churchill had presented his memorandum to the Cabinet on June 19, his predecessor as First Lord, Reginald McKenna, now Secretary of State for Home Affairs, strongly dissented and volunteered to prepare a memorandum of his own. Many in the Cabinet had not yet digested Churchill's paper and the question was adjourned.[73] Churchill's scheme involved the acceptance of the unpleasant fact that Great Britain was no

---

[71] Parkes, *British Battleships*, pp. 492–496.
[72] Churchill's memorandum, 15 June 1912.
[73] Asquith to King George, 20 June 1912, Asquith MSS, box 6.

longer able to safeguard the Mediterranean on her own, and there was strong opposition to it in the Cabinet and official circles. Lord Esher was particularly vocal, and in a series of letters to the King he advocated the necessary increase of the fleet to avoid withdrawal from the Mediterranean. He thought any attempt to rely on the naval forces of others would be illusory.[74] King George gave evidence of his concern when he directed his private secretary, Lord Knollys, to remind Asquith that he had promised, should Churchill's scheme be agreed to by the Cabinet, that it would be brought before the CID before becoming final.[75] Outside of the government, influential people such as Lord Lansdowne, Foreign Secretary in the last Conservative government, and Lord Cromer, former consul-general and de facto viceroy of Egypt, were eloquent opponents of the Admiralty's plans.[76]

Fisher returned to England in mid-June and jumped into the fray on Churchill's side. He sent Lord Stamfordham, the King's other private secretary, a copy of a paper originally prepared for Churchill in which he argued that the development of the submarine precluded the presence of heavy ships of war and the passage of trade through the Mediterranean, as well as the capture of Malta by an invading force (whose troop-laden transports would be vulnerable targets). Fisher, as might be expected, argued in favor of reducing the Mediterranean force in order to add to the North Sea margin. His theme was, "We cannot have everything or be strong everywhere." [77] Fisher also tried to see Grey at the Foreign Office, missed him, and settled for expounding his views to Sir Arthur Nicolson, another opponent of Churchill's policy. The Permanent Undersecretary thought that Fisher was considering only naval questions, and on these he could give no opinion.

Nicolson was in an awkward position over the forthcoming CID meeting, where the Foreign Office paper was on the agenda. In his opinion Churchill's recent memorandum did not remove or weaken any of the Foreign Office objections. If Grey, whose opinion was naturally decisive in Foreign Office affairs, accepted Churchill's proposals as at least a pro-

[74] Paper of late May enclosed in a letter from Esher to King George, 30 May 1912. Cited by Marder, *Dreadnought to Scapa Flow*, I, 290–291. See also Vice Admiral Sir Peter Gretton, *Former Naval Person: Winston Churchill and the Royal Navy* (London, 1968), pp. 133–134.

[75] Knollys to Asquith, 21 June 1912, Asquith MSS, box 3.

[76] Lansdowne to Cromer, 24 July 1912; Cox to Cromer, 25 July 1912; Gertrude Bell to Cromer, 12 Aug. 1912. In PRO, Cromer MSS, FO 633, vol. XXI, pp. 159–160, 164–165.

[77] Memorandum enclosed in letter from Fisher to Stamfordham, 25 June 1912, Marder, *Fear God and Dread Nought*, II, 468–469.

visional solution, it would be unseemly for Nicolson to advocate his own opinions at the meeting. He did not, however, want to remain silent, for he did not at all acquiesce in what he termed the "Malta compromise." To avoid an embarrassing situation, he was disposed not to attend the meeting.[78]

The Cabinet spent its entire sitting of June 27 on the naval problem. No conclusion was reached, and Churchill was asked to provide exact figures on British and foreign naval strength for the next three years.[79] Papers by Churchill and McKenna, refuting each other's arguments, were circulated. McKenna suggested basing the eight "King Edwards" together with the Mediterranean cruiser squadron at Malta, with the eight "Formidables" and a cruiser squadron at Gibraltar. This force would suffice in 1914 to protect Malta, Gibraltar, and the Mediterranean and Portuguese coastal trade routes against the combined Italian and Austrian fleets. McKenna claimed that the preponderance of Britain's strength in other waters was great enough to permit reinforcement in the Mediterranean if necessary. He stressed the danger of the Austrians and Italians establishing themselves off the Portuguese coast to control that vital trade route. With the Gibraltar fleet concentrated in home waters in case of war with Germany, there would be nothing to prevent them from also cutting off the North American trade route. Churchill's promise that the navy would return to the Mediterranean in force once the German fleet had been destroyed was hardly reassuring, since the Germans might well choose to remain in their harbors while Great Britain's trade was destroyed. Obviously an alliance with France was an essential feature of Churchill's strategy, and McKenna would far rather see the fleet increased in ships and men—if this were necessary, which he could not believe—than be driven by weakness into dependence on a foreign power.[80]

McKenna submitted his paper to King George who appeared to have been influenced by it. Prince Louis of Battenberg lunched with the King on June 30 and found him "in complete ignorance of the naval aspect." Prince Louis remarked that it was "sad to think that our Sailor King stands on McK's [McKenna's] level as a naval strategist," and urged Churchill to lose no time in putting his reply before the King.[81] The First Lord immediately sent copies of his relevant memoranda.

[78] Nicolson to Grey, 30 June 1912, Grey MSS, FO 800, vol. 93. The minutes of the CID meeting list Nicolson as being present.

[79] Asquith to King George, 28 June 1912, Asquith MSS, box 6.

[80] Memorandum by R. McKenna, 24 June 1912, Asquith MSS, box 107.

[81] Battenberg to Churchill, 1 July 1912; Churchill to King George, 2 July 1912; Randolph S. Churchill, Winston S. Churchill Companion Volume II, pt. 3, 1911–1914 (Boston, 1969), pp. 1584–1585.

Churchill was easily able to refute McKenna's proposals for the Mediterranean. The eight "Formidables" that the Home Secretary wanted to bring to Gibraltar would be "in circumstances of serious inferiority" in a general action when compared to the foreign dreadnoughts coming into service. This would be true even if they succeeded in uniting with the "King Edwards," a task far from easy in the face of superior strength. McKenna's dispositions would divide the British forces between two theaters of war so "as to make victory doubtful in the Northern and decisive theatre, and defeat certain in the Southern." [82] To maintain the eight "Formidables" in full commission would entail reducing to skeleton crews ships needed in home waters, particularly the armored cruisers.[83] McKenna's bugbear of the Austro-Italian interference with the Atlantic trade routes was dismissed by pointing out its obvious fallacy. The Admiralty did not think it likely that the Austrians and Italians would "run the gauntlet" of the Gibraltar submarine and destroyer flotillas to enter the Atlantic, where they would lack harbors, coal, and supplies. McKenna's reply to this was weak on its naval points and concentrated on what the Home Secretary considered the cardinal point, dependence on France for safeguarding British interests in the Mediterranean. He wanted to know what the French would ask in return, and warned that as a result British colonies and trade would "depend for their security not on British power, but French goodwill." [84]

The meeting of the CID on July 4 concerned itself exclusively with the Mediterranean. More than twenty members were present, including Fisher and A. K. Wilson. The meeting lasted nearly all day and debate was hot. Fisher reported that "McKenna and Winston were tearing each other's eyes out the whole time." [85] The First Lord defended his position, emphasizing how the building of dreadnoughts by Austria and Italy had revolutionized the situation and how the crews of the former Mediterranean battleships were needed at home. McKenna, in turn, argued that the "King Edwards" would be an adequate force in the Mediterranean for the next two years and that it was unlikely the Austrian and Italian fleets could fight as a homogeneous unit. McKenna repeatedly implied that the

[82] Memorandum by Churchill, "The Naval Situation," 25 June 1912, Asquith MSS, box 107.

[83] Actually McKenna meant the three "Formidables" (15,000 tons), completed 1901–02, and the five similar "London" class (15,000 tons), completed 1902–04. Both classes were capable of 18 knots and had an armament of four 12-inch, twelve 6-inch, and sixteen 12-pounder. Most of them had just been reduced to skeleton crews after having formed the Atlantic Fleet at Gibraltar, Parkes, *British Battleships*, pp. 403–411.

[84] Memorandum by McKenna, 3 July 1912, Asquith MSS, box 107.

[85] Fisher to his son Cecil V. Fisher, 5 July 1912, Marder, *Fear God and Dread Nought*, II, 470–471; see also Callwell, *Sir Henry Wilson*, I, 115; Maurice V. Brett and Oliver Viscount Esher, *Journals and Letters of Reginald Viscount Esher* (4 vols. London, 1934–1938), III, 100–101.

margin the Admiralty proposed to maintain in the north was excessive, stressing among other things what he considered the individual superiority of British ships over their German counterparts. David Lloyd George, Chancellor of the Exchequer, also thought the margin a large one. Lewis Harcourt, the Colonial Secretary, spoke of Churchill's scheme in relation to Mediterranean trade, possible loss of Malta, and other damage to imperial interests. General Sir John French, Chief of the Imperial General Staff, introduced the consideration that the papers prepared by the General Staff for the Malta conference had been drafted in haste and that the necessary increases in the Malta and Egyptian garrisons had been underestimated. If the fleet was withdrawn, instead of seven to eight battalions, Malta would probably require a division and most of the mobile artillery. To hold Egypt for two months against a Turkish attack, about four divisions would be needed. Churchill and Fisher were able to dispose of the argument about a threat to Malta by pointing out that the torpedo and submarine defenses would make an attack by a large force too expensive. In this they received effective support from General Ian Hamilton, who had been present at the recent maneuvers at Malta where the cruiser *Suffolk* with a battalion of the garrison aboard had been torpedoed twice by a submarine before getting close enough to land her troops.[86]

Admiral A. K. Wilson, when asked by the Prime Minister what his proposed standard for the Mediterranean had been while he was First Sea Lord, replied that he had never calculated on having to reckon with the Italians, but he had expected to reconsider the position toward the Austrians in 1913 and make whatever additions were necessary in the building program to maintain equality in battleships against Austria. Fisher considered a force equal to that proposed at Gibraltar—the Fourth Battle Squadron—sufficient, for he had confidence in the power of the submarines based on Malta, Alexandria, and Gibraltar to dominate the narrow waters; he did not believe that trade could pass through the Mediterranean in time of war in any case; and he judged by the Board of Trade memorandum that diversion to the Cape route would not be a problem. Churchill pointed out that, although the Board of Admiralty did not agree with Fisher that the submarine could deny the open waters of the Mediterranean to battleships, they did agree that in wartime it might become very precarious as a trade route. Churchill contended that, with the German fleet only twelve hours' steaming distance away, the Royal

---

[86] CID, Minutes of the 117th Meeting, 4 July 1912, pp. 6–8, 10–11, Asquith MSS, box 132. See also Fisher to Esher, 6 July 1912, Marder, *Fear God and Dread Nought,* II, 471.

Navy always had to be ready. Grey supported him against Lloyd George's doubts about the possibility of a sudden German attack, by agreeing that a diplomatic crisis could be manufactured overnight. The Foreign Secretary concurred that diplomacy could be of no help in the actual protection of the United Kingdom, which must depend entirely on the navy. But diplomacy could prevent too powerful a combination against the country elsewhere. For this it must have an effective weight behind it, and Grey suggested a one-power standard with a fleet that was free to operate in the Mediterranean as required. He added, "It would be better based on Malta, but that was not essential; freedom of movement was, and its freedom of movement should be emphasized on every occasion." [87] Churchill warned that if the Committee failed to agree to the Admiralty's margin for the North Sea, he would feel it his duty to rouse the country. Brigadier General Wilson took this as a threat that "clinched the matter." [88] The Committee came to the conclusion: "There must always be provided a reasonable margin of superior strength ready and available in Home waters. This is the first requirement. Subject to this we ought to maintain available for Mediterranean purposes and based on a Mediterranean port, a battle fleet equal to a one-Power Mediterranean standard excluding France." [89]

The outcome of the meeting represented a partial victory for both sides. Those who resolutely opposed any abandonment of the Mediterranean rejoiced that, as Esher wrote to the King, the principle of maintaining a Mediterranean fleet of battleships had been recognized, or so he thought.[90] Because the outcome was so much better than he had anticipated, General Wilson "was quite pleased, though not quite satisfied." [91] On the other side, the ebullient Fisher, writing to his son, declared that when he could get Admiral Wilson to agree with him, "we are just irresistible! . . . We just 'wiped' the soldiers clean out yesterday." To Esher he wrote, "I expect you will see that the course of action will inevitably result in what I ventured to indicate, IF ONLY the Admiralty will keep their backs to the wall, of the irreducible margin required in Home Waters." [92] This was a shrewd observation by Fisher because the details for implementing the CID conclusion were to be settled by the Cabinet and the Admiralty. At

[87] CID, Minutes of the 117th Meeting, pp. 13–14, 16.

[88] Callwell, *Sir Henry Wilson*, I, 115. Callwell quotes from Wilson's diary.

[89] CID, Minutes of the 117th Meeting, p. 16.

[90] Esher to King George, 4 July 1912, cited by Marder, *Dreadnought to Scapa Flow*, I, 294.

[91] Callwell, *Sir Henry Wilson*, I, 115.

[92] Fisher to C. V. Fisher, 5 July 1912, and Fisher to Esher, 6 July, Marder, *Fear God and Dread Nought*, II, 470–471.

first this might look like a tactical setback for Churchill, since a force equal to a one-power Mediterranean standard—meaning Austria— must certainly be more than the two or three battle cruisers that the Admiralty and Lord Kitchener had agreed upon at Malta. On the other hand, the demands of McKenna for a Mediterranean battle fleet of eight "King Edwards," with the "Formidables" and "Londons" at Gibraltar, were cast aside. Most important of all, the Admiralty had secured the recognition of a reasonable margin of superior strength in home waters as the first requirement. This left the Admiralty with much ground for maneuver: armed with the charts and statistics at their disposal, they would obviously have a major say in deciding exactly what the reasonable margin would be. Contrary to Lord Esher's belief, the Admiralty had not been specifically committed to providing battleships for the Mediterranean. In fact, right up to the outbreak of the war, the actual force maintained permanently in the Mediterranean, as opposed to squadrons detached for temporary service, was to be very close to the figures agreed upon at Malta.

The Cabinet provisionally accepted the CID conclusion the following day, and Churchill was charged with preparation of the necessary plans.[93] On July 9 the *Pall Mall Gazette* reported the CID's adoption of a one-power Mediterranean standard, perhaps justifying Fisher's suspicion of "leakage" in the Committee.[94] Speaking in Commons on July 10, Grey hinted at the policy to be adopted when he renounced any abandonment of the Mediterranean but questioned the necessity of keeping a force equal to all the other fleets. Great Britain, he argued, wants "to keep a sufficient naval force available for use in the Mediterranean at any moment to count as one of the Mediterranean Naval Powers." [95]

The CID met again on July 11. Present at this meeting were Robert L. Borden, Prime Minister of Canada, and a few members of his Cabinet. In reviewing the Mediterranean situation, Grey pointed out that England was on friendly terms with both Italy and Austria, whose interests conflicted more with each other's than with Great Britain's. Were Great Britain to be opposed in the Mediterranean by more than one power, it would be as a result of causes that would bring France in on her side. Therefore the adoption of only a one-power Mediterranean standard was justified. Churchill then surveyed the naval situation in detail for the Canadians, starting with the North Sea and eventually passing on to the Mediterranean. In discussing Austria, the crucial date cited was 1909, when that

---

93 Asquith to King George, 5 July and 10 July 1912, Asquith MSS, box 6.
94 Marder, *Fear God and Dread Nought*, II, 471 n. 1.
95 *The Parliamentary Debates* (Commons), 5th ser., XL, 1993.

country began to build dreadnoughts—an unprecedented step since Austria was not menaced in any way by sea and had no overseas possessions to guard. The first ships were begun secretly as a speculation by the shipyards and taken over by the government only after the money was voted for them. The Admiralty believed that Austria was instigated to building these ships by Germany, possibly as a return service for the help given over Bosnia and Herzegovina. Churchill admitted that he did not know "whether there is any truth in that . . . but that is the Admiralty view as to the cause of it." [96] The consequence was that Italy was also provoked into building. Although the interests of Italy and Austria were often in conflict, Italy was still a member of the Triple Alliance, probably through fear of Austria. There was no certainty that the same "terror" that forced Italy into the alliance might not, at some critical moment, also force her to honor her obligations under the treaty. Churchill concluded, "These two Powers mutually and reciprocally provoking each other—both being potential factors with which we have to deal—make a most difficult and unsatisfactory position in the Mediterranean." [97] He added that there were rumors that the Austrians were planning to lay down another four battleships. Asquith suspiciously noted that Austria only had a three-hundred-mile seacoast.

Churchill now presented his revised plans for the Mediterranean. In naval matters it was necessary to look ahead three years so that in 1915 Great Britain would have a battle squadron capable of holding its own against the naval force of any power except France. This meant there were to be available in the Mediterranean eight dreadnought class ships, either battleships or battle cruisers. The Royal Navy was not in a position to do this until 1915, for the necessary new ships were needed in home waters. But the Austrian program would also not be completed until 1915. In the interval, Churchill proposed to hold the Mediterranean with a force of four battle cruisers, whose speed would enable them to fight only if they chose to do so. The submarine and destroyer flotillas at Malta and Alexandria would be developed as originally planned. The use of battle cruisers was

[96] CID, Minutes of the 118th Meeting, 11 July 1912, pp. 4–10, Asquith MSS, box 132. The Admiralty were less than fair to the Austrians. See below, Chap. VI.

[97] *Ibid.*, p. 11. The Admiralty expected the first Austrian dreadnought to be ready October 1912; the second, April 1913; the third, April 1914; and the fourth, January 1915. The first Italian dreadnought was to be ready July 1912; the second and third, April 1913; the fourth October 1913; and the fifth and sixth (the latter very doubtful), January 1915. The actual completion dates for Austria were: first, October 1912; second, July 1913; third, June 1914; and fourth, November 1915. For Italy they were: first, January 1913; second and third, May 1914; fourth, April 1915; fifth, May 1915; and sixth, March 1916.

justified: "We think the method of confronting an enemy's battle fleet by a cruiser force of the greatest strength is the substitute for a stronger line of battle, and a far better force to have than a line of battle which is weaker than the enemy. The sure way of obtaining defeat is to have exactly the same thing as your enemy, but not quite so good or in such large numbers. If you are not in a position to prevail by simple strength the best plan is to make an original variation from the system of your probable antagonist. This is what we propose to do." [98]

Implementation of this plan under the current British building program would mean that, after the four battle cruisers went out to the Mediterranean, the Royal Navy would be approximately two ships short of the desired 3:2 margin in home waters until 1914, and one ship short after that. Churchill thought this could be tolerated for the time being, but when eight ships went out to the Mediterranean in June or December 1915 they would be three to four ships short. They would continue to be four ships short for the next few years because, though eight ships in the Mediterranean would be sufficient in 1915, probably ten would be required in 1916 or 1917. This led Churchill to a request for the laying down of three ships in addition to the program announced in March. It would be financially inconvenient for Britain to do this, and it would spur on the naval competition with Germany, but if Canada were to decide to take part in the defense of the Empire, comparisons with the German or Austrian fleets could be avoided in Parliament, and the naval increase effected in a way that would be inoffensive to the great powers.[99] Later in the year Borden did propose to the Canadian Parliament that Canada provide three dreadnoughts for imperial defense but, while the measure passed the Lower House, it was blocked in the Senate in May 1913 by the Liberal opposition, which insisted that the Canadian ships actually be built in Canada and be manned by Canadians. As suitable dockyards did not exist in Canada at the time, the issue was deadlocked, and the subject of the Canadian ships continued to be a most uncertain factor in Admiralty plans before the war.[100]

Churchill's proposal to hold the Mediterranean until 1915 with only

[98] *Ibid.*, p. 12.
[99] *Ibid.*, pp. 12–13.
[100] For discussions of the proposed Canadian contribution see E. L. Woodward, *Great Britain and the German Navy* (Oxford, 1935), pp. 391–394; Churchill, *The World Crisis*, I, 173f; Marder, *Dreadnought to Scapa Flow*, I, 297–298; Elie Halevy, *A History of the English People in the Nineteenth Century*, vol. VI: *The Rule of Democracy* (2nd rev. ed., paperback, London, 1961), pp. 608–611; Donald C. Gordon, "The Admiralty and Dominion Navies, 1902–1914," *Journal of Modern History*, 33.4 (Dec. 1961): 407–422.

four battle cruisers was not really very different from the Malta agreement with Kitchener, which called for two to three. In the Cabinet McKenna severely criticized it, and the subject was extensively discussed on July 15 and 16.[101] McKenna argued that in a war with Germany the four battle cruisers would be needed in home waters and would therefore be withdrawn, leaving Mediterranean commerce and territory unprotected or inadequately defended. Should Austria be a hostile belligerent, the four battle cruisers could not hold their own against an Austrian battle squadron of, for example, three "Radetzkys" and two or more dreadnoughts. The problem could not be answered by the battle squadron based on Gibraltar, for this was to be regarded as an essential part of the force in home waters in the event of war with Germany. A one-power standard in the Mediterranean could only be maintained by basing a battle squadron on Malta which for the time being "was equal to giving a good account of any battle squadron which, say Austria can put into the fighting line." [102] By this McKenna obviously meant several battleships.

Churchill was able to meet these objections and to satisfy the Cabinet. He assured them that in a war with Germany there would be no need to withdraw the four battle cruisers from the Mediterranean, "unless to meet some unlikely and unforeseeable emergency," and that, "in the opinion of his best expert advisers, the proposed cruiser squadron would, during the next two years, be more than a match in the Mediterranean for any force that Austria could oppose to it." Thus assured, the Cabinet unanimously approved the Admiralty proposals and also took up the question of continuing communication with the French naval and military staffs. It was to be made clear to the French government that the talks "were not to be taken as prejudicing the freedom of decision of either Government as to whether they should or should not cooperate in the event of war." [103]

In his speech in the House of Commons on July 22 Churchill stated the policy determined by the Cabinet during the debate on the supplementary naval estimates. In the debates that followed (July 22, 24, and 25) the Conservative opposition criticized his Mediterranean provisions as either inadequate or made at the expense of the North Sea margin. Particularly outspoken was Lord Charles Beresford, whose celebrated feud with Fisher while he was commander of the Channel Fleet (1907–1909) had split the service. Since his retirement he held a seat in the

[101] Asquith to King George, 16 July 1912, Asquith MSS, box 6.
[102] Memorandum by Asquith, 15 July 1912, *ibid.*
[103] Asquith to King George, 16 July 1912, *ibid.*

House of Commons and in January 1912 published an indictment of recent naval policy in a book called *The Betrayal*. He attacked Churchill and the government for leaving at this uncertain moment only one old armored cruiser, the *Good Hope*, in the Mediterranean. He questioned the suitability of battle cruisers in that sea, claiming them to be too big and powerful with immense length and area underwater, which exposed them to torpedo attack and rendered berthing and refitting at Malta difficult.[104] Beresford depreciated the value of the French navy and attacked Churchill for changing his mind on the Mediterranean after the March debates.[105] Arthur Lee, former Civil Lord of the Admiralty (1903–1905), was inclined to support the Admiralty policy as a temporary expedient, but pointed out the fallacy of using Gibraltar as a pivotal base since it was farther from Alexandria than from Rosyth and farther from the North Sea than a fleet based on Newfoundland would be from the British Isles. Consequently, a squadron based there could neither reinforce the North Sea fleet in time nor exercise any practical influence over the course of events in the most important portion of the Mediterranean.[106]

In general the Liberal press, as might be expected, received the government's naval proposals more favorably than the Conservative press, which echoed the criticism made in Parliament. Some Liberal papers, notably the *Manchester Guardian*, were alarmed at the implication of future naval cooperation with France.[107]

Thus the general lines of British naval policy in the Mediterranean, which were to last until the outbreak of war, had been established. Churchill and the Admiralty attempted in March 1912 to carry the policy begun by Fisher in December 1904 to its logical conclusion by concentrating all battleship strength close to home waters. The German Novelle, which necessitated a British increase in personnel to keep the required margin of ships in full commission, might be thought of as the immediate cause. The underlying cause was the decline in relative fighting value of the ships in the Mediterranean Fleet brought about by the construction of dreadnought-class battleships by the navies of Austria and Italy. The plan

[104] *Parliamentary Debates* (Commons), 5th ser., XLI, 882, 891. Beresford based his claim on the fact that because of refits or the summer maneuvers the other Mediterranean ships were not on station. The old (completed 1902) and ill-fated armored cruiser *Good Hope*—she went down in the battle of Coronel in November 1914 with Rear Admiral Cradock aboard—served as Mediterranean flagship in the interval between the departure of the battleships in June and the arrival of the battle cruiser *Inflexible* in late November.

[105] *Ibid.*, p. 1250. Bonar Law, opposition leader in Commons, also attacked the vacillation in policy between March and July. *Ibid.*, p. 1488.

[106] *Ibid.*, p 925.

[107] Marder, *Dreadnought to Scapa Flow*, I, 298–299.

of organization outlined by Churchill in his March statement apparently provided only for an armored cruiser squadron in the Mediterranean. But this decision had been based strictly on naval considerations. Diplomatic and imperial factors required something more and, in the face of heavy opposition from the Foreign Office and General Staff—which, with the comparatively small number of regular troops available for overseas garrisons, relied heavily on British sea power—the "Malta compromise" was reached with Lord Kitchener. This called for a large enough British force in the Mediterranean to maintain, when added to the French fleet, a clear superiority over the combined Austrian and Italian fleets. The set total was two to three battle cruisers. This was still not enough for many in the Cabinet, the Foreign Office, and the CID. It was unpleasant to realize that, after a century of naval supremacy, the Royal Navy was no longer strong enough to hold the Mediterranean alone against all rivals. The implication that to at least a certain extent British interests might have to depend on the French fleet was unpalatable.

At Sir Edward Grey's suggestion, the strength of the Mediterranean Fleet was set at a one-power standard, excluding France. Although this seemed an even greater departure from Churchill's original scheme, the Admiralty actually won the important concession that a "reasonable margin" in home waters was the first requirement. Churchill's final proposal, four battle cruisers as an interim measure until 1915 when a squadron of eight dreadnoughts would be required, was not significantly different from the Malta compromise of two to three. In fact, the first of the battle cruisers, the *Inflexible*, did not arrive in the Mediterranean until November 1912 and remained the only ship of this type on station until joined by the *Indomitable* and *Invincible* in August 1913, over a year after the plan had been adopted. There were various reasons for this: delays in the completion of the new battle cruisers *Princess Royal* and *Queen Mary* prevented release of the older battle cruisers to the Mediterranean; the *New Zealand* was temporarily absent on a world cruise; and ships were concentrated for maneuvers in home waters.[108] At the outbreak of the war the battle cruiser squadron still had only three of its allotted four ships on station.[109] Nevertheless, British interests were not unrepre-

[108] See Churchill's replies to questions in Commons, 2 June and 7 July 1913, *Parliamentary Debates* (Commons), 5th ser., LIII, 564; LV, 11.

[109] Sir Julian S. Corbett, *History of the Great War: Naval Operations* (2nd ed., London, 1938), I, 33–34. The *Indefatigable* (completed 1909) went out to the Mediterranean in December 1913, but the *Invincible* was called home the same month to have her electrical turret machinery replaced by the hydraulic system standard in the other ships. Parkes, *British Battleships*, pp. 494–496, 516.

sented during this period. Following the outbreak of the Balkan Wars, the Third Battle Squadron was ordered to the Mediterranean in November 1912, and for several months into 1913 some five or six "King Edwards" cruised the waters of the eastern Mediterranean. But this was only a temporary detachment, and the ships obviously would have been recalled at the first serious possibility of hostilities with Germany. One might question whether even four battle cruisers could equal the heavier Austrian fleet, as the Admiralty implied, but this would be speaking with the hindsight afforded by the battle of Jutland.

With the main lines of the Mediterranean reorganization established in July 1912, the Admiralty was now free to turn to the connected problem of relations with the French.

III

France: The Leading
Mediterranean Naval Power

The navy of France occupies a puzzling place in the history of that nation. Its strength often was far from negligible, and it has enjoyed its share of success as well as defeat. But its enthusiasts remained relatively small in number, and the degree of public esteem did not come anywhere near the veneration with which the Royal Navy was held in England. The Ligue Maritime et Coloniale, the French navy league founded in 1899, never approached the membership reached by the German, or even the Austrian, Flottenverein. In 1914 it numbered only 28,000. To a large extent it was preaching to those already converted and its importance in spreading naval propaganda was slight.[1] The decades after the founding of the Third Republic were difficult ones for the navy. Long the world's second naval power, France saw herself eclipsed by Germany and the United States and crowded by Japan in the early years of the twentieth century. In 1910 she still had the strongest fleet in the Mediterranean, but the building programs of Italy and Austria-Hungary represented a serious challenge. After the new British naval deployment was implemented in 1912, the strength and battle worthiness of the French fleet became of great importance to England as well as to France.

The pernicious effects of the controversy in the late 1880's over the strategical and tactical doctrines of the Jeune Ecole, compounded by the chronic ministerial instability of the Republic, were felt by the navy even after the turn of the century. The leading exponents of this school of naval strategy were Admiral Hyacinthe Aube, Minister of Marine from January 1886 to May 1887, and Gabriel Charmes, foreign affairs editor of the *Journal des débats*. The Jeune Ecole maintained that the develop-

[1] Theodore Ropp, "The Development of a Modern Navy: French Naval Policy, 1871–1904" (unpub. diss., Harvard University, 1937), pp. 416–417.

47

ment of steam as a means of propulsion and the torpedo as a weapon had rendered the old concept of a battle fleet obsolete. Large battleships would henceforth be vulnerable Goliaths when faced by modern Davids in the form of high-speed torpedo boats. A large number of these small craft could be built for the price of one battleship. This was an important factor since France did not have the means to match British shipbuilding. An enemy with a powerful battle fleet such as England could be humbled through the relatively cheap methods of the *guerre de course.* Spurred by the success of the Confederate commerce raiders during the American Civil War, Aube and his followers believed that Great Britain's weak point was her overseas commerce which could be paralyzed through the depredations of fast cruisers and torpedo boats. This would be accomplished as much by driving marine insurance rates to prohibitive heights as by actual destruction. As minister, Aube slowed the construction of battleships in order to increase that of cruisers and torpedo craft.

Opponents of the Jeune Ecole maintained that claims made for the torpedo boats (*torpilleurs*) were excessive, and that the small craft lacked the necessary sea-keeping qualities. Moreover, the development of the destroyer, originally known as a "torpedo-boat destroyer" and to this day as a *contre torpilleur* in the French navy, served as an effective counter weapon. Other technical innovations such as quick-firing light artillery, improved searchlights, and the anti-torpedo net tended to reduce the vulnerability of battleships to the torpedo boats.

The controversy over the Jeune Ecole passed beyond naval technicalities. Reflecting the political and social divisions of the Third Republic, it became interwoven, through the efforts of rival publicists, with more doctrinaire questions of republicans versus conservatives, Right versus Left, and with the rivalry between the *Journal des débats,* a partisan of the Jeune Ecole, and *Le Temps,* which favored the traditionalists and their support of the battleship. In the navy the Jeune Ecole tended to find support among the junior officers and younger men dissatisfied with the naval aristocrats and higher officers who exercised a firm grip on promotions and choice assignments. The dispute has been considered a Dreyfus quarrel without a *cause célèbre.*[2]

Some of Aube's theories were sound and many of the grievances of the younger officers were justified, but in trying to throw out all of the old school's ideas and change everything simultaneously his ministry ended in chaos. A clear reaction set in after Aube's departure. This was one of the

---

[2] *Ibid.,* p. 277. See also Henri Le Masson, *Histoire du torpilleur en France* (Paris, n.d. [1965]), pp. 31–37.

worst effects of the controversy, for the idea arose that every minister had to change something. From May 1887 to June 1902 there were sixteen ministers of marine. These frequent changes resulted in considerable confusion and worked against the development of coherent long term policy.[3]

The situation did not improve in the 1890's when deputies of the Left such as Edouard Lockroy, Georges Clemenceau, and Camille Pelletan were leading advocates of Jeune Ecole ideas. The emphasis shifted from cruiser warfare against England to reduction of the navy to a coastal defense force for use against the Triple Alliance. The money thus saved on naval expenditure, it was pointed out, could be given to the army. Advocates of this school also championed the cause of the dockyard workers, stokers, engineers, and those officers discontented with the old naval aristocracy, and called for more economical naval administration. In the agitation all elements of the Dreyfus case save anti-Semitism seemed involved.[4]

The confusion of their naval policy was reflected in French ship building. By the turn of the century the navy was contemptuously dubbed a "fleet of samples."[5] The ministry specified the general features of the design but allowed the chief engineer at each dockyard considerable leeway in working out the details. The result was that ships nominally of the same class differed in a thousand points. This system could result in progress through innovations by imaginative engineers. But any advantages likely to be derived from it were canceled by the disadvantages and delays it caused in construction. This diversity was also true of French naval artillery. The battleship *Charles Martel* (11,683 tons), launched in 1893 and completed in 1897, was a veritable artillery museum with six different calibers, plus a seventh for the ship's boats. Her 5-inch guns alone had nine types of projectiles. In the navy of 1899 there were fifteen calibers with forty-five different charges and 128 different projectiles.[6] In appearance French ships were often bizarre in the style denoted as "fierce face." The complicated superstructure of the battleship *Hoche* earned her the name of "Grand Hotel."[7] The aggressive appearance of French battleships stemmed from their "piled-up superstructure, preposterous masts, uncouth funnels,

[3] Ropp, "Development of a Modern Navy," pp. 303–305; Henri Salaun, *La Marine française* (Paris, 1934), pp. 76–78.

[4] Ropp, "Development of a Modern Navy," pp. 417–418.

[5] Henri Le Masson, *De la "Gloire" au "Richelieu"* (Paris, 1946), p. 37.

[6] Ropp, "Development of a Modern Navy," pp. 448–449.

[7] Le Masson, *De la "Gloire" au "Richelieu,"* p. 20; Parkes, *British Battleships*, p. 376. The *Hoche* (10,581 tons) dated from an earlier period having been launched in 1886 and completed in 1889. At the end of her career she was used as a target and dismayed everyone by the ease with which she sank after a few hits. See *Le Yacht,* 13 Dec. 1913, p. 799.

tumble-home sides and long ram bows, with no attempt at achieving any symmetry or balance in profile."[8] Beyond mere aesthetic considerations, the enormous superstructure presented a vulnerable target easily demolished by shell fire, and raised the ship's center of gravity. Although well armed, the French battleships had a comparatively narrow armor belt for the protection of their hulls which were dangerously exposed only a few feet above the waterline. The net effect was that if the ship rolled only 9 degrees water could enter above the belt; with the small inherent stability of these ships, even a slight amount of flooding above the belt was apt to prove fatal.[9]

The ministry of Jean de Lanessan (June 22, 1899–June 7, 1902), during which the moderate elements of both naval schools were in control, marked a turning point in the fortunes of the French fleet. Although the Pelletan ministry which followed was a serious relapse, De Lanessan's program of 1900 provided a sound basis for future development. The Conseil Supérieur de la Marine advised the minister that the composition of the fleet should be: 28 battleships, 24 armored cruisers, 52 destroyers, 263 torpedo boats, and 38 submarines or submersibles. De Lanessan accepted this view, and, taking into account those ships built or building on January 1, 1900, he proposed to lay down before January 1, 1907, 6 battleships of 14,865 tons, 5 armored cruisers of 12,600 tons, 28 destroyers, 112 torpedo boats, and 25 submarines.[10] The minister specified that the battleships should be at least as powerful as foreign contemporaries. The armored cruisers were intended to operate singly or in groups against enemy commerce, or in defense of French maritime communications. For this mission they were to be endowed with an extensive radius of action and a speed superior to foreign protected cruisers and at least equal to foreign armored cruisers. The battleships were to be laid down in groups of six and the armored cruisers in groups of three so as to create homogeneous battleship squadrons and cruiser divisions. This would reduce both the cost and the duration of their construction. The naval law which was finally promulgated on December 9, 1900, incorporated De Lanessan's proposals without, however, specifying the number of torpedo boats and submarines to be

[8] Parkes, *British Battleships*, p. 376.

[9] *Ibid.*, pp. 374, 376. This description applied to the French battleships of the 1890's. In contrast, the eight "Royal Sovereigns" (14,150 tons), launched and completed in the years 1891–1894, formed a homogeneous squadron. In both displacement and the extent of their armor protection British battleships were superior to their French contemporaries. See also Ropp, "Development of a Modern Navy," p. 432.

[10] Ropp, pp. 504, 511. The five important naval laws of 1900 covered growth of the fleet, harbor works, coast defense, colonial bases, and cables (*ibid.*; Salaun, *Marine française*, p. 48).

built.[11] At last it seemed that a clear course had been charted for the navy. Unfortunately this optimism proved to be premature.

French naval aspirations received a heavy blow when Camille Pelletan became Minister of Marine in the Radical cabinet of Emile Combes. Pelletan, a journalist of very advanced ideas, had served as *rapporteur général* in 1901 at the first congress of the Radical Socialist Party (*Partie républicain radical et radical socialiste*). This bearded, rather shaggy looking Bohemian embarked on a crusade to democratize the navy and shake its administration out of its lethargy. In doing so he often imperiled discipline. While the admirals were treated cooly, strikers from the naval dockyards were warmly welcomed. Meatless Fridays were suppressed aboard warships, a symbol of the government's militant anti-clericalism.[12] The more amusing side of Pelletan's doctrinaire approach to the navy was revealed in the names given to the six battleships laid down under the naval law of 1900. They were dubbed *Patrie, République, Démocratie, Justice, Vérité,* and *Liberté*—rather unusual names for warships. Less amusing for the navy were the effects of Pelletan's technical ideas. Although six battleships had been authorized by the law of 1900, it was still necessary that the required appropriations for each year be requested in the Chamber and Senate. But Pelletan was most unenthusiastic about battleships. The minister, not surprisingly, was a fervid believer in new weapons, notably the submarine. Following in the footsteps of the Jeune Ecole, he did not think that France could afford to keep up with England and Germany in the construction of large ships. Therefore he placed his major efforts on the construction of submarines. When Pelletan left the ministry after the fall of the Combes cabinet there were thirty-five submarines and submersibles in service or undergoing trials, and eighteen submarines or submersibles under construction. This total of fifty-three should be compared with the number recommended by the Conseil Supérieur, which was thirty-eight. However, the same error that had been made with the torpedo boats in the 1880's was repeated with the submarines. Many of them (twenty-three) were too small to render useful service at sea, even when limited to coastal defense. As is often the case with visionaries, Pelletan was correct in his broad assumption that submarines had an important future. But he failed miserably in his apprecia-

[11] Salaun, *Marine française,* pp. 49–50. The German naval law of June 14, 1900, called for a fleet in 1920 of 38 battleships, 14 large cruisers, 38 small cruisers, and 98 torpedo boats; the French would therefore be inferior in battleship strength in 1920. *Ibid.,* p. 52.

[12] Jacques Chastenet, *Histoire de la troisième république,* vol. III: *La république triomphante, 1893–1906* (Paris, 1955), 248.

tion of the immediate practical difficulties. The stage of development that this type of ship had reached in the years 1902–1905 simply did not permit them to be relied on as the principal naval weapon.[13]

The serious result of Pelletan's ideas was the delay caused in the construction of the battleships of the 1900 program. Anticipating a budgetary deficit, he tried to economize by having work on four of the ships halted. Battleships had a low priority in his plans. However, private firms had contracted to build a number of them, and had already assembled material for their construction. These firms therefore instituted legal proceedings against the government. In November 1902 the Chamber indicated strong feelings on the subject by voting that construction of the ships be continued. However, as important modifications from the original plans were made in the secondary armament of the last four ships of the class, their completion was considerably retarded. The actual completion of the "Patrie" class, France's first truly homogeneous battleship squadron, and the completion of the armored cruisers, was delayed nearly two years beyond the program date of January 1907. As a result the ships, originally conceived before 1900, were at least partially outmoded the very day they entered service.[14]

Pelletan was almost universally condemned. Some of the criticism in France may have stemmed from political prejudice. But the doubts were not limited to France; to foreign observers in 1905 the French fleet seemed of questionable value.[15] The French navy at the time of Pelletan's departure seemed to have reached the nadir of its fortunes.

The navy revised its building program under Pelletan's successor, Gaston Thomson, who held the ministerial portfolio from January 1905 to October 1908. On the advice of the Conseil Supérieur, Thomson proposed that by 1920 the French fleet be increased to: 34 battleships, 18 first-class armored cruisers, 18 second-class cruisers, 6 scouts (éclaireurs d'escadre), 109 destroyers, 170 torpedo boats, 82 offensive submersibles, and 49 defensive submarines. After objections had been raised to the second-class cruisers

---

[13] The Naval Annual, 1903, pp. 21–22; Salaun, Marine française, pp. 53–54.

[14] Salaun, Marine française, p. 54; The Naval Annual, 1905, pp. 15–16. The British contemporaries of the "Patries" were the more powerful "King Edwards." Armored cruisers were to be rendered almost obsolete as a class with the appearance of the faster and vastly more powerful battle cruisers. In sharp contrast to the turmoil in the French navy, the Germans proceeded rapidly and efficiently with their program. Between 1900 and 1905 they laid down twelve battleships and launched fourteen. The consensus of British experts placed Germany ahead of France in naval power by 1906. Marder, Dreadnought to Scapa Flow, I, 106.

[15] Ibid., I, 117–118. Fisher expressed doubts about the French navy in a letter to King Edward, 8 Sept. 1907, and to the Prince of Wales, 16 Oct. 1907. Marder, Fear God and Dread Nought, II, 130, 147–148.

as too feeble a class of warships, they were dropped from the program. The number of battleships was also raised to meet the total of the German program. Thomson's amended project of 1906 was therefore 38 battleships and 20 first-class armored cruisers. To start, Thomson obtained parliamentary approval to lay down beginning in 1906 a new class of six 18,000-ton battleships which were to be finished in 1910.[16]

At last it would seem that the navy was on the way to recovery. Unfortunately, it was now to be plagued by a series of accidents which cast fresh doubts—in both France and the rest of Europe—on the abilities of its administration and personnel. The large armored cruiser *Sully* (9856 tons) ran onto an uncharted reef off Tonkin in February 1905 and had to be written off as a total loss barely two years after her entry into service. There were fires and explosions aboard warships, and the submarine *Farfadet* was lost with all fourteen of her crew at Bizerte the same year. The cruisers *Chanzy* and *Jean Bart* were wrecked in 1907. The crowning disaster occurred in March 1907 when the battleship *Iéna* (11,-861 tons), completed in 1901, blew up in Toulon harbor with the loss of her captain, seven officers, and 110 men. The parliamentary commission which investigated the disaster was headed by former Foreign Minister Théophile Delcassé. The *Iéna* disaster was followed by a serious fire at the Toulon dockyard and the wreck of a troopship on her way to Morocco in 1908. There were other accidents during gunnery exercises. The government's naval policy and administration was the subject of an interpellation in the Chamber in October 1908. Delcassé intervened in the debates, and his criticism of Thomson was so scathing that Thomson was forced to resign.[17]

Clemenceau chose Alfred Picard as the new Minister of Marine. It was a difficult assignment. The Commander-in-Chief of the Mediterranean squadron, Vice Admiral Paul-Louis Germinet, revealed to a journalist during an interview that the military value of his warships would be compromised in time of war by the deficiencies in supplies at the ports. The admiral was relieved of his command for breach of discipline.[18] Picard was forced by Joseph Caillaux, the Minister of Finance, to reduce his requests for supplementary appropriations. In the Chamber debates on the subject in March 1909, Delcassé was able to point out contradictions

[16] Salaun, *Marine française*, pp. 56–57.

[17] Georges Bonnefous, *Histoire politique de la troisième république*, vol. I: *L'Avant-guerre, 1906–1914* (Paris, 1956), 110; Charles W. Porter, *The Career of Théophile Delcassé* (Philadelphia, 1936), pp. 277–278.

[18] Bonnefous, *Histoire politique*, I, 111. He was later recalled to serve as a member of the Conseil Supérieur.

between Picard's report and Caillaux's proposals, and to force the establishment of a new parliamentary committee to investigate naval affairs. The report of this committee the following July was highly critical of the navy's administration, particularly in regard to the insufficiency and poor quality of the munitions. French naval shipbuilding, which was scandalously slow, was also castigated, particularly because of the frequent modifications added during construction which caused innumerable delays, the defective work of the dockyards, and the poor organization of their workers. The lack of repair facilities large enough to handle the new battleships was also noted. In the bitter debates which followed, Delcassé took a prominent part in attacking Clemenceau's government over the state of the navy. These did not fail to assume a personal tone in the rough and tumble of French politics. Clemenceau well deserved his nickname of "The Tiger" for his fierceness in parliamentary debate, but this time he made the mistake of referring to the Moroccan crisis of 1905. He accused Delcassé of having led the country to the brink of war at a time when no preparations for it had been made so that the Ministers of War and Marine had to admit in cabinet that neither the army nor the navy were ready. Although this was true, it was beyond the bounds of parliamentary decency or political expediency to say so publicly, and Clemenceau's sharp tongue brought about his own fall. On July 20 the ministry was overturned.[19]

Vice Admiral Augustin Boué de Lapeyrère became Minister of Marine in the government led by Aristide Briand which followed. Lapeyrère was forced to undertake a realistic reappraisal of the current French building program. The Conseil Supérieur had recommended to his predecessor that the fleet in 1920 be composed of: 45 battleships, 12 fast scouts, 120 destroyers, and 64 submarines. The goal of this expanded program was obviously superiority over the German fleet. Armored cruisers and torpedo boats, long favorites of the French, were not included.[20] The naval General Staff realized that the Conseil Supérieur's program was beyond the resources of the nation. The requisite number of new battleships could not be built before 1920. The General Staff was therefore led to admit the impossibility of maintaining equality with the German fleet, and readjusted its goal to providing for naval supremacy in the Mediterranean over Austria and Italy combined.[21] Lapeyrère agreed and elaborated a reduced program which he hoped to see enacted into a naval law

19 Ibid., pp. 131, 134–138; Porter, Career of Delcassé, pp. 280–283.
20 Salaun, Marine française, p. 67.
21 Philippe Masson, "Delcassé, Ministre de la Marine" (Thèse de Diplôme d'Etudes Supérieures d'Histoire, n.d. [1951]), p. 51.

which would free the navy from the whims of capricious ministers like Pelletan.

The project submitted to the Chamber in 1910 called for the composition of the French fleet in 1920 to be: 28 battleships, 10 scouts, 52 destroyers, 94 submarines, 10 ships for colonial service, and a number of specialized types such as gunboats, minelayers, and minesweepers. Because of the large number of existing cruisers, construction of the scouts and colonial ships would not begin until 1917.[22] This program was more modest than the one established in 1906 and represents a reversion to the battleship strength set by De Lanessan in 1900. By forsaking equality with Germany it seemed to restrict the major role of the fleet in the future to the Mediterranean. Lapeyrère, who made a good start in getting the navy on a proper footing, was unable to get the naval law through parliament. He was only able to procure funds for the laying down of two dreadnoughts in 1910.[23] Obtaining passage of the naval law was to be the achievement of his successor, Delcassé.

Théophile Delcassé became Minister of Marine in the Monis cabinet in March 1911 and held the position in various governments until January 1913. His outstanding achievement was the naval law of 1912. But above and beyond this was the leadership and drive he brought to naval affairs and the restoration to a large degree of public confidence in the fleet. Delcassé improved collaboration between the branches of the service and the administration of the dockyards so that a considerable reduction in building time could be anticipated. His efforts for the navy were appreciated by those interested in naval affairs abroad. It was clearly recognized that the French fleet was again on the road to becoming a formidable fighting force whose avowed aim was supremacy in the Mediterranean. Naturally faults can be found with Delcassé's administration, among them the delay in construction of the badly needed scouts and other light vessels for protection against submarines. But Delcassé's achievement is even greater when measured against the disastrous powder crisis through which the navy was passing during much of his ministry.[24]

---

[22] *Ibid.*, pp. 58–60; Salaun, *Marine française*, p. 68.

[23] Salaun, *Marine française*, p. 69. The two ships, the *Courbet* and *Jean Bart*, were laid down in September and November 1910 and were the first true dreadnoughts to be built in France.

[24] Admiral G. Durand-Viel, "Delcassé et la Marine," *Revue maritime*, n.s., no. XLI (May 1923), pp. 577–605. Without diminishing Delcassé's achievements, it is only fair to add that much credit for ameliorating the length of time necessary for naval construction belongs to two engineer officers, Léon Lyasse, who served as director of the Service Technique from Nov. 1909 to Nov. 1911, and Charles Doyère who followed him. See Henri Le Masson, "Politique navale et construction de navires de ligne en France en 1914," *Revue maritime*, no. 202 (Aug.-Sept. 1963), pp. 1007–1008.

Knowing that full parliamentary discussion of the naval law would require much time, Delcassé secured approval of the first portion of it. The law of April 13, 1911, authorized the navy to lay down during that year another pair of dreadnoughts to be ready in three years, and to undertake important work at the ports especially in respect to the preparation of suitable docks at Toulon to handle the new and larger ships foreseen in the naval programs.[25] The entire naval law was finally voted by the Chamber of Deputies, despite the opposition of the Socialists, on February 13, 1912, and by the Senate on March 29. In presenting his report on this budget to the Chamber, Paul Painlevé had admitted publicly that France could not match Germany in naval armaments, and stated unequivocally that the object of the French fleet was supremacy in the Mediterranean.[26] Including the first steps in the program which had been voted in 1910 and 1911, the building tempo, with 1910 as the first year, was 2-2-3-2-2-4-0-2. Two scouts were to be laid down annually in 1917, 1918, and 1919. The age limits for the battleships were set at twenty-five years for those ships begun before 1906, and twenty years for those begun after.[27]

The year 1911 was an important one for the French navy. In addition to the arrival of Delcassé at the Ministry of Marine, the material strength of the fleet was appreciably strengthened. In the period between March and September, the six "Dantons" finally entered service. The last of the armored cruisers, the *Edgar Quinet* and *Waldeck-Rousseau*, were also completed. The addition of six battleships and two large cruisers would have been a worthy achievement for any fleet in a single year, but it was particularly welcome to the French after the gap in modern capital ships resulting from the Pelletan ministry.

The cruisers were, however, a hollow triumph. Despite their size and imposing silhouette they were undergunned with an armament of the 7.6-inch caliber, and underpowered with a maximum speed of only 23 knots. Large and expensive, they were still no match for a battle cruiser. The "Dantons," although powerful ships, were also a controversial class. Even though they were laid down after the *Dreadnought* had entered service they retained the mixed armament of the pre-dreadnought era.[28]

[25] Durand-Viel, "Delcassé et la marine," p. 583.
[26] Quoted in *The Naval Annual, 1912,* pp. 36–37.
[27] *Ibid.,* p. 40; Masson, "Delcassé," p. 60. Article 2 of the naval law provided for the replacement of any ships that were lost. Therefore a third dreadnought was laid down in 1912 to replace the *Liberté*. Salaun, *Marine française,* p. 69.
[28] The "Dantons" (18,400 tons) had a primary armament of four 12-inch and twelve 9.4-inch guns, and a speed of over 19 knots. Jane lists them as "semi-dreadnoughts." Fred T. Jane, (ed.), *Fighting Ships, 1915* (London, 1915), p. 250.

Like the two "Lord Nelsons" in the Royal Navy, they could be counted as dreadnoughts or not, depending on what the speaker wanted to prove. Their defenders maintained that they could sustain a rapid rate of fire and actually deliver each minute a broadside which was considerably superior to that of the *Dreadnought,* and only slightly inferior to that of the *Neptune,* the German "Nassau" class, and the United States *Delaware.*[29] Yet this argument could not alter the fact that by the time the six "Dantons" entered service the Royal Navy had completed ten dreadnoughts and four battle cruisers, the Germans had completed or were on the verge of completing seven dreadnoughts and three battle cruisers, the United States had completed four dreadnoughts, and Japan had launched two. Both the Italians and the Austrians had each laid down two dreadnoughts before the French began their first.[30]

It seemed as if the French navy still suffered from the burden of the past, and had again received obsolescent ships. But it must be remembered that by Mediterranean standards, as opposed to North Sea standards, the "Dantons" were still very good ships. When compared to its previous condition, the French navy was also immeasurably strengthened vis à vis its potential Mediterranean rivals by the addition of this second squadron of homogeneous ships. Extensive naval maneuvers took place at the end of the summer of 1911, and on September 4 a great naval review was held off Toulon at which President Fallières and many important members of the government and legislature were present. The Agadir crisis served to enhance the importance of this, the most impressive display of French naval strength in many years. In the judgment of the editors of *The Naval Annual* of 1912, no navy had made greater progress during 1911 than the French.[31]

Three weeks after the President's review disaster struck the French navy, and hopes for a French naval renaissance were clouded. Early on the morning of September 25 while the fleet was at anchor in Toulon, the battleship *Liberté* blew up with a tremendous explosion which also damaged nearby ships. The catastrophe left 210 dead or missing and 136 badly injured.[32] The country was shocked and outraged for the calamity was similar to that of the *Iéna* in 1907, and just a few days before the *Liberté's* misfortune a gunnery accident had taken a number of lives aboard the

[29] *The Naval Annual, 1912,* p. 38.

[30] Data from Jane, *Fighting Ships, 1915;* Parkes, *British Battleships.*

[31] *The Naval Annual, 1912,* p. 36. This was the moment when the French proposed to the British that they undertake the defense of all the Mediterranean.

[32] Jean Tonnelé, "La Catastrophe de la 'Liberté,'" *Neptunia,* no. 68 (Autumn 1962), p. 28.

cruiser *Gloire*.[33] The parliamentary commission of inquiry into the *Iéna* disaster, presided over by Senator Ernest Monis, cast doubt on the stability of the powder currently in use in the French navy, the notorious "Powder B" with amyl alcohol. The Service des Poudres, the government powder monopoly which was under the Ministry of War rather than Marine, contested this theory of spontaneous combustion.[34] The navy's committee of inquiry on the *Liberté* disaster, headed by Rear Admiral Gaschard, also implicated the suspect powder in its report. Apparently all regulations for the preservation of powder had been observed so that no responsibility fell on anyone aboard the *Liberté,* and there was no trace of sabotage. The catastrophe was traced to the ignition, most probably spontaneous, in the forward magazine of a cartridge of Powder B dating from 1906.[35]

Even before this report had been published, Delcassé ordered all munitions manufactured before 1907 to be landed and replaced by newer powder.[36] For the next few months the French were busy landing suspect lots of powder which were subjected to careful examination. Large quantities of it were dumped at sea. Delcassé also formed a committee to investigate the manufacture of the navy's powder. The report was damning to the Service des Poudres. The use of *poudre radoubée* was particularly controversial. This was the practice of refreshing powder by treating it with alcohol or ether or else mixing it with other powders. Under this system, powder labeled as having been manufactured in 1908 might contain a portion of powder manufactured as long ago as 1896.[37] In his report to the Chamber on the 1912 naval budget, Painlevé recommended that the Ministry of Marine exercise complete control over the manufacture of its own powder. This was also the decision of Delcassé who ordered the preparation of a plan for an interministerial decree giving the navy its independent powder service.[38]

The powder problem was far from being solved. During the winter of 1912 suspect powder began to appear in lots manufactured after 1908; Delcassé ordered them landed.[39] Lapeyrère, now commanding the Mediterranean forces (First Armée Navale), demanded weekly tests of powder

---

[33] *The Naval Annual, 1911,* p. 19.
[34] Tonnelé, "La Catastrophe de la 'Liberté,'" p. 28.
[35] *Ibid.* The full report is in République française, *Journal Officiel,* Suppl., 24 Oct. 1911, *Rapport de la commission nominée par le Vice-Amiral Commandant en Chef la 2e Escadre pour rechercher les causes de l'explosion de la Liberté.* A summary of the report is in *The Naval Annual, 1912,* pp. 329–331.
[36] Decision du Ministre, 11 Oct. 1911, AMF, carton BB4-2358.
[37] *The Naval Annual, 1912,* p. 331.
[38] Conférence des Directeurs Militaires, 18 May 1912, AMF, carton BB8-1716.
[39] Masson, "Delcassé," pp. 203–204.

samples and the debarkation of any lots which were suspect. Unfortunately there were insufficient quantities of the safer powder prepared with diphenylamine available to replace the munitions of certain calibers. If the fleet went north for the annual maneuvers in the summer of 1912 it would have to do so nearly devoid of munitions.[40] Powder supplies for the 12-inch guns were nearly complete but most of the powder for the 9.2-inch guns and half the powder for the 7.6-inch and 6.4-inch guns had to be landed. Of the newer and more stable powders, only 1054 tons had been received out of the 4000 tons necessary for the fleet.[41] The summer maneuvers were held in the Mediterranean, but the situation looked as if it would get worse before it improved. As tests revealed new suspect lots, ships with this powder aboard would have to hastily put into port and debark the questionable munitions. This, for example, happened to the *Vergniaud* and *Condorcet* in early June.[42]

Despite all precautions a gunnery exercise produced a new tragedy aboard the cruiser *Jules Michelet* on June 26. Explosions claiming a number of lives took place in two different turrets, for the gunnery exercise had been continued after the first accident for the purpose of maintaining discipline.[43] The British naval attaché, Captain Howard Kelly, feared public confidence in the naval administration would be completely lost if after the enormous expense involved in the withdrawal from service and destruction of old and doubtful powders the disasters continued. Parliament had accepted the powder crisis "very well" following the loss of the *Liberté* and had given the government a free hand to correct the situation. But if a great outcry were to occur, it was doubtful Delcassé could survive, and the Poincaré government itself might be in a precarious position.[44] On July 31 Delcassé ordered all powder treated by the amyl alcohol process to be disembarked. Only the D Powder, prepared with diphenylamine, was to be used in the future. All gunnery practice with suspect powder was halted.[45] This was hardly beneficial to the efficiency or morale of the fleet. The French crews, who had behaved magnificently up to

[40] Conférence des Directeurs Militaires, 7 May 1912, AMF, carton BB8-1716.
[41] Conférence des Directeurs Militaires, 18 May 1912, *ibid.*
[42] *Le Yacht,* 8 June 1912, p. 358.
[43] *Ibid.,* 29 June 1912, p. 407; *ibid.,* 6 July 1912, pp. 417–418; *The Naval Annual, 1913,* pp. 39, 380–381. June 1912 was another bad month for the French navy: on the eighth the submarine *Vendémiaire* was rammed and sunk by the battleship *St. Louis* during maneuvers off Brittany. All aboard, twenty-four officers and men, were lost. *Ibid.,* p. 39.
[44] Kelly's report enclosed in Bertie to Grey, 27 June 1912, FO 371, vol. 1368, France, no. 27406.
[45] *The Naval Annual, 1913,* pp. 380–381.

now under harrowing circumstances, began to show signs of strain. On August 13 the sudden appearance of smoke aboard the battleship *Vérité* produced a panic and the flooding of two magazines.[46] The news that Swedish and Italian powders were being tested by the navy provoked an article in *Le Temps* on September 24 calling for an end to the state monopoly of the manufacture of powder. The following day *Le Matin* published a scathing attack on the methods of manufacture used at the state powder factories.[47]

Of course other navies lost ships and lives from mysterious internal explosions both before and during World War I. The French also had no monopoly on accidents due to the hazards of the sea or human error. But the powder crisis left the French navy largely disarmed in mid-1912 after a succession of accidents traced to unstable powder. Naturally in case of mobilization much of the suspect powder would, by necessity, have been re-embarked, although it was far from certain that the official assurances of a resulting delay of only eighteen hours were correct.[48] It was only in 1913 that the production of new munitions enabled the navy to become sure of its powder.

From the standpoint of naval strategy geography has placed a heavy burden on France. Her extensive littoral faces two major bodies of water, the Atlantic and the Mediterranean. In the north the peninsula of Brittany separates the English Channel from the Bay of Biscay. Between the Bay of Biscay and the Mediterranean lies the enormous bulk of the Iberian peninsula. Toulon, the major naval base in the south, is over 1600 miles steaming distance from Brest, the major northern naval base. This is three times the distance by land.

The natural desire to obtain the advantages inherent in concentrating one's naval strength in one place always provoked the question of where. But there was another complication to the problem of a French concentration. This was the insufficient resources of the naval bases. Neither Brest nor Toulon could handle the needs of the entire fleet.[49] The problem was magnified by the growing size and complexity of warships. A certain amount of dispersion was necessary for this reason alone aside from

[46] Vice Admiral Bellue, Commander-in-Chief second squadron, to Delcassé, 17 August 1912, AMF, carton BB3-1346.

[47] Bertie to Grey, 25 Sept. 1912, FO 371, vol. 1369, France, no. 40334. *Le Yacht,* one of the leading professional journals, had been in favor of this for a long time.

[48] Masson, "Delcassé," pp. 206–207.

[49] Raoul-Victor Castex, *Théories stratégiques,* vol. IV: *Les Facteurs internes de la stratégie* (Paris, 1935), pp. 49–50.

other political and strategic factors. The French had, especially after the naval law of 1900, an elaborate series of naval bases to support the fleet, with strong offensive and defensive flotillas in both north and south as well as in their North African possessions. The system in 1902 included Dunkirk, Cherbourg, Lézardrieux, Brest, Lorient, Rochefort, Marseilles, Toulon, Bizerte, Ajaccio, and Oran. The whole, with the coastal defenses taken over by the army under the naval law of 1900, formed a complicated system of bases and major and minor refuges for cruisers and light craft. With the ripening of the friendship with England certain of the bases, particularly those in the Bay of Biscay, became redundant. The reduction of the forces at them was to bring forth cries of anguish from local interests in later years. A weak minister might be tempted to yield to such cries, with the resulting waste of resources on obsolete craft of small fighting value at ports which the changing strategical situation had rendered superfluous.[50] In 1912 a major reorganization of the flotillas took place, and those at Rochefort and Lorient were cut.[51]

The French concentration in the Mediterranean in September 1912 attracted much attention. However, like the British withdrawal of the Malta battleship squadron a few months before, it was really only the manifestation of a policy which was far from new, but one which had received new impetus when diplomatic and political factors changed England from potential enemy to potential ally. In March 1895 when the naval General Staff (EMG) gave the Conseil Supérieur de la Marine its recommendations for naval action against the Triple Alliance, the general approach was to be defensive in the Channel and offensive in the Mediterranean.[52] According to the Instructions de guerre (Feb. 27, 1897) the French planned to concentrate their Mediterranean squadron at Gulf Jouan and cruisers would seek to force the Italian fleet to action by bombarding and destroying the coastal railway between Savona and Ventimiglia.[53] An entente

[50] Ropp, "Development of a Modern Navy," pp. 522–523; Henri Bernay, "Escadres et flotilles," *Le Yacht,* 6 May 1911, p. 274. The reform of the flotillas was a frequent subject in professional journals.

[51] An exhaustive discussion is in P. Le Roll, "Le Plan d'armement de la flotte pour 1913," *Le Yacht,* 27 Apr. 1912, pp. 257–258; also *ibid.,* 5 Oct. 1912, p. 632, and 26 Oct. 1912, pp. 673–674.

[52] Memorandum by second and third sections, Etat-major général (henceforth referred to as EMG), 2 Apr. 1898, AMF, carton BB4-2680. In the event of war against England all French squadrons would be concentrated in the Atlantic and Channel ports after a number of cruisers had been detached to operate against commerce. The French fleet was to back up the threat of an invasion, with the aim of deterring use of the British army in overseas expeditions against French colonies.

[53] "Instructions pour le temps de guerre à l'Escadre de la Méditerranée, (T)," 27 Feb. 1897, AMF, carton BB4-2680. The Escadre du Nord was limited to a defensive attitude. "Instructions," 31 July 1897, *ibid.*

between the Ministers of War and Marine had been concluded on the subject, because the French army placed great stress on impeding an Italian mobilization on France's southeast frontier.[54] The Austrian fleet was apparently not considered at all.

The situation had altered to France's disadvantage by 1900 so that the deployment of her squadrons no longer corresponded to the requirements of the plan of 1897—offensive in the south, defensive in the north. The French fleet now found itself, with respect to the Triple Alliance, slightly inferior in the Channel and completely inferior in the Mediterranean. If the three best battleships were given to the Escadre du Nord it would enjoy a decisive superiority over the German fleet. The Mediterranean squadron would then have to remain on the defensive until the defeat of the German fleet permitted a concentration in the south against the Austrians and the Italians. If the present plans were to be maintained, the Mediterranean squadron should be reinforced and the struggle against Germany delayed until victory in the Mediterranean had been achieved.[55]

The Mediterranean squadron steamed north to join the northern squadron for the summer maneuvers in 1900. Vice Admiral Alfred Gervais, nominated to command the two combined squadrons, which were then known in French naval terminology as an "armée navale," asked for a copy of the current war plans. The minister, De Lanessan, told him that under the special situation in which the fleet found itself together in the north, a war with the Triple Alliance would mean a French concentration at Cherbourg. The German fleet was to be sought and destroyed. It was assumed that the Germans would follow a similar strategy thereby producing an encounter between the rival fleets in the Dover Straits. If the German fleet remained in port, a blockade of the Elbe and an occupation of Heligoland would be considered. Cruiser patrols to intercept German commerce were to be established off Lizard Point, Finistère, the north of Scotland, and Cape Clear.[56] The following year, 1901, combined maneu-

---

[54] By 1901 the Tuscan and Ligurian railway net had been extended to the point where the Italian mobilization depended far less on the coastal railway, whose destruction was henceforth considered as of secondary importance. Minister of Marine to Commander-in-Chief, Escadre de la Méditerranée, 28 Feb. 1901, AMF, carton BB-653.

[55] Note by third section, EMG, Feb. 1900, *ibid.*, BB4-2680. The French estimates were:

1895	Battle-ships	Cruisers	Destroyers	1900	Battle-ships	Cruisers	Destroyers
France	19	13	7	France	13	14	10
Triple Alliance	17	17	7	Triple Alliance	28	13	24

[56] De Lanessan to Vice Admiral Gervais, 14 June 1900, *ibid.*, carton BB4-2680. A war against England would necessitate a concentration at Brest, *ibid.* The French maneuvers added to the invasion scare in England, which was then in the midst of the Boer War. See Marder, *Anatomy of British Sea Power,* pp. 377f.

vers were held in the Mediterranean, and the French returned to their old plan of an immediate offensive in the south. If possible the Italian fleet was to be defeated before it could be joined by the Austrians. The force would move north to oppose the Germans after the decisive victory in the Mediterranean had been obtained.[57] The French in the early years of the new century were therefore still able to think of a successful offensive against either the Austrians and the Italians in the Mediterranean or against the Germans in the north. They could not, however, act against both at the same time.

The 1897 Instructions de Guerre were still in force in 1906 although the EMG had realized since early 1900 that they no longer fitted the situation. Their much delayed revision had to await a more rational deployment of French naval strength.[58] Vice Admiral François Fournier, who commanded the combined squadrons in the maneuvers of 1905 and who was then Commander-in-Chief designate in case of war, favored concentrating *all* French naval forces in the north. He feared that the northern squadron would be blockaded in Brest before being able to get underway to Oran and the Mediterranean. This apprehension was based on the belief that the Germans would pass through the English Channel at night and initiate a surprise opening of hostilities.[59] The Japanese attack on Port Arthur before a formal declaration of war was still very much on everyone's mind.

The EMG did not agree with Fournier's views.[60] In the first place a concentration in the north was unwise under the present political circumstances. The Algeciras Conference was in progress, and a naval move like this would constitute a real military demonstration which would not pass unnoticed. It would undoubtedly be exploited by the German press and would cause a sensation in Europe. Moreover to disarm the Mediterranean was dangerous for it would offer Italy "a tempting and easy prey." What was worst of all, the German fleet might be able to effect a junction with the Italian fleet. If the French fleet were concentrated at Brest it would be hard for it to intercept the Germans, and once the latter had passed Ushant, nothing could stop them from reaching the Mediterranean. With the Italian bases at their disposition they could interrupt French communications with Algeria. Tunisia would probably be attacked and taken.

[57] Third section, EMG to Commander-in-Chief, Armée navale, 17 June 1901, AMF, carton BB4-2680. Similar instructions were given to Admiral Fournier for the combined maneuvers in 1905 by the dispatch of 3 July 1905, *ibid.*

[58] Third section, EMG, "Avantages et inconvenients de la concentration des forces navales suivant qu'elles seraient concentrées dans le nord ou dans la Méditerranée, Nécessité de la concentration," 22 June 1906, AMF, carton BB4-2443.

[59] Vice Admiral Fournier to Minister of Marine, 18 Jan. 1906, AMF, carton BB4-2437.

[60] Observations by the EMG on Vice Admiral Fournier's note, Feb. 1906, *ibid.*

The French fleet would be limited to a futile blockade and demonstrations against the German coast, for it would have lost all possibility of regaining command of the Mediterranean in the face of the powerful German and Italian combination. Even if England entered the war as an ally, the French would still have every interest in letting the Royal Navy have the task of striking the first blows at sea.

Admiral Fournier clung to his views and suggested suitable pretexts for a concentration in the north. He also mentioned the difficulty of calming French, as opposed to European, public opinion if the northern coasts were stripped of major units in the face of the German menace.[61] The EMG were not convinced. In his provisional report to the permanent section of the Conseil Supérieur de la Marine the chief of the EMG, Rear Admiral M. J. C. Aubert, repeated its arguments. The French naval units presently in the north were powerless to resist the German fleet, and a concentration of force was absolutely necessary. Such a concentration had to be in the Mediterranean, and not only in case of an alliance between Germany and Italy. One could not know in advance exactly what nations would enter the war, and this deployment appeared to correspond best with the various contingencies. Aubert proposed moving the coast defense vessels from the Mediterranean to the north and the best of the battleships currently in the north to the south to form a Mediterranean force of twelve battleships. These would represent the newest and most powerful units although six of them would be kept in reserve. Aubert also called attention to the French naval division in the Far East which was impotent against the Japanese fleet. He regretted that its three good armored cruisers were not part of the Mediterranean fleet.[62] This desire to concentrate one's strength in home waters instead of dispersing it on colonial stations is of course similar to the policies of Fisher at the Admiralty in 1904.

One objection raised in the Conseil Supérieur to Aubert's proposals was that in the event of war with Germany the Mediterranean squadron would take at least eight days to complete its preparations and steam north. It might then find itself opposed to the German squadrons with its bunkers empty and its crews exhausted. This objection was met by

[61] Vice Admiral Fournier to Minister of Marine, 6 Feb. 1906, *ibid.*

[62] To support his arguments Aubert compared the strengths of the German and French fleets. By mobilizing their B category ships the Germans could have within a few days a battleship and armored cruiser force of 25 ships with 102 large-, 296 medium-, and 580 small-caliber guns. To oppose this the French had in the north, including reserves, 18 ships with 51 large-, 179 medium-, and 264 small-caliber guns. The French Mediterranean force, including reserves, consisted of 12 ships with 39 large-, 174 medium-, and 209 small-caliber guns. Rear Admiral Aubert, "Note sur la Répartition des Forces Navales," 13 Feb. 1906, AMF, carton BB4-1813.

recognizing the necessity of providing the fleet with the means for rapidly replenishing its coal supplies, at least up to the Straits of Gibraltar. It would then arrive before Brest in about the same condition as a German force coming from Wilhelmshaven.[63]

The permanent section of the Conseil Supérieur de la Marine unanimously adopted the principle of a Mediterranean concentration although it was recognized that this could be modified later should circumstances change. Only one large armored cruiser would be kept in Indo-China together with a sufficient number of smaller cruisers to outweigh the German force in the Far East. The Minister of Marine was to request the necessary funds to keep full complements at all times aboard all first line warships so that the fleet would always be ready for combat.[64]

The entire Conseil Supérieur voted in favor of concentrating all first line forces in the Mediterranean on March 31, 1906. But the Conseil's opinion and the action of the government were not always the same. It had voiced similar views in 1901, but in June 1906 the French first and second line forces were still divided between the north and the south. The EMG pleaded that advantage be taken of the presence of the Escadre du Nord in the Mediterranean for the annual maneuvers in order to detach the battleships for service in the south. Political considerations favored such a redeployment, and the idea had received favorable comment from maritime writers when it was raised in the budget proposals for 1907.[65] This time the recommendations of the EMG and the Conseil Supérieur were finally accepted. By 1907 the armored cruisers were recalled from the Far East and France's first line battleship strength was concentrated in the Mediterranean.[66]

By the summer of 1907 the EMG had formulated a number of propositions which were to serve as the basis for the new Instructions de Guerre. These were circulated for examination and comment to the vice admirals commanding the northern and southern squadrons by a secret dispatch on August 27.[67] The EMG believed that even if France was faced with

[63] Minutes, Section Permanent, Conseil Supérieur de la Marine, 16 Feb. 1906, *ibid.*
[64] *Ibid.* The German squadron in the Far East was composed of the armored cruiser *Fürst Bismarck*, a second-class and a third-class cruiser, and a number of gunboats and torpedo craft. Three second-class French cruisers of the "Charnier" class were to be sent out. *The Naval Annual, 1906*, p. 44. The fact that the Conseil favored a Mediterranean concentration was reported by the *Echo de Paris* cited in *The Times*, 16 Apr. 1906.
[65] Third section, EMG, "Avantages et inconvenients de la concentration dans la Méditerranée," 22 June 1906, AMF, carton BB4-2443.
[66] *The Naval Annual, 1907*, pp. 42–43, 45.
[67] Third section, EMG, "Note I Au sujet des Instructions de guerre des escadres," 6 Apr. 1907, AMF, carton BB4-2437.

a war against Germany alone, a Mediterranean concentration would still have been the most rational as long as the balance of naval power was not altered to her advantage. This stemmed from the fear that if some first line battleships were stationed at Brest, as was the case under the old system, the pressure of public opinion following the appearance of the German fleet in the Channel might force the Escadre du Nord to accept battle under distinctly unfavorable conditions. Moreover the presence of the French fleet in the Mediterranean while it completed its mobilization and prepared to sail north would have the advantage of allowing time for the attitudes of Italy, Austria-Hungary, and England to be clarified. The German fleet might also give some indication of whether it would try to reach the Mediterranean or remain in the north. The fleet's presence would also add to the security of the transfer of troops from North Africa to France. The EMG depreciated the material effects of the appearance of a German fleet in the Channel during the first days of a war. It would undoubtedly facilitate the free movement of German commerce, and the Germans would seek to provoke an unequal struggle with the weak forces of the Escadre du Nord. There might also be coastal bombardments and minelaying off the French ports. The mines were to be feared the most. It would, however, be a precarious command of the sea for the Germans, since they would be exposed to torpedo attack and would face the serious problem of replenishing their coal supplies. If England came into the war on France's side the employment of French naval forces would become of only secondary interest. The EMG reasoned that the Royal Navy would not need their help in defeating the German fleet, and even the participation of the French in a blockade of Germany would be more of a hindrance to the British because of the difficulties involved in signaling and recognition.

The situation from the French point of view was much brighter vis à vis Italy and Austria in the Mediterranean. After mobilization France would have a superiority of several units over each of her possible adversaries.[68] The power of the French battleships and armored cruisers which had been laid down since 1900, made this superiority qualitative as well as quantitative.

[68] Third section, EMG, "Note II Au Sujet des Instructions de Guerre des Escadres," 22 Apr. 1907, *ibid*. The French estimated the situation in 1907 as follows. France: 6 battleships, 3 armored cruisers; Italy: 4–6 battleships, 2–3 armored cruisers; Austria: 3 battleships, 1–2 armored cruisers. In 1910–11 the situation would be as follows. France: 16 battleships, 6–8 armored cruisers; Italy: 11 battleships (3 very old); 9 armored cruisers; Austria: 7 battleships, 3 coast defense battleships, 4 armored cruisers. *Ibid*.

The high speed (21 knots) of the latest Italian battleships might lead the Italians to form them into a special division to disturb French communications with Algeria and Tunisia, lay mines before French ports, and bombard coastal cities. The Italians would rely on their superior speed to avoid combat with the bulk of the French fleet. Because of this threat the six armored cruisers of the northern squadron would be especially valuable in the Mediterranean. The EMG were therefore thinking of an even further reduction of French forces in the north.

The heavy units of the Italian fleet would probably remain on the defensive in their fortified ports. The Austrian fleet had formerly been limited to a defensive role by the types of ships it possessed, but now that it had true high seas vessels it was conceivable that an Austrian squadron would attempt to join the Italian fleet. This might actually be advantageous for the French after the addition of the northern squadron to their Mediterranean forces for it would present an opportunity to decide once and for all the question of sea supremacy. It was absolutely necessary that the Italian fleet be forced out of its bases for a decisive battle, and that the French fleet not be exposed to the slow attrition inherent in the prolonged blockade of an Italian port. This might best be accomplished by the seizure of some Italian territory as a gage. The number of troops necessary for a landing on the Italian mainland were not available, but the French fleet acting under the threat of a bombardment might occupy the Bay of Cagliari and, if the requisite troops could be drawn from Tunisia, seize the city itself. Cagliari would provide a secure anchorage in a strategic position to cover Tunisia from an Austrian threat, oppose the combined Austrian and Italian fleets, or prevent such a combination if the Italian fleet was still at La Spezia.

For purposes of clarity, the possible intervention of British forces in the Mediterranean had not been considered in the plan. The location of Malta seemed to indicate the British mission to be the interruption of communications between Messina and Taranto and the blockade of the Austrian fleet in the Adriatic. At least this is what the EMG thought might be proposed to the British, if possible without revealing the plans for Cagliari. It would be in the French interest to keep these secret.

The new Instructions de Guerre for the contingency of war with Germany alone, other powers remaining neutral, were finally dispatched by the Minister of Marine in May 1908. The Mediterranean squadron was, after completing its mobilization at Toulon, to proceed to Mers-el-Kebir. Here it would refuel and be joined by the armored cruisers of the northern squadron. The northern squadron was ordered to proceed south right after the opening of hostilities with specific instructions to avoid combat with a superior force. The combined French force would then steam north, presumably receiving intelligence about the enemy fleet after entering the Bay of Biscay. The French admiral's objective was always to seek and fight the principal enemy force either after refueling at Brest, or immediately should circumstances so dictate. A close surveillance of the Strait of Dover was to be organized during the period of international tension to prevent a German surprise. The uncertain position of England would act as a powerful brake on the ardor of the German fleet and might limit its action. For this reason a German thrust to the Mediterranean was discounted. Any plans for a landing on the French coast would presuppose a period of preparations which were not likely to pass without notice, and which would be dangerous for the Germans to attempt before their fleet had won control of the sea from the French. The German action to worry about was a raid rather than a landing. This might incite public opinion and force the weak units at Brest to sortie. It was to avoid this unequal combat that the northern squadron had been ordered to the Mediterranean.[69] The fear among French admirals that public opinion might force a French squadron into an unequal combat was not without precedent. During the Lockroy ministry in 1896 it had been used to argue against a naval concentration at Brest in case of war against England.[70]

The Instructions de Guerre of 1908 applicable in case of a war against the Triple Alliance continued along the now familiar lines of an offensive in the south and a defensive in the north.[71] An eventual Austro-Italian combination was not considered dangerous since it would lack cohesion. The idea of a seizure of Cagliari as a gage was abandoned as impractical, at least before the battle assuring France command of the sea. Without sea supremacy the transport and supply of the troops from Tunisia would present serious risks, and the withdrawal from Tunisia of the troops necessary for the expedition might be detrimental to the latter's defense. Measures aimed at forcing the Italian fleet out of port were to be limited to such comparative pinpricks as the destruction of overseas cables,

[69] Instructions G1, Minister of Marine [Gaston Thomson] to Vice Admiral, Commander-in-Chief, Armée navale, 11 May 1908, AMF, carton BB4-2681. If the German fleet remained in the North Sea, Cherbourg instead of Brest was to be the principal base of operations. The French were puzzled as to what to do if they succeeded in defeating the German fleet. Only two operations against the German coast were considered possible. These were against the Isle of Sylt and the Bay of Howacht. The possible results, if successful, were not considered to be in proportion to the risks.

[70] Statement of Vice Admiral de Maigret, Minutes, Section permanent, Conseil Supérieur de la Marine, 16 Feb. 1906, AMF, carton BB8-1813.

[71] Instructions T1, Minister of Marine to Commander-in-Chief, Armée navale, 6 Oct. 1908, AMF, carton BB4-2681.

coastal railway works, dockyards, and torpedo-boat stations. As soon as possible after the opening of hostilities a cruiser division was to patrol between the Balearics and Algiers in order to intercept any German merchant vessels from the east trying to reach shelter in neutral Spanish waters.

It would now seem that the principle of a Mediterranean concentration had been firmly established, but in 1910 and 1911 French naval strategy appeared to undergo a complete reversal. Completely opposite answers were given to the old question of where the fleet should concentrate and which of the potential enemies should be faced first. Brest was named as the point of concentration by the EMG in the Instructions de Guerre of July 29, 1910. This was to be true not only in a war against Germany alone, but against the Triple Alliance as well. Only after the principal German naval forces had been destroyed would the French fleet proceed to Oran after coaling. If no junction between the Austrian and Italian fleets had yet taken place, the latter was to be considered the primary objective. The Mediterranean was retained as the original point of concentration and action only in the contingency where England was an active ally of France.[72] This general scheme remained basically the same in the instructions issued in July 1911 after Delcassé had replaced Lapeyrère as Minister of Marine. The Germans were to be met and fought if possible in the triangle Cape Lizard–Ushant–Cherbourg. Here the French fleet would be supported by the Brest and possibly the Cherbourg flotillas.[73] The peacetime deployment of the French fleet also veered north again. In the fall of 1909 the second squadron comprising the pre-1900 battleships in reserve was temporarily shifted back to Brest. The six "Patries" of the first squadron and the *Suffren* in reserve remained at Toulon. The reason given for this reversion to the pre-1906 deployment was the difficulty Toulon experienced in meeting the needs of the combined battleship and cruiser squadrons.[74] The Conseil Supérieur recommended in 1909 that the French fleet have four bases of operations for large ships. These were to be Cherbourg, Brest, Toulon, and Bizerte. Brest and Toulon were to be endowed with six large docks apiece for the simultaneous careenage of large ships of the latest type. Cherbourg and Bizerte were to have a minimum of three such docks.[75]

Under the 1911 instructions the naval commander-in-chief was to con-

[72] Fourth section, EMG, "Minutes des Instructions de guerre, du 9 Juillet 1910 remplacent les Instructions G et T envoyées le 6 Octobre 1908," *ibid.*

[73] Minister of Marine to Commander-in-Chief, Forces navales, 29 July 1911, *ibid.*

[74] Vice Admiral Aubert, "Rapport au Ministre," 7 May 1912, AMF, carton Ed-38.

[75] Minutes, Conseil Supérieur de la Marine, 27 May 1909, AMF, carton BB8-1813.

sider as his sole object the complete destruction of the enemy squadrons. As a general principle the enemy was to be hunted wherever he was, attacked, and annihilated by every possible means.[76] These instructions have a certain abstract ring about them. They seem a naval version of the French army's doctrine of the *offensive à outrance*. But the question inevitably arises as to how realistic or wise they were. Certainly they would be applicable if the French had to deal with the Italian fleet, but when applied to a possible conflict with the German navy, they seem fantastic. Even after the completion of the six "Dantons" the French fleet was decidedly inferior to the German fleet. Its six "Dantons," six "Patries," and eight to nine older battleships, after mobilization, were faced in September 1911 by a potential German force of seven dreadnoughts, fifteen pre-dreadnought battleships completed 1902–1908, and five battleships completed 1898–1901.[77] Before the month of September had ended the French navy was to lose a good battleship along with many of her crew, and the usefulness of the navy's powder, without which the fleet was practically disarmed, was to be called into question. The possibility that by 1910 the French were fairly certain Great Britain would be an ally in the event of war with Germany is not a satisfactory explanation for the Instructions of 1910 and 1911. If in 1908 the French thought that the Royal Navy would act as a brake on German action against the French coast even if Britain remained neutral, they would have had even more reason to do so in 1911. The decision to stake the fleet on an all or nothing offensive in the north against an adversary superior in number and probably in material, and renown for the excellence of his gunnery, is a difficult and puzzling one to explain. Certainly the material factor is not everything in a war, and a daring French commander imbued with the offensive spirit, as was Lapeyrère, might if blessed with a bit of luck have achieved at least a partial success. But against an adversary as technically competent as the Germans it is difficult to believe that a French naval offensive in 1911 would have met a different fate than the French army's Lorraine offensive of 1914.

With the completion of the "Danton" class battleships the French achieved, by the autumn of 1911, a de facto concentration of first-line naval strength in the Mediterranean. The entry into service of this second homogeneous squadron of battleships had been considerably delayed by the teething troubles experienced with their turbine engines, then a novel

---

[76] Minister of Marine to Commander-in-Chief, Armée navale, 29 July 1911, AMF, carton BB4-2681.

[77] *The Naval Annual, 1912;* Jane, *Fighting Ships, 1915,* pp. 121–128.

form of propulsion in the French Navy. The six "Dantons" were formed into the first squadron, based on Toulon. The five "Patries," plus the *Suffren* which was to temporarily replace the *Liberté*, became the second squadron, also based on Toulon. By a ministerial decree of October 31, 1911, the first and second squadrons were to form the First Armée Navale under the command of Vice Admiral Boué de Lapeyrère. The six old battleships based at Brest were now designated the third squadron.[78] Despite these new dispositions the July 1911 Instructions de Guerre, specifying the German fleet as the primary antagonist and calling for a Channel concentration, remained in force.

The 1911 plan was disturbing to Vice Admiral Marie Aubert when he resumed the position of chief of the EMG in February 1912, a post he had held from 1905 until October 1909 when he had been nominated to command the northern squadron. He warned Delcassé that to desert the Mediterranean in order to face the German fleet in a war in which Austria and Italy were on the German side would abandon to France's enemies the sea in which the French had the most interests.[79] It would also mean the renunciation of all communication between France and Algeria. The French mobilization order would automatically begin the movement of the nineteenth army corps from Algeria to France, and also the transport of territorial troops from France to Algeria to replace the nineteenth corps. For around a month the Mediterranean would be crisscrossed with troop transports. Moreover the French would be playing Germany's game by hastening the encounter between the two fleets, since the Germans lacked bases for coaling near the French coast. The sooner the clash between the two fleets, the greater the strength that the Germans would be able to throw against the French. Perhaps Aubert sensed the probable result of such a naval battle and, without wanting to admit openly that the fleet was not equal to the task or give the impression that it shrank from an encounter with the German fleet, he sought to alter French strategy to a more cautious and realistic approach.

Aubert also had, along with many in the French navy, a profound mistrust of Italy. French withdrawal from the Mediterranean would offer a terrible temptation to Germany's long-standing allies. Aubert feared they might wait until the French fleet had entered the Atlantic before joining the war, perhaps at the very moment when the first transports loaded with troops were leaving the Algerian coast. The French navy therefore ought to adopt the Mediterranean as its field of operations under all circum-

[78] *The Naval Annual, 1911*, pp. 17–18; *The Naval Annual, 1912*, p. 74.
[79] Vice Admiral Aubert, "Rapport au Ministre," 7 May 1912, AMF, carton Ed-38.

stances. The logical result of this would be the concentration here in time of peace of all available units. Aubert particularly meant the third squadron, for there was a strong chance it might not be able to join the First Armée Navale in the event of a Franco-German war. The German fleet required less time to steam from Wilhelmshaven to Brest than it took the third squadron to complete its crews and get underway, even assuming that the Germans did not sail before the actual declaration of war. The third squadron would be blockaded unless it sailed with incomplete crews, in which state it could only be a burden to the fleet. At the time the powder question added its influence, for the third squadron would require thirty-six to forty-eight hours just to re-embark its munitions. Aubert could not see how the isolation of the third squadron in the north corresponded to any eventuality foreseen in a war with Germany. The possibility of an English alliance added yet another argument in favor of sending it to the Mediterranean.

Aubert was not advocating that the north be left completely devoid of high seas forces. He spoke only of attaching the third squadron to the First Armée Navale. The presence of a cruiser squadron in the Channel was considered necessary to support the action of the French destroyer, torpedo boat, and submarine flotillas which might threaten an enemy fleet compelled to pass through a narrow sea. To this effect Aubert proposed that this second cruiser squadron (2e escadre légère) consist of the three "Gloires" presently in commission with full crews, and the three "Gueydons" then in reserve. The "Gueydons" would be given reduced crews as soon as sufficient personnel were available. The "Gloires" were large cruisers (9856 tons) completed 1903–1904. The "Gueydons" (9367 tons) were completed 1902–1905.[80] To surmount the difficulties of a congested Toulon, Aubert recommended the reduction and even complete cessation of new construction at this port so that all its efforts could be concentrated on maintenance of the fleet. The Bizerte dockyards should be developed so that they could alleviate Toulon's task, and the northern ports were to undertake at least some of the refits and repairs. The number of workers at Toulon might be increased by around five hundred, the force presently employed at Brest and Cherbourg to maintain the third squadron. The fleet also ought to take advantage of the private yards at La Seyne near Toulon.

Aubert's arguments were substantially the same as those he advocated in 1906. But there was the important difference that this time he did not

[80] The newest armored cruisers were naturally attached to the First Armée Navale in the Mediterranean. *The Naval Annual, 1912,* pp. 203–206.

propose steaming north to meet the German fleet once the concentration had been completed. Aside from the growing superiority of the German squadrons, naval activity in Austria and Italy also began to cause concern. In June 1912 the EMG prepared a study on the three major Mediterranean fleets at the present, at the end of 1915, and in 1920.[81] The results were alarming for the French. In June 1912 the comparison in battleships and armored cruisers showed twenty-eight for France and twenty-three for Austria and Italy. By the end of 1915 the Triple Alliance would have a slight superiority of twenty-six to twenty-four. In 1920 the battleship totals would be thirty-one to twenty-eight in favor of the Triple Alliance, and this meant including the *Suffren* and five "Patries," by then obsolescent, in the French total. Translated into terms of artillery—a common practice among naval staffs or commentators of the time—the situation at the end of 1915 would be:

| | Italy and Austria | | France | |
	Heavy	Medium	Heavy	Medium
First line	145	120	102	286
Second line	8	128	44	142
Total	153	248	146	428.

To re-establish the naval balance of power the EMG considered that it was necessary to have seven dreadnoughts in addition to those voted in the naval program of March 1912. A careful study of all available intelligence seemed to indicate a strong tendency toward further naval increases in Austria-Hungary. This would probably mean the construction of a second division of super-dreadnoughts after the four ships of the "Viribus Unitis" class had been completed.[82] The French had turned to the Mediterranean after hopes of successfully meeting the German fleet in the north had faded. But even after all the reservations that paper comparisons of this sort necessitate, it was obvious that an Austro-Italian combination would challenge this mastery of the Mediterranean which the EMG considered so vital.

Delcassé approved Aubert's plans and discussed them with the fleet commander, Admiral Lapeyrère, when the two met at Ajaccio during the July naval maneuvers. The crux of the matter was the problem of Toulon's

[81] First and fourth sections, EMG, "Etude comparée de la valeur des marines de guerre française, italienne et austro-hongroise," June 1912, AMF, carton BB7-160.

[82] First section, EMG, "Note pour le Ministre au sujet du développement de la flotte austro-hongroise," 13 Aug. 1912, AMF, carton BB7-129.

capacity to maintain the entire fleet—that was the reason a squadron of battleships had to be transferred back to Brest a few years before. After studying the problem Lapeyrère concluded that the best solution would be to permanently attach one of the squadrons to the arsenal of Sidd-Abdallah near Bizerte for all of its repairs, careenage, and provisioning. It was materially impossible to give all the fleet's work to the Toulon dockyards; it was also simpler, more logical, and more economical for each of the two ports to have exclusive charge of the ships assigned to it. The first and second squadrons could not be separated without weakening the fleet, so the choice would have to be made between the cruiser squadron and the third squadron. Lapeyrère favored the latter, for its old battleships were undoubtedly the lesser charge. Two flotillas of destroyers (fourteen) and one of submarines (six) were also to be stationed at Bizerte.[83]

Delcassé decided that the dispatch of the third squadron to the Mediterranean would take place around October 15. The squadron was to join the First Armée Navale in combined maneuvers after its arrival in the Mediterranean, following which its commander was to consider himself under Lapeyrère's orders. The cruisers remaining in the north, the second cruiser squadron, would constitute an independent naval command under Rear Admiral Favereau, who would also control the northern torpedo boat and submarine flotillas.[84] The order from Aubert to the commander of the third squadron was accidently dispatched and made public prematurely when a draft intended for the minister was sent to the squadron in September by a staff officer who had misunderstood Aubert's orders.[85]

After the third squadron had reached the Mediterranean, Lapeyrère received a set of general directives from Delcassé.[86] The commander of the fleet was informed of the precise nature of the agreements between the Ministries of Marine and War with respect to the transport of the nineteenth corps. The army wanted the navy to consecrate all its efforts to assure before all else, and at whatever cost, the transport to France of the troops from North Africa. The paramount importance attached to the security of French communications with Algeria and Tunisia led the minister to issue two directives. The first called for indirect protection of

[83] Lapeyrère to Delcassé, 31 Aug. 1912, AMF, carton BB4-2708.

[84] Delcassé to Lapeyrère, 28 Sept. 1912, *ibid.* Also third and fourth sections, EMG, Circular to Commander-in-Chief and Préfets Maritimes, 5 Oct. 1912, AMF, carton BB4-2707.

[85] Note by Admiral Lacaze (Chef du cabinet of the Minister of Marine), France, Ministère des affaires étrangères, Correspondence politique (hereafter cited as MAE), Italie-Dossier Général-Politique étrangère, carton 12.

[86] Delcassé to Lapeyrère, 11 Nov. 1912, AMF, carton Ed-38.

the transport by the acquisition as rapidly as possible of sea supremacy. This could only be obtained by destroying, blockading, or immobilizing the enemy forces. All Lapeyrère's first-line strength would be assigned this task. Delcassé's second directive called for the direct protection of the transports by five second line cruisers. Under the present conditions of French foreign policy, Austria and Italy were the two Mediterranean powers to be watched. Lapeyrère was to position himself so as to oppose the junction of their two fleets. It was not certain, however, that both would declare war against France together. Italy might possibly await events before committing herself. During the period of international tension preceding a war, Lapeyrère was to ascertain the points of enemy concentration and prepare to act against the closest enemy fleet. If he was unable to prevent a junction of the two enemy fleets he was not to hesitate in accepting combat with all the forces at his disposal. The examination of questions of detail by the EMG and Lapeyrère's own staff would probably lead to supplementary instructions. The changing political situation and more specific alliances and ententes would also add new elements for study in the formulation of Mediterranean war plans. Delcassé was probably hinting at the staff talks and diplomatic activity which were then underway between Britain and France. However, discretion was the rule in this matter, and Delcassé told the commander of the second cruiser squadron in the north that he was to act as if England would remain neutral. Should the entente take a decisive form the commander would be notified without delay.[87]

Lapeyrère's advice about basing the third squadron at Bizerte was not followed. None of the First Armée Navale's four squadrons were specifically attached to this port. Instead the minor repairs of the three battleship squadrons were to be accomplished indiscriminately at Toulon or Bizerte. In principle Toulon would be especially responsible for the major repairs and careenage of the first and second squadrons. It would also be responsible for the careenage of the third squadron, but major repairs to these old battleships would be accomplished in the northern ports. Bizerte would take care of the upkeep of the armored cruisers of the first cruiser squadron, but major work of a long duration would be done at Toulon. The munitions which it might become necessary to disembark as new lots of unstable powder were discovered would be stored at Toulon.[88]

---

[87] Delcassé to rear admiral commanding second cruiser squadron, 11 Nov. 1912, *ibid.*

[88] Aubert to Lapeyrère, 15 Nov. 1912, AMF, carton BB2-955. The many disadvantages of Bizerte as a naval base were not rectified before the outbreak of the war. See the account of the Préfet Maritime in 1914: Vice Admiral Dartige du Fournet, *A travers les mers* (Paris, 1929), pp. 239–241, 245–247.

The French redeployment of their naval forces in September 1912, like the British moves earlier in the year, was only a manifestation of policies long favored by naval leaders. By transferring the Brest squadron to Toulon, the French navy was merely reverting to the situation which existed from 1907 to 1910. But following in the wake of the Moroccan crisis, the Tripolitan war, and the British withdrawal of their Malta battleship squadron, the move caused much comment in the French and European press. The transfer was probably more important for its psychological effect than for the actual military value of the aging battleships of the Brest squadron. One significant difference between England and France did appear in the domestic reaction to redeployment. Where the withdrawal of the Malta squadron provoked a great public debate in the British press and Parliament over Mediterranean policy, the removal of practically all major naval units from France's northern and Atlantic coasts created comparatively little stir in France once its international significance had been commented on. This is probably the result of the general lack of public interest in naval affairs. The debate over the concentration, such as it was, was largely confined to a handful of interested deputies and senators, particularly those from the ports concerned, professional naval periodicals and writers, and those who made use of the issue in their political rivalries.

Le Temps greeted the concentration as conforming to theories for the best utilization of the fleet and the best solution for the security of the country. It discussed France's obligations under the Russian alliance and the entente with England, and assumed that the general duties of the British, Russian, and French fleets in case of war had been established. It would be France's task to face the left wing of the Triple Alliance represented by the fleets of Austria and Italy in the Mediterranean.[89] The assumption that the transfer was part of a concerted plan by the Triple Entente was also shared by *Le Journal* which pointed out that the old ships of the third squadron were too weak to oppose the German dreadnoughts in the north and would face the choice of either being shut up in Brest or sallying forth to die with honor.[90] The *Journal des débats* observed, correctly, that Delcassé's decision was simply a return to the situation in 1909 when Lapeyrère became naval minister. The transfer then of some of the battleships to Brest was caused by the inability of Toulon and Bizerte to maintain a large number of ships. Lapeyrère had deliberately abolished the regional nomenclature of the squadrons in

---

[89] *Le Temps*, 11 Sept. 1912. The article is also discussed in Bertie to Grey, 10 Sept. 1912, FO 371, vol. 1369, France, no. 38300.

[90] *Le Journal*, 13 Sept. 1912.

favor of numerical designations in order to emphasize the possibility of the entire fleet fighting in any area. All the squadrons had maneuvered together in 1910 and 1911, and by now the dockyard facilities at both Bizerte and Toulon had been improved.[91] Vice Admiral Germinet, the former commander of the Mediterranean squadron, in an interview given to the *Echo de Paris* described the concentration as good strategy since after the entente cordiale had become a reality the role of the French navy consisted of winning and keeping sea supremacy in the Mediterranean.[92] *Le Temps* also printed a number of interviews with several retired admirals who favored the Mediterranean concentration.[93]

The immediate opposition to a Mediterranean naval concentration came from Brest, as might have been expected. Here a committee was formed to protect the port's interests, and the local paper, the *Dépêche de Brest*, led an active campaign to get Delcassé to delay execution of the order.[94] Emile Goude, Socialist deputy from the *arrondissement* of Brest, was one of the leaders of the fight and tried to intercede with the minister. Delcassé politely informed him that the measure was dictated solely by his concern to assure the national defense under the best conditions, and that he meant to examine its repercussions with the aim of giving satisfaction to the interests of the population of Brest.[95] The Brest chamber of commerce passed a resolution calling for compensations, if the decision was not rescinded. These would take the form of assignment to the port of six armored cruisers with full crews, reinforcement of the submarine and torpedo boat flotillas, and transfer to Brest of the naval gunnery school.[96] The municipal council of Brest divided on ideological grounds. Goude and the Socialist majority condemned the Mediterranean concentration as ruinous to small merchants, harmful to recruiting in Breton districts, and provocative to other powers; the non-Socialist minority favored creation of a separate fleet for the north, an "Armée navale du Nord."[97]

---

[91] *Journal des débats*, 11 Sept. 1912.

[92] *Echo de Paris*, 13 Sept. 1912. The admiral, who once before had gotten in trouble through indiscretions to the press, again caused a minor sensation in diplomatic circles by advocating that in the event of war the Strait of Dover should be considered English and French territorial waters and the passage of neutral ships forbidden. See also Bertie to Grey, 13 Sept. 1912, FO 371, vol. 1369, France, file 38618.

[93] *Le Temps*, 18 Sept. 1912.

[94] *Ibid.*, 13 Sept. 1912; *Journal des débats*, 28 Sept. 1912.

[95] Delcassé to Goude, n.d. [Sept. 1912], AMF, carton BB4-2347.

[96] *Eclair*, 13 Sept. 1912; *Le Yacht*, 21 Sept. 1912, p. 596.

[97] *Journal des débats*, 16 Sept. 1912. At the end of October another protest meeting was held at Brest and motions were passed calling for the government to be asked to formally state the reasons for the Mediterranean concentration, and to be asked that all the special naval schools be sent north as compensation. *Le Yacht*, 2 Nov. 1912, p. 694. In 1909 the impending transfer of one of the squadrons back to the north provoked a protest meeting and similar resolutions in Toulon. *The Times*, 18 Sept. 1909.

All criticisms of the Mediterranean concentration were given great prominence in the columns of the *Eclair,* whose editor Ernest Judet waged a constant vendetta against Delcassé. He ran a highly critical series of articles under the general title of "Delcassé marin"; anything that could be interpreted in a manner hostile to the Minister of Marine was certain to be highlighted.[98] Brest also received some support from the city of Rochefort, whose municipal council passed a resolution in the latter part of October 1912 calling for an increase in the French naval program, the creation of a separate fleet for the north, and extensive defensive measures for the Atlantic coast.[99] With the passage of time the protest movement in Brest tapered off. By the middle of February 1913 the British consul was able to report that the agitation among the commercial classes in Brest and the district seemed "to have died a natural death" and that the rare references to the subject evoked "a resigned moan, with vague hopes of 'compensations.' "[100]

Although a good deal of the opposition to the Mediterranean concentration stemmed from purely local interests which would have been harmed by it or from personal animosities, this was not always the case. The move after all did leave much of France's coastline bare of serious naval defense. Probably the most influential opponent of the Mediterranean school was Jean de Lanessan, deputy from the Charente-Inférieure, a former governor general of Indo-China, and an able naval minister who had given France her first homogeneous battleship squadron. De Lanessan, it must be added, was not completely free from local interest, for he represented the *arrondissement* of Rochefort, one of the Atlantic ports whose importance and prosperity was diminished by a Mediterranean concentration. It could be argued, of course, that Rochefort's declining importance was the result of the substitution of Germany and Italy instead of England as the most probable maritime enemy rather than any specific ministerial decree. De Lanessan ridiculed the facile assumption that England would, or even could, entrust France with guarding her Mediterranean interests.[101] The principle of concentration was a wise one but it could be carried to absurd lengths. However large French interests in the Mediterranean, they were just as important and the enemy just as serious in the north.

98 *Eclair,* 12, 13, 14, 16, 22 Sept.; 1, 6, 7 Oct. 1912.

99 *Le Temps,* 24 Oct. 1912; *L'Action,* 26 Oct. 1912.

100 "Information relating to Naval Affairs in, and connected with, the port of Brest, during the period from the 1st November 1912 to the 15th February, 1913," p. 17. Enclosure in consular dispatch, Spencer Dickson to Sir Edward Grey, 21 Feb. 1913, FO 371, vol. 1642, France.

101 J.-L. de Lanessan, "L'Angleterre le voudrait-elle?" *L'Action,* 23 Sept. 1912.

De Lanessan favored the creation of a fleet for the north as well as the south, an idea reflected in the resolution of the Rochefort municipal council. He advocated the addition of eight dreadnoughts to the building program voted in 1912 so that France could have in 1920 three squadrons of six ships each available for both the north and the south. Eventually, he presented a bill to this effect in the Chamber. De Lanessan warned, in the rhetoric common among French advocates of naval expansion, that Napoleon had failed to see Trafalgar as the preface to Waterloo; he hoped that the Republic would be more clairvoyant than either Louis XV or Napoleon.[102]

Toward the end of 1913 De Lanessan assembled a book from his many articles on the subject entitled *Notre défense maritime*. In this polemical work he pictured the Mediterranean concentration as part of an evolution he had noted since 1902 which was backed by a small group of ambitious men—to whom he applied the name "Méditerranéens"—who were anxious not to separate themselves from the offices where advancements were made and where the most agreeable posts were distributed. The pleasant conditions of life in the Mediterranean as compared to the icy fogs of the North Sea and the tempestuous winds of the Atlantic, according to the former minister, were seductive considerations which were apt to rally the majority of French naval officers to the theory of a Mediterranean concentration.[103]

If it was important to protect the Mediterranean ports from the Austrians and Italians, De Lanessan argued, it was just as important to protect the Channel and Atlantic ports from the more powerful German fleet. It was a sophism to accuse the northern ports of local egoism, for France was one, and all her ports had the right of being effectively defended from the attacks of possible enemies. De Lanessan, firmly convinced that the idea of France's undertaking the defense of the Mediterranean for England, and England the defense of the Channel for France, was an illusion, wanted a French fleet of thirty-six dreadnoughts, half of which would remain in the north. The British and French fleets, in the event of an alliance, would support each other in both theaters. To support the fleets, well-provisioned bases endowed with strong flotilla defenses were necessary at Brest and Cherbourg for the Channel, Rochefort for the Atlantic, and Toulon and Bizerte in the Mediterranean. Even with a Mediterranean concentration De Lanessan doubted that it would be possible to transport the troops from North Africa to France at the beginning of or in the course

---

[102] De Lanessan, "Nos besoins maritimes," *L'Action*, 23 Nov. 1912.
[103] De Lanessan, *Notre défense maritime* (Paris, 1914), p. 153.

of a war. The political and morale state of the colonies would not permit their withdrawal, and even if it did it was doubtful if the fleet could protect the enormous convoys of transports.

Inadvertently contradicting this argument to some extent, De Lanessan raised the specter of a German amphibious assault on France's Atlantic coast. The French flotillas would not be able to stop it, and Germany might obtain a badly needed base on the Atlantic. Moreover, with the Atlantic coast almost bare of defenses there would be nothing to prevent a force of fast German battle cruisers from proceeding up the Loire and destroying the ships under construction in the dockyards at Saint-Nazaire, as well as undertaking similar operations in the Gironde. To prevent destructive raids of this sort De Lanessan advocated the creation of a force of around six battle cruisers similar to the ones that the Germans were building, as well as the strengthening of coastal defenses and the flotillas. The battle cruisers, based on Brest, should suffice to deter German operations.

Le Yacht, among the professional periodicals, strongly supported the transfer of the third squadron. The role of the French fleet was not to defend the coasts and ports directly but rather to attack and defeat the enemy fleet at sea. The handful of old battleships at Brest were no match for the German fleet but could play a useful role in the Mediterranean by helping to assure French superiority over the Austrian and Italian fleets. The old "Charlemagnes" and "Bouvets" could still put up a good show against the Italian "Saint Bons" or the Austrian "Erzherzogs." [104] As the third squadron was the slowest in the French fleet it would be best to station it at Bizerte where it might be closest to the future battlefield.[105] *La Marine française*—the old organ of Admiral Aube and the Jeune Ecole and now under the direction of Henri Michel, Radical Socialist senator from the Basses-Alpes—devoted a long and favorable study to the principle of a Mediterranean concentration. Delcassé was criticized, however, as too subordinate to England for not insisting on a reciprocal visit to Malta and Gibraltar by high French military authorities following Churchill's and Asquith's visit to Bizerte the previous June.[106]

Captain René Daveluy, one of the best-known French naval writers of

[104] Henri Bernay, "La Concentration navale française dans la Méditerranée," *Le Yacht,* 21 Sept. 1912, pp. 593–594.

[105] P. Le Roll, "La Répartition des escadres," *Le Yacht,* 12 Oct. 1912, pp. 641–642. Another favorable appreciation from the point of view of general strategy and geographical factors was given by A. Rousseau, "La Concentration dans la Méditerranée," *Moniteur de la flotte,* 21 Sept. 1912, pp. 3–4.

[106] Quoted by *Eclair,* 15 Nov. 1912. As usual, the portions critical of Delcassé were emphasized by Judet's paper.

his day, rationalized the fact, difficult to deny, that France's northern and Atlantic coasts were being left practically defenseless: he pointed out that their protection could not be assured by forces which were destined to be crushed.[107] An exchange of fire between French shore batteries and German warships could be as murderous for the latter as for the former. Daveluy doubted that Germany would immobilize an important enough portion of her army away from the decisive land theater of operations to make a German landing on the French coast a serious danger. The real damage following the appearance of a German squadron would be caused by the almost complete cessation of French maritime activity along the Channel and Atlantic coasts, and undoubtedly the population of this area would face a painful crisis. Unfortunately it was not possible to wage war painlessly, as the inhabitants of France's eastern frontiers knew only too well. The best way to diminish the suffering was to make the war as short as possible and to emerge the victor. To accomplish this one should not divide one's forces with the sole aim of distributing them equally wherever an attack was feared. On the contrary, all efforts must be concentrated on striking irresistible blows where decisive results might be obtained.

De Lanessan, as befitting a deputy representing Rochefort, questioned Daveluy's minimization of the effects of a coastal bombardment.[108] He doubted that this shelling of French cities and ports—to which no effective reply could be given—would leave the French public and army indifferent. Furthermore, Daveluy's opinion that the enemy could not spare sufficient troops for a landing on the Channel coast might be valid in respect to the Italian army and the coast of Provence, but De Lanessan believed that the German army had a sufficient numerical superiority over the French to spare several corps. It was also questionable if in a war where France was alone against the Triple Alliance the German fleet would remain content to stay locked in the North Sea while the French destroyed the Austrian and Italian fleets in the south. It seemed more probable that the German fleet, having nothing to fear in the Atlantic, would try to reach the Mediterranean even before the opening of hostilities and, together with the naval forces of Austria and Italy, attack the French fleet. The truth, sad as it was, could not escape the thoughtful. The navies of the Triple Alliance had been, were, and would be developed to such an extent

---

[107] René Daveluy, "La Concentration méditerranéene," *Moniteur de la flotte*, 30 Nov. 1912, p. 3.

[108] J.-L. de Lanessan and P. Pierreval, "Deux opinions sur la concentration méditerranéene," *ibid.*, 21 Dec. 1912, p. 3.

that it was impossible for France to think of struggling against them with the French fleet alone. This was also true for England and it was from this reasoning that the entente cordiale was born. Even with England as an ally De Lanessan did not think that France's coasts would be secure, for he doubted that the Germans were building 26,000-ton battle cruisers with a speed of 28 knots and a dreadnought's armament just to leave them confined in the Baltic or behind the fortifications of Heligoland. The implication was that they might be used for raids against French ports.

C. Pierreval, writing in the same issue of the *Moniteur de la Flotte* as De Lanessan, spoke of the morale problem that would result in the navy if the French fleet remained immobile in the Mediterranean while the decisive events of the war unfolded elsewhere. Yet such immobility was quite likely since neither of the potential foes in the Mediterranean might choose to risk its fleet in battle. Pierreval did not consider mastery of the Mediterranean essential, for he saw no reason to fear possible hostile operations against French North Africa if it had already been decided to oppose only passively similar operations against the Breton and Norman coasts. The conclusion which might be drawn from this was that France did not really need a fleet. If it was only a question of assuring the transport of the troops from North Africa to France it might be claimed that the effort was disproportionate to the result, and the expense of a fleet disproportionate to its object.[109]

Rear Admiral Darrieus, as well known as Daveluy in the field of French naval literature, and like him a follower of Mahan, also argued that German bombardments and possible landings on the French Atlantic and Channel coasts were not to be taken lightly. An unopposed promenade along the coast by the Germans would immediately result in intense public emotion, and the news, deformed and exaggerated by distance, could have a fatal result on the morale of the army. It would not be any more difficult for the German fleet, once mistress of the seas, to land large numbers of troops in Brittany or Normandy than it was for the Japanese to land men by the hundreds of thousands on the Manchurian coast. The full freedom of action of the French armies on the Vosges, as well as the atmosphere of security which was an essential condition for their planned operations on the land frontiers, required by definition that France's "blue frontiers" also be guarded.[110]

[109] *Ibid.*, pp. 4–5. C. Pierreval was supposedly the pseudonym of a "very experienced naval officer," *The Naval Annual, 1914*, p. 29.

[110] Quoted in *ibid.*, p. 33. Darrieus, a former professor of strategy and tactics at the Ecole de Guerre Navale, was the author of *La Guerre sur mer* (Paris, 1907). When Pierre Baudin replaced Delcassé as Minister of Marine in January 1913, Darrieus served as his chef du cabinet. *Moniteur de la Flotte*, 1 Feb. 1913, p. 6.

The principle of the Mediterranean concentration was upheld in the Chamber by Paul Painlevé in his report on the naval budget for 1913.[111] He also deplored the delays in completing the required work so that Toulon would be able to maintain the entire fleet, and hoped that when the first dreadnoughts entered service they would find at that port the necessary depth of water in which to maneuver instead of being restricted, as the "Dantons" were at present. Painlevé shared Admiral Aubert's opinion that if necessary the construction of large units at Toulon should be abandoned so that the dockyards could devote all their efforts to maintenance of the fleet. It was absolutely essential that the harbor be adapted without delay for the concentration of all French squadrons in the Mediterranean. Similar views were also advanced by the budget reporter in the Senate, Camille Chautemps, who also favored De Lanessan's proposal for an augmentation of the building program by eight dreadnoughts.[112] De Lanessan kept some of the controversy over the Mediterranean concentration alive in the Chamber. This was particularly true after Baudin, as Minister of Marine, proposed the suppression of the torpedo boat flotillas at Lorient and Rochefort and the submarine flotilla at La Pallice. Supported by a few deputies from the Channel and Atlantic ports, De Lanessan interpellated the Minister of Marine, and an exchange over the subject took place at the end of July 1913.[113] An anonymous article "La Manche ou la bataille?" in the *Moniteur de la Flotte*, proposing the transfer to the Mediterranean of the armored cruisers remaining at Brest, provoked a new series of polemical pieces.[114] The appearance of De Lanessan's book *Notre défense maritime* early in 1914 continued the debate, but one cannot escape the conclusion that by this time the opponents of the Mediterranean concentration were waging guerrilla warfare over a question which had long since been decided.

At least one French military writer was undisturbed about the superiority of the German navy over the French navy, for he believed that the final issue of a Franco-German war must naturally be decided on land. If anything the growth of the German fleet could be looked on with favor, for the resulting naval expenditure would check expenditure on the German

[111] Ministère de la Marine, *Rapport portant fixation de Budget Général de l'Exercice, 1913*, translated in *Journal of the Royal United Service Institution*, 57.422 (April 1913): 528–529.

[112] *Moniteur de la Flotte*, 17 May 1913, p. 3.

[113] *Ibid.*, 5 July 1913, p. 4; 2 Aug. 1913, p. 6.

[114] It appeared 20 Sept. 1913, p. 3. This was answered by C. Pierreval, "Théories et réalités," *ibid.*, 27 Sept. 1913, p. 3. The rejoinder, Anon., "Encore la Manche," *ibid.*, 14 Oct. 1913, p. 3. In favor of a concentration against Germany were: Un officier breveté, "La Manche et la bataille," *ibid.*, 18 Oct. 1913, p. 3; and C. Pierreval, "La Doctrine contre la Méditerranée," *ibid.*, 29 Nov. 1913, p. 3.

army which was already far superior to that of the French. In an application of Tirpitz's "Risk Theory" which the German admiral might never have anticipated, Charles Cormier, writing under the pseudonym Captain Sorb, deemed Germany a maritime power who was dependent on her fleet and therefore not apt to risk it lightly in a war with France if victory at sea might be too dearly bought.[115]

To a certain extent the discussions over the Mediterranean concentration or French naval strength have an air of unreality about them, for they usually centered on the hypothesis that France would have to face Germany or the entire Triple Alliance by herself. Those who constantly cited the danger of an invasion by sea because the numerical superiority of the German army would permit a sufficient number of troops to be spared for this purpose seem never to have considered the alliance with Russia and the effect the Russian army might have in offsetting this German advantage. The material effects on the war as a whole of the German fleet cruising unopposed off France's northern coasts, even if permitted by the British, were depreciated by many of the admirals, although it would hardly have been politic to proclaim publicly their cold-blooded indifference to the unpleasant consequences for the coastal population. Naturally the entrance of England into a war on the French side would have made most of the argument about the defense of the northern coasts superfluous.

The French fleet by the summer of 1912 was well on the way to recovery after the tribulations of previous years. Much might remain to be done, but by Mediterranean standards it was a formidable fighting force, and the Mediterranean was now to be its primary theater of operations. It would be misleading to excessively depreciate the French fleet through unfavorable comparison to the British and German navies. The nightmarish powder question remained but was being gradually alleviated as supplies of reliable powder became available. A naval program had finally been voted at the end of March 1912, although its adequacy was questionable in the light of Austrian and Italian naval progress.

As has been shown, the Mediterranean concentration of September 1912 was not a new policy, but was merely a reversion to one agreed upon

---

[115] Capitaine Sorb, *La Doctrine de défense nationale* (Paris, 1912), pp. 387–389. The author in discussing France's colonial defense problem mentioned the advantage for France in remaining neutral in the event of an Anglo-German conflict. At the close of such a war the fleets of both powers might well be greatly weakened. France would then find herself in an advantageous, if not preponderant, maritime position (p. 369).

by the EMG and the Conseil Supérieur de la Marine in 1906. As such, and contrary to many of the assumptions made by contemporaries, it was not immediately related to the withdrawal of the British battle squadron from Malta earlier in 1912. By itself the third squadron was worth little at Brest against the dreadnoughts of the German fleet, and had only been sent north in 1909 because of the limited capacity of Toulon for maintenance of the fleet. The French Mediterranean concentration had really been accomplished in 1911 when the "Dantons" were assigned to Toulon one by one after their entry into service. One might take a broad view and argue that indirectly the entente with England made the Mediterranean concentration possible, since the French, whether they admitted it or not, could feel sure enough of the restraining influence of the Royal Navy on the Germans to take the calculated risk of stripping the north of heavy units. But the far more immediate causes of the Mediterranean concentration were the growing inferiority of French naval strength in comparison to the German fleet and the development of far more potent Austrian and Italian naval power.

Throughout the controversy over the Mediterranean concentration the French government had a hidden asset which would have done much to satisfy most of its critics who harped on the exposed condition of the northern French coasts: the secret naval agreement with Great Britain, negotiated in the course of 1912. Although nonbinding, this agreement was of tremendous future import.

IV

The Basis of the Anglo-French Entente in the Mediterranean

In December 1911 Admiral Sir Francis Bridgeman, First Sea Lord of the Admiralty, hinted to Commander Count Legouz de Saint-Seine, French naval attaché in London, that the Admiralty would willingly consider a division of the Channel into zones of action for the flotillas of the two nations in view of a possible struggle against a common foe.[1] Presumably this reflected a desire on Bridgeman's part to revise and perhaps clarify the rather vague agreements reached by the two navies since 1906. Saint-Seine, writing in a private letter to a friend on the EMG, thought it opportune to profit from the Admiralty's good intentions and go beyond the question of coordination of flotillas to the study of possibilities for the exchange of secret information by radio, joint recognition signals, and a whole ensemble of delicate questions.[2] To his surprise he received no reply from the EMG to the British propositions which, given the existing political and military situation, one might have expected the French to jump at. After a fortnight he wrote a private letter to the chief of the first section (intelligence) of the EMG asking the reason. Saint-Seine received the reply that the chief of the EMG, Vice Admiral Paul Auvert, was an officer of the old school who thought of England as "perfidious Albion" and, lacking confidence in the British, had simply pigeonholed Saint-Seine's dispatch without the minister knowing about it.[3] As Cambon was a friend of Delcassé, the attaché used his aid in bypassing the EMG. Delcassé administered a sharp reprimand to Auvert in Saint-Seine's presence, and authorized the attaché to report directly to his office in the future con-

[1] Saint-Seine to Delcassé, 11 Dec. 1911, AMF, carton Es-10.
[2] Saint-Seine to ? [probably Capitaine de vaisseau Mornet, Chief of first section, EMG], 16 Dec. 1911, *ibid.*
[3] Memorandum by Saint-Seine, n.d. [early 1937], *ibid.* No record of this letter appears in the "Dossier Anglais."

86

cerning this subject instead of going through the usual channels.[4] In the course of January 1912 Captain Kelly also referred to the possibility of a more precise agreement in respect to the Channel. At this time Delcassé asked the British to define exactly what they wanted.[5]

Later in the month Vice Admiral Boué de Lapeyrère, now French Commander-in-Chief in the Mediterranean, expressed his own thoughts to the British on the best employment of British and French forces in the event of war. The plans of the French fleet would be greatly complicated by the question of whether or not Italy would join her Triple Alliance allies or, as Lapeyrère believed, remain aloof and "not definitely cast in her lot with either side until that side had gained some advantage." [6] With his present force of twelve battleships and six armored cruisers in full commission he could hold command of the Mediterranean, but to guarantee the safe passage of the Algerian army corps to France it would be necessary to have the six old battleships then stationed at Brest. The security of commerce in the Mediterranean could not be guaranteed without the assistance of British cruisers. Lapeyrère proposed to bar the three passages from east to west in the Mediterranean with the French destroyer, torpedo boat, and submarine flotillas. The passages in question were the channels between Cape Bon and Sardinia, Corsica and France, and the Strait of

[4]*Ibid.* The incident probably took place the last week of December. The navy's historical section prepared a historical summary of the talks with England based on the documents in the "Dossier Anglais," (carton Es-10). This 104-page typewritten summary was sent to Saint-Seine in February 1937 to enable him to corroborate it with his own account written from memory. After seeing it the former attaché put the date of the incident as December 1911 instead of January 1912 as he had originally supposed. Saint-Seine to Commandant Guichard, 5 Mar. 1937, *ibid.* There is no documentary evidence to support Saint-Seine's account which was written from memory twenty-five years after the event when he was in his early seventies. Consequently portions of his memorandum are hazy and do not always correspond exactly with known facts. It is probable, however, that some incident of this sort did occur. An event as vivid as the reprimand of a senior naval officer in his presence would naturally have made a strong impression on Saint-Seine although the details may have been blurred by the passage of time. The somewhat irregular nature of the proceedings may account for the lack of documentation.

[5] Statement by Paul Cambon quoted in Grey to Churchill, 11 May 1912, *BD*, X (pt. 2), no. 389, p. 591; note by Admiral Auvert, 17 Jan. 1912, AMF, carton Es-10. As Delcassé's instructions form the subject of this note by Auvert, the admiral definitely knew of Bridgeman's feelers at the time. Consequently it is puzzling to find Saint-Seine writing in a letter of March 21 that he had received no reply to his request for instructions concerning Bridgeman's proposals. He may be referring to the incident with Auvert which supposedly took place in December, or the EMG may never have informed him of Auvert's conversation with the British naval attaché in January. The exact progress of the Anglo-French talks in the winter of 1912 is not clear. Saint-Seine to ? [possibly Mornet], 21 Mar. 1912, *ibid.*

[6] Report of an interview with Admiral Boué de Lapeyrère, 21 Jan. 1912, Admiralty Archives, case 0091. The report is unsigned but the logical assumption is that the conversation took place with Captain Kelly, the naval attaché.

Bonifacio. He suggested that the outlet from the Adriatic be left to the British assuming—this was before the Admiralty reorganization—that there would be a squadron of battleships available at Malta. The French would act to prevent a junction between the Austrian and Italian fleets, or separated portions of the Italian fleet. In the north the French admiral deemed the Calais and Dunkirk submarine and torpedo-boat flotillas capable of effectively blocking the Strait of Dover, and thought that to insure the safe passage of a British expeditionary force another blockade should be established on the line Cherbourg-Portland by the flotillas of Brest and Cherbourg. Should Britain remain neutral in a Franco-German war, Lapeyrère feared that a German raiding force would be sent around the north of Scotland. This German force could threaten commerce or might attack Brest, possibly drawing French troops back from the frontiers.

These naval staff talks between France and England are often difficult for the historian to follow because of their secret nature and the fact that much business was handled orally, a fact which Saint-Seine stressed in his account written after the war.[7] The French records tend to be more complete than the British, particularly because few reports by British naval attachés survive for this period. These reports were usually destroyed when no longer current unless deemed of sufficient interest for a copy to have been retained by the Foreign Office and possibly reproduced in the Confidential Print.[8] It would appear from the records which survive that the naval talks remained dormant during the winter of 1912. An unsigned handwritten note in French, dated January 1912, dealing with general principles for the defense of the Channel and Strait of Dover may be found in the French archives, but no communications between the two navies appear to have occurred. One may surmise that the Admiralty were too preoccupied with their impending reorganization to spare much time for the French, and apparently never followed the lead given by Bridgeman in December or the suggestion of Delcassé to make new proposals. In fact it seems to have been the French who took up the matter again through Cambon in May.

The Admiralty had not completely forgotten the French, however, and on April 23 Churchill prepared an outline of each navy's patrol zones in

[7] Memorandum by Saint-Seine, n.d. [1937]; Saint-Seine to Cmdt. Guichard, 5 Mar. 1937, AMF, carton Es-10. The editors of the *Documents diplomatiques français* also make this point concerning oral reports of which no record remains. Ministère des affaires étrangères, Commission de publication des documents relatifs aux origines de la guerre de 1914, *Documents diplomatiques français*, third series (hereafter referred to as *DDF3*) 11 vols. (Paris, 1929–1936), III, viii.

[8] Conversation with Lieutenant Commander P. K. Kemp, R.N., 11 Oct. 1963.

the Channel, its western approaches, and the Mediterranean. As this was before the Malta meeting with Kitchener, and before the CID and Cabinet meetings which forced him to alter his plans, the First Lord indicated a very limited role for the Royal Navy in the Mediterranean, where its force was to be reduced to merely a cruiser squadron until the situation in the North Sea permitted reinforcement by a battle fleet. These cruisers were to safeguard the eastern Mediterranean from hostile raids and watch the entrance of the Adriatic. Should the Austrian fleet come out, the cruisers would "actively cooperate" with the French fleet. The French would handle the Austrians, and the Italians if they joined the Austrians, and would have "the fullest use of all British Mediterranean ports and their re-sources."[9] There is no evidence this scheme was ever communicated to the French, at least at the time it was conceived. It differs from La-peyrère's thoughts in that the British proposed to merely watch, and not to fight, the Austrian fleet.

Sir Arthur Nicolson was somewhat taken aback when Cambon broached the subject of the naval talks on May 4 and told the French ambassador that he "knew nothing absolutely" about the arrangements.[10] Grey assured the Permanent Undersecretary that the talks had begun with both his and the Prime Minister's knowledge, and that it was always understood neither government was committed to go to war. The arrangements were rather to enable the naval and military authorities to cooperate at short notice in case of an emergency.[11] Churchill indicated that the time was approaching when further conversations would have to take place, but that he would put off asking for the necessary authority for them until after the Malta meeting.[12] Cambon tried to press Grey into agreeing to a resumption of the talks, arguing that the subject concerned not the Mediterranean but the Channel, but Churchill put off Saint-Seine until after Whitsuntide when he hoped that the entire question of fleet distribution would have been solved.[13] Grey considered this "enough for the present."[14] In the light of the controversy which was shaping up over Mediterranean policy it was really the only action which the Admiralty could take in regard to

[9] Memorandum by Churchill, 23 Apr. 1912, Admiralty Archives, case 0091. The note is actually unsigned but appears to be in Churchill's handwriting and is initialed by him, as well as Bridgeman and Battenberg, the First and Second Sea Lords respectively.

[10] Nicolson to Grey, 4 May, 1912, *BD*, X (pt. 2), no. 383, pp. 582–583.

[11] Minute by Grey, 5 May 1912, *ibid.*, p. 583.

[12] Minute by Churchill, 10 May 1912, *ibid.*

[13] Grey to Churchill, 11 May 1912, *ibid.*, no. 389, p. 591; Minute by Churchill, 19 May 1912, *ibid.*, pp. 591–592.

[14] Minute by Grey, *ibid.*, p. 592.

the French, who were naturally close observers of the debate in England. Cambon thought it in France's interest that English power in that sea not be eclipsed, totally or even partially. In case of war the French navy would have enough to do in assuring communications with North Africa without having to worry about British interests in the eastern Mediterranean. He also favored including Spain in any future Mediterranean entente with England, less for the value of her small navy, than for the use of her ports and extensive coastline.[15]

Saint-Seine's long delayed meeting with Admiral Bridgeman took place on the morning of July 10, but the First Sea Lord had to confess that he could say nothing about the Mediterranean since the whole subject had escaped from the competence of the Admiralty to the wider sphere of the Cabinet and CID.[16] Saint-Seine, on Delcassé's instructions, informed Bridgeman of the plan to concentrate all French battleship squadrons in the Mediterranean. Bridgeman immediately asked if the French under those conditions considered themselves stronger than an Austro-Italian combination. Saint-Seine replied that for the present there was no doubt about it. As for the future, he mentioned that the French had seven dreadnoughts under construction and would begin four more in 1913. He also proposed a modification of the September 1911 agreement with Admiral Wilson concerning the zone of French operations in the Channel. Bridgeman agreed to have the question studied by the War Staff.[17]

The morning after Cabinet approval for the new Mediterranean dispositions had been obtained the French naval attaché met with Churchill and Bridgeman. Churchill announced that the moment had come to settle the conditions of cooperation between the two navies, but that this was a job for technicians in which he did not have to interfere. It would be handled by Saint-Seine as representative for the French navy, and Bridgeman as representative for the Royal Navy; a kind of military convention might result.[18] It is difficult to think of the dynamic young First Lord not interfering in matters as important as these, but Churchill was obviously seeking to emphasize the technical nature of the talks. He attempted to make this explicit, declaring: Saint-Seine "must clearly understand that no discussion between naval or military experts could be held to affect

---

[15] Cambon to Poincaré, 27 June 1912, *DDF3*, III, no. 145, pp. 180–181. Shortly before, Cambon had aired his ideas about Spain to Nicolson. See Grey to Bertie, 21 June 1912, *BD*, X (pt. 2), no. 395, p. 597.

[16] Saint-Seine to Delcassé, 10 July 1912, *DDF3*, III, no. 189, pp. 235–236. Cabinet approval for the new Admiralty scheme was not obtained until 16 July.

[17] No corresponding British record of this conversation has been traced. Editor's Note, *BD*, X (pt. 2), p. 599.

[18] Saint-Seine to Delcassé, 18 July 1912, *DDF3*, III, no. 207, p. 271.

in any way the full freedom of action possessed by both countries; that the basis was purely hypothetical, and that nothing arising out of such conversations or arrangements could influence political decisions. On such matters the Foreign Office alone would express the views of H[is] M[ajesty's] G[overnment]" [19] Churchill added that he desired this restriction to appear in some form in the text of the notes which were to be exchanged by the general staffs.[20]

After the necessary qualifications had been made the French attaché was treated to a confidential preview of the new Mediterranean policy which would be announced in the House on July 22. The recent efforts of the French navy were praised by Churchill along with the work of Delcassé. He also advised the French to aim at a "two power" standard in the Mediterranean: the combined fleets of Austria and Italy. Saint-Seine was shown a comparative chart of the three major Mediterranean navies which the Admiralty had prepared. After counting "modern battleships," starting with the French "Dantons," the Italian *Dante*, and the Austrian "Radetzkys," the Admiralty thought French superiority over the combined Austrian and Italian fleets was assured until March 1914, but not afterwards.[21] The French attaché told the British of Delcassé's intention to accelerate the French building program in 1913 so that two ships would be laid down in April, and two not later than September. The Admiralty also placed their intelligence about new Austrian and Italian construction at Saint-Seine's disposal.[22]

The British Government, in preparing to proceed with close naval planning with the French which might result in a convention, was obviously treading very close to a formal alliance, something it desperately wanted to avoid. The distinction between such an alliance and a military convention, which would take effect only after both governments decided that it should, was an important one, constantly stressed by the British. But

[19] Memorandum by Churchill, 17 July 1912, *BD*, X (pt. 2), no. 399, p. 600.

[20] Saint-Seine to Delcassé, 18 July 1912.

[21] *Ibid.*, pp. 271–272. Earlier in the year the Admiralty gave Asquith a similar chart which reached substantially the same conclusions. To solve the difficulty of estimating the fighting value of different ships a point system was used which assigned a numerical value to each ship based largely on firepower and armor protection. The dreadnoughts of the "Courbet," "Cavour," and "Viribus Unitis" classes each received the value of 100; the semi-dreadnought "Dantons," 75, and "Radetzkys," 70. The "Patries" and "Romas" were rated at 50, and the "Erzherzogs" at 20. The crucial question remained the dates when the Italian "Cavours" and the last of the French "Courbets" would be completed. "France, Italy, Austria. Estimated strengths in the middle of 1914," n.d. [Jan.-Mar. 1912], Asquith MSS, box 93.

[22] Memorandum by Churchill, 17 July 1912, p. 601; Saint-Seine to Delcassé, 18 July 1912. The technical discussions between Bridgeman and Saint-Seine were to begin the following week.

the talks could easily open a Pandora's box of troubles transcending mere verbal technicalities and distinctions, and involving questions in the nature of moral, as opposed to legal, obligations. Cambon and Grey engaged in some polite skirmishing over the question on July 22 when the Foreign Secretary repeated Churchill's restrictions on the nature of the talks, and the French ambassador spoke of the moral, as opposed to a formal, entente between the two countries.[23] The Admiralty proposal for the zones of action in the Channel and the Mediterranean embodied the strict and narrow British interpretation in its preamble. The agreement was to relate solely to the contingency in which Britain and France were allies in a war "and does not affect the political freedom of either government as to embarking on such a war." [24] The naval dispositions of each country had "been made independently because they are the best which the separate interest of each country suggests . . . and they do not arise from any naval agreement or convention." The Mediterranean aspects of the British proposal were extremely simple. The British would look after British and French interests to the east of Malta, and the French would do the same to the west with "combined action if possible for the purposes of general engagement," both navies enjoying the use of each other's ports if required.[25]

The text of the preamble, and not the actual naval dispositions, proved to be the difficult point in the negotiations between the two countries. Cambon warned that Premier Poincaré, who was acting as his own Foreign Minister, might not agree to the British proposition without some assurance that British aid for France's northern coasts would be forthcoming.[26] The French ambassador claimed that Churchill was incorrect in his assumption that the naval dispositions had been arrived at independently. The French fleet was concentrated in the Mediterranean, he insisted, as a result of Fisher's verbal assurances in 1907 about England taking care of the north.[27] If this preamble was retained in its present form, Cambon proposed that both governments exchange notes promising mutual consultation if either country was menaced, but Grey objected to making any engagement which could not be published. Churchill admitted that he was not aware to what extent the Admiralty had been committed by his predecessor, but he still considered his proposals perfectly fair. The French, he wrote, had not concentrated in the Mediterranean to oblige

[23] Grey to Carnegie, 22 July 1912, *BD*, X (pt. 2), no. 400, p. 601.
[24] Draft Plan for Naval Cooperation in the event of War, 23 July 1912, *ibid.*, p. 602.
[25] *Ibid.* French text in *DDF*3, III, no. 420, app. I, pp. 507–508.
[26] Minute by Nicolson, 24 July 1912, *BD*, X (pt. 2), no. 401, p. 603.
[27] Grey to Carnegie, 26 July 1912, *ibid.*, no. 402, pp. 604–605.

the British, but, realizing that they could not be effective in both theaters, they had resolved to be supreme in one, for the Germans could "easily defeat them at sea." [28] When Lord Bertie, the British ambassador in Paris, pressed Poincaré on the point, the French leader agreed that the decision of the French government about the concentration "was quite spontaneous," but that it would not have been taken if they thought English assistance would not be forthcoming in the event of a German naval attack on France's northern coasts, for then the best French ships would be required to face the Germans in the Channel. Poincaré wanted some form of declaration requiring conversations between the two governments in the event a danger to their interests appeared. Bertie advised the French not to press for this at the present since the majority of the Cabinet would not be disposed to make such a declaration. However, he asserted, as long as Grey remained Foreign Secretary they could be sure there would be no abandonment of the spirit of the Entente. Poincaré remained adamant, insisting that if the Entente did not mean England would come to France's aid in case the Germans attacked French ports, its value to France was not great. [29]

Sir Francis Bertie reported that the French, and this included such political figures as Pichon, Cruppi, De Selves and Clemenceau, in addition to Poincaré, were dissatisfied with uncertain conditions, and Bertie had been putting them off with "generalities and platitudes." Bertie, in rejecting one amendment for the naval convention's preamble which Churchill had proposed, considered Poincaré technically right in holding that "any such reservations should be placed on record by an exchange of notes or declarations or records of conversations between the *Diplomatic representatives* of the two countries." [30] The Prime Minister also agreed with Bertie that Poincaré's criticism was justified and thought it a matter of form on which the British should give way, provided Bertie could suggest something of not too formal a character. [31] Churchill expressed his concern about the moral claims France might be able to make on Great Britain in a minute to Asquith and Grey on August 23:

> The point I am anxious to safeguard is our freedom of choice if the occasion arises, and consequent power to influence French policy

[28] Churchill to Grey, 29 July 1912, *ibid.*, no. 403, p. 605.
[29] Bertie to Grey, 30 July 1912, *ibid.*, nos. 404 and 405, pp. 606–607. Poincaré's version is in Raymond Poincaré, *Au service de la France*, vol. I: *Le Lendemain d'Agadir, 1912* (Paris, 1926), pp. 215–217.
[30] Bertie to Grey, 13 Aug. 1912, *BD*, X (pt. 2), no. 409, p. 609.
[31] Louis Mallet to Grey, 23 Aug. 1912, Grey MSS, PRO, FO 800, vol. 93.

beforehand. That freedom will be sensibly impaired if the French can say that they have denuded their Atlantic seaboard, and concentrated in the Mediterranean on the faith of naval arrangements made with us. This will not be true. If we did not exist, the French could not make better dispositions than at present. They are not strong enough to face Germany alone, still less to maintain themselves in two theatres. They therefore rightly concentrate their Navy in the Mediterranean where it can be safe and superior and can assure their African communications. Neither is it true that we are relying on France to maintain our position in the Mediterranean . . . If France did not exist, we should make no other disposition of our forces.[32]

Delcassé joined those seeking an acceptable formula for the naval convention and suggested the preamble, "In the event where the defense of their interests would determine France and Great Britain, allied [*alliées*] to associate their naval forces, the following dispositions are agreed upon between: On one side the French Admiralty which will have united in the Mediterranean nearly all its battle fleet . . . On the other side the English Admiralty which will have concentrated its battle fleet in home waters." [33] Delcassé thought it superfluous to emphasize the importance of the British giving the character of a firm engagement to the military dispositions.[34] Cambon feared that the premature order transferring the Brest squadron to the Mediterranean as well as the widespread journalistic comment following its publication on September 10 would damage France's bargaining position should the impression be created that the move was a permanent one. In his opinion such a transfer would have been the principal advantage to Britain of a naval accord with France.[35] The French ambassador therefore told Nicolson on September 17 that the move was a temporary one to enable the Brest squadron to participate in Mediterranean maneuvers, and there was no intention for the present of deliberately transferring it to the Mediterranean command, at least until the French government knew exactly what their position was vis à vis the British. He repeated this to Grey two days later.[36]

Cambon's statement about the transfer of the Brest squadron was completely wrong, of course, for its commander was specifically ordered to place himself under Lapeyrère's orders following the maneuvers, and

[32] Churchill, *The World Crisis*, I, 112–113.

[33] Note by Delcassé, 1 Sept. 1912, *DDF*3, III, note 2, p. 507.

[34] Delcassé to Poincaré, 17 Sept. 1912, *DDF*3, III, no. 420, p. 506.

[35] Cambon to Poincaré, 19 Sept. 1912, *ibid.*, no. 431, pp. 523–524; Poincaré, *Au service de la France*, I, 216–217.

[36] Grey to Bertie, 21 Sept. 1912, *BD*, X (pt. 2), no. 411, pp. 611–612; 19 Sept. 1912, *ibid.*, no. 410.

the decision to effect the transfer had been made by Delcassé the previous spring. Moreover the Admiralty had been informed of this plan by Saint-Seine in July, and the latter may well have mentioned it to Cambon at the same time. It would be uncharitable, however, to accuse the veteran ambassador of deliberately attempting to mislead. He was a diplomat naturally interested in improving his bargaining position, not a naval officer, and he may well have been ignorant of the technical details of service matters or else honestly confused or forgetful about the scope of Delcassé's plans. Moreover, Delcassé's decisions were only departmental ones and could have been canceled or altered at any time by Poincaré.

It would also be wrong to judge Poincaré harshly for his stubborn stand on the matter. He had admitted to Bertie that the decision whereby the bulk of the French fleet was concentrated in the Mediterranean had been reached spontaneously, but then added that it would never have been taken if it were thought Britain would not aid France in the event of a German naval attack in the north. In this Poincaré was speaking both as a patriotic Frenchman and a politician, for he could not have looked upon unopposed German bombardments of French ports with the same calm that some French admirals apparently did. Furthermore, no matter how many plans the EMG may have formulated, they were an advisory rather than an executive body, and the navy was still subordinate to Poincaré. The admirals often worried over the pressure of public opinion forcing the fleet into an unequal combat. Poincaré therefore had the power to overrule his advisers, although his decision may well have been unwise and potentially disastrous. It is doubtful if Poincaré or Cambon fully realized, as Churchill did so clearly, what a weak hand they were playing. The actual value of the six old battleships of the Brest squadron, all dating from the 1890's, was not nearly in proportion to the fuss which was made over them.

Whatever talent he may have lacked as a naval strategist, Cambon more than compensated for by his skill as a diplomat. Apparently on his own initiative he suggested a compromise formula to serve as preamble to the naval convention. In the event of complications threatening to peace, it would call for discussions by the two governments on ways to maintain the peace or avert any attempts at aggression. Grey observed that this is what would happen under existing conditions; a suggestion with which Cambon agreed, but added that there was no written understanding about it.[37] Asquith saw no harm in the formula which he considered "almost a platitude."[38] Poincaré would have preferred to completely eliminate a preamble from the naval convention, but the ambassador

[37] Grey to Bertie, 19 Sept. 1912, *BD*, X (pt. 2), no. 410, p. 611.
[38] Asquith to Grey, 11 Oct. 1912, *ibid.*, no. 412, p. 612.

recognized that this was impossible and authorized Saint-Seine to submit Delcassé's proposal.[39] Admiral Bridgeman and Rear Admiral Troubridge, Chief of the Naval War Staff, agreed that the French text was both simpler and clearer and promised to pass it on to Churchill. Bridgeman then inquired if the French Minister of Foreign Affairs was kept informed of the progress of the naval talks, for this had not been the case with the Foreign Office. If Poincaré knew the text of all the French proposals, Bridgeman thought, it would naturally be well that Grey did too. Saint-Seine replied that he kept the French ambassador informed of his conversations with the Admiralty, and that Poincaré also knew the text of the proposals.[40] From Bridgeman's confession it would appear that, incredible as it may seem, the Foreign Office knew little if anything about the actual progress of the naval talks until Churchill sent Grey a copy of Delcassé's proposal for the preamble. This may, to a certain extent, have been deliberate in order to emphasize the purely technical nature of the talks, but it must certainly have put the Foreign Office at a disadvantage in dealing with the French. Churchill asked the Foreign Secretary's opinion as to how far Delcassé's proposal modified the original Admiralty draft, or could be accepted for a purely technical agreement. The First Lord admitted that it went "a long way towards meeting my view." [41]

Cambon continued to impress very strongly upon Grey the desirability of exchanging some statement concerning naval conversations in case of need. Grey objected that if notes were exchanged the Government would be obliged to publish them, since it could not make secret arrangements of a formal character. Grey thought that to publish an exchange of notes at that moment, with Europe unsettled by the outbreak of the Balkan Wars, would have "a very exciting effect." Cambon agreed that if anything were published it would be misconstrued, but urged that the exchange be made by letters between Grey and himself. He "could not see why an arrangement merely for consultation should be regarded as one of those binding engagements which must be published." The French ambassador agreed with Grey that his formula involved nothing which did not already exist in fact since the naval experts of the two countries were already in consultation, but thought "that some thing ought to be on record, as French Governments changed so frequently." [42]

[39] Poincaré to Cambon, 20 Sept. 1912, *DDF3*, III, no. 436, p. 530; Cambon to Poincaré, 21 Sept. 1912, *ibid.*, no. 448, pp. 544–546; Saint-Seine to Aubert, 21 Sept. 1912, *ibid.*, no. 449, pp. 546–547.

[40] Saint-Seine to Aubert, 1 Oct. 1912, *ibid.*, IV, no. 15, pp. 11–12. This would imply Cambon was informed of Delcassé's plans for the Brest squadron at the time the Admiralty was told in July.

[41] Churchill to Grey, 8 Oct. 1912, Grey MSS, FO 800, vol. 86.

[42] Grey to Bertie, 16 Oct. 1912, FO 371, vol. 1368, France, file 40010.

At the end of October a long discussion over Cambon's proposed formula took place in the Cabinet, which did not find it satisfactory since its language was "vague and open to a variety of constructions." [43] The draft of the letter which Grey proposed to send Cambon was also criticized, and to some extent modified, by the Cabinet before the Foreign Secretary could give it to the French ambassador.[44] Poincaré, when he saw it, found it a little vague but acceptable. He also wanted to add a statement that if the measures both governments decided upon following consultations in the event of danger called for action, the agreements of the general staffs would take effect.[45] The British Cabinet feared that Poincaré's proposed amendment would bind the governments to staff plans which might become impracticable in two or three years under new and changed conditions. Grey therefore suggested an alternate wording in which the staff plans would be taken under consideration and the governments would then decide what effect to give to them. Both the Cabinet and the French ambassador accepted this formula.[46] The final version of the letter which Grey wrote Cambon on November 22 illustrates the framework and restrictions under which the military conventions between Britain and France operated.

> From time to time in recent years the French and British naval and military experts have consulted together. It has always been understood that such consultation does not restrict the freedom of either Government to decide at any future time whether or not to assist the other by armed force. We have agreed that consultation between experts is not, and ought not to be regarded as an engagement that commits either Government to action in a contingency that has not arisen and may never arise. The disposition, for instance, of the French and British fleets respectively at the present moment is not based upon an engagement to cooperate in war.

> You [Cambon] have, however, pointed out that, if either Government had grave reason to expect an unprovoked attack by a third Power, it might become essential to know whether it could in that event depend upon the armed assistance of the other.

[43] Asquith to King George, 1 Nov. 1912, Asquith MSS, box 6.

[44] *Ibid.*; Grey to Bertie, 30 Oct. 1912, *BD*, X (pt. 2), no. 413, pp. 612–613; Cambon to Poincaré, 31 Oct. 1912, *DDF*3, IV, no. 301, pp. 318–322.

[45] Cambon to Poincaré, 23 Nov. 1912, *ibid.*, no. 534, p. 535. Grey to Bertie, 7 Nov. 1912, *BD*, X (pt. 2), no. 414, p. 613. As a result of the projected exchange of letters between the two foreign offices, the preamble of the naval convention itself was no longer considered necessary. "Communication de l'Amirauté Britannique," 8 Nov. 1912, *DDF*3, IV, no. 398, p. 415.

[46] Asquith to King George, 21 Nov. 1912, Asquith MSS, box 6; Grey to Bertie, 21 Nov. 1912, *BD*, X (pt. 2), no. 415, p. 614.

I agree that, if either Government had grave reason to expect an unprovoked attack by a third Power, or something that threatened the general peace, it should immediately discuss with the other, whether both Governments should act together to prevent aggression and to preserve peace, and if so what measures they would be prepared to take in common. If these measures involved action, the plans of the General Staffs would at once be taken into consideration, and the Governments would then decide what effect should be given to them.[47]

Cambon's reply to Grey the following day was couched in similar terms.[48]

Anglo-French naval planning was thus to be conducted under something short of a formal alliance, and any agreements reached would be contingent on the governments' decisions to implement them in the moment of crisis. In the previous summer, Captain Kelly, the British naval attaché in Paris, had written a lengthy and somewhat rambling paper advocating an alliance; most of his conclusions had been concurred in by Captain George Ballard, Director of Operations Division.[49] But Kelly's arguments were not very impressive to those at the Foreign Office who read his paper, and a binding engagement such as he advocated was obviously what the government was most anxious to avoid.[50] While Grey and Cambon were seeking a mutually acceptable formula in October, a prominent member of the Cabinet, Louis Harcourt, Colonial Secretary, publicly and emphatically declared: "Under existing circumstances of territory and responsibility our position in the Mediterranean must remain one of national and international importance. We shall maintain it there, both on land and on sea, to as full an extent as we have ever done in the past, and in doing so we depend on no alliance or understanding, actual or implied, but upon our own and only our own needs, and to the tactical exigencies of our own unfettered policy and discretion."[51] The Grey-Cambon exchange of letters and subsequent technical agreements certainly contradicted Harcourt in spirit, if not in fact. In retrospect Churchill

[47] *Ibid.,* no. 416, pp. 614–615.

[48] Cambon to Grey, 23 Nov. 1912, *ibid.,* no. 417, p. 615. The texts of both letters are also reproduced in: *DDF*3, IV, no. 534, app. I and II, pp. 536–538.

[49] Capt. A. H. Kelly, "A Naval View of a Franco-British Alliance," 2 July 1912, PRO, Adm 116, case 866b; Minute by Capt. Ballard, 20 July 1912, Admiralty Archives, case 0091. The paper did not reach Churchill until October, something which annoyed him a great deal. He found it "interesting." Minute by Churchill, 11 Oct. 1912, *ibid.*

[50] Minutes by George R. Clerk and Walter Langley, 5 July 1912, FO 371, vol. 1367, France, file 28419. The Foreign Office did not retain a copy of Kelly's paper.

[51] *Daily Telegraph,* 26 Oct. 1912. Enclosed with Note by Churchill on the Naval Estimates, 25 Dec. 1913, Asquith MSS, box 110. Churchill used Harcourt's statement in his struggle to prevent Lloyd George from reducing the dreadnought construction program in 1914.

was to describe the military and naval conversations with France since 1906 as having led Great Britain "into a position where we had the obligations of an alliance without its advantages." [52]

The technical discussions over Anglo-French cooperation were carried out at the same time that the diplomats concerned themselves with their wider implication. Delcassé thought that the British proposals relating to the Mediterranean which had been given to Saint-Seine in July needed to be made more precise, for the British delimitation of the Mediterranean into zones of action dealt only with commerce protection. Superiority over the Austro-Italian forces would not seem to be assured in the eastern basin of the Mediterranean solely by the British Mediterranean Fleet. Moreover the recent entente between the French and Russian navies could lead to French naval operations in this area. The method of employing the French fleet, assisted by British forces, might vary, but its objective according to Delcassé would always remain the same: the destruction of the Austrian and Italian fleets. The French considered the phrase used by the Admiralty in describing the French objective ("combined action, if possible for the purposes of general engagement") as "too vague and subject to diverse interpretations." They proposed that the command of allied forces in the Mediterranean go to a French admiral, and that of allied forces in the North to a British admiral. [53]

Saint-Seine, who presented these observations on October 1, thought that the Admiralty would not object to the French fleet operating outside the western basin of the Mediterranean in any action against the Austrian and Italian forces. The question of a Mediterranean Commander-in-Chief was a bit more difficult, for Bridgeman pointed out that, while he recog-

[52] Churchill, *The World Crisis*, 1, 205. See also Viscount Grey of Fallodon, *Twenty-Five Years* (New York, 1925), I, 93 95.

[53] Delcassé to Poincaré, 17 Sept. 1912, *DDF3*, III, no. 420, app. II, pp. 510–511. The editors of the *DDF* did not reproduce a chart found with the original document which is of great interest. It depicted the planned disposition and situation of the French fleet at the end of 1912. In the Mediterranean, the First Armée Navale numbered eighteen battleships, six armored cruisers, thirty or more destroyers and ten to twelve submarines. These forces were always ready. In reserve were the six old battleships of the third squadron which would require three days to be mobilized, a number of torpedo boats, and four or five cruisers attached to the various naval schools. Toulon and Bizerte each had nine torpedo boats (plus four in reserve) and seven submarines. In the north, the second cruiser squadron had three armored cruisers, eighteen or more destroyers, and ten to twelve submarines always ready. In reserve were three armored cruisers, two corsair cruisers, and a number of destroyers. Attached to Dunkirk were eight torpedo boats (plus five in reserve); to Cherbourg, nine torpedo boats (plus four in reserve) and six to nine submarines; and to Brest, nine torpedo boats (plus four in reserve) and five to eight submarines. Most of the French forces in reserve needed four days to be ready. "Situation de la flotte française à la fin de 1912," AMF, carton Es-10.

nized the principle of a French commander, the British Mediterranean Commander-in-Chief held the rank of admiral while Lapeyrère was only a vice admiral. Saint-Seine explained that at the moment the rank of "admiral of France" no longer existed in the French navy, but that there were actually a few grades included under the denomination of vice admiral. The French naval attaché suggested that one way to get around the difficulty would be for the British to appoint a Mediterranean Commander-in-Chief who was junior in rank to Lapeyrère. He also provided the Admiralty with a detailed timetable of French battleship construction.[54]

The Admiralty agreed in principle to the French proposals concerning the Channel on November 8, but put off the Mediterranean question so as not to delay the Channel arrangements. Troubridge also undertook to prepare a joint signal and recognition code book.[55] Throughout the autumn of 1912 the Admiralty gave priority to the arrangements for coordination of forces and the joint defense of the Strait of Dover and the English Channel, perhaps an interesting example of their scale of values for it must be emphasized that the naval talks were not being conducted in a vacuum. The international situation was extremely threatening as a result of the convulsions the Ottoman Empire was undergoing. On October 8 Montenegro declared war on Turkey, and ten days later Bulgaria, Serbia, and Greece joined her. By early November the Turkish forces had been completely defeated, and the Bulgarian army had reached the Chatalja defense line before Constantinople. It seemed highly possible that the city would fall to the Bulgarians. This raised the threat of military intervention by Russia as well as the danger of a massacre of the Christian and foreign inhabitants in the anarchy which might accompany evacuation of the city. A similar danger existed at Salonika, and the major European powers ordered warships to the area to protect their nationals if necessary. On November 3 the Turkish government granted permission for foreign warships to pass the Dardanelles, and an international fleet soon assembled at Constantinople.[56]

[54] Saint-Seine to Delcassé, 1 Oct. 1912, DDF3, IV, no. 15, pp. 12–13. The timetable is not reproduced in the DDF. It indicated that the first French dreadnoughts, the Jean Bart and the Courbet, would not enter service until October and November 1913 respectively. The last of the class, the France and the Paris, were not due until November 1914. The three "Bretagnes" were scheduled for August to November 1915. These were conservative estimates and allowed time for official trials; AMF, carton Es-10.

[55] Communication de l'amirauté britannique, 8 Nov. 1912, DDF3, IV, no. 398, pp. 415–418. Saint-Seine to Aubert, 24 Nov. 1912, ibid., no. 544, pp. 543–544.

[56] E. C. Helmreich, The Diplomacy of the Balkan Wars (Cambridge, Mass., 1938), pp. 200–201. On November 10 the Ottoman government permitted each of the powers to send a second warship to Constantinople with the understanding they would leave on the re-establishment of normal conditions. Sir G. Lowther, British ambassador to Constantinople, to Grey, 12 Nov. 1912, FO 371, vol. 1506, Turkey, file 48961.

Even before the middle of October Churchill had quietly asked Grey if the European situation had any significance from the Admiralty's point of view, adding that the fleet was not ill disposed although the squadrons were not united.[57] Grey did not think the situation serious enough to request sizeable British naval reinforcements to protect British lives and property in Ottoman ports until November 1. The Third Battle Squadron, made up of "King Edwards," was therefore ordered to proceed to Malta.[58] Press reports that the Austrian fleet had steam up ready to sail at a moment's notice for Salonika, long considered a focal point of Austrian ambitions in the Balkans, caused some concern at the Foreign Office that the Austrian ships might stay "a good deal longer than was absolutely necessary for ensuring the safety of Christians."[59] The Admiralty, in seeking Grey's views on the distribution of their Mediterranean forces, commented that it was not desirable except in grave and urgent necessity to break a battle squadron into separate units, and if there was any risk of European complications, it was unadvisable to send the whole squadron too far east.[60] A report from the British consul at Fiume that the Austrian battleships *Radetzky* and *Zrinyi* and two cruisers had sailed for Salonika caused the Admiralty to order Admiral Sir Berkeley Milne, Mediterranean Commander-in-Chief, to proceed to that port without delay, and to instruct the first division of the Third Battle Squadron to do the same without stopping at Malta.[61] The Admiralty wanted a "superior British squadron" to arrive at Salonika at the same time or as soon as possible after the Austrian ships. If the latter bypassed the Greek port, Milne was to proceed there alone and divert the battleships to Besika Bay.[62] Shortly before he sailed, the Mediterranean Commander-in-Chief detached the cruiser *Dartmouth* to sight and report the movements of the Austrian squadron.[63]

Sir Arthur Nicolson questioned the wisdom of a British counterdemonstration at Salonika in the event, which was still not certain, the Austrian squadron went there. Given the "jumpy" condition of European public

[57] Churchill to Grey, 11 Oct. 1912, Grey MSS, FO 800, vol. 86.

[58] L. Mallet to Admiralty, 1 Nov. 1912, FO 371, vol. 1503, Turkey, file 46298; Admiralty to Commander-in-Chief, Mediterranean, and Vice Admiral, Third Battle Squadron (cable), 1 Nov. 1912, *ibid.*, vol. 1504, file 46394.

[59] Minute by A. Parker on Sir. F. Elliot, British ambassador, Athens, to Grey (cable), 1 Nov. 1912, *ibid.*, vol. 1503, file 46295.

[60] Minute by A. Parker of Admiralty telephone communication, 4 Nov. 1912, *ibid.*, vol. 1504, file 46932.

[61] Admiralty to Commander-in-Chief, Mediterranean (cable), 5 Nov. 1912, *ibid.*, file 47044. As none of the battle cruisers had yet reached the Mediterranean, Milne flew his flag from the old armored cruiser *Good Hope*.

[62] Admiralty to Commander-in-Chief, Mediterranean (cable), 5 Nov. 1912, in Admiralty to Foreign Office, 6 Nov. 1912, enclosure no. 9, *ibid.*, file 47101.

[63] Commander-in-Chief, Mediterranean, to Admiralty (cable), 6 Nov. 1912, *ibid.*, enclosure no. 6.

opinion and press, he thought that ships should only be sent where wanted for protecting British life and property. Movement of the battle squadron to Salonika would be "a little theatrical and perhaps even provocative."[64] The Admiralty considered the shadowing of the Austrians by the *Dartmouth* as unnecessary, and also told Milne to hold the battleships at Mytilene ready to join him at Salonika should the Austrians arrive.[65] The other half of the third battle squadron, the second division, had coaled at Malta and was awaiting instructions on November 8. Churchill originally wanted to send them to the east coast of Greece (Nauplia) where they would be in effective supporting distance of Besika Bay.[66] Grey apparently objected to this, and the ships were diverted to the Turkish coast to Smyrna, although Churchill still considered Nauplia "quite a harmless place for them to wait at."[67]

Despite the Admiralty's apprehensions, the only Austrian naval force present at Salonika during Milne's stay was an old cruiser. The Austrian squadron which sailed for Ottoman waters during the crisis had actually been ordered to Smyrna for the protection of Austro-Hungarian subjects, and not to Salonika to establish a claim for that port.[68]

Churchill deemed it essential that the ships in the eastern Mediterranean be capable of concentrating for mutual protection, but the Admiralty did not propose to bring any of them home immediately. The First Lord considered that the force of eight "King Edwards" when united would be "largely superior to the Austrian Fleet," and was "capable of looking after itself in all probable eventualities." The margins at home were considered "sufficient in view of the steps of a precautionary character" which had quietly been taken.[69] This rapid concentration of strong naval forces in

[64] Minute by Nicolson, *ibid.*

[65] Admiralty to Commander-in-Chief, Mediterranean (cable), 6 Nov. 1912, *ibid.*, vol. 1505, file 47215. Actually two battleships of the first division, Third Battle Squadron, joined Milne at Salonika on the eighth. After the town had fallen to the Balkan forces without serious incident, Milne and the battleships were ordered to join the remainder of the first division at Besika Bay. Milne to Admiralty, 13 Nov. 1912, *ibid.*, vol. 1506, file 49933.

[66] Churchill to Grey, 8 Nov. 1912, Grey MSS, FO 800, vol. 86.

[67] Churchill to Grey, 9 Nov. 1912, *ibid*; Admiralty to Commander-in-Chief, Mediterranean (cable), 9 Nov. 1912, FO 371, vol. 1505, file 47746. Grey may have been anxious to avoid offending Greek susceptibilities, something which Sir George Elliot feared when the warships were first sent to Salonika. Elliot to Grey, 1 Nov. 1912, *ibid.*, vol. 1503, file 46295.

[68] Admiral Montecuccoli, Marinekommandant, to Rear Admiral von Chmelarž, commanding the Austrian squadron ordered to Smyrna, 3 Nov. 1912, Austria, Kriegsarchiv, Vienna, Operationskanzlei des Kriegsministeriums/Marinesektion (hereafter referred to as OK/MS), X-4/6, 1912. The Admiralty information about the composition of the Austrian force was also wrong. It numbered the three "Radetzkys," a cruiser, and two large torpedo boats. In addition to the cruiser at Salonika, another was at Besika Bay ready to proceed to Constantinople. *Ibid.*

[69] Churchill to Grey, 8 Nov. 1912, Grey MSS, FO 800, vol. 86.

the eastern Mediterranean was a striking example of the flexibility of British seapower. The "King Edwards" were pre-dreadnoughts but this was not a crippling disadvantage, for the first Austrian and Italian dreadnoughts were only just making their appearance. After all the gloomy predictions by the prophets of doom the previous summer, it is significant to find the First Lord of the Admiralty adding in a postscript, "I am not at all displeased with the naval position." [70]

France also ordered ships to the Levant in case of disturbances on the different points of the Ottoman coast where there were French interests. Poincaré was mindful of the somewhat sensitive relations between France and Italy arising out of incidents of the Tripolitan War, but considered the signature of a peace treaty between the Italians and Turks as ending the risk that French naval movements in these waters would provoke inopportune comment. In line with traditional French interests he wanted part of the French force to pay special attention to Beirut. [71] The French force which sailed for the Levant on October 31 consisted of three large armored cruisers, detached from the Mediterranean fleet, under the command of Rear Admiral Dartige du Fournet, who subsequently became the senior naval officer in the international fleet assembled at Constantinople. The hasty departure of the division combined with the powder crisis which still plagued the French navy forced the admiral to sail with incomplete munition stocks aboard his flagship the *Léon Gambetta*. This was hardly a satisfactory situation for a flagship about to enter a war zone, and at Syra the other two cruisers in the division were ordered to transfer some of their munitions to the *Gambetta*. [72]

Poincaré, well informed as to the naval movements in the Levant, was anxious that France not be taken unawares and wanted the navy to be prepared should it become necessary to send additional ships so as to constitute "a naval force more in agreement with the role that our country may eventually be called to play on the coast of Asiatic Turkey." [73] Delcassé considered sending another division of three armored cruisers and cabled Toulon to secretly prepare the necessary munitions. [74] This would

[70] *Ibid.* Later in the month the Admiralty obtained Foreign Office approval for the quiet and slow withdrawal of the Third Battle Squadron from the eastern Mediterranean to Malta. The Earl of Onslow, private secretary to Nicolson, to Nicolson, 19 Nov. 1912, FO 371, vol. 1506, file 49561.

[71] Poincaré to Delcassé, 27 Oct. 1912, AMF, carton BB3-1341.

[72] Rear Admiral Dartige du Fournet to Delcassé, 4 Nov. 1912, *ibid.*, carton BB3-1346. After the cruiser had been in Constantinople for a few weeks additional munitions reached her by means of the French naval tanker *Rhône*, which passed through on her way to the Black Sea. Dartige du Fournet to Delcassé, 2 Dec. 1912, *ibid.*

[73] Poincaré to Delcassé, 19 Nov. 1912, AMF, carton BB7-160.

[74] Minute by Delcassé, 21 Nov. 1912, *ibid.* The French also had a few old small cruisers in the Levant.

mean that practically all the Mediterranean fleet's armored cruisers would be in the Levant. The actual number of ships in the eastern Mediterranean fluctuated according to the circumstances of the Balkan Wars, but the French were always careful to match the movements of other powers. In January 1913, for example, a report that the Italians were about to send two armored cruisers east caused the Quai d'Orsay to ask the Minister of Marine to prepare similar measures.[75]

In the final month of 1912 the warships of many nations cruised the waters of the eastern Mediterranean or anchored in the Golden Horn at Constantinople. In addition to the major Mediterranean powers and Russia, there were cruisers from the United States, Holland, Spain, and Rumania. But the most important of the visitors, and of the greatest significance for the future, was undoubtedly the naval force which had been dispatched by Germany. This was the new battle cruiser *Goeben* and the equally new fast light cruiser *Breslau*. Together with a pair of old training cruisers and an old third-class cruiser they formed the Mittelmeerdivision under the command of Rear Admiral Trummler.[76] The 23,000-ton *Goeben* was a magnificent example of German shipbuilding; with her primary armament of ten 11-inch guns and speed thought to be in excess of 27 knots, she was easily the most imposing warship in the Levant.[77] The impression made on the Ottoman government was particularly profound, much to the chagrin of Admiral Dartige du Fournet who sadly felt the eclipse of "the old and glorious French Navy behind a navy born 40 years ago." [78] The German Naval Staff sorely missed the *Goeben* and *Breslau* in the North Sea and, given the naval strength of Germany in relation to Great Britain and the possibility of a worsening in the political situation, proposed that they be brought back from the Mediterranean as soon as circumstances permitted.[79]

Considering the large number of foreign warships present at Constantinople, courtesy calls undoubtedly took up much of each captain's time. Relations between the French and German crews were not marked by the formal politeness that officers might often have used to hide their real feelings, and brawls occurred at both Constantinople and Smyrna. Since

[75] Jonnart to Baudin, 25 Jan. 1913; Paléologue to Baudin, 31 Jan. 1913, AMF, carton BB3-1357.

[76] *Nauticus, 1913; Jahrebuch für Deutschlands Seeinteressen* (Berlin, 1913), pp. 47–48; Hermann Lorey, *Der Krieg in den türkischen Gewässern* (Berlin, 1928), p. 1.

[77] Bompard, ambassador, Constantinople, to Poincaré, 17 Dec. 1912, enclosed in Poincaré to Delcassé, 23 Dec. 1912, AMF, carton BB3-1341.

[78] Dartige du Fournet to Delcassé, 16 Dec. 1912, AMF, carton BB3-1346.

[79] Admiral von Heeringen to Kaiser Wilhelm, 17 Dec. 1912, PRO, German Naval Archives Microfilmed at the Admiralty, London, for the University of Cambridge and the University of Michigan (hereafter referred to as GFM), *Admiralstab der Marine Abteilung B*, reel GFM 27/19 [frame numbers illegible]. See also Walther Hubatsch, *Der Admiralstab* (Frankfurt, 1958), p. 152.

the provocation seemed to be on the part of the French, they were embarrassing enough to warrant the Foreign Minister's attention.[80] At Smyrna the French and German commanders provisionally agreed to give their men liberty on alternate days when their ships were together in the same port.[81] There were other incidents at Constantinople which the French admiral found somewhat moving. While passing certain groups of sailors ashore from the *Goeben,* he was on occasion cordially greeted in French and even heard the words "Vive la France" discreetly pronounced by men whom he assumed to be from Alsace or Lorraine.[82]

It was against this background of Balkan turmoil, naval movements in the Levant, the London ambassador's conference, and the ever present threat of international complications that the British and French naval staffs prepared their plans for cooperation during the autumn and winter of 1912–1913. The Count de Saint-Seine appears to have been the hardworking intermediary at this stage of the negotiations. It was not until January that serious discussions began in regard to the Mediterranean. Prince Louis of Battenberg, now First Sea Lord of the Admiralty, was in favor of cooperation with the French naval forces, but not—unless circumstances required it—on the same field of battle. As far as possible the cooperation was to be strategical and not tactical: the French would be charged with defeating the Italian fleet as well as the protection of convoys and commerce in the western basin of the Mediterranean; the British would assume similar duties in the eastern basin and would also immobilize or combat the Austrian fleet. Prince Louis admitted that if the Austrians and Italians succeeded in joining their fleets, the French and the British would be obliged to effect their own combination, but he was still against any conference between the British Mediterranean Commander-in-Chief and his French counterpart. He feared that such a meeting, even if given the appearance of a fortuitous encounter in neutral waters, would attract too much attention. It was preferable that the broad lines of the plan be settled by the general staffs, and that the commanders in the Mediterranean be responsible only for the details of execution.[83]

Anglo-French cooperation in the Mediterranean was the subject of a

[80] Dartige du Fournet to Baudin, 17 Feb. 1913, AMF, carton BB3-1353; Minister of Foreign Affairs to Minister of Marine, 23 Apr. 1913, AMF, carton BB3-1357.

[81] Dartige du Fournet to Minister of Marine, 17 Mar. 1913, AMF, carton BB3-1353. The behavior of the crew of the *Jurien de la Gravière* at Smyrna provoked scathing comments from Kaiser Wilhelm on the appalling state of French discipline. Captain H. Watson, naval attaché, Berlin, to Sir E. Goschen, 12 May 1913, *BD,* X (pt. 2), no. 475, p. 700.

[82] Dartige du Fournet to Minister of Marine, 6 Jan. 1913, AMF, carton BB3-1353.

[83] Saint-Seine to Aubert, 22 Jan. 1913, AMF, carton Es-10. With an eye to the unsettled international situation Battenberg also asked that work on the signal code for the allied fleets be expedited.

strategical game played at the Royal Naval War College at Portsmouth in the autumn of 1912. A copy of the instructions to the Mediterranean Commander-in-Chief which the officers attending the course had proposed was forwarded to the Chief of the Naval War Staff for comment. The officers assumed that the primary objective of both governments would be the safe passage of troops from Algeria to the south of France. The main British force was to be located between Sardinia and Bizerte so as to protect the French lines of communication from the fast armored cruisers of the Italian fleet.[84]

Churchill disagreed strongly with the tone of these proposed instructions, which he did not think stressed with sufficient clearness and emphasis his principles of Mediterranean strategy. He considered Malta the best base from which the British fleet could assist the French in the passage of their army, join them in a decisive action against the Italians, and watch the Adriatic to prevent the Austrians joining their allies. If, as was much less likely, the Austrians came out and turned eastward, it would be in the British interest to allow them to proceed as far as possible, for the longer they had been at sea, and the farther they were from their bases, the more favorable would be the conditions under which they could be engaged, and the more complete their ruin if defeated. Churchill stressed the importance of not weakening the British force, limited as it was in the Mediterranean, by dispersing cruisers to protect British trade in the eastern basin, unless of course the Austrians had already succeeded in detaching equal forces from the Adriatic, in which case the deductions from both forces would be equal. In that event he cautioned against letting the Austrian cruisers rejoin their main fleet while the British force was still scattered. He concluded: "The British Fleet concentrated in the neighborhood of Malta with its left hand in touch with the French, offers the highest strategic advantages, and so long as superior Franco British forces are in this position, the eastern basin of the Mediterranean will either be perfectly safe for British commerce, or the Austrians will have committed themselves to an eccentric movement of a most hazardous nature, for the sake of which the chances which it offers of any temporary or incidental injury to local British trade or interests will be well worth putting up with." [85]

Battenberg fully concurred with Churchill and considered it the business of the French to protect their transports from Italian ships, while England's concern was to contain the Austrian fleet in the Adriatic. He thought it faulty strategy to begin the transportation of large and helpless military

[84] Enclosure, Jackson to Troubridge, 29 Nov. 1912, Admiralty Archives, case 0091.
[85] Minute by Churchill, 9 Dec. 1912, *ibid.*

forces across a sea of which the command is in doubt, but presumed that the dire necessity of the French army left no choice. The naval dispositions which the French would make to protect this transit would also serve to protect British trade between Gibraltar and Malta. In his opinion the best protection for British trade between Malta and Port Said, and between the Dardanelles and Malta, would be to hunt down any Austrian commerce-destroying cruisers issuing from the Adriatic.[86]

Most of these points, as well as those previously mentioned to Saint-Seine, were incorporated in a draft project given by the Admiralty to the French naval attaché in February 1913.[87] According to the plan, if an attempted junction of the Italian and Austrian fleets rendered the concept of distinct areas of French and British operations impracticable and necessitated close tactical contact, there would still be no endeavor to form the two allied fleets into a single line of battle. Instead "they should operate separately but in mutual support, relying on their common signal book and pre-arranged means of communication, by sight or sound, to ensure this being carried out successfully." The initial points of concentration would be Malta for the British and Toulon for the French, unless intelligence reports showed the Italians mobilizing at Taranto, in which case the French might concentrate at Bizerte. Changes in the composition and strength of the British forces in the Mediterranean would be communicated to the French through the British naval attaché in Paris. When acting as allies all naval harbors and bases of each country would be at the disposal of the other, and mutual assistance in regard to fuel, provisions, docking, and repairing was envisioned.

There were two important British reservations in the draft plan submitted to the French. The Admiralty expressly stated: "The North Sea will be the decisive theatre of naval operations, and it is absolutely essential that Great Britain should have complete freedom to concentrate such forces in that area as are necessary to defeat the enemy. The British therefore cannot enter into any arrangement specifying that the British Mediterranean Squadron shall be kept at any permanently fixed standard. But it will be the aim of British policy in practice to maintain in peace and war such a force in the Mediterranean as should be able with reasonable chances of success to deal with the Austrian fleet should it emerge from the Adriatic." If the British government were compelled through a situa-

---

[86] Minute by Battenberg, 27 Dec. 1912, *ibid.* Battenberg assumed that the Suez Canal would be neutral and that this neutrality would be maintained by the Egyptian government. Consequently no British warships could operate within the three-mile limit of Port Said or Suez.

[87] "F.010—Joint Action in the Mediterranean," 10 Feb. 1913, *DDF*3, V, no. 397, app. II, pp. 486–487.

tion arising in or near the North Sea to withdraw so many ships from the Mediterranean that those remaining no longer sufficed to act independently against the Austrian fleet, they would join the French Mediterranean fleet and act under the French admiral's orders, but "always on the understanding that they are subject to recall at any time to England should circumstances require it." By this, Saint-Seine observed, the Admiralty reserved the right to withdraw every ship down to the last destroyer from the Mediterranean.[88] He considered it a confession of impotence which must have been costly to Anglo-Saxon pride, but which created a heavy burden for the French, since they had to envisage the possibility of being left to their own resources against the united Austrian and Italian fleets with the sole advantage of having the use of Malta as a base. According to Battenberg, Churchill had previously exposed this plan to Poincaré and Delcassé and obtained their agreement in principle.[89]

At the same time that he handed Saint-Seine a copy of the draft plan, Battenberg proposed a meeting between himself and Le Bris, new chief of the EMG, in Paris. As he intended to travel absolutely incognito, he wanted to avoid both the Ministry of Marine and the British embassy, where he might be recognized. Prince Louis, anxious to avoid journalist conjectures and considering his hotel an imprudent meeting place, tentatively suggested Captain Kelly's quarters. Saint-Seine, however, proposed a room at the Franco-American bank in the Place Vendôme (where his brother was an officer) for a rendezvous most likely to go unnoticed.[90]

The secret meeting between Prince Louis and Vice Admiral Pierre Le Bris took place on March 12. In those portions of the discussion dealing with the Mediterranean, Battenberg indicated that it was preferable that only the admirals commanding in the Mediterranean know the definitive text of the agreements. He pointed out that because the British were especially concerned with destruction of the Austrian fleet and policing of the eastern Mediterranean, they would not be able to assure the surveillance of the passages leading from the eastern basin to the western basin; this might be of consequence for the security of the French troop transport.[91] Prince Louis also thought that it would be well if both navies

[88] Saint-Seine to Aubert [?], 14 Feb. 1913, *DDF3*, V, no. 397, pp. 483–484.

[89] *Ibid.* An editor's note mentions that no documents relating to this have been found.

[90] *Ibid.*

[91] Section historique, French navy, "Pourparlers et conventions franco-anglais relatifs aux operations dans la Manche et la Pas-de-Calais." Unpublished study, n.d., p. 55. Found in AMF, carton Es-10. No specific document is cited in the study on the Le Bris–Battenberg meeting and no corresponding record found in the Admiralty MSS, possibly because, as Saint-Seine frequently stated, much which transpired was purely oral.

exchanged frequent visits in both the north and the Mediterranean. To avoid arousing foreign susceptibilities these should be accomplished by small groups of ships and without showy receptions. He preferred that the regular exercises not suffer from this. There were, he thought, many advantages to be hoped for from the visits and the exchange of ideas among officers.

On April 4 Saint-Seine reported that the Admiralty considered the agreements concerning the defense of the Strait of Dover (F.06), the defense of the western Channel (F.07), and joint operations in the Mediterranean (F.010) as definitely secured (*acquis*).[92] They had also approved the naval convention on cooperation in the Far East which had been signed January 27 by the local commanders, Admiral Alfred Winsloe for Great Britain, and Rear Admiral Henri Calloch de Kérillis for France.[93] The signal code book for the allied fleets had been sent to the printers; this had been prepared with the utmost secrecy by the Admiralty.[94] The signal book, along with the war orders for the contingency of an alliance with France, were to be sealed and distributed to the appropriate commanders with instructions to open only when so ordered.[95] Sir Edward Grey agreed with Churchill's approval of the Admiralty instructions to the naval commanders since it was clearly stipulated that they were provisional, and that in an emergency the government or the Admiralty must decide what effect to give them.[96]

By the spring of 1913 the two nations had therefore reached a series of agreements which could serve as the basis for cooperation in the event of war. The Mediterranean convention tended to be vague on the details of tactical, as opposed to strategic, cooperation, but those dealing with the Channel and the Strait of Dover were fairly specific in defining respective responsibilities. The restricted nature of the theater of operations lent itself to this, if it did not necessitate it. Agreements on specific points of detail would continue until the outbreak of the war.

Although the general lines of the entente had been established, both the British and French navies still had their own problems to resolve. For

[92] Saint-Seine to Aubert [Le Bris], 4 Apr. 1913, *DDF*3, VI, no. 198, pp. 247–248. Texts in *DDF*3, V, no. 397, app. I–III, pp. 485–490.

[93] *DDF*3, VI, no. 198, pp. 247–248. For the text see De Kérillis to Baudin, 31 Jan. 1913, *DDF*3, V, no. 303, app. I–IV, pp. 385–389.

[94] Admiral Jackson to Capt. S. R. Fremantle, president of signal committee, 12 Feb. 1913, Admiralty Archives, case 0091.

[95] Unsigned note [probably by Admiral Jackson], 15 Mar. 1913, *ibid*. The Mediterranean Commander-in-Chief was to receive a copy of F.010 which was to be his general war orders; *ibid*. See also editor's note, *BD*, X (pt. 2), p. 694.

[96] Grey to Churchill, 11 Apr. 1913, *ibid*., no. 472, p. 695; Churchill to Grey, 10 Apr. 1913, *ibid*, no. 471, p. 695. A printed set of instructions for use of the signal code, dated 10 Aug. 1913, may be found in Admiralty Archives, case 0091.

Great Britain, attractive though the idea of exerting maritime pressure in the Mediterranean might have been, it would remain a secondary theater almost totally dependent on the situation in the North Sea for the force which could be spared for it. The French realized this, and also that the new dreadnoughts coming out of the Austrian and Italian yards were threatening their own predominance in an area they considered essential. In the year before the outbreak of the World War the French turned to face this challenge by the Triple Alliance.

V

The Entente at Work

In the summer of 1913 the French navy, now concentrated in the Mediterranean for almost a year, cast longing eyes northward toward the coast of Brittany. The transfer south of the third squadron had, it will be remembered, produced an angry outcry in the northern ports. It was claimed that the people of Brittany suffered a material prejudice and considerable morale discomfort from the absence of major naval forces. Breton sailors were unable to visit their homes frequently, and perhaps as a result voluntary engagements among the maritime population of the north declined. This was disturbing: the navy was suffering a personnel shortage in this period, and Bretons furnished the major part of the new contingents.[1] On the other hand, recruiting was very limited along the Provençal coast. The navy, anxious occasionally to show the people of Brittany and the north an important fraction of the fleet, proposed that the "Patries" of the second squadron be allowed to make a temporary visit, and asked the Minister of Foreign Affairs if the state of international relations would permit this.[2] Aside from being a possible stimulus to recruiting, it would be good for the morale of the crews, who would be able to see their families without the expense of the long trip from Toulon to the north, and good experience for officers and men in navigation outside of the Mediterranean. As the British had just withdrawn part of their Mediterranean naval force for maneuvers, the Minister of Marine presumed that the political situation had eased. The question was considered important enough to be deferred for the Conseil Supérieur de la Défense Nationale.[3]

---

[1] Pierre Baudin, "Rapport de presentation," Conseil Supérieur de la Défense Nationale, 28 June 1913, AMF, carton Es-23.

[2] Baudin to Pichon, 17 June 1913, DDF3, VII, no. 143, p. 154.

[3] "Annotation du Départment," 21 June 1913, ibid., p. 155.

The Conseil met June 28 with Poincaré presiding. It had little difficulty in agreeing that the principle of a Mediterranean concentration should be maintained, and that a permanent return of the third squadron to the north was out of the question. Pierre Baudin, Minister of Marine, revealed that this squadron lacked part of its crews and that he intended transforming it into a school division. Lapeyrère, who was also present, claimed its battleships were indispensable in the Mediterranean, for even after counting them the French had only nineteen battleships against twenty-two for the Austrians and Italians. Baudin admitted that a recent study showed that the force which was to visit the north would, once there, require twelve days to return to the Mediterranean and coal. Its trip could only be justified if there were no chance of a conflict during its absence. Stephen Pichon, Minister of Foreign Affairs, and Maurice Paléologue, Director of Political Affairs at the Quai d'Orsay, immediately warned of the critical events in southeastern Europe where the second Balkan War was about to erupt, and where the question of the Aegean Islands would soon come to the fore. It seemed clear that British and French forces were required at full strength in the Mediterranean. Poincaré concurred, and also agreed with Eugène Etienne, Minister of War, who argued that such a naval move coming so soon after the President's visit to England might be taken as a change of orientation in French foreign policy. The French President disclosed that during his recent state visit to England he had mentioned the idea of a temporary detachment of a battleship squadron from the Mediterranean to Churchill, who appeared notably unenthusiastic. He concluded that the naval visit to the north should be postponed until the Balkan countries accepted arbitration and the international situation clarified itself, and that no preparations for the trip were to be undertaken because of possible indiscretions.[4]

In early July Churchill reciprocated Baudin's previous hospitality at Toulon and invited him to the Home Fleet's maneuvers in the Channel where he witnessed a gunnery exercise from the bridge of the super-dreadnought *Orion*. While both were aboard the Admiralty yacht *Enchantress*, Baudin asked Saint-Seine to bring up the French plans for the northern cruise. When the attaché did a few days later he found Battenberg undisturbed by it. With the exception of the battle cruiser *Inflexible*, now Mediterranean flagship, and the armored cruiser *Black Prince*, the Admiralty intended to bring all large units home from the Mediterranean for summer maneuvers, and Prince Louis did not think that in the present

---

[4] Procès-verbal, Conseil Supérieur de la Défense Nationale, 28 June 1913, AMF, carton Es-23.

state of relations between the great powers the French plans need modify the Admiralty's dispositions.[5]

Before receiving Saint-Seine's report of this conversation, Le Bris, who knew of the British intention to bring home the "King Edwards" of the Third Battle Squadron, became anxious lest the measures taken independently by both countries reduce Anglo-French naval strength in the Mediterranean below that of the Triple Alliance. He suggested to the Foreign Minister that they propose to the British that the portion of the Mediterranean convention dealing with the notification of withdrawal of forces be extended to peacetime.[6] Pichon agreed to this and after the Balkan situation had improved, finally approved the visit to Brittany of the second squadron with the provision it be made absolutely clear to the Admiralty that the absence of the ships was only temporary, and that they would return to the Mediterranean by the end of September.[7] Cambon dutifully informed the Foreign Office of the move; the Admiralty, having learned of it through Saint-Seine, was not surprised.[8] Le Bris could not promise the return of the ships to Toulon before the middle of October, but this was considered acceptable. The second squadron accompanied by two armored cruisers and two flotillas of *torpilleurs* left for its deferred visit to the northern ports on August 23.[9] The great pains to which the French went to stress that the displacement was only temporary are interesting. Perhaps it stemmed from the thought, and possibly even fear, that the Mediterranean concentration was their major attraction to Great Britain as a potential ally.

The agreement between the British and French concerning the Mediterranean had been designated War Orders Number 2 and dispatched to

[5] Saint-Seine to Le Bris [?], 9 July 1913, AMF, carton Es-10.

[6] Note by Le Bris, 11 July 1913, *DDF*3, VII, no. 344, pp. 380–381. An undated copy of this is also in Admiralty Archives, case 0091.

[7] Pichon to Baudin, 31 July 1913, *DDF*3, VII, no. 504, p. 545; Pichon to Cambon, 31 July 1913, *ibid.*, no. 505, pp. 545–546; Baudin to Pichon, 9 Aug. 1913, *ibid.*, no. 591, p. 630; Pichon to Cambon, 11 Aug. 1913, *ibid.*, VIII, no. 9, p. 12; Pichon to Baudin, 11 Aug. 1913, AMF, carton BB4-2357. Bulgaria signed an armistice with her Balkan foes July 31. The Treaty of Bucharest was concluded August 10.

[8] Fleuriau, first secretary, French embassy, London, to Pichon, 20 Aug. 1913, *DDF*3, VIII, no. 56, p. 63.

[9] Le Bris to Pichon, 14 Aug. 1913, AMF, carton BB4-2357. After the plan became known to the public the Minister of Marine was besieged by deputies and senators clamouring for the ships to call at their districts; *ibid.* The visit was not an unmixed blessing for the crews, since the delay due to the international situation caused the voyage to occur during the normal leave period, thus upsetting many plans; *Le Yacht*, 23 Aug. 1913. The second squadron was to repeat the visit in August and September 1914, but the war intervened. The tour of the northern ports may well have become an annual event in the French navy. See Pivet, chief of the EMG after May 18, 1914, to Lapeyrère, 8 July 1914, AMF, carton SS-A-132.

the British Mediterranean Commander-in-Chief on May 1, 1913. The older orders for the contingency in which Britain would fight alone became War Orders Number One; these were obviously out of date following the recent displacements.[10] During their revision the War Staff revealed lingering doubts about abandoning the Mediterranean under any circumstances. The War Staff wanted a reconsideration of reinforcing the Mediterranean if Austria, or Austria and Italy, joined Germany in a war against Britain alone, since neither would initially affect the situation in the North Sea, which would remain favorable to the British. The staff also argued against concentrating the Mediterranean Fleet at Gibraltar even in the desperate contingency where Britain faced the entire Triple Alliance alone. At Gibraltar the fleet would cease to be an appreciable threat to enemy communications and coasts, or a deterrent to enemy overseas expeditions. The fleet, if it remained at Malta, would occupy a position analogous to the German fleet at Wilhelmshaven, that is, although inferior to the enemy, forcing the latter to constant vigilance. The Mediterranean Fleet of battle cruisers and cruisers had the advantage of speed and any reinforcements should be equally fast ships. The War Staff thought that if the battle cruiser *New Zealand* and cruiser *Shannon* were sent out at the end of 1913 in addition to the ships already proposed, the Mediterranean squadron would consist of ten very fast ships equal to meeting the seven battleships and one heavy cruiser the Austrians would be likely to use outside of the Adriatic in 1914.[11]

Churchill did not agree. He held to his view that if faced by the Austrians and Italians the Mediterranean squadron should concentrate at Gibraltar without delay and avoid being cut off at Malta or prevented from going into the Atlantic. The "worst thing in the world" would be for reinforcements to arrive at Gibraltar only to find the Mediterranean squadron had been intercepted and forced to fight separately.[12] The new Mediterranean War Orders No. 1 therefore provided for a concentration at Malta only if Austria alone was hostile. The Mediterranean squadron was to watch the Adriatic until strong enough for battle and consider making use of an advanced temporary base in the Ionian Islands or on the Greek and Albanian coast. War against the entire Triple Alliance would mean concentration at Gibraltar until reinforced, leaving only the flotillas at

---

[10] Milne to Admiralty, 9 Aug. 1913, Adm 137, vol. 819.

[11] War Staff, "Notes on War Orders No. 1 for the Mediterranean," 18 June 1913, *ibid.*

[12] Churchill to Battenberg, 15 Aug. 1913, Adm 137, vol. 819.

Malta. This situation was, however, "not considered reasonably probable" since French assistance "is almost a certainty." [13]

Churchill was favorable to a reinforcement of the Mediterranean destroyer flotilla which was then composed of ten "River" class destroyers plus one in reserve. In 1912 the First Sea Lord had proposed raising its strength to twenty. At the time Churchill preferred waiting until more of the newer destroyers then under construction entered service. This was anticipated by late 1913 or early 1914, and the First Lord was therefore now ready to reconsider raising the strength of the Mediterranean flotilla.[14] But the plan was deferred again because of lack of sufficient crews to man the vessels. It was considered out of the question to reduce the North Sea preponderancy over Germany in destroyers, then less than 25 percent (89:69), to provide men for the Mediterranean.[15]

Temporary displacements of sizable forces to the Mediterranean were, however, possible. In June 1913 the ever imaginative Churchill conceived the idea of a powerful fleet detached from home waters effecting a sudden and swift concentration in the Mediterranean some time during the month of November. Here it would maneuver together with the regular Mediterranean Fleet in the area between Gibraltar and Malta. The First Lord justified his plan by claiming: "It is an important feature in our present policy to show the great mobility of the Fleet, and to make it impossible for any Foreign Power to calculate the force that may be brought against them in the Mediterranean. Some very interesting operations might be planned about the Balearic Islands. The advantages to the Fleet from the point of view of training and relief from duties in Home Waters have often been impressed upon me by you [Battenberg] and your predecessors. There is no reason why these political benefits should not be combined with potential and strategic advantages." [16] Churchill also proposed that the next year, subject of course to the foreign situation, general maneuvers of the whole Eastern Fleet take place in Australian waters. He hoped this would stimulate naval preparations in both Australia and New Zealand. With the great fleets Britain was maintaining in commission, Churchill believed she had "the means alike of puzzling our European competitors and educating the British Empire."

---

[13] Mediterranean War Orders No. 1, 20 Aug. 1913, *ibid.*
[14] Churchill to Battenberg, 25 June 1913, Adm 116, case 3089.
[15] Report by Capt. Ballard, 7 July 1913, *ibid.* At the outbreak of the war the Mediterranean destroyer flotilla consisted of sixteen "Beagles." Marder, *Dreadnought to Scapa Flow*, II, 21, 25 n. 3.
[16] Churchill to Battenberg, 7 June 1913, Adm I, box 8333.

Captain Ballard, Director of the Operations Division, prepared the plans to implement the First Lord's ideas. He assumed that in time of war the principal British effort would be directed toward preventing the Austrians from attacking their eastern trade route. Here the proximity of the Austrian bases and the superior strength of the Austrian torpedo craft would render a close watch of the Adriatic entrance difficult, if not impossible, for the force which was currently at the disposal of the Mediterranean Commander-in-Chief. For purposes of the maneuver Gibraltar would represent the Adriatic base of the Austrian or "Red" fleet. The "Blue" fleet, to be played realistically by the Mediterranean Fleet, would start the problem at Port Mahon or Palma which would represent Malta. Red's object would be to cruise the area between the third and fifth meridian, east longitude, without being brought to action until compelled to return to Gibraltar to coal; Blue's object would be to bring Red to action as soon as possible.[17] It is interesting to note that the Austrian fleet was given no other role than that of operating against the British trade routes. The possibility that the Austrians might attempt to join the Italian fleet, the contingency which haunted the French and was often represented in their maneuvers, seems not to have been considered.

A substantial force was to be detached from home waters for the maneuvers, the most important portion being four dreadnoughts of the first division, First Battle Squadron.[18] At the last minute the entire affair was almost canceled because of an apparent discrepancy in the Admiralty estimates of the ratio of strength between the British and German forces in the North Sea. The figures which had been agreed upon in August showed eighteen British against twelve German dreadnoughts and battle cruisers for the month of November. But the estimates prepared on October 24 by the intelligence division showed a ratio of 19:16—a superiority of 15 instead of 50 percent.[19] For a while there was a flurry of cables between Churchill, away at the moment aboard the *Enchantress*, and Battenberg at the Admiralty over how the mistake had arisen. The technicalities of the problem revolved around the recent commissioning of the German battle cruiser *Seydlitz* and the fact that three German dreadnoughts were undergoing trials after commissioning, whereas the commissioning and

[17] Memorandum by Capt. Ballard, 3 July 1913, *ibid.* To add to the realism, part of Red's force would have to leave Gibraltar with only 60 percent coal to represent the limited radius of action of the Austrian "Erzherzogs." Red would also have a strong enough destroyer force at Gibraltar to make it too risky for Blue to attempt a close watch.

[18] Minute by Battenberg, 8 Aug. 1913, *ibid.*

[19] Minute by Churchill, 25 Oct. 1913, *ibid.*

trials of two British dreadnoughts were delayed. Churchill was ultimately able to conclude that, counting completed ships only, the ratio was 19:13, approximately a 50 percent superiority. The maneuvers could therefore proceed as originally proposed.[20] This minor flap clearly shows where the Admiralty's real concern was. Sizable forces may have cruised the Mediterranean during the Balkan Wars—although it might be pointed out that the battle squadron involved was composed of pre-dreadnoughts—and impressive maneuvers might be held to awe potential enemies with the flexibility of British sea power, but the real emphasis was, and would remain, the North Sea. In the Mediterranean naval convention with France, the Admiralty reserved the right, as Saint-Seine put it, to withdraw the last destroyer from the Mediterranean if necessary.

Before the brief scare over the Mediterranean naval maneuvers, Churchill told Grey that it had been possible to send so great a fleet only because of the lateness of some of Germany's projected ships. The Admiralty could not tell when it would be able to send so large a force again without prejudice to the 50 percent preponderance.[21] The occasion came sooner than expected, for shortly afterwards it was learned that a pair of the latest German dreadnoughts would begin a two-month cruise in the Atlantic in January 1914. The Admiralty decided to take advantage of this by sending four super-dreadnoughts of the Second Battle Squadron on a similar cruise to the Mediterranean. This would afford a welcome change to the officers and men without disturbing margins in home waters.[22] Once again the North Sea was given precedence over the Mediterranean.

According to the Cabinet decisions of 1912 the battle cruiser force stationed in the Mediterranean was only an interim measure until the Cabinet's resolution to maintain a one-power standard in that sea could be carried out. Originally the Admiralty assumed that, given a favorable situation in 1915 and providing that Austria did not increase her building program, no construction in addition to the established British program would be necessary. The gift of the *Malaya* and the three Canadian dreadnoughts would make up the Mediterranean deficit.[23] The rejection on May 30, 1913, of Borden's naval proposals by the Canadian Senate upset this plan. To counteract its effects the Cabinet decided in early June to ac-

[20] Battenberg to Churchill, 26 Oct. 1913; Memorandum by Capt. H. F. Oliver, 27 Oct. 1913; Minute by Churchill, 28 Oct. 1913, *ibid.*

[21] Churchill to Grey, 21 Oct. 1913, Grey MSS, FO 800, vol. 86.

[22] Churchill to Grey, 4 Dec. 1913, *ibid.*

[23] Memorandum by Churchill, "Naval Requirements," 29 Nov. 1912, Asquith MSS, box 108.

celerate the construction of the three ships of the 1913–14 program, that is, to begin their construction as early as possible so that they would be ready at the same time as the Canadian dreadnoughts would have been. The Admiralty thought this would provide a delay of seven or eight months during which Borden could renew his proposals, while the necessary margin of naval strength in the autumn, winter, and spring of 1915–16 would be maintained.[24]

By the end of 1913 the Canadian dreadnoughts had still not materialized, and Churchill, in presenting the next year's naval estimates to the Cabinet, felt obligated to remind his colleagues that it would not be possible to carry out the decision to maintain a one-power standard in the Mediterranean unless these ships or their equivalents had been built by the end of 1916 or the beginning of 1917.[25] Until then a "containing force" of fast battle cruisers and armored cruisers would be kept in the Mediterranean. In 1914 this force would consist of four battle cruisers, four armored cruisers, four modern light cruisers, and a new flotilla of sixteen destroyers ("Beagles") to be based on Malta. Should the Germans keep the *Goeben* in the Mediterranean, the British forces there would be reinforced by the battle cruiser *New Zealand* as soon as the new battle cruiser *Tiger* joined the fleet at the end of 1914. This force would not fulfill a one-power standard, but it would make Great Britain a "formidable factor for diplomatic purposes," and if joined to the French fleet, "a decisive reinforcement." As long as the speed of this force was greater than any other equal force, Churchill thought there was no danger of its being cut off and destroyed in detail. For this reason the Admiralty did not propose to send out any of the older battleships for they would ruin the speed of the Mediterranean Fleet and add little to its effective strength. As a result there were no capital ships available to permanently reinforce the Mediterranean until the *Malaya* was ready in the autumn of 1915, but as long as the understanding with France remained unimpaired the delay would "not necessarily be injurious."

Churchill was not being completely frank with his colleagues. Despite his talk of a "decisive reinforcement" to the French fleet the Admiralty were anxious to avoid tactical cooperation with the French as far as possible. Should the French be challenged by the Austrians and Italians

[24] Statement by Churchill, 17 July 1913, *Parliamentary Debates* (Commons), 5th ser., LV, 1486; Memorandum by Churchill, 10 Jan. 1914, p. 6, Asquith MSS, box 25. An Italian plan to build an additional four super-dreadnoughts aggravated the Mediterranean situation. See Marder, *Dreadnought to Scapa Flow*, I, 314.

[25] Memorandum by Churchill, "Naval Estimates, 1914–1915," 5 Dec. 1913, p. 7, Asquith MSS, box 109.

in a great naval battle, it was rather hazy exactly how this "decisive reinforcement" would be accomplished. Yet once the first Austrian dreadnoughts were in service, the ability of Admiral Sir Berkeley Milne's forces to handle the Austrian fleet by themselves was questionable, and a combination with the French might become imperative. Milne himself in the spring of 1914, estimating comparative strengths in the Mediterranean on July 1 of that year, considered that after detaching a sufficient force to protect British commerce against the Mittelmeerdivision, he would have to be reinforced by four battleships of the "Orion" class or similar, four cruisers of the "Minotaur" class or similar, and six or seven light cruisers in order to meet the Austrian fleet "with a reasonable prospect of success." [26]

The subject of the 1914–1915 naval estimates produced a heated dispute between Churchill and Lloyd George, Chancellor of the Exchequer and leader of those who sought to lower the estimates, particularly to reduce the dreadnought building program for that year from four to two.[27] In justifying his proposals during the controversy, which threatened to break up the Cabinet, Churchill was able to make effective use of the 1912 CID decisions and pledges of the government, particularly those of Harcourt, concerning the maintenance of the British position in the Mediterranean.[28] The Admiralty were bound by Cabinet decisions in questions of policy, Churchill insisted, and if standards were changed the Admiralty could readjust its calculations, but the government and not the Admiralty would have to take the responsibility for changing the standards. The government would then be exposing itself to opposition charges of bad faith which, Churchill clearly implied, would be justified. The Admiralty suggested that two ships of the 1914–15 program be laid down as soon as possible, so as to be ready by the second quarter of 1916. This would secure the Mediterranean position until the end of the first quarter of 1917, and Borden would have another twelve months to get his naval proposals through the Canadian parliament. If he succeeded it might be possible to retard the battleships of the 1915–16 program by an amount equal to the accelerations of the two previous years. If the Canadian dreadnoughts still were not authorized, the Mediterranean position could be secured after the first quarter of 1917, in the absence of fresh Austrian

[26] Milne to Admiralty, 4 Apr. 1914, Adm 137, vol. 819.
[27] For the Cabinet dispute see especially Marder, *Dreadnought to Scapa Flow*, I, 316f.
[28] Churchill, "Naval Estimates 1914–15," 10 Jan. 1914, p. 6. Churchill also frequently cited Austrian and Italian naval plans. See also Marder, *Dreadnought to Scapa Flow*, I, 323.

and Italian construction, by accelerating one ship of the 1915–16 program. By then Churchill thought it was also possible that the progress of naval science, particularly in the field of submarine construction, would permit a new view of the whole naval situation.[29]

The decision finally reached was a compromise. The four dreadnoughts were retained in the building program for that year and the Admiralty's proposals for acceleration were accepted, but a number of light cruisers and torpedo boats for harbor defense were cut.[30] In his speech introducing the estimates to the House of Commons, Churchill promised that before the end of 1915 a battle squadron of six dreadnoughts and two "Lord Nelsons" would replace the battle cruisers based at Malta.[31]

The ability of the French navy to fulfill the major role now allotted to it in the Mediterranean was still a matter of concern at the beginning of 1913, despite the evident improvement under Delcassé's administration. The naval balance of power between the French fleet on one side, and the Austrian and Italian fleets on the other, was a close and delicate one to begin with, and there was no guarantee that the French in a moment of crisis would be able to employ all the strength theoretically at their disposal. In late February 1913, Admiral Lapeyrère reported confidentially to Pierre Baudin—who had replaced Delcassé as Minister of Marine a month earlier—that at the moment, the First Armée Navale could count on only thirteen of its eighteen battleships, four of its six armored cruisers, thirty-one of its thirty-four destroyers, and eleven of its seventeen submarines.[32] The reasons for this were varied, involving the need for repairs and detachments made for service in the Levant during the Balkan Wars. The situation was worst in the third squadron where half of the old battleships could not be used before major repairs had been undertaken.

The fleet was also hampered by a shortage of trained personnel, especially in the cadres of experienced petty officers, whose posts were often occupied by ordinary sailors.[33] The personnel shortage placed a great strain on the reduced crews during naval maneuvers. It was a strain which Lapeyrère feared they might not be able to stand for several weeks in

[29] Memorandum by Churchill, "Naval Requirements 1914–15," 6 Feb. 1914, pp. 2–4, Asquith MSS, box 110.

[30] Marder, *Dreadnought to Scapa Flow*, I, 325–326.

[31] Statement by Churchill, 17 Mar. 1914, *Parliamentary Debates* (Commons), 5th ser., LIX 1929–1930.

[32] Lapeyrère to Baudin, 22 Feb. 1913, AMF, carton BB3-1353.

[33] *Ibid.* In the customary "Rapport de prise de commandment" which captains filed on assuming command of a new ship, the personnel shortage was frequently noted. For example, the battleship *Démocratie* in May 1913 lacked 143 of her official complement of 730, and the battleship *Vergniaud* was short 119 men in October 1913.

a real war.[34] To fill the gaps in the crews of the more modern battleships, the suppression of the third squadron was considered. Admiral Le Bris questioned the effect that this might have on public opinion after all the arguments advanced for its transfer to the Mediterranean the previous year.[35] But, with the first dreadnoughts, the *Jean Bart* and *Courbet*, expected by the end of 1913, the decision to disband the third squadron was taken. The First Armée Navale was reorganized into two squadrons of eight battleships each. The first squadron was to consist of the dreadnoughts and the "Dantons," and the second squadron the "Patries" plus an independent division (Division de complément) composed of the older battleships *Suffren, Gaulois,* and *Saint Louis*, drawn from the third squadron. The third squadron's other ships were formed into a training division.[36] The squadron whose transfer to the Mediterranean had aroused so much comment in 1912 therefore ceased to exist, and half its ships assumed the more prosaic duties of naval schools.

In the face of growing naval competition in the Mediterranean an augmentation of the French program of 1912 became highly desirable to the EMG.[37] Paul Painlevé, in his report to the Chamber on the naval budget for 1913, advocated an acceleration of the French building program and the supplementary construction of six battle cruisers by 1920.[38] The battle cruiser was a class of warship not represented in the French navy. A few months later, Camille Chautemps, reporter on the naval budget to the Senate, went even further. He invited the government to submit proposals for the construction before 1920 of eight additional battleships. These were to be fast enough to fulfill the tactical role given to armored cruisers or battle cruisers in other navies.[39]

Baudin was successful in obtaining an acceleration of the building program. Under Etat A of the naval law of 1912 only two battleships were to be laid down in 1913. The government was now authorized by Article 9 of the financial law of July 30, 1913, to lay down four that year.[40] These

[34] Lapeyrère to Baudin, 7 July 1913, AMF, carton BB4-2708.
[35] Conférence des Directeurs, 17 Apr. 1913, AMF, carton BB8-1716.
[36] *Le Yacht*, 11 Oct. 1913, p. 638; *Moniteur de la flotte*, 27 Dec. 1913, p. 3.
[37] First section, EMG, "Nouvelle extension du programme naval de l'Autriche-Hongrie, ses conséquences au point de vue de l'équilibre méditerranéen," Nov. 1912, AMF, carton BB7-192. The recommendation was for the French building program to be supplemented by six battleships, seven battle cruisers and ten scouts.
[38] *The Naval Annual, 1913*, p. 33; P. Claude, "La Budget de la Marine à la Chambre," *Le Yacht*, 22 Feb. 1913, p. 113; Henri Bernay, "L'Augmentation du programme navale," *Le Yacht*, 26 Apr. 1913, pp. 257–258.
[39] *Moniteur de la flotte*, 17 May 1913, p. 3.
[40] Henri Le Masson, "Politique navale et construction de navires de ligne en France en 1914," *Revue maritime*, no. 202 (Aug.-Sept. 1963), p. 997. Two were laid down in April and two in October.

ships, of the "Normandie" class, were scheduled for completion from May 1916 to June 1917. Their outstanding feature was the somewhat daring arrangement of the primary armament in quadruple gunned turrets. A fifth "Normandie," the *Béarn*, was begun in January instead of October 1914 as had originally been planned. This acceleration of the program by nine months was partially explained by Le Bris' decision to reorganize the fleet into squadrons of eight instead of six ships. As the maneuvering characteristics of the "Normandies" were to be similar to those of the "Bretagnes," already under construction, a homogeneous squadron could be formed from the five "Normandies" and three "Bretagnes." [41] Although four out of the five "Normandies" were near launching at the outbreak of the war, they were fated never to be completed. The mobilization of the dockyard workers paralyzed work at the beginning of the war, and later, after they had been launched, the more pressing and often conflicting demands of the armies for material and munitions kept work on them at a minimum.[42]

Vice Admiral Le Bris, who remained chief of the EMG until May 18, 1914, worked hard at obtaining an increase in the building program in the months before he left office.[43] In June 1914 the Ministry of Marine prepared a carefully worded bill to be brought before the chambers later that year. It was to be presented as a simple rectification of the law of 1912 in order to bring the text of the law into accord with the current situation. By changing the legal age of replacement for the "Dantons" and "Patries" from twenty-five to twenty years, it would ultimately have led to a French fleet in 1925 composed of four squadrons totalling thirty-two capital ships with a primary armament of 13.4-inch to 15-inch guns, plus the four "Jean Barts" with their 12-inch guns.[44] One of the four squadrons would have been a "fast squadron" composed of eight *cuirassés rapides*, literally "fast battleships," for the EMG was thinking of interpreting the scouts (*éclaireurs d'escadre*) which were specified in the naval law of 1912 not in terms of light cruisers, as was common at the time, but rather in terms of large warships of 28,000 tons, 13.4-inch guns, and a speed of 26–27 knots. These ships were to be more heavily armored than the battle cruiser type, and akin to the British "Queen Elizabeth" class in their con-

[41] *Ibid.*, pp. 997–998.

[42] H. Le Masson, "Les Cuirassés à tourelles quadruples de la classe normandie," *Revue maritime*, no. 203 (Oct. 1963), pp. 1178, 1183–1184. The "Normandies" (24,-800 tons) were to have 12 13.4-inch and 24 5.5-inch guns, and a speed of 21 knots. The *Béarn*, last of the class, was finally launched in 1920 to clear the slip. She was eventually completed as an aircraft carrier; *ibid.*, p. 1189.

[43] Le Masson, in *Revue maritime*, no. 202, p. 999.

[44] *Ibid.*, pp. 1003–1005.

ception.[45] The French also intended to continue the use of the as yet untried quadruple gunned turret in the "Lyon" class of battleships which were to have followed the "Normandies" under the building program.[46]

In the year before the outbreak of the World War the French navy had therefore replied to the challenge of the Triple Alliance in the Mediterranean by an acceleration of its building program, and was about to seek parliamentary approval for a substantial increase to its strength in future years. Whether or not such approval would have been obtained is an open question, for the war began before the proposals could be considered.

During the first half of 1914 the French navy repeatedly attempted to strengthen, and even extend, its agreements with the Royal Navy. The latter naturally deftly sidestepped any overt attempt which might be interpreted as extending the entente beyond the narrow limits set in the Grey-Cambon exchange of letters. In the process the French revealed a certain degree of suspicion toward their ally who politely refused any project with the slightest flavor of an alliance. In January 1914 the French military attaché in Vienna reported disturbing impressions gathered from conversations with British naval officers about a withdrawal by the Royal Navy to Gibraltar in the event of war. Saint-Seine suspected that these were only private opinions. Admiral H. B. Jackson, chief of the Admiralty War Staff, flatly denied the rumors and reaffirmed that the base of operations for the Mediterranean Fleet was, and would remain, Malta.[47] To emphasize his point, he showed the French naval attaché a copy of the Admiralty instructions to the Mediterranean Commander-in-Chief dated May 5, 1913. Saint-Seine found that these conformed absolutely in spirit, and very closely in text, to the Mediterranean accord between the two admiralties. Jackson also reassured the French that in 1914 Britain would not need to make use of the reservation—so suspect to the French— that ships would be withdrawn from the Mediterranean for the North Sea if necessary. On the contrary, the Royal Navy would probably be

[45] Le Masson, "La Difficil gestation du croiseur léger français, 1910–1926" (pt. 1), *Revue maritime*, no. 199 (May 1963), p. 588; and "Des cuirassés qui auraient pu être . . .," *ibid.*, no. 204 (Nov. 1963), pp. 1291–1309. The "Queen Elizabeths" (27,-500 tons) belonged to the 1912 program and were laid down between October 1912 and October 1913. They were armed with 8 15-inch and 16 6-inch guns. Although originally designed for 25 knots, 24 was about the best obtained. Parkes, *British Battleships*, pp. 562–565.

[46] Le Masson, "Des cuirassés qui auraient pu être . . .," p. 1296. The *Lyon, Lille, Duquesne,* and *Tourville* (29,000 tons) were to have been laid down in 1915 with a primary armament of 16 13.4-inch guns in four turrets. Details of their protection had not been decided before the outbreak of the war.

[47] Saint-Seine to Le Bris, 18 and 22 Jan. 1914, AMF, carton Es-10.

able to reinforce the Mediterranean in 1914, although this would not be true for the following winter. However, Jackson insisted, sea supremacy in the Mediterranean was so important to the British Empire that they would stretch their sinews to the breaking point before abandoning it.

Toward the latter part of January, Lieutenant Bergasse du Petit Thouars, a staff officer attached to the operations section of the EMG, visited London to discuss with Saint-Seine a number of points of detail which remained to be settled with the Admiralty. At the same time he brought a letter from Le Bris in which the admiral stressed the importance of mutual exchange of information on the Austrian and Italian fleets. To facilitate this he proposed that Code BG, the signal code for the allied fleets, be placed in service aboard the *Inflexible* and *Courbet,* the respective Mediterranean flagships, in time of peace, and that an exchange of radio communications take place whenever the French or British Commander-in-Chief thought it useful.[48] This would involve the employment of a code which had been prepared for use in the event of naval cooperation in war, cooperation which could only take place after the British government had so agreed. It is not surprising that the French naval attaché found the First Sea Lord decidedly unenthusiastic when approached on the subject. Prince Louis also could not see the advantages in Le Bris' proposal, for Code BG was simple enough in its mechanics to be put into service without preliminary practice.[49] He agreed to the proposals about exchange of naval intelligence, but preferred that it continue to take place by means of the naval attachés. As Saint-Seine had anticipated, he was officially informed the following day that the British government had not "authorized the Admiralty to do more than prepare for an alliance between the two countries, and that it considered the actual use or practice with our joint signal books would go beyond that stage of preparations, and is therefore inadmissible."[50] Saint-Seine privately wrote Admiral Jackson that he was not surprised, and that he was sorry the suggestion had been made by the French for he did not "clearly see what useful purpose it could serve."[51]

The Admiralty's reservation of the right to withdraw all British ships from the Mediterranean weighed heavily on Le Bris' mind because of the

[48] Le Bris to Saint-Seine, 23 Jan. 1914, *ibid.* A copy may also be found in Admiralty Archives, case 0091.

[49] Saint-Seine to Du Petit Thouars, 28 Jan. 1914, AMF, carton Es-10. Battenberg did agree to take up the subject with Churchill.

[50] Jackson to Saint-Seine, 29 Jan. 1914, Admiralty Archives, case 0091. Also enclosed in Saint-Seine to Le Bris, 30 Jan. 1914, AMF, carton Es-10.

[51] Saint-Seine to Jackson, 30 Jan. 1914, Admiralty Archives, case 0091.

uncertainty it created. He could not rely absolutely on British assistance even should the British government decide to enter a war as France's ally. Battenberg, when he learned of these fears through Saint-Seine, repeated the assurances that Jackson had given shortly before. The reservation which was the source of so much worry to the French had been inserted in the agreement only after long and difficult discussion by the Board of Admiralty, but it was necessary to subordinate the Mediterranean to the North Sea in order to maintain a sufficient margin over the German fleet. Prince Louis, like Jackson, saw no difficulty in maintaining at Malta a British force strong enough to keep the Austrians in check in 1914, but considered 1915 a delicate year, for it was then the Royal Navy would suffer from the absence of the Canadian dreadnoughts, and the ships whose construction had been accelerated to offset them would not enter service until 1916.[52]

It was primarily the present and future situation in the Mediterranean that Le Bris wanted to be the subject of the conversations which he proposed at the beginning of February to hold in London with Battenberg. At first Battenberg said that he would be glad to see Le Bris and did not anticipate any difficulty obtaining the necessary authorization from Churchill who would probably like to be present at the talks. He did, however, suggest that the talks be postponed until after the naval budget for 1914–15 had definitely been drawn up.[53] But just three days later Saint-Seine was summoned to the Admiralty by telephone in order to have Battenberg politely advise against the expediency of Le Bris' visit to London. Prince Louis based this on his belief that the majority of the Cabinet, with the exception of Asquith, Grey, and Churchill, were strongly in favor of the traditional policy of "splendid isolation," and opposed any engagement with a continental power. He assumed, quite incorrectly, that only a few in the Cabinet knew a naval and military convention with France existed. If certain ministers learned of it, Battenberg was convinced the Admiralty would immediately receive a formal order to cease all conversations with the French and tear up all the arrangements which might have been made. In the interest of these arrangements the most extreme prudence was therefore necessary, and Prince Louis thought that no matter what precautions were taken it would probably be difficult to throw the British reporters off the scent. He could not receive Le Bris at the Admiralty or at his home, and he was too important a personage for a visit to Le Bris' hotel to pass unnoticed. If news of their meeting were

[52] Saint-Seine to Le Bris, 10 Feb. 1914, AMF, carton Es-10.
[53] Saint-Seine to Le Bris, 7 Feb. 1914, *ibid.*

published, it would be "a veritable catastrophe." Battenberg suggested that when he passed through Paris incognito, as he expected to do on a trip to the Continent in May, he would be happy to see Le Bris "sheltered from the curiosity of the British Ministers." [54]

Cambon, who was kept informed by Saint-Seine of the conversations with the Admiralty, was quickly able to verify that Battenberg had been mistaken about the Cabinet's knowledge of the naval and military conventions. Saint-Seine thought his error could be explained by the fact that Prince Louis was not First Sea Lord when the communication in question took place, and also by the atmosphere of suspicion and distrust at the Admiralty in regard to certain radical members of the Cabinet. Although Saint-Seine did not mention it in his report and could not have known its full import, the Cabinet crisis over the 1914–15 naval estimates undoubtedly aggravated this situation. But if the First Sea Lord had been mistaken on a factual point, Cambon believed that his opinion on the question should be taken by the French as a warning to be very prudent and very discreet. He too advised against a visit to London by Le Bris, which if it became known would create difficulties for the Admiralty. In fact this is exactly what Battenberg said when Saint-Seine told him of his error and he had verified the French version.[55]

Le Bris apparently interpreted Battenberg's objections to his visit as indicative of a cloud on the entente cordiale, an opinion which Saint-Seine definitely did not share. Saint-Seine was personally convinced that the ideas of Asquith, Grey, and Churchill in regard to France had not changed, and he took advantage of his close and frank relations with Battenberg to mention Le Bris' fears. The First Sea Lord assured him that he was correct about the sentiments of the ministers, and added his own opinion that the imprudent words of Lloyd George had overexcited the zeal of those ministers who desired a rapprochement with Germany, but these numbered no more than three or four in the Cabinet.[56]

These events during the early months of 1914 were only minor irritations, but they served as a reminder to the French that no matter how frequent or intimate the communications between the naval staffs were, it was important that they be carried out discreetly. In the middle of April the French prepared a list of fourteen points, mostly technical, which remained to be resolved with the Admiralty. Among the most important was the

---

[54] Saint-Seine to Le Bris, 10 Feb. 1914, *ibid.* There is no evidence as to what extent, if any, Churchill was involved in the decision.

[55] Saint-Seine to Le Bris, 13, 18, and 24 Feb. 1914, *ibid.*

[56] Saint-Seine to Le Bris, 24 Feb. 1914.

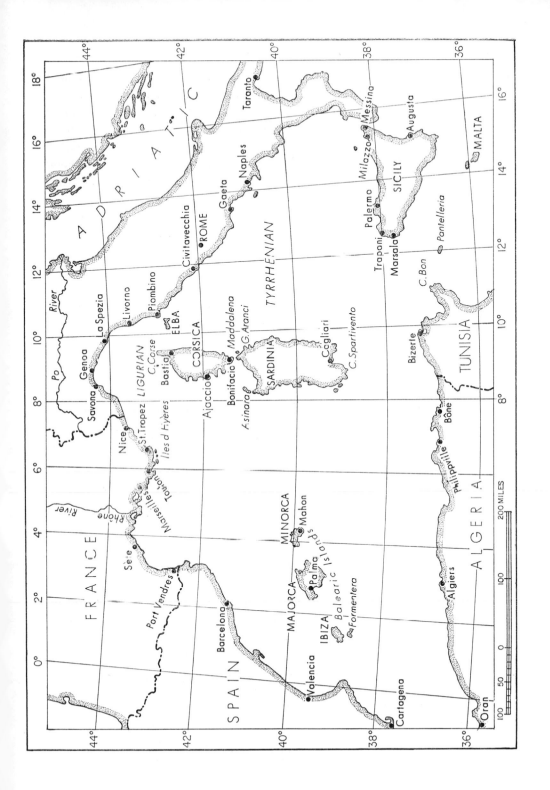

proposition for an addition to the Mediterranean convention concerning the German battle cruiser *Goeben* which had remained in the Mediterranean after the conclusion of the Balkan Wars. Since the British had stationed battle cruisers in the Mediterranean, and the French had none of this class, the French suggested that the British battle cruisers from the very beginning of hostilities be given the mission of destroying the *Goeben* and other fast German cruisers which were by far the most dangerous threat to the transfer of the nineteenth army corps.[57]

Le Bris also wanted to return to his proposal of January 24 concerning use of the allied code and exchange of intelligence. He felt the British had "evaded" the question since they did not seem to realize that the exchange of information proposed concerned the position of enemy ships, rather than information of a general character which was independent of the time factor. He thought the French could return to the subject without seeming to bring up something which had been rejected if they spoke in explicit terms of information concerning the location of enemy ships during the period of international tension preceding and at the very beginning of hostilities, and proposed the transmission of this information from one Commander-in-Chief to the other by the special code.[58]

Le Bris tried to give his projected meeting with Battenberg in Paris a more normal character and avoid enveloping it in mystery, but Prince Louis would have none of it. He preferred to remain incognito even if he was not going to meet Le Bris because of the number of people in Paris he wished to avoid and, most important of all, because Churchill had only consented to the interview on the condition that it not become known. Battenberg suggested that Le Bris' private home serve as the meeting place, and that he meet Vice Admiral Louis Pivet, who had been designated Le Bris' successor as chief of the EMG when the latter left to take command of a squadron.[59]

It is not known whether Le Bris and Battenberg discussed at their meeting the new French proposals concerning the employment of the British battle cruisers or the use of the code to transmit intelligence in

[57] Unsigned note, "Situation des questions non encore résolues à la date du 15 avril, 1914," AMF, carton Es-11. The note appears to be in Le Bris' writing.
[58] *Ibid.*
[59] Saint-Seine to Le Bris, 6 and 17 May 1914, AMF, carton Es-10. Unfortunately I was unable to find any record of the meeting, which was to take place June 2, in either the French or British naval archives. According to a marginal comment on the list of unresolved questions, presumably prepared by Le Bris on April 15, Prince Louis was to receive a copy of the instructions to the Commander-in-Chief of the French Mediterranean fleet in case of an English alliance. The instructions to the British Mediterranean Commander-in-Chief were to be requested in exchange. "Situation des questions non encore résolues," AMF, carton Es-11.

time of peace. The proposals were, however, incorporated in a ministerial dispatch of June 14, a copy of which was left with Battenberg by Saint-Seine. The Admiralty readily agreed on the question of the battle cruisers, and promised that in case of war under the conditions specified in the Mediterranean convention the battle cruisers would immediately attempt to bring the German cruisers in the Mediterranean to battle.[60] But on the question of the direct exchange of information by the Mediterranean Commander-in-Chief before the government decided the convention would take effect, the Admiralty remained adamant. They cited Sir Edward Grey's repeated declarations in public that no secret agreement existed which restricted or hindered the freedom of the government or Parliament to decide if Great Britain would take part in a European war. The Admiralty considered that in time of peace any exchange of information concerning warships of possible adversaries must be limited to the naval general staffs. Admiral Jackson privately commented, when he delivered the official reply, that the existence of secret communications between the two naval commanders would not escape the attention of interested parties for long, and exposure would lead to difficulties it was wiser to avoid. However, all British intelligence concerning movements of ships of the Triple Alliance was placed at Saint-Seine's disposal, and in case of international tension this information would be made available upon its reception for the French attaché to cable to his superiors.[61]

Until the outbreak of the war the naval conversations between the two countries never lost their character of an illicit relationship. Admiral Le Bris showed signs of resentment over this aura of mystery which required meetings in borrowed offices and at private homes. It was obviously no secret that relations between the two countries were warm. The public visits of leading political personalities, such as Poincaré to England at the end of June 1913, as well as the visits of British naval units to French ports with their accompanying banquets, speeches, and toasts all received full press coverage. So too did Churchill's visits to French naval bases and Baudin's appearance at British naval maneuvers. But the Admiralty were extremely careful to keep the actual communications between the technicians, as opposed to the ceremonial appearances of public figures,

---

[60] Saint-Seine to Gauthier [Minister of Marine], 22 June 1914, AMF, carton Es-10. Saint-Seine included an abbreviated translation of the Admiralty reply dated 20 June and bearing Jackson's signature.

[61] *Ibid.* The Admiralty kept their word. During the crisis preceding the war, when Saint-Seine asked to be kept informed of German movements in the Mediterranean, he was told "That was understood" ("C'est une affaire entendue"), Saint-Seine to ?, 27 July 1914, *ibid.*

as secret as possible. To facilitate this they required these communications to be effected through the naval attachés. There was no mystery among the other foreign attachés in London about the fact that Saint-Seine enjoyed a favored position at the Admiralty. Saint-Seine appears to have been the principal intermediary in these exchanges; the role of Captain Kelly in Paris is less clear, although it may well have been more extensive than surviving records indicate.[62]

By July 1914 the French navy was therefore in the position of having accomplished much in the way of preparation for possible cooperation with the Royal Navy, especially in respect to codes and signals as well as the defense of the Channel. But the fear persisted that in the absence of a firm British commitment it might be left to face the Triple Alliance by itself in the Mediterranean. The uncertainty was twofold: whether the British government would choose to enter a war; and if it did join the French, whether it would maintain a significant force in the Mediterranean.

At the same time the French were seeking to tighten the entente with England and increase their own naval strength, they were also faced with the problem of how to utilize most profitably their naval forces in the Mediterranean once the concentration here had been effected. In this problem the questions of how to assure the safe return of the troops from North Africa and destroy the enemy naval forces occupied the most important place.

Following the transfer of the third squadron from Brest to Toulon, Delcassé issued his general directives for the French Mediterranean Commander-in-Chief in a dispatch dated November 11, 1912. These called for the indirect protection of the transport of the nineteenth army corps to France by an immediate offensive leading to the destruction of enemy naval forces. In addition Lapeyrère was given the detailed plans of the "Transport Spécial," the code name for the transfer of the corps, to supplement these directives and aid him in formulating his own plan. He was also advised of the Anglo-French convention concerning the Mediterranean with the request that his chief of staff be the only other person informed of it.[63] Recent intelligence concerning the Italian navy showed a tendency toward abandonment of the northern ports of the peninsula

[62] In his journal Kelly refers to having obtained approval in the summer of 1913 for providing the Admiralty with information concerning landing facilities in French ports which might be utilized by a British expeditionary force, and speaks of making frequent visits to these ports. H. Kelly, "Journal as Naval Attaché," pp. 39–40, Kelly MSS.

[63] Baudin to Lapeyrère, 30 Mar. 1913, AMF, carton Ed-38.

in favor of a concentration in the ports of the south, particularly Taranto; this would greatly facilitate a junction between the Austrian and Italian fleets. The French Commander-in-Chief was advised to take this into account in drawing up his plans. Since the summer of 1912 the EMG had been busy organizing a special intelligence service on the Austrian and Italian navies, and an inventory had been made of all documents on hand dealing with a war against these two powers.[64] Mobilization plans for the port of Toulon were revised with the object of enabling the units of the First Armée Navale to complete their preparations in the shortest possible time. The organization of a net of coastal radio stations to permit the fleet to remain in secure contact with distant units was studied, and a monthly bulletin issued concerning foreign radio transmissions. At certain coastal stations an interception service was instituted to monitor these transmissions and, possibly, decipher them.

Lapeyrère, upon whose shoulders would rest the responsibility of leading the bulk of the French naval forces, was a vigorous champion of the offensive. In his plan of operations against Austria and Italy he made the ruthless destruction without delay of any enemy force or unit afloat an axiom. He prefaced his plans by declaring that, as a partisan of the offensive at any cost, his first act would be to bring out from Toulon all available forces at the very beginning of hostilities and lead them on a sweep through enemy waters "in order to hinder his mobilization and fight to the death [*combattre à outrance*] at their first appearance any of his naval forces that would venture out of their ports, either to meet us, or to attempt to effect their junction with the allied fleet." [65]

Lapeyrère intended to order immediately the first and second squadrons accompanied by two flotillas of destroyers into the Gulf of Genoa to watch the approaches to La Spezia and establish a blockade of that port if necessary. One of the destroyer flotillas was to cut the cables from Elba and nearby islands to the mainland, and also to mine the Piombino Channel. A flotilla of submarines and one of torpedo boats were to be stationed at Bastia or Villefranche, the minelayers supported by the armored cruisers of the second cruiser division would proceed to Bonifacio. The latter group was to blockade the enemy forces in Maddalena by means

---

[64] Fourth section, EMG, "Programme d'Entraînement de la Ière Armée Navale," 19 July 1913, *ibid*. The EMG were anxious to improve the flow of this information to the fleet. They also sought more sophisticated intelligence about potential enemy weaknesses in addition to the usual technical data about naval construction and ship movements. For example, they were most interested in consular reports concerning the large quantities of coal Italy was forced to import. Fourth section, EMG, "Note pour . . . Chef de la Ière Section, EMG," 21 June 1912, AMF, carton Ed-37.

[65] Lapeyrère to Baudin, 1 Sept. 1913, *ibid*.

of mines, eventually mining the entire Straits of Bonifacio. The cruisers would then rejoin the Commander-in-Chief and might be ordered to do so earlier if necessary. The armored cruisers of the first cruiser division were to reconnoiter the Italian coast from Piombino to the Strait of Messina, destroying any enemy forces found afloat. They were then to patrol the northern entrance of the strait to prevent any surprise by an enemy force coming from the Adriatic or the Gulf of Taranto. For their mission they would be accompanied by colliers, with whom a rendezvous would be set, and if possible by a group of torpedo boats with good endurance. On their way south the cruisers were to search the Bay of Naples, reporting or destroying according to the situation any enemy ships found there.

The third squadron had not been disbanded when Lapeyrère first formulated his plans. He intended this force to proceed to Bizerte when it was ready. This would have been a few days later than the rest of the fleet because of the necessity of completing its crews. It would be accompanied by a destroyer flotilla and on its way south would search the western and southern coasts of Sardinia to make sure there was no enemy force hidden in the various bays, particularly at Cagliari. Following this, the squadron was to patrol the waters between Cape Bon and Sicily to prevent any enemy force entering the Tyrrhenian Sea and surprising the French fleet from the rear, or operating against Bizerte or the Algerian coast. Lapeyrère realized that at full draft the old battleships of the third squadron were badly prepared for combat since their armor belt would be only slightly above the waterline. To lighten them and expose more of the armor protection, their coal provision was to be reduced. The obvious disadvantage to this was a corresponding reduction in their radius of action. They were therefore given a mission which would keep them near their base of operations, in this case, Bizerte.[66]

Lapeyrère also planned to use two steamers belonging to the Cie. Générale Transatlantique, the *Provence* (13,750 tons, 22 knots) and the *Lorraine* (11,869 tons, 21 knots), which were under contract for use as auxiliary cruisers in case of war. They were to patrol the Strait of Messina and passages to the south of Sicily, searching all vessels met along the east coast of Corsica and Sardinia on their way to and from their base of operations which was Toulon.[67]

Lapeyrère recognized that the Italians, anxious to effect a junction with the Austrian fleet, might have concentrated their forces before the outbreak of hostilities to the east of Sicily, notably at Taranto. In this

[66] *Ibid.*
[67] Lapeyrère to Captain, *Provence*, 27 Jan. 1914, AMF, carton A-89.

case the dispositions against La Spezia outlined above would not be completely wasted for they would assure the French that the Tyrrhenian was free of enemy forces. The main French effort, however, would be brought around south of Sicily to establish a blockade of Taranto and a close watch by cruisers over the Strait of Otranto, the entrance to the Adriatic. The forces blockading Taranto would include the two battleship squadrons and two destroyer flotillas, to be joined as soon as possible by the armored cruisers of the first cruiser division. The latter would participate along with the cruisers of the second cruiser division in the patrol of the Strait of Otranto to prevent any surprise from the Adriatic to the blockading force. If the presence of the submarine forces from Bastia or Villefranche before La Spezia was judged no longer necessary, they would be sent to Bizerte to await further orders. Lapeyrère thought operations in the Adriatic itself should only be conducted after the Tyrrhenian and Ionian were purged of enemy forces. Even then, this narrow sea, with numerous islands offering protection to submarines and torpedo boats, should be penetrated only with the greatest circumspection. A base of operations as close as possible to the Strait of Otranto would have to be chosen in order to permit the best utilization of the small units which would play a dominant role in the search for the enemy and the destruction of his flotillas. The French Commander-in-Chief considered the support of a repair ship absolutely indispensable to his fleet for these operations. There should be a minimum of four colliers per squadron so that two were always at the appointed rendezvous while the other pair were coaling. The fleet also needed at least four tankers.[68]

Le Bris criticized certain aspects of Lapeyrère's scheme, particularly the operations against La Spezia, for he did not consider it likely that the war would break out suddenly enough for the principal Italian units to be shut up in that port.[69] Moreover it would be dangerous to blockade La Spezia with the battleships of the first and second squadrons, for they would be exposed to attack by submarines from that port. At the present moment French naval forces were sufficient to struggle under favorable conditions against the naval forces of Austria and Italy, even united, but it was necessary that they not be exposed to loss or immobilization while conducting secondary operations. The operations against La Spezia, if enemy forces were found there at the beginning of hostilities, would best be left to the submarine and torpedo boat flotillas. Similarly, the potential

[68] Lapeyrère to Baudin, 1 Sept. 1913, AMF, carton Ed-38.
[69] Note by Le Bris [?], n.d., *ibid.* This critique is unsigned but is written on stationery imprinted "Chef d'Etat-Major Général" in what appears to be Le Bris' handwriting.

gain of blockading Maddalena was not sufficient to justify exposing the cruisers of the second cruiser division to submarine attack in Le Bris' opinion. There were also not apt to be any large enemy ships at Naples, and the cruisers of the first cruiser division would probably find only torpedo boats and submarines. A submarine ambush was likely should they make a prolonged stay in the bay. Nevertheless Lapeyrère's plan was approved in January 1914, at which time he was told that commencement of the transfer of the nineteenth corps would be advanced from the fifth to the third day of mobilization according to the latest army plans. The vigorous and immediate offensive which Lapeyrère had decided upon was considered the best means of covering the operation.[70]

This was certainly the consensus among the officers of the Ecole Supérieure who had studied the problem of a war against Austria and Italy employing the naval force available to each power in the spring of 1913. A majority of these officers also envisaged a surveillance of La Spezia by the submarines based at Bastia or Villefranche, but Taranto was considered too far from Bizerte for submarines to maintain a continuous watch. For these small craft, far more than for the squadrons of the line, all offensive conceptions were limited by the need for a nearby base. Floating depot ships, colliers, tankers, and special scouts to reconnoitre for submarines (convoyeurs de sous marins) were needed in sufficient numbers in order to increase the radius of action of the underwater craft. The construction of fleet submarines—submarines capable of operating together with the fleet—was recommended; this would require greatly increased surface speed and range. New aircraft were also to be given greater range, and the organization of an aerial reconnaissance service with either a floating or land base was recommended. In the event of an English alliance Malta could be used as a base for light craft for operations against Messina or Taranto. And the British submarines stationed at Malta might relieve French submarines in their blockade. However all officers firmly opposed attempting to tie British and French forces to close tactical cooperation. This was something the Austrians and Italians would be forced to resort to, and it was considered as leading to difficulties compromising the success of the operations.[71]

In summary, Lapeyrère and what appears to be a majority of senior French naval officers were convinced that a vigorous offensive against the

[70] Fourth section, EMG [Le Bris or Minister of Marine] to Lapeyrère, n.d. [The order is endorsed "Written in Jan. 1914"], AMF, carton BB4-2708.
[71] Fourth section, EMG, "Analyse des travaux des officiers élèves de l'Ecole Supérieure en 1913," enclosed in Le Bris to Lapeyrère, 18 Mar. 1914, AMF, carton A-132.

Austrian and Italian forces at the beginning of hostilities offered the best chance of success, and that it would be a mistake for the French to wait in port for enemy provocations or a junction of the enemy squadrons. Instead the French fleet was to take up its position before the hostile ports to attack or blockade the enemy in order to reduce him to inaction at the very beginning of the war and prevent the concentration of his forces. This was the object of Lapeyrère's plans, and he believed it gave France every chance of becoming mistress of the seas in the shortest possible time.[72] The plan was primarily concerned with Italy as the potential enemy. Austria and possible operations in the Adriatic were barely mentioned. This is somewhat surprising, for given the existing political and diplomatic situation Austria was far more likely than Italy to be an adversary. But the proximity of Italy and her commanding geographical position on the flank of the line of communications to North Africa, as well as her larger and therefore potentially more dangerous forces, caused French eyes to be riveted on her during this period.

One problem in French Mediterranean war plans that was never fully resolved is to what extent the doctrine of an immediate offensive coincided with the transfer of the nineteenth corps, the strategic object of the French army. The transfer of the corps from Algeria to France had been the subject of discussion and controversy between the Ministries of War and Marine for more than forty years before the outbreak of the First World War. It was first raised in 1868 when the Ministry of War proposed the establishment of a special commission to settle the details of the transport.[73] The question was taken up again in 1876 when the navy placed ten ships at the disposal of the Ministry of War for the purpose of the transfer. In 1883 the Ministry of Marine announced that these would no longer be available because of commitments in the Far East. Consequently some twenty-six commercial ships, mostly belonging to the Cie. Générale Transatlantique and chartered directly by the Ministry of War, were assigned to the operation. At this point direction of the operation passed out of the hands of the navy, which was content to supply advice on the best routes for the convoys. The correspondence between the two ministries between 1887 and 1900 shows that the navy, after presenting objections of a strategical order, disinterested itself in the "Transport Spécial," the material means to assure it, and its protection.

[72] Lapeyrère to Baudin, 1 Sept. 1913, AMF, carton Ed-38.
[73] L. Decoux, "Note sur le 'Transport Spécial,'" 4 May 1913, p. 1, AMF, carton Eb-120. Unpublished study at the Ecole Supérieure de Marine made at the suggestion of, and with the dossier supplied by, the EMG.

The fundamental objection of the navy to involvement in the plan was expressed in 1892 by Admiral Dupont, then assistant chief of the EMG, when he maintained that the French fleet must remain concentrated and always ready for a rapid offensive. The admiral asserted that destruction of the enemy squadrons had to come before any other consideration: after this had been achieved everything would become simple; until then everything would remain difficult if not impossible.[74] In addition to the strategic argument against beginning the transport before freedom of the seas had been assured, the navy objected to being deprived of the fast steamers employed in the transfer of the troops since it intended to use these vessels as auxiliary cruisers. This objection, however, was of a secondary nature and varied in intensity over the years according to the relative speed of merchant steamers and warships. In May 1891 the two ministries seemed in agreement that the transport of the troops must be rapid so that the best Mediterranean steamers could be quickly returned to the navy. The navy, with neither transport nor escort to furnish, would have its war fleet available at the outbreak of hostilities. The operation was to be effected by the Ministry of War alone at the moment it considered opportune without the least relation between the operations of the squadrons of the line and the movements of the convoy.[75]

The Ministry of War showed signs of uneasiness over the security of the transports in both March 1892 and December 1894 when it requested that a few cruisers be assigned to the operation, either for direct protection or to watch the movement of enemy ships between the Balearics and Algiers. The Ministry of Marine refused, the matter became deadlocked, and the Ministry of War gave up the idea of obtaining naval protection until 1906. In June 1900 General Louis André, Minister of War, indicated that the transport was no longer obligatory at the beginning of hostilities, but would eventually take place at an undetermined date if the sea was free and the defense of the nation required it. Therefore the required transports must be left at the disposal of the Ministry of War as long as the latter deemed them useful. In September of the same year the navy formulated its objections anew, this time declaring that it was up to it to take the operation in hand and choose the most favorable moment to effect the transfer. In November 1902 General André informed the Ministry of Marine that the use of the nineteenth corps in Europe had ceased to be

[74] *Ibid.*, p. 7.
[75] *Ibid.*, pp. 2–3. The convoy routes were decided on the suggestion of the Cie. Générale Transatlantique and only communicated to the navy as a matter of information. In general, they hugged the Spanish coast. This had been suggested by the navy in 1887.

part of the army's plans, but in 1906 the matter was taken up again. After the law reducing compulsory military service to two years was voted the Ministry of War became preoccupied with increasing the number of first-line effectives, which had become insufficient. Consequently army War Plans XV (1906) and XVI (1909) included the transport of approximately 35,000 men and their equipment. The objections of the navy remained unchanged.

France's military position and the disposition of her forces was scheduled to be the subject of a meeting on January 9, 1912, of the Conseil Supérieur de la Défense Nationale, the council—composed of the President of the Republic, the most important ministers, the major service chiefs, and the leading civil servants—which had been formed in 1911 to discuss major questions of national defense. The projected transfer of the nineteenth corps formed an important part of this session. In a note prepared by the Minister of Marine on the collaboration between the fleet and the army, the navy's position was forcibly stated.[76] Only after the Minister of Marine had given the government the assurance that the enemy forces had been reduced to impotence could the departure of the convoys be ordered.

In the contingency where the Triple Entente was at war with Germany and Austria alone, the fleet was considered strong enough to destroy the Austrian fleet and destroy or blockade any German vessels that might be found in the Mediterranean at the beginning of the war. The period of time necessary to achieve mastery of the sea might therefore not exceed by very much the time required to complete the mobilization and embarkation of the corps from Algeria. An important exception to this, and one of the greatest future import after the arrival of the *Goeben* in the Mediterranean, would be the stationing of German battle cruisers in the area.[77] In the situation where Italy would join Austria and Germany, it would not be prudent, according to the navy, to count on the nineteenth corps in France in the first weeks of the war. The navy felt confident of the issue of an encounter with the united Austro-Italian fleet, but the decisive naval battle would not suffice to insure the freedom of the seas since delays would be caused by the necessity of blockading or destroying all surviving enemy light and flotilla vessels. Moreover, the years 1913–1916 would be a critical period because of the increase in Austrian and Italian dreadnought strength; thus the minimum time necessary for ob-

[76] "Note remise par le Ministre de la Marine," 3 Nov. 1911, Section d'études, Conseil Supérieur de la Défense Nationale, "Note de Presentation," app. VI, 9 Jan. 1912, AMF, carton Es-23.

[77] The EMG had sadly concluded it might only be possible to blockade them after they ran out of coal.

taining sea supremacy would undoubtedly grow, delaying the transport even further. In case France and Germany were engaged in war alone, the transport might be effected on the condition that German forces were prevented from entering the Mediterranean, but in case France had to face the entire Triple Alliance by herself it would be expedient not to count on the nineteenth corps in plans for the European theater. Moreover it would be imprudent to strip the Mediterranean colonies of their garrisons under those circumstances. In these various contingencies, the intervention of Spain was not considered, since her negligible naval power would not appreciably affect the principal struggle. However her coastline might afford facilities for enemy vessels operating against the troop convoys. In that event the delay necessary before the transport could begin would be increased slightly.[78]

The army's plans for the transport established in 1909 were criticized as being too complicated.[79] The navy considered that letting each transport when ready sail by itself at full speed offered the best chance of success. The grouping of the steamers into convoys presented the drawbacks of delays in departure, reduction of speed to that of the slowest ship, and in case of surprise by the enemy, a concentration of risks. Moreover, the protection each of the convoys would receive from the one second-line cruiser allotted to it was illusory, and the five cruisers involved in the operation would be lost to the fleet for the impending naval battle.

The Ministry of War recognized the difficulties inherent in the transport, but was determined to run the risk because of the absolute necessity of facing the Germans with all available first-line troops. It therefore insisted that the navy adhere to the decisions and plans of 1909. According to the army, in case of war the simple objective of France and her allies consisted in crushing Germany, and to this effect troops assigned to secondary theaters, notably the Italian and Spanish frontiers, were to be reduced to a minimum. Moreover, it was likely that Italy would remain neutral. She was apparently absorbed in the Tripolitan expedition, and bound to France by the secret agreement of 1902. There were also signs that her policies were directed more against Austria, her nominal ally, than against France. For example, the forces used in the Tripolitan expedition were drawn largely from units stationed in Piedmont while the garrisons on the Austrian frontier remained complete. The army admitted that it was not impossible that Italy would declare against France after the first great battles if she found it in her interest to do so, and maintained

---

[78] This note was drafted during the period of Franco-Spanish friction over Morocco.
[79] "Résumé de l'Instruction du 16 février 1909," *ibid.,* app. VIII.

that precautionary measures were necessary on the alpine frontier. Spain might also be tempted to enter the war against France, but her forces were too limited to cause serious danger.[80] Like the navy the army was uncertain about Italy, but unlike the navy it was almost completely absorbed by the German problem.

During the actual discussions by the Conseil, the army, through Alexandre Millerand, Minister of War, revealed itself as confident that the troops of the nineteenth corps would not be missed in Algeria.[81] The French *colons* would furnish a contingent of at least 60,000 territorials or reservists which, when added to the 25,000 troops of the active army which would be retained in Algeria and Tunisia, would assure the protection of North Africa. Eventually the garrison in Algeria would also be reinforced by nine infantry battalions and three artillery batteries of territorials from France. The Moroccan Expedition, however, was currently absorbing around 40,000 men whose absence would be felt in France and Algeria. One result of this was a reduction in strength of the mobilized nineteenth corps from twenty-eight to twenty-one battalions of infantry.[82]

Both the Minister of War and General Joffre, chief of the army General Staff, recognized that the navy's warships had better things to do than to escort convoys, and Joffre suggested that if the transports sailed independently they would stand a better chance of escaping enemy destroyers. They would undoubtedly run risks, but such was the law of war and the essential thing was to effect the transport at whatever cost. Delcassé did not raise any objection in principle to Joffre's proposal, and promised the navy would do its best to diminish the risks run by the transports, for it was more a question of reducing risks than of eliminating them completely. The French squadrons of the line, the battleships and latest armored cruisers, would naturally not be available for protection of the transports, but the torpedo boat and submarine forces might contribute to it, along with the Toulon flotillas watching the passage between that port and Corsica, the Corsican flotilla barring the Strait of Bonifacio, the Tunisian flotilla watching the passage between Bizerte and Sardinia, and the Oran detachment watching the entrance to the Mediterranean from Gibraltar.

[80] "Note de Presentation," *ibid.*, pp. 3, 12. Austria was considered an almost certain ally of Germany in case of war.

[81] Procès-Verbal, Conseil Supérieur de la Défense Nationale, 9 Jan. 1912, *ibid.*

[82] The nineteenth corps when mobilized would also be reduced to seven instead of eight cavalry squadrons, and seven instead of nine mounted batteries. An independent brigade of Chasseurs d'Afrique, also destined for transport to France, was reduced from eight to six squadrons. "Effectif du troupes mobilisées dans l'Afrique du Nord," "Note de Presentation," app. IX, *ibid.*

Joffre was extremely confident the transports would be able to pass without accident, even if the French did not have sea supremacy. As the line of rail transport for the nineteenth corps ran along the length of the coast, he would not be unduly disturbed if the transports were forced to land, or even run aground, at various points along the southern coast of France. The general was asked if the nonarrival of the corps would create a gap in the French line. He replied that even without it he would not hesitate to push forward vigorously. At the moment the corps was destined to reinforce the French left, but in the next plan it would constitute independent divisions to be used where required.

In summing up the navy's case, Vice Admiral Paul Auvert, then chief of the EMG, seemed almost to be washing his and the navy's hands of the matter. He pointed out that none of the measures involving use of the submarine and torpedo boat flotillas could actually prevent enemy torpedo boats from sinking the transports. One could not compare the situation to the late eighteenth century, as some had tried to do, when Bonaparte had been able to cross the Mediterranean to Egypt despite the Royal Navy. At that time there were no submarines or high-speed torpedo boats to worry about. The navy had done its duty in warning of the dangers, Auvert concluded, and would do everything possible to facilitate the operation, but the risks remained high. The Conseil unanimously gave an affirmative answer to the double question of whether, in the most probable eventuality of France and England against Germany and Austria, the transport of the nineteenth corps should be effected as soon as that corps was mobilized; and whether if Italy joined the enemy this transport was to be effected before all else and at whatever cost, the Navy making in this case every reservation on the security of the transport, even if it consecrated all its efforts toward assuring that security.[83]

During the meeting Joffre had hinted at a new mobilization plan which the army General Staff was working on. This was the celebrated Plan XVII under which the French army was to begin the war.[84] Its fundamentals were presented to the Conseil Supérieur de la Guerre on April 18, 1913. The army General Staff (EMA) believed that the thrust of the Balkan peoples had modified to a certain extent the European equilibrium. The

[83] The original text of the question to be posed before the Conseil omitted the final reservation by the navy. The head of the third section, EMG, was, however, a member of the Conseil's Section d'études and insisted on its insertion so that the navy would not be rendered responsible for the security of an operation which it considered acceptable only after the acquisition of sea supremacy. Auvert to Delcassé, 6 Jan. 1912, ibid.

[84] For a summary of Plan XVII see J. J. C. Joffre, The Personal Memoirs of Joffre. Translation by Col. T. Bentley Mott (New York, 1932), I, pp. 89f.

Balkan events reduced the amount of support Germany could expect from Austria-Hungary, who would now be compelled to detach more forces to watch her southern frontier. This combined with the rebuilding of the Russian army and the maritime rivalry between England and Germany tended to lean the balance of power toward the side of the Triple Entente. Germany, however, was seeking to redress the balance and regain superiority by augmenting the number of her effectives and increasing the speed of her concentration. It was therefore against the northeastern frontier of France that the strongest thrust could be expected at the beginning of the war. The EMA therefore considered the northeast the most important theater of operations, and thought that the number of troops employed there, particularly of the active army, could not be too numerous.[85]

Although Italian interests were opposed to those of France in the Mediterranean, her latent hostility to Austria in the Adriatic probably counterbalanced this. The EMA believed that Italy would remain neutral until after the first battle, and then probably intervene on the side where she felt able to satisfy her wants. However, even should she enter the war against France at once, the action would not be felt until the end of the first month because of the slowness of her mobilization. Geography favored France: the neutrality of Switzerland forced the Italians to operate in a mountainous region with fairly well defined avenues of approach. The French would have to prevent the enemy breaking out of this area and exercising an influence on the campaign against Germany. This could be accomplished by reserve divisions, supported by fortifications barring the major passes and roads. Although the French were numerically very inferior to the invaders, the terrain was such that if the defenders could not halt the invasion indefinitely, they could force the Italians to advance with extreme caution and very slowly.[86]

The improved state of French relations with Spain permitted the protection of the Pyrenees to be reduced to simple surveillance. The EMA was equally unconcerned about the old fear of an invasion by sea. In the north this would be limited to raids, and would constitute a diversion which would not be a serious danger or exercise grave repercussions on

---

[85] France, Etat-Major de l'armée, Service Historique, Vincennes, third bureau, EMA, "Plan XVII-Bases du Plan," Conseil Supérieur de la Guerre, Séance du 18 Avril 1913, no. CXLIII, p. 41.

[86] *Ibid.*, p. 42. In addition to the fortress garrisons, only four reserve and one territorial division were assigned to this theater (p. 45). Should Italy adopt a benevolent attitude, it was planned to form the fortress garrisons, which were of the active army, into a division for use in the northeast (p. 72).

the general development of events or the ultimate outcome of a war. Coastal defense must therefore be accomplished with the strictest economy. It would consist of a *défense fixe,* the garrisons of fortifications at major ports, and a *défense mobile,* entrusted to territorial divisions which would repulse any landing between fortified coastal points. This *défense mobile* would be relatively strong between Calais and Boulogne, and between Dieppe and Le Havre and thence to the Cotentin Peninsula.[87] An Italian landing on the coast of Provence—which would enable the invading force to turn the line of the Alps—would be prevented by the fleet concentrated in the Mediterranean. In this strategic picture the veteran troops from Algeria and Tunisia, judged to be invaluable in the crucial battles on the northeastern frontier, would form two autonomous divisions, the thirty-seventh and thirty-eighth, to be used where most needed. The two divisions would land at Marseilles on the seventh to ninth day after mobilization. Taking into account possible delay and congestion on the line of transport, the EMA expected them to arrive in the region between Toul and Epinal on the morning of the sixteenth day, and in the zone of concentration to the north of Toul on the morning of the seventeenth day.[88]

The navy thought this operation with its fixed timetable risked paralyzing the offensive action of two thirds of the French fleet. In April 1913 the chief of the EMG ordered the Ecole Supérieure de Marine to prepare a special study on the "Transport Spécial" which the navy might use to bolster its arguments.[89] Lieutenant Laurent Decoux, the officer charged with the study, examined the various methods by which the convoys might be secured, directly or indirectly, and concluded that none would be effective until France had acquired sea supremacy.[90] He did not believe, and he had a good deal of company among contemporaries in this, that thirty-four to thirty-seven transports could be effectively screened from a swarm of torpedo boats, and he ridiculed the proposal to permit the transports to sail independently and take advantage of neutral Spanish coastal waters in their route. The high speed of enemy cruisers or torpedo boats and the slight respect apt to be shown Spanish neutrality in a major war rendered their safety illusory. Certainty of victory in battle over the combined Austrian and Italian fleets rested less on the material strength

---

[87] *Ibid.,* pp. 75–77. Only six territorial divisions were assigned to the Pyrenees, and the Atlantic and Channel coasts. Of these, three were in the north. A few additional territorial units were also available from the general reserve (p. 45).

[88] *Ibid.,* pp. 14, 51.

[89] Le Bris to director of l'Ecole Supérieure de Marine, 8 Apr. 1913, AMF, carton Eb-120.

[90] Decoux, "Note sur le 'Transport Spécial,'" *ibid.*

of the French forces, which at the moment were scarcely equal to their potential enemies and would soon become inferior, and more on the inherent advantage of the French concentration, cohesion, state of training, and above all, offensive spirit. Therefore nothing should distract from the attack which the French intended to push to the limit at the beginning of a war. Even if the transport should succeed, the question might be raised if it was worth the possible loss of a naval battle. Decoux concluded that the Conseil de la Défense Nationale would have to compare the eventual influence on the battlefield of the detachments of the nineteenth corps with the psychological effect on the army and the nation of the news of a great naval victory at the beginning of the war.

Lapeyrère advanced substantially the same arguments and insisted that the naval Commander-in-Chief not only be consulted on the date of the transport, but that the operation take place only on his proposal and at the moment he judged opportune.[91] The navy could not accept a fixed date for the transport that was determined solely by the requirements of the army's mobilization, taking no account of the maritime circumstances prevailing at the time. Lapeyrère doubted that the nation had imposed such large sacrifices on itself for the benefit of the navy in order to see it reduced to the role of a convoy escort. Furthermore he wanted the number of ports of embarkation in Algeria reduced from five to three, with none to the east of Phillippeville because of the proximity of Sardinia and Sicily, which were potential bases for hostile forces. The convoy leaders should also not be restricted to arrival at one port, but should be able to land their troops at Toulon, Marseille, Sète, or even Port Vendres if circumstances required it.[92]

The Minister of Marine backed Lapeyrère's views, and the question was again submitted to the Conseil Supérieur de la Défense Nationale on May 17, 1913. At the meeting the Ministry of War declared itself willing to lighten the navy's task by having the transports sail independently instead of in escorted convoys, but it insisted that there could be no delay in the date fixed for the transport to begin. In an argument which was difficult to answer, the army declared that the fate of France's coasts, overseas

[91] Lapeyrère to Baudin, 2 May 1913, AMF, carton A-89. Lapeyrère learned the detailed plan for the transport only in Dec. 1912 when the cruisers assigned to cover it were placed under his orders. Delcassé to Millerand, 9 Dec. 1912, AMF, carton Eb-120; Millerand to Delcassé, 19 Dec. 1912, *ibid.*; Delcassé to Lapeyrère, 30 Dec. 1912, *ibid.*

[92] Lapeyrère to Baudin, 2 May 1913, AMF, carton A-89. The admiral also proposed a substantial increase in the protection to be given the convoys. This would include cruisers, at least two flotillas of destroyers, and even a battleship squadron should one be available.

possessions, and even the fleet itself, depended in the final reckoning on the result of the great battles which would take place on the northeastern frontier. It would be a grievous mistake to renounce the use of the crack troops of the nineteenth corps in this battle which might determine the very existence of the country.[93] The Conseil decided to maintain their decision of January 9, 1912, concerning the transport.

Shortly after the meeting, Premier Louis Barthou ordered the Ministries of Marine and War to undertake a joint study of the problem of the "Transport Spécial." [94] Throughout the fall of 1913 and the winter of 1914, the two departments worked on the details of implementing Plan XVII. The army accepted the navy's proposals concerning the Algerian ports of embarkation which were reduced to three: Oran, Algiers, and Phillippeville. Only a few units were to embark at the last, and no steamer with a speed of less than 12 knots was to be used in the transport.[95] In the final version of Plan XVII, which was to take effect on April 15, 1914, the transports would sail alone on fixed dates at full speed in a direct line toward the port of Sète.[96] If necessary, the captains could divert their ships to either Marseille or Port Vendres. The only deviation from the plan permitted was the formation of convoys should these be judged essential, but it was specifically noted that their formation must not cause any appreciable delay. A total of thirty-seven steamers were involved, chartered from three of the major Mediterranean steamship lines. They were to sail from the Algerian ports between the third and seventh day of mobilization, and would carry a total of 26,160 officers and men, and 4289 horses.[97] In addition to this, 4507 officers and men and 106 horses were to be carried from Corsica (Ajaccio) to Marseille between the fifth and eleventh day of mobilization by slower steamers not utilized for the Algerian troops. The EMA had no specific provision in Plan XVII to transfer territorials from France to Algeria, although this might take place at a later date if necessary.[98]

[93] Section d'études, Conseil Supérieur de la Défense Nationale, "Rapport de presentation," 17 May 1913, AMF, carton Es-23.

[94] Etienne to Baudin, 16 June 1913, AMF, carton Eb-120. To save time, the first assistant chief of the EMA, General de Castelnau, worked directly with Le Bris.

[95] Castelnau to Le Bris, 14 Oct. 1913, *ibid*. The possibility of shortening the sea voyage by landing troops in Spain and utilizing Spanish railways was also discussed. For the Spanish question see below, pp. 284f.

[96] Le Bris to Lapeyrère, 7 Apr. 1914, *ibid*.

[97] Fourth bureau, first section, EMA, "Plan XVII—Transports par mer . . . en cas de Mobilisation Générale," 25 Mar. 1914, app. IV, "Table de Fractionnement," *ibid*. From the tables accompanying the plan, it would appear that not all these ships had a speed of at least 12 knots.

[98] Minister of War to Minister of Marine, 4 Apr. 1914, *ibid*.

The security for the transport would be obtained indirectly by the offensive of the French fleet at the beginning of hostilities.[99] This would be supplemented by the formation of a special division composed of the old battleship *Jauréguiberry* and seven old armored and protected cruisers under the command of the rear admiral commanding the Mediterranean instruction division, and subject to Lapeyrère's authority.[100] This division was to concentrate to the southeast of the Balearics and east of the Algiers-Toulon line so as to be midway between the Provençal and Algerian coasts. Its mission was: (1) to supplement the convoy's security by advising the captains of the best routes to follow to avoid the enemy, (2) to stop suspicious vessels, and (3) to combat any enemy cruisers, scouts, or torpedo boats trying to reach the transports.[101]

Rear Admiral Gabriel Darrieus, who would lead the special division, was invited to submit his comments and detailed proposals concerning its role. Darrieus, one of the most articulate officers in the French navy, did exactly that, echoing the navy's long-standing objections to transport of the corps before command of the sea had been assured.[102] The German battle cruiser *Goeben* currently posed the greatest threat to the transports, and the old ships allotted to the special division were no match for her. In Darrieus' opinion the best way to minimize risks would be to form the transports into two successive convoys under the direct protection of his division. The fleet's offensive might keep the principal enemy forces away, but the transports would still be exposed to the depredations of enemy cruisers and torpedo boats. Even when concentrated the special division would not be a match for the German Mittelmeerdivision, but the sacrifice of the old cruisers might enable the transports to scatter and perhaps reach the shelter of a Spanish port. To reduce the risks of the operation to an acceptable level it was necessary to strengthen the special division by the addition of the old battleships *Charlemagne* and *Gaulois* which present plans had placed in a "Division de Complément" at the disposal of the Mediterranean Commander-in-Chief. This force would be

[99] Le Bris to Lapeyrère, 7 Apr. 1914, *ibid.*

[100] Le Bris to rear admiral commanding Medit. instr. div. (Darrieus), 7 Apr. 1914, *ibid.* The division was a heterogeneous collection of old ships to be drawn from the schools, reserve, Moroccan division, and Levant service. The arrival date of the ships detached from the Levant was most uncertain, and the rear admiral commanding was told to expect only six of his eight ships to join him around the fourth day of mobilization.

[101] Exactly how the transports were to be advised is uncertain for they lacked the secret codes. Therefore any radio messages would have had to be carefully edited to avoid giving the enemy useful intelligence.

[102] Rear Admiral Darrieus, "Propositions relatives au 'Transport Spécial,'" n.d., enclosed in Lapeyrère to Gauthier, 28 July 1914, *ibid.*

too inferior in speed to the *Goeben* to afford truly effective protection, but its concentrated gun power might at least make the Germans more circumspect.

As one would expect Lapeyrère fully agreed with his subordinate. During the height of the July crisis, on the very day when Austria-Hungary declared war on Serbia, he forwarded a copy of Darrieus' memorandum to the Minister of Marine, repeating his old proposals concerning the transport. If, for reasons which he could not appreciate, the government persisted in effecting the transfer without waiting for his approval, he proposed that the Division de Complément when mobilized be added to the special division, thus making a total force of six battleships.[103] He also insisted that the transports be formed into successive convoys, and that the number of ports of embarkation be reduced to two: Oran and Algiers. In his opinion any other procedure was an adventure with which he did not desire to associate himself.

The exasperation which Lapeyrère's letter must have caused at the Ministry might well be imagined. Gauthier, the minister, recalled to Lapeyrère that he had claimed the previous year that he could detach none of his forces for the purpose of escorting the convoy, and it had been admitted that the navy accepted no responsibility for the security of the transport. The Minister of War had decided to accept the risks, a detailed plan had been formulated, the navy had added the special division to aid in the transport, and the details of the plan had been given to Lapeyrère on April 7. The obligation of the transports to proceed at full speed excluded the idea of a convoy. Since April 7 Lapeyrère had sent no observation on the plan. It was not possible at this late stage to modify the plans resulting from the collaboration of the two ministries following the decision of the Conseil Supérieur de la Défense Nationale—a decision in which the navy had neither taken the initiative nor accepted the responsibility. If war broke out, Lapeyrère was ordered to exert all his efforts toward assuring the success of Plan XVII.[104]

The attempt by the Mediterranean Commander-in-Chief to alter a mobilization plan whose detail had been the object of careful collaboration between the two ministries for almost a year does not present a very complimentary picture of French naval preparations on the eve of the war, especially since the question had been under discussion for the past forty years.[105] Unfortunately, at this moment of crisis the navy also lacked

---

[103] Lapeyrère to Gauthier, 28 July 1914, AMF, carton A-89.

[104] Gauthier to Lapeyrère, 30 July 1914, AMF, carton Eb-120.

[105] Joffre also made a last-minute decision: to recall in case of mobilization part of the troops from Morocco. Those drawn from eastern Morocco would embark at Oran for Sète, and those drawn from western Morocco would embark at Casablanca for

a strong hand at the helm in Paris. The Minister of Marine, a genial senator from the *département* of Aude, was infamous for his lack of knowledge concerning naval affairs. He did not prove up to the strain of war and was replaced shortly after its outbreak.[106]

For more than three years preceding the war the French forces in the Mediterranean had been under the command of one man: Vice Admiral Boué de Lapeyrère. Early in his career Lapeyrère was dubbed by Admiral Courbet the bravest of his captains in the China squadron.[107] Captain Kelly, the British naval attaché, knew him as a "fine figure of a man, with a ferocious expression . . . a kind heart, and . . . a very fine seaman." [108] The general picture of the French Mediterranean Commander-in-Chief is of an ardent and energetic officer with a passion for the sea. By nature and temperament Lapeyrère was well suited to carry out the prevailing French naval doctrine of an immediate and rigorous offensive to achieve sea supremacy through the destruction of the enemy squadrons. After the uncertain years through which the French navy passed at the beginning of the century, Lapeyrère shaped the major portion of its forces into a fine fighting instrument. Although he was recognized as authoritarian, the fleet had confidence in him and morale was high on the eve of the war.[109]

But there was another face to the coin. Lapeyrère's emphasis on squadron warfare in which long lines of dreadnoughts would be ranged against one another, and his preoccupation with complex and difficult evolutions necessary to maneuver large numbers of fast moving ships so that the maximum fire power could be brought to bear on the enemy once contact had been made, prepared the French navy for a type of warfare which it was not destined to meet. In this failing, of course, he was joined by the majority of naval leaders of his time. As a former Minister of Marine he

Bordeaux. This modification does not appear to have caused undue difficulty. Joffre to Gauthier, 29 July 1914, AMF, carton Eb-120; Gauthier to Minister of War, 30 July 1914, *ibid.*; Minister of War to Minister of Marine, 1 Aug. 1914, *ibid.* A good and very complete study of the problem based on official sources is Lieutenant de vaisseau Laurin, "Le Transport du 19me corps et des troupes coloniales en 1914" (unpublished study, Ecole de Guerre Navale, Session 1930–1931), esp. pp. 10–12, AMF.

106 Gauthier had, except for a few days, been minister since April 1914. During the crisis his erratic behavior—ranging from failure to issue important orders to overzealous demands that the *Goeben* be attacked before the outbreak of war—alarmed the cabinet. See Poincaré *Au Service de France*, vol. IV: *L'Union sacrée, 1914* (Paris, 1927), 509–510; Adolphe Messimy, *Mes souvenirs* (Paris, 1937), pp. 155–156; Dartige du Fournet, *A travers les mers*, pp. 247–249.

107 R. de Belot and A. Reussner, *La Puissance navale dans l'histoire*, vol. III: *De 1914 à 1959* (Paris, 1960), p. 26.

108 Kelly, "Journal as Naval Attaché," pp. 29–30, Kelly MSS.

109 Admiral Daveluy, "Marine et marins d'hier-XXVI," *Revue maritime*, no. 214 (Oct. 1964), p. 1222; Belot and Reussner, *La Puissance navale dans l'histoire*, III, 26.

was inclined to treat the directives of the chief of the EMG rather cavalierly; he tended to obey only the minister, and rather grudgingly at that, as events on the eve of the war showed. He regarded himself as senior to the chief of the EMG, and in some cases this was true in respect to rank.[110] Lapeyrère was also criticized as being too narrow in his vision and unable to see the larger strategic picture. There is perhaps some justice in this. As a sailor he appreciated far more than the General Staff of the army the terrible dangers to which the unprotected transports laden with helpless troops were exposed while crossing a sea where enemy naval forces might be lurking. Joffre seems incredibly sanguine about the "Transport Spécial" and casual in his acceptance of risks in an area which was really beyond his special competence. It must also be granted that in his objections to the transport Lapeyrère was merely reflecting long-standing policy of the Ministry of Marine. Yet it cannot be denied that in his single-minded concentration on the offensive and almost fanatical desire to bring his squadrons to grips with the Italian fleet, he distorted the relative importance to France of the land battles on the northeastern frontier, for which every available man was desperately needed, and a possible and by no means certain naval encounter with Austria and Italy. In this distortion he had a good deal of company in both the fleet and the Ministry itself.

In fairness to Lapeyrère it should be stressed that the command structure of the French navy and the channels of communication between the EMG and the fleet left much to be desired. The relationship between the government, the EMG, and the naval Commander-in-Chief was never clearly defined.[111] According to Admiral Louis Pivet, Le Bris' successor as chief of the EMG, Victor Augagneur, who had replaced Gauthier early in the war as Minister of Marine, thought that the role of the EMG was to prepare for war in time of peace and then, when war came, to disappear. In fact, during the mobilization fifteen out of seventeen junior officers on the EMG left for various naval units.[112] The poor French staff coordination combined with the somewhat hazy plan for Anglo-French cooperation in

[110] Masson, "Delcassé Ministre de la Marine," pp. 187–188. Lapeyrère was also supposed to have relied very little on his own staff. Masson is perhaps too harsh in some of his criticism about the admiral's neglect of the technical services. In his reports on naval maneuvers, Lapeyrère constantly stressed the need to remedy many of these deficiencies. Admiral Daveluy, who was under his authority during the war, presents a more favorable picture. Daveluy, "Marine et marins d'hier-XXVI," p. 1226.

[111] Masson, "Delcassé Ministre de la Marine," p. 187; A. Reussner and L. Nicolas, *La Puissance navale dans l'histoire*, vol. II: *De 1815 à 1914* (Paris, 1963), p. 241.

[112] Belot and Reussner, *La Puissance navale dans l'histoire*, III, 21. See also Adolphe Laurens, *Le Commandement navale en Méditerranée* (Paris, 1931), pp. 9–10.

the event of war help to account for some of the confusion involved in the escape of the *Goeben* and *Breslau* in the early days of the war. Le Bris may well have had a good point in his desire for regular radio communications between the two Mediterranean Commanders-in-Chief before the outbreak of war, but of course other and perhaps more important political, as opposed to military, factors prevailed.

Lapeyrère was denied the opportunity of leading the French fleet into a decisive battle, an event toward which he had devoted so much preparation. The declaration of neutrality by Italy and the wise decision by the Austrian fleet not to venture out of the Adriatic in the face of overwhelming Anglo-French naval strength completely changed the situation. In fact the EMG had no real plan for war against Austria alone.[113] When the prewar plans and preparations of the Austrian and Italian fleets to join their fleets under the command of the Austrian Admiral Anton Haus in an attempt to wrest sea supremacy from the French are taken into consideration, one may say that the defection of Italy from the Triple Alliance made Lapeyrère one of the great "might-have-beens" of naval history.[114]

[113] A. Thomazi, *La Guerre navale dans l'Adriatique* (Paris, 1927), p. 38.

[114] Lapeyrère retained naval command in the Mediterranean until October 1915, when, disillusioned by the changed conditions of naval warfare, and exhausted after four years of command, he asked to be relieved. Belot and Reussner, *La Puissance navale dans l'histoire*, III, 54.

VI

A New Factor in the Mediterranean: The K.u.K. Kriegsmarine

Even among historians mention of the Austro-Hungarian navy is apt to provoke smiles amid images of a Ruritanian situation complete with elaborately bemedaled officers bearing grandiose titles, a bathtub fleet, and in general a comic opera atmosphere. In one sense this is hardly surprising, for both Austria and Hungary have long been cut off from the sea, and the K.u.K. Kriegsmarine disappeared along with the empire it so faithfully served over fifty years ago. With the passage of time the ranks of its surviving veterans are rapidly being depleted. The flags, portraits, and models in the Marinesaal of the Vienna Heeresgeschichtliches Museum are today almost reassuring signs that it actually existed. Nevertheless in the years immediately preceding the First World War the Austro-Hungarian fleet became a serious and disturbing factor in the Mediterranean, and its activity was deemed important enough to influence the dispositions of the world's largest navy.

The history of the Austrian navy was not devoid of success in the nineteenth century. Austrian warships participated in the international squadron which seized Saida and Saint Jean d'Acre from the forces of Mehemet Ali in 1840. The Austrian fleet was badly shaken by the revolutions of 1848–49 and its main base was shifted from Venice, henceforth considered too Italian, to Pola in 1850. By 1853 German had replaced Italian as the service speech (*Dienstsprache*). Archduke Ferdinand Max, brother of the Emperor Franz Joseph, served as Marinekommandant from 1854 to 1864. During this period the first five armored ships were launched (1861 and 1862), and a separate Ministry of Marine was established (1862). The navy's independence did not survive by long the departure of the archduke for his ill-fated career as Emperor Maximilian of Mexico. In 1865 the navy came under the administration of the Marinesektion of the Kriegsministerium, and remained in this position until the collapse of the empire.[1] During the war with Denmark in 1864, the small Austrian squadron, assisted by a few Prussian ships, distinguished itself in naval action off Heligoland. Its commander, Commodore Wilhelm Tegetthoff, was to become Austria's greatest naval hero by leading her fleet to its most famous triumph at the battle of Lissa in 1866, one of the few bright moments for Austrian fortunes in that disastrous year.

The cumbersome constitutional arrangement under which the Austro-Hungarian Empire was governed affected the fortunes of the navy. By the *Ausgleich,* or compromise of 1867, Austria and Hungary became two separate and equal states each possessing its own constitution, parliament, ministry, administration, and courts. The two halves of the kingdom were tied together in the person of the Emperor, whose titles included "Emperor of Austria and Apostolic King of Hungary," and by three common ministries, Foreign Affairs, War, and Finance. The legislative power of the Austrian Reichsrath and the Hungarian Parliament over the common ministries was exercised by the Delegations, two sixty-member bodies elected by each of the parliaments. To demonstrate their absolute equality the Delegations met alternately in Vienna and Budapest. However, they sat separately, and transacted business in their own languages. Communications between the two were conducted in writing, and the proposals of the government were laid before both at the same time by the common ministers. The question of which proportion of the common expenses each half of the monarchy would bear, the so-called "Quota," had to be negotiated every ten years and was the source of endless friction between the Austrians and Hungarians.[2]

The sensitivity of the Hungarians toward their position as absolute equals in the Dual Monarchy led in 1889 after much controversy to the title of the common fleet and army being changed from Imperial-Royal (*kaiserlich-königlich* or K.K.) to Imperial and Royal (*kaiserlich und königlich* or K.u.K.).[3] The naval ensign, however, remained the red-white-red flag with the crown and Austrian coat of arms under which the fleet

[1] Walter Wagner, *Die Obersten Behörden der k. und k. Kriegsmarine, 1856–1918* ("Mitteilungen des Österreichischen Staatsarchivs"), Ergänzungsband VI (Vienna, 1961), pp. 49f.

[2] Frederic Austin Ogg, *The Governments of Europe* (New York, 1913), pp. 509f. The Hungarian contribution was originally 30 percent. By the agreement of 1907, it was 36.4 percent.

[3] *Ibid.,* p. 510 n. 1. Institutions which were strictly Austrian in character, such as the *Landwehr,* remained "k.k." Those that were Hungarian, such as the *Honvéd,* were "k.u." (*königlich ungarisch*) or "m.k." (*magyar királyi*). Like the German navy, warships were designated as S.M.S. or *Seiner Majestät Schiff.*

had traditionally served. In contrast, the merchant flag was half Austrian, and half the red, white, and green of Hungary with the crown of Saint Stephen.

The navy became keenly aware of the disadvantages of its subordinate position in the Kriegsministerium as its requirements and expenditures grew after the turn of the century. This was particularly true in regard to the discrepancy between the full responsibility of the Marinekommandant, who was also chief of the Marinesektion, to the Emperor for the condition of the fleet, and his technical lack of responsibility to the Delegations. But proposals in 1912 for the creation of a separate Ministry of Marine faltered over the fear that, with four common ministries, the Hungarians might demand equality of nomination for subjects of both halves of the monarchy, and possibly the transfer of two of the ministries to Budapest.[4]

The K.u.K. Kriegsmarine, with its crews drawn from various parts of the Dual Monarchy, was an interesting example of a relatively successful multinational force. Entire regiments of the army might have been drawn from the same district with most of the men speaking the same language, but this was certainly not true of the navy, where each warship could be a floating Habsburg empire in miniature. Naturally the bulk of the crews came from areas adjacent to the Adriatic. Croatians formed the largest national group, constituting well over 30 percent of the navy's personnel. They were followed by Magyars, Germans, and Italians. Czechs varied between 7 and 11 percent of the crews; the other nationalities had a very small representation.[5] Among the crews the Germans and Czechs tended to enter the mechanical and electrical services, or the heavy artillery. Dalmatians constituted a large proportion of the stokers. They were in general physically suited for the service and volunteered much more readily for it.[6] A French naval attaché found the Austrian sailors

---

[4] Wagner, *Die Obersten Behörden,* pp. 89, 131 n. 1.

[5] According to the *Jahresbericht der Marineverwaltung,* of the 3810 recruits in 1910 approximately 32 percent were Croatians; 23.7 percent Germans; 17.4 percent Hungarians; 15.2 percent Italians; and 6.6 percent Czechs. Cited by *Marine Rundschau,* June 1912, p. 834. These figures naturally varied from year to year. Three years later the French naval attaché reported the composition of the personnel as of January 1, 1913, to be: 34.6 percent Serbo-Croatian; 20.8 percent Hungarian; 14.7 percent Italian; 12.5 percent German; and 9.3 percent Czech. Faramond to Minister of Marine, 1 Dec. 1913, AMF, carton BB7-92.

[6] K.u.K. Matrosenkorpskommando, "Bericht," 10 Apr. 1912, Vienna, Kriegsarchiv, Militärkanzlei Erzherzog Franz Ferdinand (hereafter cited as MKFF), Mm 59, 1912. See also Hans Hugo Sokol, *Österreich-Ungarns Seekrieg, 1914–1918* (Vienna, 1933), p. 37.

well turned out, with both more initiative and a more alert air than their German counterparts. On the other hand, they were less healthy with a much higher incidence of tuberculosis and syphilis.[7]

Given the polyglot nature of the crews, it is not surprising that the study of languages was an important part of the Austrian naval officers' training. The officers were predominantly German with a Magyar and Croatian minority. The majority of the executive branch were graduates of the naval academy at Fiume. This branch tended to preserve its social exclusiveness through the limited number of places available at the naval academy, the importance given to German in the entrance examination, and the preference given to the sons of naval and military men. Entry into the executive branch was also possible through the *Adria* training establishment, a group of hulks at Pola. Petty officers were more apt to become officers if they were bachelors. If married, their wives were carefully scrutinized for social acceptability. At least some foreign observers considered the structure of the various Austrian training establishments and their courses of instruction as out of proportion to the relatively modest needs of the Austrian fleet.[8] Undoubtedly the officer corps of the Austrian navy considered itself a small but elite group. Admiral Nicholas Horthy, later to be Regent of Hungary, remembered that in 1882, the year he entered the naval academy at Fiume, approximately 42 out of 612 candidates were accepted, and more than one third of these dropped out during the four-year program. The ideal for the corps was set by the school's lofty motto, "Above life stands duty."[9] The K.u.K. Kriegsmarine was one of the most effective of Habsburg institutions and enjoyed a good reputation abroad for the economy and method of its administration which was thought to obtain much value from the relatively small amounts of money spent.[10] The navy also seemed relatively immune from the dissolving currents of nationalism which plagued so much of the Dual Monarchy, and it was not until the World War that serious incidents

[7] Faramond to Minister of Marine, 23 Dec. 1910, AMF, carton BB7-129.

[8] Captain Don Augusto Miranda and Lieutenant D. Manuel Andujar, "Organization of the Naval Schools of Germany and Austria," translated from the Spanish *Revista General de Marina*, Nov. 1911, in *Journal of the Royal United Service Institution*, 56.422 (Sept. 1913): 1172–1175.

[9] Admiral Nicholas Horthy, *Memoirs* (New York, 1957), p. 13. The original was "Höher al das Leben steht die Pflicht."

[10] A. H. Burgoyne (ed.), *The Navy League Annual, 1911–1912* (London, 1911), p. 48; O. T. C., "The Austrian Army," *The Westminster Review*, 179.2 (Feb. 1913): 124.

occurred, the most famous of which was the February 1918 mutiny at Cattaro.[11]

Support of the navy was slight in the last part of the nineteenth century. Vice Admiral Wilhelm von Tegetthoff, the victor of Lissa, was named Marinekommandant in March 1868 and held the position until his death in April 1871. Tegetthoff wanted a fleet of fifteen armored ships and twenty-four cruisers, but his ideas met with little sympathy at the court or in the government. Although an imposing memorial, still to be seen, was erected in Tegetthoff's honor at the Praterstern in Vienna, neither he nor his successors were able to arouse interest in the fleet, and the naval budget in 1897 was only slightly higher than it was at the time of his death.[12] In 1898 Admiral Hermann Freiherr von Spaun, Marinekommandant from 1897 to 1904, presented a building program to be spread over ten years which would give the fleet fifteen battleships, seven large and seven small cruisers, and appropriate supporting units. However, the Hungarian Delegation consented to vote only for annual proposals, and refused to approve a ten-year program. Between 1898 and 1907 the Austrians built only six battleships and three cruisers.[13]

In direct contrast to the situation in Germany the navy received scant support from the court. Emperor Franz Joseph regarded Austria as primarily a continental power and took little interest in naval or maritime affairs. Admiral Rudolf Graf Montecuccoli, Marinekommandant from 1904 to 1913, complained in 1910 about what he considered the Emperor's aversion toward the navy.[14] Archduke Franz Ferdinand, heir to the throne, once asked the Emperor, who invariably appeared in military uniform, why he never wore a naval uniform. Somewhat bemused, the old Emperor replied that he had never been given any rank in the navy, and did not consider himself capable of managing even one of his grandson's paper boats in a fountain.[15]

Archduke Franz Ferdinand was the direct opposite of his uncle in regard to naval affairs. In 1892–93 he had been on a world cruise aboard

[11] Arthur J. May, *The Hapsburg Monarchy* (Cambridge, Mass., 1960), p. 452; Horthy, *Memoirs*, pp. 87–90; Sokol, *Österreich-Ungarns Seekrieg*, p. 37. For wartime unrest see Sokol, pp. 450f.

[12] Sokol, *Österreich-Ungarns Seekrieg*, p. 20; v.D., "Der Ausbau der österreichisch-ungarischen Flotte," *Marine Rundschau*, April 1911, p. 461.

[13] Commandant Davin, "La Marine austro-hongroise," *Questions Diplomatiques et coloniales*, no. 300 (16 Aug. 1909), pp. 210–211.

[14] Leopold von Chlumecky, *Erzherzog Franz Ferdinands Wirken und Wollen* (Berlin, 1929), pp. 43–44.

[15] Lieutenant General Baron von Margutti, *The Emperor Francis Joseph and His Times* (London, 1921), pp. 114–115.

the cruiser *Kaiserin Elisabeth,* and in 1902 was given the rank of admiral, the highest naval rank attained by an Austrian archduke. He became patron of the Austrian Navy League in 1908. The Archduke had his own Militärkanzlei under the leadership of Major von Brosch-Aarenau, and later Colonel Carl von Bardolff. Through this body, which had no statutory existence, he became one of the best informed men in the Dual Monarchy and eventually sought to intervene in many government matters.[16] His frequent distaste with the methods by which affairs were conducted led to a certain amount of friction between the Belvedere—the Archduke's residence in Vienna and general name given to his supporters—and the circle around the old Emperor.[17] In the person of Franz Ferdinand the Kriegsmarine probably enjoyed the most energetic and influential patron in its history, although there undoubtedly were times when the Archduke's intervention into questions of naval administration might have been regarded by the admirals as a rather mixed blessing.[18] Franz Ferdinand was also an admiral in the German navy and attended its autumn maneuvers in 1911 as a guest of Kaiser Wilhelm. On his return he requested that accommodations be created for his special use aboard the *Viribus Unitis* similar to those the German Emperor had aboard the battleship *Deutschland.* He also wanted a motorboat for his personal use which could be hoisted aboard any warship he boarded, and that one of the future scout cruisers be fitted as his yacht in peacetime, but so constructed as to be rapidly convertible for wartime duties.[19]

The Austrian Navy League, which patterned itself on the much larger German organization, began modestly with thirty-nine members in September 1904. The original title was "Verein zur Forderung zu der österreichischen Schiffahrt," with the subtitle "Österreichisches Flottenverein"; the subtitle eventually became its regular name.[20] Its initial progress was slow but at the general meeting in 1910 the president, Graf Josef Thun-Hohen-

16 Chlumecky, *Erzherzog Franz Ferdinands Wirken,* pp. 43–44; Horthy, *Memoirs,* p. 62; Theodore von Sosnosky, *Franz Ferdinand* (Munich, 1929), pp. 113–114; Joseph Redlich, *Emperor Francis Joseph of Austria* (New York, 1929), p. 493; M. von Auffenberg-Komarów, *Aus Österreichs Höhe und Niedergang* (Munich, 1921), pp. 230–231; Carl Freiherr von Bardolff, *Soldat im Alten Österreich* (Jena, 1938), pp. 118, 143.

17 Redlich, *Emperor Francis Joseph,* pp. 494–495; Bardolff, *Soldat im Alten Österreich,* p. 107 n. 1; Sosnosky, *Franz Ferdinand,* pp. 119–120; Margutti, *Emperor Francis Joseph and His Times,* pp. 132f.

18 For problems over the creation of the fleet inspectorate in 1912 and reorganization in 1913 see Wagner, *Die Obersten Behörden,* pp. 89f.

19 Unsigned memorandum, n.d. [late 1911 or early 1912], MKFF, Nm 23, 1912. Various plans for the cruiser-yacht were under consideration at the time of the Archduke's assassination.

20 Friedrich Wallisch, *Die Flagge Rot-Weiss-Rot* (Graz, 1956), pp. 214–216.

stein was able to report 4389 members.[21] Later in the year Prince Alfred von und zu Liechtenstein was nominated to the presidency by Archduke Franz Ferdinand. The Flottenverein's monthly organ, *Die Flagge*, carried a constant stream of articles in favor of developing both the navy and the Austro-Hungarian merchant fleet, as well as descriptions of the Adriatic coast and islands which it dubbed "the Austrian Riviera," and summaries of articles and books on maritime subjects that had appeared abroad. Any 20 members could form a branch or *Ortsgruppe*, and by May 1911 there were 72 of these with over 12,700 members. The *Ortsgruppen* were not limited to the Dual Monarchy and a number began to appear among Austrian subjects living abroad. The rapid growth of the 1910–1911 period continued in the following year with membership doubling by the end of May 1912 to 26,532. By May 1913 memberships totaled 35,800. The Flottenverein's growth rate slowed toward the end of 1913, but on the eve of the war it could claim 44,617 members.[22]

With the first division of Austrian dreadnoughts under construction by the spring of 1912, the Flottenverein set as its goal the replacement of the obsolete "Monarch" class battleships by a modern division of dreadnoughts. The Flottenverein included this in a petition to the Austrian Delegation in May 1912, and the proposal formed the major part of its propaganda for the next two years.[23] Archduke Franz Ferdinand, as patron of the league, took more than a friendly interest in its activities. He approved the plans for its propaganda campaign in the summer of 1912, which included the extensive use of printed materials, often in languages other than German, and helped to arrange for the printing to be done at cost at the state press, the Hof- und Staatsdruckerei in Vienna, thus lowering the printing costs by around 50 percent.[24] The Marinesektion in August gave the Flottenverein a subvention of 400 kronen for its propaganda campaign.[25] The Flottenverein also received 500 kronen from the

[21] *Die Flagge*, June 1910, p. 2. All membership figures cited are from this source.

[22] *Ibid.* Aug. 1914, p. 248. During the war memberships climbed, to over 70,000 in February 1917, but these statistics published by the Flottenverein must naturally be treated with caution and reflect perhaps the pressures of abnormal events and the stimulus of wartime patriotism.

[23] "Petition der Österreichischen Flottenverein," 2 May 1912, copy in Kriegsarchiv, Vienna, Präsidialkanzlei des Kriegsministeriums/Marinesektion (hereafter cited as PK/MS)-XV-9/8, 1912.

[24] Unsigned letter to MKFF, 28 July 1912, MKFF Nm/39, 1912; Lieutenant Uhlič (naval aide-de-camp to Franz Ferdinand), report, 24 July 1912; Militärkanzlei to Österreichischen Flottenverein and K.K. Hof- und Staatsdruckerei, 31 July 1912, MKFF, Mm/39, 1912.

[25] PK/MS to Flottenverein, 26 Aug. 1912, PK/MS-XV-9/8, 1912.

Marinesektion as a subsidy for *Die Flagge* in April 1911, and another 500 for the same purpose in October of 1912.[26]

These signs of official support are small. And the extent of the Flottenverein's influence is difficult to judge. Its membership claims should be interpreted as presenting as favorable a picture as possible. The Vicomte de Faramond, French naval attaché in both Germany and Austria-Hungary, reported that its influence was not great, and that no public authorities outside the Marinesektion showed any sympathy for it. State employees were not encouraged to join and were, in fact, even discouraged. In Faramond's opinion the ground was not as favorable to the development of maritime ambitions in Austria as it was in Germany, and the Austrian people, lacking the military temperament of the Prussians, were not anxious to add to their tax burden.[27] The amount of support the Flottenverein actually had in official circles is not easy to gauge. In February 1912 a circular letter to army corps commanders was prepared by the Minister of War commending the Flottenverein to their favorable attention, and suggesting they request their officers to pave the way for the formation of new *Ortsgruppen* by providing suitable, presumably favorable, information when the occasion presented itself. These propsals were sharply criticized by General Friedrich von Georgi, the Austrian Minister for National Defense (*Landesverteidigung*).[28] But whatever the extent of the Flottenverein's influence in official circles, and the depth and degree of its public support, it did manage to arouse at least some interest, if only to refute its propaganda, in a field which had been almost totally neglected in the past. The rise in its membership coincided with the rise in Austro-Hungarian naval activity in the years preceding the war.

The period during which the K.u.K. Kriegsmarine vastly increased its fighting potential and aroused the attention and anxiety of the naval staffs of Europe occurred during the administration of Vice Admiral Rudolf Graf Montecuccoli who served as Marinekommandant and chief of the Marinesektion from 1904 until his retirement at the age of seventy in February 1913. Montecuccoli was the son of an army officer and a mem-

[26] Flottenverein to Marinesektion, 15 and 25 Oct. 1912, *ibid.* In 1914 the Austrian krone was worth approximately 20 cents (U.S.).

[27] Faramond to Minister of Marine, 13 Apr. 1912, AMF, carton BB7-92. As De Faramond spent the majority of his time in Berlin and not Vienna, he too must be treated with care as a critic. In depreciating the role of the Archduke in the Flottenverein, De Faramond, or his source, was quite wrong.

[28] Auffenberg, circular letter to corps commanders, 21 Feb. 1912; Remarks by General Georgi to above, 11 Mar. 1912, PK/MS-XV-9/8, 1912. The whole question of the Flottenverein and Austrian naval development is worthy of further study.

ber of a noble family with roots in both Austria and Italy. He himself had been born in Modena while it was still under Habsburg rule. As a young ensign he fought in the battle of Lissa aboard a wooden frigate, and in 1900 he commanded the Austro-Hungarian squadron in Chinese waters during the Boxer Rebellion. With his white beard and short stocky figure, Montecuccoli presents almost a comic appearance when photographed in full dress with admiral's cocked hat and epaulets, but the old admiral was recognized as extremely talented in the more political aspects of his career, propagandizing for the navy, and above all, obtaining money in unprecedented amounts for the fleet.[29] The French naval attaché found him a "charming old man," with a fine political sense, though he doubted that Montecuccoli had the physical ability to withstand the strain of long periods of activity as Commander-in-Chief in time of war.[30] There was at least some discontent with Montecuccoli in the fleet itself, although it is difficult to say how deep it was. Shortly after the admiral's retirement an Italian naval officer whose ship visited Gravosa for a few days reported that the former Marinekommandant was frequently mentioned by older as well as young officers in terms which left little doubt how much he was disliked in naval circles.[31] He was, however, successful in defending naval interests in Vienna.

In 1906 the Marinesektion prepared a memorandum on the necessity of strengthening the fleet through accelerating the replacement of obsolete vessels. Printed by the state press, it was circulated to high officials including the army's General Staff. At that time the Austrian battle fleet was oriented toward coastal defense. It consisted of the three "Monarch" class battleships (5550 tons) launched in 1895–96, and the three "Habsburgs" (8208 tons) launched 1900–02. In 1907 the last of the three larger "Erzherzogs" (10,433 tons) was due to enter service. In tonnage, firepower, and radius of action, these ships were outclassed by their foreign contemporaries. Their low freeboard also prevented them from effectively using all their armament in the open sea. The Austrian navy clearly realized this, as well as the fact that the "Monarchs" could hardly even be counted

[29] For interesting, but unfortunately completely noncritical, sketches of Montecuccoli's career see Heinrich Bayer von Bayersburg, *Österreichs Admirale, 1867–1918* (Vienna, 1962), pp. 118–122; Wallisch, *Die Flagge Rot-Weiss-Rot,* pp. 208f.

[30] Faramond to Minister of Marine, 23 Dec. 1910, AMF, carton BB7-129.

[31] Tenente di Vascello R. Mancini to Chief of the Naval Staff, 24 May 1913, Ufficio Storico della Marina Militare, Rome (hereafter cited as USM), cartella 229/4. The Austrian officers were also highly critical of their government's other policies, especially in internal affairs. It is an isolated incident and one wonders how prevalent the attitude was in the rest of the navy.

as battleships. The situation in regard to cruisers was equally grim. Unlike other great powers the protection of overseas colonies was not one of the reasons for which a strong navy might be advocated, but the Marinesektion believed that on purely military grounds, and in the interests of her own preservation, a strong navy was required by the Dual Monarchy. The primary mission of this fleet was the protection of her coastline, and the hindrance of hostile sea action which could influence the military situation on land. The fleet might also protect Austro-Hungarian economic interests and subjects abroad.[32]

The Marinesektion realized that under the present lamentable ratio of strength the offensive would remain in the hands of the enemy. Once a hostile fleet had gained sea supremacy in the Adriatic, and with the remains of the Austrian fleet blockaded, the enemy would be able to aid unhindered the aspirations of Austria's southern neighbors in the Dual Monarchy's coastal areas with arms, munitions, and possibly even irregular troops. This would force detachments from the Austrian army to counter the threat. The enemy would also be in a position to occupy Austrian ports and territory and capture the defenseless steamers of the Österreichischen Lloyd and other shipping companies. In conclusion, the Marinesektion claimed that they had neither the desire to vie with any other emerging sea power nor the intention to give the fleet a mission beyond the scope of coastal defense, but that this mission could not be fulfilled until the obsolete and worthless material had been renewed.[33]

The intention to build ships the equal of their foreign contemporaries became manifest in the next class of Austrian battleships, the "Radetzkys." When the *Erzherzog Franz Ferdinand,* first of the class and appropriately named after the navy's powerful patron, was launched on September 30, 1908, one Austrian naval historian considered the modern nucleus of the navy to have been born.[34] The "Radetzkys" (14,226 tons), with their armament of four 12-inch and eight 9.4-inch guns, a speed of 20.5 knots, and a range of 5600 miles, represented a clean break with past Austrian tradition.[35] Their armament was strong enough to class them as semi-dread-

[32] Kriegsministerium, Marinesektion, *Denkschrift über Die Notwendigkeit der Verstärkung der k.u.k. Flotte durch Beschleunigung der Erforderlichen Ersatzbauten,* n.d. [1906], pp. 1, 3–5. Copy in Kriegsarchiv, Generalstabe (hereafter referred to as GSTB) -141.

[33] *Ibid.,* pp. 10–11, 19. Although no potential enemy is mentioned by name, Italy and Serbia are obviously implied. The Austrians estimated the naval ratio of strength between themselves and Italy as 1:2.24-2.5 in their disfavor; *ibid.,* p. 8.

[34] Sokol, *Österreich-Ungarns Seekrieg,* p. 24.

[35] *The Naval Annual, 1910,* p. 39.

noughts, and one could argue that in the brief period between their completion and the entry into service of the French "Dantons" they were the most powerful warships permanently stationed in the Mediterranean.

The next logical step was the construction of true dreadnoughts. During the Bosnian crisis with its threat of war, the fleet had been mobilized, and the unsettled conditions were naturally favorable for additional expenditure on armaments. The fact that the first Italian dreadnought was laid down in July 1909 and that others were expected to follow made the problem acute. Montecuccoli was reported ready to present a naval program to the Delegations in the fall of 1909, but this was deferred largely because of the incessant political crisis in Hungary where the year 1909 passed without even the vote of a budget.[36] The possibility that the Austrians might build dreadnoughts outside of the budget and without the approval of the Delegations was a lively topic of discussion in naval and diplomatic circles in the winter of 1909–10. Austria, like Germany, surrounded her naval affairs with a good deal of secrecy, and the naval attachés in Vienna found themselves confronted by a wall of polite vagueness in their contacts with Austrian naval authorities. It was forbidden to move about Pola with a camera, and foreigners in Austrian ports, particularly the naval attachés, were subject to discreet but constant surveillance.[37] Authorizations to visit naval establishments had a way of getting tangled and interminably delayed in bureaucratic red tape, and requests for official but nonclassified manuals were often returned with the polite reply that the "edition was exhausted."[38] One has only to think of the suspicion that the Germans were secretly accelerating their building program which resulted in the naval scare of 1909 in England to have an idea of what, to admittedly a far lesser extent, the atmosphere was like among those who were most concerned with the Mediterranean naval situation.

The projected construction of dreadnoughts before the approval of the Delegations was exposed by the Socialist *Arbeiter Zeitung* in April 1910, and the full discussion of the matter—in which *Die Zeit* and the *Reichspost*, the latter generally thought to be the organ of Franz Ferdinand, gave their full approval to the construction—appeared to the French ambassador to confirm the authenticity of the story.[39] All sorts of rumors floated about including one published by the British service journal the *Naval and*

[36] *Ibid.*, p. 38; Ogg, *Governments of Europe*, p. 504.

[37] Faramond to Minister of Marine, 23 Dec. 1910, AMF, carton BB7-129; and 5 May 1913, carton BB7-92.

[38] Amiral de Faramond, *Souvenirs d'un attaché naval en Allemagne et en Autriche, 1910–1914* (Paris, 1932), pp. 27–28.

[39] Crozier to Minister of Foreign Affairs, 18 Apr. 1910, AMF, carton BB7-129.

Military Record that a secret agreement between the German Kaiser and Archduke Franz Ferdinand called for the purchase of two of the projected four dreadnoughts by the German government should the Austrian parliament refuse the necessary appropriations.[40] On May 19 the Minister of Finance, Leon Bilinski, was directly interpellated about the dreadnoughts by a Social Democrat deputy. Bilinski denied that the Austrian government had any official knowledge of the subject or that any engagement for the necessary expense had been undertaken, and added that the present state of finances forced the government to extreme prudence.[41]

In October Montecuccoli disclosed to the Delegations that two slips had become vacant at the yards of the Stabilimento Tecnico Triestino in July 1909, and that the company had asked for additional naval orders. The Marinekommandant replied that he was not authorized to give such orders despite the urgent need for new battleships. The Stabilimento Tecnico then offered to build two warships on its own account in order to avoid having to lay off its skilled workers, and asked the Marinesektion to provide the necessary plans. The latter, in view of what it considered the feverish activity in foreign yards, feared that it was lagging behind and accepted the offer. The first dreadnought was laid down in July 1910, and the second a month later. Montecuccoli pointed out the advantage of this plan whereby the navy would have two dreadnoughts well on the way to completion should the Delegations grant the necessary appropriations, instead of having to wait three years for the construction of the warships after the money was voted. The admiral stressed that no price had been agreed upon and no installment had been paid by the government. In his opinion the budgetary rights of the Delegations had therefore been respected. He added that he had no intention of requesting an extraordinary credit for the ships in the budget of 1910, for their bill would not be presented until the spring of 1911. Montecuccoli also announced his intention of presenting a long-term program in the budget of 1911, and mentioned sixteen battleships, a force similar to the one Tegetthoff had favored, as the minimum strength of Austria-Hungary at sea.[42]

[40] *Naval and Military Record*, 27 Apr. 1910. Extract cited by first section, EMG, 30 Apr. 1910, AMF, carton BB7-129. A similar story that the Austrian dreadnoughts were actually destined to fight England, and had been laid down on the specific request of the German Kaiser who supposedly had Franz Ferdinand under his domination, also reached the French naval attaché in Rome. Barrère to Minister of Foreign Affairs, 30 May 1910, *ibid.*

[41] Crozier to Minister of Foreign Affairs, 24 May 1910, MAE, Autriche-Hongrie, vol. NS-25.

[42] Saint Aulaire (chargé d'affaires, Vienna) to Minister of Foreign Affairs, 26 Oct. 1910, AMF, carton BB7-129; a translation of Montecuccoli's speech before the Delegations from *Die Zeit*, 20 Oct. 1910, was enclosed; *The Naval Annual, 1911*, p. 29.

Montecuccoli wanted, by 1920, sixteen battleships, twelve cruisers, twenty-four destroyers, seventy-two torpedo boats, and twelve submarines, with an age limit of twenty years for battleships, fifteen years for cruisers and destroyers, and twelve years for torpedo boats. His immediate request in 1911 was for a special appropriation of 312.4 million kronen to be divided over six years for the construction of four dreadnoughts, including the two laid down the previous summer, three scout cruisers of 3500 tons, six destroyers of 800 tons, twelve torpedo boats, and six submarines.[43] These proposals met with strong opposition in the Hungarian Delegation, particularly the intention to build all four dreadnoughts in Austrian yards. The Hungarians insisted that Hungarian industry receive orders amounting to the same proportion of total naval expenditures that their half of the monarchy contributed to the common defense: 36.4 percent. The Hungarians also demanded that one of the projected dreadnoughts be built at the Danubius yard near Fiume, then part of Hungary. They made these two conditions a *sine qua non* of their vote for Montecuccoli's budget.[44] The Marinekommandant was obliged to agree to this, thereby exposing himself to attacks in the Austrian Delegation where he was accused of inflating the proportion of Hungarian orders in order to obtain their vote. For a brief time rumors were rife that Montecuccoli would be compelled to resign, but he managed to weather the storm, and the naval budget including the special appropriation for new construction was voted without modification by the Delegations at the end of February 1911.[45]

The first of the dreadnoughts, named *Viribus Unitis* after the motto of the Emperor, was launched at Trieste on June 24, 1911. She was christened by the Archduchess Maria Annunziata, sister of Franz Ferdinand, who was also present for the gala occasion. The "Viribus Unitis" class (20,000 tons), with their primary armament of twelve 12-inch guns, were easily the most powerful ships ever built in the Dual Monarchy. They were also the first Austrian battleships with turbine engines, with a designed speed of 21.5 knots.[46] The *Viribus Unitis* entered service before the Italian *Dante Alighieri*, thereby becoming the world's first battleship with triple-gunned

[43] *The Naval Annual, 1911*, pp. 30–31; v.D., "Der Ausbau der österreichisch-ungarischen Flotte," *Marine Rundschau*, April 1911, p. 463.

[44] Faramond to Minister of Marine, 24 Dec. 1910, 3 Mar. 1911, AMF, carton BB7-92. Danubius is the short name generally given to Ganz und Comp.—"Danubius", Maschinen-Waggon-und Schiffbau-Aktiengesellschaft whose yards were located at Bergudi near Fiume.

[45] Crozier to Minister of Foreign Affairs, 2 Mar. 1911, AMF, carton BB7-129; v.D., "Der Ausbau der österreichisch-ungarischen Flotte," *Marine Rundschau*, April 1911, pp. 472–475; *Le Yacht*, 18 Mar. 1911, p. 165.

[46] *The Naval Annual, 1912*, p. 52.

turrets. Heavy artillery for these ships was provided by the Skoda works in Pilsen, and armor plate came from the Wittkowitz works in Moravia.[47] The second of the dreadnoughts, the *Tegetthoff*, was launched in March 1912 with Franz Ferdinand again present in Trieste for the event.[48] Work on the *Tegetthoff* was delayed by heavy storms and a tidal wave, which also affected progress on the *Prinz Eugen*, which was laid down in January 1912 on the slip vacated by the *Viribus Unitis*.[49]

The progress of the last of the four at the Danubius yards was a sad contrast to the efficiency of the Stabilimento Tecnico. Danubius had no prior experience with ships of this size, and at the time the Hungarian Delegation forced the concession of the dreadnought contract to it the firm did not even have a slip suitable for its construction. The Hungarian government assisted Danubius with 3 million kronen in the firm's acquisition of additional land and in the expensive excavations necessary to prepare the new slips, part of which had to be carved from rocky and difficult terrain.[50] It was also necessary to install costly shops and equipment. Not until January 1912, almost a year after the Delegation's vote, was the yard able to lay down the dreadnought.[51] Hungarian chauvinism on this point had proved to be expensive. Danubius was plagued by innumerable delays as well as labor troubles. Archduke Franz Ferdinand, no friend of Magyar pretensions, followed the slow progress with an unfriendly eye and received regular reports through his Militärkanzlei on the reasons for the delay. He looked into the possibilities for pressuring Danubius without arousing the ire of the Hungarian government and the risk of reducing grants for future naval expenditure.[52] For those reasons it was necessary for the Archduke to request the governor of Trieste to try and persuade a Social Democratic deputy not to bring up in parliament the embarrassing subject of Danubius' tardiness.[53]

[47] The French naval attaché reported that the Rothschild bank in Vienna owned half the stock of Wittkowitz and gave financial support to the speculative building of the first pair of dreadnoughts before the approval of the Delegations; French naval attaché to Minister of Marine, 15 May 1910, AMF, carton BB7-129.

[48] Faramond to Minister of Marine, 30 Mar. 1912, AMF, carton BB7-129. The Italian naval attaché was conspicuous by his absence, presumably because of the memories the name invoked.

[49] *The Naval Annual, 1912*, p. 52. The *Prinz Eugen* was launched 30 Nov. 1912.

[50] *The Naval Annual, 1911*, pp. 29–30; Sokol, *Österreich-Ungarns Seekrieg*, pp. 26–27; Faramond to Minister of Marine, 24 Dec. 1910, 28 Jan. 1911, 3 Mar. 1911, AMF, carton BB7-92.

[51] Lieutenant Menier (assigned to the Whitehead factory at Fiume for the receipt of torpedoes) to Minister of Marine, 4 Nov. 1912, *ibid.*; *The Naval Annual, 1912*, p. 52.

[52] Report by Lieutenant Uhlič, 24 Apr. 1913, MKFF-41-31/2, 1913; report by Militärkanzlei, 9 Apr. 1913, MKFF-41-31/3, 1913.

[53] Bardolff to Prince Hohenlohe, 1 May 1913, MKFF-41-31/4, 1913.

In recognition of the battleship's Hungarian connection she was named *Szent István,* a minor setback to Franz Ferdinand who originally proposed to the Emperor the name of the eighteenth century Austrian military hero Laudon.[54] It is hardly surprising that the Archduke did not attend the launching ceremonies which took place in January 1914, almost two years after work was begun, and that he deleted the traditional word of praise for the shipyard from a copy of the speech to be delivered at the launching which was submitted for his approval.[55] The *Szent István* was unfinshed when the war began and had to be towed from the unprotected harbor of Fiume to Pola for completion.[56]

With the construction of the first dreadnoughts the K.u.K. Kriegsmarine ceased to be a purely Adriatic factor and a matter of concern to Italy only. The British ambassador in Vienna in January 1911 privately sought to ascertain the coal carrying capacity of the new dreadnoughts. His unnamed informant reported that it was not considered excessive for their tonnage, but was probably sufficient to enable them to reach the North Sea without coaling.[57] This fact was important, for the suspicion persisted in Great Britain that in building dreadnoughts the Austrians were merely acting as agents for the Germans. This idea appeared during the House of Commons debates over Mediterranean policy in the summer of 1912 when Balfour alluded suspiciously to Austria having only 300 miles of coastline, and was also held by Brigadier General Wilson, Director of Military Operations, who persisted in viewing Austria-Hungary as a docile dependent of Germany despite the attempts of the British military attaché in Vienna to dissuade him.[58]

This view is understandable from a superficial glance, but it completely overlooks Austria's own apprehensions and ambitions, not to mention a certain measure of chauvinism fired by the diplomatic success of the Bosnian annexation. The counterargument could be made that the Germans would have gained more if the Dual Monarchy concentrated on her land

[54] Bolfras to Bardolff, 10 June 1913, Kriegsarchiv, Vienna, Militärkanzlei Seiner Majestät des Kaisers und Königs (hereafter cited as MKSM) -66-5/12-2, 1913; Report by Bardolff, 14 and 24 Apr. 1913, MKFF-41-2/6, 1913.

[55] Report by Bardolff, 3 and 8 Jan. 1914, MKFF-41-6/1, 1913; report by Uhlič, 19 Jan. 1914, *ibid.*

[56] Sokol, *Österreich-Ungarns Seekrieg,* pp. 179–180. An unlucky ship, the *Szent István* was torpedoed and sunk by an Italian torpedo boat (MAS) off Premuda in June 1918.

[57] Extract from Sir F. Cartwright to Nicolson, 19 Jan. 1911, Grey MSS, FO 800, vol. 86. Reginald McKenna, then First Lord of the Admiralty, read the extract. J. E. Masterton Smith to Tyrrell, 30 Jan. 1911, *ibid.*

[58] Col. Sir Thomas Montgomery-Cuninghame, *Dusty Measure: A Record of Troubled Times* (London, 1939), p. 91; see above pp. 40–41.

armaments; this could lighten the German burden on the eastern front. One is more inclined to agree with the French ambassador Philippe Crozier who did not detect the hand of Germany in Austrian shipbuilding at all, but viewed it as the natural desire of the Austrian government to keep its naval forces on a par with those of Italy. Crozier thought that Germany had only to let her allies alone and secretly delight in their private naval race which served to augment the force of the Triple Alliance in the Mediterranean, where it might be possible one day to turn Italian irredentism from Austria and Trieste toward Tunis or even Corsica. His conclusion was that it was more important than ever to maintain France's indisputable naval predominance in the Mediterranean in order to keep Italy from temptation.[59]

Montecuccoli's statements left little doubt to foreign observers that the first dreadnoughts were part of a wider program. The heir apparent's known interest in the fleet, added to the advanced age of the Emperor, seemed to confirm this. The Vicomte de Faramond, the French naval attaché, speculated that paradoxically the Austro-Italian naval rivalry might have the result of leading to a rapprochement between the two. He thought the day both their fleets grew to the point where a combination of the two might give them mastery of the Mediterranean would be the day when Austrian and Italian policy became clearly anti-French. It would therefore be folly, he argued, for France to aid Austria's efforts by allowing them to use the Paris money market should they wish to float a loan to defray naval expenses.[60] Future events were to show that there was some substance to his fears.

Although Austria-Hungary had the nucleus of a modern fleet under construction in 1912, the K.u.K. Kriegsmarine was thwarted in its efforts to give its expansion the rapid and regular character which distinguished the German program. Responsible for this were both the financial condition of the Dual Monarchy, and the peculiar constitutional arrangement which required the consent of the Hungarian as well as the Austrian government in matters relating to the common army and navy. The navy was sorely pressed for funds to meet its regular needs despite the generous appropriation for new construction voted in February 1911. An agreement in 1910 between General Franz von Schönaich, the Common

[59] Crozier to Minister of Foreign Affairs, 24 May 1910, MAE, Autriche-Hongrie, vol. NS-25. Additional support for minimizing the role of Germany may be found in Gunther Helbing, "Die deutsche Marinepolitik 1908–1912 im Spiegel der österreichisch-ungarischen Diplomatie," *Marine Rundschau*, Beiheft 6, Oct. 1961, p. 32.

[60] Faramond to Minister of Marine, 23 Dec. 1910, AMF, carton BB7-129.

Minister of War, and the Delegations had set the annual increase in the regular naval budget for a ten year period at only 1.5 million kronen, although Montecuccoli had originally requested a 6.5 million annual increase. The sum was insufficient, and in the course of 1911 the navy exceeded its appropriations by around 3 million kronen. Both the Austrian and Hungarian Ministers of Finance were completely unsympathetic to Montecuccoli when the budget for 1912 was discussed at a meeting of the common ministers. Count Alois von Aehrenthal, who presided, agreed with them in considering this an internal matter for the Kriegsministerium to be settled between the Marinekommandant and Minister of War.[61]

Part of the navy's difficulty stemmed from the rising cost of maintaining ever larger ships, a problem all contemporary navies faced. For example, the "Erzherzogs" cost approximately 1,138,000 kronen per ship a year to maintain, the "Radetzkys" 1,411,000, and the *Viribus Unitis* 2,040,000.[62] Montecuccoli's independent contracting of debts with the yards and banks led to a sharp disagreement between himself and the Minister of War in March 1912. The minister, in a rather pointed manner, reminded the Marinekommandant of his constitutional responsibility as Minister of War for matters affecting the common military forces. He ordered the navy not to undertake, without his prior consent, any financial obligations which would exceed budgetary provisions or involve expenditures not specifically approved by the Delegations. The minister also sought to require a regular financial accounting from the Marinesektion. The ensuing controversy, in which the Militärkanzlei of the Archduke intervened on the side of the navy, pointed out the desirability of creating an independent Ministry of Marine.[63]

Admiral Montecuccoli, in a memorandum for the Emperor on Austrian and Italian provisions for the Adriatic submitted in March 1912, demonstrated the need for a new building program requiring an extraordinary appropriation of around 464 million kronen, and including four 24,500 ton dreadnoughts as well as fortifications at Sebenico.[64] The Emperor did not think that the time was ripe for these proposals because of the financial

[61] Protokoll, Ministerrates für gemeinsame Angelegenheiten, 6 Dec. 1911, pp. 268–271, Austria, Haus-, Hof- und Staatsarchiv, Vienna, Politische Archiv (hereafter cited as HHSA) -XL-310.

[62] Montecuccoli to Berchtold, 10 July 1912, PK/MS-XV-7/8, 1912.

[63] Wagner, *Die Obersten Behörden*, p. 87.

[64] Montecuccoli, "Militarische-maritimen Vorsorgen Österreich-Ungarns u. Italiens in der Adria," 13 Mar. 1912, OK/MS-VI-1/3, 1912. Montecuccoli wanted to build four dreadnoughts, five cruisers, twelve destroyers, twenty-four torpedo boats, six submarines, three colliers, and a floating dock. For the Danube he wanted four monitors and four patrol boats.

situation, and suggested that they be deferred until a more favorable moment.[65]

When the naval estimates for the following year were discussed by the common ministers in July 1912, the Marinekommandant had sharply curtailed his plans. Title VII of the budget, which covered new construction, contained a request for an appropriation of 24 million kronen as the first installment for the construction of a new dreadnought. The proposal met the firm opposition of the Hungarians. László Lukács, the Hungarian Minister-President, claimed that it had been with the greatest difficulty that he, while Finance Minister, had been able to obtain consent from the Hungarian legislature for the earlier program. At the time he had solemnly promised that the program would be maintained and no new obligations undertaken. The naval demands were accompanied by a military request for an extraordinary grant of 250 million kronen to be used mostly for artillery, fortifications, and aircraft. The Hungarian Finance Minister, Johann Teleszky, pointed out the difficult financial situation of the Hungarian government which needed 250 million to cover its own obligations. He feared the military demands would burden the securities market to such an extent that further engagements could not be taken. Teleszky also feared that publication af a new naval program would close the French money market to not only Austro-Hungarian government bonds, but other industrial issues as well. Bilinski, the Common Finance Minister, disagreed, and the navy received strong support from the Foreign Minister, Graf Leopold Berchtold, who indicated the precarious nature of the international political situation. His support led the Austrian members of the council to agree, although reluctantly, to the military and naval proposals.[66]

Both Lukács and Teleszky remained adamant, contending that the pro-

[65] Bolfras to Montecuccoli, 11 Apr. 1912, *ibid.* A draft of what was obviously a formal report (*Vortrag*) which the Marinekommandant intended to submit to the Emperor in favor of his program is to be found in the Sonder Reihe of the Operationskanzlei. Included among the proposals was one to raise new construction to 70 million kronen. Italian naval construction was used to justify the proposals. The document bears no OK/MS number and, except for the year, no date, although "January" appears to have been erased. There is no indication of the background of this plan although its provisions are similar to those of the Promemoria on the Adriatic situation submitted to the Emperor in March. OK/MS-Sonder Reihe.

[66] Protokoll, Ministerrates für gemeinsame Angelegenheiten, 8 July 1912, pp. 433f, HHSA-XL-310. A brief discussion of financial relations between France and Austria-Hungary is in Herbert Feis, *Europe the World's Banker, 1870–1914* (New Haven, 1930), pp. 201–209. Berchtold's view of the foreign situation, but not the discussion of the naval and military proposals, is printed in Ludwig Bittner and Hans Uebersberger, ed., *Österreich-Ungarns Aussenpolitik: Von der Bosnischen Krise 1908 bis zum Kriegsausbruch 1914*, 9 vols. (Vienna, 1930) (hereafter cited as *OeU*), vol. IV, no. 3612, pp. 254–257.

posed increases would hurt the Hungarian government party by giving the opposition the chance to accuse them of breaking their promises. Teleszky did not think any appropriation for new dreadnoughts could be voted until 1916 when the present building program, as far as its financial aspects were concerned, would be finished. The Hungarians therefore insisted that the first installment for the dreadnought be stricken from the estimates. They did agree to substitute the sum of 4.6 million kronen as the first installment on the construction of two new colliers.[67] Berchtold warned that within two years the Triple Alliance would expire and that one could not foresee what the political situation would be then. In view of the rapid development of the already numerically superior Italian navy, the Foreign Minister explained, it was necessary to look to the future lest one day Austria be judged impotent in the Adriatic. In an appendix to the minutes of the meeting, Admiral Montecuccoli added a formal protest that he could defend the reduced naval budget before the Delegations only on the express command of the Emperor.

Montecuccoli sought the influence and support of Archduke Franz Ferdinand in getting the entire question discussed again by the common ministers before the budgetary proposals were submitted to the Delegations in the fall.[68] He also asked Berchtold to sound the Emperor's opinion concerning his protest which had been added to the minutes of the last meeting.[69] Franz Ferdinand agreed to help him and directed the Marinekommandant to prepare a report for the Emperor which amplified the military and political consequences of the reduction of naval appropriations and elimination of the battleship.[70] Berchtold informed Montecuccoli that at the moment the question did not appear to him sufficiently clarified to permit a final decision. He raised the possibility that both governments might still be able to satisfy the navy's needs in the course of the year, or at the beginning of the following year.[71] Berchtold's solid support of the naval and military requests earned him the personal thanks of Franz Ferdinand.[72]

Montecuccoli's report was shown to the Archduke's Militärkanzlei before it was submitted to the Emperor on July 27. In it the Marinekommandant stressed the urgent need for the prompt replacement of the obsolete "Monarch" class in view of the rapid expansion of the navies of

---

[67] Protokoll, Ministerrates für gemeinsame Angelegenheiten, 9 July 1912, HHSA-XL-310.

[68] Montecuccoli to MKFF, 14 July 1912, PK/MS-XV-7/8, 1912.

[69] Montecuccoli to Berchtold, 10 July 1912, *ibid.*

[70] MKFF to Montecuccoli, 17 July 1912, *ibid.*

[71] Berchtold to Montecuccoli, 23 July 1912, *ibid.*

[72] Hans Hugo Hantsch, *Leopold Graf Berchtold* (Graz, 1963), I, 281–282.

neighboring states. Because of the length of time necessary to build a large warship, this replacement would have to start right away. A slip had been vacant at the Stabilimento Tecnico since the *Tegetthoff* had been launched the past winter, and another would soon be freed by the launching of the *Prinz Eugen*. It was very unhealthy for the shipbuilding industry to have periods of stagnation between large orders; such idle periods also increased the price of construction. Montecuccoli therefore requested the Emperor to use his influence to obtain a renewal of the financial discussions by the common ministers with the idea of increasing the sums allotted to the navy.[73] Montecuccoli's efforts were successful, and Berchtold was able to inform the common ministers in September that the Marinekommandant would present new proposals at their next meeting.[74]

Austro-Hungarian naval development naturally provoked a certain amount of pamphlet literature, most of it pro since it was the supporters of the navy who sought to change public indifference. In August 1912, however, a pamphlet appeared which was hostile in tone. The author of *Die Probleme der österreichische Flottenpolitik*, supposedly an Austrian mariner, argued that a fleet of dreadnoughts for the protection of the Austrian coast was completely useless. A comparatively cheap fleet of coastal-defense ships, fast cruisers, and torpedo boats would make it impossible for the Italians to attempt a landing since they could not protect their transports from Austrian torpedoes. A victory at sea would bring Austria no essential advantage, according to the pamphleteer, and Italian control of the sea need not be feared.[75] Colonel Bardolff, head of Franz Ferdinand's Militärkanzlei, reported that the author was not a mariner and that Skoda, whom the author attacked, had tried to bribe him with 20,000 kronen to abandon the brochure, but the most they could secure from him was the addition of a chapter titled "Why after all" (*Warum doch*) and the motto "Aut Caesar, aut nihil." The Marinesektion did not have legal grounds to propose a confiscation, but according to Bardolff a series of counter articles were in the course of preparation by various writers on naval affairs. In a marginal comment Franz Ferdinand described Skoda's action as a wholly objectionable procedure, noting that the payment of hush money suggests a need for secrecy.[76]

---

[73] Vortrag by Montecuccoli, 27 July 1912, PK/MS-XV-7/8, 1912.
[74] Protokoll, Ministerrates für gemeinsame Angelegenheiten, 14 Sept. 1912, p. 525, HHSA-XL-310.
[75] Anonymous, "Weshalb bauen wir Dreadnoughts?" *Der Morgen*, 12 Aug. 1912; clipping enclosed with report by Bardolff, 15 Aug. 1912, MKFF-Mm/ 94, 1912.
[76] Report by Bardolff, 15 Aug. 1912, and marginal comment by Franz Ferdinand, *ibid.*

The following month a retired naval officer, Rear Admiral Franz Mirtl, published a pamphlet entitled *Unsere Flotte sinkt* in which he criticized the system of budgeting for the navy, advocated the creation of a fleet of sixteen dreadnoughts with supporting ships, and proposed an increase of the annual provision for renewal of the fleet from the present 20 to 80 million kronen. The pamphlet was to be handed to all Austrian deputies and sent to over three hundred Austrian and Hungarian newspapers and periodicals for review. The publisher was also working on a Hungarian translation.[77] The Archduke's Militärkanzlei added their support by drawing the pamphlet to the attention of the editors of a number of newspapers and periodicals associated with the Archduke, such as the *Reichspost* and *Österreichische Rundschau,* and requesting the widest possible publicity and favorable comment.[78] Later in the fall Rear Admiral Mirtl was to be honored by an audience with the Archduke who wanted personally to thank him for his work.[79]

The meeting of the common ministers on October 3 took place in the shadow of the impending Balkan upheaval. Admiral Montecuccoli, who in July had asked for only the first installment for a dreadnought, now presented a program calling for a special appropriation of 170 million kronen to be distributed over a period of three years. Its most important provision was for the construction of two 24,000–25,000 ton dreadnoughts with 14-inch guns (35 cm) to replace two of the obsolete "Monarchs." Montecuccoli also asked for 6.5 million kronen to supplement the funds provided in 1911 for construction of six submarines. The extra money was necessitated by the increasing size and cost of submarines. He also wanted funds for a 40,000 ton floating dock, two monitors and two patrol boats for service on the Danube, the replacement of six outmoded torpedo boats, and a half million kronen for the naval flying service.[80] This request, which accompanied even heavier army demands, took the Austrians—who had been inclined to favor the navy in July—somewhat aback. Graf Karl Stürgkh, the Austrian Minister-President, asked for time to consult his colleagues.

When the ministers met again on October 8 the Hungarians proposed a sharp curtailment of the naval requests. Their reasons were twofold. First came the condition of the Hungarian state finances, and second

[77] Report by Bardolff, 19 Sept. 1912, MKFF-Mm/94, 1912. Bardolff gives no indication who provided the financial backing for this.

[78] MKFF to *Reichspost, Österreichische Rundschau,* and so forth, 22 Sept. 1912, *ibid.*

[79] MKFF to Mirtl, 22 Oct. 1912, *ibid.*

[80] Protokoll, Ministerrates für gemeinsame Angelegenheiten, 3 Oct. 1912, p. 552, HHSA-XL-310.

came the inability of the Hungarian government on tactical political grounds to propose anything to the Hungarian deputies but short-term appropriations based on a momentary crisis. This was due to the government's past declarations on the subject. Both Lukács and Teleszky maintained their contention that construction of a second dreadnought division, as well as the floating dock, could begin only after the first dreadnoughts had been paid for. To expedite this they were willing to accelerate the payment schedule for the appropriation of 312 million kronen voted in 1911. The last installments, which originally were due in 1915 and 1916, would be paid in 1913 and 1914, thus clearing the way for new dreadnought construction in 1915. In addition they agreed to provide the money for the smaller units (torpedo boats, monitors, and submarines) which the Marinekommandant had requested.[81] The Austrian ministers also favored a reduction in the navy's demands, at least in slowing the schedule of payments if not in the total number of units, but not as drastic a reduction as the Hungarian proposal. Berchtold again supported the navy. He observed that the Triple Alliance would soon expire, and that the recent concentration of the French fleet at Toulon had caused concern in Italy. If the development of the Austrian fleet were retarded, Berchtold feared that the Italians, after comparing the naval strength of Austria and France, would come to the conclusion that they would find no support from their allies against the French threat and therefore back the stronger power. In the Foreign Minister's opinion, if they wanted to keep Italy in the Triple Alliance, they also had to be able to protect her vital interests in Alliance questions.

In the long and acrimonious debates over the naval and military requests the Hungarians held fast to their position. The only additional concession Montecuccoli was able to obtain was 8.5 million kronen for the dock.[82] This raised the total grant for the navy to 26 million kronen, to be paid over a two year period. When he presented this program to the Delegations, Montecuccoli was authorized to say that he would promptly put forward proposals for the construction of a second dreadnought division once the present dreadnought construction was paid for, and that the government had taken note of his intention.[83]

Both Berchtold and Bilinski thought that the commencement of the second dreadnought division seemed secure for 1915.[84] This may have

[81] Protokoll, Ministerrates für gemeinsame Angelegenheiten, 8 Oct. 1912, pp. 588f, *ibid.*

[82] Ibid., p. 597.

[83] Protokoll, Ministerrates für gemeinsame Angelegenheiten, 9 Oct. 1912, p. 600, *ibid.*

[84] Vortrag by Bilinski, 10 Oct. 1912, PK/MS-XV-7/8, 1912.

been true, but the decision of the ministers constituted another defeat for the Marinekommandant. The construction of the replacements for the "Monarchs" and their subsequent entry into service would be delayed by one and possibly two years. The acceleration of credits in payment for the first four dreadnoughts was merely a bookkeeping device of little practical value to the navy since the ships were already in varying stages of completion, and would have joined the fleet before all installments for their construction had been paid. Montecuccoli recognized this and promised the Archduke he would take advantage of every opportunity to alter the decision of the ministers and obtain the financial means to build the ships. But the admiral realized that within his own sphere of action he could not fully exploit such an opportunity, and he requested Franz Ferdinand's support and intervention in behalf of his efforts.[85]

The essentially passive attitude of watchful waiting that the Marinekommandant proposed to adopt was not warmly received in the Archduke's Militärkanzlei where Colonel Bardolff advised Franz Ferdinand against doing Montecuccoli's dirty work. Bardolff thought that if the admiral was unable to obtain a reversal of the ministerial decision he should resign in protest. Bardolff also recommended that he be told to prepare a new report for the Emperor citing the impossibility of further delay, and presenting concrete proposals on possible means to commence the new construction in 1913.[86] The Archduke considered that the reaction of the Delegations to new naval proposals would be favorable, and asked Montecuccoli to arrange yet another meeting of the common ministers as soon as possible to discuss naval credits. He feared that by waiting for the next session of the Delegations most of 1913 would be wasted, and the resulting unemployment of the large slips at the Stabilimento Tecnico might mean the loss of that firm's cadre of trained personnel.[87]

When the common ministers met on January 11, 1913, to discuss the extraordinary appropriations necessary for the partial mobilization of Austrian forces during the Balkan Wars, Montecuccoli asked them to permit the new construction to take place in 1914 instead of 1915. They evaded the issue by deciding that this should be brought up during the deliberations over the budget for 1914.[88]

In the latter part of February Admiral Montecuccoli, upon reaching the age seventy, retired after nearly fifty-four years of service. The morning

[85] Montecuccoli to MKFF, 30 Oct. 1912, *ibid.*
[86] Report by Bardolff, 3 Nov. 1912, MKFF-Mm/100, 1912.
[87] Bardolff to Montecuccoli, 6 Dec. 1912, PK/MS-XV-7/8, 1912.
[88] Protokoll, Ministerrates für gemeinsame Angelegenheiten, 4 Jan. 1913, p. 837, HHSA-XL-311.

of his birthday the German Emperor sent a ship made of flowers and decorated with the German flag.[89] The new Marinekommandant and chief of the Marinesektion was Vice Admiral Anton Haus. He was a man of many accomplishments, a gifted linguist, fond of music, and author of a text on oceanography and marine meteorology. In 1907 he acted as an Austrian delegate to the Hague Peace Conference. Haus filled with distinction some of the navy's most important posts, and had long been regarded as Montecuccoli's successor.[90] Within the navy he was extremely popular and enjoyed the complete confidence of the officers, being regarded as more competent in technical matters than Montecuccoli. There was, however, some apprehension that he would not prove as adept as his predecessor in managing the Delegations and the other more political aspects of his position.[91] In August 1913 the Marinesektion was reorganized and the office of the Marinekommandant was shifted from Vienna to Pola. Haus remained chief of the Marinesektion, but was represented at its headquarters on the Marxergasse in Vienna by a deputy (*Stellvertreter*) Rear Admiral Karl Kailer von Kaltenfels.[92]

With a formal grant for new construction apparently out of the question for 1913, the idea of speculative building before the approval of the Delegations, as had been done in 1910, was taken up again. As early as January 1912 the Marinesektion issued a formal denial to a rumor that a financial consortium was building dreadnoughts for the navy. The denial served the tactical advantage of enabling the Marinekommandant to take the position that he was not involved. The Marinesektion intended to send a representative to any such negotiations about speculative building which might actually follow.[93] The truth of the rumors which were then current is difficult to establish. There was talk at the time that some of the stories were at least partially connected with maneuvers on the Vienna stock exchange.[94]

There was constant suspicion abroad that the Austrians would secretly

[89] Report by Bardolff, 21 Feb. 1913, MKFF/41-1/3-2. For Montecuccoli's farewell speech to the fleet see Bayer von Bayersburg, *Österreichs Admirale, 1867–1918*, pp. 121–122.

[90] Heinrich Bayer von Bayersburg, *Unter der k.u.k. Kriegsflagge* (Vienna, 1959), pp. 7f. In May 1916 Haus was raised to the rank of Grossadmiral, Austria's first and last.

[91] Report by Lieutenant Mancini, 24 May 1913, USM, cartella 299/4; Faramond to Minister of Marine, 23 Dec. 1910, AMF, carton BB7-129, and 5 May 1913, carton BB7-92.

[92] Wagner, *Die Obersten Behörden*, pp. 95–98; Sokol, *Österreich-Ungarns Seekrieg*, p. 31; Faramond to Minister of Marine, 24 Jan. 1914, AMF, carton BB7-129.

[93] Report by Bardolff, Jan. 1912, MKFF-Mm/10, 1912.

[94] *Ibid.*; Report by Bardolff, 22 Feb. 1912, *ibid.*

begin work on the ships before appropriations were voted. In November 1912 Captain Courtenay Stewart, the British naval attaché, reported that, although he could discern no signs of the commencement of another ship on the vacant slip at Trieste, he believed that an arrangement similar to the previous one existed between the firm and the Marinekommandant.[95] On December 7, 1912, a somewhat sensational article appeared in the *Daily Telegraph* exaggerating the state of advancement of Austrian naval construction and anticipating the imminent laying down of new dreadnoughts on credit. This provoked a denial by the *Fremdenblatt,* considered to be the organ of the Austrian Foreign Ministry, which termed the construction of ships on credit without the sanction of the Delegations as completely out of the question. At the Foreign Office Sir Eyre Crowe considered the statement to be ridiculous for it had actually happened two years before and would "no doubt be done again." [96] Only the stubbornness of the Hungarian government was to prove him wrong.

By March 1913 the *Viribus Unitis* was in service, the *Tegetthoff* was close to completion, and the *Prinz Eugen* had been launched. With no appropriation by the Delegations for major new construction in 1913 the Stabilimento Tecnico was therefore faced with the necessity of discharging its skilled workers or detailing them to minor work with a corresponding reduction in their pay, thus risking the loss of their skilled workers to the busy Italian yards. Consequently the Stabilimento Tecnico, together with Skoda and Wittkowitz, proposed to build a dreadnought on their own account which could be taken over by the navy when the necessary funds were voted. To facilitate this the firms requested plans and specifications from the Marinesektion, but specifically agreed that this was not to be considered a formal order and that the Delegations' right to decide on the subject was not prejudiced.[97] Before the firm's offer had been received, Franz Ferdinand, who learned of the plan, advised Admiral Haus that it would be "superfluous and inopportune" to inform the government of the proposed action.[98] Haus did not feel himself in a position to follow this advice, for on assuming office he had explicitly promised to keep the government informed of even nonbinding negotiations on this subject so as to avoid future embarrassments. He doubted that the commencement

---

[95] Extract of Stewart's report in Cartwright to Grey, 30 Nov. 1912, FO 371, vol. 1298, Austria-Hungary, file 52451. Stewart's movements were restricted and he was unable to visit the naval ports.

[96] Cartwright to Grey, 10 Dec. 1912; Minute by Sir Eyre Crowe, 12 Dec. 1912, *ibid.*

[97] Joint Proposal by Stabilimento Tecnico, Skoda and Wittkowitz, 18 Apr. 1913, MKFF-41-2/4-8, 1913.

[98] Bardolff to Haus, 8 Apr. 1913, MKFF-41-2/4-3.

of a dreadnought would remain unnoticed. He was particularly concerned about this because he hoped to be able to induce Danubius to undertake a similar speculation.[99] In a private letter to Rear Admiral Kailer, Haus revealed his intention of obtaining as much preliminary support as possible, starting with the Emperor, in anticipation of a negative Hungarian reaction.[100]

When the proposal was presented, the Austrian government gave a generally favorable reply. The Austrians did insist that the technical aid the Marinesektion would give the yards in enabling them to work at full capacity be recognized in the final price, and in more favorable terms for payment.[101] The reply of the Hungarian Finance Minister, however, was a categorical refusal based on both economic and political grounds.[102] Haus tried to overcome Hungarian Minister-President Lukács' opposition in an hour-long conference, and had an even longer session with Teleszky. But he was unsuccessful in both cases. Berchtold, who made a special trip to Budapest for the purpose, was equally unsuccessful. Even the Emperor, whose support Haus had sought the day before Teleszky was due for an audience, could not budge the Hungarian. At a meeting of the common ministers on May 14 Admiral Haus and the Austrian and common ministers tried for more than three hours to convince Lukács and Teleszky that speculative construction by the yard was not a formal order and that the constitutional proprieties were therefore observed. The Hungarians merely dug in their heels.[103]

Haus believed that the strategic situation was critical enough to justify this acceleration of the building program. At the meeting of the common ministers Haus argued that France's open claim to hegemony in the Mediterranean had pushed Italy into Austria's arms, had forced her to recognize the necessity of cooperation at sea in order to protect Italy against a landing attempt and hinder the transport of French troops from Africa. This would free more Italian troops to support Germany who, in turn, could then give more support to Austria. Although Haus did not mention it, he undoubtedly had at the back of his mind the negotiations for the Triple Alliance naval convention which were then in progress. Berchtold was also a strong supporter of additional naval construction, for if one could not be certain that three years hence Austria-Hungary would be at war, one could also not guarantee the opposite. He described

[99] Haus to MKFF, 10 Apr. 1913, MKFF-41-2/4-4, 1913.
[100] Haus to Kailer, 9 Apr. 1913, Kriegsarchiv, Vienna, Nachlass Kailer, B/242.
[101] Enclosure 3 in Haus to MKFF, 22 May 1913, MKFF-41-2/4-8.
[102] Teleszky to Bilinski, enclosure 4, *ibid.*
[103] Haus to MKFF, 22 May 1913, *ibid.*

the Balkan upheavals and change of occupants of part of the North African coast as giving a new physiognomy to all Mediterranean politics. England, he observed, had once stood morally on the side of the Triple Alliance, but as the result of the "Einkreisungspolitik" of King Edward had transferred most of her Mediterranean force north; the few ships that remained had to be considered alongside the French in the hostile grouping. Berchtold declared that relations with Italy could be described as cordial and it was hoped they would remain that way, but in the future the Balkan states could no longer be treated as a *quantité négligeable,* especially Greece who was on the verge of becoming a sea power. The Foreign Minister concluded with a warning against indulging in illusions about the foreign situation. Bilinski, the Common Finance Minister, showed a somewhat more ambivalent attitude toward the Italians. For him a strong fleet was necessary either to face a disloyal Italy, or to be a desirable ally for her.[104]

The Hungarians were particularly sensitive about what they considered infringements of their rights in questions regarding the common affairs of the Dual Monarchy, and they still smarted over the methods used by the Marinesektion to commence dreadnought construction in 1910. The Hungarian Delegation which met in Vienna in the fall of 1912 had passed a resolution specifically forbidding the army and navy to take even preliminary steps toward matters involving financial commitments without the consent of both governments, and this resolution was repeated by the Hungarian Delegation in the fall of 1913 and the spring of 1914.[105] For Lukács and Teleszky, no matter how the joint proposal by the Stabilimento Tecnico, Skoda, and Wittkowitz was cloaked, it was still an order for new dreadnoughts, and they felt unable to defend it before the Hungarian parliament. Teleszky called the acceleration of payments for the first dreadnought division the limit of the Hungarian government's concessions. He also objected to using private financial resources for state purposes while the economy was suffering from lack of necessary capital. Lukács argued that if matters were so pressing that they could not wait the seven months until the Delegations met again, then constitutional forms should be observed and the Delegations immediately summoned. The meeting concluded with the unequivocal statement by the Hungarians that they would

[104] Protokoll, Ministerrates für gemeinsame Angelegenheiten, 14 May 1913, pp. 1116–1117, 1120–1122, HHSA-XL-311. Haus exaggerated by using the figure of 100,-000 for the French North African troops.

[105] K.K. Hof- und Staatsdruckerei, *Resolution der einberufenen Delegation des ungarischen Reichstages,* 11 Oct. 1912, *Protokollspunkt* 6. Copy in PK/MS-XV-7/3, 1912; 20 May 1914, Protokollspunkt 103, PK/MS-XV-7/3, 1914.

consider the news of the Marinesektion's delivery of plans to the Stabilimento Tecnico an order, and would draw the necessary consequences from it. This implied that the Hungarian government would resign.[106]

Shortly after this futile meeting Haus made a final effort to secure the Emperor's intervention. In this he was supported by General Bolfras, head of Emperor Franz Joseph's Militärkanzlei, who told Colonel Bardolff that he knew the Emperor favored pressing the construction.[107] But when the old Emperor merely promised to continue his efforts to get the Hungarian government to agree, offering the vague hope that he might eventually succeed, Haus felt that all his resources for implementing the plan had been exhausted. It was slightly consoling that the conviction had apparently taken root among both governments that the "Monarch" class would have to be replaced. The fiscal administration of the Dual Monarchy planned to advance the beginning of the budgetary year 1915 to July 1 1914; this raised the possibility that the new construction might thus be advanced by some six months. In the meantime, the Marinekommandant proposed to prepare the preliminary drafting for plans and specifications.[108]

During the summer of 1913 Haus carried out his intention of giving the Stabilimento Tecnico, Skoda, and Wittkowitz the general lines of the new dreadnoughts, but presumably not the actual plans, so that they would be in a position, he hoped, to begin construction around a month and a half after a formal order was placed, and to complete work within three years.[109] The new battleships were to have 14-inch (35 cm) cannon in place of the 12-inch guns of the first Austrian dreadnoughts. In June 1913 Haus engaged in confidential negotiations with Skoda on the subject. The firm was to begin preliminary work on the larger caliber artillery at its own risk. In January 1914 Haus was able to report they would be able to deliver the first 14-inch gun turret the following August.[110]

In autumn of 1913 Haus presented his new building program, which required a special appropriation of 426,836,000 kronen. This would provide for the construction of four dreadnoughts to replace the three "Monarchs" and the *Habsburg*, three 4800-ton cruisers, six destroyers, two Danube monitors, and a supply ship. In speaking of the urgent need to replace the "Monarchs," Haus probably echoed the thoughts of many foreign observers when he declared that no one in the world understood why they were

---

106 Protokoll, Ministerrates, 14 May 1913, pp. 1123–1125, 1128.

107 Report by Bardolff, 17 May 1913, MKFF-41-2/4-7.

108 Haus to MKFF, 22 May 1913, MKFF-41-2/4-8.

109 Protokoll, Ministerrates für gemeinsame Angelegenheiten, 3 Oct. 1913, p. 1162, HHSA-XL-311.

110 Haus to MKFF, 3 Jan. 1914, MKFF-62-2/2.

waiting.[111] This time both governments approved the requests, as the Marinekommandant anticipated, but he was frustrated in his desire to fulfill the program as rapidly as possible because of the stringent financial controls attached to the grant. These required yearly expenditures to agree with the yearly installments (to be paid monthly) provided by the special appropriation, and excluded the payment of penal interest.[112] This would have caused construction to drag at an excessively slow pace if all four ships were laid down at the same time. The commencement of the second pair of dreadnoughts therefore had to be postponed until the end of the second credit year. The payments were to be spread over five years, but the installment for the first credit year (1914–15) was only 45 million kronen because of the necessity of paying off the remainder of the 312 million voted in 1911. Haus intended to lay down the first pair of dreadnoughts immediately after the formal vote of the Delegations. This was far from all the Kriegsmarine would have desired. Franz Ferdinand realized that the rigid financial controls binding annual expenditure to annual appropriations would mean that the program could not be completed until 1918–19. He asked Haus to do everything possible to shorten this by at least a year.[113]

The new program was formally presented to the Delegations in the spring of 1914 and approved without difficulty the end of May. The first of the 24,500-ton dreadnoughts, armed with ten 14-inch guns, was to be laid down at the Stabilimento Tecnico in September, and the second in October.[114] At last it seemed as if the obsolete "Monarchs" would be replaced. But the war broke out in August. In February 1915 at a meeting of the common ministers the navy declared itself ready to delay using the special credit for the duration of the war. Rear Admiral Kailer, representing Haus, insisted that the Marinesektion did not consider the credit annulled but merely deferred. The ministers, however, decided the question would remain in abeyance until after the war when the program would be revised and new proposals submitted to the Delegations.[115] By then, both the Dual Monarchy and its fleet had ceased to exist.

The projected Austrian program was the subject of conflicting reports by the British and French naval attachés, who informed their respective admiralties in the spring of 1914 that they believed the new dreadnoughts

111 Protokoll, Ministerrates für gemeinsame Angelegenheiten, 3 Oct. 1913, p. 1161.
112 Haus to MKFF, 3 Jan. 1914.
113 Bardolff to Haus, 23 Jan. 1914, *ibid.*
114 Sokol, *Österreich-Ungarns Seekrieg*, pp. 21–22, 24–25; *Le Yacht*, 6 June 1914, pp. 357–358; *ibid.*, 20 June 1914, p. 388; *ibid.*, 1 Aug. 1914, p. 484; Faramond to Minister of Marine, 15 July 1914, AMF, carton BB7-92.
115 Protokoll, Ministerrates für gemeinsame Angelegenheiten, 3 Feb. 1915, p. 368, HHSA-XL-312.

might already have been begun.[116] It was the familiar story of suspicions concerning secret building and apprehensions that the Marinesektion would repeat its coup of 1910. Actually the expansion of the K.u.K. Kriegsmarine had been slow and painful with the Hungarian government acting as a constant brake. It had taken two years of struggle to obtain the appropriations to replace the obsolete "Monarchs," and even then financial restrictions meant the new dreadnoughts would probably not be finished until the end of 1918. At that time, using Austria's own standard of the "Radetzkys" as the first really modern ships, the Kriegsmarine would have only eleven of the sixteen units Montecuccoli set as its goal. But slow as the progress might have been, this total would include eight dreadnoughts which, joined to the ten the Italians were expected to have within five years, was more than enough to worry the French.[117] Winston Churchill also thought, in view of the new Austrian and Italian plans, that it was necessary for the Cabinet to review the situation in the Mediterranean and decide on general policy at an early date.[118]

The dictates of geography and its own small numerical strength in the first decade of the new century confined the wartime role of the K.u.K. Kriegsmarine almost entirely to the Adriatic. In case of war with the Dual Monarchy's Balkan neighbors—*Kriegsfall B*—the land locked position of Serbia and all but a small portion of Montenegro would limit the navy to cooperation with the army in the vicinity of Cattaro in repelling a possible Montenegrin invasion. The navy's job would be to shell the batteries on Mount Lovćen which dominated Cattaro, and evacuate isolated coastal garrisons in the area which might be cut off during the early part of the war. The monitors of the Danube flotilla would naturally work closely with the land forces. In case of war with Russia (*Kriegsfall R*) or with Italy (*Kriegsfall I*), the action of the fleet would be dependent on the circumstances prevailing at the time.[119]

---

[116] Extract from Report by naval attaché, Vienna, 24 Mar. 1914, in Admiralty circular, "Austro-Hungarian and Italian Shipbuilding Programmes," 21 Apr. 1914, PRO, Cab. 37/119; Admiralty circular, "Austro-Hungarian New Naval Programme," 6 May 1914, *ibid.*

[117] Faramond to Minister of Marine, 7 May 1914, AMF, carton BB7-92; Dumaine (French ambassador, Vienna) to Minister of Foreign Affairs, 4 June 1914, *ibid.*

[118] Minute by Churchill 26 Apr. 1914 to Admiralty circular, "Austro-Hungarian Programmes," 21 Apr. 1914, PRO, Cab. 37/119.

[119] K.u.K. Chef des Generalstabes, "Grundlagen für die Anfängliche Tätigkeit des k.u.k. Kriegsmarine in falle einer Alarmierung oder Mobilisierung gültig vom 1 Marz 1911 für den Kriegsfall 'B', Kriegsfall 'I' oder 'R'," 8 Dec. 1910, OK/MS-IX-9/2, 1910; "Grundlagen für die Anfängliche Tätigkeit gültig ab 1 Marz 1913," 9 Dec. 1912, OK/MS-IX-9/2, 1912; "Grundlagen für die Anfängliche Tätigkeit gültig vom 1 Apr. 1914," 5 Dec. 1913, OK/MS-IX-9/2, 1914.

Traditionally the Italian fleet was the obvious potential enemy. But in 1904 the tonnage of the Italian fleet was more than double that of the Austrian fleet.[120] As a result of this adverse ratio of strength the Austrians considered out of the question a confrontation by their own force with the full strength of the Italian fleet. The Austrian fleet, secure in its fortified base at Pola, would be held ready to exploit any diversion or momentary weakening of the enemy force, although raids against suitable objectives on the Adriatic coast of Italy were also to be considered.[121]

General Conrad von Hötzendorf, chief of the army General Staff, in an exchange of ideas with Montecuccoli in 1907 on the navy's role in *Kriegsfall I,* listed as highly desirable the destruction of the railways the Italians would use for mobilization, as far as this was possible by maritime means.[122] Equally important was the frustration of similar Italian efforts against Austria in the Gulf of Trieste. Conrad was also anxious to counter possible Italian maritime threats to the seaward flank of the Austrian army. The general was inclined to consider the protection of the Dalmatian coast of only secondary importance, an opinion Montecuccoli did not share. The navy relied on coastal steamers to bring reservists from Dalmatia to Pola in the event of mobilization, and these could not be exposed to enemy capture at the beginning of hostilities.[123] The admiral thought that with the long stretch of the Dalmatian coast stripped of Austrian offensive forces the Italians would find it much easier to operate against the flank and line of communications of the Austrian army in the Quarnero or Gulf of Trieste. Montecuccoli therefore advocated fortification of Sebenico as a secure naval base in middle Dalmatia. Austrian naval forces based here could threaten the flank of an advance up the Adriatic by the Italian fleet. Moreover, the Marinekommandant considered Pola a "mousetrap" relatively easy for a superior fleet to blockade. On the other hand, the geographical configuration of Sebenico made a blockade possible only through employment of the greater portion of the enemy fleet. This would naturally facilitate Austrian counter measures against maritime threats to the flank of their own army in the north. Montecuccoli was to advocate a base at Sebenico until his retirement. He also wanted the peacetime strength to be raised so as to enable a more rapid mobilization for he was

[120] Operationskanzlei, Marinesektion, "Vergleich der beiderseitigen Streitkräfte," Mar. 1904, OK/MS-Sonder Reihe. The Marinesektion's estimates of total tonnages were Austria: 114,291; Italy: 272,329. This was a ratio of 1:2.38.

[121] Operationskanzlei, Marinesektion, "Defensiv- und Offensiv-Aufgaben der k.u.k. Flotte," n.d. [1904], *ibid.*

[122] Conrad to Montecuccoli, 5 Apr. 1907, OK/MS-IX-9/1, 1907.

[123] Montecuccoli to Conrad, 26 Apr. 1907, OB/GSTB-38.

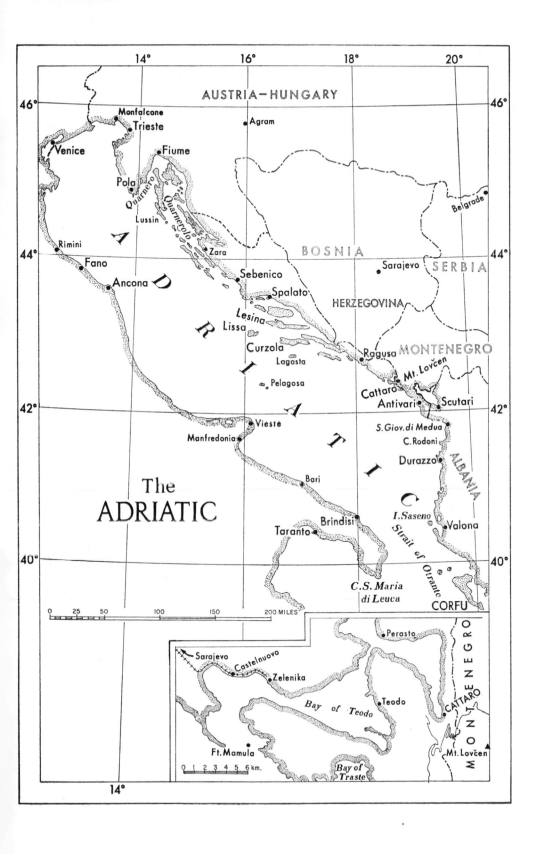

The
ADRIATIC

convinced that success at sea was possible if he could fall on the Italians before the bulk of their forces had time to appear in the Adriatic.

The Austrians continued to concern themselves with questions inherent in a "small" war of raids and counterraids, surprise attacks, operations on the flank of the land armies, and above all the disruption of the enemy's mobilization and protection of one's own. In April 1910 Conrad offered to place a small contingent of troops at the navy's disposal for a raid on the Italian Adriatic coast.[124] He and Montecuccoli agreed upon the railway bridge over the Cesano Torrente, nine miles southeast of Fano, as a suitable target for the Austrian force which was to be carried in two destroyers.[125]

During these discussions Montecuccoli renewed his emphasis on the value of Sebenico and pointed out the advantage of keeping a portion of the Austrian ships maintained in a reserve status here. In case of mobilization they could be manned by reservists from Dalmatia; this would save the men the hazardous sea journey to Pola. The Marinekommandant also thought that the mobility inherent in a modern fleet did not lend itself to a concrete plan of operations. In a genuine sea war, especially in the relatively small area of the Adriatic, the surprise raid would be the norm, and Montecuccoli predicted that as a rule one would be faced with situations which developed suddenly and which would require immediate decisions. He held that in these circumstances the fleet with the advantage would be the one which mobilized the fastest, and which in peacetime had acquired the highest degree of skill and training for its officers and men. This was especially true for a small fleet like Austria's which could only offset its numerical weakness through the technical competence of its crews. Montecuccoli therefore stressed the importance of maintaining the largest number of units possible in permanent commission, a question which was linked with increasing the navy's peacetime effectives.[126]

In March 1912 Admiral Montecuccoli submitted to the Emperor a lengthy memorandum on Austrian and Italian military and maritime provisions for the Adriatic.[127] The Marinekommandant believed that the latent conflict of interest between the two countries could lead to hostilities overnight, and that the only possibility of preventing war was a fleet nearly

124 Conrad to Montecuccoli, 22 Apr. 1910, OK/MS-IX-9/1, 1910.

125 Montecuccoli to Conrad, 24 May 1910, Conrad to Montecuccoli, 5 Aug. 1910, Montecuccoli to Conrad, 17 Aug. 1910, *ibid.*

126 Montecuccoli to Conrad, 24 May and 17 Aug. 1910, *ibid.*

127 "Militarisch-Maritimen Vorsorgen Oesterreich-Ungarns und Italiens in der Adria," 13 Mar. 1912, OK/MS-VI-1/3, 1912.

equal to that of Italy, always battle-ready, supported by fortified bases, and ready for any eventuality in the Adriatic. It was not certain that the final decision in a war with Italy would easily be achieved by the land forces, for the numerous fortifications the Italians had erected on their frontier would hardly permit a rapid advance by the Austrian army. The time necessary to reduce these works might allow a decisive action against the Austrian fleet and subsequent maritime threats to the flank and possible troop landings in the rear of the advancing Austrian army. With Austria no longer master of the Adriatic, a rapid advance on land would be rendered more difficult. Moreover even a decisive victory by the Austrian army could only obtain a peace on the basis of the status quo ante; thus the Dual Monarchy would have lost her fleet without any compensation for the sacrifice of men or money. The situation in the Adriatic which the Marinekommandant sketched was almost entirely to the disadvantage of Austria-Hungary. Naturally Montecuccoli was making the best case for his claims by painting the worst possible picture, but his memorandum is an interesting example of the disadvantages the Austrian navy believed it faced in a war with Italy.

The Italian fleet in the Adriatic enjoyed the use of four fortified harbors: Venice, Ancona, Brindisi, and Taranto. Taranto fulfilled all the requirements of a naval base and, according to Montecuccoli, so would Venice after dredging operations were completed. He considered Ancona and Brindisi, if not yet of full value, as nevertheless well protected operational bases. Austria-Hungary, in comparison, possessed only two bases (*Kriegshäfen*): Pola and Cattaro. Cattaro was insufficiently protected and dominated by Montenegrin batteries on Mount Lovčen. The fortifications on the land side of Pola also did not correspond to requirements. And it was steadily becoming apparent that Pola was too small to serve as the sole fitting-out harbor and operational base for the fleet as well as the main supply center. Austria was also inferior to Italy in number of light craft, torpedo boats, and destroyers. The Italians considered the irregular configuration of the Austrian side of the Adriatic as an advantage for the Dual Monarchy, but Montecuccoli turned it into a disadvantage. Montecuccoli claimed that the Italians, with 700 nautical miles of Adriatic coastline to protect, had 18,071 men including auxiliaries available for coastal defense. The Austrians, with 1100 nautical miles of coastline (3300 including the islands), had only 7299 men including auxiliaries available for the same purpose.

The Marinekommandant grossly overestimated the speed with which the Italian dreadnoughts projected or under construction would enter service, and also included in the Italian totals obsolete battleships which were no longer likely to be a serious menace. The results were a projected Austrian inferiority in terms of tonnage of 1.7:1 at the end of 1912, 1.6:1 at the end of 1913, and 1.8:1 at the end of 1914. Actually, if one counted recent capital ships, and particularly firepower, this Italian lead would be sharply reduced. In fact—although Montecuccoli did not mention it or possibly could not realize its full implications through lack of intelligence concerning the Italian fleet—the Austrian navy, thanks to delays in Italian shipbuilding, actually had a slight lead in terms of dreadnoughts at the end of 1913. The *Viribus Unitis* entered service before the Italian *Dante Alighieri,* and the *Tegetthoff* joined the fleet approximately ten months before the Italians could complete their next dreadnought.

In his memorandum for the Emperor, Montecuccoli also renewed his proposals for the creation of a fortified naval base at Sebenico. Here even inferior Austrian forces operating among the islands under cover of night would be able to attack superior Italian forces and return to the safety of their fortified base by day. They would constitute a threat in the rear of any Italian forces operating in the northern Adriatic against Pola. One dominant anxiety emerges from Montecuccoli's lengthy arguments to the Emperor in favor of Sebenico. This is the fear that the fleet would lose its freedom of movement by being blockaded in Pola by superior forces. Montecuccoli believed that the geographical configuration of the great Austrian war port made it relatively easy to block its entrances by mines which would retard the entry and exit of Austrian warships. For a weaker fleet which would seek to profit from momentary enemy weaknesses, this was clearly an intolerable disadvantage. The Marinekommandant's plans for Sebenico also included fortifications on the island of Lissa which would serve as an advance bulwark for the Sebenico area. The fortifications involved an expenditure of 60 million kronen. These were linked with the proposal for a building program, including the four dreadnoughts to replace the "Monarchs," that would have cost 464 million kronen. It was hardly surprising Franz Joseph thought that, chiefly on financial grounds, the present moment was scarcely suited for the realization of Montecuccoli's proposals. The Emperor suggested that they be deferred until the proper moment when their success seemed assured.[128] Although some funds were eventually voted for the development of Sebenico, they were nowhere near what Montecuccoli had suggested, and the port remained largely a flotilla base at the outbreak of war.[129]

[128] Bolfras to Montecuccoli, 11 Apr. 1912, OK/MS-VI-1/3, 1912.
[129] Sokol, *Österreich-Ungarns Seekrieg,* pp. 34–35.

The Balkan Wars in the autumn of 1912, and the threatened fall of Constantinople which might have resulted in Russian intervention, forced the Austrian navy to consider other maritime foes than the Italians. The Operationskanzlei examined the possibility of the Russian Black Sea fleet being able to force the passage of the Bosporus and Dardanelles without serious casualties and in violation of treaty stipulations. Once in the Mediterranean it might unite with the Greek fleet, the only Balkan navy worth considering. The prospect of such a combination did not alarm the Austrians unduly, for they considered themselves both quantitatively and qualitatively superior, except for the number of destroyers.[130] Counting the tonnage of completed ships only, the ratio of strength between the Austrian and the combined Greek and Russian Black Sea fleet was 1.3:1 in Austria's favor. But if the Russian Baltic fleet was taken into considera tion the ratio became 1:1.74 to Austria's disadvantage. The appearance of the Russian Baltic fleet in the Mediterranean was not likely if Germany held to her alliance obligations and refused to give Russia an assurance of strict neutrality. But should it attempt to reach the Mediterranean, the Austrian objective was the destruction of the enemy forces before it arrived. An advance by the Austrian fleet into the Aegean would be dependent on the neutrality of Great Britain and France. If it occurred the fleet train might be accompanied by an expeditionary force of approximately division strength to seize the islands of Corfu and Milos to serve as advanced bases. Because of the Austrian inferiority in destroyers, special precautions would have to be taken at night, and action by the bulk of the fleet would be limited to daylight hours.

This memorandum, which was far from a concrete plan, is interesting for its idea in this case of an offensive by the fleet into the Aegean against the naval force of a major power. It reflects the growth in strength of the Kriegsmarine which could now turn its attention away from the narrow confines of the Adriatic. But judging from the records which have survived, the Kriegsmarine's major concern before the war was with Italy.

The exact ratio of strength between the two fleets is difficult to determine because of the wide variations in displacement, firepower, and armor pro tection between different ships which diminish the value of numerical or even tonnage comparisons. Certainly the Italian "Saint Bons" and "Brins" were superior to their Austrian contemporaries, the "Habsburgs" and "Erzherzogs," with the "Monarchs" far behind. With the entry into service of the "Radetzkys" in 1910–11, the Austrians greatly improved

---

[130] Österreich-Ungarn, Russland und Griechenland," n.d. [1st half of 1913], OK/ MS-1/ g.v., 1913. The Russian and Greek destroyer superiority was 27 to 19.

their position, for these were more powerful ships than the much delayed Italian "Romas" which had entered service between 1907 and 1909[131] In terms of capital ships one might almost say that delays in Italian construction gave the Austrians a slight superiority at the end of 1913.[132] At the outbreak of the war they were roughly equal, and by 1915 the Italians would regain a clear lead. The relatively slow progress by which the Austrian building program voted in 1914 was to have been executed would have made it extremely difficult for the Austrians to catch up even had the war not broken out. But this discussion refers only to battleship strength. In terms of armored cruisers, destroyers, and torpedo boats the Italians were definitely superior.[133] Their fleet was undoubtedly the stronger, and only construction delays had brought their battleship lead temporarily into question. The Austrian navy had the cloud of the larger Italian building program hanging over its future.

As the two fleets were destined never to meet in a battle where the squadrons of one would be ranged against the squadrons of the other, it is difficult to make comparisons in seamanship, efficiency of crews, and skill of their leaders. In the actual war which was to follow both sides could claim successes and failures. However, one thing is certain. In the years immediately preceding the outbreak of the World War the K.u.K. Kriegsmarine, slow and painful as its progress might have been, had become a force to be reckoned with.

[131] It is interesting to refer to the scale of merit which the Admiralty had devised for the Mediterranean fleets. This made the "Cavours," *Dante Alighieri*, and *Viribus Unitis* approximately equal at 100. The "Radetzkys" were ranked at 70; the "Romas," 50; the "Erzherzogs," 20; the "Brins," 40; the "Saint Bons," 30; and the "Habsburgs" and "Monarchs," 15. Admiralty Chart, "France, Italy, Austria, Estimated Strengths," n.d. (early 1912), Asquith MSS, box 93.

[132] The *Viribus Unitis* entered service in Oct. 1912; the *Dante Alighieri* in Jan. 1913; the *Tegetthoff* in July 1913; the *Leonardo da Vinci* and *Giulio Cesare* in May 1914; and the *Prinz Eugen* in June 1914.

[133] The Italian advantage in modern armored cruisers was 7 to 2.

VII

Italy: The Second Mediterranean Power

Italy's geographical position automatically gives her a prominent role in any discussion of Mediterranean affairs. The boot-shaped peninsula with the island of Sicily at its toe juts into the Mediterranean almost dividing the eastern from the western basin; and the island of Sardinia occupies a central position in the western basin. In 1912 the young nation, after only half a century as a unified state, was considered a restless and disturbing factor seeking somewhat belatedly her share of overseas colonies in Tripoli and Cyrenaica, and ready to expand her economic activity across the Adriatic to Albania and into the Aegean and Anatolia.

The technical daring of Italian naval engineers and the relatively large sums of money the kingdom spent on her fleet kept the Italian navy constantly in the eyes of European naval staffs. In the 1870's and 1880's the Italian fleet actually ranked third in tonnage behind the navies of Great Britain and France. The names of Vice Admiral Saint Bon and Inspettore del Genio Navale Benedetto Brin, both Ministers of Marine a number of times in the years 1873–1898, are associated with this period of maritime prominence. The 11,000-ton *Duilio* and *Dandolo*, launched in 1875 and 1878 respectively, and the 13,800-ton *Italia* and *Lepanto*, launched in 1880 and 1883, placed Italy in the vanguard of naval design. The Italian navy also placed great emphasis on speed in their warships.[1]

The primary object of the Italian navy was the protection of Italy's lengthy coastline with its numerous exposed cities. During the period of tension with France in the 1880's anxiety over an invasion from the sea

---

[1] Ufficio Storico della Marina Militare [Ammiraglio di Squadra, r.n. Giuseppe Fioravanzo], *La Marina Militare nel suo primo secolo di vita, 1861–1961* (Rome, 1961), pp. 20–24; Georgio Giorgerini and Augusto Nani, *Le Navi di linea italiane, 1861–1961* (Rome, 1962), pp. 99–113, 117–122; Ropp, "Development of a Modern Navy," pp. 137–138, 179–180, 291–293.

also increased because of the natural restrictions the alpine frontier would have placed on an invading army. The Italian navy, however, failed to maintain its position among the world's fleets, and by the end of the nineteenth century it had tumbled to seventh place. There were various reasons for this including the economic crisis at the end of the century, the reduction in naval and military expenditures after the disastrous Adowa campaign, the development of quick-firing artillery which rendered the *Italia* and *Lepanto* obsolete, and of course the great increase in naval activity by other and often wealthier powers. The Italians had also failed to budget sufficient sums for maintenance and upkeep of their fleet.[2] Recognizing Italy's naval weakness, and in order to protect the long Italian coastline from French attack, Benedetto Brin, Minister of Marine, in the latter part of 1889 broached the subject of an alliance with England to the British ambassador. The British were quite aware of Italian difficulties, and later, in a memorandum of 1896, the Director of Military Intelligence argued against a British guarantee of the Italian coast on the grounds that the value of the Italian fleet as a reinforcement would not be equal to the additional duties incumbent on the Mediterranean Fleet in undertaking to safeguard Italian ports.[3]

In a period when warships absorbed ever growing amounts of steel in their armor belts and heavy cannon, the development of the Italian navy was hampered by a lack of both iron ore and coal deposits within the confines of the Italian kingdom. By the outbreak of the First World War Italy was forced to import approximately 10 million tons of coal per year. In 1885 Benedetto Brin introduced legislation to foster the shipbuilding and metallurgical industries and gave generous advances and orders at high prices to the infant steel works established by a group of Italian companies at Terni (the Società Alti Forni Fonderie e Acciaierie di Terni) for the manufacture of armor plate.[4] He was also successful in getting Armstrong of England to establish an ordnance factory at Pozzuoli, and in promoting mergers of the Italian firms of Ansaldo and Guppy with the English firms of Maudslay and Hawthorn, respectively, for the production of propulsion machinery. By the early years of the twentieth century the major Italian metallurgical and shipbuilding firms had formed an industrial

---

[2] Ufficio Storico, *La Marina nel suo primo secolo*, p. 18; Osvaldo Paladini, "The Italian Navy," *The Naval Annual, 1906*, pp. 164, 166–167; Umberto Guglielmotti, *Storia della Marina italiana* (Naples, 1959), pp. 52–53; Ropp, "Development of a Modern Navy," pp. 382–383, 471.

[3] Marder, *Anatomy of British Sea Power*, pp. 141–143; D.M.I., "Memorandum on Naval Policy," 13 Oct. 1896, reproduced in Marder, App. III, p. 577.

[4] Shepard B. Clough, *The Economic History of Modern Italy* (New York, 1964), pp. 393 n. 27, 87f.

complex enjoying both state support and foreign participation.[5] In 1903 Armstrong and Ansaldo associated themselves in what was to be an unsuccessful and short-lived alliance. To strengthen its competitive position Ansaldo concluded agreements with Schneider et Cie. of France for the manufacture of ordnance and munitions. The Terni steel works, with whom the great shipbuilding firm of Orlando was associated, affiliated with Vickers in 1905 in an agreement by which the British firm promised to give the new company the benefit of its experience and design in providing similar armaments to those produced in England. The group, the Società Italiana di Artiglieria ed Armementi Vickers-Terni, erected an ordnance factory near La Spezia.[6]

The ingenuity of Italian naval engineers again aroused interest abroad when Colonel Vittorio Cuniberti contributed an article to the 1903 edition of Jane's *Fighting Ships* proposing a warship with an all big-gun armament and a speed superior to its contemporaries. This was of course the essence of the *Dreadnought*, and Cuniberti's ideas probably influenced Fisher to a considerable extent.[7] The Italians themselves did not immediately adopt the dreadnought type, but Cuniberti was responsible for the design of the "Regina Elena" class. These ships, projected around the turn of the century, were the result of Italy's membership in the Triple Alliance, and were designed with the idea of the French navy as their primary adversary. The Italians realized that they would not be able to wrest control of the sea from the French; but they did want units capable of contesting France's free use of the sea. They needed ships more powerful than French armored cruisers, and faster than French battleships. The four "Regina Elenas" (c. 12,700 tons) with a primary armament of two 12-inch guns and a speed of 21–22 knots were a result of this concept. These ships were relatively lightly armored, and some naval experts were reluctant to consider them true battleships. Their long period of construction diminished their value; when they finally entered service in 1907–08, their armament was generally recognized at inadequate.[8]

---

[5] Jack La Bolina, "Naval and Maritime Industries in Italy," *The Naval Annual, 1908*, pp. 160–161; Richard A. Webster, "Autarky, Expansion, and the Underlying Continuity of the Italian State," Paper read at the American Historical Association Convention, 30 Dec. 1964, pp. 3–5, 7–8.

[6] Clough, *Economic History of Italy*, p. 91; J. D. Scott, *Vickers—A History* (London, 1962), pp. 84–85. On English and French capital invested in Italy see also W. W. Gottlieb, *Studies in Secret Diplomacy during the First World War* (London, 1957), pp. 224–225; Feis, *Europe the World's Banker*, pp. 235–242.

[7] Marder, *Dreadnought to Scapa Flow*, I, 13 n. 6; Giorgerini and Nani, *Le Navi di linea italiane*, p. 8.

[8] *Ibid.*, pp. 170, 174–175.

The excessive length of time it took Italian yards to complete ships, as well as other charges of maladministration, formed the subject of an exhaustive inquiry in 1905–06 by a parliamentary commission. To the charge that inferior armor plate was being accepted from Terni in order to promote private industry, the navy replied that the Terni armor was much cheaper than that produced by Krupp, and the resistance of the plate, if not as good, was sufficient when put to a reasonable test.[9] Despite the criticism, Vice Admiral Carlo Mirabello, Minister of Marine from 1903 to 1909, continued development of the fleet. The naval law of July 2, 1905, provided for completion by 1910 of three large armored cruisers of the "Pisa" class (10,000 tons), ten destroyers, fifteen high-seas torpedo boats, and seven submarines.[10] Italy became one of the dreadnought powers with the naval law of June 27, 1909, which provided a series of steadily increasing appropriations for the expansion of the fleet by four dreadnoughts, three scout cruisers, twelve destroyers, thirty–forty torpedo boats, and twelve submarines.[11] The first dreadnought, the *Dante Alighieri* (19,500 tons), was laid down in June 1909, a year before the first French or Austrian dreadnoughts. The ship was to be capable of 23 knots; to save weight she was designed with four triple-gunned turrets, a novel conception at the time. The heavy artillery was provided by Armstrong-Pozzuoli, but was not ready until a year after the contract date.[12] As a result the ship was not ready until January 1913, after the Austrian *Viribus Unitis,* but before the French *Jean Bart* and *Courbet.*

The *Dante's* design followed the principles of Saint Bon and Brin in sacrificing protection to firepower and, above all, to speed. She was therefore criticized as being too lightly armored for a dreadnought, and remained the sole specimen of her type. The three other ships of the 1909 program, the *Conte di Cavour, Caio Giulio Cesare,* and *Leonardo da Vinci,* belonged to the improved "Cavour" class (23,088 tons) laid down in the summer of 1910. They had the heavier armament of thirteen 12-inch guns and more extensive armor protection. At the time of their commencement they were among the most powerful warships in the world but were quickly surpassed by the British "Orions" and the American *Texas.* Compared to their archrivals of the "Viribus Unitis" class, the "Cavours" were

[9] *The Naval Annual, 1906,* pp. 22–23; Ufficio Storico, *La Marina nel suo primo secolo,* p. 25.

[10] This was in addition to warships already under construction. V.D., "Italiens Flottenbaupolitik und das italienische Marine budget 1911/1912," *Marine Rundschau,* Aug. 1911, p. 985; Paladini, "The Italian Navy," p. 166.

[11] V.D., "Italiens Flottenbaupolitik," p. 987; *The Naval Annual, 1910,* p. 35.

[12] Giorgerini and Nani, *Le Navi di linea italiane,* pp. 184–187.

better armed (thirteen as opposed to twelve 12-inch guns), faster by at least one knot (21.5 knots), enjoyed a better radius of action and better accommodations for their crews, and were more suited to distant operations in the open sea. On the other hand, they were inferior in armor protection, secondary armament, and maneuverability.[13] In 1911 it was decided to add another two dreadnoughts to the program. The design chosen for the "Duilio" class (22,964 tons) was essentially the same as for the "Cavours" except for a heavier caliber secondary armament. The *Caio Duilio* and *Andrea Doria* were laid down in February and March of 1912 respectively.[14] By the spring of 1912 the Italian navy therefore had six dreadnoughts in varying stages of completion, and this alone made it an important factor in the calculations of naval staffs concerned with the Mediterranean. Added to this was the expectation that the Italians would begin still more and larger dreadnoughts with a heavier armament.[15]

The Italian dreadnought building program was fulfilled far more slowly than had originally been intended. Given the past performance of Italian yards, which were even slower than their much criticized French counterparts, it is somewhat difficult to understand why this came as a surprise to the naval staffs. The difficulty revolved less around the work in the yards themselves than around the supply of heavy cannon, turrets, and armor plate. The Italian steel industry was simply not up to the task. Terni had contracted to deliver 550 tons of armor plate per month for the *Cesare* and *Leonardo Da Vinci* starting in March 1911. By October of that year, they were already behind by 1700 tons.[16] This caused the navy to turn to foreign sources. An order for 4100 tons of plate was given to an American consortium formed by the Carnegie and Bethlehem Steel companies, but the plate supplied by Bethlehem proved unsatisfactory and its return entailed further delay.[17] There were also delays of a year in the delivery of the 12-inch cannon, a problem the *Dante* had previously ex-

[13] *Ibid.*, pp. 194–196, 198.

[14] *Ibid.*, pp. 205–208. Both the "Cavours" and the "Duilios" were also criticized for inadequate armor protection. See also J. V., "Les Cuirassées italiens type 'Conte di Cavour,'" *Le Yacht*, 1 June 1912, pp. 340–341.

[15] Sir Rennell Rodd, "The Annual Report for 1911," p. 33, enclosed with Rodd to Grey, 10 Feb. 1912, FO 371, vol. 1383, Italy, file 6027.

[16] Lieutenant de vaisseau d'Huart, French naval attaché in Rome, to Minister of Marine, 10 Mar. 1913, AMF, carton BB7-126. Similar problems in the delivery of armor plate had delayed the armored cruisers *San Giorgio* and *San Marco. The Naval Annual, 1910*, p. 36.

[17] D'Huart to Minister of Marine, 10 Mar. 1913, AMF, carton BB7-126; K.u.K., Chef des Generalstabes, "Jahresbericht über die Wehrmacht Italiens, 1913," Dec. 1913, p. 68, OK/MS-X-1/4, 1913. An overestimate of Italian capabilities is in *The Naval Annual, 1912*, pp. 335–337. See also *The Naval Annual, 1913*, pp. 46–47, 387–388; *The Naval Annual, 1914*, pp. 40–41.

perienced. These orders had been split among three companies: Vickers-Terni was to provide the cannon for the *Cavour* from their ordnance factory at La Spezia; Armstrong-Pozzuoli, the cannon for the *Cesare;* and Vickers and Armstrong in England, the cannon for the *Da Vinci.* Delivery of the heavy artillery for the "Duilio" class was also greatly retarded, and the *Andrea Doria* ultimately received the armament intended for the *Cavour.*[18]

In March 1913 the Minister of Marine, Vice Admiral Leonardi Cattolica, clashed with his predecessor, Admiral Bettolo, in the Senate over the responsibility for delays in naval construction. Bettolo blamed faulty coordination of technical and administrative functions; in reply the minister pointed to the weaknesses of Italian industry. Cattolica also considered the division of responsibility resulting from partial contracts for the same unit as a source of delay.[19] The chief of the Italian naval General Staff (Capo di Stato Maggiore), Vice Admiral Rocca Rey, also feared that future orders for new construction to Italian firms would not offer the proper guarantee of promptness. Moreover he advocated the complete independence of Italian firms from foreign firms because deliveries by the foreign firms were often excessively delayed, and he suspected these delays were not always due to purely incidental causes.[20] Lieutenant D'Huart, the French naval attaché, believed that part of the trouble was tardy placement of orders by the naval administration. D'Huart made a specialty of carefully analyzing Italian naval budgets, and in his opinion the real responsibility for the delays rested with the previous ministers, Admirals Mirabello and Bettolo, who entered into a naval program without having seriously studied it from the financial point of view. Consequently, while Italian naval progress was being admired abroad, the Italian navy was actually living on day to day expedients until the budget of 1913–14. D'Huart, who was an admirer of Cattolica, termed Italian budgets particularly confusing because of de facto subsidies which did not necessarily appear in the budget, and budgetary anticipations on the part of the naval administration. For example, the *Duilio* and *Doria* are first mentioned in the budget for 1913–14 although they were laid down in February and

---

[18] Giorgerini and Nani, *Le Navi di linea italiane,* pp. 197, 208. The *Cesare* and *Da Vinci* were completed in May 1914, but the *Cavour* was not ready until April 1915. The *Duilio* was finished in May 1915 and the *Andrea Doria* in March 1916.

[19] D'Huart to Minister of Marine, 20 Mar. 1913, AMF, carton BB7-126.

[20] Vice Admiral Rocca Rey, "Relazione di S.E. il Capo di Stato Maggiore circa il lavoro compiuto dallo Ufficio di Stato Maggiore della Marina dal Settembre 1911 al Marzo 1913," Mar. 1913, USM, cartella 286/6.

March of 1912, and the materials for their commencement assembled the previous fall. The naval budget traditionally seemed too low for the work on hand, and D'Huart considered them to be only the first approximation of expenses.[21]

Whatever the cause of the delays, the result was that the Italians lost their early lead over the Austrians in dreadnoughts, actually fell behind in 1913, and did not catch up again until the spring of 1914 nor move ahead until 1915.

With the exception of Japan and Russia, the Italian navy had the distinction of being the only major fleet to actually engage in a war in the decade prior to 1914. Italy's long-standing ambitions in Tripoli and the natural Turkish resistance to them, coupled with the favorable diplomatic situation from the Italian point of view following the Moroccan crisis, led to the outbreak of the Libyan War on September 29, 1911. With the tonnage of the Turkish fleet barely one seventh that of the Italian, and even this in a much lower state of efficiency, there could be no question of a major encounter at sea. The bulk of the Turkish fleet took refuge behind the Dardanelles, and the Italians occupied themselves in neutralizing the assorted gunboats and torpedo boats that remained dispersed about the Turkish empire.[22] Scattered actions took place at Prevesa in the Adriatic, where Austrian diplomacy sharply curtailed Italian activity; at Beirut, where the Italian action also offended neutrals; and in the Red Sea. The initial concern of the Italian navy was the landing of the expeditionary corps at Tripoli, where it provided the traditional offshore bombardment and landing parties for the capture of that port, and later Tobruk, Derna, Benghazi, Homs, and other points along the Tripolitan and Cyrenaican coast.

With the failure to achieve peace after the seizure of the coastal points, the Italian army found itself engaged in wearisome guerrilla warfare as it tried to extend its control to the barren interior. The campaign absorbed a considerable body of troops. By December 1911 over 76,000 officers and men were committed in Libya. By the middle of January 1912 the

[21] D'Huart to Minister of Marine, 1 Mar. 1913, AMF, carton BB7-126; 20 Jan. 1912, 10 Apr. 1912, 10 Aug. 1912, 20 Dec. 1912, carton BB7-125. The British naval attaché also commented on the preliminary work for the *Doria* and *Duilio* in advance of the official laying down. Naval attaché report in Rodd to Grey, 26 Feb. 1912, FO 371, vol. 1383, Italy, file 10541.

[22] Short accounts are in Ufficio Storico, *La Marina nel suo primo secolo*, pp. 119–129; Commander C. N. Robinson, "The Turco-Italian War," *The Naval Annual, 1912*, pp. 146–174; *The Naval Annual, 1913*, pp. 189–200; H. W. Wilson, *Battleships in Action* (London, n.d.), I, 266–274.

total had grown to over 84,200, and there was still no prospect of peace.[23] The Italians therefore turned their attention to the Aegean in an effort to force the Turks to terms. In April an Italian squadron dueled with Turkish batteries at the Dardanelles: at the end of the month and in the first part of May Italian forces seized Rhodes, Stampalia, and other islands in the Dodecanese. On the night of July 18–19 Captain Enrico Millo led five torpedo boats in a daring raid through the Dardanelles. Although he failed to reach the Turkish fleet, secure behind its boom defense, Millo was able to bring his forces back unscathed. The incident produced no military advantages but served as a tonic for Italian public opinion. These operations off the Dardanelles had less desirable consequences for the Italians by involving them with the great powers whose trade was threatened by a Turkish closure of the Straits.[24]

In its efforts to control contraband and prevent the smuggling of arms and ammunition to Turkish and Arab forces fighting in the interior of Libya, the Italian navy earned itself the unpopularity among neutrals normal to a blockading force. Probably the most serious incidents occurred in January 1912 over the French mail steamers *Carthage* and *Manouba*. On January 16 the *Carthage*, belonging to the Cie. Générale Transatlantique, was stopped off Sardinia by the old Italian torpedo cruiser *Agordat*. The *Carthage* was carrying an airplane destined for a French citizen in Tunis which the Italians feared would wind up in Turkish hands. The ship was taken to Cagliari and later released. On January 18 the *Agordat* stopped the *Manouba* of the Cie. Navigation Mixte, and she too was taken into Cagliari. The *Manouba* carried twenty-nine members of the Turkish Red Crescent, and the Italians suspected them of actually being officers and soldiers. The Turks were removed and the *Manouba* eventually allowed to depart. The firm demand of Poincaré and the French parliament that they be returned to French jurisdiction and the jingoistic tone adopted by the French press caused much ill feeling in Italy. Although the Italians released the Turks and agreed to submit the *Carthage* and *Manouba* incidents to the Hague Court for arbitration, the affair was a nasty break in the relatively good Franco-Italian relations that had prevailed since the Barrère-Prinetti agreements of 1902. The French had appeared as bullies in Italian eyes, and the frequent talk in France about naval su-

[23] Comando del Corpo di Stato Maggiore [Army], Ufficio Coloniale, "Specchio della forza del Corpo di occupazione della Libia all data del 10 Dicembre 1911," p. 8; "Specchio della forza alla data del 15 Gennaio 1912," pp. 6–9, USM, cartella 271/1.
[24] Ufficio Storico, *La Marina nel suo primo secolo*, pp. 127–128; William C. Askew, *Europe and Italy's Acquisition of Libya* (Durham, N. C., 1942), pp. 201f.

premacy in the Mediterranean was resented. The incidents undoubtedly pushed Italy temporarily closer to her Triple Alliance allies.[25]

The protracted Italian and Turkish negotiations eventually culminated in the formal signature of a treaty of peace at Lausanne on October 18, 1912.[26] The Libyan War obviously would have been impossible for Italy without her navy. At the end of May 1912 there were 91,405 officers and men in Tripolitania and Cyrenaica, and another 8878 in the Dodecanese.[27] The navy was therefore responsible for the safe transport and supply of approximately 100,000 men. If the war had brought it little glory in terms of combat at sea, the navy had nonetheless been constantly employed in the less glamorous but equally important functions of sea power.

For more than a year the fleet had been engaged in continuous steaming. Given the nature of the war, the heaviest burden had fallen on the light craft, whose machinery showed signs of excessive wear.[28] The navy therefore needed a period of rest during which material could be repaired, personnel reorganized, and training resumed. Officer instruction courses, for example, had been suspended during the war.[29] Both officers and men had gained much practical experience, but it was not always the sort which would be useful in a war against a maritime power. The French naval attaché—who was inclined to be somewhat patronizing toward his Italian colleagues—thought the Libyan War had deceived them by giving capital importance to secondary aspects of the profession such as combined operations with the army, landing parties, and coastal bombardments, while other subjects had suffered. D'Huart believed that success in these secondary operations had given the Italians an exaggerated con-

25 *Ibid.*, pp. 149–154, 156–159. Other incidents off Tunisia followed at the end of January, including the seizure of the French steamer *Tavignano* in what might have been Tunisian coastal waters. The Italians also agreed to arbitrate this. The Italians, frustrated at the continuance of the war, believed that supplies were reaching the interior of Libya from across both the Tunisian and Egyptian frontiers. *Ibid.*, pp. 154–156, 147–149.

26 A secret treaty signed at Ouchy on October 15 contained the real settlement. In brief, the Turks recognized Italian sovereignty over Libya, and the Italians recognized the spiritual primacy of the Sultan as Caliph. The Italians would evacuate the Dodecanese as soon as all Turkish forces had been withdrawn from Libya. *Ibid.*, pp. 243–245.

27 Comando del Corpo di Stato Maggiore, Ufficio Coloniale, "Specchio No. 11 indicante la force mobilata ripartita fra i vari presidi della Libia e dell'Egeo," n.d. [31 May 1912], p. 7, USM, cartella 271/1.

28 Ufficio Storico della R. Marina [Capitano di vascello G. Almagià and Capitano di corvetta A. Zoli], *La Marina italiana nella grande guerra*, vol. 1: *Vigilia d'armi sul mare* (Florence, 1935), pp. 11–12; Commandante Guido Po, *Il Grande Ammiraglio Paolo Thaon di Revel* (Turin, 1936), p. 50.

29 Vice Admiral Thaon di Revel, "Relazione sintetica sull'opera svolta dal 1 Aprile 1913 al 1 Ottobre 1915," 1 Oct. 1915, p. 1, USM, cartella 1451/740.

fidence in their aptitude and training, and a real maritime war would be a painful awakening.[30] Rear Admiral Paolo Thaon di Revel, Capo di Stato Maggiore from April 1913 until October 1915, recognized this when he assumed office, but also faced the problem that the Balkan crisis, and the continuing military requirements of the guerrilla war in Libya, which dragged on after the treaty of peace, did not permit the Italian navy to resume its normal life until the summer of 1913.[31]

The Libyan War occurred during the period when Rear Admiral Pasquale Leonardi Cattolica was Minister of Marine. Cattolica, who held the portfolio from April 1910 until July 1913, was a scholarly and jovial Neapolitan. He belongs to the type of reforming administrator who came into office during the decade before the First World War. Fisher and Churchill in England, Delcassé in France, Grigorovitch in Russia, and to a somewhat lesser extent Montecuccoli in Austria-Hungary were the leading examples. As the Italian navy declined in world rank in the 1890's, the judgments of foreign observers about its efficiency were far from complimentary.[32] Its somewhat leisurely training persisted into the twentieth century, with the number of ships in full commission greatly reduced six months out of the year. The units commissioned in the spring would undertake a cruise to the Levant, conduct gunnery exercises, add somewhat heterogeneous new elements for summer maneuvers, and then return to La Spezia to wait for the following year, during which time much of the training gained might be lost. Cattolica changed all this, reorganizing the squadrons so as to enable ships and men to spend more time at sea in full commission.[33] He improved conditions of pay, pension, and advancement for all ranks, and sought to rejuvenate the somewhat formalist and senescent higher command with more active and younger leaders. This was largely accomplished through a pruning of the officer corps with compulsory retirements.[34]

Compulsory retirements naturally aroused a good deal of discontent, and the procedures and decisions of the selection committees involved in the promotions and retirements were not infallible. There were some who

[30] D'Huart, "Rapport annuel, 1912," 30 Dec. 1912, AMF, carton BB7-125.

[31] Thaon di Revel, "Relazione sintetica," 1 Oct. 1915, p. 1. See also Admiral Alfredo Acton, "La Marina di guerra, 1900–1925," *Rassegna Italiana,* 16.91 (Dec. 1925): 746–747.

[32] For reports by British naval officers in 1892 see Marder, *Anatomy of British Sea Power,* pp. 172–173. For the situation in 1896–1897 see *ibid.,* p. 271.

[33] D'Huart, "Rapport annuel, 1911," 20 Jan. 1912, AMF, carton BB7-125. Also Sir R. Rodd, "Annual Report for 1911," 10 Feb. 1912, p. 33, PRO, FO 371, vol. 1383, file 6027.

[34] D'Huart, "Rapport annuel, 1913," 30 Dec. 1913., AMF, carton BB7-126.

questioned the wisdom of many of the retirements at a time the navy was thought to suffer from a shortage of officers. The minister was also criticized for his lack of enthusiasm for the new construction demanded by the Lega Navale, the Italian naval league, and other navalists, however well grounded on financial and technical reasons his actions might have been.[35] The minister's position was undermined as his enemies grew. A former minister, Vice Admiral Bettolo, was now head of the Lega Navale and one of those pressing for new construction. In the Senate Cattolica faced increasing opposition from retired admirals and others hurt by his policies. Within the fleet itself he was most commonly criticized as being more of a scholar than a sailor, and lacking in an appreciation of the real needs of the navy. He was also accused of wanting character, and of having sacrificed the navy during the Libyan War to the exigencies of the President of the Council of Ministers, Giovanni Giolitti. This charge actually reflected frustration over the restriction of naval activities because of diplomatic considerations. The Senate, which had approved the naval budget in May by a vote of 72–45, passed Cattolica's bill for the reorganization of naval personnel by a scant 58–56 in June. A disastrous blow to his prestige occurred when one of the admirals he had retired assaulted him in the street and was ultimately given only a suspended sentence.[36]

Cattolica resigned July 29, 1913, and Giolitti immediately chose as his new Minister of Marine Rear Admiral Enrico Millo, hero of the Dardanelles raid and one of the youngest flag officers in the navy. Giolitti may not have been entirely free from cynicism in this choice, for Millo was likely to follow Cattolica's policies, but with his war record would be popular with the public and strong vis à vis the navy, yet sufficiently weak vis à vis Giolitti.[37] After nearly a year as minister, Millo's personal position had

[35] *Ibid.;* Korvettenkapitän Johannes Prince von und zu Liechtenstein, Austrian naval attaché in Rome, to Marinekommandant, 1 July 1913, OK/MS-X-1/2, 1913. Liechtenstein apparently did not completely share his French colleague's high regard for Cattolica.

[36] D'Huart to Minister of Marine, 10 Aug. 1913, AMF, carton BB7-126; Liechtenstein to Marinekommandant, 30 July 1913, OK/MS-X-1/1, 1913; K.u.K. Chef des Generalstabes, "Jahresbericht über die Wehrmacht Italiens, 1913," 21 Dec. 1913, p. 35, OK/MS-X-1/4, 1913; Luigi Albertini, *Venti anni di vita politica*, pt. I: *L'Esperienza democratica italiana dal 1898 al 1914*, II (Bologna, 1951), 223–224.

[37] D'Huart to Minister of Marine, 10 Aug. 1913, AMF, carton BB7-126. The Austrian naval attaché reported the rumor, particularly strong in nationalist circles, that Giolitti had become alarmed at the growing opposition to Cattolica and chose Millo in order to win nationalist votes for his government. Liechtenstein to Marinekommandant, 30 July 1913. The Austrian ambassador also reported that a friend of Cattolica's who was threatened with bankruptcy received a letter from the minister concerning anticipated orders by the navy for shipbuilding materials. The individual attempted to use the letter to obtain bank credit and the affair became known, making Cattolica's resignation unavoidable. Méry to Berchtold, 31 July 1913, HHSA, XI-148.

weakened. The departure of Giolitti from office in the winter of 1914 left him somewhat in the air, and his relatively young age and junior rank raised eyebrows in the Italian Senate and among flag officers in the navy. In professional circles he was criticized for losing himself in questions of detail with matters never coming to a head.[38] Shortly after the outbreak of war and the declaration of Italian neutrality Vice Admiral Leone Viale became minister.

The war with Turkey quickly revealed to the Italian navy its deficiency in light vessels. The complete lack of scouts prevented enemy movements from being followed immediately, and necessitated long and useless precautionary measures against possible attacks by Turkish torpedo boats. The lack of light craft to serve as escorts or scouts forced the use of large units for these tasks, resulting in an unjustified expense and a dangerous division of force. The scarcity of destroyers, and the small displacement of those which were available, imposed a heavy burden on these ships and caused excessive wear to their machinery. Admiral Rocca Rey, chief of the naval General Staff, therefore recommended that construction of large destroyers of at least 800 tons proceed at the same pace, if not actually precede, that of the dreadnoughts.[39] The admiral realized that Italy did not have the financial means to emulate Great Britain, Germany, and Japan in the construction of battle cruisers, nor did he consider them necessary for his country's Mediterranean objectives. He therefore advised that all efforts be concentrated on providing the Italian fleet with a nucleus of dreadnoughts and the necessary number of light units. At least ten protected cruisers of around 3,000 tons especially adapted for colonial service were also needed.

Rocca Rey pointed to the development of the Austro-Hungarian fleet as the principal concern. He argued that Italy ought never fall behind in total number of ships, and that each Italian ship should always be more powerful than a similar Austrian ship. The chief of the naval General Staff wanted the Italian building program to be aimed at assuring as soon as possible a fleet of sixteen battleships, with nothing older than the two "Brins" (completed 1904–1905); eight scouts; and twenty-four destroyers. And Rocca Rey's predecessor had estimated the previous July that seventy-two coastal torpedo boats and forty-six submarines would be needed for

[38] D'Huart to Minister of Marine, 30 June 1914, AMF, carton Ea-139.
[39] Vice Admiral Rocca Rey to Minister of Marine, 12 Dec. 1911, USM, cartella 204/2.

coastal defense.[40] To achieve this strength, after taking into account those modern vessels in service or under construction, it would have been necessary to provide for the construction of an additional four dreadnoughts, five scouts, fourteen destroyers, twenty-six submarines, and seven colonial ships. Rocca Rey knew that the Italian yards were saturated with work and could not build the desired number of ships in a short time, even if parliament were to provide the necessary funds. He therefore scaled down his immediate requirement to three scouts, fourteen destroyers, twelve submarines, and two colonial ships.[41] The reduction in the number of submarines by more than half was justified by the slight probability that Italy would find herself faced with an Adriatic and Tyrrhenian war—that is, against both Austria and France—at the same time. The Comitato degli Ammiraglio accepted Rocca Rey's proposed structure for the fleet and advised that the navy in achieving it always endeavor to maintain a superiority over the Austrians of at least two dreadnoughts and a corresponding number of scouts and destroyers with the object of remaining the second Mediterranean naval power.[42]

Approximately a week before the treaty of peace with Turkey was signed Admiral Rocca Rey prepared a lengthy memorandum for Giolitti on the naval situation. In it he claimed that the advantage Austria-Hungary derived from the configuration of the Adriatic coast resulted in the fundamental principle that even with parity in the number of ships, valor and ability of personnel, and distribution of armaments and material, the Italians would always be inferior to the Austrians. This was because of the necessity of the Italian fleet to remain at sea for long periods of time exposed to the ambushes and attacks of torpedo boats hidden along the Istrian and Dalmatian coasts, and the obligation of dividing its forces after a few days for coaling. The Austrian fleet, concentrated among the islands, would be able to remain united and ready to pounce upon the

[40] They were to be deployed thus: six submarines and twenty torpedo boats at Venice; four submarines and four torpedo boats at Ancona; six submarines and four torpedo boats at Brindisi; six submarines and twelve torpedo boats at Taranto; six submarines and twelve torpedo boats at Messina; six submarines at Naples; six submarines and eight torpedo boats at Maddalena; and six submarines and twelve torpedo boats at La Spezia. *Ibid.*

[41] *Ibid.* He had, however, received funds from the Ministry of the Treasury for the construction of the two "Duilios" which would shortly be officially laid down.

[42] "Organico della Flotta approvato dal Comitato degli Ammiragli nel febbraio 1912," n.d., USM, cartella 260/4. The planned totals were: sixteen battleships, eight scouts, twenty-four squadron destroyers, seventy-two torpedo boats (including high-seas torpedo boats and 300–400-ton destroyers), twenty-five submarines, and ten colonial ships.

Italian forces at the opportune moment. These considerations had led the naval staff to recommend to the Commissione Suprema per la Difesa dello Stato in a session at which Giolitti presided at the end of 1908, that the Italian fleet be maintained in the proportion of 2:1 over the Austrian.[43] It was not possible to attain this. The Stato Maggiore, calculating the respective tonnages and number and caliber of cannon, estimated the ratio between the two fleets to have fallen to 1.24:1 in Italy's favor in 1904, and then to have climbed to 1.8:1 in 1908. With the "threatening impetus" given to the Austrian navy by the work of Montecuccoli, the ratio fell to 1.5:1 in 1911 and would be only 1.3:1 and 1.2:1 in 1913 and 1914, respectively, when the Austrian dreadnoughts entered service.[44] Other considerations such as the defensive qualities of the Austrian ships, the distribution of their artillery, and the building by the Austrians in homogeneous groups of three or four, were notable advantages for the Austrian fleet. In October 1912 the chief of the naval General Staff did not hesitate to consider the Austrian fleet equal, if not superior, to his own in its material. He claimed this was in direct opposition to the opinion prevalent in Italy, which considered the Italian navy incontestably superior to that of Austria.

With the laying down of the *Duilio* and *Doria* the Italians had hoped to achieve a slight superiority over the Austrians at the end of 1914. But the fact that the *Dante* would enter service later and the *Viribus Unitis* earlier than anticipated, a situation which was evident in October 1912, and the obvious intention of the Austrians to replace the three "Monarchs" in the near future, threatened Italian hopes of maintaining a lead. Assuming that the *Duilio* and *Doria* would be completed by 1915–16, the Stato Maggiore feared that six Italian dreadnoughts might be faced by seven Austrian dreadnoughts.[45] At this date the *Filiberto* and *Saint-Bon,* roughly

[43] Ufficio del Capo di Stato Maggiore, "Promemoria sulla potenzialità della Marina rispetto a quella austro-ungarica e alla nuova situazione Mediterranea," 9 Oct. 1912, USM, cartella 331/3. The report to the Commissione is in Ufficio Storico, *La Marina italiana nella grande guerra,* I, 260–261.

[44] "Promemoria sulla potenzialità della Marina," 9 Oct. 1912. These calculations coincided with the Austrian estimate of 1.25:1 in 1905–06. It is interesting to compare, however, Montecuccoli's thoughts on a war with Italy and his calculation of the future ratio of strength which he presented to the Emperor in March 1912. The Austrian estimates are completely at variance with those of the Italians; they foresaw an Italian superiority of 1.7:1 at the end of 1912, 1.6:1 at the end of 1913, and 1.8:1 at the end of 1914.

[45] "Promemoria sulla potenzialità della Marina," 9 Oct. 1912. The Italians obviously expected the Austrians to lay down the substitutes for the three "Monarchs" in 1913 and probably could not have known the extent to which efforts of the Marinesektion to accomplish this had been frustrated by the Hungarians, nor the slow fulfillment of the Austrian program the rigid financial controls necessitated once approval had been obtained.

contemporary with the "Monarchs," would also have to be replaced. The efficiency of all other Italian units, when compared to their Austrian opposites, had also been impaired by the rigors of a year of war. In addition to the wear on their machinery, the life of their heavy artillery had been shortened. In general the fleet required a period of extensive repair to its engines and boilers, replacement of worn barrels of its heavy artillery, and the replenishment of depleted munitions. Surveying the situation, the Stato Maggiore concluded that the fleet would need to have ready an additional four dreadnoughts in 1918–19, two to replace the *Filiberto* and *Saint-Bon,* and two to maintain superiority over the Austrian fleet. They also recommended that provision for the additional dreadnoughts be made immediately, since experience with the present building program showed the necessity for preparing studies and ordering the required materials for large ships well in advance. The Stato Maggiore assumed that the projected ships of both nations would be roughly equal in power, armor, and speed, and that the Italians would then have ten dreadnoughts against seven for Austria, giving a ratio of 1.43:1. Actually it would have been lower, 1.25:1, for the Austrians eventually decided to replace the *Habsburg* at the same time as the three "Monarchs."

Admiral Rocca Rey estimated that he would need three scout cruisers, two of which were urgent, to maintain a sufficient lead over the Austrians. The Austrian *Admiral Spaun* was already in service, and three other modern scout cruisers were under construction. Of the Italian scout cruisers, the *Quarto* was in service and two more would be ready in 1913. Rocca Rey also cited the need for at least four colonial ships, two for Tripolitania and two for Cyrenaica, and restated the necessity of reinforcing the worn-out torpedo boats. Torpedo boats would be particularly valuable in Adriatic operations. Outmoded artillery defending the fleet's bases had to be replaced, and their defenses against submarines improved. It was also necessary to create a coastal aviation service and imitate other nations in a more extensive use of submarines to defend the long Italian coastline.

The bulk of this memorandum, which Rocca Rey prepared near the close of the Libyan War, concerned the relation of the Italian fleet to the Austrian, and clearly revealed his and the Stato Maggiore's anxiety over the narrowing gap between the strength of the two. But the Adriatic was no longer their sole preoccupation, for the acquisition of Libya and the development of the Entente Cordiale in the Mediterranean had created a new political situation in which the British and French naval forces might weigh heavily in case of a European war. The Capo di Stato Maggiore concluded that whatever Italy's future policy, her fleet must be strong enough to have a deterrent value.

The possibility the Italian navy would be involved in a war against France on the side of the Triple Alliance increased during the winter and spring of 1913 as negotiations for a new Triple Alliance naval convention were in progress. The plans for the 1913 naval maneuvers which Rear Admiral Thaon di Revel, new Capo di Stato Maggiore, presented for ministerial approval had a decidedly anti-French tone. They were to be held in the Tyrrhenian with Maddalena playing a central role, and one of the strategic themes involved the interception of a simulated convoy heading from North Africa to Toulon.[46]

Revel, a member of a distinguished Piedmontese family whose father had been a minister to King Carlo Alberto, had assumed office on April 1, 1913. He was one of those mentioned by the French naval attaché as representative of a new spirit in the Italian navy.[47] The future ratio of the Italian navy to its possible rivals, Austria and France, was not very reassuring to the new head of the Stato Maggiore. Using the year 1918 as a term of reference, he posed as a premise the absolute necessity that the fleet be maintained at a minimum of 60 percent of the French fleet and four thirds that of Austria.[48] This was certainly less than the 2:1 ratio which had been recommended in 1908, but Revel thought it could be accepted given the present improved relations with Austria and the tightening of the bonds of the Triple Alliance.

By Revel's calculations the ratio of French dreadnoughts to Italian would be 2.9:1 in 1918; the Austrians would have an advantage of 1.45:1. Only in terms of large destroyers would the Italians have their desired 60 percent ratio to the French fleet. They would have the necessary fourth-thirds superiority over Austria in large destroyers and submarines, and a slight superiority in pre-dreadnoughts and torpedo boats. Revel's conclusion was an Italian requirement by 1918 of no fewer than nine dreadnoughts in addition to those presently projected or under construction. He considered this minimum program perfectly feasible through the commencement of four ships (including the three Type "L" already projected for the near future) in 1913, two in 1914, three in 1915, and three at the beginning of 1916. This was certainly an ambitious program far in advance of Italy's past performance in shipbuilding. But Revel had definitely

[46] Revel to Minister of Marine, Apr. 1913, USM, cartella 303/2. Instructions to Commander-in-Chief, First Squadron, Apr. 1913, *ibid.*

[47] D'Huart, "Rapport annuel, 1913," 30 Dec. 1913, AMF, carton BB7-126; D'Huart to Minister of Marine, 30 June 1914, AMF, carton Ea-139.

[48] Revel to Minister of Marine, 25 July 1913, USM, cartella 331/3.

overestimated the number of dreadnoughts available to Austria and France in 1918. By his calculations the French would have had twenty-six dreadnoughts, which was an absurdly high figure since the French program of 1912, even after its acceleration, had as its goal twenty-eight first-class battleships in 1920. This total included six "Dantons" and five "Patries," thus leaving only seventeen dreadnoughts, or possibly twenty after the acceleration of the French program. Unless Revel counted the "Dantons" and "Patries" as dreadnoughts it is difficult to account for his mistake save as a deliberate exaggeration. Even then one might have argued about counting the semi-dreadnought "Dantons," and by no stretch of the imagination could the "Patries" be considered dreadnoughts.[49] The estimate of thirteen probable Austrian dreadnoughts in 1918 is also too high. Even if the three "Radetzkys" are considered dreadnoughts, the Austrians would not have had more than ten or eleven. It is of course easy with the benefit of hindsight to criticize the Stato Maggiore for what are apparently sloppy calculations. One must remember the atmosphere in which these prewar naval rivalries took place. The fear that a rival would secretly lay down ships or accelerate his program was a very real one, and the commencement of new construction in advance of budgetary provisions had occurred in both Italy and Austria. It was therefore simple, if not tempting, for a naval staff to overestimate a rival's strength and even capacity.

Revel was initiating a new emphasis in Italian naval policy when he proposed a notable increase in the number of large destroyers and submarines from the total recommended previously by the Comitato degli Ammiragli. The latter had specified twenty-four large destroyers and twenty-five submarines. Revel wanted, in addition to the twenty-four or twenty-five coastal submarines which would be assigned to the defense of naval bases, another sixteen large submarines to cover the Ligurian coast, and twenty-four large submarines for offensive operations in the western basin of the Mediterranean. Counting those submarines under construction and excluding the three oldest submarines already in service, Revel's plans would have meant the construction of an additional three small submarines for coastal defense, and forty large submarines suitable for long range operations. He also wanted the number of destroyers in the proposed establishment (*Organico*) of the fleet to be more than doubled to sixty-four. This would have entailed an additional thirty-four destroyers

---

[49] If the "Dantons" and "Patries" are included as eleven of the presumed twenty-six French dreadnoughts in 1918, Revel's figure becomes plausible. In mid-1913 there were four "Courbets," and three "Bretagnes," in varying stages of completion. Therefore the projected "Normandies" and "Lyons" would account for the remaining eight.

(800–1000 tons) by 1918 over and above the number existing or under construction. To provide the necessary funds Revel was willing to forego the further building of scout cruisers. In the Italian theater of operations, he thought that the scouting duties normally given to cruisers could be assumed by large destroyers without excessive inconvenience. In addition, auxiliaries, which had given good service in the Libyan War, could be used for scouting. Revel was also willing to make do for a few years with old ships for colonial service and, save for those units already under construction, refrain from building any vessels especially for this purpose. The funds thus saved could be applied to destroyers and submarines.[50]

Revel's plans are most interesting for their large provision for submarines, a service which had generally been neglected by the Italians until then, according to the French naval attaché.[51] The fact that the bulk of these were destined either for the protection of the Ligurian coast or for offensive operations in the western basin of the Mediterranean also indicates that the Italian navy during the summer of 1913 was apparently taking quite seriously its possible obligations under the Triple Alliance.

This anti-French orientation was also manifest in a September 1913 memorandum on Maddalena, which Revel considered likely to be one of the first French objectives in case of hostilities because of its strategic importance and proximity to the Corsican coast. He deemed it urgent that the island's defenses be improved, since they were essentially in the same condition as when first set up thirty years before. The artillery of the defensive works was outmoded, and the works themselves were sited too close to the anchorage of the fleet. The ability of the Italian navy to make use of Maddalena in time of war was of vital importance to Revel: its location and double exits made it the sole position that would permit a struggle for control of the Tyrrhenian and western Mediterranean against a superior fleet. Its strategic position was very different from the other Italian bases, since it was a position of maneuver without any possible substitute, rather than a center of refuge. Revel believed that, given their inferiority of naval force, without the support of Maddalena Italy's fate on the sea must be considered highly precarious.[52]

Lieutenant General Alberto Pollio, chief of the army General Staff,

[50] Revel to Minister of Marine, 25 July 1913, *ibid.*

[51] D'Huart to Minister of Marine, 20 Mar. 1913, AMF, carton BB7-126; "Rapport annuel, 1913," 30 Dec. 1913, *ibid.*

[52] Revel, "Promemoria sulla Piazza di Maddalena," 3 Sept. 1913, USM, cartella 2390/10. Revel did not mention it in his memorandum, but the island was also to serve as a base for operations by the Austro-Hungarian and German naval forces in the Mediterranean under the Triple Alliance naval convention concluded the previous June.

warmly supported Revel's desire to increase submarine strength. Pollio, a firm champion of the Triple Alliance, was appalled at the anticipated ratio of submarine strength between Italy and France in 1920 (3.75:1), for he considered submarines an indispensable weapon for a nation with the weaker fleet and a long and exposed coastline. He was particularly concerned over the vulnerable state of Genoa and other maritime centers on the Tyrrhenian, and called the immediate acquisition of an adequate number of submarines not only justified but imperative. Aside from the material effects of an unexpected attack on the coastal cities, the morale effect produced on the entire country would be disastrous and might thereby influence land operations. Pollio went so far as to advocate the renunciation of some of the costly colossuses which would henceforth form part of the fleet in order to obtain the necessary means for submarine defenses.[53]

Revel agreed with Pollio about the battleships to a certain extent. Because of the complex and varied needs of the fleet in regard to training, secure bases, and docking and supply facilities, he concluded that until the naval budget rose beyond 230 million lire, no more than 46 percent or 105 million could be spent on new construction. Of this total a maximum of 80 million should be for battleships and no less than 25 million for smaller craft.[54] Revel suspected that the decisive battle at sea might not occur in the first few days of a war. A momentary tactical inferiority to the enemy might require a period of delay during which time the fact that the Italian squadron was ready to follow-up a fortunate torpedo attack might restrain an enemy from operating against the Italian coast, or else force him to pay for his boldness. To purge their own waters of enemy torpedo boats and secure the movements of their warships, the Italian torpedo boats and submarines would not remain in their bases but would be employed intensively from the very beginning of hostilities, particularly if the combat took place in the Adriatic. There would undoubtedly be frequent encounters with inevitable losses, and it was therefore necessary that the Italians have at least as many of these small units as the enemy they were likely to face. Revel had closed a memorandum the previous month with the statement that the question of maritime defense imposed the dilemma of either adapting the naval preparations—with the consequent financial burden—to foreign policy, or else harmonizing the policy with the armaments which financial means permitted. He now pointed out that an expensive battleship represented a considerable portion of a

---

[53] Pollio to Revel, 24 Mar. 1914, USM, cartella 323/8.
[54] Revel to Minister of Marine, 27 Apr. 1914, USM, cartella 331/3. The lire in 1914 was worth approximately 20 cents (U.S.).

fleet's offensive power, and that the loss of a single one to a submarine or torpedo boat would not be compensated by an analogous loss to the enemy as might be the case in a regular battle. Revel stressed the technical progress of submarines and torpedoes, as well as the vulnerability of large ships to underwater weapons. He therefore favored a battleship of not more than 26,000 tons and costing less than 80 million lire.

Revel and Pollio were actually objecting to the design for the next group of Italian super-dreadnoughts, ultimately called the "Caracciolo" class. Their plans had been the subject of lengthy discussion and much controversy since 1910. They were originally to have had 14-inch guns, a larger caliber than the 12-inch weapons of the first Italian dreadnoughts, and in February 1912 their displacement was specified as 27,000–29,000 tons, with a speed of 23–25 knots.[55] By 1913 the decision was taken to increase the caliber of their armament to 15-inches, and the final project accepted in 1914 was for a 34,000-ton super-dreadnought with eight 15-inch guns and a designed speed of 28 knots. The Italian navy was following its past tradition of technical daring, for these ships, roughly analogous to the British "Queen Elizabeths," would have had the most powerful armament in the Mediterranean. Their French and Austrian contemporaries were to have either 13.4-inch or 14-inch guns and would be a few knots slower. However, like the French "Normandies" and "Lyons," and the Austrian "Ersatz Monarchs," the four "Caracciolos" were destined never to be completed.[56] Lieutenant General Edgardo Ferrati of the Naval Engineers, who was responsible for the project, had planned an even larger ship, but had to scale it down as a result of strong opposition based on cost, which might have reached 120 million lire, and the adequacy of Italian docks and bases to handle the mammoth. Cuniberti, now a Major General in the Naval Engineers, was one of the strongest opponents of the huge ship, and enlisted the support of General Ugo Brusati, King Victor Emmanuel's aide-de-camp, who interceded with the sovereign on his behalf.[57] Cuniberti had been far from happy over the time lost to the navy because of the battleship dispute and repeated changes of plan. He favored a 25,000-ton 25-knot project, and remained opposed to the final choice of his rival Ferrati's more ambitious project.[58]

[55] Comitato degli Ammiragli, "Programma Tecnico Militare per il Progetto delle Navi Maggiori da Battaglia," Feb. 1912, USM, cartella 260/4.

[56] Giorgerini and Nani, *Le Navi di linea italiane*, pp. 213–214, 216–218.

[57] Cuniberti to Brusati, 21 Mar. 1913, Archivo Centrale dello Stato, Rome (EUR) (hereafter cited as ACS), Carte Brusati, cartella 10/VII-3-43; Cuniberti to Brusati, 30 May 1913, *ibid.*, cartella 10/VII-1-41.

[58] Cuniberti to Brusati, 30 Oct. 1913, *ibid.*, cartella 10/VII-3-43.

The cost of the scaled-down "Caracciolos" would still be in the neighborhood of 100 million lire each, and this did not sit well with Revel who wanted a more generous portion of the naval budget applied to submarines and destroyers. During the period of Italian neutrality after the European war had broken out, he proposed that Giuseppe Orlando, whose firm was not scheduled to begin construction of the fourth and last ship in the class until the end of 1915, be asked to agree to the construction of a ship for only 80 million. It would retain the armament of eight 15-inch guns, but displacement and cost would be reduced by giving it a lower speed and less extensive armor plate. The 20 million saved could provide four 680-ton destroyers and eight 250-ton submarines.[59] However, the new Minister of Marine, Vice Admiral Leone Viale, did not consider it opportune to give up the construction of the fourth "Caracciolo," but declared his intention to attribute a larger portion of future budgets to the construction of destroyers and submarines.[60]

In the fall of 1914 the Stato Maggiore suspected that whatever the outcome of the war the naval balance in the Mediterranean would be violently disturbed, and the close balance which prevailed before the war between the British and French forces on one side and the Austrian and Italian on the other would be lacking. An Entente victory might see France predominant in the Mediterranean and possibly the French flag in Syria as a reward for her sacrifices. A German victory with consequent domination in the Balkans would make Germany a Mediterranean power where her fleet, supported by Turkey's, might become more powerful. Moreover the war, with its weakening of both victor and vanquished, would not render a new conflict less possible if Italian weakness permitted the anticipation of an easy victory. Italy therefore had to bend every effort after the war and in the period 1916–1920 to maintain a force proportionately inferior to her present force in regard to the battle squadron, and superior in respect to destroyers and submarines.[61]

While Revel was less enamoured of the battleship and perhaps paid more attention than some of his contemporaries to the destroyer and submarine, this interest tended to take the form of opposing excessive expenditure on what he considered abnormally large dreadnoughts rather than a significant de-emphasis of the dreadnought itself. Revel still feared that after a period of maximum efficiency in 1915–1916 when the last of

[59] Revel to Viale, 24 Sept. 1914, USM, cartella 331/3.
[60] Viale to Revel, 10 Oct. 1914, *ibid.* The ship was laid down in Oct. 1914 but work was suspended in 1916.
[61] Unsigned memorandum, "La Situazione navale italiana nel 1916–1920," 12 Oct. 1914, USM, cartella 296.

the 12-inch gun dreadnoughts entered service, the fleet would pass through a grave crisis in the years 1916–1918 when no large unit would reinforce it until the "Caracciolos" entered service in 1918. He estimated that the fleet in this period would be three dreadnoughts short of the desired 1.33:1 predominance over Austria, and five dreadnoughts short of the required .6 proportion to France.[62] He therefore proposed that Italy acquire two or three dreadnoughts abroad. This was a much more realistic appraisal and a considerable reduction from his request for nine the previous year. Revel thought that the *Rivadavia* and *Moreno,* two dreadnoughts under construction in the United States for the Argentine government, might be purchased, and he recommended them from the technical point of view.

On the destroyer question Revel advised the construction or acquisition of thirty-six including, possibly, those currently being built at the Pattison Yards near Naples for Rumania. His object was to form twelve destroyer flotillas of six units each by 1918. In view of Italy's exposed coastline and in the interest of economy, Revel was ready to reduce the number of desired long-range submarines. He now wanted the immediate acquisition or construction of twenty-four coastal submarines of around 300 tons to be ready if possible in 1916. His immediate requirement for offensive, long-range submarines was only twelve. However, if the experience with this type of submarine proved to be favorable it would be followed by a second series of twelve. If it was not favorable, coastal submarines would be substituted. It should be remembered that these were merely plans, and that the experiences of the war modified the number and type of vessels that actually entered service with the Italian navy.[63]

The studies and plans made by the Italian navy for possible operations against their Austrian ally and traditional rival are dominated by the conviction that the geography of the Adriatic basin with the numerous islands and the irregular configuration of the Dalmatian coast was entirely favorable to the Austrians. The Austrians, secure from surprise behind the natural defensive line Pola-Sebenico-Cattaro, could undertake operations against the Italians at the best time or place. This was the premise stated by Vice Admiral Giovanni Bettolo, Capo di Stato Maggiore from April 1907 until May 1911, in a study on war against Austria written in 1909.[64] The Italian side of the Adriatic was devoid of natural protection,

[62] Revel to Minister of Marine, 7 Nov. 1914, USM, cartella 331/3.
[63] Ufficio Storico, *La Marina nel suo primo secolo,* pp. 27–28.
[64] "Studio di preparazione militare marittima per un conflitto armato contro l'Empero Austro-Ungarico," n.d. [1909], pp. 4f, USM, cartella 296.

and the great naval bases of Venice and Taranto were considered too eccentric to adequately cover it. Brindisi was a port it would be opportune to fortify and provision because of its position in relation to the probable line of Italian operations, and the short railway connection uniting it to Taranto. Bettolo believed the attitude of the Austrian fleet would be one of waiting in a fortified base for an opportunity to attack the Italian fleet. The Italian fleet would be held under the threat of attack, and forced to keep to sea under difficult conditions. The Italians must therefore undertake a diversionary action to force the enemy to come out for a decisive battle which would give the victor command of the sea.

Admiral Bettolo did not believe that coastal bombardments by the Italians would have the desired effect, nor would the results be commensurate with the risks involved. Most of the Dalmatian coast was of minor importance, and Fiume was too well protected because of its proximity to Pola. Trieste was an attractive target, but operations in the Gulf of Trieste were perilous, and to reach it the fleet would have to traverse the length of the Adriatic exposed to torpedo boat attacks from the Dalmatian coast. Even if they succeeded in provoking an encounter in the Gulf of Trieste, Bettolo thought the Italians would be at a disadvantage after the battle. The Austrians would have Pola to fall back on while the Italians would have Venice. But the logistical and strategic capacity of Venice was far inferior to that of Pola. Some form of territorial occupation would be preferable, and Bettolo discussed the possibility of seizing and using as a temporary base one of the more southerly islands off the Dalmatian coast, notably Lesina or Curzola.[65]

Bettolo was a firm believer in the value of a commercial blockade of the Strait of Otranto to cut off trade from Trieste and Fiume with the Mediterranean. Aside from the financial damage this would cause to the enemy, he believed the blockade would make a profound impression on public opinion and might affect the loyalty of the Dalmatian region to the central government. Moreover the imposition of such a blockade would signify virtual control of the sea; this could be tolerated by the enemy fleet only at the expense of its own dignity and the morale of its crews. Closure of the sea routes to Austro-Hungarian ports would therefore constitute a diversionary action with nearly certain results, and the almost inevitable encounter would take place under conditions more favorable to Italy since

[65] *Ibid.*, p. 10. A staff officer had previously prepared a study on the occupation of the valley of Cittavecchia on the island of Lesina to serve as a temporary base: "Formazione d'una base navale passeggera su territorio nemico," enclosure V: "Studio in caso di conflitto fra l'Italia e l'Austria," 14 Sept. 1907, USM, cartella 199/5.

the Austrians would be forced to operate in the southern portion of the Adriatic far from their main base of operations.[66]

Bettolo realized that the cities of the Adriatic coast were exposed to raids, and that Venice, Ancona, and other minor ports might be attacked before the fleet could concentrate. Venice, in addition to naval considerations, had its own importance as a military camp threatening the flank of an enemy army advancing in the Po valley. But Bettolo concluded that the defense of Venice ought to be based on itself. He absolutely opposed the fleet dispersing and wearing itself out rushing to the defense of whatever locality might be threatened. Its primary objective must be the destruction of the enemy fleet. Once this was achieved the defense of the coast would implicitly follow. The bulk of Italy's first-line force would therefore concentrate at Taranto, and then operate in the triangle Brindisi-Viesti-Cattaro. To guard against enemy raids, or force the employment of more considerable forces in them, the four armored cruisers of the "San Giorgio" class would cruise from Viesti northward. Ancona would be the northern limit of their operations so that the fleet would not be deprived of their services. This flying squadron was to avoid becoming engaged with a superior force. The defense of the coast between Ancona and Venice would be left to torpedo boats and submarines.[67]

The more elaborate and detailed war plans which the Stato Maggiore prepared on Bettolo's directive also considered the possibility that the Austrian fleet would concentrate at Cattaro and assume the offensive with an attack on Brindisi or an advance into the Ionian in an attempt to defeat the Italian squadrons either before they had completed their concentration at Taranto, or as they entered the Adriatic should their concentration already have taken place.[68] This contingency could not be dismissed because of the aggressive tradition left the Austrian navy by Tegetthoff, the recent speeches of Montecuccoli, the current building program, and the fact that the Austrian fleet had concentrated at Cattaro during the Bosnian crisis in 1908. Obviously the bases of Taranto and Brindisi would have to be kept at full efficiency, completely garrisoned, and with sufficient material to supply the fleet, which should concentrate at Taranto during the period of diplomatic tension.[69] On receipt of intelligence that the Austrian fleet was at Cattaro, it would be necessary for scouts based on Brindisi to watch the enemy and inform the Italian Commander-in-Chief of his movements.

[66] Bettolo, "Studio," pp. 11–12.

[67] *Ibid.*, pp. 13–15, 23–27.

[68] Ufficio di Capo di Stato Maggiore, "Appendice alle 'Considerazioni Generale sopra un conflitto armato in Adriatico,'" n.d. [1909–1911], pp. 1–2, USM, cartella 312.

[69] *Ibid.*, p. 2.

Once concentrated, the Italian fleet would establish a distant blockade of Cattaro should the Austrian fleet still be there. The Italians would be based on Brindisi for supplies. Along with the establishment of the blockade, the Italians planned a secondary operation to destroy the coastal railway linking Cattaro to the rest of Austria-Hungary.[70] An Austrian attack on Brindisi was not feared. Brindisi was 108 miles from Cattaro and 146 miles from Taranto. If the Italian scouts were efficient in reporting the Austrian movements, the Italian fleet could reach Brindisi a few hours after the enemy, and it was assumed Brindisi could offer sufficient resistance in the meantime. Should the Austrians enter the Ionian the problem was simplified for the Italians who would try to separate them from their bases before attacking. Bettolo's plan appears to have been kept up to date through appendices and annotations in 1911 and 1913.[71]

The Stato Maggiore also studied the possibility of a maritime expedition of at least corps strength against the Austrian Empire once control of the sea had been won, but this was largely from a strictly nautical point of view regarding feasible landing sites.[72] The possibilities were: Trieste and the Bay of Muggia for a corps cooperating with an advance by the Italian army over the eastern frontier; Gravosa-Ragusa for an operation in southern Herzegovina, particularly in cooperation with concurrent action from across the Montenegrin and Serbian borders; Cattaro, for a combined action with the fleet to deprive the Austrians of the naval base; and Spaleto, which was rejected because of various natural difficulties. In the course of 1909 the Ministers of Foreign Affairs and War also assigned the army General Staff the task of planning for the mobilization of an army corps destined eventually to land in Eastern Europe.[73] These amphibious operations were merely staff studies naturally dependent on winning supremacy at sea. Given these plans—which involved avoiding a commitment of the bulk of

[70] *Ibid.*, pp. 5–6. The plan was for three "Garibaldis" (armored cruisers), four destroyers, and some torpedo boats to land about three hundred men—sailors, sappers, and infantry—to destroy a section of the Cattaro railroad in the section Ragusa Vecchia–Castelnuovo. Allegato all' Appendice, "Azione contro la ferrovia Ragusa Vecchia–Castelnuovo," *ibid.*, pp 9–11.

[71] Enclosure III concerning the Adriatic coast of Italy bears an annotation dated 1911; enclosure VIII concerning procedures for economical use of engines is dated 13 Feb. 1913; enclosure X contains the order of battle for 1913. The dossier containing the plan is dated 1914 and there are various annotations in what appears to be Revel's handwriting.

[72] Capitano di corvetta P. Orsini, "Studio summario circa una spedizione marittima dall'Italia contro l'Empero Austro-Ungarico," Mar. 1909, USM, cartella 119.

[73] Comando del Corpo di Stato Maggiore, Riparto Operazioni, Ufficio Coloniale to Capo di Stato Maggiore (Marina), 8 July 1909, USM, cartella 119/7. The question of a special corps for operations in Eritrea was also studied. Memorandum by Pollio, 28 Feb. 1909, *ibid.*

the fleet in the northern Adriatic and an attempt to draw the Austrian fleet out of Pola to the southern Adriatic for the decisive battle—the general form the maritime war actually took when Italy entered the struggle in 1915 can hardly be surprising.

During and after the Balkan Wars with their accompaniment of shifting and disputed boundaries the Italian fleet was used to underscore Italian diplomacy in much the same way as the fleets of other powers. Italian interests were particularly concentrated on Albania, and intervention at Valona was seriously contemplated in the spring of 1913.[74] The Marquis di San Giuliano, Minister of Foreign Affairs, consulted the chiefs of both the army and navy general staffs on the most desirable borders to claim for the new state in the peace negotiations. The navy's position was to extend the boundary of Albania as far south as possible so that the Albanians would share domination of the internal basin of Corfu with the Greeks. The logic behind this was simple. The navy was anxious to prevent the establishment of a foreign naval base close to the Strait of Otranto and considered Greece far more likely than Albania to develop naval power.[75] When it became apparent that the more extreme claims advanced on behalf of Albania could not be sustained for political reasons, the Stato Maggiore advised insisting on the proposal for the neutralization of the Corfu Channel.[76]

The Austro-Hungarian government, which had its own ambitions about eventually bringing Valona and the Corfu Channel within its sphere of interest, was equally concerned with the neutralization of the Corfu Channel. The Marinesektion considered the monarchy's position as a great power, as well as its economic well-being, dependent on the assurance of open communications between the Adriatic and the Mediterranean under all circumstances.[77] The two allies therefore reached an agreement between

[74] Ufficio Storico, *La Marina italiana nella grande guerra,* I, 19–21, 40f. For the tangled diplomatic background see Helmreich, *Diplomacy of the Balkan Wars,* esp. ch. XIV.

[75] Rocca Rey to Minister of Marine, 17 Mar. 1913; ACS, Presidenza Consiglio, Gabinetto, Atti 1913 (hereafter cited as Presidenza Consiglio), fascicolo 9/2.

[76] Revel to Minister of Marine, 12 Apr. 1913, enclosed with San Giuliano to Giolitti, 14 Apr. 1914, *ibid.* The army General Staff did not consider a guarantee of neutrality by the powers to be enforceable in time of war. Comando del Corpo di Stato Maggiore, Riparto Operazioni, Ufficio Coloniale, "Promemoria circa la proposta neutralizzazione del Canale di Corfu," 3 Apr. 1913, *ibid.* The protracted correspondence is also summarized in Ufficio del Capo di Stato Maggiore, IV Riparto, "Riassunto di lettere e dispacci del Marzo al Aprile 1913, riguardi la frontiera Greco-Albanese," Aug. 1919, USM, cartella 288/1. A small collection of documents relating to the subject is reproduced in Ufficio Storico, *La Marina italiana nella grande guerra,* I, 389–396.

[77] Report PK/MS no. 3402, 22 July 1913, "Korfu Channel," 31 July 1913, MKFF/41-60, 1913. On the Austrian navy's own aspirations for Valona see draft memorandum by the Marinekommandant to the Minister of Foreign Affairs, n.d. [late 1912], MKFF, Mm/107, 1912.

themselves on a neutralization project to be presented for the approval of the other powers.[78] The islands of Corfu and Paxio along with their dependencies and territorial waters extending six miles out to sea, the Corfu Channel between 39°5' and 40° north latitude, and a zone along the mainland side of the channel six nautical miles wide were to be considered neutral. No naval or military force, except that which was strictly necessary to maintain public order and collect state revenues, was to be stationed there. No fortifications or military harbors were to be erected in the enumerated territory.[79]

The British Foreign Office objected to certain points in the Austro-Italian proposal, and the Admiralty were not ready to admit that territorial waters could extend beyond three marine miles.[80] The British and French differed in their proposed reply, but the issue was not a burning one and it was not until July 1914 that Serge Sazonov, Russian Foreign Minister, suggested the French and Russian ambassadors in London meet with Grey to draft a formal reply.[81] All three were soon at war with Austria-Hungary.

The question of the neutralization of the Corfu Channel, as well as the disputed southern boundary of Albania, was linked to the Aegean islands. The Italians had occupied the Dodecanese during the Libyan War. And a number of islands had been seized by the Greeks in the Balkan War which followed. The Italian action in the spring of 1912 provoked a warning from the Admiralty that possession by Italy of naval bases in the Aegean would imperil the British position in Egypt, cause the loss of British control over the Black Sea and Levant trade at its source, and in war expose the route to the east via the Suez Canal to the operations of Italy and her allies. Admiralty policy in the past had been based on the condition that British interests in the eastern Mediterranean could be threatened only by hostile fleets operating from countries a thousand miles distant from the area, and that the movements of these fleets could be observed and controlled by British forces based on Malta. The cardinal factor of this condition was that no strong naval power should permanently occupy any territory or

[78] San Giuliano to Millo, 3 Dec. 1913, USM, cartella 298/1. On the potential threat to Austrian and Italian operations by Greek destroyers and submarines, possibly assisted by a British flotilla in the event of war, see the interesting dispatch by the British naval attaché in Rome, Captain W. H. Boyle, enclosed with Rodd to Grey, 16 Dec. 1913, *BD*, vol. X (pt. 2), no. 439, p. 641.

[79] "Projet concernant la Neutralisation du Canal de Corfu," communicated by the Austro-Hungarian embassy 22 Dec. and the Italian embassy 24 Dec. 1913, FO 371, vol. 1656, Greece, file 57763.

[80] Admiralty [O. Murray] to Foreign Office, 24 Jan. 1914, FO 371, vol. 1995, Greece, file 3849; Grey to Bertie, 2 Mar. 1914, *ibid.*, file 3334.

[81] Bertie to Grey, 19 Mar. 1914, *ibid.*, file 12283; Cambon to Grey, 9 May 1914, file 21036; Cambon to Grey, 7 July 1914, file 30880; Foreign Office to Cambon, 27 July 1914, *ibid.*

harbor east of Malta capable of being transformed into a fortified naval base. Therefore the occupation by Italy or any other naval power of any of the Aegean islands was strenuously opposed. The potential danger was increased by the withdrawal of British battleships from the Mediterranean.[82]

Under the terms of the peace treaty with Turkey the islands were to be evacuated by the Italians once all Turkish troops and officers had departed from Libya. Given the circumstances of the guerrilla war the Italians found on their hands as they sought to consolidate their control over the new colony, this provision was subject to endless dispute. The Italians claimed Turkish soldiers were involved in the fighting. The situation was aggravated by the Balkan upheavals during which the Greeks seized other Aegean islands, and the Italians stayed on, to the intense suspicion of Britain and France. San Giuliano clearly realized that unless circumstances changed it would not be possible for Italy to keep any of the islands because of the opposition of the Triple Entente. Moreover if the principle that none of the great powers draw territorial advantages from the Balkan crisis was broken, the results would be threatening for European peace. The probable advantages gained by possession of some of the islands would thus be minor compared to the peril for Italy's major interests. San Giuliano thought Giolitti was in a better position than he to prepare public opinion for relinquishing the islands. He was afraid that Austria might use a prolonged occupation of the islands to claim some compensation. He also warned that all their political expedients would not suffice to guarantee Italian interests in the anticipated debacle of Asiatic Turkey if they were not linked to and publicized by serious economic activity in the zone the Italians coveted.[83]

San Giuliano favored the eventual evacuation of the islands as a means for obtaining advantages from either Greece or Turkey.[84] He was looking beyond the Dodecanese toward the creation of an Italian economic sphere of influence in Asia Minor, and realized that he would probably have to reach an agreement with Austria who had shown interest in the same zone as the Italians.[85] While reducing the size of Italy's zone, this would offer the advantages of introducing Austria-Hungary as a new political and military factor in the Mediterranean to oppose French or Anglo-French

[82] Admiralty memorandum [Rear Admiral E. T. Troubridge], "Italian Occupation of Aegean Islands and Its Effect on Naval Policy," 20 June 1912, Admiralty Archives case 0091.

[83] San Giuliano to Giolitti, 17 July 1913, ACS, Carte Giolitti, busta 29, fascicolo 90.

[84] Memorandum by San Giuliano, n.d. [19 Aug. 1913], *ibid.*

[85] San Giuliano to Giolitti, 21 Aug. 1913, *ibid.*

hegemony, increase Italian influence in both the Triple Alliance and the Triple Entente, guarantee Italy against French oppression, and distract Austria from the desire for absolute predominance in the Adriatic. For San Giuliano possession of part of the coast of Asiatic Turkey with its corresponding hinterland was more important to Italy as a coefficient of the balance of power in the Mediterranean than as a necessary colonial possession. Libya, Somalia, and Eritrea were more than sufficient for Italy's economic potential for many years.[86]

In connection with these ambitions in Asia Minor, an Italian cruiser was directed in September 1913 to survey the coast of Turkey between the Gulf of Mendelyah and Alaja and subsequently to visit the ports of Malori and Marmaritza and the coast from Cos to Alaja.[87] French and British plans to cruise in the Mediterranean in November led San Giuliano to believe it a mistake for the Italian fleet to be represented at Rhodes by only a single warship, and after correspondence between the Ministries of Marine and Foreign Affairs, a naval division commanded by the Duke of the Abruzzi was ordered to Rhodes and Anatolia for a goodwill visit.[88] San Giuliano did not think that Italian public opinion would permit any ministry to evacuate the Dodecanese without some material and moral satisfaction which would assure Italian interests and prestige in the Mediterranean, and he intended to use the islands as a lever to obtain this.[89]

It would seem that the Admiralty's fears about a naval base in the Aegean were groundless and that the Italians actually intended to retrocede the islands to Turkey as San Giuliano had always affirmed in his conversations with the British and French ambassadors. But if the islands themselves were to be returned to Turkey, the Italians still intended to develop a net of interests in them, and the Ministry of Marine wanted these to include a coaling station.[90] For this purpose the navy recommended

---

[86] San Giuliano to Garroni, Italian ambassador, Constantinople, 10 Sept. 1913, *ibid.*

[87] San Giuliano to Millo, 22 Sept, 1913, and Millo to Commander of *Amalfi*, 30 Sept. 1913, USM, cartella 318/2; San Giuliano to Millo, 22 Oct. 1913, cartella 286.

[88] San Giuliano to Millo, 25 Oct. 1913, and Millo to Commander-in-Chief, Second Squadron, 26 Oct. 1913, *ibid.* San Giuliano's letter to Millo and the Duke of the Abruzzi's account of the rather chilly meeting with the French squadron off Rhodes—the French seemed on the verge of steaming past without saluting the Duke's flag until the latter saluted first—are reproduced in Ufficio Storico, *La Marina italiana nella grande guerra*, I, 398–399.

[89] San Giuliano to Tittoni, ambassador in Paris, 28 Dec. 1913, ACS, Carte Giolitti, busta 15, fascicolo 21. Later in 1914 Garroni advised against linking the question of concessions in Asia Minor with the evacuation of the Dodecanese and the alleged Turkish nonfulfillment of the Treaty of Lausanne. See Garroni to San Giuliano, 19 July 1914, Ministero degli affari esteri, *I Documenti diplomatici italiani* (hereafter cited as *DDI*), 4th ser., vol. XII (Rome, 1964), no. 357, pp. 235–238.

[90] San Giuliano to Millo, 5 June 1914, USM, cartella 335/4.

the island of Leros where coaling stations were to be established at Laki on the southwest coast and Parthani on the north. (Both anchorages were needed so as to prevent a rival power obtaining the other in the future.) Admiral Millo was willing to leave to the Ministry of Foreign Affairs the task of determining under what legal form the concessions might be obtained. He forwarded sketches and maps indicating likely sites for the installations, and referred to the two anchorages as forming the embryo of an eventual Italian support base (*base di appoggio*) in the Aegean.[91] A confidential agent, Baron Giuseppe Lazarrini, was sent to the Dodecanese to sound out the proprietors of the land in which the navy was interested. Lazarrini was to correspond with the Ministry of Marine by cypher, and San Giuliano emphasized that it was necessary for the Foreign Ministry to remain absolutely extraneous to the mission.[92]

Lazarrini left Rome for the Dodecanese June 30 and returned July 24. In this fateful month during which the great powers drifted toward war, Lazarrini concluded a few preliminary contracts subject to the confirmation of the Italian government for the rental of land on Leros at both Laki and Parthani, and prepared a report of more than twenty typewritten pages on the Dodecanese. Lazarrini admitted he was speaking as a layman judging the case without any knowledge of secret diplomatic agreements and obligations which could prejudice the question. He recommended a minimum number of islands that Italy endeavor to keep. These included Leros and the islands inseparably linked to it from the military point of view: Lipos and Patmos to the north, and Calimnos to the south. The little group of islands was reminiscent to Lazarrini of the small islands closing the Zara Channel off Dalmatia. With their numerous harbors, bays, and gulfs, they were well adapted to ambushes, would permit ships to slip easily from one sea to another, and dominated the shortest maritime route between Constantinople, Smyrna, and the Suez Canal. Lazarrini believed that Leros by itself would be only an indifferent port, but joined to the surrounding islands, it would form a far from negligible system of naval bases which, though not another Malta, would always be sufficient in pro-

[91] Millo to San Giuliano, 13 June 1914, *ibid.;* Millo refers to a letter of 23 April in which he advanced these views. An unsigned and undated note of the naval staff refers to Parthani as a coaling station for light craft and torpedo boats, and Laki for large ships; USM, cartella 335/4. The sites had already been surveyed by an Italian naval vessel; Report of R.N. *Dandolo,* no. 96, RR, 2 May 1914, *ibid.*

[92] San Giuliano to Millo, 18 June 1914, *ibid.* The Foreign Ministry assumed the expense of the mission aside from the cost of the voyage which would be partially reimbursed. See also "Appunti consegnati al cifrario Mengarini B.L. al Barone Lazarrini il 30 Giugno 1914," *ibid.*

portion to Italy's interests and future in the Levant.[93] Lazarrini had hardly returned when the European war broke out and the kingdom of Italy declared her neutrality.

One of the four contracts Lazarrini had signed involved the subletting of land belonging to the Monastery of Patmos on the bay of Parthanisis. The monastery subsequently protested that its tenant had no right to sign such an agreement. This brought the matter to the attention of the Italian military authorities on Rhodes who were somewhat piqued because Lazarrini had been very vague to them on the nature of his mission.[94] The correspondence thus generated gave Revel the opportunity to press the new Minister of Marine, Vice Admiral Viale, for a decision.[95] Revel approved the provisional contracts and Lazarrini's conclusions concerning the Cos-Patmos chain, but doubted some of the suggestions the baron had made concerning the use of the other islands, particularly Nisero and Piscopi, as bargaining points. If Italy wanted only to procure a good permanent military position in the Aegean, Revel thought the Cos-Patmos chain would suffice, and he was disposed to abandon all the other islands if necessary, including Rhodes. However, if the government wanted to take into consideration economic and sentimental factors as well as strictly military ones, Revel advised keeping the chain from Rhodes to Patmos, for the abandonment of Nisero and Piscopi would create a gap from which nothing but harm would come.[96] Sidney Sonnino, who had replaced San Giuliano as Foreign Minister after the latter died in October, agreed to assume the burden of the rents for the property in question, but repeated the condition that the Foreign Ministry remain apparently extraneous to the question.[97]

There is a wide disparity between the ambitions of Revel and Lazarrini in the Dodecanese and the rental of some land on Leros for the eventual creation of a coaling station. It is also interesting to watch these ambitions

[93] "Relazione della missione eseguita nel Dodecanneso dal Barone Lazarrini," n.d. [July 1914], pp. 5–7, USM, cartella 335/4. The chain Lazarrini recommended also included Cos, Cappari, and the minor islands of Levita and Candeliusa.

[94] Regio Commissariato per l'Amministrazione delle Isole dell'Egeo, to Minister of War, 21 Sept. 1914, and Minister of War to Minister of Marine, 1 Oct. 1914, USM, cartella 335/4.

[95] Revel to Minister of Marine, 17 Oct. 1914, and Viale to Revel, 20 Oct. 1914, *ibid.* Viale seemed equally in the dark on Lazarrini's mission which had been arranged before he assumed office.

[96] Revel to Viale, 4 Nov. 1914, *ibid.* In Revel's opinion Simi could probably be excluded as too close to the Anatolian coast, and Stampalia, Caso, and Scarpanto could be abandoned as having neither military nor economic value.

[97] Sonnino to Viale, 28 Nov. 1914, and Viale to Revel, 5 Dec. 1914, *ibid.*

expand from a few anchorages on Leros to the Cos-Patmos chain, and then to the Rhodes-Patmos chain or the majority of islands in the Dodecanese. Exactly how much opposition the erection of an Italian coaling station on Leros—which was San Giuliano's modest objective in the spring of 1914—would have met on the part of Great Britain and France once it became public cannot be known. By the time the Italian Foreign Ministry approved the provisional contracts for the rental of the necessary land, both nations were involved in a war in which Turkey, to whom the Italians were bound by treaty to return the islands, had joined the opposing side. It was therefore an open question.[98]

With her long coastline and populous ports exposed to attack, and her navy notably weaker than that of a suspicious and none too friendly France, the extent to which Italian naval forces could have been committed away from home in adventures among the Dodecanese in case of war with a major maritime power is questionable. The memoranda of Admirals Rocca Rey and Thaon di Revel seem primarily concerned with more immediate problems in the Adriatic or Tyrrhenian. Captain Boyle, the British naval attaché, believed that acquisition of Tripolitania and Cyrenaica had actually weakened Italy by increasing her dependence on the sea and vulnerability to naval attack. He indicated the fallacy of the popular assumption that because Italy held both shores of the central Mediterranean she would be able to control it: this would require a fleet strong enough to deny passage to the ships of two powers, Great Britain and France, who had excellent bases adjacent to the waters in dispute.[99] At the end of 1912 the French naval attaché also reported that the Italian fleet could not think of engaging the French fleet without risking a disaster because of the numerical and technical inferiority of its ships and the state of its training, which had fallen off during the Libyan War. Moreover, at the moment, Taranto was unable to serve as sole naval base thereby forcing a dangerous division of forces between it and La Spezia.[100] This confident French attitude was manifest in the offensive strategy Lapeyrère intended to employ: coming to grips with the Italian fleet as soon as possible should Italy and France find themselves on opposing sides in a war.

A year later, however, the French attaché sounded a note of alarm. He

---

[98] In a note to the Italian ambassador, Churchill indicated that the attitude of the Admiralty toward Italy as a potential ally, and not a potential foe through membership in the Triple Alliance, was changed. See Imperiali to San Giuliano, 28 Aug. 1914, *DDI*, 4th ser., vol. I, no. 474, pp. 260–262; San Giuliano to Imperiali, 29 Aug. 1914, *ibid.*, no. 497, p. 275; San Giuliano to Tittoni and Carlotti, Italian ambassador to St. Petersburg, 25 Sept. 1914, *ibid.*, no. 803, pp. 475–477.

[99] Report by Capt. Boyle in Rodd to Grey, 16 Dec. 1913, *BD*, X (pt. 2), pp. 640–642.

[100] D'Huart to Minister of Marine, 30 Dec. 1912, AMF, carton BB7-125.

still considered the Italian navy clearly behind the French at approximately the state the French found themselves in 1906. But, he added, if one took account of the distance the Italians had already come, it was necessary for the French to be on guard in the future and to keep their lead. He warned that by 1917 an Italian fleet led by vigorous new chiefs, and with a dozen dreadnoughts based on Maddalena, might constitute a danger.[101] This danger might have materialized sooner if the Italians, instead of being forced closer to the Triple Entente powers by their maritime vulnerability as the British naval attaché and many others in England confidently believed, turned toward close naval cooperation with their Austrian rival and ally whose fleet was no longer to be disdained. This is exactly what had already happened in the spring and summer of 1913. By the outbreak of the World War the Triple Alliance had a naval convention and elaborate plans for joint operations in the Mediterranean.

[101] D'Huart to Minister of Marine, 30 Dec. 1913, AMF, carton BB7-126.

VIII

The Triple Alliance Naval Convention of 1913

A combining of the naval forces of Italy and Austria-Hungary was a contingency that deeply preoccupied the naval staffs of Great Britain and France. Although such a combination was frequently mentioned during the discussions on Mediterranean naval policy which accompanied the major Anglo-French redeployment in 1912, its possibility in the event of war did not become real until the following year. On the whole the naval aspects of the Triple Alliance appear to have been rather neglected. Perhaps this was a reflection of the comparative lack of interest in maritime affairs which prevailed among these powers, with the obvious exception of Italy, until almost the end of the nineteenth century. After prolonged negotiations a naval convention outlining cooperation at sea in the event of war against France and Russia was signed at Berlin on December 5, 1900.[1] Somewhat unrealistically each fleet was assigned a separate zone of operations in which it was to obtain control of the sea and prevent the union of enemy forces so as to defeat them separately. The German zone included the Baltic, North Sea, English Channel, and Atlantic Ocean adjacent to Europe; the Austrian zone, the Adriatic up to the parallel of Santa Maria di Leuca; and the Italian zone, the western basin of the Mediterranean from the Straits of Gibraltar to the line Cape Santa Maria di Leuca—Ras el Tin (Cyrenaica). The Mediterranean to the east of this

[1] A. F. Pribram *The Secret Treaties of Austria-Hungary*, Eng. ed. by Archibald Cary Coolidge, II (Cambridge, Mass., 1921), 87–88, 115. Pribram was unable to locate this treaty in the State Archives; *ibid.*, p. 115. See also Sokol, *Österreich-Ungarns Seekrieg*, p. 43. A copy may now be found in the archives of Archduke Franz Ferdinand's Militärkanzlei. See MKFF/41-25/6, 1913. Italian documents on the 1900 convention are in USM, cartella 176/2. The text of the treaty has been printed by G. Ducci, "Accordi e convenzioni durante la Triplice Alleanza," *Rivista marittima*, 68.3 (Mar. 1935): 282–287.

line was considered a common zone for Austria and Italy. The supreme command in case of joint operations was determined by seniority and size of force, and in any case normally belonged to the commander of the nationality in whose zone the operations occurred.[2] Such joint operations were mentioned in only the vaguest of terms.

The Italians originally wanted to include the eastern Mediterranean in the Austrian zone. The Austrians rejected this, claiming that the types of ships in their fleet restricted it to a defensive attitude in the Adriatic. Even within the Adriatic the Austrians were reluctant to commit themselves to anything beyond the defense of their own coast, although they accepted in principle the idea of cooperation with Italian forces left there for coastal defense.[3] This was little help to the Italians who would be faced by a superior French force in the Tyrrhenian, and Rear Admiral Grenet, the Italian naval delegate to the conference which drew up the treaty, proposed that a study be made into the possibility of uniting the fleets of all three countries to prevent the French from defeating each of them separately. He was particularly interested in obtaining German naval support in the Mediterranean if it appeared at the beginning of hostilities that the greatest French naval effort would be concentrated in the south. But Vice Admiral Otto von Diederichs, chief of the Admiralstab was unenthusiastic about the idea, and doubted that a combined fleet of this size would have the means to support itself outside of its own waters. He claimed that Germany's naval strength was not yet sufficient for her to detach part of her fleet to the Mediterranean, and then blockade or destroy the French forces in the north with the units remaining at her disposal. Reinforcement of the Italians in the Mediterranean was not possible for the next three or four years, and even then it would be totally dependent on the French deployment.[4]

The convention included the usual provisions about reciprocal use of each other's ports, requisition of merchant shipping, and relations between allied ships outside of the Mediterranean. A commission met in Rome the following summer to discuss a common cipher and recognition signals. By October 1901 a signal code for the allied fleets had been prepared. In 1901 and 1902 the three navies traded intelligence, mostly on the French

[2] Ducci, pp. 273–275, 282–284; Sokol, *Österreich-Ungarns Seekrieg*, p. 43.

[3] Processo verbale, "Commission chargé d'établie des règles générales pour l'emploi des flottes des nations de la Triple Alliance en temps de guerre," 5 Nov., 8 Nov., 10 Nov. 1900, USM, cartella 176/2. The commission met at the offices of the Admiralstab under the presidency of Vice Admiral Otto von Diederichs and included army as well as naval representatives from the three nations.

[4] *Ibid.*, 10 Nov., 12 Nov., 14 Nov. 1900.

and Russian fleets, and in these and following years the commanders of allied ships in Chinese waters also exchanged communications with each other.[5]

The naval convention of December 1900 continued in force until November 1913, but within a few years of its signature it was already a dead issue, something to be mentioned in standing orders for ships on foreign stations and to be stored securely in embassy safes and accounted for in annual inventories. After the initial exchange of information there are few documents relating to it in the archives. This is hardly surprising, for the cooperation envisaged was largely ephemeral. Collaboration between the Italians and the Austrians outside of the Adriatic had been rejected by Austria, and the passing of naval superiority from France to Germany paradoxically lessened the likelihood of significant German support to Italy in the Mediterranean. This was because of the effect German naval development had on Great Britain and the ensuing Anglo-German naval competition which concentrated the attention of both fleets on the North Sea. As a result, and despite the concern of the British and French naval staffs, the Italians in the summer of 1912 were still left to face the weight of the French fleet by themselves in the Tyrrhenian, at least as far as a formal naval convention was concerned.

In 1900 the Italians were certainly more interested in obtaining German rather than Austrian naval support. Given the nature of the Austrian fleet, whose most important units were then the coastal defense battleships of the "Monarch" class, this is understandable. The Austrians themselves were quite ready to admit their maritime limitations and disclaimed a more ambitious role for their fleet. But there is a vast difference between the capabilities of the "Monarchs" and dreadnoughts like the *Viribus Unitis* which were entering service in the summer of 1912. The German Admiralstab naturally watched Austrian naval development with benevolence, and in 1909 spoke of it as a threat to British lines of communication in the Mediterranean which would relieve pressure on their own fleet in the North Sea.[6] Two years later the German naval attaché in Vienna happily spoke of the possibility, in the event of war, of the Austrian fleet, joined with the requisite number of transports, being directed against Egypt, which he considered the weakest point in the British position. He regarded the projected withdrawal of the British battle squadron from

---

[5] "Triplice Codice di Segnali," Rome, 1901, USM, cartella 295/1, 180/2, 180/3; "Signal Codex für Verbundeten," GFM 26, reel 61, frame 297, 301f.

[6] Memorandum by chief of the Admiralstab, 20 Apr. 1909, GFM 26, reel 68, frame 661–668.

Malta in the spring of 1912 as leaving the Austrian fleet free for action in the Eastern Mediterranean.[7] That summer the Kaiser, in speaking of the British and French naval displacements to Count Hieronymus Colloredo-Mannsfeld, the Austrian naval attaché in Berlin, stressed the importance of a common advance by the Austrian and Italian fleets. He hoped that the future development of the Austrian navy would meet with no interruption and exuberantly spoke of "ejecting" (*hinauszuwerfen*) the English and French from the Mediterranean.[8] The Kaiser's motives at that particular moment were transparent, for with characteristic loquaciousness he freely expressed to the Austrian officer his resentment and low opinion of Churchill. He described the First Lord of the Admiralty's removal of naval forces from the Mediterranean as an unsuccessful effort to intimidate Germany out of plans for naval expansion.

By 1913 the situation had also changed for Italy, who drew somewhat closer to the Triple Alliance as the result of the Tripolitan War. Italian ties to the Triple Alliance had been weakened by the Barrère-Prinetti agreements of November 1902 in which Italy agreed to remain neutral in case France was the object of direct or indirect aggression, or in case France declared war as a result of direct provocation. The terms of the Triple Alliance specified Italian assistance to Germany only in the event of an attack without direct provocation. However the interpretation of exactly what constituted "direct provocation" was naturally subject to Italy's discretion, and the Franco-Italian accords of 1902 might be considered a violation of the spirit, if not the letter, of the Triple Alliance.[9]

But a distinction must be made between the Triple Alliance itself, which was renewed in December 1912, and the separate military and naval conventions which were to take effect only after the *casus foederis* had arisen. Moreover, the Italian naval and military chiefs pursued their preparations in ignorance of the exact terms which bound them to their allies. When General Pollio, chief of the Italian army General Staff, asked the terms of the Triple Alliance, he was merely told that the treaty contained no military clauses which he needed to know, and that naturally he would be informed with priority by the government whenever the probability of a war presented itself.[10] If the actions of both the Italian military and naval staffs sometimes seem overenthusiastic and at variance with Italian di-

---

[7] Naval attaché, Vienna (Graf Posadowsky) to Staatssekretär, Reichsmarineamt, 12 Aug. 1911, GFM 26, reel 94, frame 79; 12 Apr. 1912, frame 85–86.

[8] Colloredo-Mannsfeld to Marinesektion, 20 Aug. 1912, PK/MS-XII-2/1, 1912.

[9] Fay, *Origins of the World War*, I, 146–148.

[10] San Giuliano to Giolitti, 7 Dec. 1912, ACS, Carte Giolitti, busta 12, fascicolo 9; San Giuliano to Spingardi (Minister of War), 10 Dec. 1912, *ibid.*

plomacy and public opinion, it is well to bear in mind this lack of communication.[11]

The incidents arising out of the Libyan War, notably the *Carthage* and *Manouba* affairs, while minor in themselves, jarred Italian confidence in friendship with France and "left a sense of mortification and disappointment" which required considerable time to remove.[12] It was this residue of ill feeling in June 1912 which led Sir Rennell Rodd to warn that if British interests in the Mediterranean were left to France, as the impending naval redeployment seemed to indicate, the prospect of Italy becoming the "mere vassal of the Triple Alliance" was greatly increased through lack of a balancing weight to the unpopular but feared Germany and Austria.[13]

News in 1912 of the planned concentration of French battleships in the Mediterranean also created a strong impression in Italy, which the German and Viennese press sought to exploit by insinuating that the measure was especially directed against the Italians. The French chargé d'affaires in Rome cautioned of the danger that the imprudent language of portions of the French press, in which certain editors spoke chauvinistically and tactlessly of "l'empire de la Méditerranée" played the game of Italy's allies.[14] Poincaré quickly sought to convince the Italians of the defensive nature of the projected naval displacement, and informed them its sole object was to assure the transport of troops from Algeria in the event of war with Germany.[15] San Giuliano appeared to accept these French promises about respecting the legitimate interests of Italy and denials of any intention of turning the Mediterranean into a "French lake." He replied to the French chargé that his government did not see in the French naval measures any suspicious intention in its regard.[16] He was also inclined to dismiss the value of the six old battleships involved in the transfer, and told Baron Ludwig von Ambrózy, First Councillor of the Austro-Hungarian embassy, that he considered them only a symptom of the warlike current in the French Republic and the ambitions of Poincaré.[17]

When speaking with the First Councillor, the Italian Foreign Minister

[11] For a discussion of this point see Albertini, *Origins of the War*, I, 564–565. The situation was also far from perfect in France where Joffre had not learned of the 1902 Prinetti-Barrère accords until June 1909, and as a result of his ignorance maintained an important and useless army in the Alps. Joffre, *Personal Memoirs*, I, 37–38.

[12] Rodd to Grey, 5 Feb. 1912, FO 371, vol. 1368, France, file 5861.

[13] Rodd to Grey, 24 June 1912, *BD*, vol. X (pt. 2), no. 396, p. 598.

[14] Laroche to Poincaré, 13 Sept. 1912, *DDF3*, vol. III, no. 397, pp. 485–486; 14 Sept. 1912, no. 400, p. 489.

[15] Poincaré to Laroche, 15 Sept. 1912, *ibid.*, no. 403, p. 492.

[16] Laroche to Poincaré, 17 Sept. 1912, *ibid.*, no. 413, pp. 500–501.

[17] Ambrózy to Berchtold, 24 Sept. 1912, *OeU*, IV, no. 3840, p. 468.

made a revealing reference to the Triple Alliance naval convention. San Giuliano asked Ambrózy if he knew anything about this, and indicated he had somewhat vague memories of having read it about four years before. At that time he had told the former Austrian ambassador it was a plan for defeat because of the provision for separate naval action which exposed each fleet to destruction in detail by the superior French.[18] The somewhat startled Ambrózy could only ask the Austrian naval attaché, Prince Liechtenstein, about the alleged convention. From him he learned that such a convention actually existed and was still in force.

The position of the Austrian naval attaché, Korvettenkapitän Johannes Prince von und zu Liechtenstein, was a delicate one owing to the traditional rivalry between the nominally allied countries. Liechtenstein noted the friction with France and the talk in the Italian press over the strength of the united Austrian and Italian fleets compared to the French. He observed that, while the traditional concern over maintaining superiority in the Adriatic remained, the Italians now had the new and additional problems of protecting the Tripolitan coast and the security of communications between the new colony and the homeland.[19] The growth of the idea of cooperation with the Austrian fleet as the best protection for Italy's Mediterranean position was also remarked, presumably with satisfaction, by the German ambassador in Rome. On the other hand, the German naval attaché reported in October 1912 that within the Italian navy itself he had heard up to then only timid support for joint action with Austria.[20]

It would be a mistake to exaggerate the extent of the desire for cooperation between Austria and Italy, a desire which was publicly aired by the deputy Frederico di Palma in the *Rivista nautica*. It would also be wrong to minimize the depth of the mutual fear, suspicion, and rivalry which still existed between the two neighbors. In August 1912 the French naval attaché could discern no evidence of any staff conversations between the two navies, and his personal impression was one of great suspicion between the two. He considered the growth of the Italian fleet an autonomous effort and not in liaison with any external influences.[21] Jules Laroche, the French chargé d'affaires, considered the relative success of those who sought to profit from the *Carthage-Manouba* incidents as short-lived and

[18] *Ibid.*, pp. 468–469.
[19] *Ibid.*, pp. 469–470; Liechtenstein to Marinesektion, 9 Aug. 1912 and 16 Sept. 1912, OK/MS-X-1/2, 1912.
[20] Jagow, German ambassador to Rome, to Bethmann Hollweg, 27 Oct. 1912, *GP*, XXX (pt. 2), no. 11271, pp. 558–559; Rheinbaben, naval attaché, Rome, to Tirpitz, 18 Oct. 1912, GFM 26, reel 90.
[21] D'Huart to Minister of Marine, 20 Aug. 1912, AMF, carton BB7-125.

already crumbling, and that enlightened Italians would realize that the best guarantee for the security of their new possessions must come from the powers bordering the Mediterranean, and not from allies seeking to introduce themselves there.[22] In the long run the French diplomat might have been right, but he had underestimated the degree of Italian resentment against France which was still evident long after the *Carthage-Manouba* incidents.[23] It was not only these two incidents which soured relations between the two nations, but rather what King Victor Emmanuel termed the vexatious attitude of French officials which "savoured rather of want of manners." The King complained to the British ambassador that "France could never accept Italy as one of the great powers and always treated her as an inferior." [24]

Wounded national pride may be an intangible difficult to measure, but it played its role in estranging Italy from France and diverting a certain amount of rancor which would naturally have been directed against Austria-Hungary. The ambivalent nature of Italy's relations with her Triple Alliance allies and the powers of the Triple Entente was, in view of her relatively powerful fleet, one of the primary sources of instability in the Mediterranean naval situation before the World War.

The first move toward a revision of the now dormant naval convention apparently came from the Italian side, through the army's Capo di Stato Maggiore, Lieutenant General Alberto Pollio. Pollio, who was well known in military circles for his publications on military history, became chief of the General Staff in June 1908 while still one of the more junior divisional commanders.[25] In the 1880's he had served as military attaché in Vienna and was married to a Viennese. Pollio was considered one of the leading friends of the Triple Alliance in Italy, and like many of his fellow officers was particularly impressed by German military power.[26] Before the renewal of the Triple Alliance General Helmuth von Moltke, chief of the German General Staff, had suggested an exchange of views, and Pollio's representative, Colonel Vittorio Zupelli, arrived in Berlin early in December 1912. He brought bad news for the Germans. The heavy military drain of the Libyan colony would make it impossible for the third Italian army, in the event of war against France, to be sent through

[22] Laroche to Poincaré, 30 Sept. 1912, *DDF*3, vol. III, no. 484, pp. 581–582.
[23] See Rodd's comments on the renewal of the Triple Alliance, Rodd to Grey, 9 Dec. 1912, FO 371, vol. 1384, Italy, file 53326.
[24] Rodd to Grey, 29 Jan. 1913, Grey MSS, FO 800, vol. 63.
[25] Adriano Alberti, *L'Opera di S.E. il Generale Pollio e l'esercito* (Rome, 1923), p. 5.
[26] Lieutenant Colonel de Gondrecourt, French military attaché, Rome, to Minister of War, 20 Sept. 1913, *DDF*3, VIII, no. 174, p. 236.

the Tyrol to the upper Rhine as foreseen by a previous agreement dating from January 1888. On the other hand, the Italians did intend to assume the offensive across the Alpine frontier and, if sea supremacy was wrested from the French, land in Provence and advance up the Rhône valley.[27] This news left the Germans with the impression Italy would remain neutral at first in the event of war between the great powers, and in practical terms it meant a loss to Moltke of five army corps and two cavalry divisions.[28] Pollio, giving official form to Zupelli's verbal communication, in a letter dated December 21 assured Moltke that Italy would mobilize at once if the *casus foederis* were verified, and would assume an energetic offensive across the Alps to tie down as many French troops as possible. He also mentioned the possibility of a landing in Provence and concluded, in agreement with the chief of the Italian naval staff, that a revision of the naval convention of 1900 was necessary.[29]

This change in Italian plans was conveyed by Lieutenant Colonel Alberico Albricci, the Italian military attaché in Vienna, to General Conrad von Hötzendorf, who was recalled on December 12 as chief of the Austrian General Staff. As far as Conrad was concerned this merely confirmed anew his low evaluation of the Italian ally.[30] He was notorious for his anti-Italian views and had been dismissed as chief of the General Staff the previous year because of them.[31] These views were widely held in the Austrian army. General Moritz Freiherr von Auffenberg, the common Minister of War, expected the Italians "to blow up like a powder keg against us on the outbreak of war"; and the Evidenzbureau of the General Staff in its annual report on Italy spoke of the Tripolitan War opening a valve through which a fanatical hatred against the Austrian monarchy discharged, and also warned that many Italians were convinced war against Austria was unavoidable.[32] Feldmarschalleutenant Blasius von

[27] *Ibid.*, p. 20 n. 1; Wolfgang Foerster, "Die deutsch-italienische Militärkonvention," *Die Kriegsschuldfrage*, 5.5 (May 1927): pp. 398–399. A detailed summary of published material on Italy's military relations with her allies is in Albertini, *Origins of the War*, I, 535–559.

[28] Von Kiderlin to Jagow, 18 Dec. 1912, *GP*, XXX (pt. 2), no. 11286, pp. 574–575; Moltke to Bethmann Hollweg, 30 Dec. 1912, *ibid.*, no. 11287, p. 575.

[29] Pollio to Moltke, 21 Dec. 1912, enclosed in *ibid.*, p. 576.

[30] Feldmarschall Conrad [Franz, Graf Conrad von Hötzendorf], *Aus meiner Dienstzeit, 1906–1918* (5 vols., Vienna, 1921–1925), II, 393–394; "Note des Chefs des Generalstabes," 19 Dec. 1912, *OeU*, V, no. 4984, p. 176.

[31] Conrad, *Aus meiner Dienstzeit*, II, 281f; Report by Major Grafen von Kageneck, military attaché, Vienna, 18 Nov. 1911, *GP*, XXX (pt. 2), no. 11238, p. 520, and 1 Dec. 1911, pp. 525–526.

[32] Von Tschirschky, ambassador to Vienna, to Bethmann Hollweg, 18 Nov. 1911, *ibid.*, no. 11235, pp. 514–515; Evidenzbureau des k.u.k. Generalstabes, *Jahresbericht über die Wehrmacht Italiens, 1911*, 31 Jan. 1912, p. 2, copy in OK/MS-X-1/4, 1912.

Schemua, who served as chief of the General Staff during Conrad's absence in 1912, was more diplomatic than his predecessor, but he did not hesitate to tell the German military attaché that he did not entirely trust the Italians, and that in the case of a general mobilization during the Balkan crisis there could be no thought of withdrawing the two strong corps from Austria's southern frontier.[33]

Despite the grave suspicions of their army colleagues, and undoubtedly their own as well, the Operationskanzlei of the Marinesektion had seriously studied the strategic possibilities of an Austrian-Italian naval combination even before Pollio's suggestion for a revision of the existing naval convention reached them. In October 1912, probably motivated by the Balkan crisis, the Operationskanzlei prepared a memorandum for the Marinekommandant on the naval aspects of a conflict between the Triple Entente and the Triple Alliance. The Austrians considered the French fleet superior to the united Austrian and Italian fleets, but not to the degree that a successful offensive by them was out of the question. Whether the combined fleets would immediately undertake such an offensive or assume a defensive attitude until a favorable moment presented itself was dependent on the British strength in the Mediterranean. Should the Dardanelles be opened to the Russian Black Sea fleet, the naval superiority of the Triple Entente would be such that a joint action with the Italians could be considered only under especially favorable circumstances.[34] The Operationskanzlei thought an attempted union with the Italian fleet should be axiomatic if it was judged this would fulfill their main objective, protection of the Austro-Hungarian coast and trade, better than operating by themselves. The combined fleets were to seize every possible opportunity for an energetic offensive in regard to stimulation and support of rebellious movements in enemy colonies, hindering the projected troop transport from these colonies, and cutting off enemy trade, particularly British food supplies passing through the Suez Canal. Other objectives included a combination against portions of the enemy fleets, particularly the British detachment, protection of their own coast, and covering Italy's African possessions whose defection was to be feared. The Austro-Hungarian navy had certainly traveled a long way in its strategic thinking in the dozen years since 1900 when it refused to commit itself outside of the Adriatic or even beyond its own coast.

[33] Report by military attaché, Vienna, 27 Sept. 1912, *GP*, XXXIII, no. 12179, p. 126, and 13 Nov. 1912, no. 12370, p. 328.

[34] Operationskanzlei, Marinesektion, "Triple entente gegen Dreibund," Oct. 1912, OK/MS-1/G.V., 1913. The estimated ratio in tonnage for 1913 between the Triple Entente and the Triple Alliance in the Mediterranean was 1.5:1 excluding, and 1.8:1 including, the Russian Black Sea fleet.

The Operationskanzlei judged Taranto to be the harbor which corresponded best to both offensive and defensive needs, and Maddalena to be
suited as a base for armored cruisers and flotillas which would operate
against the French troop transport and conduct diversionary operations
against the southern coast of France. The Austrians recognized that a
lack of armored cruisers, particularly the battle cruiser type, was the main
strategic and tactical weakness of the allied fleets. They favored a prompt
increase in the number of Austrian dreadnoughts in order to complete
the transformation of the K.u.K. Kriegsmarine from a defensive force to
a high seas fleet capable of fighting far from its own coast.

The Marinekommandant, Admiral Montecuccoli, added his own conclusion to the Operationskanzlei study. He advocated, first of all, striving
for the quickest possible union with the Italian fleet in order to destroy
the enemy fleet. If that was not successful, he thought the Ionian Sea the
position from which the Adriatic and Tyrrhenian could be equally protected. A concentration in the Augusta-Syracuse area would make it
possible to block the Malta Channel, thus cutting off the western basin
of the Mediterranean from the eastern. Montecuccoli thought the condition of the fleet after a naval battle would determine whether it was necessary to call at Taranto, and that in certain cases Corfu would also be
important.[35]

At the end of 1912 the German ambassador in Rome submitted a careful
analysis of Italian military strength which concluded, in agreement with
the Italian General Staff, that after subtraction of the forces in Libya,
Italy was not in a position to send an expeditionary corps to the Rhine.
The recent Italian decision was therefore seen to be less a concealed attitude of reserve and more an open admission of weakness, particularly
a lack of officer strength.[36] While this represented a setback for the Germans as far as land operations were concerned, the Italian proposal for an
alteration in the naval convention presented an opportunity which they
were quick to grasp. On January 3 Colonel Erich Ludendorff of the General Staff met with Vice Admiral August von Heeringen, chief of the
Admiralstab, and showed him a copy of a memorandum on the Mediterranean which the German General Staff had sent to the Austrian General
Staff. Von Heeringen found the situation depicted in the paper much too
favorable for the Triple Alliance, particularly that part pertaining to
British naval strength in the Mediterranean. He also had no great hopes
for a significant Italian landing attempt in the south of France. Ludendorff

[35] Marginal comment by Montecuccoli, 29 Oct. 1912, *ibid.*
[36] Jagow to Bethmann Hollweg, 31 Dec. 1912, *GP*, XXX (pt. 2), no. 11288, pp.
577–579.

acknowledged both objections at once, but thought one had to encourage the Austrians somewhat in the question of an agreement with Italy. He observed that the General Staff had a great interest in the destruction of the French troop transports. Ludendorff also doubted an Italian landing in Provence, and indicated that the General Staff placed little value on the Italian offensive against the French frontier which could be easily stopped in a region where routes of advance were few, blocked by French fortifications, and some of the roads were covered by snow most of the year.[37]

Moltke informed Pollio of his favorable attitude toward a new naval convention, and indicated that the strength of German naval participation in the Mediterranean was dependent on the attitude of England. He also emphasized his interest in preventing the transport of French troops from North Africa which he estimated, somewhat excessively as it turned out, at two army corps.[38] Moltke told the German military attaché in Rome that it would be highly desirable for Italy to make the necessary proposals toward a naval convention for joint operations which would facilitate both the prevention of the French transport, and a landing on the French coast.[39]

The Kaiser authorized Von Heeringen to approach the Austrian naval attaché on the subject also. The naval attaché, Colloredo-Mannsfeld, was told that only joint action by Austria and Italy could prevent the transfer of the French troops, since the German fleet would be completely tied up by the British. Von Heeringen pointed out Austria's interest in the question: if the French did not succeed in strengthening their army, greater German strength could be turned toward the east thus relieving the pressure on the Austrian army. The Austrian officer asked about the *Goeben,* sent to the Mediterranean during the Balkan crisis, which the French had nothing to match. Von Heeringen told him that the question had already been considered, but owing to the small number of battle cruisers a ship like the *Goeben* would be missed in the North Sea. He also disclosed that the Admiralstab scarcely included the Russian Black Sea fleet in its calculations. The military value of this force was very small because of the

---

[37] Admiralstab, "Änderung des Dreibundabkommens vom 1900—Besprechung mit Oberst Ludendorff vom Generalstab, am 3/I 13," GFM 26, reel 61, frame 87. The Austro-Italian strength was assumed to be numerically slightly superior to the French, but based on smaller ships. The British force in the Mediterranean was assumed to be not in a position to hamper the exit of the Austrian fleet from the Adriatic. Memorandum, "Die strategische Lage in Mittelmeer in einen Kriege der Dreibunds gegen Frankreich und England," *ibid.*, frame 92–95.

[38] Moltke to Pollio, 9 Jan. 1913, quoted in Foerster, "Die deutsche-italiensche Militärkonvention," pp. 400–401.

[39] Moltke to Major von Kleist, 9 [?] Jan. 1913, GFM 26, reel 61, frame 89–90.

poor discipline of its crews and its obsolete ships, and its employment in the Mediterranean, even if it was possible for it to pass the Dardanelles, was highly improbable. Colloredo-Mannsfeld sensed a certain anxiety on the part of the Germans that the Austrian fleet would be limited to a defensive role in the Adriatic.[40]

On January 18 Emperor Franz Joseph authorized the competent Austro-Hungarian authorities to begin discussions on the questions raised by the German Admiralty.[41] Montecuccoli ordered Haus to report exactly which units of the fleet and its train were suitable for operations outside of the Adriatic.[42] The Marinekommandant decided that for the operations in question the fleet would have to be strengthened by six or seven colliers with a collective coal capacity of 30,000 tons, a steamer equipped with a freezing compartment to serve as a victualing ship, and a tanker. In view of the urgency of the matter, Montecuccoli recommended that the necessary steamers be guaranteed from domestic shipping companies, two fully laden colliers be set enroute from England to Pola and be held ready there until further notice, and that a steamer of the Austrian Lloyd be kept clear for loading at Pola as a munitions ship in case of mobilization.[43] These measures were reported to Archduke Franz Ferdinand as facilitating a possible combination with the Italian fleet. The heir to the throne, expressing his characteristic suspicion of Italy, wrote across Colonel Bardolff's report that he took note of the matter but would not mix in it.[44] Montecuccoli was able to obtain Count Berchtold's agreement to his collier proposal, and on January 30 the Emperor gave his approval.[45] Shortly afterwards the steamer *Nippon* (6500 tons) was chartered from the Austrian Lloyd, and the *Francesca* (5300 tons) from the Austro-America Line. In early May the easing of the political situation made their maintenance at Pola seem no longer necessary, and they were returned to their owners.[46]

The readiness of the chief of the Austrian General Staff to consider joint

---

[40] Colloredo-Mannsfeld to Marinesektion, 11 Jan. 1913, *OeU*, V, no. 5333, pp. 418–420. Shortly afterwards, Prince Henry of Prussia also spoke at length on Austro-Italian cooperation, maintaining that the situation was much more advantageous for the Triple Alliance in the Mediterranean than in the North Sea. Colloredo-Mannsfeld to Marinesektion, 26 Jan. 1913, OK/MS-1/G.V., 1913.

[41] Bolfras to Montecuccoli, 18 Jan. 1913, *OeU*, V. no. 5468, Beilage 1, p. 504.

[42] Montecuccoli to Haus, Res. Nr. 2/M.K., 18 Jan. 1913, G.V./ (nicht protokolliert). Haus, as Commander-in-Chief designate in time of war, had also been told the provisions of the 1900 naval convention the previous December. Montecuccoli to Haus, 7 Dec. 1912, PK/MS-8-4/13 Separat.

[43] Montecuccoli to MKSM, 23 Jan. 1913, OK/MS-IX-9/3, 1913.

[44] Marginal note by Franz Ferdinand to Bardolff's report of 25 Jan. 1913, MKFF/41-23, 1913.

[45] Montecuccoli to MKSM, 27 Jan. 1913, OK/MS-IX-9/3, 1913; Bolfras to Montecuccoli, 30 Jan. 1913, *ibid.*

[46] Haus to MKSM, 8 May 1913, *ibid.*; Bolfras to Haus, 9 May 1913, *ibid.*

operations with the Italians outside of the Adriatic was gratifying to the Germans, although the naval attaché in Vienna, Freiherr von Freyberg, could not refrain from commenting on the change in Conrad, who at the beginning of the Tripolitan War used all his influence in favor of a preventative war against Italy. Conrad did have some reservations over the safety of the Adriatic coast should the Russian Black Sea fleet break out of the Dardanelles after the Austrian fleet had left the Adriatic, but the Marinesektion was inclined to dismiss the danger, and thought the obsolete naval units to be left behind sufficient to protect the coast.[47] Montecuccoli did intimate that the question of command was apt to cause difficulties.[48] In order to facilitate agreement among the three allies, and also to expand the talks to questions involving land operations should progress be made in naval matters, Moltke sent Major General Graf von Waldersee, Oberquartiermeister I of the General Staff, on a confidential mission to Rome and Vienna in the middle of January. Waldersee was furnished with naval documents for the talks; a close understanding between the German army and navy staffs existed over his mission which Waldersee admitted was unusual for the time and which did not last.[49]

Waldersee, who stayed at the home of the German military attaché in Rome in order to make his presence as inconspicuous as possible, suggested to Pollio that Italy immediately take the initiative in approaching Austria for a more detailed naval agreement. The Italian general expressed his satisfaction that such an initiative would be favored in Berlin and well received by Austria. After a delay of a few days Pollio obtained King Victor Emmanuel's approval for the general outline of the approach to Austria. To avoid friction with the Austrians over the question of command, Pollio promised Waldersee that every willingness to oblige would be shown. He added that the present division into zones of operations would be omitted, and all details settled for the operations. Pollio did caution that the forthcoming change in the office of chief of the Italian naval staff would delay the proposals to be made to the Austrians. He again mentioned the possibility of an Italian landing on the Provençal coast and showed a surprising lack of concern over the British navy whose Mediterranean force he hoped to settle with before it could unite with the French. He had a very unfavorable opinion of the French fleet, not only because of the powder question, but also in regard to the quality of

[47] Freyberg to Tirpitz, 15 Jan. 1913, GFM 26, reel 94, frame 103–104.
[48] Freyberg to Tirpitz, 27 Jan. 1913, GFM 26, reel 61, frame 111.
[49] Graf Waldersee, "Von Deutschlands militärpolitischen Beziehungen zu Italien," *Berliner Monatshefte,* 7.7 (July 1929): 641–642; Foerster, "Die deutsch-italienisch Militärkonvention," pp. 401–402.

its officers and the spirit of its crews. Despite the considerable requirement in troops which the defense of Italy's long coastline necessitated, and the fact that the British fleet would be counted on the opposing side, Pollio thought that the combined fleets of Italy and Austria could be in a position to turn aside any serious threat to the Italian coast. This caused Waldersee to comment in his report to Moltke that one could not completely depart from the thought that fear of the English fleet was employed when the occasion demanded as a political necessity in Italy. Waldersee left Rome with the best impression of Pollio, and thought there could be no doubt he was a supporter of the Triple Alliance who saw the welfare of his country in the holding down of France.[50]

Waldersee found both Conrad and Montecuccoli receptive toward an Italian initiative for joint fleet action, but the Austrian chief of the General Staff took little trouble to conceal his skepticism about Italy. Conrad had full confidence in Pollio personally, but doubted the leading Italian politicians' loyalty to the Triple Alliance.[51] Franz Ferdinand had agreed to the projected convention, but only on the condition that it was valid solely for Triple Alliance matters and not for a one-sided conflict between Italy and France.[52] The Archduke's acceptance must have been reluctant, and indeed Colonel Bardolff had recommended it on practical grounds. Bardolff argued that as long as they could not expect quiet on their eastern or southeastern frontier, it was necessary to come to terms with Italy. The head of the archduke's Militärkanzlei concluded that one could not make war on all fronts and cited the French proverb "Qui trop embrasse, mal étreint." [53] He also added that a paper liaison with Italy would make naval construction comprehensible to friends of the Triple Alliance. One could tear up the paper when it was no longer convenient, but one would still have the ships.

Montecuccoli told Waldersee that he too did not have a very high opinion of the French fleet, although recently more was being done for it. He also hoped that the British force in the Mediterranean could quickly be mopped-up (*aufräumen*). Montecuccoli was anxious to arrive at an agreement with the Italians on provisions for coaling during the operations. He added that it seemed desirable that this question be raised in Rome by Germany. Waldersee thought this issue could be used to give the Italians a nudge should the naval talks be delayed. Moltke's emissary left

[50] Report by Waldersee to Moltke, 29 Jan. 1913, reproduced in Waldersee, "Von Deutschlands Beziehungen zu Italien," pp. 643–646.

[51] Conrad, *Aus meiner Dienstzeit*, III, 86–88, 92, 153.

[52] *Ibid.*, p. 81.

[53] Report by Col. Bardolff, n.d. [20 ? Jan. 1913], MKFF/Nb/N-240, 1913.

Vienna with the impression that Montecuccoli, who had grown up in Modena, could not entirely suppress a certain mistrust of Italy. This was directed not at the men governing at the moment, but rather at Italian public opinion. Waldersee's experiences in Rome and Vienna convinced him that Germany would have to provide the impetus in keeping the affair moving and the allies united. The presence of more German ships in the operations also appeared desirable; in fact Montecuccoli had particularly welcomed the idea of assistance from German scout cruisers.[54]

The Germans did not envisage a very large role for themselves in the Mediterranean, and only those ships already there at the outbreak of hostilities would be considered for the joint operations. Under normal circumstances this number would not be great, and during the summer half-year the Mediterranean was generally empty of German warships. The Admiralstab expected to recall the *Goeben* and *Breslau* after the Balkan crisis eased; a special detachment of naval force was not likely to replace them in the foreseeable future because of the ratio of strength in the North Sea.[55] Freiherr Werner von Rheinbaben, the German naval attaché in Rome, who appears not to have been informed of the 1900 convention when he assumed his duties, hoped that the project for joint operations would also lead to Krupp's participation in the provision of new 15-inch cannon for the Italian navy.[56] On February 10 the attachés in Rome and Vienna were cabled not to undertake anything for the moment, but the enthusiastic Rheinbaben reported that prior to the receipt of these orders he had already gotten the matter going again by his unofficial initiative with Cattolica's naval secretary at the Ministry of Marine.[57] Rheinbaben, whose correspondence indicates a certain rivalry with Major von Kleist, his military colleague, was impatient at the delay ostensibly caused by the change in naval chiefs of staff, and insisted that the local methods required gentle prompting.[58]

The eager Germans had to wait two months after Waldersee's visit for the expected Italian initiative to occur. Thaon di Revel did not replace Rocca Rey as Capo di Stato Maggiore until the middle of March, and not officially until April 1. In the meantime Rheinbaben was given favorable

[54] Waldersee, "Von Deutschlands Beziehungen zu Italien," pp. 647–649.
[55] Admiralstab to Moltke, 12 Feb. 1913, GFM 26, reel 61, frame 118.
[56] Rheinbaben to Capt. ?, 22 Jan. 1913, *ibid.*, frame 116–117.
[57] Admiralstab to attachés, Rome and Vienna, 10 Feb. 1913, *ibid.*, frame 123; Rheinbaben to Chief of Admiralstab, 11 Feb. 1913, *ibid.*, frame 126–127.
[58] *Ibid.*, frame 127; Rheinbaben to Capt. ?, 18 Feb. 1913, *ibid.*, frame 127–129. By the middle of March he was able to report working in the closest understanding again with Von Kleist. Rheinbaben to Chief of Admiralstab, 18 Mar. 1913, *ibid.*, frame 139.

assurances by Count Tosti di Valminuta, the minister's naval secretary, Leonardi-Cattolica himself, and of course Pollio who claimed that he had to proceed with a certain tact until Revel took office.[59] The Italians hinted that a special staff officer would soon be sent to Vienna; Rheinbaben suggested the officer also be sent to Berlin. This provoked a cable from the chief of the Admiralstab for Rheinbaben to explain himself, for Admiral von Heeringen thought it would be sufficient for the Germans merely to receive a report of the Austro-Italian agreement. He also did not think that a complete abrogation of the 1900 convention was necessary, but rather the establishment of suitable provisions for joining the fleets.[60] Rheinbaben explained that the visit of the Italian officer to Berlin was desirable to clarify the question of future German strength in the Mediterranean. While this was not apt to be large, Waldersee had thought it best to exaggerate it somewhat along with the possibility of its operating under Italian command in order to make the matter more palatable to the Italians. Rheinbaben also added his personal opinion that because of a certain mistrust of Austria which lingered in Italian naval circles, it was extremely desirable for Germany to serve as an intermediary in order to prevent the convention from existing merely on paper.[61]

Count Tosti told Prince Liechtenstein that one ought not to wait until the army general staffs had stipulated something for the navies, that the navies ought to reach an agreement directly among themselves.[62] The Marinesektion, however, advised the Austrian naval attachés in both Berlin and Vienna that while such talks were very desirable, it was expected that the Italian government would take the initiative in the matter.[63] The hiatus in naval conversations did not extend to military matters. Early in February Lieutenant Colonel Carlo Montanari brought the skeptical Conrad two letters from Pollio and discussed with him the Italian view of the military situation and plans for an offensive in case of war with France. Montanari made a good impression on Conrad, but Conrad could not help noting that the Italian dispositions were also suitable for action against Austria-Hungary.[64]

[59] Rheinbaben to Capt. ?, 8 Mar. 1913, *ibid.*, frame 133–134, and 19 Mar. 1913, frame 143–144.

[60] Chief of Admiralstab to Rheinbaben, 14 Mar. 1913, *ibid.*, frame 135.

[61] Rheinbaben to Chief of Admiralstab, 18 Mar. 1913, *ibid.*, frame 137–139.

[62] Liechtenstein to Capt. Rodler [?], 9 Feb. 1913, OK/MS-2/G.V., 1913; Liechtenstein to Marinesektion, 6 Feb. 1913, *OeU*, V, no. 5696, p. 651, and 25 Feb. 1913, no. 5940, pp. 821–822.

[63] Montecuccoli to attachés, Rome and Berlin, 24 Feb. 1913, OK/MS-2/G.V., 1913; report by Col. Bardolff, 15 Feb. 1913, MKFF/41-25/3, 1913.

[64] Conrad, *Aus meiner Dienstzeit*, III, 89–91. For a complete account of the military aspect of these negotiations see the works of Conrad, Waldersee, and Foerster.

The Italian naval General Staff was far from idle in the period following Count Waldersee's visit, and the assurances given to the Austrian and German attachés had not been deceptive. On January 28 Rocca Rey forwarded to Pollio a preliminary memorandum on the fundamental criteria for joint naval action and a new convention. If these met with Pollio's approval, Rocca Rey's directives for a complete study would follow.[65] The Stato Maggiore believed that the allied fleets should be obligated to concentrate their action wherever the enemy was located since their principal objective was to destroy the major enemy fleet. The support each allied fleet gave to the common action ought to be limited only by essential needs for coastal defense. The natural field of action for the German fleet was outside of the Mediterranean where it could cooperate with the allied fleets by preventing a complete concentration in the Mediterranean by the enemy. The Mediterranean was the natural field of action for the Austrian and Italian fleets and ought not to be subdivided into secondary zones reserved for each of the two navies. Each of the two allies should regulate the initial disposition and subsequent movements of its fleet so as always to be ready to oppose every possible enemy maneuver with a joint force at least equivalent in power.[66]

The Stato Maggiore derived the following obligations from these principles: (1) in case of the threat of an enemy concentration in the western or central Mediterranean, the Austrian fleet ought to share in the common defense with a force of not less than two principal first-line divisions dispatched to Italian bases in the Tyrrhenian; and (2) in case of the threat of an enemy concentration toward the Adriatic, the Italian fleet would send an equivalent force to its own bases in the Ionian or those in the Adriatic which would be assigned to it. As it was natural to suppose that each nation would participate with a preponderant force where its major interests were threatened, the logical consequence was always to attribute the supreme command to the nation which brought a larger force to the joint action. It was obvious to the Italians that in any war in which they were likely to be involved as a member of the Triple Alliance the western Mediterranean would witness the principal enemy concentration. The Stato Maggiore therefore had to persuade the Austrians to risk the major portion of their fleet outside of the Adriatic and, by implication, under Italian

[65] Rocca Rey to Pollio, 28 Jan. 1913, USM, cartella 295/2. See also Mariano Gabriele, "Origini della Convenzione Navale Italo-Austro-Germanica del 1913," *Rassegna Storica del Risorgimento*, no. III (1965), pp. 325–344, and no. IV, 489–597. Gabriele has published extensive extracts from the Italian naval archives.

[66] Rocca Rey, "Azione Commune delle Flotte Alleate nel caso di Guerra della Triplice," 28 Jan. 1913, USM, cartella 295/2.

command. In view of the experience of 1900, this would put to a major test Austria-Hungary's readiness to cooperate.

Pollio submitted the Stato Maggiore's preliminary study to the King. While awaiting royal approval the staff prepared another study on the effective support which the Austrian fleet might render to the Italians.[67] They considered that in a war against the Triple Entente the task of Italy would be localized against France, and that the outbreak of hostilities would be so rapid that England would not have time to recall her Mediterranean squadron. They would therefore have to face a French force augmented by this British Mediterranean force, which would largely compensate for any gap in the French fleet caused by the detachment of ships for the protection of the French Atlantic coast or the French North African Empire. The geographical situation of Austria and Italy made it obvious that Austria ought to dispatch the maximum possible force outside of the Adriatic. Should Austria not agree to this concept of complete naval cooperation, she would risk having to bear the brunt of an assault by the French fleet after the French, victorious over the isolated Italians, advanced into the Adriatic.

After discussing the probable French courses of action, the Italian naval staff easily reached the conclusion that their fleet and their Tyrrhenian coast would be the principal French maritime objective in the Mediterranean. In this region was the nucleus of Italy's national and industrial life; here too was the national capital, a short distance from the sea. The entire Ligurian coast guarded the rear and assured the supply of the vast Lombard and Piedmont region, and the movements of the Italian army operating on the French frontier would be paralyzed if command of the coastal road and ports of Savona and Genoa was not absolutely guaranteed to Italy. It was illogical to assume the French would act primarily against the distant eastern shore of the Adriatic. Command of the Adriatic could not benefit France by paralyzing the internal life and military operations of the Dual Monarchy. France's most likely secondary maritime objective would be the transport of troops from North Africa. As these were probably destined for use against Germany rather than Italy, the Stato Maggiore argued that the secondary maritime objective of France was actually directed against Germany. The logical result of this was that Austrian naval support in the Mediterranean would help Germany as well as Italy.

[67] Stato Maggiore, "Memoria No. 1 a S.E. il Capo di Stato Maggiore della Marina circa il modo come si presenta il problema di una cooperazione della flotta austro-ungarica," 28 Mar. 1913, USM, cartella 295/3.

A comparison of the rival naval forces in the Mediterranean reinforced the belief of the Stato Maggiore in the necessity of cooperation with Austria. They realized that Italy by herself could not hope to equal French naval construction, and that at the moment the French fleet was nearly equal to that of Austria and Italy combined, and much superior in submarines. Taking the British Mediterranean force into consideration, the Austrian and Italian fleets even when united would not be equal to the Triple Entente in the Mediterranean for at least ten years. Intervention by the Russian Black Sea fleet could not be dismissed a priori and would constitute a grave threat which would place the naval superiority of the Triple Entente beyond discussion. In this case the sole ally of Austria and Italy would be the time factor: the Stato Maggiore thought it would take not less than a week for the Russians to reach the western Mediterranean, coal, and be ready for battle. This interval should be exploited by the allies to seek and defeat the French fleet, whose destruction ought to be their principal maritime objective, before it could be joined by the Russians.[68] The Stato Maggiore also used this study to advance their claim for greater naval effort by talking in terms of Italy's fulfillment of her obligations under the Triple Alliance. If the combined forces of that alliance were inferior at the moment to the Triple Entente in the Mediterranean, no blame could be given to Austria because of her recent naval effort. The same could not be said of Italy. If Austria should refuse to risk her fleet in the western Mediterranean, arguing that she had provided her fleet for the defense of her own coast and not to compensate for the deficiency in Italian power, Italy would find herself in an extremely perilous position.

The general conclusion of the Italian naval staff was that the amount and type of support by the Austrian fleet was a direct function of the war plan to be adopted; and vice versa, the determination of that plan must necessarily rest upon an exact knowledge of the limits within which Austria intended to aid the attainment of the maritime objectives of the Triple Alliance in the Mediterranean, as well as upon intelligence gathered on the intentions and war plans of the Triple Entente and the policy and

[68] The Stato Maggiore estimated the comparative war value of battleships and armored cruisers as follows.

	1913	1914	1915
France	14,340	15,201	17,126
Austria and Italy	13,171	14,133	18,528

This was based on the formula war value $= 1,000 \times 25 - E/25 \times D/20,000$. D $=$ displacement; E $=$ the number of decades after the ship was laid down. The Russian Black Sea fleet for the years in question was valued at: 1145, 1013, and 900. *Ibid.*, App. A.

attitude of Spain and Russia. The general form Austrian aid should take after a reasonable provision for the defense of her own coast should be: (1) The dispatch of available battleships to the upper Tyrrhenian to join the Italians in defeating the French fleet and winning command of the sea; (2) the dispatch to the lower Tyrrhenian of available torpedo and light craft to cooperate with the Italian navy in operating against troop convoys from Algeria, and checking possible concentrations of enemy forces in Bizerte, Malta, or Algerian ports; and (3) cooperation with the Italian fleet in eventual operations aimed at neutralizing the naval bases of Tunisia, Algeria, and Malta.

Pollio was not anxious for the Minister of Marine to participate in the formulation of plans for Austrian cooperation, although he realized Revel's subordinate position as head of an office within the Ministry. He reasoned that if the Minister of Marine came into the affair, the Minister of War would have to be admitted as well. The intervention of the ministers, and possibly even the ministries, would result in too many people knowing the naval dispositions in the event of war. Pollio therefore proposed to General Brusati, the King's senior aide-de-camp, that once he and Revel agreed to the general principles of cooperation with Austria and the King had given these his approval, a special officer be sent to Vienna.[69] Pollio's formal proposal for a naval conference was sent to Moltke and Conrad and promptly accepted toward the end of March.[70] In preparing for the negotiations Revel thought it indispensable to know if the text of the Triple Alliance contemplated in general terms a military accord between the signatory powers, especially between Austria and Italy in regard to the Mediterranean. He therefore asked Leonardi Cattolica to obtain the necessary information from San Giuliano.[71] The Foreign Minister replied in general terms about consultation among the allies if one was threatened, and thought it implicit in the spirit of the treaty that in case of war the allies would cooperate with all their land and sea forces in the manner the respective military authorities judged most suitable to assure common victory.[72] Once again, however, a major service chief remained in the dark as to the exact nature of Italy's diplomatic obligations.

In anticipation of the negotiations with Austria the Stato Maggiore pre-

[69] Pollio to Brusati, 18 Mar. 1913, ACS, Carte Brusati-10/VII-3-43, no. 465; and 25 Mar. 1913, no. 469.

[70] Conrad to Haus, 27 Mar. 1913, OK/MS-3/G.V., 1913; Von Heeringen to Rheinbaben, 27 Mar. 1913, GFM 26, reel 61, frame 144. Von Heeringen added that the dispatch of an Italian officer to Berlin was therefore unnecessary.

[71] Revel to Leonardi Cattolica, 7 Apr. 1913, USM, cartella 286/3.

[72] San Giuliano to Leonardi Cattolica, 10 Apr. 1913, USM, cartella 296. Revel had already learned this verbally from the Minister of War. Revel to Leonardi Cattolica, 10 Apr. 1913, USM, cartella 286/3.

pared another detailed study on the three possible attitudes their eastern neighbor could take: cooperation in the western Mediterranean with all of her fleet; cooperation with part of her fleet; or refusal to cooperate outside of the Adriatic. The last attitude would put Italy's back to the wall and force her to choose between sacrificing for a more powerful fleet or changing her foreign policy. If the Austrians agreed to help with all of their fleet, the concentration in the upper Tyrrhenian at La Spezia or Maddalena which had been foreseen in the previous staff study, and which was naturally and strategically correct, was on close examination of logistical and tactical requirements not possible. The union with the Austrian fleet would have to be accomplished at Messina. To defend the upper Tyrrhenian the Italians realized that paradoxically they would be obliged to steam south to reach their indispensable objective, the union of the allied fleets. Their northern coast would therefore be at the mercy of the enemy for a few days. The Stato Maggiore remarked that this unpleasant truth demonstrated that their maritime position in the Triple Alliance was defective because of either the large gap in their naval preparations or a great misunderstanding. The first could be filled only by strengthening the fleet, the second could be remedied only by changing policy. A policy change, the Stato Maggiore admitted, perhaps somewhat bitterly, was beyond the scope of their memorandum.[73]

The contingency that the Austrians would cling to the 1900 naval convention which had never been abrogated and concede nothing more to the Italians than assistance in the defense of their Adriatic coast was one which would place Italy in the greatest peril. The old naval convention had been established at a time when France was the sole foreseeable enemy and England was in "splendid isolation." All this had changed. For Italy heroically to consecrate her fleet to certain defeat at the hands of the superior Anglo-French coalition would be admirable when it was a question of defending her own territory, her own existence, her own national honor. But, the Stato Maggiore argued, it would be absurd to sacrifice everything merely to second the policy of another power in an unnecessary war desired by that power.[74]

The Stato Maggiore were of course ignorant of the text of the Triple Alliance where article VII provided Italy an escape from exactly this situation. They therefore had little hesitation in criticizing their government's

[73] Stato Maggiore, "Memoria No. 2 a S.E. il Capo di Stato Maggiore della Marina circo il modo come si presenta il problema di una cooperazione della flotta austro-ungarica," 2, 6, 8, Apr. 1913, pp. 3–4; 8–9; 12–13, USM, cartella 295/4.

[74] *Ibid.*, p. 29.

foreign policy, although they admitted that this was beyond their competence. The Stato Maggiore argued that the navy could not be indifferent to any aspect of the problem and that the policy of a country was generally based on military and naval preparations. They questioned whether Italian policy was in harmony with her military and naval establishment, and whether the latter was capable of assuming all the obligations which the country in its confidence had bestowed on it. The reply to that double question might be uncertain, but one thing was certain, according to the Stato Maggiore. At the moment the necessary harmony between naval force and foreign policy appeared insufficient since they had just demonstrated that in case of war Italy would be overwhelmed. The Stato Maggiore concluded their lengthy memorandum with the unequivocal statement "Either transform the navy, putting it in relation to policy; or change policy, putting it in relation to the navy." [75] This blunt warning was applicable only to the contingency where the Austrians refused naval cooperation. The Stato Maggiore were to show themselves quite ready to be completely accommodating when the opposite proved true. But there was a definite difference in tone between this coldly analytical study and the enthusiastic and less critical spirit with which Pollio approached relations with Italy's allies.

Admiral Thaon di Revel was obviously a realist worried over his country's exposed position in the event of hostilities with the great maritime powers. He told Rheinbaben, the German naval attaché, that he had no immediate fear of the danger of war with France, but that the French recently had become so self-assured and chauvinistic, especially under President Poincaré, that one must be prepared for anything.[76] Revel had been cordial but much more reserved two days before when Prince Liechtenstein paid his respects to the new Capo di Stato Maggiore. To Liechtenstein's disappointment he mentioned nothing of the naval convention. The Austrian officer was chagrined because both German attachés were apparently better informed than he was about the plans of his own government, and were freely giving their unsolicited opinion that a naval convention between Austria and Italy was as good as signed.[77]

Lieutenant Colonel Graf Stanislaus Szeptycki, Prince Liechtenstein's military colleague at the Austro-Hungarian embassy in Rome, took an exceptionally dim view of his Italian allies. He reported that they had only renewed the Triple Alliance in order to gain six years security from attack

[75] *Ibid.*, pp. 29–30.
[76] Rheinbaben to Chief of Admiralstab, 7 Apr. 1913, GFM 26, reel 61, frame 151.
[77] Liechtenstein to Capt. Rodler [?], 6 Apr. 1913, OK/MS-2/G.V., 1913.

by Austria in which to strengthen themselves on land and sea, and as coldly reckoning *Realpolitiker* would leave Austria the moment they saw no interest to themselves there. He also warned that the naval convention would reveal much that had been unknown to the Italians.[78] Colonel Szeptycki's opinions by themselves were not unusual, and his report not very important. Nevertheless, a copy of it went to Franz Ferdinand's Militärkanzlei, and the Archduke ordered copies to be forwarded to both the Ministry of Foreign Affairs and the Marinesektion. The Marinesektion absolutely disagreed with this view. They claimed that the strategical situation dictated the use of Italian operational bases so that actually the Italians would be the ones who would reveal more.[79] Liechtenstein, who had few illusions as to the warmth of Italian public opinion toward Austria, considered it to be seeing ghosts to attribute to some Machiavellian plan Italy's perfectly comprehensible desire to enter into a naval convention in view of the various French voices which had publicly predicted an easy destruction of the separate Austrian and Italian navies in case of war.[80]

The Italian naval staff officer entrusted with the delicate mission of conducting the preliminary negotiations for a new naval convention with the Austrians was Commander (Capitano di fregata) Angelo Ugo Conz, fluent in German, former head of the intelligence section of the Stato Maggiore, and a trusted aide of Revel. In order to awaken Austrian interest in the new naval convention Revel instructed Conz to present its advantages from the point of view of the Triple Alliance as a whole rather than just Italy. Conz was to use the by now familiar argument of a French naval defeat freeing more Italian troops to operate against France or land at the mouth of the Rhône, thus diverting French forces from Germany and thereby freeing more German troops to aid Austria. In brief, the picture the Italians painted was: Austria would send her fleet to the western Mediterranean and be compensated by one or more German army corps on the Russian frontier; Italy would send one or more army corps to the mouth of the Rhône and be compensated by Austrian naval aid in the upper Tyrrhenian; and Germany would send one or more army corps to help Austria against Russia and be compensated by having one or more Italian army corps land in southern France.[81] Revel ordered Conz to make a

---

[78] Report by military attaché, Rome, 29 Mar. 1913, *OeU*, V, no. 6366, p. 1100.

[79] Marinesektion to Chief of Generalstab, 13 Apr. 1913, *ibid.*, VI, no. 6609, p. 141. Original documents based on Haus's minute are in OK/MS-5/G.V., 1913. See also Conrad, *Aus meiner Dienstzeit*, III, 290.

[80] Liechtenstein to Marinesektion, 21 Apr. 1913, OK/MS-IX-9/3, 1913.

[81] Thaon di Revel, "Istruzioni per la missione preliminare a Berlino e a Vienna per la convocazione della Conferenza di Vienna," 20 Apr. 1913, USM, cartella 295/5.

brief visit to Berlin before proceeding to Vienna in order to get German consent for this method of presenting the argument so that they would be able to speak to the Austrians in the name of Germany as well as Italy. As a rule, Conz was to request the maximum in order to obtain whatever he could. Pollio also gave him a letter of introduction to Moltke.[82] Until now the major impetus in the preliminaries for the new naval convention had come from the army rather than the navy in all three countries. With Conz's departure for Berlin, the navy resumed direction of the affair.

Conz arrived in the German capital on April 26 and was received by the new chief of the Admiralstab, Admiral Hugo von Pohl, three days later. Von Pohl agreed that the Italian line of reasoning corresponded fully to the strategical and tactical criteria of the Admiralstab. The admiral was to discuss the question the next day with the Kaiser, but he assured Conz that Germany associated herself completely with Italy, and that their logic was so cogent it would be difficult for the Austrians to evade it. He also introduced Conz to Captain (Kapitän zur See) Paul Behncke and Commander (Korvettenkapitän) Erich Köhler, the Admiralstab officers with whom he was to work out the details of their agreement in the next few days. Conz considered what he termed the Italo-German bloc as definitely constituted, barring unforeseen events.[83] He may not have known that the following morning Behncke and Köhler summoned Colloredo-Mannsfeld in order to learn the Austrian point of view so that it could be taken into consideration in their talks with Conz. The Austrian attaché, however, was unable to reply with more than generalities through lack of information. The Germans told him that the German forces in the Mediterranean in the event of war would not proceed to the Adriatic first, but rather directly to the rendezvous point in a southern Italian harbor. On the sensitive question of the supreme command Germany would take no position except to insist that the German force be placed directly under the supreme commander.[84]

The Admiralstab repeated to Conz their particular interest in the French convoys and spoke vaguely of the second phase of a war in which, after command of the sea had been won, an intensive *guerre de course* would be conducted against English trade in the eastern Mediterranean, including the obstruction of the Suez Canal. Conz was unable to see Moltke, who was away at Karlsbad, but did meet with General Waldersee, Moltke's

[82] Moltke to Pollio, 18 Apr. 1913, USM, cartella 296; Pollio to Revel, 21 Apr. 1913, *ibid;* report by naval attaché, Rome, 22 Apr. 1913, *OeU*, VI, no. 6711, p. 211.

[83] Conz to Revel, 29 Apr. and 2 May 1913, USM, cartella 296; Conz, "Relazione al ritorno della missione preliminare per la convocazione della Conferenza di Vienna," 14 May 1913, pp. 1–2, USM, cartella 295/6.

[84] Report by naval attaché, Berlin, 30 Apr. 1913, *OeU*, VI, no. 6832, pp. 297–298.

temporary substitute, who was of course well informed about the subject. Waldersee indicated that the General Staff was greatly preoccupied with the problem of coal since English supplies would naturally be cut off in a war. Germany would put her Westphalian mines at the disposal of her allies along with trains to carry the coal to Genoa or La Spezia. However, Waldersee pointed out that this traffic could not begin until after the first period of mobilization, with its massive troop movements by rail, had been completed. Moreover a fully laden train could carry at the maximum 1000 tons of coal, a trifle for an entire fleet. Waldersee therefore thought it necessary for sufficient coal stocks to be established so that the allied fleets could act without recourse to Germany for at least one month.[85]

Waldersee advised Conz to proceed directly from Berlin to Austria for, as he put it, in general one was inclined to be a little suspicious in Vienna, and if Conz returned to Rome before proceeding there his trip to Berlin would suggest a private accord.[86] Conz followed Waldersee's advice and went directly to Vienna despite the threatening international situation resulting from the Scutari crisis and alleged Montenegrin insults to Austrian officials.[87] Through the efforts of Colonel Albricci he was received by Admiral Haus on the afternoon of May 5.

Haus was extremely cold and reserved and claimed that the present political situation did not allow time to initiate new studies, that he was about to move to the squadron in order to assume command, and that in any case a decision as radical as the employment of the fleet in the Mediterranean was beyond his power and could only be taken by Conrad, the chief of the General Staff, after having obtained the consent of the Emperor and Archduke Franz Ferdinand. Conz replied that he was aware of the gravity of the moment, and it was exactly because they should not be caught unawares by unexpected events which might arise out of the present crisis that it seemed as urgent in Berlin as in Rome to know if the Austrian fleet would cooperate in the Mediterranean in the event of war with France or Russia. He argued that Germany and Italy were already in agreement and, without going into details, wanted only to know if the Austrian answer was yes or no so that no time would be lost in making the

[85] Conz, "Relazione al ritorno," enclosure 1: "Punto di vista Germanico," pp. 1–3, USM, cartella 295/6; Conz to Revel, 3 May 1913, USM, cartella 296.

[86] Conz, "Relazione al ritorno," pp. 2–3. Conz also took advantage of his presence in Berlin to enter into an agreement with Kapitän zur see Tapken of the intelligence section of the Admiralstab for the exchange of information on France, Russia, and England, joint action for the repression of espionage, and equal participation in the expense of important documents. Conz to Revel, 16 May 1913, USM, cartella 296.

[87] For background see Helmreich, *Diplomacy of the Balkan Wars,* ch. XIV, esp. pp. 320f.

necessary provisions. Haus, after a long pause, asked Conz if he was authorized to present the Italian point of view in detail, and then arranged for him to do this the following day before a conference of senior officers over which the Marinekommandant presided.[88]

In a private meeting after Conz's exposition, the Austrian naval officers whom Haus had summoned approved the Italian point of view. But Haus privately warned Conz that, while he was personally pleased by Italy's initiative and had supported it with all his power at the conference, a serious obstacle would be met in the person of Franz Ferdinand. He added that Conrad was extremely jealous of his prerogatives over both land and sea forces as chief of the General Staff, and that it would be best for Conz also to request an interview with him. Conz had already asked Albricci to obtain such an audience on the following day. However he said nothing of this and with unabashed flattery asked Haus to obtain one for him, explaining that for reasons of discipline and protocol he had not dared to take such a step except through the Marinesektion. Haus seemed pleased by the little white lie, became less reserved, and arranged for Conz and Albricci to dine with some senior Austrian naval officers that evening. During the meal, at which the atmosphere became gradually less diffident, then cordial, and in the end open, the Marinesektion informed Conz of the hour set for his audience with Conrad—which naturally coincided with the one already fixed by Albricci.[89]

Conrad, who had previously learned of Conz's impending arrival through both Waldersee and the Marinesektion, questioned the Italian officer on how the Italians would provide for the defense of their troops in Libya in the event of war. He implied that an exit of the Austrian fleet from the Adriatic ought not to serve as a compensation for deficiencies in the Italian fleet caused by units detached for Tripolitan waters. The chief of the General Staff may have been somewhat out of his element in discussing naval affairs, and Conz was easily able to turn aside his argument. He replied that the troops in Libya would be considered interned, and that in any case a naval defense of Libya was impossible because of the lack of suitable bases or supplies. Therefore the sole means of defending Libya as well as the troops stationed there was by winning control of the sea. Conz dismissed Conrad's apprehensions about the Russian Black Sea fleet by pointing out its scant value and the ten to twelve days—a slightly higher figure than previously cited by the Stato Maggiore—he claimed it

[88] Conz, "Relazione al ritorno," pp. 3–4, USM, cartella 295/6.
[89] *Ibid.*, pp. 5–6. Conz reported that the following day the rigorous surveillance by plainclothes police to which he had been (or thought he had been) subjected ceased.

would take to reach the theater of operations and be ready for battle. Conz handled the objection to leaving the Adriatic completely unprotected by promising that the obsolete Italian units and coastal torpedo boats unable to fight in the first line in the Mediterranean could join with their Austrian counterparts in barring the entrance to that sea.[90]

Conrad submitted the proposal for the naval convention in an audience with the Emperor on May 9 and received his approval for the principle of a union of the fleets in the vicinity of Messina for the purpose of defeating the Mediterranean forces of France and her allies.[91] When the news of Franz Joseph's approval reached the Marinesektion, Conz was surrounded by unusual affability complete with mutual congratulations and fraternal phrases and speeches in the Venetian-Dalmatian dialect by admirals and senior officers. A conference to settle the details of the convention would convene in Vienna at the end of May. To Conz it seemed as if the heir to the throne had been bypassed, and indeed he had been told that Franz Ferdinand was away from the capital on a hunting party in Styria.[92] Haus did not report the May 6 meeting with Conz and the discussion at the Marinesektion to the Archduke's Militärkanzlei until May 9, the date of Conrad's audience with the Emperor.[93] Though no proof exists, one has at least some suspicion that this delay may not have been entirely accidental. When Franz Ferdinand did learn of the forthcoming conference with the Italians he ordered that every Austrian officer who was to participate be instructed not to say too much to the sly (*schlauen*) Italians.[94] The Marinesektion promised to adhere scrupulously to the Archduke's wishes. Bardolff suggested that a copy of the instructions for the Austrian delegate be submitted for the Archduke's inspection. Franz Ferdinand added a somewhat irate minute to this proposal concerning his having to speak to the perpetually reserved Marinesektion about reporting everything and

[90] *Ibid.*, pp. 6–7; Conrad, *Aus meiner Dienstzeit*, III, 307–308.

[91] Conrad to Haus, 10 May 1913, OK/MS-6/G.V., 1913. A copy of the principles approved by the Emperor was also given to Conz. USM, cartella 295/6.

[92] Conz, "Relazione al ritorno," pp. 7–9, and enclosure 2, "Punto di vista Austriaco," pp. 1–2, *ibid.* Conrad's audience was originally scheduled at Schönbrunn for the eighth, but for reasons unknown to Conz was put off until the ninth. Freyberg, the German naval attaché, also reported that according to one authority, perhaps the same source that Conz mentioned, the Archduke to all appearances had been completely excluded from the matter because of his anti-Italian sentiments. Freyberg to Von Pohl, 18 May 1913, GFM 26, reel 61, frame 166–167.

[93] Haus to MKFF, 9 May 1913, MKFF/41-25/6, 1913. Haus also said nothing about his talk with Conz on the fifth. The Militärkanzlei stamp is dated 10 May as is Bardolff's report.

[94] "Höchste Bemerkung Seine kaiserlichen Hoheit," report by Bardolff, 10 May 1913, *ibid.*

not always considering him as a distinguished foreigner.[95] Bardolff was careful to specify that the desired instructions be submitted before the beginning of negotiations.[96]

The Marinesektion intended to leave the initiative at the conference with the Italians.[97] Captain (Linienschiffskapitän) Alfred Cicoli, designated to become head of the Operationskanzlei, was the Austrian officer entrusted with the negotiations. The directions he received, duly submitted to the archduke in advance, reflected a very cautious approach to the entire question. In general the Austrians intended to preserve the convention of 1900 largely unchanged, and add a supplementary convention containing an operational plan. They realized that it would be better to eliminate the old system of zones of operation, but they decided to retain them to serve as a basis for settling the difficult question of command. They proposed an unimportant modification of the Italian zone in Italy's favor. The dividing line would extend from Santa Maria di Leuca to not Ras el Tin but the eastern frontier of Libya. This of course merely reflected Italy's acquisition of the new colony. As the question of command had caused the most trouble in 1900, the Austrians decided to leave unchanged the provisions about it in the old treaty.[98] This gave the supreme command to the senior officer of the nation in whose zone operations took place. Since the Austrians agreed to send their fleet out of the Adriatic, this implied they were ready to place it under Italian command, unless they intended to propose an additional subdivision of the Tyrrhenian into zones.[99]

The Austrians participating in the conference were ordered to be extremely reticent in the establishment of technical details of the convention. On the question of wireless techniques, Cicoli was told to say nothing about Austrian arrangements and, on the other hand, attempt to learn something about those of Austria's allies. The exchange of service publications was to be limited, at least on the Austrian side, to unimportant matters and under no circumstances involve reserved internal matters. This suspicious Austrian attitude also applied to the preparation of a new signal code book for the allied fleets. The Austrians were aware that this was likely to prove a lengthy undertaking most conveniently left to one navy

[95] Minute by Franz Ferdinand to Bardolff's report, 17 May 1913, *ibid.*

[96] MKFF to Marinesektion, 21 May 1913, *ibid.*

[97] OK/MS to naval attaché, Rome, 20 May 1913, OK/MS-1/G.V., 1913.

[98] OK/MS, "Referat zur Revision und Ergänzung des Marineübereinkommens von Jahre 1900," Beilage to Marinesektion to MKFF, 24 May 1913, MKFF/41-25/6, 1913.

[99] I found no evidence the Austrians were planning to propose an additional subdivision of the zones. Material found in the Austrian archives seems to indicate the old zones, slightly altered as mentioned above, were to have been retained.

rather than a short conference. Realizing that the navy preparing the book would be at a disadvantage—since the compilers might unwittingly divulge some of their own signal and maneuver norms—they thought it wise to assign the project to Italy or Germany.[100]

The problem of the supreme command of the allied fleets was mutually regarded as the most important question.[101] So far it had been touched on only gingerly by each of the parties. It cast a heavy shadow over the impending Vienna Conference for it was the one issue that was most likely to frustrate the plans for cooperation, especially in the light of the always sensitive Austrian-Italian relationship. The Italians felt that they had a strong claim to the supreme command, for they would be contributing the major portion of ships and men, placing their naval bases and coal deposits at the disposition of the allies, and operating in a sea where their annual maneuvers were held and which was therefore thoroughly familiar in innumerable ways to their commanders. On the other hand the Italians realized that the Austrians were stripping their own coast of a fleet which was intended to protect it and which was the fruit of financial sacrifices over the years. They were sending this force far away to face heavy risks as a contribution to the Triple Alliance. Their only compensation would be assistance on land against Russia, which would come as a result of a successful maritime operation. As Revel put it, since the Austrians were gambling everything at sea on a single card, they could not be blamed if they wanted to entrust that card to a man of their own choice, the leader of their fleet Admiral Haus. Moreover Haus, a full admiral, could not be placed under the orders of an Italian Commander-in-Chief who was only a vice admiral.

Revel was therefore ready to propose that Italy on her own initiative offer the supreme command to Admiral Haus. He was not being purely altruistic: the move at the beginning of the conference would have the tactical advantage of creating a favorable terrain for Italy during the discussion of all the other questions. However, the Italians would insist that the supreme command should not become an exclusive privilege of the Dual Monarchy, and that in the future, when they too had officers with the rank of full admiral, it might also be given to an Italian.[102] The Italians also hinted to the Austrian naval attaché in Rome that a settlement of the final details of the convention might be left to personal conversations between Haus and Revel.[103]

[100] OK/MS, "Referat zur Revision," MKFF/41-25/6, 1913.

[101] Revel to Brusati, 8 May 1913, ACS, Carte Brusati/10/VII-3-43, no. 487.

[102] Revel, "Studi preparatori per i lavori della conferenza," n.d. [May 1913], USM, cartella 295/7.

[103] Liechtenstein to Marinesektion, 26 May 1913, OK/MS-2/G.V., 1913.

Conz, who had made an excellent impression on both the Germans and the Austrians, again represented his country at the naval conference, arriving in Vienna on June 1.[104] Compared to the imposing collection of army and navy officers who had prepared the 1900 convention, the group which assembled at the Marinesektion on Marxergasse was small. Aside from Conz and Cicoli, who represented the Italian and Austrian navies respectively, there was only Commander (Korvettenkapitän) Erich Köhler of the German Admiralstab accompanied by Lieutenant Commander (Kapitänleutnant) Alfred Saalwachter, a signals expert. Lieutenant Commander (Linienschiffsleutnant) Alfred Suchomel of the Austrian navy acted as secretary. The day before the first session Haus assembled all the participants for a speech of welcome during which he made the unexpected announcement that he would not be able personally to direct the work of the conference because of a serious abdominal operation he was to undergo within a few days. Afterwards he asked Conz to a private meeting during which he brought up the question of the supreme command. He indicated that the candidacy of the Duke of the Abruzzi would be acceptable and that he was ready to fall back on the concept of command by zones in order to prevent his own person from becoming an obstacle to prompt agreement. Conz interpreted this somewhat unexpected revelation to anxiety that Italy would be intransigent over the question, and a desire to let it be understood that the Duke of the Abruzzi, but only the duke, would arouse no Austrian opposition. Conz restricted himself for the moment to his usual flatteries, but was glad to note privately that the suspicion of the Austrians seemed finally to have vanished.[105]

On the following morning, immediately before the first session of the conference, Rear Admiral Karl Kailer von Kaltenfels, the representative of the Marinekommandant in Vienna, also engaged in some polite fencing with Conz over the question of the supreme command. Kailer pushed the candidacy of the Duke of the Abruzzi so openly that the Italian delegate was somewhat embarrassed, and both men were obviously happy when it was time to enter the conference room.[106] Luigi di Savoia, Duke of the Abruzzi, a vice admiral in the Italian navy, and well known for his many voyages, polar explorations and mountaineering activities, appears to have been one Italian officer who enjoyed an excellent reputation among the

104 Haus to Revel, 10 May 1913, USM, cartella 296; Pohl to Revel, 31 May 1913, *ibid.*; Pollio to Revel, 26 May 1913, *ibid.*; Liechtenstein to Marinesektion, 28 May 1913, OK/MS-IX-9/3, 1913.
105 Conz to Revel, 2 June 1913, USM, cartella 296.
106 Conz to Revel, 4 June 1913, *ibid.* Conz refers to Abruzzi's candidacy as unacceptable for reasons which Revel knew, but unfortunately does not elaborate.

ruling circles of Austria-Hungary. Even Emperor Franz Joseph in an audience with the new Italian naval attaché some months later remarked about the Duke, "There is a capable leader!" [107] However, for reasons which remain obscure, Abruzzi's candidacy was unacceptable to the Italians.[108] Conz gathered that the Austrians were giving them the choice of either Haus or Abruzzi, or command by zones, which he interpreted as including a possible subdivision of the Tyrrhenian with an infinity of muddles and complications. He therefore saw no way out except to emphasize Haus's candidacy, which he did during the first session, clothed in appropriate terms of loyalty to the Triple Alliance and suitable reservations about the possibility of an Italian Commander-in-Chief in the future. Cicoli, who presided, lacked the authority to abandon the concept of command by zones, and was obliged to adjourn the conference until the following day.[109]

The following morning the Marinekommandant sent a message graciously accepting the honor of the supreme command in the event of war. The concept of zones for operations had been abandoned, and the Italians and Germans had gained one of their principal points. The Austrian and Italian fleets might be combined. At the same time the most difficult of the problems had been successfully resolved. Conz wrote privately that everyone was "radiant with delight," and probably he alone suffered from anguish of the heart. However, he realized that reason ought to prevail over sentiment. From the private letters with which Conz kept Revel informed of the progress of the conference it is apparent that he had few illusions about his Austrian allies, despite his outward, carefully measured, cordiality. The Italian officer wryly noted that the numerous paintings, prints, and etchings of the Battle of Lissa which had formerly adorned the rooms and corridors of the Marinesektion had all been replaced with innocuous travel scenes before his return. Upon reflection, Conz thought Haus—who enjoyed an excellent reputation—was the best solution. The state of the sixty-two-year-old admiral's health made it quite possible that his command would not be of long duration, and then Italy would have a free hand. Moreover the principle of an Italian as the next Commander-in-Chief had been affirmed, and Conz believed their gesture over Haus

[107] Report by Capitano di corvetta Winspeare, 21 Oct. 1913, USM, cartella 279/1. Admiral Daveluy, the French liaison officer attached to the Duke of the Abruzzi during the war also described him as a real and effective chief who inspired confidence in his captains; report by Daveluy, 9 June 1915, AMF, carton Ea-136.

[108] Conz to Revel, 4 June 1913, USM, cartella 296.

[109] Verbali, 3 June 1913, USM, cartella 295/9. As had been previously arranged, Köhler strongly supported the Italian proposals while taking no stand on the question of the supreme command.

had made them the masters of the conference on all other points. He concluded that relations between the two countries had acquired a cordial character which it otherwise would have been impossible to hope for, and which responded, if not to their hearts, certainly to their more vital interests.[110]

The work of the conference proceeded slowly with what amounted to a regular routine. The Italian delegate was generally asked to present his government's views; this he was well equipped to do, thanks to the careful preparatory studies of the Stato Maggiore. The Italian ideas, administered in small doses by Conz, were almost all accepted in the end.[111] Messina was preferred to Taranto as the concentration point. The latter was an additional 200 miles from the Tyrrhenian, while the former was half way between the Adriatic and the upper Tyrrhenian. To prevent cluttering the harbor of Messina with too many ships and to enhance secrecy, the Italians wanted the Austrians to coal at Augusta. Conz explained that this secrecy was important should the allies in a period of diplomatic tension attempt to combine before the outbreak of hostilities. News of the Austro-Italian movements might provoke a declaration of war by the enemy. The Germans were not pleased over the Italian plan to keep a special division of four battleships (two "Brins" and two "Bons") in the upper Tyrrhenian, but Conz justified this by claiming the slower speed of the old ships would delay the movement of the rest of the fleet southward to the rendezvous, while the four battleships would hinder French action against the undefended Ligurian coast and could join the allied fleet on its advance northward, possibly drawing the French fleet after them.[112] The participants did not hesitate to discuss the contingency in which the British Mediterranean squadron was included in the enemy fleet.

Haus underwent surgery on June 9 for the removal of part of his large intestine and a stomach tumor which proved benign. By the time the conference ended he was on the way to recovery. The allies reached agreement far more easily then they may have anticipated. The Italians proved successful in getting the best Austrian torpedo craft outside of the Adriatic, and in retaining complete freedom of action for their special battleship division in the upper Tyrrhenian without having to make a similar con-

---

[110] Verbali, 4 June 1913, *ibid.;* Conz to Revel, 4 June 1913. The assignment of the supreme command to Haus was, in the light of subsequent events, a sensitive point among Italian writers after the war when the existence of the naval convention became public; it became the source of apologetic writing emphasizing the more Machiavellian aspect of the Italian action. See for example Po, *Thaon di Revel,* pp. 53f; Alberti, *L'Opera di Generale Pollio,* pp. 21–22.

[111] Conz to Revel, 9 June 1913, USM, cartella 296.

[112] Verbali, 7 and 9 June 1913, USM, cartella 295/9.

cession to the Austrians in the Adriatic.[113] The very old "Sardegna" class battleships were also free from any obligation under the convention, and the Italians planned to use them for the defense of Genoa. Here the Italians claimed they would protect the flank of any army operating against France.[114] Operations against the French convoys, the primary concern of the Germans, were discussed at length, but Conz did not think that the idea of Cagliari as a base and an Italian commander for the undertaking had been assimilated yet.[115]

Conz complained about the slow procedure of the conference and the difficulty in getting the others to accept new ideas quickly. He mentioned the daily series of why's and how's, and the way the Italians seemed to provide the leadership.[116] His implication was clearly that his Austrian colleagues were at best slow-witted. He undoubtedly did not realize Cicoli had been specifically ordered to let Conz keep the initiative. After lengthy discussions on commerce warfare, the use of auxiliary ships, and signal matters, the allies wound up the conference on June 23.[117] The Admiralstab accepted Cicoli's not so innocent proposal that Saalwachter prepare the signal book because of his experience in this field and presence at the conference.[118] Saalwachter was also to prepare a "field map" of the Mediterranean which was to be divided into small numbered zones in order to facilitate the transmittal of orders and information. This would be particularly useful in reconnaissance work by scout cruisers. The convention was signed by all the delegates and was then to be submitted to the three sovereigns.[119]

To the relatively small number of people involved in the conclusion of the new naval convention, the situation must have seemed greatly changed from that at the turn of the century. The Austrians and Italians had actually agreed to cooperate in a joint action. The Austrians were willing to risk their fleet outside of the Adriatic, and the Italians agreed to an Austrian Commander-in-Chief. For the German Admiralstab, it must have seemed almost too good to be true. Cynics might have wondered if the convention would have the necessary vitality or if it would remain largely a piece of paper like the old agreement of 1900.

[113] Conz to Revel, 9 and 14 June 1913, USM, cartella 296.
[114] Verbali, 13 June 1913, USM, cartella 295/9.
[115] Verbali, 14 June 1913, *ibid.*; Conz to Revel, 14 June 1913, USM, cartella 296.
[116] *Ibid.*
[117] For the full discussion on commerce warfare and auxiliary ships see Verbali, 16 June 1913, USM, cartella 295/9.
[118] Verbali, 17, 18, 20 June 1913, *ibid.*
[119] Verbali, 23 June 1913, *ibid.* Completion of annexes I and II of the supplementary convention, which involved technical and logistical matters as well as regulations for the requisition of merchant ships, was to be arranged between the admiralties at a later date. Cicoli to Marinesektion, 23 June 1913, OK/MS-7/G.V., 1913.

IX

The Triple Alliance
in the Mediterranean

The bulk of the difficult work in preparing the new naval convention had been accomplished by the time Conz and Köhler bade farewell to their Austrian allies in Vienna. There remained only the task of tidying up the agreement and obtaining the sovereign's consent. Over the summer of 1913 the Italians proposed certain modifications to the text of the convention, largely in the interests of maintaining secrecy. These were accepted by the Austrians and Germans without undue difficulty.[1] The Admiralstab did not think any of their own suggestions for a different wording of the text were important enough to warrant the delay resulting from a proposal for changes although the Italians would have been willing to accept them.[2] Emperor Franz Joseph, last of the three sovereigns to ratify the convention, gave his approval on October 12 and the convention went into effect November 1.[3]

The naval convention actually consisted of two parts: the convention itself, a general agreement which was not likely to require frequent revision; and a supplementary convention (*Zusatzübereinkommen*) which formed the basic outline of a plan for joint operations in the Mediterranean, the details of which could be changed by the admiralty staffs on mutual understanding.[4] The convention specified that the supreme com-

---

[1] Revel to Kailer, 2 July 1913, USM, cartella 295/11; Kailer to Revel, 2 Aug. 1913, *ibid.*

[2] Köhler to Conz, 11 July 1913, *ibid.*; Revel to Kailer, 22 Aug. 1913, *ibid.*; Kailer to Revel, 2 Sept. 1913, *ibid.* One point the Admiralstab raised referred to mention of only the French fleet, and not the British, in the text. Köhler thought the phrase "defeat of the enemy fleets" which was in the convention implied the British as well as the French, and would therefore suffice. Köhler to Cicoli, 11 July 1913, OK/MS-13/G.V., 1913.

[3] Bolfras to Haus, 12 Oct. 1913, OK/MS-22/G.V., 1913.

[4] The complete text including the German version is reproduced in A. F. Pribram, *The Secret Treaties of Austria-Hungary*, Eng. ed. by A. C. Coolidge, I (Cambridge, Mass., 1920), 282–305. The Italian text is in Ufficio Storico, *La Marina italiana*, I, 158–174.

mand could be entrusted to either an Austrian or Italian admiral. Should he become incapacitated in the course of joint operations, the officer next below him in rank, or if there were two officers of equal rank, the commander of the larger force, would assume command until a new supreme commander was named.

The supplementary convention named Haus Commander-in-Chief. He was to be given an Austrian and an Italian chief of staff with the rank of Linienschiffskapitän or Capitano di Vascello, and an admiralty staff officer from each of the three countries. The two chiefs of staff and the German Admiralstab officer would be directly subordinate to the Commander-in-Chief; it was considered desirable for the Commander-in-Chief to establish personal relations with his chiefs of staff in time of peace. Signal, wireless, and clerical personnel would be assigned as required. In general the subordinate units (squadrons, divisions) would be constituted from ships of the same nationality. In the event of war the Austrian and Italian fleets would assemble as quickly as possible in the neighborhood of Messina and complete their supplies. The anchorage of the Italian fleet was between Milazzo and Messina; the Austrian fleet, at Augusta. At the same time German ships in the Mediterranean would attempt to reach Gaeta or, in the event of unfavorable sea conditions, Naples to complete their supplies. If this was impossible they would join the Commander-in-Chief near Messina. The Italians if necessary would keep a special division in the Tyrrhenian and deploy part of their torpedo flotillas and minelayers to Cagliari and Trapani.

The objective of the Commander-in-Chief was "the securing of naval control in the Mediterranean through the swiftest possible defeat of the enemy fleets." If part of the French fleet was at Bizerte, the Commander-in-Chief would attempt to deal separately with the scattered portions. Minelayers and torpedo boats from Trapani might possibly be used to hold those enemy forces at Bizerte. Light units of the western Ligurian coastal defense might act against a French force steaming eastward from Toulon. The main action was to take place and a decision was to be reached as soon as possible so that Russian forces from the Black Sea would not have time to interfere. It was left to the discretion of the supreme commander whether or not to conduct simultaneously with the main operation secondary actions against French troop convoys or portions of the enemy coast.

The Italians were responsible for the preparation and provisioning of Augusta, Gaeta, and Messina in time of peace. They would be compensated by the Austrians and Germans for supplies used. Any supplies remaining after the Austrian fleet left Augusta would be removed or destroyed to forestall capture by the enemy. The Italians were also to prepare bases for further operations. These were: La Spezia for their own forces; Maddalena for the Austrians and Germans; and Trapani, Cagliari, and sites on the western part of the Ligurian coast for light units. In addition to the fuel stocks, Maddalena was to be provisioned with one month's rations for the Austrian fleet. The Austrian and German forces left in the Adriatic would assemble in the Gulf of Cattaro, and the Italians at Brindisi. Operations would be commanded by the highest ranking allied naval officer, who was subject to the orders of the supreme commander. The supreme commander could withdraw from or reinforce the Adriatic forces as the situation required.

The French were expected to commence troop convoys from North Africa within three days after mobilization. The Italians were therefore immediately to establish a patrol of fast auxiliary cruisers off the North African coast. To supplement this, operations by light warships from Cagliari and later Maddalena were contemplated. The joint operations against the convoys were to be directed from Cagliari by an Italian commander directly subordinate to the supreme commander, who might, if need be, also dispatch fast cruisers to hinder the convoys. Auxiliary cruisers were to be used against enemy commerce, and it appeared advantageous to establish a patrol off both the Suez Canal and the Dardanelles upon the outbreak of hostilities. The bases contemplated for operations in the eastern Mediterranean were Taranto, the vicinity of Messina, and Tripoli and Tobruk on the Libyan coast. A separate agreement for the requisitioning of allied merchant vessels for war purposes was to be concluded. Messina and Maddalena were designated as bases for supply ships of the Austrian fleet. German ship owners would be instructed to send any of their ships in the Mediterranean on the outbreak of war to Italian ports, mail boats to La Spezia if possible and others to Taranto or any port except Genoa.

The naval force Admiral Haus would command in the event of war was an impressive one on paper. It was specified for 1914 in annex I of the supplementary convention. The Italian contribution was: three dreadnoughts; four pre-dreadnoughts ("Regina Elenas"); seven armored cruisers; four scout cruisers; twenty-six destroyers; twenty-four 250-ton torpedo boats; and thirty smaller 33-knot torpedo boats. Steaming from the Adriatic to join them would be the Austrian force of: three dreadnoughts; three semi-dreadnoughts; six pre-dreadnoughts; two armored cruisers; four scout cruisers; eighteen destroyers; and twelve torpedo boats. Under favorable circumstances this combined force would be joined by the Italian special division of four pre-dreadnoughts and one scout cruiser; these would be retained initially in the upper Tyrrhenian. Haus would also have the assistance of those German ships stationed in the Mediterranean; in the summer of 1913 they numbered one battle cruiser and three scout cruisers. The defense of the Adriatic was left to the obsolete Austrian "Monarchs," ten old Austrian and Italian cruisers, and the older destroyers and torpedo craft of each fleet, plus whatever old German cruisers or school ships happened to be in the Mediterranean. In comparison, the French would have had a maximum of four dreadnoughts in service by the fall of 1914, plus twelve first-line semi-dreadnoughts or pre-dreadnoughts, and at least six old battleships. After all allowances are made for a paper force which had never actually worked together, one must admit that the Triple Alliance at the very least would have posed a serious challenge to the Triple Entente in the Mediterranean.

Revel was realistic enough to realize that the language of the supplementary convention in regard to naval operations was merely an outline, and that it was desirable, if not imperative, that he discuss the joint operations with Haus in person. How could this meeting be arranged without arousing foreign curiosity? Revel's solution was that they meet at an opportune moment in a Swiss or German location, or perhaps a large Italian city such as Turin or Milan.[5] Haus agreed, taking care to secure the Emperor's consent first. He was, however, unable to leave Vienna until the end of the autumn session of the Delegations in which the new naval program was to be presented. Haus therefore suggested that Revel choose a city in Switzerland; the Austrian admiral would be accompanied only by his adjutant Captain Josef Rodler, who was to become his chief of staff in the event of war. Immediately before the close of the Delegations Haus promised to inform Revel of his readiness to leave Vienna with a cable signed "Antonio." Revel chose Zurich and agreed to cable Haus the date of his arrival there; the message would be signed "Paolo." He was to be accompanied only by Conz and planned to register at the Hotel Bauer du Lac under the name of "Paul de Reyard."[6] The Delegations lasted longer than was anticipated, and the meeting between Antonio and Paolo apparently did not take place until just before Christmas 1913.[7]

The records of this meeting between the two admirals who within a

[5] Revel to Haus, 20 Oct. 1913, OK/MS-25/G.V., 1913.

[6] Haus to Revel, 17 Nov. 1913, *ibid.*; Revel to Haus, 26 Nov. 1913, OK/MS-27/G.V., 1913.

[7] Haus to Revel, 4 Dec. 1913, *ibid.* Haus was to use his own name at the hotel. His cable to Revel indicating his readiness to leave Vienna is dated 17 Dec.; Haus to Revel, 17 Dec. 1913, USM, cartella 296.

year and a half were to oppose each other in the Adriatic are unfortunately fragmentary. The exact date of the discussions and how long they lasted is not recorded, although both men sent a joint message to their German colleague Von Pohl on December 21. Their talk was not limited to the single contingency of a war by the Triple Alliance against the Triple Entente. Revel made a note to bring to Zurich his intelligence on the fortifications in the Gulf of Piraeus in connection with a possible blockade of Greece, along with information on precedents set by past blockades of that country. At Zurich Haus and Revel agreed that in the event of a joint blockade the Austrian fleet would patrol the zone from Corfu to Cape Maleas, and the Italian fleet would take a position to the east of them. At the time both the Austrian and Italian governments were embroiled with the Greeks over the boundaries of Albania, and this probably accounts for the discussion of the subject.[8]

In Triple Alliance matters Haus expressed his concern that while the combined fleets hurried northward after having coaled in Sicily, the French would proceed southward to the west of the screen formed by Corsica and Sardinia, turn Cape Spartivento, and unite with a French force coming from Bizerte and probably the British force from Malta. Once this combination had been effected the enemy force might turn in pursuit of the Austro-Italian fleet, which would also be exposed to surprise attacks on its flank from the Strait of Bonifacio, and submarine attacks on the line Cape Corso–Piombino. Haus was therefore anxious to bar the Straits of Bonifacio with submarines to prevent the passage of an enemy force and, vice versa, to guarantee his own passage from east to west across the Gulf of Maddalena to avoid being caught in the Tuscan archipelago. Both admirals discussed at length the problems of reconnaissance and transmittal of intelligence in these waters, and also the possibility of using their own submarines on the line Cape Corso–Elba against a French fleet moving to the east of Corsica.

If the French fleet passed to the west and south of Sardinia to unite with a force from Bizerte or Malta the role of the torpedo craft concentrated at Cagliari would be transformed. They would no longer be directed only at the French convoys, but would now strike at the French fleet on its way south. The torpedo craft at Trapani could also act against a force coming from Bizerte and Malta to join the main French fleet to the south of Sardinia. The two admirals therefore gave consideration to the torpedo craft

---

[8] Unsigned memorandum on stationery of "Il Capo di Stato Maggiore della Marina," n.d., *ibid.* The account of the meeting is based on this memorandum. For diplomatic background see Helmreich, *Diplomacy of the Balkan Wars*, pp. 429f.

to be detached from their main fleet for assignment to Cagliari and Trapani. They spoke of a flotilla of six for Cagliari and eight to twelve for Trapani. They discussed various defensive tactics and weapons which might be used against the numerous French submarines including the primitive idea of firing machine guns at periscopes. Haus did not favor this tactic.

The talks at Zurich ranged over the topics of tactical evolutions for the combined squadrons; provisions for coaling the Austrian fleet at Augusta; the possibility approximately two weeks after mobilization of material reinforcements for the Austrian fleet coming by sea from Pola to Venice, and then by rail from Venice to La Spezia or another Italian port; signal matters; night formations for the combined fleet; the marking of anchorages at Maddalena; and the possibility of mining Port Mahon if Spain's attitude made it necessary. Revel apparently thought it advisable for the combined fleet to show itself at Naples before proceeding northward in order to calm the population. He also thought it necessary to conduct a war game in the western basin of the Mediterranean and the Tyrrhenian to test some of the strategies and planned to do this during the autumn maneuvers of 1914.

Haus and Revel deliberated whether or not to use the magnificent German battle cruiser *Goeben* against the French convoys, or as a large armored cruiser in their own fleet in the anticipated naval battle. Haus would have preferred to keep her for the naval battle so as to have an additional dreadnought; the *Goeben's* speed enabling her to be used in a detached division would have been a great advantage. However it was apparently decided that it would be better to use her initially against the convoys, and only in the second phase of operations with the fleet. In attacking the convoys she would be supported by the light Italian units at Cagliari. The two admirals also agreed to try and obtain from Germany two destroyers with a large radius of action to support the *Goeben's* mission. They proposed this in the joint letter to Von Pohl.[9]

Von Pohl, not surprisingly, agreed with the decision to allow the *Goeben* full freedom of action against the French convoys at the beginning of hostilities, but regretted that it was not possible to send suitable German destroyers to support her in the Mediterranean. Support of this sort would have to be drawn from the allied fleets. Until a personal encounter could be arranged with Haus and Revel, Korvettenkapitän von Arnim, Köhler's successor on the Admiralstab, was to act as liaison officer and settle, among

---

[9] Haus and Revel to Von Pohl, 21 Dec. 1913, *ibid.* The two extended their best wishes to Von Pohl for the new year and hoped that 1914 would offer the opportunity for a similar meeting with the chief of the German Admiralstab; they regretted that the need for absolute secrecy and the pressure of time made it impossible to include him in the Zurich meeting.

other points, the question of requisition by Austria and Italy of German merchant ships.[10] The Admiralstab also cabled to the commander of the Mittelmeerdivision the information that his main objective would be the French convoys, with Maddalena as his main concentration point *(Hauptaufmarschplatz),* and Cagliari as his secondary base *(Nebenstutzpunkt).*[11]

The topic of the requisition of German merchant shipping in the event of war was probably the most important business handled by Von Arnim during his special mission to Vienna and Rome in April 1914. The Austrians did not show great interest in the question.[12] The Germans provided the Italians with a list of merchant ships which might normally be found in the Mediterranean, along with detailed annotations concerning speed, wireless equipment, mountings for cannon, and provisions for minelaying gear.[13] The Italians were particularly interested in the 20-knot Hamburg-Amerika Line steamers *Königin Luise* and *Kaiser* (both ca. 20,000 tons) for use as minelayers. As these ships were normally in the Mediterranean only during the winter months on cruises to the Riviera, the Italians requested to see their plans so as to determine if the amount of work necessary for their conversion to minelayers was proportionate to the limited probability the ships would be available for use. The Italians were also interested in the 18-knot Norddeutscher Lloyd steamers *Berlin* and *München* (both ca. 17,324 tons) which were assigned the Genoa–New York service. The Stato Maggiore were careful to specify that they did not want them as auxiliary cruisers for use against enemy commerce off the Dardanelles or Suez Canal, as had been specified in the supplementary convention. The Italians intended, instead, to use the two ships as scouts in the northern Tyrrhenian to keep the allied fleet informed as it moved northward from Messina. They requested the plans for the two ships and also authorization for their examination by Italian authorities.[14] A protocol on the rules for requisition was signed by Conz and Von Arnim on April 29, and after technical modifications the allies exchanged German and Italian translations initialed by the staff chiefs at the end of June.[15] Von Pohl also sent the plans for the *Königin Luise, Kaiser,* and *Berlin,* the last

---

[10] Von Pohl to Haus, 5 Jan. 1914, OK/MS-G.V. (nicht protokolliert); Von Pohl to Revel, 6 Jan. 1914, USM, cartella 296.

[11] 17 Jan. 1914, GFM 26, reel 61, frames 323, 326–328.

[12] "Protokoll, über die Frage der Ueberlassung und Benützung deutscher Handels schiffe durch Österreich-Ungarn," 20 Apr. 1914, OK/MS-11/G.V., 1913. See also GMF 26, reel 61, frame 394–395.

[13] List of German ships annexed to Von Pohl to Revel, 15 Apr. 1914, USM, cartella 296.

[14] "Protocollo Speciale, circa la requizione," 29 Apr. 1914, *ibid.*

[15] Conz-Arnim Protokoll, 29 Apr. 1914, GFM 26, reel 61, frame 417-421; Von Arnim to Conz, Cicoli, 18 June 1914, *ibid.*, frame 449-451; Revel to Haus, 30 June 1914, OK/MS-11/G.V., 1913; Rodler to Revel, 8 July 1914, *ibid.*

a sister ship of the *München* which had not yet been completed. The plans reached Rome in late July and the German naval attaché did not hand them to Revel until the evening of the twenty-ninth.[16] By then the hour was late indeed, and events were shortly to make the entire matter of academic interest only.

Both the Austrians and the Germans provided the Italians with the technical and logistical requirements of their forces in the Mediterranean. This included information on the handling qualities (especially the diameter of the turning circle) of their warships. The information was to be used in compiling the squadron maneuvers of the allied fleet.[17] The most ambitious project was the preparation of the signal book by the Germans. This occupied the winter and most of the spring of 1914. The German edition, the *Triplecodex,* was endorsed "To be opened only on command of the Admiralstab in case of war," and was printed by the Reichsdruckerei in Berlin shortly before the outbreak of the war.[18] The Italian translation was nearing completion in July, but printing was delayed by the departure of Conz's confidant at the Ministry's press. Because of the necessity for secrecy it had not been possible to give the job to anyone else in Rome. Conz therefore proposed to Von Arnim that the Reichsdruckerei print the Italian translation in Berlin at Italy's expense.[19]

The Germans agreed to print the Italian version, suggesting that the manuscript be brought to Berlin by an Italian officer who was prepared to stay for about six weeks.[20] Conz had not yet proposed the matter officially to his own superiors, and the outbreak of the war and Italy's decision to remain neutral naturally ended the project. A total of 736 copies of the German edition of the *Triplecodex* were printed, 420 of which were delivered to the Austrians. The latter reported on August 22 that distribution to their fleet had been completed except for a cruiser in the Far East.[21] By then the matter was another dead issue, for the code was obviously known to the Italians who had participated in its preparation. With bureaucratic tidiness the Austrians asked for the bill in August 1914, and the Germans, after taking around seven months to present it, duly collected 4775 marks

[16] Von Pohl [?] to Revel, 18 July 1914; GFM 26, reel 61, frame 507; report by naval attaché, Rome, 30 July 1914, *ibid.*, frame 508-509.

[17] Köhler to Conz, 11 Nov. 1913, USM, cartella 296; appendix II to supplementary convention, copy in USM, cartella 295/10; various Austrian worksheets in OK/MS-G.V. (nicht protokolliert); German information on maneuvering qualities dated 23 Feb. 1914, and Austrian information dated 26 Feb. 1914 in USM, cartella 298/1.

[18] A copy is in USM, cartella 286/3.

[19] Conz to Von Arnim, 13 July 1914, GFM 26, reel 61, frame 504-505.

[20] Von Arnim to Conz, 17 July 1914, *ibid.*, frame 506.

[21] OK/MS[Haus] to Von Pohl, 22 Aug. 1914, OK/MS-17/G.V., 1914.

from the Marinesektion in April 1915 as Austria's share of the expense.[22] Less than a month later Italy entered the war on the side of the Entente.

A steady flow of intelligence, mostly on the French and British navies, circulated among the naval staffs of the Triple Alliance in the year before the outbreak of the war. The Austrians participated in this with, for example, a report on French convoy plans and a list of French steamers available for troop transport which they sent to both the Germans and Italians in July 1913.[23] But from the records surviving in the archives, the volume of information originating from Vienna does not appear to be anything like the traffic between Rome and Berlin in the summer and autumn of 1913. Starting in April 1913 a regular correspondence exists between Kapitän zur See Tapken, *Abteilungschef* of the intelligence section of the Admiralstab, and his Italian counterpart, Capitano di corvetta Ettore Rota, and above all the ubiquitous Conz. Both staffs faced a minor crisis in May 1913 when someone writing from Ala on the Austro-Italian frontier tried to extort money from Tapken for documents it was feared had been stolen from the mails.[24] The affair was not lacking in some of the attributes of a swindle, since the unknown correspondent collected money for a trip to meet Tapken and then never appeared. After the identities of those involved had been discovered, the Germans decided not to take action so as to avoid public scandal.[25]

Tapken visited Rome early in October 1913, and his correspondence with Conz came to assume a friendly and frank character. The two men even discussed their relations with an agent in France, a certain Rosse or Rosso, who at one time worked with both the Germans and Italians and whose usefulness in Toulon had been curtailed by the "very well organized" French security police. Tapken, who needed an agent in northern France, thought of sending Rosso and offered to share the information received with Conz. Tapken eventually sent the man to Dunkirk, but feared the agent had deduced the close relationship between the Germans and the Italians.[26] Conz tried to convince him that this could not be true and

[22] Chief of Admiralstab (Bachmann) to Haus, 24 Mar. 1915, OK/MS-1/G.V., 1915; receipt from Admiralstab, 30 Apr. 1915, *ibid.* Revel sent the Stato Maggiore's sole copy to the Duke of the Abruzzi, then Commander-in-Chief, Italian naval forces, the month before Italy entered the war. Revel to Abruzzi, 20 Apr. 1915, USM, cartella 286/3.

[23] Cicoli to Conz, 15 July 1913, USM, cartella 296; Behncke to Cicoli, 19 July 1913, OK/MS-16/G.V., 1913.

[24] Tapken to Conz [?], 24 May 1913, USM, cartella 298/1; Tapken to Conz, 27 May 1913, *ibid.*; Conz to Rota, 29 May 1913, *ibid.*

[25] Tapken to Rota [?], 25 June 1913, *ibid.*; Rota to Tapken, 28 June 1913, *ibid.*; Tapken to Conz, 29 Oct. 1913, *ibid.*

[26] Tapken to Conz, 20 Sept., 25 Oct., 1 Nov., and 12 Dec. 1913, *ibid.*

that Rosso was merely fishing and trying to increase his importance in order to obtain a higher price for his services. In a phrase that revealed something of the amateurish quality of this espionage, Conz warned his German colleague that Rosso "must not be regarded as a complete gentleman" and needed to be knocked in the head from time to time.[27] Among the more serious items the Germans passed to the Italians was a copy of the dispatch from their naval attaché in London commenting on the heavy traffic between the British and French admiralties, the special privileges of the French naval attaché, and his frequent trips to Paris, but concluding that a formal naval convention between the two countries did not yet exist, nor was there any intention to conclude one.[28] The Italians, for their part, lent to the German naval attaché in Rome a series of reports from their naval attaché in London. Rheinbaben considered this particularly advantageous, for he assumed the Italian attaché in London would have an easier time obtaining information than his German colleague.[29]

In the summer and fall of 1913 there were a number of visits to Germany by leading Italian figures. King Victor Emmanuel aboard the royal yacht *Trinacria,* escorted by the armored cruiser *Amalfi,* visited Kiel for the *Kielerwoche* regatta. The appearance of the Italian ships was "scandalous" and made a very unfavorable impression on the spit and polish Germans, or at least so the Austrian naval attaché claimed.[30] The Duke of the Abruzzi, accompanied by an aide, the Italian naval attaché in Berlin, and of course Conz, attended German naval maneuvers in the North Sea in September and ended his visit in Germany by breakfasting with the Kaiser at Potsdam.[31] The Kaiser, in addition to making political capital, hoped to benefit German industry by the tightening of military ties with Italy. As the German naval attaché in Rome frequently told Conz, the Kaiser was anxious for Krupp to replace Schneider in the provision of cannon for the new Italian dreadnoughts, and hoped to arrange something by means of the firm of Orlando.[32] General Pollio attended the German army maneuvers

[27] Conz to Tapken, n.d. [Dec. 1913], *ibid.*

[28] Report by naval attaché, London, 18 Sept. 1913, enclosed in Tapken to Conz, 13 Oct. 1913, *ibid.* The report is printed in *GP*, XXXIX no. 15621, pp. 134–135.

[29] Rheinbaben to Tirpitz, 24 Sept. 1913, GFM 26, reel 90, frame nos. illegible. Rheinbaben mentions Chilean and Brazilian officers as major sources of information for the Italian attaché in London. This lends weight to Admiralty objections over foreign officers serving in the Royal Navy. See below pp. 321–323.

[30] Einsichtsakt der Marinesektion, 18 July 1913, MKFF/41-25/7.

[31] Colloredo-Mannsfeld to Marinesektion, 10 Sept. 1913, OK/MS-X-2/2, 1913. The Austrian naval attaché had to rely on scanty press reports for his information about the maneuvers.

[32] Conz to Revel, 15 July 1913, USM, cartella 296. Conz says he kept quiet during the frequent advances by the German naval attaché not wishing to put his nose into matters which did not concern him.

in Silesia in September. Here he met Conrad who was also invited. He made a good impression on Conrad and on the Germans, who commented on his knowledge of military history and admiration for Frederick the Great.[33] At least outwardly Italy seemed closer to the Triple Alliance in 1913 than had been the case for a number of years.

Revel had departed from his secret meeting with Haus in Zurich with the idea of putting some of their discussion to the test during the annual maneuvers of the Italian navy. The Capo di Stato Maggiore therefore prepared an elaborate plan for the maneuvers to be held in the autumn of 1914 which was frankly designed to approximate as much as possible the conditions of a war with France in which England would not remain neutral, but would lend only limited aid to France in the Mediterranean, and where the Italian fleet would be supported by the Austrians as well as the German Mittelmeerdivision. The first of the strategic themes involved the simulated passage of an enemy convoy from North Africa to France.[34] The second theme involved a blockade of Maddalena by a superior enemy force and was designed to test the logistic capacity of that base as well as the effectiveness of the defensive and counteroffensive action of Italian submarines. The great care taken to simulate the conditions of a war in which Italy was a member of the Triple Alliance and the particular attention devoted to Maddalena in what presumably would have been an expensive war game is another indication that the Italian navy, whatever its private doubts and the subtle maneuvers of Italian diplomats and politicians, was completely serious about honoring its obligations to its allies. But then it would have been folly for the Stato Maggiore to act otherwise.

The German presence in the Mediterranean was another disturbing factor in the naval balance of power. The dictates of geography obviously limited the German Mediterranean force. Yet given the very close ratio of strength between the Austro-Italian and the French fleets, and the inclusion in the Mittelmeerdivision of a powerful battle cruiser such as the *Goeben*, Germany's potential contribution to her allies was far from negligible. The *Goeben* and the fast new scout cruiser *Breslau* were

[33] Before the maneuvers Pollio visited the East Prussian battlefields. Waldersee, "Von Deutschlands Beziehungen zu Italien," pp. 651–655; Conrad, *Aus meiner Dienstzeit*, III, 432–433; Helmuth von Moltke, *Erinnerungen, Briefe, Dokumente* (Stuttgart, 1922), p. 375.

[34] Revel, "Relazione al Ministro," 23 Apr. 1914, USM, cartella 315/9. Certain Italian ports would represent French bases, for example La Spezia and Trapani would simulate Toulon and Bizerte, respectively.

originally sent out in November 1912 during the Balkan Wars to join a handful of old cruisers and school ships in the protection of German interests in the unsettled eastern basin of the Mediterranean. To the dismay of Tirpitz and the Admiralstab, who wanted these fine ships back in the North Sea, both the *Goeben* and the *Breslau* remained in the Mediterranean after the older German warships returned home. In April 1913, with the *Breslau* fully occupied with the Montenegrin blockade, another two scout cruisers, the *Strassburg* and the *Dresden,* were sent to help in the protection of German interests in the waters of the Levant.[35]

The commander of the Mittelmeerdivision, Rear Admiral Trummler, recommended on April 26 that the German forces in the Mediterranean, assembled only temporarily into a division, be united into a permanent divisional command (*Divisionskommando*). The idea appealed to the Kaiser, who in a concluding remark to Trummler's report wrote that he was in agreement with the suggestion, and ordered that the necessary budgetary proposals be prepared for the Reichstag. He spoke enthusiastically of the political and diplomatic advantages to be gained, remarking that the Mittelmeerdivision would reduce England's hypnotic gaze in the North Sea and divert her attention to other waters. Tirpitz, however, advised leaving the present displacement as it was, for he thought formal measures could easily give rise to misunderstandings and misconceptions, and he also did not see how the autumn reliefs could be accomplished. The Kaiser apparently agreed with this modification of his proposals.[36] Baron Hans von Wangenheim, the German ambassador at Constantinople, feared that Trummler's initiative in using his ships on the Syrian coast to develop German interests might prove dangerous. Wangenheim thought such activity should be limited to those points to be included in Germany's sphere of interest in a future partition of Asia Minor.[37] The previous month Wangenheim had vetoed a proposal by Trummler to take the *Goeben,* then part of the international fleet at Constantinople, through the northern

[35] Colloredo-Mannsfeld to Marinesektion, 7 Apr. 1913, OK/MS-X-2/2, 1913. This force, the *Goeben* and three scout cruisers, was the one listed for Germany in annex I of the supplementary naval convention in the absence of specific information on the composition of the Mittelmeerdivision in 1914; Pribram, *The Secret Treaties of Austria-Hungary,* I, 305 n. 1.

[36] Editor's note with Wangenheim to Jagow, 10 Apr. 1913, *GP,* XXXVIII, no. 15293, pp. 20–21.

[37] Wangenheim to Jagow, 10 Apr. 1913, *ibid.* Trummler's ideas about Syria were apparently based on a conversation, or his own interpretation of a conversation, with Admiral Sir Berkeley Milne at the funeral of King George of Greece. The British Mediterranean Commander-in-Chief supposedly recommended that Germany be prepared to send ships to Syria. See Jagow to Prince von Lichnowsky, 6 Apr. 1913, *ibid.,* no. 15289, pp. 17–18; Wangenheim to Auswärtige Amt, 9 Apr. 1913, *ibid.,* no. 15290, pp. 18–19; Lichnowsky to Auswärtige Amt, 12 Apr. 1913, *ibid.,* no. 15292, p. 19.

approach of the Bosporus in order to familiarize his crew with those waters. After a thorough examination of the relevant treaty stipulations, the ambassador concluded it was likely to lead to undesirable political consequences and was best avoided.[38]

The *Strassburg* and the *Dresden* were brought home in September 1913, but the *Goeben* and the *Breslau* were to remain throughout the autumn.[39] This decision to keep the *Goeben* in the Mediterranean made the question of her repair an urgent one. She had been built by a private firm, Blohm and Voss of Hamburg, and her guarantee expired before the end of August necessitating an inspection of her turbines by that date. The terms of the guarantee as well as the peculiarity of her turbine plant made it necessary for the work to be performed under the direction of German naval officials; representatives of Blohm and Voss probably would also be present. As the floating dock at Pola was one of the two in the Mediterranean which could handle the *Goeben*, the Germans asked if the necessary work could be undertaken at Pola before August 27. The Austrians consented.[40] The time the *Goeben* spent under overhaul at Pola also gave Korvettenkapitän Wilhelm Busse, chief of staff of the Mittelmeerdivision, an opportunity to confer with Haus. Despite her impressive appearance, the *Goeben* actually suffered from serious defects. She had been sent to the Mediterranean before the completion of her trials and her boiler tubes leaked badly, reducing her speed and radius of action. The Germans planned to replace her with the battle cruiser *Moltke* in a transfer to be effected October 4, 1914, at Algeciras. Rear Admiral Wilhelm Souchon, who assumed command of the Mittelmeerdivision in October 1913, arranged for repair of his flagship's boiler tubes by German workers at Pola after learning of Franz Ferdinand's assassination, which he anticipated would lead to complications that could involve Germany.[41]

According to the standing orders for ships outside of home waters, all German ships in the Mediterranean in the event of war were to unite with allied naval forces utilizing every opportunity on the way to damage

---

[38] Wangenheim to Trummler, 12 Mar. 1913, GFM 26, reel 50 (frame no. illegible); Trummler to Admiralstab, 13 Mar. 1913, *ibid.*

[39] *Marine Rundschau,* Nov. 1913, p. 1332; *Nauticus, 1914,* p. 38. The *Strassburg* had accompanied the detached battleship division on its cruise to South America and was scheduled to return to the Mediterranean in the summer of 1914. *Ibid.*

[40] Ministry of Foreign Affairs to Marinesektion, 7 Aug. 1913, PK/MS-XII-2/11, 1913; Matte E. Mäkelä, *Souchon der Goebenadmiral* (Braunschweig, 1936), p. 37.

[41] Lorey, *Der Krieg in den türkischen Gewässern,* pp. 2–3; W. Souchon, "La Percée de S.M.S. 'Goeben' et 'Breslau' de Messine aux Dardanelles," in E. von Mantey, ed., *Les Marins Allemands au Combat,* French translation by R. Jouan and Y. de Jonchay (Paris, 1930), pp. 32, 34–35.

French commerce and communications with North Africa.[42] If difficulties appeared in reaching an allied harbor, the commanders were to attempt to reach the Atlantic if the conduct of cruiser warfare appeared promising there. Commerce warfare could only come into consideration in the eastern Mediterranean where, however, French commerce was small. If England joined the ranks of the enemy the British grain steamers from India and the Black Sea, which carried around 49 percent of England's wheat imports, would become another objective. German ships sallying out from the Mediterranean to the Atlantic as well as German cruisers already in the Atlantic were to concentrate on French convoys from the west coast of Morocco to Bordeaux. The new standing orders for 1914 were simpler, but contained a statement about the possibility of the French convoys heading for Spanish harbors. The destruction of this transport was now named as the main objective of the German naval force in the Mediterranean.[43]

In the course of cruising the Mediterranean Souchon met Haus at Pola in October 1913 and the Duke of the Abruzzi at Alexandria in December, had an audience, in January 1914, with King Victor Emmanuel in Rome, and also met with Admirals Millo and Thaon di Revel.[44] Souchon was anxious to know what Italian or Austrian destroyers would be attached to his force, and which of the light forces at Cagliari were to work with him. He thought it necessary either for them to be placed directly under him, or for an exact agreement on their tactics to be reached before hostilities. Souchon was also anxious to have colliers in the western Mediterranean, possibly south of the island of Formentera in the Balearics, to provide logistical support for his operations against the convoys.[45] Admiral von Pohl expected that the questions about the allied forces would be clarified in discussions with Austrian and Italian authorities. He intimated to Souchon that the Germans would try to have the Italian force intended for operations against the convoys placed under German leadership. Souchon was told he would have to make his own coaling arrangements in the Mediterranean, for the German colliers would probably be employed for the cruisers in the Atlantic.[46] Revel was eager to discuss the operations against the convoys with the Germans in order to define and coordinate the role

---

[42] Der Chef des Admiralstabes der Marine, *O-Befehle für die Auslandsschiffe (Auslands-O-Befehle)* (Berlin, 1913), GFM 27, reel 19.

[43] *O-Befehle für die Auslandsschiffe (Auslands-O-Befehle)* (Berlin, 1914), *ibid.*

[44] His personal impressions of the Italian leaders are in Souchon to Kaiser Wilhelm, 25 Jan. 1914, GFM 26, reel 51. See also Souchon, "La Percée de S.M.S. 'Goeben,'" pp. 33–34; Lorey, *Der Krieg in den türkischen Gewässern*, p. 3; Mäkelä, *Souchon*, p. 37; Ufficio Storico, *La Marina italiana nella grande guerra*, I, 175.

[45] Souchon to Von Pohl, 12 Mar. 1914, GFM 26, reel 61, frame 353-354.

[46] Von Pohl to Souchon, 8 Apr. 1914, *ibid.*, frame 354-355.

of the torpedo craft at Cagliari and auxiliary cruisers at Palermo.[47] However, he probably would not have been happy about placing them under German command.

The Admiralstab, as revealed in a memorandum dated July 3, 1914, were in complete disagreement with their Austrian and Italian allies on a number of points concerning operations in the Mediterranean.[48] This was particularly true in the estimate of the French fleet's probable course of action. The Germans believed—correctly—that the French would seek a decisive battle with the allied fleet for control of the sea with or without the support of England. Haus and the Italians thought the French would avoid an encounter as long as they were alone and devote their attention to attacking the Italian coast and attempting to win a strong point on Sardinia. This expectation of a French appearance in the Ligurian had resulted in the detachment of the special division of four old pre-dread-noughts in the hope of diverting the French from the Italian coast to a blockade of the Italian warships in Maddalena. The Germans, however, feared that the special division would be cut off and destroyed without fulfilling its mission. The preoccupation with the Ligurian had led to an allied plan for an advance by the combined fleet northward from Messina. The Admiralstab argued cogently that an advance northward to the west of Sardinia, rather than along the Italian coast, offered the best chances for success. They also deplored what they surmised as a tendency for the Austrians to look with mixed feelings on an offensive use of their own fleet far from home waters and to regard Austria-Hungary as the party making the concessions while Italy, in comparison, had not offered or could not offer enough.

The Germans wanted to put on a firm footing plans for the cooperation of the allied light units at Trapani and Cagliari with the Mittelmeerdivision against the French convoys. However, neither Haus nor Revel thought it expedient to place these forces under German command. Haus held that the Italian light forces were intended before all else to guard the approaches to the Tyrrhenian. In view of their relatively small number one could not count on their use against the French transports. The allied Commander-in-Chief designate was therefore against the establishment of any further plans for the undertaking. Revel, on the other hand, was in favor of clarifying these operations against the convoys, although not anxious for them to be under German command. This was a question which it was

[47] Revel to Von Pohl, 29 Apr. 1914, USM, cartella 296.
[48] Admiralstab, "Denkschrift über die Kriegführung des Dreibundes gegen Frankreich und England im Mittelmeer," 3 July 1914, GFM 26, reel 61, frame 467f.

considered best to leave to a personal encounter between the Capo di Stato Maggiore and Souchon. In view of this divergence of allied opinion in which Germany's allies manifestly showed relatively less interest in the primary German goal in the Mediterranean, the Admiralstab concluded that aside from the two destroyers definitely promised by the Italians, they could not safely count on the support of any of the allied light forces against the convoys. The Italians themselves were not yet sure which destroyers they would offer, but were considering the assignment of two as yet uncompleted 800-ton ships with a large radius of action.

The question of cruiser warfare against enemy commerce in the eastern Mediterranean was another subject which the Admiralstab realized was somewhat up in the air. Both the Austrians and Italians were apparently ready to use auxiliary cruisers in support of their fleets in the western Mediterranean, but the eastern basin was another question. The Germans considered the Italian attitude that they had neither sufficient money nor men to outfit auxiliary cruisers for services which would benefit all of their Triple Alliance partners as a typical example of the lack of unity in the interests of the Mediterranean allies. In this they considered the Italians to be merely more outspoken than the Austrians, and they realized that methodical cruiser operations in the eastern Mediterranean could be considered only in the second phase of a war when sufficient Austrian and Italian auxiliary cruisers were free.

Thus a year after the Triple Alliance naval convention had been concluded at Vienna, and barely a month before the European conflagration, the Admiralstab were far from happy over the plans for joint operations in the Mediterranean, but the comparatively small German contribution must naturally have reduced the weight of their opinion. The old curse of any alliance, a wide disparity of interests among its members, was highly evident.

In the talks preceding the Triple Alliance naval convention the Italians had mentioned a landing on the Provençal coast of France as one of the benefits which might be derived from supremacy in the Mediterranean. One might question if such an amphibious assault was ever a serious possibility. The problem was naturally interwoven with the Italian army's plans in the event of a war with France. The existing plan for an offensive by the Italian army over the northwest frontier had not met with universal acceptance. Lieutenant General Luigi Cadorna, Commander-in-Chief designate of the army, and ultimately Pollio's successor as chief of the General Staff, expressed to both Generals Brusati and Spingardi his opposition toward getting fruitlessly entangled in the Alps.[49] In a study prepared in the spring of 1913 for Pollio, Cadorna argued in favor of sending the largest possible portion of the army to the Rhine, which he considered the main theater of a war, and favored treating the Alps as a secondary theater.[50] At the German maneuvers the following September Pollio agreed to request the King's permission to send two cavalry divisions and eventually three to five infantry divisions through the Tyrol to southern Germany.[51] Pollio justified this to San Giuliano on the highly realistic grounds that a future war would be decided on the Franco-German battlefield, and Italy ought therefore to influence the result here. If most of their army remained unemployed, Italy would risk a disaster if Germany were defeated, while if the Germans were victorious they would be entitled to only a minor portion of the fruits of victory. Pollio added that if the French, contrary to all expectations, turned their main force against Italy, the Germans promised to send two army corps and some regiments of fortress artillery to their assistance, placing them under Italian command.[52]

Pollio secured the King's consent to send two cavalry divisions to the Rhine, and a new round of staff talks began to plan the movement. Actually, Moltke thought the cavalry would arrive too late to be employed as scouts and would therefore present no positive advantages. He thought it impolitic to decline them, however, and hoped they might be the vanguard for Italian infantry.[53] Italian forces stationed in Libya and the Aegean Islands at the beginning of 1914 numbered 69,000, of whom approximately 11,500 were native troops.[54] Though substantial, this total was almost half that of the forces employed in the Libyan War, and Pollio was soon able to think of restoring Italy's military commitment to Germany closer to what it had been before the colonial venture. In February of 1914 he obtained permission to add three army corps, or a total of six infantry divisions, to the cavalry force to be sent to the Rhine.[55] In March General Luigi

---

[49] Cadorna to Brusati, 26 May 1913, ACS, Carte Brusati/10/VII-1-41; Cadorna to Spingardi, 26 May 1913, *ibid.*

[50] Cadorna, "Studi sulle operazioni militari alla frontiera N.-O.," 26 May 1913, *ibid.*

[51] Conrad, *Aus meiner Dienstzeit,* III, 433; Waldersee, "Von Deutschlands Beziehungen zu Italien," pp. 652–655; Foerster, "Die deutsch-italiensche Militärkonvention," p. 404.

[52] San Giuliano to Giolitti, 2 Nov. 1913, ACS, Carte Giolitti, busta 11, fascicolo 1.

[53] Foerster, "Die deutsch-italiensche Militärkonvention," p. 404; Conrad, *Aus meiner Dienstzeit,* III, 498–501, 752–753; Waldersee, "Von Deutschlands Beziehungen zu Italien," pp. 656–659.

[54] Comando del Corpo di Stato Maggiore, Ufficio Coloniale, "Specchi indicata la forza mobilita riparita fra i vari presidi della Libia e dell'Egeo alla data del 1 gennaio," [1914], p. 31, USM, cartella 307/1.

[55] Conrad, *Aus meiner Dienstzeit,* III, 599–600.

Zuccari, who was designated to command these forces, conferred with Moltke in Berlin. Moltke learned that the Italian army corps could not arrive until the nineteenth day of mobilization, and would not be ready until the twenty-second day. However, as Moltke told Conrad, he hoped that the military decision would have been reached by the twenty-second day. He therefore concluded that he would have to begin the war as if the Italians were not expected.[56]

Pollio's plans did not cease with assistance to Germany on the Rhine. In April 1914 he suggested to Major von Kleist, the German military attaché in Rome, sending Italian troops to help Austria against Serbia. This was a suggestion which almost caused the German officer to fall off his chair, and Kleist speculated on whether the Italians were looking for a thank you in the way of Trieste or the Trentino.[57] Pollio also spoke of the ring around the Triple Alliance being tightened from year to year and alluded to the example of Frederick the Great in 1756 and a preventative war. Moltke discussed Pollio's hints with Conrad at their meeting at Karlsbad in May, and the Austrian on his return to Vienna ordered a staff study of the possibility of using Italian troops in Galicia against the Russians, or against Serbia. Nevertheless he remained skeptical about the Italians. He told Moltke that Pollio was only one man and he might not be there tomorrow.[58] Pollio was, of course, only a technician speaking of technical matters, and his agreements would take effect only when the Italian government decided the *casus foederis* of the Triple Alliance—of whose exact text Pollio was ignorant—had arisen.[59] Pollio was not to be present at the great military test for which he had steeled himself. On July 1, only a few days after the assassination of Franz Ferdinand, he died suddenly of a heart attack.[60] With his death the Triple Alliance lost one of its most loyal and important adherents in Italy at the very moment it most needed such support.

The project of an Italian landing on the coast of Provence must be seen against this background of the probable dispatch of Italian troops to the

---

[56] *Ibid.*, pp. 609–610. The cavalry divisions would arrive on the tenth day. The Italians hoped to be able to shorten the transport about five days by April 1915.

[57] Foerster, "Die deutsch-italienische Militärkonvention," p. 407.

[58] Conrad, *Aus meiner Dienstzeit*, III, 670, 671, 673.

[59] For an interesting discussion of this point see Albertini, *Origins of the War*, I, 564–565; Alberti, *L'Opera di Generale Pollio*, pp. 19, 29; Gaetano Salvemeni, *La Politica estera dell'Italia* (Florence, 1944), pp. 198–201. Also see above p. 223. On the purely military nature of the Italo-German staff talks from the German side see Waldersee, "Von Deutschlands Beziehungen zu Italien," p. 660.

[60] Report by Szeptycki, 8 July 1914, OK/MS-X-1/4, 1914; Méry to Berchtold, 16 July 1914, Nr. 32/P, HHSA, Politische Archiv XI-150, folio 28–29.

Rhine in the event of war with France. During the preliminary negotiations for the new naval convention the Italians had repeatedly spoken of a seaborne invasion of France, followed by an advance up the Rhône valley threatening the rear of the French forces on both the Italian and German frontiers. Naturally this operation would be totally dependent on winning sea supremacy in the Mediterranean. A very detailed study of such an invasion was actually prepared along with a tentative plan for its execution. The landing force was to include five army corps and two cavalry divisions, making a grand total of 217,000 officers and men, 60,000 horses and mules, 10,000 wagons, and numerous automobiles and bicycles. Its transport would require five separate echelons of which the first would have to be not less than an army corps and cavalry division, or 46,000 officers and men, and 14,000 horses and mules.[61] Approximately seventy steamers would be required for each echelon. There would be three ports of embarkation: Genoa, La Spezia, and Livorno. After an exhaustive study of the French coast, the point where the landing would take place was narrowed to three possibilities: the Gulf of Fos, near the mouth of the Rhône; Marseille; and the Gulf of Saint Tropez. The choice recommended was Saint Tropez largely because this would necessitate the convoys spending only one night at sea, thus reducing the dangers of collision and attack by enemy torpedo boats.

From Saint Tropez the army could take the entrenched camp of Nice from the rear, and march on Marseille, masking Toulon and Hyères on its left with sufficient troops to prevent the besieged from disturbing its flank. Once Marseille was captured, it could be used as a base instead of Saint Tropez, and the army would be free to advance up the Rhône valley into the heart of France.[62]

Protection for the large Italian convoys was of critical importance, especially since the Stato Maggiore considered the French to have surpassed other European navies in the construction and employment of submarines. To minimize danger from French forces which might remain after the decisive naval battle, the convoys would steam as far from the enemy coasts as possible, or midway between the coast of Provence and Corsica. In the days immediately preceding the departure of the first echelon,

61 Comando del Corpo di Stato Maggiore, Ufficiale di Marina, "Operazioni di Sbarco in Provenza," fascicolo I, "Composizione delle Spedizione—Divisione in Scaglioni," n.d. [1913–early 1914], pp. 1–2, USM, cartella 295. The plan consisted of nine parts. Each bears the signature of Capitano di fregata A. Capon, who is listed in the *Annuario Ufficiale della Regia Marina 1914* as liaison officer with the army General Staff.

62 *Ibid.*, fascicolo II, "Quadri di Imbarco," pp. 1–2; fascicolo III, "Scelta dei porti di Imbarco," pp. 1–4; fascicolo IV, "Scelta del Punto di Sbarco," pp. 27–29.

offensive operations, particularly against torpedo boat and submarine installations, would be conducted along the Provençal and Corsican coasts. In addition, a blockade of the fortified naval bases of Nice, Villefranche, Hyères, Toulon, Marseille, Ajaccio, and Porto Vecchio would be established. It was obvious that the Italian fleet, even before the losses that might result from a naval battle, was hardly numerous enough to undertake such an ambitious task by itself. The cooperation of the Austrian navy was as indispensable to the realization of the landing in Provence as it was to winning sea supremacy. The Italian fleet would provide the escorts for the convoys since most of the transports were to be Italian. The Austrians were to maintain the blockades against French bases. The risks of the entire operation were certainly not minimized in this study, and its feasibility was directly linked to the naval power still available to the Austrian and Italian fleets after the decisive battle for naval supremacy in the Mediterranean.[63]

The Stato Maggiore calculated that it would take approximately fifteen days to assemble the requisite steamers in the ports of embarkation, an operation which could not begin until control of the sea was obtained. It would require another ten days to prepare the transports to receive the troops, animals, and equipment, and an additional five days to embark them. The five echelons could only be landed in Provence two and a half or three months after the order to concentrate the steamers had been issued. The time necessary to win control of the sea from the French had to be added to this. Under the most favorable of circumstances, this could not take less than one month. Therefore the advance of the invading troops could only be effectively pushed approximately four months after the opening of hostilities. Delays due to weather and unfavorable sea conditions might further prolong the operations.[64] The plan of course presupposed that the Austrians and Italians would be victorious at sea and the French unable to repel the landings.

The common opinion among military circles before 1914 was that the decision in a Franco-German war would be reached, probably on the Rhine, long before four months had elapsed. During this period the Italian army would have had no weight in the general operations, and the forces in the Alps would probably not even be successful in drawing French troops from the main theater of operations. Therefore, despite the enormous risks and large expense of an attempted landing, the Italians would probably not be compensated by tangible results. It was certainly not

[63] *Ibid.*, fascicolo VII, "Navigazione-Protezione del Convoglio," pp. 2, 4–5, 19–20, 23.
[64] *Ibid.*, fascicolo IX, "Conclusione," pp. 1–3.

foreseeable that Italian forces in the Alps would succeed in breaking the French defensive line and emerge into the Rhône valley. With Germany victorious on the Rhine, Italy would thus have contributed only a minimum share to the outcome of the war and would be treated in proportion at the conclusion of peace.[65]

This staff study could hardly have aroused much enthusiasm for the landing in Provence. Moreover, the entire project rested on the far from certain prerequisite that sea supremacy could be obtained, and the neutrality of England was cited as essential to such a naval success.[66] An Italian amphibious assault on Provence does not, therefore, appear to have been a strong probability. Given the fear of being shut out of a future peace conference or limited to meager gains, a possibility Pollio had already expressed to San Giuliano, it is not surprising that the Italian army preferred to concentrate on transporting troops over the Tyrol to the assistance of their allies.

The French government learned of the conclusion of the Triple Alliance naval convention through an allusion to it in an Italian diplomatic dispatch which was intercepted in October 1913.[67] The question of French apprehensions that Italy had entered into secret military and naval agreements directed against them was merged into the larger diplomatic issue of a Mediterranean agreement between Great Britain, France, and Italy. Efforts to reach such an agreement before the outbreak of the war proved unsuccessful.[68] The French therefore remained extremely suspicious of the repeated assurances by San Giuliano and other Italian officials that the Triple Alliance had been renewed without modification.[69] San Giuliano blandly assured the French ambassador in Rome, Camille Barrère, that any documents which the French claimed to have that proved supplementary

[65] *Ibid.,* pp. 4–5.

[66] *Ibid.,* fascicolo VII, p. 21. This reservation about British neutrality was probably Capon's personal opinion; it may not have been completely shared by Revel.

[67] The French apparently learned the Italian cipher and were able to decode cables to the Italian ambassador in Paris. Reference to the naval convention was made by the Duke d'Avarna, Italian ambassador in Vienna, in a message to San Giuliano which the latter transmitted to Tittoni in Paris. San Giuliano to Tittoni, 28 Oct. 1913. French translation in MAE, Correspondence Politique, Italie-Politique étrangère, Dossier général II, carton 12, folio 417.

[68] For the British view with cross references to the *DDF* see *BD,* X (pt. 2), ch. XCVI, pt. 2, pp. 620–654. A general discussion is in Albertini, *Origins of the War,* I, 565–571; Askew, *Europe and Italy's Acquisition of Libya,* pp. 220–223, 245–247.

[69] Rodd to Grey, 13 Jan. 1914, *BD,* X (pt. 2), no. 440, pp. 642–643; Rodd to Grey, 22 Apr. 1914, *ibid.,* no. 442, pp. 644–645; Grey to Rodd, 6 May 1914, *ibid.,* no. 446, pp. 649–650; Doumergue to Ambassadors to Rome, Berlin, St. Petersburg, Vienna, Constantinople, 11 Dec. 1913, *DDF*3, VIII, no. 612, p. 767; Doumergue to Barrère, 18 Dec. 1913, *ibid.,* no. 643, p. 805.

clauses had been added to the Triple Alliance with special reference to the Mediterranean were forgeries. He added that there was no military protocol among the allies concerning France, although the Italian General Staff had naturally envisaged all eventualities, as undoubtedly did the French General Staff. San Giuliano insisted that there was no agreement against France, that the Triple Alliance was defensive, and that the 1902 Franco-Italian accords had the same extent and value as when they were concluded.[70]

The statements of San Giuliano were so positive that both Sir Rennell Rodd and Sir Edward Grey were inclined to believe them. Grey, anxious to help restore better feeling between France and Italy, was ready to continue impressing upon the French that the Italians had assured them the reports about a Triple Alliance agreement concerning the Mediterranean were a myth.[71] The French naturally could not specify the exact nature of the intelligence they had, nor how they had obtained it, but their suspicions were not dispelled.[72] San Giuliano was technically correct in his assertions, insofar as they referred to the Triple Alliance itself, which was defensive. He had hinted at the General Staff preparing for all eventualities, but had attempted to minimize this. The naval convention was this sort of technical agreement, not taking effect until the Triple Alliance itself took effect. But certainly the joint Italian, Austrian, and German planning, like the Anglo-French staff talks, was something a bit more than mere contingency plans compiled by the General Staff of *one* country and subsequently buried in its own files. San Giuliano was treading a narrow line between truth and its opposite, and the suspicions of the French were perfectly comprehensible.

A month after the actual signature of the Triple Alliance naval convention the French naval attaché in Rome reported that he did not believe in an agreement between the Austrian and Italian staffs, but admitted that one might be possible someday under German auspices. By December of 1913 he was reporting an evident reorientation of the Italian fleet northward toward the La Spezia–Maddalena system.[73] Admiral Le Bris, possibly informed of the intercepted Italian documents, considered this displace-

[70] Private memorandum by Sir Rennell Rodd, 16 Feb. 1914, Grey MSS, FO 800, vol. 64; Rodd to Grey, 16 Feb. 1914, *ibid.;* Barrère to Doumergue, 18 Feb. 1914, *DDF3*, IX, no. 324, pp. 417–418.

[71] Rodd to Grey, 28 Apr. 1914, Grey MSS, FO 800, vol. 64; Grey to Rodd, 8 May 1914, *ibid.*

[72] Jules Cambon, ambassador to Berlin, to Doumergue, 30 Mar. 1914, *DDF3*, X, no. 48, pp. 68–69. For a French idea of the provisions of the Triple Alliance see Note du Département, 30 Nov. 1913 [?], *ibid.*, VIII, no. 557, pp. 703–704.

[73] D'Huart to Minister of Marine, 27 July and 10 Dec. 1913, AMF, carton BB7-126.

ment of the center of action of the Italian fleet as of considerable importance to the French navy, and pressed Lieutenant d'Huart for more information.[74] The Vicomte de Faramond, French naval attaché in Austria and Germany, had also been sending disturbing reports to which were added such open manifestations of Italian ties to the Triple Alliance as the presence of the Duke of the Abruzzi and Pollio at German maneuvers. Faramond thought it Germany's design to make Italy the advanced sentinel of the Triple Alliance in the Mediterranean. There were other danger signs, such as the increase in the Austrian fleet and the fact that the Austrian navy had begun to change the color of its ships from dark green, suitable for operations on the Adriatic coast, to light grey, which diminished the visibility of a warship on the high seas. This and the apparent permanence of the Mittelmeerdivision, joined to the seeming movement of the Italian point of concentration northward from Taranto, seemed to indicate a plan for naval action by the Triple Alliance against France.[75] Faramond thought that the Kaiser and Victor Emmanuel had established the basis of a plan for common action when the Italian sovereign visited Kiel during *Kielerwoche,* and believed that on the outbreak of war French submarines would find the *Goeben* at Maddalena.[76] The Italian fleet was France's primary naval objective in the Mediterranean in the event of a war against the Triple Alliance, and the French Commander-in-Chief, Admiral Lapeyrère, certainly had few fears of an attempted combination by the Austrian and Italian fleets. All his efforts had been bent toward preparing for the decisive naval battle which he assumed must occur.

As the July crisis of 1914 moved toward its climax, Revel, whom Souchon had considered unaware of the gravity of the international situation, proposed to the Minister of Marine that certain precautionary measures be taken.[77] He cabled the naval Commander-in-Chief of the first and second squadrons as well as the commanders of the naval bases to quietly take preparatory measures to facilitate prompt and efficient mobilization, and also to guard against espionage and nocturnal surprise.[78] Sealed orders were sent to various naval and maritime authorities with instructions they be opened only on mobilization at the outbreak of war, and destroyed after reading. If mobilization did not occur, they were to be returned

[74] Le Bris to D'Huart, 10 Feb. 1914, *ibid.,* carton Ea-136; D'Huart to Minister of Marine, 20 Feb. 1914, *ibid.*

[75] EMG, "Autriche-Hongrie, Bulletin Annuel de 1913," n.d. [Feb. 1914], *ibid.* On the color of Austrian warships, see *Rivista Marittima,* 47.3 (Mar. 1914): 511.

[76] Faramond to Minister of Marine, 11 Apr. 1914, *DDF3,* X, no. 99, pp. 162–163.

[77] Souchon, "La Percée de S.M.S. 'Goeben,'" p. 35; Revel to Millo, 29 July 1914, USM, cartella 323/8.

[78] 29 July 1914, *ibid.*

unopened to Revel.[79] Revel reported to the Austrian naval attaché that the first and second squadrons were fully ready for war; the first was enroute to Taranto from Brindisi, and the second was at Gaeta. He said that the coal deposits at Augusta were complete along with colliers and lighters, but that oil stocks were not at the desired point. However, there were 10,000 tons of oil at Messina. Revel added that Conz, who had been given a tour of sea duty in the spring, was expected in Rome the following day, and in the event of war would be attached to Admiral Haus.[80] The declaration of Italian neutrality on August 2 rendered these arrangements meaningless.

One uncertainty in the Mediterranean was removed shortly before the outbreak of the war. On July 26 Rear Admiral Behncke, representing the Chief of the Admiralstab, told the Austrian naval attaché that in the event of a war in which England remained neutral, the offensive action of the German fleet in the first period of the war would be limited to operations against the Russians in the Baltic. The sending of additional forces to the Mediterranean was not considered opportune. They reasoned that the attitude of England was at best not completely reliable, and that the greatest caution was always necessary. The Germans must be careful to avoid anything which would hurt England's susceptibilities. The British might quietly watch a conflict between the French and Austro-Italian fleets in the Mediterranean, but would certainly look askance and possibly intervene if the German fleet entered this area.[81] Actually, as far back as 1909 this same concern over the British had even led the Germans to give up the idea of an offensive action by their fleet against the French coast.[82] The old French nightmare of the German fleet established in Italian bases therefore had no basis, and even their Atlantic and Channel coasts were more secure than they might have realized.

To one endowed with hindsight there is something slightly unreal about the elaborate preparations by the Triple Alliance for naval operations in the Mediterranean. The naval convention was known only to a handful, and relations between Austria and Italy were never more than correct during

---

[79] Covering letter from Revel, 29 July 1914, *ibid.*, cartella 295. I found all these orders but one unopened with their seals intact at the USM in April 1964. The exception was the envelope for the commander of the maritime defense of Messina which had been opened by order on August 2, 1914, and subsequently destroyed.

[80] Naval attaché, Rome, to Marinesektion, 29 July 1914, OK/MS-G.V. (nicht protokolliert).

[81] Report by naval attaché, Berlin, to Marinesektion, 27 July 1914, reproduced in Conrad, *Aus meiner Dienstzeit*, IV, 277–278. The dispatch did not reach Vienna until the thirty-first.

[82] Admiralstab, "Denkschrift über den O-Plan im Kriege gegen Frankreich," 9 May 1911. Admiralty, London, Univ. of Cambridge and Univ. of Michigan Microfilming Project no. 2, reel 8, frames 96, 104–110.

this period. The relatively small number of staff officers involved in these matters worked together cordially, at least on the surface, and as their work progressed might even have acquired a certain respect, if not liking, for each other. On a popular level Austria-Hungary remained the traditional enemy for Italians and was generally disliked. San Giuliano's explanation of the renewal of the Triple Alliance had been greeted "in frigid silence" by the Italian Chamber of Deputies, while the attack upon the alliance by the Republican Deputy Salvatore Barzilai "was received with prolonged applause from almost all quarters." [83] At the very moment the sovereigns of the Triple Alliance powers were in the process of ratifying the naval convention, the decree by Prince Hohenlohe, Austrian governor of Trieste, against the employment of Italian citizens by the municipality exasperated Italian opinion. This, added to the traditional rivalry with Austria in the Balkans, particularly in Albania, diverted much of the resentment that had been aroused by France and Poincaré the previous year.[84]

Prince Liechtenstein, the Austrian naval attaché, had few illusions about the feelings of Italians toward Austria after a rash of street demonstrations in May 1914.[85] The previous year, in September 1913, he himself had become involved in an incident, quickly hushed, when he boarded an excursion steamer from Cittavecchia to the Gulf of Aranci hoping to catch a distant glimpse of the naval gunnery exercises which were being held there. Liechtenstein had been asked to show his papers, and had to return aboard the same steamer without landing, although accounts which inevitably found their way into the press hinted at something far more serious—for example, an arrest for spying—without naming the Austrian attaché.[86] The incident was minor, and Liechtenstein was probably innocent of exceeding the bounds of "espionage" normally expected of any attaché, since he was merely traveling aboard a public excursion steamer. However the affair was indicative of the real relations between the two countries who had only just concluded a convention for naval cooperation. The somewhat bemused French naval attaché received the impression that only Liechtenstein's high social rank saved him from being expelled.[87]

A similar example of the sensitive relations between the two allies oc-

---

[83] Rodd [H. Dering] to Grey, 19 Dec. 1912, FO 371, vol. 1384, Italy, file 54939.

[84] Albertini, *Origins of the War*, I, 524–526; Albertini, *Venti anni di vita politica*, pt. 1, vol. II, pp. 444–449.

[85] Liechtenstein to Marinesektion, 10 May 1914, PK/MS-XII-1/1, 1914.

[86] Liechtenstein to Marinesektion, 3 Sept. 1913, PK/MS-XII-1/1, 1913; Ambrózy to Berchtold, 3 Sept. 1913, *ibid.*

[87] D'Huart to Minister of Marine, 20 Nov. 1913, AMF, carton BB7-126.

curred in February 1914 in relation to the international escort for the Prince of Wied on his way to assume the Albanian throne. The Prince was to board a yacht provided by the Austrians at Trieste, but it was feared that the entry of the Italian scout *Quarto*, designated to be part of the escort, into the harbor would provoke Irredentist demonstrations. The Italian government, which officially attempted to maintain a scrupulously correct attitude in regard to the Irredentist question, was afraid that a harsh repression of demonstrations by the Austrian police would further damage relations with their ally. Despite all precautions, Prince Hohenlohe could not guarantee there would be no demonstrations, and the *Quarto* therefore joined the Prince's escort at sea.[88] Circumstances such as these were hardly conducive to a cordial alliance.

The Italian officers present at *Kielerwoche* in 1913, particularly the captain of the *Amalfi*, amused Faramond by the resigned attitude with which they accepted the attentions of the Germans.[89] Captain Boyle, British naval attaché in Rome at the time, found the Italian Ministry of Marine pro-British, and noted that confidential information found its way to the embassy.[90] After the outbreak of war "there was no doubt about where the sympathies of the Italian Navy lay," and on occasion Captain Boyle received useful information on the movements of an Austrian submarine.[91] Naturally all of these were minor incidents, and the circles involved in naval affairs were narrow. The attachés, upon whose reports the naval staffs relied a good deal, were a small group in these years, and not entirely free from prejudice. The complex of conflicting fears, ambitions, and jealousies make an evaluation of Italy's place in the Triple Alliance difficult. This uncertainty over the Italians also accounts for much of the instability in the Mediterranean naval situation. The Triple Alliance naval convention did exist; communications between the Austrian, Italian, and German naval staffs did take place; coal stocks for the Austrian fleet were assembled at Augusta; and the Italian navy was prepared to honor its obligations should the need arise. Although the British were always less concerned over the attitude of Italy, the French, with their preponderant interests and vulnerability in the Mediterranean, fully expected something like the Triple Alliance naval convention and made it the basis of their

---

[88] Millo to San Giuliano, 12 Feb. 1914, USM, cartella 320/1; Millo to Captain, *Quarto*, 21 Feb. 1914, *ibid.*; Winspeare, Italian naval attaché, Vienna, to Minister of Marine, 25 Feb. 1914, USM, cartella 318/3; Einsichtsstück des Präsidiums des k.k. Ministeriums des Innern, 24 Feb. 1914, PK/MS-XII-1/2, 1914.

[89] Faramond, *Souvenirs d'un attaché navale*, pp. 118, 129–130.

[90] The Earl of Cork and Orrery to me, 9 Oct. 1963.

[91] Admiral of the Fleet, the Earl of Cork and Orrery, *My Naval Life* (London, 1942), p. 85.

naval preparations. Any other attitude would have been dangerous to their national security. The Triple Alliance naval convention, despite its ultimate futility, has its place in naval history.

X

Spain and Russia:
Ambitious Naval Powers

The position of Spain among the great powers of Europe in the first decade of the twentieth century was very different from that of the mighty kingdom which had sent out the imposing Armada in the sixteenth century. What remained of the old Spanish Empire had been virtually wiped out in 1898 as a result of the war with the United States in which the bulk of the Spanish navy was destroyed. In the early years of the new century Spain was practically defenseless at sea, with one obsolete battleship and (in 1908) three armored cruisers whose long period of construction rendered them obsolete before they even entered service, four protected cruisers, two of which had been the gift of Spanish residents in Latin America, and a few destroyers, torpedo boats, and gunboats.[1] There were serious doubts that Spain, plagued by chronic internal instability, could even retain what remained of her island possessions. Great Britain and France were specifically concerned over the possibility Germany would be able to acquire either the Canary or Balearic islands. Britain and France began negotiating with Spain early in 1907, and in May, shortly after a visit to Carthagena by King Edward VII, the three countries, in an exchange of notes, promised to preserve intact their rights over their island and maritime possessions in the Mediterranean and that part of the Atlantic adjacent to Europe and Africa. Should the status quo be threatened, the three powers agreed to consult among themselves on the measures to be taken. This Mediterranean accord of 1907, which was published, was generally recognized as anti-German in object.[2]

Spain's imperial ambitions had not died as a result of the disasters of

---

[1] *The Naval Annual, 1912,* pp. 234–235.

[2] Pierre Renouvin, *Les Questions méditerranéennes de 1904 à 1914* (Paris, 1958), pp. 17–18; Renouvin, *Histoire des relations internationales,* VI (Paris, 1955), 220. The notes are reproduced in *BD,* VII, nos. 39, 40, 41, pp. 32–34.

1898. The long Spanish occupation of the Presidios on the Moroccan coast, as well as the geographical proximity of this land, made Spain's interest in it perfectly comprehensible. The European crisis which had resulted over Morocco and the international conference about the issue at Algeciras, the agreements and constant friction with the French over division of the territory, and the somewhat humiliating tutelage which lay behind the Mediterranean accords, with their suggestion that Spain could not hold what was rightfully hers, must have emphasized to the Spanish the disadvantages of maritime impotence. In this heyday of navalism the Spanish fleet had sunk to the level of that of Turkey or Greece. Almost a decade after the war with the United States, in November 1907, a modest naval program was presented to the Cortes by the Conservative Prime Minister Antonio Maura. Maura explained that the government wanted to establish the basis of future maritime power in order to protect itself from attack. The project was approved in January 1908 and the Spanish navy began its slow recovery.[3]

The naval law of January 7, 1908, provided for the construction of three battleships, four gunboats, three destroyers, and twenty-four torpedo boats. These were to form the nucleus of a new Spanish fleet.[4] British firms played a large role in this regeneration of the Spanish navy. The company formed for the execution of the building program, La Sociedad Española de Construccion Naval, was one in which Vickers, Armstrong, and John Brown had 24.5 percent of the issued capital. Moreover, Vickers' Spanish subsidiary, La Placienca de las Armas, which had been small and unprofitable and which Vickers' had considered closing in 1903, benefited from large orders from La Sociedad. (La Sociedad, however, still had not been able to repay the majority of its debt to Vickers when the war broke out in 1914.)[5] The prominent role of Vickers was the subject of attacks in both the Cortes and the Spanish press, less perhaps because of the firm itself than the unpopularity of expenditure on a new squadron. In 1909 there was additional legislation to foster maritime activity by means of state subventions.[6]

A British design was chosen for the Spanish dreadnoughts, the first of which, the *España*, was laid down at Ferrol in December 1909, and launched in February 1912. The 15,700-ton *España* and the two others

[3] Albert Mousset, *L'Espagne dans la politique mondiale* (Paris, 1923), p. 144; J. C., "Lettre d'Espagne," *Journal des débats*, 21 Feb. 1913.

[4] *The Naval Annual, 1908*, pp. 45–46; *The Naval Annual, 1909*, pp. 41–42.

[5] Scott, *Vickers—A History*, p. 84.

[6] M. Carbonnier, "L'Espagne maritime," *Revue maritime*, Dec. 1913, pp. 367–378; *ibid.*, Jan. 1914, p. 44.

of her class were somewhat smaller than contemporary dreadnoughts, with a primary armament of eight 12-inch guns.[7] The second dreadnought, the *Alfonso XIII,* was launched at Ferrol in May 1913, and the third ship, the *Jaime I,* was laid down in 1912 on the slip vacated by the *España.*[8] Spain's young and ambitious sovereign, Alfonso XIII, regarded a good squadron of Spanish dreadnoughts as a support for France and England in guarding the Mediterranean. In the spring of 1912 the King in an audience with the French naval attaché outlined his plans for new naval construction to follow completion of the 1908 program. This would include another three dreadnoughts of 20,000 tons armed with eight 13.4-inch guns. Alfonso would have preferred 25,000-ton ships with 15-inch guns, but realized that budgetary considerations and the lack of adequate docking facilities prevented this.[9]

The new Spanish naval proposals underwent repeated alterations by successive ministers of marine. The bill which was finally presented to the Cortes in May 1914 provided for three dreadnoughts, the first to be laid down upon the launching of the *Jaime I* and to enter service in 1918. The second would be laid down in 1917 as soon as the first had been launched. An annual appropriation of 36 million pesetas was provided for nine years to be used exclusively for new construction with the reservation that Spanish industry was to be employed as much as possible. Particular efforts were to be made toward manufacturing heavy artillery and armor plate in Spain so that, with the exception of patented equipment, the dreadnoughts to be commenced in 1917 would be entirely the product of Spanish industry. In addition to the dreadnoughts, a 1000-ton "scout" (really a large destroyer) was to be ready by 1917, with another to follow. The Spanish navy was also to have three submarines by 1918, with another three to be commenced before that date. Eighteen of the twenty-four torpedo boats specified in the law of 1908 were to be transformed into destroyers of the "Bustamente" class, and provision was made for improvements to the harbors of Ferrol, Cadiz, and Carthagena.[10] In June 1914 King Alfonso told the French naval attaché that his aim was to lay down a new dreadnought every two years.[11]

[7] *The Naval Annual, 1910,* pp. 60–61; *The Naval Annual, 1912,* pp. 66–67; report by British naval attaché, Capt. Kelly, 12 Feb. 1912, PRO, FO 371, vol. 1475, Spain, file 9013.

[8] *The Naval Annual, 1914,* p. 63. The *España* was completed late in 1913, and the *Alfonso XIII* in 1915. Deliveries of British armor and cannon for the *Jaime I* were stopped after the outbreak of hostilities, and the ship was not completed until after the war.

[9] D'Huart to Minister of Marine, 25 May 1912, AMF, carton BB7-130.

[10] Report by military attaché, Madrid, Lt. Col. Tillion, 18 May 1914, AMF, carton Ea-78.

[11] D'Huart to Minister of Marine, 15 June 1914, *ibid.*

This rebirth of Spanish naval power inevitably attracted attention in continental naval periodicals. Maritime commentators did not fail to point out the possible significance of a Spanish squadron of eight or nine dreadnoughts in the delicate Mediterranean balance of power.[12] However, the realities of the Spanish situation were apt to be quite different from the speculations in naval periodicals. The new Spanish program was not to be completed until 1924, and both the French naval and military attachés, as well as the British naval attaché, doubted that Spanish industry would be in a position to provide armor plate and cannon within three years as the program specified. Moreover the sums provided for the improvement of the ports were inadequate to create three effective naval bases and might better have been concentrated on one. Among Spanish naval officers, at least those with whom the French naval attaché came into contact, the program was considered insufficient, and one officer complained that they were falling to the rank of Turkey.[13]

There was some doubt whether the Spanish would have the trained personnel necessary to handle large modern warships when the new ships were ready. Captain Kelly found a "marked lack of zeal even among the younger officers" while the senior officers appeared too old and apparently physically unable to stand the strain of active command.[14] Lieutenant d'Huart, for his part, found the Spanish officer corps to be unimaginative and lacking in curiosity about the methods of their foreign contemporaries. He theorized that with a relatively secure career, the Spanish officer was exempt from the shock of emulation and, with rare exceptions, saw no need to change. D'Huart thought that within the Spanish kingdom both Liberal and Conservative politicians, as well as the general public, were disinterested in the navy. The credits to renew the fleet had been voted to please the King, and were in no way part of a broader political conception.[15] The navy was also top-heavy with admirals. In the Executive branch there were some 21 officers of flag rank as compared to only 162

[12] See for example the lengthy series by M. Carbonnier, "L'Espagne Maritime," *Revue maritime,* Apr. 1913, pp. 32–41; May 1913, pp. 175–184; July 1913, pp. 40–49; Aug. 1913, pp. 184–193; Sept. 1913, pp. 315–324; Oct. 1913, pp. 32–41; Nov. 1913, pp. 188–196; Dec. 1913, pp. 366–375; Jan. 1914, pp. 37–45; O. Guethénoch, "La Renaissance de la marine espagnole," *Le Yacht,* 18 Oct. 1913, pp. 669–670; V, "Die französischen-spanischen Beziehungen," *Die Flagge,* Apr. 1914, pp. 24–25; *Marine Rundschau,* May 1914, pp. 705–706.

[13] Report by Tillion, 18 May 1914, AMF, carton Ea-78; D'Huart to Minister of Marine, 15 June 1914, *ibid.*

[14] Report by Kelly, 12 Feb. 1912, FO 371, vol. 1475, file 9013. Kelly admitted, however, that while he was at Ferrol three Spanish warships which had entered the harbor at night in bad weather were apparently well anchored on station the following morning.

[15] D'Huart to Minister of Marine, 10 July 1912, AMF, carton BB7-130.

lieutenants and 100 sublieutenants. Of the admirals, only two actually commanded at sea, and they had been appointed to their positions when too old and lacking in practice because of long periods of shore duty. Training was nearly nonexistent, D'Huart reported. There was no gunnery practice with reduced charges. Pieces larger than 6 inches in caliber were fired on the average only three times, and smaller pieces only ten times, every six months. The torpedo boats were in commission only three months out of the year.[16]

These observations were not merely reflections of the prejudices of hypercritical or condescending foreign observers. They were shared by King Alfonso himself. The King recognized the need for specialists' schools and, for example, intended to transform the obsolescent cruiser *Reina Regente* into a true gunnery school.[17] Alfonso complained that Spanish naval officers had the habit of considering their profession merely as a way of making a living. Lieutenant d'Huart, with whom Alfonso had a number of lively and characteristically candid conversations, received the impression after a few visits to Spain that the King had evaluated the situation accurately, but that any reforms were stymied by the whole of the administrative machinery. To take strong action would require smashing the bureaucracy, and the King did not want to smash it.[18]

The Spanish navy, therefore, in the years immediately before the outbreak of the war was only just beginning to recover from a situation that could hardly have been weaker. It would have required a number of years of uninterrupted development to prepare the navy to play a significant role in the Mediterranean. Moreover the war broke out before the Cortes could consider the new naval program, and in the autumn of 1914 the Minister of Marine presented a more limited program eliminating new dreadnought construction and providing instead for four rapid cruisers, six destroyers, twenty-eight submarines, three gunboats, eighteen smaller ships, and improved defenses against mines and submarines.[19]

Although Spain's naval power was negligible during this period, her geographical position closing the western basin of the Mediterranean, and her strategically located island possessions, the Balearics, gave her an importance out of proportion to her material strength. Spain's young King

---

[16] D'Huart to Minister of Marine, 10 July 1913, *ibid.* In August 1911 a mutiny, apparently anarchist inspired, had also been nipped in the bud aboard the old training ship *Numancia*. Report by military attaché, 14 Aug. 1911, *ibid.*

[17] D'Huart to Minister of Marine, 10 Nov. 1913, *ibid.*

[18] D'Huart to Minister of Marine, 15 June 1914, AMF, carton Ea-78.

[19] Hardinge to Grey, 9 Nov. 1914, FO 371, vol. 2104, file 72571.

Alfonso XIII was anxious for his country to play a greater role in Mediterranean affairs, and showed a marked preference for Great Britain and France among the rival diplomatic systems. Alfonso had a lively interest in naval and military affairs and displayed a charming frankness in his conversations with foreign diplomats and naval and military attachés. In May 1912 he told Lieutenant d'Huart that his policy was to march in accord with France and England, and in September of the same year the Spanish ambassador in London reported that the King had definitely chosen to throw in his lot with the Entente powers.[20]

The Moroccan question, however, was a great barrier to a closer understanding between France and Spain. During the Moroccan crisis of 1911 the Spanish government had been afraid that France and Germany might reach an agreement between themselves at Spain's expense and in disregard of the 1904 treaty between Spain and France. The Spanish therefore tended to look to Great Britain for support.[21] Throughout most of 1912 the French and Spanish were engaged in negotiating a precise delimitation of their respective zones in Morocco and, not surprisingly, this proved difficult. There were Frenchmen who were anxious to grant a reasonable settlement to Spain. These included Léon Geoffray, ambassador at Madrid since 1910, and Clemenceau, the latter on grounds of general policy and the necessity of Spanish friendship in case of a general conflict. Others, including Joseph Caillaux, who was Premier in late 1911, could not see the importance of Spain to France. Caillaux told the British ambassador that Spain had only been important to Britain during the Napoleonic Wars because "the Emperor was fool enough" to attack her.[22] During the Agadir crisis itself, the French army General Staff had been prepared to act against Spain if necessary, and spoke to their naval colleagues about a bombardment of Barcelona, which it was hoped might stimulate an insurrection in Catalonia.[23]

Poincaré saw no inconvenience in Spain being associated in any conference on pending questions in the Mediterranean, but only after the negotiations over Morocco had been successful.[24] King Alfonso let it be

[20] D'Huart to Minister of Marine, 25 May 1912, AMF, carton BB7-130; Minute by Sir Eyre Crowe, 14 Sept. 1912, FO 371, vol. 1475, file 39582.

[21] M. de Bunsen, annual report, Spain, 1911, 24 Apr. 1912, pp. 19–20, *ibid.*, file 17898.

[22] *Ibid.*, p. 19; Bertie to Tyrrell, 1 Jan. 1912, Grey MSS, FO 800, vol. 52; Bertie to Grey, 5 Jan. 1912, *ibid.*

[23] Conversation between Capitaine de frégate Lanxade, Chief of the third section, EMG, and Lt. Col. Halluin, Chief of the the third bureau, EMA, 6 Sept. 1911, AMF, carton Es-10.

[24] Poincaré to Geoffray, 18 June 1912, *DDF3*, III, no. 116, p. 140; Bertie to Grey, 20 Sept. 1912, Grey MSS, FO 800, vol. 52.

known to the Russian government that he was interested in seeing his country enter the Triple Entente after the signature of a Moroccan treaty, and asked the Russians to act as his exponent with the French.[25] Geoffray advocated circumspection on this subject for he was not anxious to see France become involved in new difficulties with Germany over Spain's uninspiring African colonies of Rio Muni or Fernando Poo.[26] Poincaré preferred that any understanding with Spain include England as well as Russia, and be limited to the Mediterranean. He was thinking of an agreement whereby the British and French navies were given use of the Balearics in the event of war.[27]

The Spanish also showed interest in participating in any conference arising out of the eastern question, and during the Balkan crisis a Spanish cruiser was actually sent to Constantinople. Spain's interest in this portion of the world was rather tenuously justified by the presence in the Balkans of colonies of Jews, originally of Spanish origin, but expelled from Spain centuries before.[28] The Spanish also approached the Russians on this subject, noting the advantages of another vote on the side of the Triple Entente in any international conference.[29] This transformation of Spain to a possible ally undoubtedly provoked a request from the French navy for additional information on Spanish military organization. In the absence of a permanent naval attaché accredited to Spain, the French military attaché in Madrid reported that he thought Spain could "render appreciable support," and that after the necessary deductions had been made for the Moroccan garrisons and the maintenance of internal order, the Spanish army had sufficient artillery, service, and engineer units to dispatch three army corps, 90,000–100,000 men, for operations abroad.[30] The French ambassador in Berlin, Jules Cambon, thought this force would be an appropriate one by its nature for guarding the Alpine frontier with Italy, thereby releasing additional French troops for service in the east.[31]

The Royal Navy was also extremely interested in Spain. On their way back from the Malta conference with Kitchener, Asquith and Churchill had conferred at Gibraltar with the British ambassador to Spain. The First Lord of the Admiralty, undoubtedly preoccupied with Mediterranean problems and the difficulty of sparing adequate naval strength for that

[25] Poincaré to Geoffray, 7 Oct. 1912, *DDF*3, IV, no. 85, p. 76.

[26] Geoffray to Poincaré, 11 Oct. 1912, *ibid.*, no. 124, pp. 118–121.

[27] Bertie to Grey, 10 Oct. 1912, Grey MSS, FO 800, vol. 52.

[28] Geoffray to Poincaré, 29 Nov. 1912, *DDF*3, IV, no. 594, pp. 612–613.

[29] Buchanan to Grey, 8 Dec. 1912, Grey MSS, FO 800, vol. 73.

[30] Major Paris to Minister of War and EMA, second bureau, 28 Nov. 1912, EMA, Attaché Militaire-Espagne/4 bis.

[31] Jules Cambon to Poincaré, 22 Dec. 1912, *DDF*3, V, no. 108, p. 130.

sea, was emphatic in declaring that Spain ought not to be treated as a negligible quantity.[32] Near the end of 1912 the Admiralty War Staff produced a memorandum on the value of Spain to the Triple Entente. They pointed out that in a war with the Triple Alliance, even with command of the sea in the Mediterranean, the British and the French would be hampered in any supplementary action since all available army strength would be required on the French frontier. Spain as an active ally could provide a force of 50,000 men which, carried in French and British transports, could strike at any point along the Sicilian, Sardinian, or south Italian coast. The Admiralty believed a mere knowledge of the existence of this force "would introduce a fresh element into the situation which Italy could not afford to ignore" and might eventually help to weaken her adhesion to the Triple Alliance.[33]

From a strictly naval point of view, too, Spain was valuable as a British ally. The handful of cruisers her fleet did possess could be used to assist British cruisers in protecting the important trade routes which passed near the Spanish coast. Perhaps even more important in its strategical implications would be the right to use Spanish ports. The Admiralty were particularly interested in Ceuta as a complementary base to Gibraltar for light vessels, torpedo boats, and submarines charged with guarding the entrance to the Mediterranean. Carthagena and Cadiz would facilitate covering both eastern and western approaches to the Straits of Gibraltar. The Canary Islands were well placed to afford coaling and repair facilities to British merchantmen and cruisers on the important trade routes between Europe and South America, the west coast of Africa, the Cape, Australia and New Zealand. Ferrol might provide similar facilities for the trade route passing Cape Finisterre. The Balearics would be particularly useful in covering the transport of troops from French North Africa. The transport might also be partially accomplished by means of Spanish railways.[34] Thus the men responsible for guiding the world's most powerful navy were for a variety of reasons far from depreciating the value of Spanish friendship.

King Alfonso's flirtations with Great Britain and France were likely to have practical value for the latter. In March 1913 the King told both Geoffray and Lieutenant Colonel Tillion, the French military attaché, that in the event of war the French would not have to leave any troops guard-

[32] Geoffray to Poincaré, 14 June 1912, *ibid.*, III, no. 102, p. 127.
[33] Admiralty War Staff, "Spain and the Triple Entente," 24 Dec. 1912, p. 1. Copy in FO 371, vol. 1753, Spain, file 7900.
[34] *Ibid.*, pp. 2–6.

ing the Pyrenees.[35] The successful conclusion of a Franco-Spanish treaty over Morocco at the end of November 1912 had freed Alfonso for the state visit to Paris which he desired to make. The Spanish King's visit took place in May 1913 at which time Alfonso presented the Collar of the Order of the Golden Fleece to President Poincaré. During his private conversations with Poincaré, Alfonso again mentioned his decision to side with the Triple Entente in the event of a war with Germany, which he considered both inevitable and close. He offered France the freedom to use the Balearics as a base of operations, and the use of Spanish railways to repatriate the troops from North Africa, thus shortening the potentially hazardous sea journey.[36] Alfonso wanted two Spanish army corps, which he would command in person, to fight alongside the French armies. He declared that the war he predicted was likely to extend to all of Europe, and that if Spain did not play a role she was lost and would fall back for an indefinite time into internal quarrels. The Spanish King mentioned Portugal as an answer to Poincaré's question about possible compensations for Spanish sacrifices, a suggestion that caused the French President to remark that England would never consent to anything affecting the independence of Portugal. Poincaré thanked Alfonso for his overtures and promised to have them studied by the military and naval staffs.[37]

Maurice Paléologue, then Director of Political Affairs at the Quai d'Orsay, approached the chief of the army General Staff for his opinion on the Spanish overtures. Joffre thought they appeared to be of only mediocre interest. In case of a Franco-German war he believed the transport of the North African troops could easily be effected by sea to Marseilles or Port Vendres, for the French navy would assure absolute supremacy in the western Mediterranean. On the other hand, Joffre

[35] Geoffray to Minister of Foreign Affairs, 18 Mar. 1913, DDF3, VI, no. 21, p. 42; Tillion to Minister of War, 22 Mar. 1913, ibid., no. 50, p. 73.

[36] Maurice Paléologue, Au Quai d'Orsay à la veille de la tourment, Journal 1913–1914 (Paris, 1947), p. 127; Pichon to Delcassé, 21 May 1913, DDF3, VI, no. 582, pp. 674–675.

[37] Paléologue, Au Quai d'Orsay, pp. 127–129. Paléologue, who dates this conversation May 8, claims Alfonso replied unhesitatingly to Poincaré's question about compensation with the phrase the annexation of Portugal (p. 128). This may be slightly dramatized. The version Bunsen received from Geoffray, and had himself heard the King allude to in the past, referred more gently to an Iberic Union under the Spanish crown. Bunsen to Grey, 19 May 1913, FO 371, vol. 1753, file 24158. Poincaré, in his memoirs published in 1926 while Alfonso still reigned, mentions nothing of the Spanish overtures and, in fact, states that except for the subject of collaboration in Morocco, no political discussion took place. Raymond Poincaré, Au service de la France, vol. III: L'Europe sous les armes, 1913 (Paris, 1926), p. 208. This is clearly refuted by Pichon's dispatch to Delcassé of May 21, but Pichon does not mention anything concerning Portugal, a subject about which there is discreet silence in the DDF.

thought the transport by rail across Spain would take much longer and would be much more hazardous. He wondered how much confidence they might have in the ability of the Spanish administration to assure the regular dispatch of the trains, protection of the routes, and subsistence of the troops. Joffre was anything but anxious for the two Spanish army corps to fight alongside his armies. He believed that the Spanish yielded to no one in courage and endurance, but their military instruction was very backward, their general staff were crassly ignorant, their armament was very different from that of the French and would greatly complicate his supply services, and Spanish haughtiness would create difficulties in the overall conduct of operations. Although Joffre promised to submit the question to the Conseil Supérieure de la Défense National, Poincaré, Paléologue, and Paul Cambon decided at a meeting on May 11 that Alfonso's overtures had little value except for the implied intimacy of their relations with Spain. Cambon showed some surprise over the peremptory and negative opinion of Joffre, but he categorically rejected the idea of Portugal, traditional ally of England, as a price for Spanish military cooperation.[38]

The idea of using the Spanish railways was brought up in the meeting of the Conseil Supérieure de la Défense Nationale on May 17 during a discussion of the transport of the North African troops in the event of mobilization. Both the Ministries of War and Marine were to examine the subject in concert, but the fourth bureau of the EMA formulated a number of objections. If the French troops were disembarked between Carthagena and Alicante safety at sea might be enhanced, but the use of the Spanish railways presented serious disadvantages. For much of its length up to the frontier the line ran along the coast and was therefore exposed to enemy attack. The Spanish were short of rolling stock and the difference in gauge between the French and Spanish lines made it difficult for the French to equip them.[39]

General Castelnau, assistant chief of the army General Staff, reported to Admiral Le Bris in October 1913 that, owing to difficulties with Spanish railways, a landing at Carthagena, Alicante, or Valencia would result in a marked delay in arrival of the troops in the zone of concentration. On the other hand, a landing farther north along the Spanish coast at Barcelona would be feasible. Before proceeding with further study the army General Staff wanted to ask the Naval Staff what advantages from the point of view of security of the transports Barcelona would offer in place

38 Paléologue, *Au Quai d'Orsay*, pp. 128–129.
39 Joffre, *Personal Memoirs*, I, 99–100.

of Marseilles or Sète.[40] Admiral Le Bris replied that from the navy's stand-point Barcelona would be preferable as a port of debarkation in default of one farther to the south. The navy, preoccupied with the many perils to which the troop transports would be exposed at sea, was naturally in favor of the Spanish route. The route was more removed from the potential enemy bases, and being shorter, it meant less time at sea and was easier to cover. Algiers, for example, was approximately 440 miles from Marseilles and 400 miles from Sète, but was only 280 miles from Barcelona and 190 miles from Carthagena. Admiral Le Bris therefore asked that the Spanish alternative be given favorable mention in the report to be submitted to the Conseil Supérieure de la Défense Nationale.[41]

In the absence of a firm agreement, which might well have taken the form of an alliance, it is difficult to see how the army General Staff with its rigid mobilization timetables could have seriously considered putting the arrival of the troops of the nineteenth corps at the mercy of Spanish goodwill and the efficiency of the Spanish railway authorities. The proposal, which was ultimately abandoned, is another example of the fundamental divergence of views between the French army and navy over the transport of troops from North Africa.[42]

The question of Spanish intervention in Portugal, plagued with disorder since the overthrow of the House of Braganza in 1910, was destined to remain a purely hypothetical one. Bunsen and his successor at Madrid, Sir Arthur Hardinge, were inclined to view the matter as a private speculation on the part of King Alfonso rather than a serious intention of the Spanish government.[43] It is interesting to note that Grey's attitude was not categorically negative, as was assumed by continental statesmen. The British Foreign Secretary was not sure that Britain "should necessarily intervene," but he was inclined to doubt Spain had sufficient strength to annex Portugal.[44]

Alfonso, as he told the French ambassador, did not abandon his ideas

---

[40] Castelnau to Le Bris, 14 Oct. 1913, AMF, carton Eb-120.

[41] Le Bris to Joffre, 7 Nov. 1913, *ibid*. There is reference to the possibility of a supplementary inquiry on the Spanish railways at the request of the fourth bureau in an intelligence report on the subject dated 11 Nov. 1913, "Chemin de fer: ligne Cerbère-Barcelone-Carthagène," EMA, second bureau, Espagne, carton 14.

[42] Joffre, *Personal Memoirs*, I, 99–100.

[43] Bunsen to Grey, 19 May 1913, FO 371, vol. 1753, file 24158; Hardinge to Grey, Jan. 1914, Grey MSS, FO 800, vol. 76.

[44] Grey to Hardinge, 9 Feb. 1914, *ibid*. During a visit to London in July 1913 King Alfonso hinted that continued Portuguese unrest might necessitate Spanish intervention. Grey warned him of the difficulties involved, but hedged on what the British attitude would be. Grey to Bunsen, 31 July 1913, *ibid*., vol. 87. Similar advice was given by Churchill who met the King on a visit to Spain in April 1914. Hardinge to Grey, 19 Apr. 1914, FO 371, vol. 2104, file 17547.

easily, and in July 1913, a few months after his visit to France, he returned to the subject of utilization of the Spanish railways by the French army. This time the Spanish King tried a different tack. He revealed to Geoffray that he was studying modification of the Spanish railway gauge to the continental width. The King hinted that France might contribute to the financing of such a conversion. Geoffray limited his reply to a comment on the commercial value of the plan.[45]

Poincaré was scheduled to reciprocate Alfonso's visit to France with a state visit of his own in the fall. This was to be climaxed by a Franco-Spanish naval demonstration at Carthagena. Poincaré did not know how far the Spanish government concurred in the King's sentiments, but thought it might be possible to bring about arrangements between the French and Spanish naval and military authorities similar to those existing between the French and the British.[46]

In a conversation with the Spanish ambassador on September 2, Grey depreciated an alliance between France and Spain as not necessary to intimate relations between the two nations. He thought that an open alliance between the two would be presumed to be against Germany and would therefore be provocative; the Germans might attempt some countermove to either test or to break it.[47] The press in both France and Spain became carried away with the prospect of Poincaré's impending visit, although Paléologue told Sir Francis Bertie that he doubted the Spanish government was willing to conclude any formal agreement. Bertie remarked that at the moment there was not the same prejudice in France as in England against secret treaties or agreements when they were in the national advantage, and that the French government would not risk a provocation of Germany by a public treaty involving the sort of agreement Bertie suspected Poincaré wanted to attain. The fact that Germany could not reach Spain except by sea past the coasts of France and England enabled the Spanish, according to Bertie, "not to have the same terror of Germany as some other Powers" if French and possibly British aid could be relied on.[48]

Alfonso expressed a desire that a British ship be present at the Carthagena naval review.[49] To make certain that the Spanish ambassador had not misunderstood Grey's conversation with him on the subject of a

---

[45] Geoffray to Pichon, 18 July 1913, *DDF3*, VII, no. 416, p. 452.

[46] Bertie to Grey, 25 July 1913, Grey MSS, FO 800, vol. 53.

[47] Grey to Rennie, councillor, British embassy, Madrid, 15 Sept. 1913, FO 371, vol. 1754, Spain, file 41436.

[48] Bertie to Grey, 2 Oct. 1913, Grey MSS, FO 800, vol. 53.

[49] Crowe to Admiralty, 6 Oct. 1913, FO 371, vol. 1754, file 45470; Nicolson to Grey, 5 Oct. 1913, Grey MSS, FO 800, vol. 93.

Franco-Spanish alliance, Sir Arthur Nicolson on October 6 repeated to Merry del Val that, while Grey had depreciated a public alliance as provocative, he had no wish to depreciate "contingent arrangements." The Spanish ambassador replied that his government had no desire to make an alliance, but was willing to give the French such assurances and possible facilities as to allow them to remain perfectly tranquil over their western frontier. He added that he had informed his government that under certain contingencies the passage of French troops through Spain would be viewed favorably, as Grey had hinted. Nicolson replied that "contingent arrangements were entirely a matter for France and Spain to settle and presumably they would not be made public." [50] From this bit of diplomatic fencing it seems certain that the Spanish, at least as far as their ambassador in London was concerned, had correctly interpreted the British hint.

Poincaré's state visit to Spain was the occasion of talks between General Hubert Lyautey and Spanish military authorities on the possibility of concerting their actions in Morocco. Probably the most impressive of the public ceremonies was the naval review at Carthagena on October 10, after which Poincaré sailed for home aboard the French battleship *Diderot*. In addition to the Spanish warships—among which the new dreadnought *España* must have been a source of special pride to King Alfonso as symbolic of Spain's renascent sea power—there were four French "Dantons" accompanied by a pair of destroyers, and the British battle cruiser *Invincible*.[51] The presence of the British warship enabled Alfonso and Poincaré to send a joint cable thanking King George, and served to underline Spain's friendship with the Triple Entente. However, the visit did not result in any written undertaking. The usual platitudes were included in the joint press communiqué about a perfect concordance of views in all political, economic, and commercial questions discussed by the representatives of the two countries.[52] Alfonso and the Spanish Prime Minister did give formal verbal assurances concerning Spanish neutrality and the safety of France's Pyrenees frontier. Alfonso also repeated his offer of Spanish railways for transport of French troops in the event of German aggression. This time he added the qualification that the Cortes' authoriza-

[50] Nicolson to Grey, 6 Oct. 1913, *ibid.*

[51] Poincaré, *Au service de la France*, III, 286–298; *Le Yacht*, 18 Oct. 1913, pp. 670–672. An amusing account by the captain of the *Invincible* is Admiral Sir Henry Pelly, *300,000 Sea Miles* (London, 1938), pp. 125–126.

[52] Bertie to Grey, 11 Oct. 1913, FO 371, vol. 1754, file 46398; Bunsen to Grey, 13 Oct. 1913, *ibid.*, file 46984, 46985, and 13 Oct. 1913, file 47155.

tion was needed. The King solemnly assured Poincaré that in any case "you will never have to fear a stab in the back on our part." [53] Poincaré and Pichon departed confident that Spanish facilities would be offered if necessary.[54]

There was another naval objective associated with Poincaré's visit. This did not involve questions of the Triple Entente, for if anything the British were the leading rivals of the French in this respect. Poincaré wanted to discuss the participation of French industry in the renewal of the Spanish Navy. The French, who had built some of the older Spanish warships, including the battleship *Pelayo*, resented the fact that British firms played the predominant role in execution of the Spanish naval law of 1908. In May 1912 D'Huart had suggested that the French attempt to profit from the improvement in diplomatic relations with Spain to obtain naval orders, particularly for submarines, in which the great French armament firm of Schneider et Cie. was interested.[55] The question had been the subject of a special communication from Admiral Aubert to the Quai d'Orsay, and the Foreign Ministry instructed the French ambassador in Madrid to raise the matter with the competent Spanish authorities. The Spanish assured Geoffray that Schneider's propositions would be taken into account.[56] The Quai d'Orsay suggested that Poincaré remind the Spanish of this promise during his visit, since the construction of Spain's first submarines would constitute a legitimate compensation for Schneider after the rejection in 1908 of its proposals for executing the Spanish program.[57]

Both Geoffray and the French military attaché in Madrid thought it would be advantageous if French naval units visited Spanish waters more frequently—as the Royal Navy did—in order to stimulate orders for French industry.[58] In June 1914 D'Huart reported that the current Minister of Marine was against giving La Sociedad, in which Vickers had a leading interest, a monopoly of Spanish naval construction, and that the contest for submarines was now between French and German types. Should the balance weigh in favor of Germany, the French naval attaché

[53] Poincaré, *Au service de la France,* III, 295–296.

[54] Bertie to Grey, 14 Oct. 1913, FO 371, vol. 1754, file 47155; Bertie to Grey, 13 Oct. 1913, Grey MSS, FO 800, vol. 53.

[55] D'Huart to Minister of Marine, 25 May 1912, AMF, carton BB7-130.

[56] P. de Margerie, assistant director for Europe, Quai d'Orsay, to Minister of Marine, 27 Aug. 1912, *ibid.*

[57] Note pour le Ministre, 4 Oct. 1913, *DDF3,* VIII, no. 253, p. 318. Of the ten submarines the Spanish projected, Schneider proposed to furnish two completed and build the other eight in Spain.

[58] Tillion to Minister of War, 21 Jan. and 12 Feb. 1914, EMA, Attaché Militaire, Espagne/4 bis.

was confident that a *haute intervention* would re-establish things in favor of French industry.[59]

Competition for Spanish orders may have had at least some role in Vickers' championship of a Spanish proposal in June 1914. According to Vickers, the chief of the Spanish artillery, General Gonzalez, called on them with royal authorization to propose that in return for information on the British 15-inch gun, which might be adopted for ships of the new Spanish program, the Royal Navy would be permitted to use the docks built or about to be built at Ferrol and Carthagena and to draw on Spanish stocks of 15-inch ammunition in time of war if necessary. Vickers argued that it would not be until autumn of 1917 that the first of the new Spanish ships entered service therefore lessening the need for secrecy about the guns, and that compliance with the request for information would make Spanish adoption of a German or French gun most unlikely.[60]

The Admiralty considered Spanish docking facilities "almost worthless in peace," and unusable in war if Spain were neutral; they also could not count on the reserves of guns and ammunition in Spain. Nevertheless they were disposed to grant the request to strengthen British industry against foreign competition. The Admiralty also thought this would encourage Spain to associate herself in case of war with the Triple Entente, but wanted Grey's opinion, assuming he would prefer the question to be handled by the Admiralty War Staff rather than more formal diplomatic correspondence.[61] The Foreign Office considered the Admiralty letter rather vague.[62] Grey did not object to the particular agreement regarding the 15-inch gun, but wanted more precise information regarding further discussions about Spain's attitude in a war before approving even informal conversations with the Spanish.[63] Within a few days, Britain was at war.

Despite the exchange of visits by the French and Spanish heads of state, there was still no formal alliance between the two countries on the outbreak of the war. Alfonso's attitude remained friendly and he repeated to the French ambassador the assurances given the previous year.[64] Aside from conversations about Morocco, there do not appear to have been any staff talks between the French and Spanish similar to those held between the French and the British. One might say that a form of entente did

---

[59] D'Huart to Minister of Marine, 20 June 1914, AMF, carton Ea-78.

[60] Vickers Ltd. to Admiralty, 16 June 1914, FO 371, vol. 2104, file 33642.

[61] Admiralty [W. Graham Greene] to Foreign Office, 23 July 1914, *ibid.*

[62] Minute by Crowe, 26 July 1914, *ibid.*

[63] Foreign Office [Crowe] to Admiralty, 30 July 1914, *ibid.*

[64] Albert Pingaud, "Alphonse XIII et la France en 1914," *Revue des deux mondes*, 1 May 1931, pp. 194–202.

exist, based almost entirely on King Alfonso's verbal assurances as to Spain's benevolent neutrality. But the King was not the Spanish government, and there were Spanish politicians and members of the cabinet who feared the German reaction to overt support for France.[65] Geoffray thought that an English initiative was necessary to reassure the Spanish, but Grey had depreciated a formal alliance. The French themselves were loath to become involved with Germany over Spain's African colonies, such as they were. Alfonso's ideas about Portugal may also have had a dampening effect for the French as likely to lead to complications with England. To this must be added the traditional Spanish isolationism and preoccupation with internal problems, as well as some support for the Triple Alliance in Spain. Such support was particularly strong in the army.[66]

Grey had hinted that secret staff arrangements would arouse no British opposition, but these apparently did not materialize. Whatever the Spanish government or General Staff might have thought about this, it seems obvious that the French were not particularly interested in pushing the matter. This was probably because of the lack of enthusiasm of Joffre and the French General Staff for either the Spanish railway net or the prospect of Spanish troops fighting alongside the French army. The French navy believed differently and might have been the driving force behind any Spanish project, but the disagreement between the two services over the transport of the troops from North Africa in case of mobilization was fundamental. Whatever the benefits, which were somewhat debatable, the General Staff was not likely to base its detailed mobilization plans for the troops of the nineteenth corps on the willingness of the Spanish to consent to the use of their facilities in a moment of crisis. Spain in the years before the First World War remained, along with her navy which was only just beginning its recovery, a minor though potentially important factor in the Mediterranean situation.

At the opposite end of the Mediterranean from Spain the shadow of another renascent naval power began to grow in the years 1912–1914. Imperial Russia was technically not a Mediterranean power. She had a fleet in the adjacent Black Sea, whose narrow exits were held by another

[65] Geoffray to Pichon, 16 Oct. 1913, *DDF3*, VIII, no. 338, pp. 424–426.

[66] Renouvin, *Les Questions méditerranéennes*, p. 39; Mousset, *L'Espagne dans la politique mondiale*, pp. 170–171; Paul Herre, *Die Kleinen Staaten Europas und die entstehung des Weltkrieges* (Munich, 1937), pp. 73–77, 78–79; Adolf Hasenclever, "Zur Geschichte der spanisch-französischen Beziehungen vor Ausbruch des Weltkrieges," *Berliner Monatshefte*, 14.9 (Sept. 1936): 729–732; Albertini, *Origins of the War*, III, 691–693; Salvador de Madariaga, *Spain: A Modern History* (New York, 1958), pp. 311–315.

power and closed to Russian and other warships by treaty stipulations. But as a complete Turkish collapse appeared imminent following the disasters of the Balkan Wars, and as Russian naval strength began to grow in both the Baltic and the Black Sea, it was inevitable that she would have at least some influence on the Mediterranean situation. Russia had enjoyed a far higher position than Spain in the ranks of the world's naval powers and her potential for the future was clearly much greater. On the eve of the First World War she had embarked on a large building program and her increasing maritime power would inevitably have played a role beyond the confines of the Black Sea or the Baltic if only by the mere fact of its existence.

The disastrous Russian naval losses in the Russo-Japanese War of 1904–1905 left the Black Sea fleet—which was unable to exit—untouched in its material strength. But the *Potemkin* mutiny of June 1905 and the unwillingness of the crews of other ships in the fleet to suppress it showed the unreliability of the personnel. The Russians were slow to begin a new naval program after the war. Proposals by the government were rejected by the Duma which insisted on a complete reorganization of the naval administration before any reconstruction; there were sterile quarrels over the wisdom of expenditures on harbors and dockyards as well as designs adopted by the navy; the question was raised whether or not the future Russian naval force should be purely defensive; and there were other demands that all future building be effected within Russia.[67] Such capital ship construction as there was proceeded very slowly, largely on modified ships laid down before or during the Russo-Japanese War. The backwardness of Russian industry also hampered progress. When the 17,200-ton *Andrei Pervozvannyi* and *Imperator Pavel* finally entered service with the Baltic fleet in 1910–11 they had been under construction for almost eight years. A similar period of construction was required for the 12,733-ton Black Sea battleships *Evstafi* and *Ioann Zlatoust* which also entered service in 1910–1911, and were really modified versions of the *Potemkin* (now renamed *Panteleimon*).[68] The ships were clearly out of date. Although this was not yet of vital importance in the Black Sea, it was for the Baltic

[67] *The Naval Annual, 1907*, pp. 30–31; *The Naval Annual, 1908*, pp. 36–37; *The Naval Annual, 1909*, pp. 29–30; *The Naval Annual, 1910*, pp. 43–45; *The Naval Annual, 1911*, pp. 35–38; Charles E. Adams, "Der Wiederaufsteig der russischen Kriegsmarine in den Jahren 1905–1917," *Marine Rundschau*, 61.1 (Feb. 1964): 16; N. Monasterev and Serge Terestchenko, *Histoire de la marine russe,* trans. Jean Perceau (Paris, 1932), pp. 272–274.

[68] Adams, "Der Wiederaufsteig," pp. 16–17; Henri Bernay, "La Reconstruction de la flotte Russe," *Le Yacht*, 15 July 1911, pp. 433–434; *The Naval Annual, 1912*, pp. 53–54.

where the Russian ships compared unfavorably with their German contemporaries.

The fortunes of the Russian navy improved considerably with the arrival of Vice Admiral Ivan K. Grigorovitch to the office of Minister of Marine in April 1911. Grigorovitch was a capable and energetic officer who doggedly set out to simplify procedures and streamline the almost legendary complications of the Russian Admiralty, as well as to define responsibility and increase decentralization. Under Grigorovitch more time was also devoted to training and gunnery practice. The Admiral himself set the example as a hardworking officer, arriving punctually in his office each morning at nine in what the British naval attaché described as an example perhaps more respected than admired by some subordinates.[69]

Admiral Grigorovitch was successful in obtaining appropriations from the Duma in June 1911 for badly needed capital ship construction. Major construction included four 23,000-ton dreadnoughts of the "Gangut" class for the Baltic; and three 22,500-ton dreadnoughts of the "Imperatritsa Maria" class, nine destroyers, and six submarines for the Black Sea. These units were merely the first part of a long range program put forward in 1910, but not accepted by the Duma, which foresaw in 1920 a Baltic fleet of eight dreadnoughts and battle cruisers, twenty cruisers, thirty-six destroyers, and twelve submarines, and a Black Sea fleet one and one-half times the combined naval strength of Turkey, Bulgaria, and Rumania.[70] Russian naval plans went beyond this goal. The Russian naval attaché in London told Churchill in October 1911 that they were looking forward to a Baltic fleet of sixteen dreadnoughts with eight other battleships in reserve by 1930. Moreover, the Russians expected that some of the dreadnoughts then building in England for South American countries or Turkey might come on to the market through a change of policy or failure of contracted conditions. The Russian government was prepared, with British approval, to buy such units within three days. The Russian attaché also hinted that Admiral Grigorovitch might visit England for, among other things, the purpose of placing orders with British yards.[71]

In the spring of 1912 the proposals for a new Russian building program aroused a strong current of opposition both in and outside of the Duma.

[69] Adams, "Der Wiederaufsteig," pp. 18–20; EMG, "Bulletin Annuel-Russie, 1912," AMF, carton Ea-160; Commander H. Grenfell, "Report on Russian Naval Progress for 1912," 8 Jan. 1913, FO 371, vol. 1743, Russia, file 1685.

[70] *The Naval Annual, 1912*, p. 54; Walter Hubatsch, "Die russischen Marine im deutschen Urteil 1890–1914," *Das deutsche Bild der russischen und sowjetischen Marine*, Beiheft 7/8 of *Marine Rundschau* (Frankfurt am Main, 1962), p. 37.

[71] Churchill to Grey, 28 Oct. 1911, Grey MSS, FO 800, vol. 86.

Opponents claimed that the Russian Baltic fleet would always be outclassed by the Germans so that money spent on naval construction would be thrown away and would delay the realization of social reforms. Opponents of the naval proposals, generally on the Left and including the Octobrists, favored a purely defensive fleet of small units instead of one composed of dreadnoughts. Those favoring the naval proposals maintained that a moderate fleet in the Baltic was necessary for Russia's position as a great power and the security of the capital and northern coasts. The arguments of Foreign Minister Sazonov in a closed session of the budget committee of the Duma were reported to have convinced some of the Octobrists to vote for the naval proposals despite the opposition of prominent members of the party. The measure passed by a narrow vote of 26–19.[72] After a lengthy secret session of the Duma on June 19, the bill was passed by the surprisingly large majority of 228–71. The bill, known as the Small Shipbuilding Program, provided funds for the period 1912–1917 to be used for four battle cruisers, eight light cruisers, thirty-six destroyers, and eighteen submarines. Of this number, two of the light cruisers and six of the submarines were destined for the Black Sea, and two of the light cruisers for the Far East; the remainder of the force, the largest portion, was for the Baltic. Also included in the bill were heavy expenditures on harbor works and auxiliary ships.[73] It was generally assumed that this Small Shipbuilding Program was, as its name implied, the fore runner of a larger program. Although the government had promised that the Duma would not be asked for additional sums during the next five years, the British naval attaché estimated that provision for new ships could be made before 1918 out of the large ordinary naval estimates.[74]

Russian shipbuilding gained by the association of foreign firms with Russian yards. In the north, Schneider collaborated with the Putilov Works, and was reported to be building its own yard at Revel. The German firm of Schichau intended to establish a yard at Riga through a Russian intermediary, and other French, British, and German firms gave technical assistance.[75] In the Black Sea, the British firm of John Brown advised the Russian yard Bunge and Ivanov at Nikolaev. In preparation for dreadnought construction the yard was furnished with new shops and

[72] O'Beirne, councillor of embassy, St. Petersburg, to Grey, 12 June 1912, FO 371, vol. 1470, Russia, file 25622.

[73] Grenfell, British naval attaché, to O'Beirne, 22 June 1912, ibid., file 27675. See also Hubatsch, "Die russischen Marine," p. 38; The Naval Annual, 1913, pp. 55–59.

[74] O'Beirne to Grey, 25 June 1912, FO 371, vol. 1470, Russia, file 27674.

[75] EMG, "Bulletin Annuel-Russie, 1912," AMF, carton Ea-160; Buchanan to Grey, 31 Oct. 1912, FO 371, vol. 1470, file 46618; Le Yacht, 18 Jan. 1913, p. 45.

railway connections as well as the latest machinery. Vickers acquired an interest in the Ateliers et Fonderies de Nicolaïeff, also known as the Franco-Belgian Company, where it exercised technical supervision over dreadnought construction.[76]

The keels of the first Black Sea dreadnoughts, the *Imperatritsa Maria* and the *Imperator Alexander III*, were laid at Bunge and Ivanov on July 14, 1912. Commencement of the third ship, the *Ekaterina II*, was delayed, partially through an apparent error on the part of Vickers in preparing the slip.[77] The Russian Ministry of Marine was reported to be dissatisfied with Vickers over the English firm's carelessness as well as the delay in preparing and submitting plans for the ship. The Foreign Office asked the Admiralty to unofficially let Vickers know of Russian displeasure.[78] Vickers was also involved in a dispute over the large armored cruiser *Rurik* which had been built in England for the Russian government. The ship was not accepted by the Russians as ready for use until two years after the contract date and Vickers was therefore penalized. Admiral Grigorovitch and the Imperial Auditor General became involved in their own controversy over the subject of how large Vickers' fine should be. The Minister of Marine favored a much lower sum than the Auditor General, and this exposed him to attacks by his enemies on account of the unsatisfactory experiences with the firm in the past. To complicate matters there was also the threat of a scandal over alleged favoritism to Vickers because of a reported entry in the accounts of Vickers' Russian subsidiary concerning the sum of 100,000 rubles "expended at the Ministry of Marine."[79]

In October 1912 Vickers lost a tender for construction of two 4300-ton

[76] Grenfell to Buchanan, 4 Sept. 1912, FO 371, vol. 1469, Russia, file 3774. *The Naval Annual, 1912*, p. 54; Anon., "La Marine russe-sa situation actuelle," *Moniteur de la Flotte*, 10 Aug. 1912, p. 3; Anon., "Russian Naval Progress," *Army and Navy Gazette*, 13 June 1914, pp. 542–543; Scott, *Vickers—A History*, p. 85.

[77] Grenfell to Buchanan, 4 Sept. 1912. Both the *Naval Annual, 1913* (p. 57) and Jane, *Fighting Ships, 1915* (p. 325), list the *Imperator Alexander III* and *Imperatritsa Maria* as having been laid down in October 1911. The British naval attaché did report that a large amount of material was prepared beforehand, which may account for the discrepancy. The *Naval Annual* also reports the *Ekaterina II* as having been laid down in September 1912, though Grenfell thought it unlikely construction could begin before 1913. The "Imperatritsa Marias" were slightly smaller "Ganguts" armed with twelve 12-inch guns and had a speed of 21 knots (Jane, p. 325).

[78] Grenfell to Buchanan, 4 Sept. 1912; minutes by Louis Mallet and Arthur Nicolson, *ibid.*; L. Mallet to Secretary to the Admiralty, 23 Sept. 1912, *ibid.*

[79] Buchanan to Grey, 31 Oct. 1912, FO 371, vol. 1470, file 46618; Grenfell to Buchanan, 31 Oct. 1912, *ibid.*; Grenfell to Buchanan, 2 Oct. 1912, FO 371, vol. 1469, file 41946. Grenfell refers to a board member of Vickers named "Mr. Sakharov" who supposedly served as intermediary. This is probably the legendary Basil Zaharoff. See Scott, *Vickers—A History*, p. 81.

fast light cruisers to the German firm of Schichau, despite what the British firm claimed were more advantageous terms. When the British ambassador remarked on the singularity of building cruisers in the country against whom they might one day have to fight, Sazonov replied that they were unimportant vessels and that the Russian government wanted them delivered quickly.[80] Schichau probably would have been able to deliver the ships eighteen months sooner than a Russian yard and at less cost. However, the action probably diminished the Duma's confidence in Grigorovitch, who during the debate over the naval law had spoken of a policy of shipbuilding in Russia. The two cruisers were scheduled for completion by the autumn of 1914, but were taken over by the Germans on the outbreak of the war and served against the Triple Entente as the *Elbing* and *Pillau*.[81]

The construction in Russia of large warships was considered by some, including the British naval attaché, to involve a "gigantic" waste of money and to open infinite opportunities for secret commissions and peculation. According to Commander Harold G. Grenfell construction costs in Russia would run about 60 percent higher than in England. One criticism of the Russian program was that the country was not yet in the industrial, technical, and economic position to expend efficiently the huge sums (£14 to 15 million annually) on shipbuilding to which it had committed itself for a number of years. If new yards were created for the program, serious economic loss would eventually result through their disuse once demand for warships tapered off as the naval program was completed. Moreover, the new Russian warships would still be outclassed by foreign contemporaries because of the longer Russian building time.[82] In half the number of cases the works where the destroyers and submarines were to be built had still to be erected at the end of 1912. The ceremony of formally laying down the keels of the "Borodino" class battle cruisers for the Baltic fleet was held on December 19, 1912, but according to Commander Grenfell appearances were deceiving for the slips to build them were not yet complete, and the first deliveries of materials were not expected before the spring of 1913.[83]

Whatever success the Russians might have had in the material devel-

[80] Buchanan to Grey, 31 Oct. 1912.

[81] Grenfell to Buchanan, 31 Oct. 1912, FO 371, vol. 1470, file 46618.

[82] Grenfell to O'Beirne, 22 June 1912, FO 371, vol. 1470, file 27675.

[83] Grenfell, "Report on Russian Naval Progress for 1912," 8 Jan. 1913, FO 371, vol. 1743, file 1685. The four "Borodinos," which were to be over 32,000 tons, armed with twelve 14-inch guns, and a speed of 27–28 knots, were destined never to be completed.

opment of their fleet, they would still be faced with the problem of personnel. The unsound administrative traditions of the past weighed heavily on the Russian navy, and the British naval attaché considered it questionable whether the officers would submit to the long periods of constant effort and frequently monotonous work necessary for the attainment of efficiency. While many of the officers were "intelligent and keen," they were "drawn entirely from a class in which the sense of responsibility is a less noticeable feature than its love of pleasure; a class whose conception of integrity, in both private and official relations, possibly is not quite the same as generally accepted by Western nations. Young officers, accustomed nightly to sit in the cafés-chantant of Kronstadt and St. Petersburgh until the early hours of the morning, who—badly paid as they are—help to support the most numerous and most expensive *demi-monde* in the whole of Europe, can hardly be expected to give much time or trouble on the following day to the tamer business of instructing, or superintending the instruction of, recruits taken from an illiterate inland peasantry, or, indeed, to any other duty." [84] The German naval attaché in St. Petersburg in 1911 also commented on the numerous deficiencies of the Russian officer corps. [85]

Training in the Russian navy was hampered by the long winter in the north and the narrow tideless waters of the Baltic. Moreover, conditions of service and pay were so unattractive that it was extremely difficult to get men qualified in the specialties to re-engage; because of the low general level of technical education they could always receive higher wages on shore. [86] Memories of the *Potemkin* affair were fresh, and the threat of incipient mutiny still hung over the Russian fleet in 1912. In the spring there was unrest in the Baltic fleet. Over the summer widespread arrests were made in the Black Sea fleet. Martial law was declared in Sevastopol following the uncovering of a plot to seize the ships and their treasure, murder the officers, and sail to a foreign port. About 200 arrests were made and very bad feeling was reported to prevail among the lower ratings of the fleet; most of the discontent revolved around poor food and treatment. [87] Eventually 142 men were tried, and 123 found guilty and handed various sentences including seventeen executions. The

---

[84] Grenfell to O'Beirne, 22 June 1912.
[85] Cited by Hubatsch, "Die russischen Marine," p. 28.
[86] Grenfell to O'Beirne, 22 June 1912.
[87] O'Beirne to Grey, 12 May 1912, FO 371, vol. 1469, file 20817; Grenfell to Buchanan, 21 Aug. 1912, FO 371, vol. 1470, file 35876; Acting Consul General, Odessa, F. Watson, to Grey, 23 Aug. 1912, *ibid.*, file 36297; Watson to Grey, 26 Aug. 1912, *ibid.*, file 37928.

publication of the sentences provoked sympathy strikes in the capital. Ultimately the sentences of six of those condemned to death were commuted to life imprisonment. About 400 sailors were transferred from the Black Sea to the Baltic or the Far East.[88]

Both the French and British naval attachés concluded that serious disaffection was prevalent in the Russian fleet, and consequently Commander Grenfell thought that "a heavy discount must continue to be made upon its paper value, as an opponent or as an ally." [89] This situation was not apt to improve. Although the crews remained outwardly calm the following year, they were always exposed to revolutionary propaganda. This was aggravated by the influx of mechanics and engineers who had worked in the factories around St. Petersburg and often held more advanced ideas than the largely illiterate sailors.[90] In September 1913 the Baltic fleet visited Great Britain and France. The Russian officers and men generally made a good impression by their bearing and conduct, but there was evidence that all was far from well: the squadron was reported to have left a large number of deserters behind.[91]

Whatever the difficulties involved in her naval renaissance, Russia's present plans would bring her a relatively large number of modern ships, and Hugh O'Beirne, Councillor of the British embassy at St. Petersburg, thought the Russian fleet would have to be taken seriously by the German General Staff.[92] This view was shared by Prince Louis of Battenberg. In a private letter to the Prime Minister accompanying O'Beirne's dispatch concerning approval of the naval proposals by the budget committee of the Duma, Prince Louis wrote that he could not help feeling the new third squadron created by Germany was partly intended to contain the Russian ships if need be, and that "the threat of a Russian fleet, even in small numbers, should in time, ease the situation for us in the North Sea." [93] Battenberg judged by the Kaiser's remarks to him the preceding year that Wilhelm was much more disturbed at Britain's friendship with Russia than with France. Prince Louis added that while the Russians had "so far shown little aptitude or understanding for warfare at sea," the few higher commanders who came out of the last war creditably were at the Admiralty, and the new

---

[88] Consul General Smith, Odessa, 11 Nov. 1912, *ibid.*, file 48471; Grenfell to Buchanan, 14 Nov. 1912, *ibid.*, file 48946; Consul General Smith, Odessa, to Grey, 9 Dec. 1912, *ibid.*, file 52996.

[89] Grenfell, "Report on Russian Naval Progress for 1912," 8 Jan. 1913, FO 371, vol. 1743, file 1685; EMG, "Bulletin Annuel-Russie, 1912," AMF, carton Ea-160.

[90] EMG, "Bulletin Annuel de 1913-Russie," *ibid.*

[91] *Le Yacht,* 18 Oct. 1913, p. 674.

[92] O'Beirne to Grey, 25 June 1912, FO 371, vol. 1470, file 27674.

[93] Battenberg to Asquith, 28 June 1912, Asquith MSS, box 24.

ships when built "would constitute a force no one could neglect." Prince Louis also thought that the Black Sea fleet "could easily be made to act as a check upon any Turkish movement towards Egypt." He believed that Sweden would remain neutral despite German attempts to woo her and strong Swedish sentiment against Russia, reinforced by sympathy with Finland.

The Germans were not blind to Russian naval activity, and in November 1913 their naval attaché in Russia warned of having to reckon with a strong Russian Baltic fleet in the future.[94] The news of the Franco-Russian naval convention in the summer of 1912 was also disturbing. At the end of 1912 the Admiralstab recognized that the light forces which it had formerly intended to leave in the Baltic in the event of war were insufficient. The Germans therefore decided to transfer the older portions of their battle fleet to the Baltic, although it was deemed too costly to seek a decision by means of an offensive into the Gulf of Finland.[95] The problem of the Russian fleet was discussed at length in an anonymous article in the authoritative German naval periodical *Marine Rundschau* in April 1914. The writer concluded that while much had been done for the Russian fleet, much still remained to be accomplished, and that the fleet would be an important political factor.[96]

The role of the Russian Black Sea fleet and the Straits question were naturally bound closely together. The latter was a complex diplomatic problem which lies beyond the scope of this study. An obvious assignment for the Black Sea fleet was the maintenance of Russian maritime supremacy in that sea, and this was endangered by Turkey's acquisition of dreadnoughts constructed in foreign yards. Therefore, regardless of the status of the Straits, the acceleration of naval construction at Nikolaev became of vital importance for the Russians.[97] On a broader scale, and of importance for French dispositions in the Mediterranean, was the Franco-Rus-

[94] Hubatsch, "Die russischen Marine," pp. 33–34.

[95] *Ibid.*, pp. 34–35. A more detailed discussion of the problem is in Hubatsch, *Die Admiralstab*, pp. 152–156.

[96] G., "Der Wiederaufbau der russischen Flotte," *Marine Rundschau*, Apr. 1914, pp. 495–496.

[97] Important memoranda on the Straits question from the naval and military point of view are in "Meinung des Admiralstabes in der Frage der Meerengen," 7 July 1911, *Die Internationalen Beziehungen im Zeitalter des Imperialismus: Dokumente aus den Archiven der Zarischen und der Provisorischen Regierung* (hereafter cited as *Int. Bez.*), Otto Hoetzsch, trans., 11 vols. (Berlin 1931–1942), 3rd series, I, no. 231, pp. 293–294; report by Minister of War Suchomlinov, 11 Aug. 1911, *ibid.*, no. 310, pp. 375–378; Chief of Russian Admiralty Staff to Minister of Marine, 15 Nov. 1912, *ibid.*, vol. IV, no. 374, pp. 364–369.

sian naval convention of July 16, 1912. Before this the naval potential of the alliance between France and Russia had been neglected. The French did not appraise the Russian fleet very highly and had been reluctant to rely much upon it. A nonbinding naval convention had been concluded in December of 1901, but this merely outlined a division of activity between the fleets in case of a war against England.[98] The situation had changed when Vice Admiral Prince Lieven, Chief of the Russian Admiralty Staff, Vice Admiral Aubert, and the Ministers of Marine Delcassé and Admiral Grigorovitch signed the new convention. Paléologue represented the Quai d'Orsay in the negotiations, and the convention was confirmed by the signatures of Poincaré and Sazonov when Poincaré visited St. Petersburg in August.[99] The convention itself was a fairly general one for cooperation between the two fleets when the *casus foederis* arose, prepared for by regular conferences between the naval staffs in time of peace.[100]

The exact way this naval cooperation might be accomplished was the subject of a series of secret talks between Prince Lieven and Admiral Aubert in July prior to signature of the convention. A handful of officers of the EMG were present, along with the Russian naval attachés in London and Paris. Both parties were careful to specify they were not binding their governments in any way. Prince Lieven explained that the maintenance of Russian naval supremacy in the Black Sea was necessary for the secure transport of troops and supplies indispensable for operations on land. With this aim in mind, Russia intended to maintain a naval force in the Black Sea superior by at least one half to any fleet Turkey might put into the line. However, the Russians feared the situation would completely change if the Austrian or Italian fleet, or both, passed through the Dardanelles with the connivance of the Turks. It was this threat of Triple Alliance naval superiority in the Black Sea that the Russians wanted their French ally to counteract.[101]

The French were careful to cite the special obligations the Anglo-French entente might impose on their fleet; these would affect any question of

[98] Ropp, "Development of a Modern Navy," pp. 390–392, 529–531; Marder, *Anatomy of British Sea Power*, p. 399 n. 12.

[99] Izvolski to Neratov, 18 July 1912, *Un Livre Noire: Diplomatie d'avant-guerre d'après les documents des archives Russes* (Paris, 1922–1923), I, 296–299; report by Sazonov to Tsar, 4 Aug. 1912, *ibid.*, II, 339.

[100] "Projet de convention navale franco-russe," 16 July 1912, DDF3, vol. III, no. 206, p. 270. See also V. Egorief and E. Schvede, "La Convention navale de 1912 et les relations navales Franco-Russes au cours de la guerre mondiale," *Les Alliés contre la Russie* (Paris, n.d. [1926]), pp. 54–60.

[101] Vice Admiral Aubert and Prince Lieven, "Ière echange de vues stratégiques entre le Chef d'EMG de la Marine Impériale Russe et le Chef d'EMG de la Marine Française," 16 July 1912, MAE, Russie, vol. NS-41.

sending the French Mediterranean fleet in pursuit of an Austrian or Italian force attempting to reach the Black Sea. Prince Lieven, in turn, was hardly encouraging about the aid the Black Sea fleet might give to the French. Under present circumstances he did not believe this fleet could operate in the western basin of the Mediterranean. In his opinion it was not enough to pass the Straits once; the line of communications must be assured. Russian operations in the Mediterranean could only be envisaged after the occupation of at least one side of the Straits. From the various contingencies the two naval staff chiefs discussed, it appeared as if a concentration of French naval forces at Bizerte at the beginning of hostilities would by virtue of its intimidating effect on Austria and Italy be the most useful strategic French measure for Russia.

Prince Lieven discussed the possibility that the Baltic fleet might operate in the Mediterranean, and asked if Bizerte could serve as its base of operations, emphasizing that its ships would probably rely heavily upon oil instead of coal. Aubert replied that until then the Ministry of Marine had been concerned at Bizerte only with the needs of the French fleet, whose large ships employed coal almost exclusively. The question would therefore have to be studied along with information as to the exact fuel requirements of the Russian ships in order to determine the level of the stocks to be maintained. The two admirals considered radio communications between Bizerte and Sevastopol and the usefulness of a joint code. Aubert declined a Russian request for a French naval demonstration off the coast of Sweden in order to divert the attention of that country from Finland, where a Russian army corps was immobilized on the Swedish frontier. He pointed out that the French had to concentrate in the Mediterranean leaving little for the north. Aubert and Lieven agreed that the Baltic ought to be discussed with the British along with Mediterranean problems. Prince Lieven emphasized that only in 1916–17 would the Russian Baltic fleet be ready to undertake any offensive action. He summarized the ideas of the Russian Admiralty staff as: (1) France would assure freedom of the seas in the Mediterranean; (2) England would have the same job in the North Sea; and (3) Russia would do the same in the Baltic and also the Black Sea if she had to deal with only Turkey. The two staffs also concluded an agreement for the exchange of intelligence.[102]

Prince Lieven told Alexander Izvolski, Russian ambassador in Paris, that his conversations with the French EMG had been most advantageous for Russia. The French had shown themselves willing to facilitate Russia's

[102] "Convention pour l'echange des renseignements entre la Marine Russe et la Marine Française," 16 July 1912, *ibid.*

hegemony in the Black Sea by exerting pressure on the fleets of Russia's potential enemies through a concentration of their own forces more toward the east at Bizerte. Prince Lieven added that this involved no counter obligation on Russia's part.[103] Actually the French had promised nothing they did not intend to do in the first place. Aubert had spoken of Bizerte as a concentration point primarily in reference to the apparent choice by the Italians of Taranto as their principal base.[104]

The idea of Russia assuring command of the sea in the Baltic seemed more in the nature of a pious wish rather than a reality, and while Poincaré was in Russia in August he asked Sazonov if the Russians intended to ask the Royal Navy for assistance in the north, something which the French could not give. This seemed like a hint, and Sazonov thought the matter needed a detailed discussion.[105]

In May 1913 Vice Admiral Le Bris, now chief of the EMG, accompanied by a few staff officers traveled to St. Petersburg to continue the conversations begun the previous year. In general, Prince Lieven and Le Bris maintained the dispositions of 1912, but their attention was especially drawn to the necessity of coordinating the rapid transmission of precise intelligence about the fleets of the Triple Alliance. It was recognized as highly desirable that the Russians establish a powerful radio post in the Baltic to ensure communications with France. The possibility that circumstances would permit the Russian Black Sea fleet to pass the Straits was discussed, and both staff chiefs agreed it would be of interest for the naval staffs to study in what manner the French fleet, without sacrificing any of its objectives in the Mediterranean, might combine its action with that of the Black Sea fleet in order to facilitate the strategic concentration of allied forces in the Mediterranean.[106]

It was Russia's turn to come to Paris in May 1914. Prince Lieven had died in March of that year, and Vice Admiral A. I. Rusin now led the Russian staff officers who met with Vice Admiral Pivet, the new chief of the EMG. The French had a number of points they wanted to raise with the Russians. These included: the force which the Russians might send out of the Black Sea to the Mediterranean, so that the French could prepare for its provisioning; the apparent new reorientation of the Italian fleet toward La Spezia, Maddalena, and the north; and Russian plans for the employment of the Baltic fleet. The French also wanted to study the

---

[103] Izvolski to Neratov, 18 July 1912, *Livre Noire*, I, 297–298.
[104] "Ière Echange de Vues Stratégiques," 16 July 1912.
[105] Report by Sazonov to Tsar, 4 Aug. 1912, *Livre Noire*, II, 339–340.
[106] Procès-Verbal, 31 May 1913, AMF, carton Es-9. This record of the conversations bears both Prince Lieven's and Admiral Le Bris' signatures.

establishment of a joint surveillance of the Triple Alliance fleets, particularly in regard to Austria. They were thinking in terms of agents in Taranto, Brindisi, Denmark, and Sweden, and wanted to know what the Russians had done in this respect.[107]

During the discussion on June 22 Admiral Rusin reaffirmed the necessity for Russia of security in the Black Sea. He believed that the Austrian fleet would be increased and its construction accelerated, and also that the Entente could count on the neutrality of Rumania.[108] Admiral Pivet asked if the Russians might send ships out of the Black Sea now that their fleet there was being greatly increased. Rusin replied that ships from the Baltic might be sent instead, and that he believed they would have battleships in the Mediterranean in one and one half to three years, including 32,000-ton 28-knot ships.[109] Rear Admiral de Bon, assistant chief of the EMG, remarked that it would then be necessary to organize the resources of Bizerte. To this observation, Admiral Rusin replied that the question could be stated more specifically the following year. Pivet and Rusin concluded another convention for the exchange of intelligence, as well as a protocol for the embarkation of officers in each other's warships, since embarkation of Russian officers in the French submarine flotillas had proved advantageous. They also agreed to have their staffs work out as soon as possible the details of a convention for the reciprocal use of naval bases in the event of war.[110]

This last meeting of the French and Russian naval staffs before the war is interesting because of Admiral Rusin's allusion to the new battle cruisers of the Baltic fleet operating in the Mediterranean. But the completion of these ships (never to be achieved) was still a long way off in the summer of 1914, and the idea certainly involved great practical difficulties. The question naturally arises whether the Russians really would have risked their best units far from the Baltic; and if they did, how this force might succeed in leaving the Baltic and passing around the Danish peninsula in the face of a hostile German fleet which was likely to be superior in strength and hardly indifferent to the Russian action.

The Russians also hinted at future operations in the Mediterranean by the Black Sea fleet, but they were actually far from certain of control of

[107] Unsigned and untitled memorandum of what appears to be the French agenda for the meeting with Admiral Rusin, n.d., AMF, carton Es-9.

[108] Procès-Verbal, 22 June 1914, *ibid.* These notes are fragmentary, obviously written in haste by one of the participants in the conference.

[109] *Ibid.* Actually these specifications fit the battle cruisers of the "Borodino" class.

[110] Admiral Pivet and Admiral Rusin, "Convention pour l'Echange de Renseignements entre la Marine Russe et la Marine Française," 23 June 1914, and "Protocole du 23 Juin 1914," AMF, carton Es-9.

the Black Sea against the rising naval power of the Turks. Turkey had one powerful dreadnought under construction in England which was scheduled for completion in the summer of 1914. A similar unit was planned for the future. At the end of 1913 the Turks purchased a dreadnought building in England for the Brazilian government. This raised the prospect of two dreadnoughts, each more powerful than anything in the Russian Black Sea fleet, entering service by the autumn of 1914.[111] Furthermore, there were two dreadnoughts building for Chile in England, and two for Argentina in the United States. The Russians were afraid that one or more of these ships would also fall into Turkish hands, and Sazonov instructed the Russian ambassador in Paris to see if French financial assistance might be obtained in getting the Chilean ships for Greece.[112] The emphatic denial by a representative of Armstrong that the Turks would purchase the dreadnought they were building for Chile must have been scant consolation to the Russians.[113]

Admiral Grigorovitch received extremely alarming reports from his intelligence sources at the beginning of 1914 that the Turks had purchased one of the Argentine dreadnoughts. Counting the dreadnoughts the Ottoman government already had, plus the more advanced Chilean ship, it was highly possible they would be able to put into service between the end of 1914 and the middle of 1915 four dreadnoughts, which would represent a force approximately six times the power of the existing Russian Black Sea fleet. With this unfavorable ratio, no tactical superiority on the part of the Russians could alter the situation, and the Turks would enjoy command of the sea. Grigorovitch pointed out that the Russian Black Sea dreadnoughts, whose construction at Nikolaev was to be accelerated, could not be placed into service until the end of 1915. Even then sea supremacy would not be regained if the three Russian dreadnoughts faced four Turkish ships. Turkish command of the sea would clearly prejudice Russia's interests in the Straits question, and any thought of a sortie against Constantinople would have to be abandoned. The maritime communications

111 The Russian Black Sea fleet consisted of only two battleships completed since the Russo-Japanese War, the obsolescent *Ioann Zlatoust*, and *Evstafi*. There were also five older battleships, two of scant value by 1913 and none in any way comparable to even the earlier dreadnought types. *The Naval Annual, 1912*, pp. 230–231.

112 Sazonov to Izvolski, 2 Jan. 1914, F. Stieve, ed., *Der Diplomatische Schriftwechsel Iswolskis, 1911–1914* (Berlin, 1924), IV, nos. 1202, 1204, pp. 13, 14; Izvolski to Sazonov, 3 Jan. 1914, *ibid.*, no. 1205, p. 14. The preceding year the Russians had tried to induce the French to hamper the purchase in France of four destroyers by Rumania. Neratov to Izvolski, 28 Jan. 1913, *ibid.*, vol. III, no. 703, p. 42; Izvolski to Sazonov, 29 Jan. 1913, *ibid.*, no. 704, p. 43.

113 Russian chargé, London, to Sazonov, 5 Jan. 1914, B. Siebert, ed., *Graf Benckendorffs Diplomatischer Schriftwechsel* (Berlin, 1928), III, no. 1025, pp. 240–241.

of the Russian army in the Caucasus would be threatened, and there would be the danger of a Turkish landing on its flank. The flank of the main Russian armies would also be exposed if the coast from Odessa to Sevastopol was not secured. Grigorovitch hinted at possible internal political repercussions if the Russian fleet was again defeated, particularly by the Turks. To avoid these dangers, Admiral Grigorovitch recommended the purchase by Russia if possible of the Argentine and Chilean dreadnoughts. After their acquisition, if the Russians succeeded in solving the difficult diplomatic question involved in bringing the ships through the Straits into the Black Sea, Turkish hopes for naval supremacy would be decisively broken, since there were no further foreign dreadnoughts on the market, and Russia's own building program would begin to have its effect. If it proved impossible to pass the ships through the Straits, they would still be useful either in the Baltic or as the nucleus for a Russian Mediterranean squadron.[114] Sazonov agreed with Grigorovitch's proposal, and the Russian naval attaché in the United States began his attempts to purchase the Argentine ships; the Russian chargé d'affaires in Buenos Aires was ordered to support his efforts.[115]

The situation in the Black Sea was discussed at length in a special conference held by the Russians on February 21 in order to consider the naval and military preparations necessary should circumstances require an expedition to seize the Straits. Sazonov presided over the group which included naval and military experts as well as the Russian ambassador at Constantinople. A representative of the Russian Admiralty staff revealed that special measures had been taken to hasten the completion of the dreadnoughts *Imperatritsa Maria* and *Imperator Alexander III* so that both would be ready for service by the fall of 1915 instead of the beginning of 1916. The third dreadnought, the *Ekaterina II,* was to be ready by the end of 1915, and the navy intended to begin construction of a fourth ship of the class, subsequently named the *Imperator Nikolai I,* to enter service in 1917. A squadron of four dreadnoughts would thereby be constituted.[116]

The Turkish government was reported to be aiming at building a squadron of six dreadnoughts, but Admiral Grigorovitch told the members of the special conference that the Russian Admiralty deemed the realization of this program to be very uncertain. In any event, Grigorovitch declared, his department was planning the construction of a second dreadnought

[114] Grigorovitch to Sazonov, 6 Jan. 1914, *Int. Bez.,* 1st series, I, no. 50, pp. 45–47.
[115] Sazonov to Grigorovitch, 20 Jan. 1914, *ibid.,* no. 55, p. 53; Sazonov to Russian chargé, Buenos Aires, 25 Feb. 1914, *ibid.,* no. 325, p. 324.
[116] Journal einer Sonderkonferenz, 21 Feb. 1914, *ibid.,* no. 295, pp. 293–294.

squadron for the Black Sea. Moreover by acquisition of the dreadnoughts building in foreign yards for Argentina and Chile the Russians would hasten the strengthening of their own fleet and make a rapid increase of the Turkish fleet impossible. Sazonov was particularly pleased that these South American dreadnoughts might serve in the Mediterranean where they could divert Turkish sea power from the Black Sea. The conference closed by recommending a number of preparatory measures to be taken in case an expedition to the Straits became necessary. These included the provision of suitable transports, and an acceleration of the planned mobilization and transport of the expeditionary corps.[117] Grigorovitch's proposal for the construction of the additional dreadnought as well as smaller vessels for the Black Sea was presented to the Duma on March 31, and a large appropriation was voted April 10.[118]

Any thoughts the Russians might have had about forming a Mediterranean squadron in the near future were probably frustrated when the Argentine government declined to sell the two ships building on their account in the United States.[119] Sazonov was still anxious to prevent these ships from being purchased by anyone else, and tried to get a promise from the Argentines that should the question of their transfer arise in the future the Russians would receive preference.[120] The Russians were also after the Chilean dreadnoughts building at Armstrong's yard in England, and made a substantial offer for them. Sir Charles Ottley of the firm notified the Admiralty, who passed the information on to the Foreign Office where Grey minuted, "We cannot object and need of course say nothing." [121] It was doubtful, however, that Chile would consent to sell her dreadnoughts if Argentina did not dispose of hers.[122] The Russians tried to link the question with a demonstration before the British of an airplane designed by the Russian aviation pioneer Igor Sikorski. The Russian government said that although the plane represented a valuable secret they would allow the demonstration in consideration of their friendly relations

---

[117] *Ibid.*, pp. 294–296.

[118] *Int. Bez.*, 1st series, II, no. 123, pp. 121–123; Note a, p. 431. See also Grigorovitch to Sazonov, 10 July 1914, *ibid.*, IV, no. 170, pp. 166–167. Also to be completed by 1917 for the Black Sea were an additional two cruisers, eight destroyers, and six submarines; *ibid.*, I, no. 295, p. 294.

[119] Bachmetjew, ambassador to Washington, to Sazonov, 10 Mar. 1914, *ibid.*, I, no. 418, p. 418, 14 Mar. 1914, II, no. 11, p. 8; and 19 Mar. 1914, nos. 51, 53, p. 40.

[120] Sazonov to Bachmetjew, 23 Mar. 1914, *ibid.*, no. 64, p. 51. These were the ships Revel recommended the Italians purchase after the war had broken out. See above p. 208.

[121] J. Masterton Smith to Tyrrell, 13 Mar. 1914, Grey MSS, FO 800, vol. 87; Minute by Grey, *ibid.*

[122] Russian chargé, Buenos Aires, to Sazonov, 19 Apr. 1914, *Int. Bez.*, 1st series, II, no. 241, pp. 245–246.

with England, but they hoped in turn for British support in the negotiations for the purchase of the Chilean dreadnought. The British replied that they were quite ready to comply with Russia's desire, but unfortunately had not been successful in inducing Chile to sell the ships, and had only received the assurance they would not be sold to anyone else.[123]

The Russians were persistent in their efforts to acquire the Chilean *Almirante Latorre,* and her less advanced consort *Almirante Cochrane,* working through their envoys in South America and ambassador and naval attaché in London.[124] At one point it seemed that the Russians would be successful in purchasing the *Almirante Cochrane,* which was not expected to be ready before August 1916. Although the Chilean Minister of Marine approved the sale, it was apparently blocked by the Chilean envoy in London, and the Russians requested Grey's assistance in influencing this diplomat.[125] Grey had previously promised the Russian ambassador he would do this, but Count Benckendorff noted that the real difficulty resided in the fact that the Chilean minister in London opposed not only the sale to Russia, but any disposal of the ship at all.[126] The Russians were to remain frustrated in their efforts to get the Chilean dreadnoughts, which were ultimately taken into British service after the war had broken out.

The Russian government was anxious to enter into naval conversations with the British as well as the French. Sazonov had touched on the subject of naval arrangements during his visit to Great Britain in September 1912, and the Tsar spoke of the same subject in an audience granted the British ambassador on April 3, 1914.[127] The idea of nonbinding, informal conversations similar to those already held with the French found some favor in the Foreign Office, notably with Crowe and Nicolson. Grey thought that, if France approved, the Russians might be informed of what had passed between the British and French military authorities, but that it was best to postpone discussion of anything as long as they could.[128] The French were anxious to give the Anglo-Russian entente a more precise form, and Paléologue, now French ambassador at St. Petersburg, told

[123] Sazonov to Grigorovitch, 27 Apr. 1914, *ibid.,* no. 306, p. 300; Buchanan to Nicolson, 16 Apr. 1914, *BD,* X (pt. 2), no. 538, p. 785.

[124] Chargé, Buenos Aires, to Sazonov, 23 May 1914, *Int Bez.,* 1st series, vol. III, no. 71, p. 64; Sazonov to Benckendorff, 24 May 1914, *ibid.,* no. 74, p. 66; Benckendorff to Sazonov, 25 May 1914, *ibid.,* no. 77, p. 67.

[125] Naval attaché, London, to Chief of Admiralty Staff, 6 June 1914, *ibid.,* no. 175, p. 159; Foreign Ministry to Benckendorff, 12 June 1914, *ibid.,* no. 221, pp. 205–206; Saint-Seine to Minister of Marine, 2 June 1914, AMF, carton Ea-160.

[126] Benckendorff to Sazonov, n.d. [13 June 1914], *Int. Bez.,* 1st series, vol. III, no. 230, p. 210.

[127] Viscount Grey of Fallodon, *Twenty-Five Years* (New York, 1925), I, 287–288; Buchanan to Grey, 3 Apr. 1914, *BD,* X (pt. 2), no. 537, pp. 780–781.

[128] Minutes by Crowe, 8 Apr. 1914; Nicolson, n.d.; Grey, 16 Apr., *ibid.,* p. 783.

Buchanan that Poincaré was likely to bring up the matter when Grey accompanied King George on a state visit to Paris later in April.[129] Paléologue was sending favorable reports of Russian naval activity to his own government.[130] The subject was raised by Premier Gaston Doumergue when Grey visited Paris. Eventually the British somewhat reluctantly agreed to the naval conversations, largely with the idea of placating Russia.[131]

Grey anticipated little of practical value from the talks since it would not be safe for the British fleet to enter the Baltic until the end of a war when they were practically victorious.[132] The Admiralty could hardly have been enthusiastic about any agreements with the Russians since Commander Grenfell's reports from St. Petersburg were as disquieting as ever. The naval attaché reported that there was small chance of the new naval program being completed by 1917, and even if "by some miracle" it was, the state of Russian training and naval administration was such that Germany's old battleships and the four earlier dreadnoughts of the "Nassau" class would amply suffice to mask any sea power Russia was likely to possess before 1918.[133] The Russians, on the other hand, were convinced of the importance of coordinated but separate actions by the allied fleets. They also wanted to secure some compensation for drawing part of German sea power toward themselves. They were still particularly anxious that the Austrian fleet might attack them in the Black Sea; they therefore wanted the British to detach a sufficient number of ships to assure the naval supremacy of the Triple Entente in the Mediterranean, at least until their own fleet was strong enough to undertake this role. Moreover, the Russians wanted their warships to use British bases in the eastern Mediterranean. They were also interested in the establishment of a common signal code, periodic talks between the staffs, and an exchange of intelligence.[134]

The impending naval talks between the British and the Russians were revealed to the Germans who leaked the news to the press, creating em-

[129] Buchanan to Nicolson, 16 Apr. 1914, *ibid.*, no. 538, p. 784.

[130] Paléologue to Doumergue, 13 Apr. 1914, *DDF3*, X, no. 100, pp. 164–165; 21 May 1914, no. 268, p. 409; 27 May 1914, no. 290, pp. 431–432.

[131] Grey to Bertie, 1 May 1914, *BD*, X (pt. 2), no. 541, pp. 787–788; Grey to Bertie, 21 May 1914, *ibid*, no. 543, pp. 789–790; Grey, *Twenty-Five Years*, I, 273–274, 277–278.

[132] Grey to Bertie, 1 May 1914, *BD*, X (pt. 2), no. 541, pp. 787–788.

[133] Grenfell to Buchanan, 19 Mar. 1914, *ibid.*, no. 531 enclosure, pp. 771–772.

[134] Record of a conference between the Admiralty Staff and the Foreign Ministry, 26 May 1914, *Int. Bez.*, 1st series, III, no. 86, pp. 73–75.

barrassing questions for Grey to answer in the House of Commons.[135] The Admiralty were disposed to wait in the matter until Battenberg's proposed visit to Russia in August 1914, but Sazonov begged the British ambassador to let the talks begin at once. He said that Captain Volkov, the Russian attaché in London, had the full confidence of his government and all necessary instructions. The Tsar also requested that the preliminary conversations begin immediately so that Battenberg could give the arrangements finishing touches on his visit.[136] However Churchill claimed that, although one conversation had already taken place and another would soon occur, the Russian naval attaché was neither sufficiently informed nor possessed of authority to discuss matters of such consequence with Battenberg, and at best could only listen and report to his government. The First Lord concluded that no real progress would be made until "a conversation takes place between equals." [137] Less than a month later, Great Britain and Russia found themselves allies in a war.

The war broke out long before the Russian naval program had begun to produce tangible results. Only some of the Black Sea dreadnoughts, and none of the ambitious "Borodino" class battle cruisers of the Baltic fleet —which might have operated in the Mediterranean—were ever completed. The Imperial Russian navy was destined to be shattered by war and revolution. The *Imperator Alexander III*, under a different name, eventually reached the Mediterranean as the largest of the remnants of Baron Wrangel's White Russian squadron. The dreadnought was interned at Bizerte in 1920 along with a few smaller warships left from the Tsar's Black Sea fleet.

The practical influence of the Russian navy on the Mediterranean naval situation was small in the years immediately preceding the World War. Probably only the Austrians were even a little concerned about it. But the Russians had embarked upon a great naval building program. They had also spoken of a Mediterranean squadron. Russian naval power was still a distant cloud on the Mediterranean horizon in 1914 but, even after all the many Russian difficulties are taken into account, it might well have played a much larger role in future years.

---

[135] Goschen to Grey, 23 May 1914, *BD*, X (pt. 2), no. 544, pp. 791–792; editor's note, *ibid.*, pp. 800–801; statement by Grey in Commons, 11 June 1914, *ibid.*, no. 548, p. 801; Grey, *Twenty-Five Years*, I, 278–279.

[136] Naval attaché in London (Wolkow) to Chief of the Admiralty Staff, 6 June 1914, *Int. Bez.*, 1st series, III, no. 175, pp. 159–160; editor's note, *BD*, X (pt. 2), pp. 812–813; Buchanan to Grey, 25 June 1914, *ibid.*, no. 556, p. 812.

[137] Churchill to Grey, 7 July 1914, *ibid.*, no. 559, p. 814. See also Grey, *Twenty-Five Years*, I, 274–275; Serge Sazonov, *Fateful Years: 1909–1916* (London, 1928), pp. 129–133.

XI

The Greek and Turkish Navies:
A Balkan Naval Race

While the navies of the great powers prepared for the decisive battle in the Mediterranean that all assumed would follow soon after the outbreak of hostilities, a miniature naval race was taking place in the Aegean. The competition between Greece and Turkey seems almost a parody of the one between the larger nations. At times the rivalry appeared to hang on a single ship rather than a ratio of strength. Certainly the numbers of warships involved were small, at least until 1914, although both sides had far-reaching ambitions which their impoverished countries could ill afford. Unlike the great powers, neither Greece nor Turkey could build her own warships, and so Athens and Constantinople became a favorite hunting ground for agents of the major shipbuilding and armament firms. The orders the agents competed for must have been lucrative, judging from the energy with which they were pursued. Though the material strength of the Greek and Turkish navies was but a fraction of the larger fleets, their rivalry underlined the potential danger of a war that would ultimately involve a great power. In the delicate naval balance between the Triple Alliance and Triple Entente in the Mediterranean, the Greek and Turkish naval race was yet another unsettling factor in an unstable situation.

The Turkish fleet had declined steadily from the dominant position in the Black Sea that it had held during the Russo-Turkish War of 1877–1878 —although the situation then was more the result of Russian weakness than Turkish strength. In the early years of the twentieth century the Ottoman navy was in pitiful shape, and could hardly be considered a serious fighting force. Turkish impotence at sea was of some significance to the great powers because of the strategic importance of the Straits. Shortly after the Young Turk Revolution of 1908 a British admiral received the task of reorganizing the Turkish navy. The British hoped this naval mis-

314

sion would be able to exert some political influence, counter German activity, and obtain construction orders for British firms.[1]

Rear Admiral Sir Douglas Gamble was appointed to head the mission in December 1908. Gamble found his job "an awful task & a thankless one. I mean one never sees any radical change or improvement—and it requires a man in strong health and full vigour to stand the disappointments and continued grind . . . They are talking very big about a programme of construction, & the engagement of the officers I want, but nothing practical has been done & until the actual steps have been taken I cannot believe in any of their promises or assurances." [2] Discouraged, and with the climate at Constantinople affecting his health, Gamble submitted his resignation in February 1910.

In April 1910 Gamble was succeeded by Rear Admiral H. P. Williams. Williams too found the position a difficult one, and at the end of his appointment wrote: "I do not think that anyone who has not experienced service at the Turkish Admiralty at this period can have any idea of the difficulties I have had to struggle against in the face of German intrigue and the opposition of nearly all senior officers to any reform at the Admiralty or Arsenal." [3] Initially the British admiral was hampered by the fact the Turkish and French copies of his contract specified his title as "conseiller technique," while his Foreign Office letter of appointment referred to him as "naval adviser." The former would have been considered a specialist whose opinion was consulted only in technical matters, whereas the latter was an adviser and assistant in all matters. Williams therefore had some difficulty in asserting himself.

Admiral Williams got on well with the Turkish Minister of Marine who was in office on his arrival, but trouble developed when this official was replaced, "probably due to foreign intrigue," by two successive ministers who were both German-trained army officers. They were assisted by a permanent secretary to the Turkish Admiralty, a rear admiral with "very strong German proclivities." Williams found that Turkish senior officers considered all responsibility rested with the Minister of Marine, and would neither deal with papers themselves nor state their opinion for fear of having it brought against them. The system was highly centralized. For exam-

[1] Marder, *Anatomy of British Sea Power*, pp. 153, 401–402; Marder, *From the Dreadnought to Scapa Flow*, I, 301–302; for a description by the British naval attaché in 1904 see Mark Kerr, *Land, Sea and Air* (London, 1927), pp. 122–126; see also the report by the commander of the British stationnaire in Constantinople for 1907, "Turkish Naval Policy and Armaments," 1907, *BD*, V, pp. 40–42.

[2] Gamble to W. Graham Greene, Secretary to the Admiralty, 27 Jan. 1910, PRO, Adm I, box 8192.

[3] Report by Williams, 29 Apr. 1912, FO 371, vol. 1487, file 22853.

ple, the organization and victualing of the fleet was based on the supposition that it would be in touch with Constantinople, and therefore that daily ration papers and monthly pay lists could be taken to the Admiralty for correction. When Williams ended his tour of duty in the spring of 1912, there was no provision for providing a bread and meat ration at sea, although one was issued daily in harbor. Turkish crews at sea had to rely on biscuit, olives, and bread.[4]

In the summer of 1910, the Turks, possibly alarmed at reports that the Greeks were acquiring a large new armored cruiser, began negotiations in Germany for the purchase of two old battleships. The Turks complained that the British government refused to sell them a modern ship, but Williams prevailed on them to bid for the *Triumph* and *Swiftsure,* the pair of battleships originally built for Chile and purchased by the Admiralty during the Russo-Japanese War to forestall acquisition by a European power. However, the best the British would offer were two old "Royal Sovereigns," and the Turkish government therefore purchased in August 1910 the 9,900-ton *Kurfürst Wilhelm* and *Weissenburg* which had both been launched in 1891, and were practically at the age for replacement under the German naval law. The two ships—renamed the *Kheyr-ed-Din Barbarossa* and *Turgut Reis*—required a total crew of 1100 men which, in the absence of sufficient personnel in the naval barracks, had to be provided from the squadron by drawing a large proportion of the relatively trained ratings from each ship and replacing them with raw conscripts, while the oldest ships were reduced to skeleton crews. A similar problem occurred in autumn of 1910 when four 620-ton destroyers purchased from the German firm of Schichau arrived in Turkish waters.[5]

Williams thought that the purchase of German ships would increase the difficulties of the British officers.[6] At the request of the Turkish Minister of Marine he tried to arrange for a number of Turkish officers to be sent to England. Williams was not blind to the advantages this might offer in "getting a firm hold on the service."[7] Between 1910 and the spring of 1912 approximately forty Turkish officers attended British naval schools, and about a dozen more were at the works of private firms in England.

Admiral Williams believed that a large flotilla of destroyers and torpedo boats, constantly employed, offered both the best means of defense for Turkey, and the best means to teach responsibility to a large number of

---

[4] *Ibid.*
[5] *Ibid.;* see also *The Naval Annual, 1911,* p. 53.
[6] Williams to Troubridge, 16 Aug. 1910, Grey MSS, FO 800, vol. 86.
[7] Report by Williams, 29 Apr. 1912.

officers. However, the Turks argued that they wanted battleships, which is understandable given the prevailing climate of opinion in naval circles of this era. Williams was forced to give way to prevent the ships being built in Germany. In the summer of 1911 Armstrong and Vickers each received a Turkish contract for a 23,000-ton dreadnought. Williams had originally proposed a smaller 16,000-ton design which he considered most suitable to Turkish requirements, but this had been changed to a design to equal the most powerful foreign contemporaries. The first of these dreadnoughts, the *Reschad V* (later the *Reschadieh*) was laid down by Vickers in August 1911; it was to carry ten 13.5-inch guns and have a speed of 21 knots. The *Reschad V*—which undoubtedly would have been one of the most powerful warships in the Mediterranean—was costly. Williams noted with disgust that he had been unable to obtain money for the training of mechanics, the increased length of service for petty officers and valuable men, and the modern training of officers. The Turkish navy seemed to be making the mistake, not unusual among minor fleets, of concentrating all its resources on the acquisition of powerful material strength without taking sufficient care to ensure the trained personnel necessary to man the ships.

Admiral Williams' frequent clashes with the Turkish Minister of Marine created a good deal of alarm at the Foreign Office. Grey thought the Admiral was "really doing harm to our interests there," and feared the Turks might be so disgusted they would not ask for anyone else once Williams' contract ran out. He suggested to the First Lord of the Admiralty that they think of a tactful way of putting the matter before Williams and getting him to resign.[8] Sir Gerald Lowther, British ambassador in Constantinople, had a "heart to heart talk" with Williams, who "did not seem to realize the situation."[9] However, as the differences between Williams and the Turkish Minister of Marine were to a great measure personal, and as the minister's position was none too secure, Lowther advised postponing any decision about inviting the British admiral to resign. Grey agreed, especially since Lowther did not think the present Minister of Marine would appoint a senior British officer in Williams' place.[10]

Aside from the British missions at Constantinople, there were other naval ties between Great Britain and Turkey. In January 1912, at the request of the Turkish government, the Admiralty nominated engineer

[8] Grey to McKenna, 12 Apr. 1911, Grey MSS, FO 800, vol. 86.
[9] Lowther to Tyrrell, 11 Apr. 1911, *ibid.*, FO 800, vol. 79.
[10] Lowther to Grey, 23 Apr. 1911, *ibid.*; minutes by Mallet and Grey, n.d., *ibid.*; Lowther to Grey, 28 Apr. 1911, *ibid.*

officers to supervise construction of the dreadnought at Armstrong's. The officers were to be paid by the Turkish government and were directly responsible to it.[11] The Turks assumed the Admiralty would see to it that the armor plate and all materials employed in the work were in accordance with specifications.[12] The Admiralty, however, took the position that they were unable to give these assurances, but that if the Turks would furnish certain technical information they would undertake such tests as were practical. The Turks replied that it was exactly this information that they were unable to furnish, and the matter reached a deadlock. Grey thought the Turks were justified and the question serious enough for the Foreign Office to intervene. He cautioned the Admiralty that a refusal to meet the wishes of the Ottoman government in this subject might seriously diminish the likelihood of similar orders for British firms in the future, and might have unfortunate political effects in checking the recent improvement in Turkish feeling toward England. After reconsideration, the Admiralty agreed to conduct such tests as necessary.[13] The Turks, manifesting a good deal of confidence in the Admiralty as well as some of the shrewdness of Eastern traders, also submitted a list of ammunition supplies, and inquired whether the prices indicated were similar to those charged the Royal Navy. After almost two months delay, and following a reminder from the Turks, the Admiralty finally replied.[14] One gets the impression that the Admiralty considered the Turkish requests for information or advice at best a nuisance and were indifferent to the diplomatic aspects of the situation.

The war with Italy was a painful lesson to the Turkish government on the value of sea power. They were unable to communicate directly with Libya, for the Italian navy had unchallenged command of the sea route, while access by land was blocked by British-controlled Egypt. The bulk of the Turkish fleet was forced to shelter behind the guns of the Dardanelles, and those small units caught outside were quickly mopped-up. The Turks impotently watched the Italians occupy the Dodecanese Islands, just off the Anatolian coast. While the war dragged on during the winter of 1912, the Ottoman government indicated that it was thinking in terms of a naval program of no less than six dreadnoughts. Admiral Williams

[11] Greene to Foreign Office, 3 Jan. 1912, FO 371, vol. 1486, Turkey, file 438.
[12] Tewfik Pasha to Grey, 18 Jan. 1912, *ibid.*, file 2651.
[13] L. Mallet to O. Murray of the Admiralty, 4 Mar. 1912, *ibid.*, file 7877; Greene to Foreign Office, 2 Apr. 1912, *ibid.*, file 14320; Tewfik Pasha to Grey, 18 Apr. 1912, *ibid.*, file 16465.
[14] Tewfik Pasha to Grey, 16 Mar. 1912, *ibid.*, file 11662; Greene to Foreign Office, 10 May 1912, *ibid.*, file 2008.

did not approve of this, and advised a goal of a fleet superior to that of Greece and nothing more. He warned that it was a waste of money to enter into competition with a strong naval power—say, Italy or Russia in the Black Sea—unless the Turks could be fairly certain of fighting on terms of equality when the program was finished. Williams therefore strongly recommended a reduction in the number of battleships in the program.[15]

The Turks, however, were determined on battleships. The Ottoman Staff Office prepared, for submission to the Ottoman Council of Ministers, a program of naval construction which would have provided for the creation of a battle fleet through heavy expenditure over a period of four to five years. Such a fleet, they maintained, was necessitated by the extent of the Turkish coastline, over 11,000 miles. Moreover, a battle fleet would enable Turkey to cooperate with possible allies in the eastern Mediterranean, act as a check on foreign powers anxious to further political or economic aims, and combat effectively adjacent powers with expanding naval programs. The program was an ambitious one and included six dreadnoughts including the one under construction, four scout cruisers, twenty destroyers, six submarines, two minelayers, a repair ship, a school ship, and a large graving dock to handle the dreadnoughts. In justification of their program, the Ottoman Staff Office argued that: "The disaster in Tripoli has been the result of the weakness of the fleet, and to ensure against similar accidents occurring in our distant possessions such as those in the Persian Gulf and Red Sea, which are closely bound up with our national existence, a sufficient naval force must be provided to enable us to affect the balance of European power."[16] Turkish naval power would also: (1) deny Crete, which was deemed essential to the preservation of Ottoman rights in the Mediterranean, the opportunity of placing itself under another power; (2) decrease Greek hopes that other powers in their own interest would render financial or other assistance; (3) lessen the possibility of pressure from the Black Sea in case of war with Bulgaria; (4) assist in securing Turkish economic and military interests in the Black Sea and Asia Minor; and (5) render Turkey's Adriatic coast less liable to attack.

Admiral Williams' critique of this program tended to be limited to technical points, including a recommendation for an increase in the number of

[15] Williams to Ottoman Minister of Marine, 11 Feb. 1912, enclosed in Lowther to Grey, 12 Feb. 1912, FO 371, vol. 1486, file 7057.

[16] Translation of the Proposed Ottoman Program of Naval Construction, enclosure No. 1, Lowther to Grey, 11 Mar. 1912, *ibid.*, file 11454.

scouts and second-class cruisers, and the possible substitution of battle cruisers for two of the dreadnoughts.[17] He still favored small craft as the best school for officers and men, but found the "commercial competition has now become so keen and manufacturers are so strongly represented by their Governments, that their claim appears to entirely override every other consideration." Williams pointed out that it was dangerous to British interests to transfer on short notice to another power—especially to one that could not properly manage them—modern battleships requiring British or allied ships of the same caliber to mask them. Williams' remarks about government support of armaments manufacturers could be taken as a slap at the Foreign Office, with whom he appears to have had his difficulties. At the same time he was condescending toward the Turks, as is revealed in his complaint that "ignorant Turks were clamouring for Dreadnoughts in the shortest possible time, and our Government so strongly represented English manufacturers, that I had to give way and could only try and see that the best article was supplied." [18]

The desire of British industry for sales to the Ottoman government and the best interests of the Turkish navy, and perhaps the Royal Navy as well, may not have always coincided, quite apart from any broader question of international stability. On the other hand, the temper of the times was such that dreadnoughts had immense prestige as a decisive weapon, and the desire of the Turks to acquire them was so strong that Schichau, Krupp, or some other foreign yard would probably have secured the order if Armstrong and Vickers did not. One could hardly blame Williams or the Foreign Office for preferring a British firm.

The troubled relations between Williams and the Turkish Minister of Marine had led to Foreign Office fears that the admiral would not be replaced by a British officer when his contract expired. In September 1911 the British were alarmed at reports that the Turkish naval attaché in Berlin, supposedly an anglophobe, was pressing his government to obtain German officers for the Turkish torpedo flotilla on the grounds the Turkish navy used German-made torpedoes. Both Williams and the British ambassador made representations to the Grand Vizier on the subject, and shortly afterwards the Minister of Marine told Lowther that the idea had been abandoned.[19] Williams' contract was to expire in April 1912, and at the beginning of that year an inquiry was sent to the British ambassador in Constantinople concerning his successor. Before Lowther's reply could

---

[17] Williams to Ottoman Minister of Marine, 22 Feb. 1912, *ibid.*, enclosure No. 2.
[18] Report by Admiral Williams, 29 Apr. 1912, FO 371, vol. 1487, Turkey, file 22853.
[19] *Ibid.*; Lowther to Grey, 25 and 28 Sept. 1911, Grey MSS, FO 800, vol. 79.

reach the Foreign Office, there was fresh concern over reports in the German press that negotiations were in progress between the Ottoman government and the German Admiralty for the services of a well-known senior German naval officer.[20] Lowther's reply, however, was reassuring when it arrived, for the Turkish Minister of Marine had told the British ambassador that he recognized the need for British officers even though the requirements of neutrality kept them ashore for the duration of the Italo-Turkish War. Lowther was specifically told that the Ottoman government wanted Williams to be succeeded by an Englishman, and the ambassador concluded there was nothing in the German press reports.[21]

The Turks indicated a strong desire for the return of Admiral Gamble. Gamble, however, did not want the appointment.[22] The Admiralty were characteristically leisurely in their reply to the question of Williams' successor. It took almost a month for Gamble's rejection of the offer to reach the Foreign Office. The question became urgent at the beginning of March, when Williams was officially informed that his and the other British officers' contracts would not be renewed.[23] One Foreign Office official was moved to comment that the Admiralty were "extremely tiresome in this as in all other matters relating to the Turkish naval construction," and were thereby "simply playing into the hands of Germany." [24] He recalled a similar situation in 1842 when Moltke replaced a British officer sent out to reform the Turkish army. After a new round of telephone calls between the Foreign Office and the Admiralty, a successor was found. Churchill proposed Rear Admiral Arthur H. Limpus.[25] The Turks, after regretting that Gamble would not return, accepted Limpus and gave him the freedom to select his staff himself. Limpus chose three naval officers and a staff paymaster to serve as secretary; the Admiralty approved of the loan of the officers to the Turkish government.[26]

A delicate diplomatic problem arose when a number of the Turkish officers being trained in England completed their training and were scheduled to return home. Grey asked the Turks for assurances that the officers

[20] Memorandum by L. Mallet, 6 Jan. 1912, FO 371, vol. 1487, Turkey, file 1330; Goschen to Grey, 27 Jan. 1912, *ibid.*, file 3870, and 27 Jan. 1912, file 3899.

[21] Lowther to Grey, 27 Jan. 1912, *ibid.*, file 3938, and 30 Jan. 1912, file 4280.

[22] Lowther to Grey, 31 Jan. 1912, *ibid.*, file 4469; O. Murray to Foreign Office, 21 Feb. 1912, *ibid.*, file 7709.

[23] Lowther to Grey, 3 Mar. 1912, *ibid.*, file 9274.

[24] Minute by A. Parker, 4 Mar. 1912, *ibid.*

[25] Churchill to Grey, n.d. [received 7 Mar. 1912], *ibid.*, file 10647; Grey to Lowther, 8 Mar. 1912, *ibid.*

[26] Lowther to Grey, 13 Mar. 1912, *ibid.*, file 11464, 19 Mar. 1912, file 11908, 8 Apr. 1912, file 14612, and 19 Apr. 1912, file 16496; Greene to Foreign Office, 24 Apr. 1912, *ibid.*, file 17400.

would not be employed for the duration of the current hostilities with Italy. The Turkish government agreed, but requested that no publicity be given to it.[27] The Admiralty were far from happy over the training of foreign officers in the Royal Navy. In the spring of 1912 an inquiry resulting from a Turkish naval lieutenant's apparent acquisition of classified information on fire control methods and instruments, always a sensitive subject, led to the calling of a special conference, to which the Foreign Office was invited to send a representative. The conference reviewed the entire practice of training foreign officers.[28] In the spring of 1912 Turkey supplied the largest contingent of these officers with nine aboard British ships and nine in British dockyards.[29]

In July 1894 the Admiralty had decided to end its former practice of allowing officers of smaller navies to serve on British ships, but by 1902 had been forced for political reasons to make exceptions in the case of Japan. The Japanese had been followed by Chinese. Then commercial as well as political considerations led to Chilean, Brazilian, Turkish, and Greek officers attending British naval schools or serving on warships. Naturally it required constant vigilance to insure that confidential information was not divulged, and this was particularly difficult in the close confines of a warship at sea. The officers who examined the question in the spring of 1912, after analyzing the advantages and disadvantages of the system, concluded that "whatever advantages may accrue to this country politically or commercially, we cannot afford to give away the information we do or to run the risk of much that is treated as confidential falling into the hands of a possible enemy." The conference therefore recommended that when the foreign officers currently serving completed their training, no more be embarked on British warships. The increasing requirements in accommodations aboard modern warships could be offered as an excuse. On the other hand, it was agreed that foreign officers might still be received in courses on shore provided confidential material had been excluded from the syllabus. The only possible exception to this would have been a country in a definite alliance with England, such as Japan.

Grey agreed to these proposals, which almost immediately effected

---

[27] Grey to Lowther, 22 May 1912, FO 371, vol. 1494, Turkey, file 18695; Lowther to Grey, 16 June 1912, *ibid.*, file 25539.

[28] Admiralty to Foreign Office, 24 Apr. 1912, PRO, Adm I, box 8308. In the spring of 1912 a missent letter which came into the Admiralty's hands seemed to indicate that a Chilean officer serving aboard a British warship in 1909 and 1910 might have sold information. Churchill to Grey, 12 May 1914, Grey MSS, FO 800, vol. 87; Grey to Churchill, 15 June 1914, *ibid.*; Steel, of the Admiralty, to Tyrrell, 17 July 1914, *ibid.*

[29] Report of Conference, 24 June 1912, Appendix, Adm. I, box 8308.

Turkey.[30] Limpus requested that a number of Turks be permitted to serve for a few months aboard the *Orion* or *Monarch*, similar vessels to the Turkish dreadnought under construction, so as to have "some faint idea" of the work they would have to do when their ship was completed.[31] The Admiralty, acting under the new policy, refused to do more than allow the Turks to attend the gunnery school on shore. They did, however, permit another group of Turkish officers to stay an additional two months after their training had ended in order to be present for firing exercises.[32]

The Balkan Wars broke out before the treaty of peace between Italy and Turkey had been signed, and the whole problem of Turkish naval officers in England was raised anew. Once again the Turkish ambassador promised that those officers continuing their instruction in England would not take part in hostilities if recalled to Constantinople before the end of the war.[33]

Greece was yet another small nation seized with the idea of creating a strong navy in the years before World War I. For the Greeks, however, bitter rivalry with the Turks and the inherent instability of the Balkans, along with unresolved territorial ambitions, were powerful incentives toward heavy expenditure on naval armaments. The Greeks had a reputation of being good seamen, although their tiny navy had not been used efficiently in the disastrous war with Turkey in 1897, when the larger Turkish fleet was practically incapable of putting to sea.[34] A decade later the Greek navy was still a small force of ancient gunboats and torpedo boats whose principal units were three small French-built coastal defense ships (5000 tons), launched in 1889–1890, and reconstructed 1897–1900. By the end of 1908 the fleet had been reinforced by four British-built and four German-built destroyers. In October 1909 the navy was shaken by a brief mutiny. On the whole, however, 1909 was a favorable year, for before it had ended a large (9956-ton) armored cruiser building at the Orlando yard in Livorno had been purchased. Part of the funds for the purchase came from the legacy of a Greek millionaire, Giorgio Averoff, who had left a large sum in his will for the purpose of increasing the navy.

30 Foreign Office to Admiralty, 30 July 1912, PRO, Adm. I, box 8308.

31 Limpus to Greene, 3 July 1912, *ibid.* This was unofficial since the official request would have had to be made through diplomatic channels.

32 Admiralty to Limpus, 15 Aug. 1912, *ibid.*; Greene to Foreign Office, 15 Aug. 1912, FO 371, vol. 1497, Turkey, file 34589.

33 Tewfik Pasha to Grey, 18 Oct. 1912, FO 371, vol. 1494, file 43869; Grey to Tewfik Pasha, 8 Nov. 1912, *ibid.*, file 45580; Tewfik Pasha to Grey, 15 Nov. 1912, *ibid.*, file 48854.

34 Wilson, *Battleships in Action,* I, 111–112.

The cruiser, named in his honor, was launched in March 1910 and completed in 1911.[35]

The acquisition of the *Averoff* by the Greek navy presumably induced the Turks to purchase the two old German battleships in 1910. The Greeks, in turn, attempted to buy two old French battleships, such as the *Brennus* which had been launched in 1891. However Admiral Lapeyrère, then Minister of Marine, refused to sanction the sale. He claimed that the insufficiency of French naval construction made it unwise to diminish the fleet by two such battleships which, though old, still had real military value.[36] Though thwarted at obtaining the French battleships, the Greeks received another form of naval assistance the following year. In the spring of 1911 a British naval mission under Rear Admiral Lionel G. Tufnell went out to assist in the reorganization and development of the Greek fleet, and in July 1911 permission was granted for ten Greek sublieutenants to come to England for the purpose of attending gunnery, torpedo, or navigation courses.[37] A pair of submarines were also ordered in France from Schneider.

With the Turkish order for a dreadnought in the summer of 1911, the Balkan naval race began to grow hot, and the Greek government invited tenders to be submitted in 1912 for a battle cruiser, destroyers, and torpedo boats. The representatives of European and American shipbuilding and armament firms were drawn to Athens like the proverbial bees to honey. Nine of the French yards formed a consortium to seek naval orders abroad, the Association des Chantiers de Construction Navale pour la Recherche à l'Etrangère de Commandes de Bâtiments de Guerre, under the presidency of Florent Guillain, a retired engineer and former deputy and Minister of Colonies. Poincaré thought that this association would facilitate the efforts of the French minister in Athens on behalf of French industry since he would no longer have to hold a balance among competing French firms.[38] The Quai d'Orsay collaborated very closely with Guillain, instantly transmitting to him the advice of Gabriel Deville, French minister in Athens, and, relaying to Deville the requests of the consortium. Almost inevitably, certain French yards complained that British firms were getting preferential treatment because of the presence of the British naval mission. Deville also mentioned what he considered the contrary ten-

---

[35] *The Naval Annual, 1907*, pp. 37, 277; *The Naval Annual, 1908*, pp. 44–45; *The Naval Annual, 1909*, p. 40; *The Naval Annual, 1910*, p. 58.

[36] Lapeyrère to Minister of Foreign Affairs, 8 Dec. 1910, AMF, carton BB7-130.

[37] Elliot, "Annual Report for Greece, 1911," p. 12.

[38] Poincaré to Deville, 26 Jan. 1912, MAE, Grèce, vol. NS-41.

dencies of Admiral Tufnell whom he suspected of being energetically encouraged by Zaharoff of Vickers.[39]

Actually Rear Admiral Tufnell was in a difficult position. Perhaps the role of any adviser to a foreign navy is difficult, for his very presence with its implication of tutelage might easily be resented by the officers of the country he is advising. Tufnell was naturally on the committee examining tenders for the battle cruiser, but he found the Greeks decidedly opposed to everything British. After the first round of proposals had been examined, the Greeks prepared more precise specifications and asked for fresh tenders. There had been no consultation with the British advisers on these specifications, and Tufnell found his opinion disregarded and his proposals thwarted. (On the other hand, Sir Francis Elliot, British minister at Athens, did not think the admiral was self-assertive enough.) [40] By then Armstrong was the only British firm still interested in the battle cruiser. Sir Edward Chichester, late of the Royal Navy and currently interested in Armstrong, was in contact with the Foreign Office over the question. Tufnell, who had managed to learn the prices of the tenders submitted, reported Armstrong to be higher than some of the other competitors, but some in the Foreign Office thought that Britain had done so much lately for the Greek navy in lending officers that they had some ground for urging the order be given to a British firm.[41]

On the other side of the Channel, the French firm Chantiers et Ateliers de St. Nazaire (Penhoët) was also very anxious for the battle cruiser order, but had an order from the French government for a 25,000-ton dreadnought too, and estimated that the preliminary work on this would take eight to ten months. Guillain wondered if it would be possible to help things to drag; but if the negotiations would not take eight to ten months, he thought it preferable to forgo the largest portion of the Greek program, the battle cruiser, if the Greeks would promise to give France the orders for the destroyers and torpedo boats. If, however, France's rivals got the smaller orders, Guillain wanted every effort made to obtain the battle cruiser as compensation.[42]

Both Great Britain and France were destined to be disappointed on the

---

[39] Paléologue to Deville, 10 Feb. 1912, *ibid.*; Deville to Minister of Foreign Affairs, 22 Feb. 1912, *ibid.*; Soc. anony. de Travaux Dyle & Bacalan to Conty (Minister plenipotentiary), 6 Mar. 1912, *ibid.*

[40] Elliot to Grey, 3 May 1912, FO 371, vol. 1381, Greece, file 19628. The requirement was for a 13,500-ton ship armed with six 14-inch and eight 6-inch guns, with a speed of 21.5 knots to be ready in twenty-six months.

[41] Elliot to Grey, 24 May 1912, *ibid.*, file 22836; Minute by R. P. Maxwell, Senior Clerk, *ibid.*

[42] Guillain to Poincaré, 20 June 1912, MAE, Grèce, vol. NS-42.

question of Greek naval orders in the year 1912. The first bad news came at the end of June when the Greeks decided to order two 750-ton destroyers and six 125-ton torpedo boats from the German firm of Vulkan. The destroyers were to be delivered in the remarkably short time of three to four months. This was possible because the German government, for whom they were originally intended, consented to relinquish them to Greece. The representative of the British firm of Thornycroft, which built large numbers of destroyers, did not see how Vulkan could make a profit at the price quoted. The deal led to speculation that the German government had relinquished the ships as a result of a secret agreement between Greek Prime Minister Eleutheros Venizelos and the Kaiser when the two had met at Corfu earlier in the year. It was also suggested that the ships might be defective or insufficient.[43] According to Chichester, one British firm, Hawthorn-Leslie, which had been in on very favorable terms, was so incensed that they would ask for Tufnell's recall. There were some at the Foreign Office who would have liked to get rid of Tufnell, who was considered "anything but a success," but they did not see how it could be done since the admiral had a contract with the Greek government.[44] The French minister in Athens, in accounting for the failure of the three French firms that had tried for the smaller Greek units, was forced to admit that on certain points the French tenders did not respond to the conditions of the program, and were less advantageous than Vulkan either on displacement and price or on the time required for delivery. However, Deville concluded that serious competition was scarcely possible given the facilities apparently accorded to the Vulkan yards by the German Admiralty.[45]

The greatest of the disappointments for the British and French occurred in the latter part of July when the order for the battle cruiser also went to Vulkan, who had apparently offered the lowest price. The artillery and armor plate for the ship were to be furnished from the United States by the Bethlehem Steel Company. The British firms involved in the competition believed it would be impossible for Vulkan to supply the ship at the price quoted without the government's support. They suspected that the German government would cover any losses incurred just to get possession of the market.[46] However, Lambros Coromilas, the Greek Foreign Minister, complained of the high price quoted by the British firms and

[43] Deville to Poincaré, 30 June 1912, *ibid.;* Elliot to Grey, 29 June 1912, FO 371, vol. 1381, Greece, file 28426.

[44] Chichester to Norman, 22 July 1912, FO 371, vol. 1381, file 31274; Minute by Maxwell, *ibid.*

[45] Deville to Poincaré, 30 June 1912, MAE, Grèce, vol. NS-42.

[46] Deville to Poincaré, 26 July 1912, *ibid.;* Elliot to Grey, 27 July 1912, FO 371, vol. 1381, file 3241.

blamed this on the "ring" of armor plate manufacturers in Britain, attributing the cheapness of the German offer to the adoption of American-made armor. Venizelos also denied that the order was given as a result of German political pressure.[47] The disappointed representatives of some of the British firms in Athens doubted that delivery of the battle cruiser could be made within six months of the stipulated period, or that the ship as designed would be a satisfactory seagoing and fighting unit.[48] Actually they were proved right, for in December 1912 the order placed with Vulkan for the battle cruiser, named the *Salamis*, was modified. Elliot remarked that this "renders the previous so-called competition still more of a farce." [49] Admiral Tufnell was to comment later that it would have been impossible to build a seaworthy ship according to the designs proposed by the Greek Ministry of Marine, and the British firms had been frank in saying so. The Germans, in contrast, agreed to build "the proposed abortion" and, according to Tufnell, after getting the contract succeeded in altering it to a feasible design in a larger and more expensive ship.[50] This still could not alter the fact that, despite the presence of a British naval mission, and a French military mission with the Greek army, the Germans had walked off with the orders for the Greek building program.

The French minister at Athens warned his government that French firms could scarcely expect to succeed in the future if they did not change their methods, particularly in regard to their refusal to submit to the common rules established by the Greeks, and their failure to meet deadlines for tenders. Deville was indignant over the suggestion of helping things to drag, but he loyally bent all his efforts toward getting a contract for a French firm for the refit of the three old "Hydra" class coast defense ships. The Greeks were ready to give the job to the Forges et Chantiers de la Méditerranée, but the diplomatic tension preceding the outbreak of the Balkan Wars suspended the talks. The Greek government naturally did not want to be deprived of the ships in the event of war.[51] The war

[47] W. Seeds to Grey, 1 Aug. 1912, *ibid.*, file 33260; Elliot to Grey, 27 July 1912, *ibid.*, file 32742.

[48] Elliot to Grey, 27 July 1912, *ibid.*, file 32741.

[49] Elliot to Grey, 25 Dec. 1912, *ibid.*, file 55766. The displacement of the *Salamis* was to be raised to 19,500 tons, and her armament increased to eight 14-inch and twelve 6-inch guns, her armor protection extended, and her speed increased to 24 knots.

[50] Elliot to Grey, 2 May 1913, FO 371, vol. 1650, Germany, file 21138. The *Salamis* was not completed when the war broke out. Deliveries of her artillery and armor from the United States were stopped, and the cannon were eventually used on British monitors; Jane, *Fighting Ships, 1917*, p. 422.

[51] Deville to Poincaré, 26 July 1912, MAE, Grèce, vol. NS-42; Halgouët to Poincaré, 27 Sept. 1912, *ibid.*

also frustrated Greek plans to have necessary repairs to the *Averoff* effected at Malta. The Admiralty were ready to agree, but as the Balkan crisis developed the Foreign Office withheld a definite reply to the Greeks until it became certain they would be belligerents.[52] The Greeks were successful in getting the two destroyers purchased in Germany out to the Aegean in time for their use in the war, a justification of their preference for the earliest possible delivery. They also purchased four large destroyers which had been built in England for the Argentine goverment; these joined the Greek fleet just after the war broke out.[53]

The British officers in the naval mission to Greece were not on the active list of the Royal Navy, while those in the naval mission to Turkey were. This fact was the subject of a press campaign by the enemies of Venizelos who attacked the idea that "worn out naval pensioners" were good enough for Greece. Undoubtedly the polemic, stemming largely from Greek politics, created a good deal of unfair prejudice against Tufnell (who personally supported a Greek application for additional officers from the active list).[54] Tufnell's role is difficult to assess largely because of the intrigues that might have surrounded him, but shortly after the outbreak of the Balkan War the Greek Minister of Marine in submitting a naval bill publicly paid tribute to the British naval mission and its chief for the progress of the fleet under their guidance. Elliot called remarkable Tufnell's success in overcoming the obstacles and jealousies of his first year. He attributed the success to the tact and unostentatious hard work of Tufnell and his staff.[55] This was no doubt somewhat to the surprise of the Foreign Office, and must mitigate the earlier unfavorable reports, as well as the disgruntled comments by disappointed representatives of shipbuilding yards.

The Balkan Wars found Great Britain in the somewhat embarrassing position of having a naval mission on each of the opposing sides, and questions were naturally raised in Parliament. The British naval mission in Turkey followed the precedent set during the Libyan War when the officers continued at their posts on the understanding they would take no part in hostilities, and "that their services were not calculated to assist the belligerent in the war." [56] The contract of the officers lent to the Greek

[52] Gennadius, Greek minister, London, to Grey, 21 Sept. 1912, FO 371, vol. 1381, file 40001; Greene to Grey, 4 Oct. 1912, *ibid.*, file 4717.

[53] *The Naval Annual, 1913*, p. 72.

[54] Elliot to Grey, 27 July 1912, FO 371, vol. 1381, file 32743.

[55] Elliot to Grey, 18 Oct. 1912, *ibid.*, file 45217.

[56] Statement by Grey in the House of Commons, 17 Oct. 1912. Excerpt from Hansard and supporting Foreign Office minutes in FO 371, vol. 1494, file 44786.

government was to be terminated in the event of war between Greece and any other power. However the Greek government desired Tufnell and most of his officers to remain and resume their work after the war. They made a similar request in respect to the French military mission. The naval mission was therefore authorized to stay, subject to the same restrictions as their colleagues in Turkey.[57]

Grey was far more cautious in the case of Rear Admiral Sir Douglas Gamble, who had formerly been head of the naval mission to Turkey and who had turned down an opportunity to return a few months before. Gamble was now very anxious to be attached to the Turkish fleet during the war, since the Greek and Turkish navies seemed evenly matched and the operations promised to be of interest. Churchill knew that Gamble was *persona gratissima* to the Turks, and thought that his appointment would be a considerable compliment to them without special significance to the rest of Europe; he pointed out that it could be balanced by the attachment of an officer to the Greek fleet. Although Churchill said he was inclined against the idea, he thought he should inform Grey of this opportunity of pleasing the Turks without giving offense to anyone else.[58] Grey, however, was afraid that Gamble's attachment to the fleet he had formerly trained would be misconstrued.[59]

The Greek and Turkish fleets were well matched, at least on paper. Greece was the only one of the Balkan allies to possess a navy of any importance, although Bulgaria did have an old gunboat and six relatively modern French-built torpedo boats. On the whole, the Greek navy was somewhat more modern than the Turkish, with the armored cruiser *Averoff,* three very old coast defense ships, fourteen destroyers, six of which had only just arrived, a submarine, and a number of older torpedo boats and gunboats. The Turkish navy possessed four or five old battleships, two modern protected cruisers, eight destroyers, and six or seven torpedo boats. Although the Turkish battleships, particularly the two purchased from Germany in 1910, were superior to the three old Greek coast defense ships, they had neither the speed of the *Averoff* (23–24 knots) nor the range of her armament. The *Averoff* was probably the finest ship in either fleet.

The Greek was by far the more active navy, even after the conclusion

[57] Elliot to Grey, 18 Oct. 1912, FO 371, vol. 1519, Turkey, file 43911; Minute by R. G. Vansittart, 19 Oct. 1912, *ibid;* Bertie to Grey, 28 Oct. 1912, *ibid.,* file 45633; O. Murray to Grey, 1 Nov. 1912, *ibid.,* file 46304.

[58] Churchill to Grey, 16 Oct. 1912, Grey MSS, FO 800, vol. 86.

[59] Minute by Grey, *ibid.*

of peace with Italy permitted the Turks to risk their ships outside of the Dardanelles. The best portion of the Greek fleet under Rear Admiral Paul Condouriotis, supported by a sufficient number of transports provided by the Greek merchant marine, occupied most of the Aegean islands. On the night of October 31 a Greek torpedo boat succeeded in penetrating Salonika harbor and torpedoing an old Turkish guardship. The Turkish fleet, employed at first in the Black Sea, was later shifted to the Dardanelles, and in December and January sortied for a few brief engagements, skirmishes rather than battles, in which the Turkish ships generally retired behind the forts of the Dardanelles after exchanging fire with their opponents. Marksmanship on both sides left much to be desired, although the Greeks improved far more than the Turks. In January 1913 the Turkish cruiser *Hamidieh* slipped out of the Dardanelles for a long raid in the Mediterranean and Red Sea, and did not return to Constantinople until August 1913. This was probably the most enterprising maritime action on the Turkish side.[60] The Balkan Wars, unlike the Russo-Japanese War or the Spanish-American War, presented little in the way of naval operations to interest foreign observers.

If the naval operations of the Balkan Wars were of little interest in themselves, the same cannot be said of the possible repercussions of the wars on the naval balance of power in the Mediterranean. Much uncertainty stemmed from the question of what form, if any, future Turkish naval development might take. Work on the large dreadnought *Reschad V* was suspended during the war (the second dreadnought forseen in 1911 was never begun), and there was some doubt the Ottoman government, which at one time had seemed on the verge of collapse, would be able to pay for completion of the ship.[61] This might have placed a large and powerful vessel on the international market. But an even greater source of instability to the Mediterranean balance of power was the South American naval race.

The Latin American republics had also caught the fever of naval competition. Brazil set off the race in 1907 when she ordered from Vickers two 19,000-ton dreadnoughts armed with twelve 12-inch guns. The ships, the *Minas Geraes* and *São Paulo,* were in service by 1911. The Argentines took up this challenge and after extensive negotiations with the major ship-

[60] C. N. Robinson, "The Balkan War," *The Naval Annual, 1914,* pp. 155f. For another short account of the war see Wilson, *Battleships in Action,* I, 274–281.

[61] Parkes, *British Battleships,* pp. 597–599; *The Naval Annual, 1913,* p. 75; *Le Yacht,* 23 Nov. 1912, p. 749.

building yards on both sides of the Atlantic finally ordered early in 1910 a pair of 27,000-ton dreadnoughts in the United States. The ships, the *Moreno* and the *Rivadavia*, were also to be armed with twelve 12-inch guns. The *Moreno* was built by the New York Shipbuilding Company, Camden, New Jersey, and the *Rivadavia* by the Fore River Company, Quincy, Massachusetts. While Chile, the third of the major South American states prepared to enter the race, Brazil ordered yet another dreadnought from Armstrong which was to have the largest number of heavy guns on any warship afloat. The *Rio de Janeiro*, laid down in September 1911, was to be 27,500 tons and carry fourteen 12-inch guns. Then Chile, to top this, ordered two dreadnoughts from Armstrong, the *Almirante Latorre* and the *Almirante Cochrane*, which were to be 28,000 tons, and armed with ten 14-inch guns.[62]

Thus there were six extremely powerful warships—the *Reschad V* and five South American dreadnoughts—in British or American yards which might come on to the market at any time as a result of the inability of the governments which had ordered them to pay, or a waning desire to continue the heavy financial sacrifices necessary for expensive symbols of prestige. The sudden acquisition by a single power of all or even some of these ships might have been enough to tip a delicate balance of power such as that which prevailed in the Mediterranean. The South American dreadnoughts were therefore yet another uncertain and disturbing factor.

The Turks, far from wanting to dispose of their ship, seemed bent on just the opposite. On November 1, 1912, during the Balkan War, they were reported by Lowther to be attempting to purchase the two Argentine dreadnoughts, for which they were willing to pay a large sum in cash. This was a report which sounded "rather fantastic" to one Foreign Office official.[63] Yet three weeks later the Turkish ambassador in London told Nicolson that the Argentines were prepared to sell both dreadnoughts for £5 million and asked whether the Admiralty could state if the vessels were in every way efficient and well built. The Admiralty, however, declined to express an opinion on ships building in foreign yards.[64] The French ambassador in Constantinople, Maurice Bompard, also reported that the Turks would purchase one of the Argentine ships, and that Buckman Pasha, an American engineer created admiral by the former sultan

[62] Parkes, *British Battleships*, pp. 602–607.
[63] Lowther to Grey, 1 Nov. 1912, FO 371, vol. 1520, Turkey, file 46185; marginal comment by Vansittart.
[64] Memorandum by Nicolson, 21 Nov. 1912, FO 371, vol. 1521, Turkey, file 49895; Greene to Foreign Office, 11 Dec. 1912, *ibid.*, file 53034.

Abdul Hamid, was supposed to be involved in the transaction. There was also an alleged plan to bring the ship to the Dardanelles with a mercenary crew.[65] The French ambassador in Washington replied to the Quai d'Orsay's queries that the ships apparently were for sale, while the French naval attaché in the United States reported the Argentine ships were experiencing difficulties with their turbines as well as delays in deliveries and a number of other troubles, and that early in December 1912 a letter from a yacht broker in New York had mentioned the subject of a possible sale. As far as the attaché could discover, similar circulars had been sent to the Spanish legation and the German embassy. He also observed that delivery of the more advanced ship of the pair could not possibly be made before the summer.[66] The Italian chargé d'affaires in Washington had also been approached by a New York maritime broker on the question. However, Admiral Cattolica did not deem it opportune to try for the ships.[67] Two years later, after the European war had broken out, Admiral Thaon di Revel was to reverse this position and strongly support their acquisition.[68]

Reports concerning these Argentine dreadnoughts were often distorted by distance, and the number of powers who might conceivably have been interested in getting them added to the confusion. Rear Admiral Dartige du Fournet, commander of the French naval forces in the Levant and senior naval officer of the international fleet at Constantinople, reported that the Americans had supposedly offered to sell a dreadnought to the Turks, and bring it and some destroyers, fully armed and with crews, out to Constantinople, fighting the Greek fleet and bombarding Piraeus on the way. He had also learned that the Turks apparently attempted to buy the *Goeben*.[69] On January 24, 1913, Admiral Montecuccoli asked the German naval attaché in Vienna if he had heard that the Russians intended to buy the Brazilian dreadnought building in England. The Marinekommandant added that since the Brazilians might not sell unless the Argentines sold

[65] Bompard to Minister of Foreign Affairs, 7 Dec. 1912, MAE, Turquie-Politique étrangère, Marine, vol. III.

[66] Jusserand to Poincaré, 8 Jan. 1913, *ibid.*; Benoist d'Azy; "Note au sujet des Bâtiments Argentins en Construction aux Etats-Unis," 8 Jan. 1913, *ibid.*

[67] San Giuliano to Leonardi Cattolica, 9 Dec. 1912, USM, cartella 279/2; Leonardi Cattolica to San Giuliano, 11 Dec. 1912, *ibid.*

[68] See above, p. 208. In June 1912 the German naval attaché in Rome had reported that representatives of the Italian government had left for England and the United States to purchase dreadnoughts under construction. This report, apparently false, may have stemmed from the activities of the Italian navy in respect to the use of British cannon and American-made armor plate in the Italian program. Rheinbaben to Tirpitz, 8 June 1912, GFM 26, reel 90, frame 698.

[69] Dartige du Fournet to Minister of Marine, 6 Jan. 1913, AMF, carton BB3-1353.

their ships, it was not impossible Russia intended to acquire the Argentine dreadnoughts as well.[70] Probably the most implausable rumor was the one which reached the Vicomte de Faramond at the end of January. The French naval attaché to Germany and Austria had heard from one of his colleagues that the British yard building the dreadnoughts for Turkey had recently offered to sell these ships to Austria.[71] Although Faramond passed on the story "with all reserve," it is an example of the climate of opinion in naval circles at the time.

The British Admiralty—at what must have been approximately the same time they received the Turkish inquiries on the *Rivadavia* and *Moreno*—became alarmed over the future of the *Reschad V.* In a confidential letter to the Foreign Office on December 10, 1912, the Admiralty claimed it had been represented to them that the Turkish government might sell the dreadnought for financial reasons. As the ship had been constructed to Admiralty specifications, to a large extent under the supervision of Admiralty officers, and would be very formidable when completed, the Admiralty did not think the *Reschad V* should be allowed to pass into the hands of another foreign power. However, they had no power to exercise any option in regard to the transfer of the ship to another owner or any means of preventing the ship's departure from British ports, except in cases covered by the Foreign Enlistment Act. The Admiralty therefore thought the case could be dealt with only by direct representation confidentially to the Turkish government. To show their earnestness in the matter they offered to negotiate for the purchase of the ship if the Turks showed any disposition to part with her. The real source of the Admiralty's anxiety was apparent in their statement: "looking to the quality and power of the 'Mohamed Reshad V' and the special assistance and supervision given by British officers in her construction it would be a serious detraction from the relative strength of the British Navy if she came into the possession of a formidable rival such as Germany. For this reason . . . it should be made clear to the Turkish Government that should they decide to retain the ship now strong exception would be taken by H.M. Government if within the next four years they should transfer her to a First Class Naval Power without previous communication to H.M. Government." [72] The Foreign Office decided on a less formal course: Nicolson privately approached Tewfik Pasha, the Turkish ambassador, for assurances that if the Ottoman government decided to sell the ship they would first

[70] Report by naval attaché, Vienna, 27 Jan. 1913, GFM 26, reel 61, frame 109.
[71] Faramond to Minister of Marine, 29 Jan. 1913, AMF, carton BB7-92.
[72] O. Murray to Foreign Office, 10 Dec. 1912, FO 371, vol. 1522, Turkey, file 52889.

offer it to the British. The Turks replied, as their other activities seemed to indicate, that there had never been any intention of selling the ship, and that on the contrary they wanted to increase their naval forces.[73]

The Admiralty were also concerned about Greek naval development. Battenberg thought it "undesirable from every point of view" that Greece should have important naval units like the *Salamis*.[74] On the other hand Churchill considered it important for British interests that Greece be in a position to defend her recent gains among the Aegean islands, for it was desirable for strategic reasons that these islands be either Turkish or Greek and not even temporarily under the control of Italy or Austria. The First Lord wanted as the opportunity presented itself to discourage the Greeks from building capital ships and encourage development of strong torpedo flotillas instead. Greek financial resources were insufficient for the creation of battle or cruiser squadrons capable of effectively opposing Austria or Italy. Nor were such ships thought necessary to deal with "any inefficient, badly-handled, capital ships" the Turks might acquire in the near future. A powerful torpedo flotilla would not require excessive expenditure compared to the resources of Greece and nothing could be more conducive to the effective defense or neutralization of Greek waters, "nor could the Greek navy adopt any form which would be more capable of lending support to the British Mediterranean squadrons." A number of torpedo craft could be obtained for the price of one capital ship, and the increasing power of torpedoes and danger of underwater attack would be an "immense deterrent" to a power like Austria with a few costly and powerful units. Churchill ordered the Admiralty War Staff to prepare a paper containing these arguments which could be given to the Greeks at an opportune moment. He wanted to persuade Greece to cancel the order for the battle cruiser and spend the money, even in Germany if unavoidable, on destroyers and submarines.[75]

The memorandum prepared by the Admiralty War Staff was the work of Captain Ballard, Director of Operations Division. Ballard, while keeping Greek interests in mind, did not want to neglect British interests either, for it was always possible bad relations might develop between the two in the future. Therefore the development of the Greek navy ought to be kept to lines which would threaten British interests least. Even three

---

[73] Minutes by Grey and Nicolson, *ibid.*; Nicolson to Tewfik Pasha, 15 [?] Dec. 1912, *ibid.*, file 54573; Tewfik Pasha to Nicolson, 18 Dec. 1912, *ibid.*

[74] Minute by Battenberg to a paper by Admiral Troubridge on Greek naval strength, 31 Dec. 1912, Adm. 116, case 3098.

[75] Memorandum by Churchill, 2 Jan. 1913, *ibid.*

or four small fast cruisers would, if British hands were full elsewhere, add to anxieties over trade routes in the eastern Mediterranean, while torpedo craft and submarines tied to the coasts and islands would pose less of a danger.[76] The Admiralty's advice to Greece, therefore, had its less altruistic side, summed up by Admiral Jackson along the lines of the fewer battle-ships possessed by Mediterranean powers, the better.[77]

British attempts to limit Greek or Turkish naval development had certain dangers. Admiral Limpus, for example, feared the Turks would lean more toward Germany and possibly employ German naval instructors if after the Balkan Wars had ended the British government did not sell them two pre-dreadnoughts, either the *Triumph* and a "Royal Sovereign" or two "Royal Sovereigns," at a price competitive with a German offer for two old battleships, and also agree to allow approximately thirty Turkish naval officers to train in England.[78] This question revealed a difference of opinion between Churchill and Battenberg. Battenberg did not favor the sale, and hoped that the naval mission itself might be withdrawn from Constantinople, for he thought the Turkish navy "hopeless." He considered "the rising sea power of Greece as much more worthy" of British care and assistance, and hoped a naval mission of active service officers would re-place the retired officers currently in Athens.[79] Churchill, on the other hand, favored both the retention of the Turkish naval mission and the sale of two "Royal Sovereigns," the money received being used to pur-chase airships. The Board of Admiralty decided to offer two "Royal Sov-ereigns" to the Turks after the conclusion of peace, but deemed it impossible to spare a more recent ship. Less than two years before Admiral Williams had found the Turks unreceptive to the "Royal Sovereigns," and there is no indication the proposal came to anything in 1913.[80] Perhaps the Turks had more attractive alternatives in the South American dread-noughts.

On one point Battenberg had his wish. The Greek government did not renew the contracts of Admiral Tufnell and his officers, and in place of them requested officers from the active list. The Admiralty agreed to this, and at the end of the summer of 1913 Rear Admiral Mark Kerr went out

[76] Ballard to Chief of Staff, 7 Jan. 1913, *ibid.*

[77] Minute by Jackson, *ibid.* The detailed technical arguments are in the paper, Admiralty War Staff, "Remarks on Shipbuilding Policy for Greece," 7 Jan. 1913, *ibid.*

[78] Limpus to Churchill, 12 Mar. 1913, quoted by Marder, *Dreadnought to Scapa Flow*, I, 302–303.

[79] Minute by Battenberg, 27 Mar. 1913, quoted *ibid.*, p. 303.

[80] *Ibid.* This decision was communicated to Limpus April 3, and Marder reports nothing further about it in the Admiralty records.

to Athens as head of a new naval mission. Kerr very quickly gave some realistic advice that was not necessarily pleasing to Greek ears. He told Venizelos that large battleships were useless in the narrow waters of the Aegean, and suggested that the battle cruiser under construction in Germany be sold. Aside from two or three armored cruisers of 10,000–12,000 tons, Kerr favored a Greek fleet of three light cruisers, thirty-four destroyers and twenty submarines, plus an air service, radio stations, and nets to destroy enemy submarines. Venizelos claimed that it would be difficult to convince Greek naval officers of this since they, not surprisingly, wanted a regular battle fleet.[81]

The French in the summer of 1913 were also considering the possibility of sending a naval attaché to Athens. Their purpose was largely commercial: if the French minister was assisted by a senior French naval officer he would be better equipped to fight German naval influence in the question of future shipbuilding contracts. This question was discussed by the French cabinet. Baudin, then Minister of Marine, offered to attach an officer to the legation in Athens in view of the benefits French industry might derive.[82] Pichon, Foreign Minister, agreed, for quite aside from the commercial question, the extent of the Greek coastline in the Adriatic and the Aegean, the development of her merchant marine following the annexation of Salonika and Kavalla, the necessity for Greece to develop a fleet to protect her flag, and the presence of a British naval mission of not less than seventeen members were all elements tending to make Athens a choice post for observation and information.[83] Capitaine de vaisseau Charles Didelot, the French officer chosen for the mission, was ordered to attempt to neutralize as much as possible the effects of German influence and, while maintaining cordial relations with the British naval mission, to endeavor to prolong the tradition of reserving to French industry an important part in the formation of the Greek navy.[84] At the same time the French shipbuilding yards decided to entrust their interests in Greece to a single representative, an improvement, according to the French chargé d'affaires in Athens, over the unseemly competition in the past.[85]

[81] Elliot to Grey, 12 May 1913, FO 371, vol. 1655, Greece, file 23053, and 13 May 1913, file 23054; Admiralty to Foreign Office, n.d. [received 21 June 1913], *ibid.*, file 28420; Elliot to Grey, 26 Sept. 1913, *ibid.*, file 44815; Kerr, *Land, Sea and Air*, pp. 180–181. A copy of Kerr's proposal is enclosed with Elliot to Grey, 25 Mar. 1914, FO 371, vol. 1994, Greece, file 14846.

[82] Unsigned note, 30 Aug. 1913, MAE, Grèce, vol. NS-43. Baudin to Minister of Foreign Affairs, 15 Sept. 1913, *ibid.*

[83] Minister of Foreign Affairs to Minister of Marine, 18 Sept. 1913, *ibid.*

[84] Baudin to Capt. Didelot, 8 Oct. 1913, *ibid.*, vol. NS-44.

[85] Halgouët to Pichon, 6 Oct. 1913, *ibid.*, vol. NS-43.

Vicomte de Poulpiquet du Halgouët, the French chargé d'affaires in Athens, tried to throw a dash of cold water on over optimistic evaluations of the Greek navy in case that country joined the Triple Entente. He pointed out that in the last war the role of the transports borrowed from the merchant marine had been more considerable than that of the military fleet, whose exploits had been inflated by the press. Moreover, Greece's adversaries in 1912–1913 could not be compared to the ones which might be faced should she join the Triple Entente. Halgouët thought that the idea of a powerful Greek navy in the future was a mirage because of the financial difficulties of the country. The price of one dreadnought was equivalent to around one quarter of the annual receipts, and even where large ships were acquired through French assistance, their maintenance would present great difficulties.[86]

Despite their financial difficulties, the Greeks maintained their naval ambitions. King Constantine told Captain Didelot in Didelot's first audience that he did not share the views of Admiral Kerr concerning the future naval program. The King preferred dreadnoughts to armored cruisers, and believed that only capital ships could assure Greek naval superiority over Turkey. He claimed that this opinion was shared by Venizelos, as well as the Greek Minister of Marine, and the majority of Greek naval officers.[87] Captain Didelot did not see in this ambitious program, though, a sizable role for French industry. The higher prices of the French yards, the pressure of the British naval mission, and the foot in the door gained by Vulkan through previous orders were all factors which seemed to leave little room for the French. The Greeks already had one battle cruiser building in Germany, and there was the possibility they would acquire one of the South American dreadnoughts building in England. Didelot did not think the state of Greek finances permitted them to think seriously of a third dreadnought, and therefore saw no chance for French industry to obtain an order for a large unit except by linking it to a Greek loan to be floated in France.[88]

Any attempts Admiral Kerr might have made to discourage the Greeks from huge and expensive ships were almost certain to be frustrated by

[86] Halgouët to Pichon, 12 Oct. 1913, MAE, Italie-Politique étrangère, Dossier général, II.

[87] Didelot to Minister of Marine, 27 Oct. 1913, AMF, carton BB7-130; Kerr was later to write that the King converted to his views, but it is not clear when. Kerr, *Land, Sea and Air*, p. 180.

[88] Didelot to Minister of Marine, 24 Oct. 1913, MAE, Grèce, vol. NS-44. The Greeks also planned to order two scout cruisers and four destroyers in England. Annex to Minister of Foreign Affairs to Minister of Marine, 14 Nov. 1913, *ibid.*, vol. NS-43; resumé of attaché report of 22 Nov. 1913, *ibid.*

the preoccupation in Greece, as reflected by the press, with Turkish naval preparations. The Balkan Wars had left a residue of bitter feeling and unsettled issues between the two countries, of which the most notable was the future of the Aegean islands. This was a question in which maritime power might play an obvious role. The *Reschad V* was scheduled for completion by September 1914, whereas the *Salamis* would not be ready until the spring of 1915. There would consequently be a period of approximately nine months during which the Turks would have, at least on paper, naval superiority, and a certain nervousness was evident on the part of the Greeks. Rumors again circulated that Greece was seeking to purchase foreign battleships.[89] Venizelos also asked that the Admiralty permit six submarines to be built in England for the Greek navy based on Admiralty designs. Admiral Kerr strongly supported this proposal, and indicated that the type in question would be the British "E" class whose design would be five years old by the time the submarines would be delivered to the Greeks, thus depreciating the confidential nature of the plans. Kerr pointed out the idea's commercial advantage in view of the Greek plans for new construction and their intention to standardize armaments and machinery.[90] The Admiralty, after lengthy deliberation, decided in the latter part of December 1913 to agree to the submarines being built by Vickers for the Greeks.[91] By this time, the subject was of minor interest to the Greeks since it appeared as if the Turks would obtain yet another nearly completed dreadnought.

Despite their disastrous defeats in the Balkan Wars, or possibly because of them, the Ottoman government was determined to press Turkish naval development with the purchase of completed ships abroad as a shortcut. In June 1913 the commander of the German Mittelmeerdivision told the British military attaché in Constantinople that the Turks had offered to buy the *Goeben*. Grey personally thought the idea of Turkey buying battleships was a waste of money, and the Foreign Office asked the Admiralty whether such advice should actually be given to them.[92] The Admiralty replied that they too considered torpedo boats more suitable than battleships for the Turks, and also less of a threat to British interests. This advice was given the Turks through both the British ambassador in Constantinople and the Turkish ambassador in London.[93] Naturally it

[89] Prince E. Fürstenberg, Austrian minister, Athens, to Berchtold, 25 Oct. and 29 Nov. 1913, copy in OK/MS-X-8/1, 1913.

[90] Kerr to Greene, 18 Oct. 1913, FO 371, vol. 1656, Greece, file 57193.

[91] Greene to Foreign Office, 19 Dec. 1913, *ibid.*

[92] Lowther to Grey, 7 June 1913, FO 371, vol. 1781, Turkey, file 26664; minute by Grey, *ibid.;* Mallet to Admiralty, 17 June 1913, *ibid.*

[93] Greene to Foreign Office, 10 July 1913, *ibid.;* Grey to Marling, 24 July 1913, *ibid.,* file 31917.

was not followed. By October 1913 the British naval attaché in Rome was reporting the possible sale by the Italian navy to the Turks of the large armored cruiser *Pisa* and the small cruiser *Libia*.[94] But the real crisis was to come when the Brazilian government decided to sell the *Rio de Janeiro*.

This decision by Brazil to part with the dreadnought under construction at Armstrong's Elswick yard on the Tyne touched off a scramble among the minor, and some not so minor, naval powers to acquire the ship. The *Rio de Janeiro* was an extremely powerful warship; a few years later when she took part in the battle of Jutland as the Royal Navy's *Agincourt* witnesses were to describe the sheet of flame from her broadside of fourteen 12-inch guns as awe inspiring.[95] But the great excitement over the transfer of this single warship is indicative of the naval fever of the time. Admiral Limpus told the British ambassador in Constantinople that the Turks were worried the Greeks would buy the *Rio* and he wondered if it was possible for Britain to buy the ship herself.[96] On November 17, 1913, the Board of Admiralty discussed the possible purchase of the *Rio de Janeiro* by a foreign government, but "decided that circumstances in the knowledge of the Admiralty did not justify special action."[97] Yet the following day the Admiralty informed the French naval attaché that the Italian government was negotiating with Armstrong for the ship; this the Admiralty feared would break the present balance in the Mediterranean. They also reported that Russia did not want to purchase the ship, and Greece could not. The Admiralty said, however, that it had arranged that the contract would not be signed for a few days thereby leaving the French navy time to purchase the ship should they judge it useful.[98]

The consternation this news must have caused the French government may be imagined, given the French suspicions over Italy's role in the Triple Alliance and preoccupation with securing the Mediterranean for the passage of the troop convoys in the event of mobilization. Pichon begged Cambon to delay the sale to Italy until the cabinet could consider the matter.[99] The French decided not to buy the ship themselves, but rather to advance the necessary funds so that Greece could acquire it; the amount was to be included in the Greek loan then under negotiation

---

[94] Captain Boyle to Dering, 18 Oct. 1913, FO 371, vol. 1846, Turkey, file 47836. The *Libia* originally had been under construction in Italy for the Turkish government and had been taken over by the Italian navy following the outbreak of the Tripolitan War.

[95] Parkes, *British Battleships,* p. 603.

[96] Mallet to Grey, 27 Oct. 1913, FO 371, vol. 1846, file 48915.

[97] Board minutes, 17 Nov. 1913, PRO, Adm. 167/41.

[98] Cambon to Minister of Foreign Affairs, 18 Nov. 1913, MAE, Turquie-Marine, vol. III.

[99] Pichon to Cambon, 21 Nov. 1913, *ibid.*

in Paris.[100] The French again pleaded for time. Battenberg told the French naval attaché the bill of sale was to be signed on the twenty-fourth, but that he would attempt to delay this. The Foreign Office also wanted to know if the French government was in agreement with the Greeks over the purchase of the ship, since past negotiations between the Greeks and Armstrong seemed to have been aimed solely at preventing the purchase of the ship by Turkey, and these talks had been interrupted and apparently not resumed.[101] Churchill had the Foreign Office informed that it was regarded as most important that Greece should purchase and not Italy. The Admiralty were also in contact with Armstrong over delaying the signature.[102] On November 24 Athos Romanos, the Greek minister in Paris, told Pichon that while he had in the past spoken only in a personal capacity of French financial aid for the purchase of the *Rio de Janeiro,* he had now been directed by his government to request that support officially. However, before Greece could get the requisite sum it was necessary for the government to accept all the French conditions for the loan and also to find a bank to cover the advance. This required time, and Pichon and the French Minister of Finance had to rely on the Admiralty to delay Armstrong.[103] In the end, the negotiations for an Italian purchase of the ship apparently proved abortive, for nothing further appears in either the French or British files on the subject.[104]

It is difficult to establish exactly what happened during the month of December 1913 when Greece, Turkey, Brazil, and Armstrong negotiated

[100] Pichon to Cambon, 22 Nov. 1913, *ibid.*

[101] Cambon to Pichon, 23 Nov. 1913, *ibid.*

[102] Admiralty to Foreign Office, 23 Nov. 1913, FO 371, vol. 1656, file 53327; memorandum by Crowe of conversation with Fleuriau, French chargé, 24 Nov. 1913, *ibid.;* minutes by Clerk, Grey and Crowe, 24 and 25 Nov. 1913, *ibid.;* Cambon to Pichon, 24 Nov. 1913, MAE, Turquie-Marine, vol. III.

[103] Unsigned memorandum, "Communication de M. Romanos," 24 Nov. 1913, *ibid.;* Pichon to Cambon, 25 Nov. 1913, *ibid.*

[104] Italy's role in this question is still not clear. I could find no evidence in the Italian naval archives that the Italian Ministry of Marine tried to purchase the *Rio de Janeiro,* although this obviously would not exclude the possibility they did. Lieutenant d'Huart, the French naval attaché in Rome, suggested that rumors Italy would purchase the dreadnought may actually have originated in a bitter rivalry between the major Italian shipbuilding yard Ansaldo—which was associated with Schneider for the manufacture of cannon—and the group including Orlando, Vickers-Terni, Armstrong, and the Banca Commerciale. Orlando may have proposed purchasing the *Rio* to prevent Ansaldo from obtaining the complete contract, including artillery and armor plate, for the fourth "Carraciolo" in the new Italian program. Ansaldo had already obtained the complete order for one of the "Carraciolos," including artillery, and Orlando was alleged to have felt its share of the program was insufficient. D'Huart pointed out that the "Carraciolos" were to have 15-inch cannon while the *Rio* was armed with 12-inch cannon so that her purchase would have been a regression for the Italians. D'Huart presents no documentary proof for his report. D'Huart to Minister of Marine, 10 Dec. 1913, AMF, carton BB7-126.

over the sale of the *Rio de Janeiro.* The Greek interests appear to have been entrusted to their consul general, Stavridi, who claimed Lloyd George and Churchill had told him the Bank of England would advance the necessary sum of money to buy the ship if it could be guaranteed the French loan would be issued.[105] Grey knew nothing about the proposed arrangements with the Bank of England but saw no reason to doubt them.[106] However, when the dust had settled it was the Turkish government which emerged with the *Rio de Janeiro,* which they later renamed *Sultan Osman I.* A French bank, Périer, provided the necessary funds for the Turks, much to the chagrin of the French government, and the transfer took place December 29 despite last minute appeals by Venizelos.[107]

The Greek minister in London implied that the ship had been lost because of lack of money, thus tending to shift responsibility on to the French. However the French chargé d'affaires in London claimed to have learned "from a good source" that the Greek government had sufficient funds on deposit for around six months in a city bank, and Fleuriau suspected the Greeks had tried to use French interest in the fate of the dreadnought to obtain better conditions for the loan to be floated in Paris. Fleuriau was inclined to put the real responsibility in the affair on Armstrong, whom he suspected of having connived with Vickers and Périer for the Turks to get the ship in exchange for the concession Armstrong and Vickers had obtained for the reorganization of the Ottoman dockyards.[108] The preceding autumn Sir Vincent Caillard, formerly a British representative on the Ottoman Debt Commission and currently a director of Vickers, and Rear Admiral Ottley, a retired naval officer who was a director of Armstrong, had gone to Constantinople and succeeded in reaching an agreement with the Turks whereby the British firms would modernize the Ottoman dockyard at Constantinople and erect an arsenal together with a floating dock in the Gulf of Ismid.[109]

Wherever the responsibility lay, the Turks now had two dreadnoughts. Not content with this, they ordered a third ship from Vickers a few months later. The contract for this dreadnought, named the *Sultan Mehmed Fatieh,* was not signed until July 16, 1914, and the ship was to be ready

[105] Granville to Montgomery, 6 Dec. 1913, Grey MSS, FO 800, vol. 53. The problem was complicated by a ministerial crisis in France.

[106] Grey to Granville, 9 Dec. 1913, *ibid.*

[107] Cambon to Doumergue, 28 Dec. 1913, MAE, Turquie-Marine, vol. III; Deville to Minister of Foreign Affairs, 28 Dec. 1913, *ibid.;* Fleuriau to Minister of Foreign Affairs, 29 and 30 Dec. 1913, *ibid.*

[108] Fleuriau to Doumergue, 30 Dec. 1913, *ibid.*

[109] Mallet to Grey, 6 Nov. 1913, FO 371, vol. 1846, file 50485, 25 Nov. 1913, file 54147, 3 Dec. 1913, file 54559; and 8 Dec. 1913, *BD,* X (pt. 2), no. 407, p. 362.

in twenty-two months.[110] The Greeks therefore faced, in addition to the danger period between the completion of the *Reschadieh* (formerly *Reschad V*) and *Sultan Osman I* and their own *Salamis,* the disconcerting possibility that in less than three years their single battle cruiser might have to contend with three Turkish dreadnoughts.

The Greeks reacted quickly to news of the *Rio de Janeiro's* sale. Barely two days after the Turks obtained the ship, the Greek Minister of Marine asked Captain Didelot to cable his government for information as to which French yard could immediately begin construction of a 20,000-ton dreadnought similar to the *Salamis,* and what would be the minimum period of construction from the time the yard received the order and the plans.[111] The French shipbuilding consortium was only too happy to begin construction of such a ship for the Greeks without delay, and promised to furnish it in the same period of time as the German yards. They offered to do the same with any smaller units in the Greek program, hoping by this to make orders in France for all material a condition of the Greek loan.[112] Deville reported from Athens a few days later that the Greeks were attempting to acquire two battleships from a foreign fleet, possibly Germany.[113] It is hardly likely the Greeks would have been able to obtain anything but a very old ship from any of the European powers. On the other hand, there were still the other South American dreadnoughts, and it was possible that Brazil's action in disposing of the *Rio de Janeiro* might induce Argentina and Chile to sell their large and costly units.

The situation continued to cause all sorts of rumors to circulate. In London Cambon heard one to the effect the Italians were negotiating with Brazil for the *São Paulo* and *Minas Geraes.* He also claimed to know that despite denials the Greek government was trying to get one of the Argentine ships in the United States. Cambon observed that the fact such powerful vessels would be on the market was of a nature to disturb the maritime powers.[114] It was undoubtedly this situation Churchill had in mind when he wrote during the Cabinet controversy over the 1914–15 estimates: "Besides the Great Powers, there are many small States who are buying or building great ships of war and whose vessels may by pur-

---

[110] Djemal Pasha, *Memories of a Turkish Statesman* (New York, 1922), pp. 94–95; Jane, *Fighting Ships, 1917,* p. 435.

[111] Deville to Minister of Foreign Affairs, 31 Dec. 1913, MAE, Grèce, vol. NS-44.

[112] Monis, Minister of Marine, to Minister of Foreign Affairs, 6 Jan. 1914, *ibid.;* note from Association des Chantiers de Construction Navale, 7 Jan. 1914, *ibid.*

[113] Deville to Minister of Foreign Affairs, 7 Jan. 1914, *ibid.*

[114] Cambon to Doumergue, 7 Jan. 1914, *ibid.,* Turquie-Marine, vol. III.

chase, by some diplomatic combination, or by duress, be brought into the line against us. None of these Powers need, like us, Navies to defend their actual safety or independence. They build them so as to play a part in the world's affairs. It is sport to them. It is death to us." [115]

The Russians, for their part, feared the Turks would succeed in purchasing more of the South American ships, particularly the Chilean *Almirante Latorre* building at Armstrong's yard. They suggested the French give the Greeks financial aid in obtaining this ship.[116] The French promised to do this although Paléologue emphasized to the Russian ambassador in Paris that it had not been through lack of funds that the Greeks lost the *Rio*. Moreover, a representative of Armstrong denied the Turks intended to purchase a Chilean ship.[117] Soon the Russians themselves began negotiating for first the Argentine ships, and then the Chilean.

Venizelos was scheduled to visit London and Paris in January 1914, and naval questions must have formed a substantial portion of the problems he expected to deal with. The French were eagerly awaiting him and, particularly in the event of a Greek loan, they were anxious to obtain before the Greek Prime Minister left for London a minimum order for French yards of a dreadnought, four destroyers, and four submarines. Schneider already had two submarines under construction, and could deliver them nine months before similar foreign units.[118] Schneider claimed they had heard the British naval mission was trying to orient the Greeks toward British-built craft despite the excellent performance of the pair of French submarines already in Greek service. They therefore requested the Quai d'Orsay to induce the Greeks to at least agree to study their proposals.[119]

Any entente which may have existed between the British and French navies had practically no effect on the keen rivalry between the armaments firms of the two nations for Balkan naval orders. Captain Didelot spoke of a struggle for maritime influence in Athens—ruthless though carried out in an atmosphere of extreme courtesy—in which French industry had more to fear from the British than the Germans, and where the efforts of the

[115] Churchill, *The World Crisis*, I, 175.

[116] Sazonov to Izvolski, 2 Jan. 1914, *Diplomatische Schriftwechsel Iswolskis*, vol. IV, nos. 1202, 1204, pp. 13, 14; Russian note verbale, 3 Jan. 1914, MAE, Turquie-Marine, vol. III.

[117] Izvolski to Sazonov, 3 Jan. 1914, *Diplomatische Schriftwechsel Iswolskis*, vol. IV, no. 1205, p. 14; Etter, Russian chargé, London, to Sazonov, 5 Jan. 1914, *Diplomatische Schriftwechsel Benckendorff*, vol. III, no. 1025, pp. 240–241.

[118] Unsigned note, 10 Jan. 1914, MAE, Grèce, vol. NS-44. See also "Note du Département," paragraph 9, n.d., DDF3, IX, no. 37, p. 45.

[119] Schneider & Cie. to Minister of Foreign Affairs, 13 Jan. 1914, MAE, Grèce, vol. NS-44.

British were powerfully seconded by the chief of the naval mission.[120] Gaston Doumergue, now Premier and Minister of Foreign Affairs, could not be accused of neglecting the interests of French industry. He invited Guillain, president of the shipbuilders' consortium, to lunch in order to present him to Venizelos, and then arranged for a meeting on January 16 of Venizelos, Guillain, and Louis Aubin, an engineer who was a director of the consortium and had been out to Athens the previous spring seeking orders. Venizelos pointed out that he needed to find a completed battleship in view of the Turkish acquisition of the *Sultan Osman,* but he agreed to order a new dreadnought in France if he was unsuccessful. Venizelos explained that if he succeeded in buying a completed battleship the need to husband Greek finances would lead him to defer for awhile the construction of a new unit.[121] Venizelos was so precise on this point that Guillain feared he already had a battleship in hand and, worried because the Greeks had just ordered four destroyers in England, he asked Doumergue to obtain a firm promise before the Greek loan was floated on the French market that the largest portion of the secondary units in the Greek program would be ordered in French yards.[122]

At this time Captain Didelot reported the departure from Athens of a British naval engineer on a secret mission to England to order the first of a projected pair of Greek scout cruisers, and four 1,000-ton destroyers. Fearful that the orders were slipping out of French hands, Didelot thought the French should claim the battleship, all future submarines, and a share of the destroyers, and use the Greek loan as the one weapon available to oblige the Greeks to depart from the partiality they had shown for British and German yards.[123] The Greeks actually purchased the pair of submarines Schneider had under construction, and the French hoped to receive an order for the other four the Greeks were contemplating. In this they expected a struggle, for Admiral Kerr was supporting the British design, and King Constantine and the German minister were reported to be partial to Krupp's proposals.[124] In a conference held at the Quai d'Orsay with the Greek minister in Paris and an official of the National Bank of Greece, the

---

[120] Didelot to Minister of Marine, 15 Jan. 1914, *ibid.*

[121] Unsigned memorandum from the Cabinet du Ministre de Marine, "Visite de M. Aubin," 14 Jan. 1914, AMF, Carton Ea-116; Guillain to Doumergue, 16 Jan. 1914, MAE, Grèce, vol. NS-44.

[122] *Ibid.* See also Note du ministre, 17 Jan. 1914, *DDF3,* X, no. 94, p. 109; editor's note, *ibid.,* p. 228 n.l. It was also proposed that Greece seek to acquire four destroyers which French yards were building for the Argentine government. However, these ships were eventually taken over by the French navy on the outbreak of the war.

[123] Note du département, 16 Jan. 1914, *DDF3,* IX, no. 89, p. 104.

[124] Unsigned note, 16 Jan. 1914, MAE, Grèce, vol. NS-44; unsigned note, 24 Jan. 1914, *ibid.*

Greek delegates promised that any naval construction based on the French loan would be shared between France and England.[125]

The French consortium were ready to cater to Venizelos' desire to husband Greek finances. Guillain announced that to overcome Greek objections on this account, the French yards were willing to begin construction of a dreadnought immediately, and defer the first payments by a few months.[126] Aubin informed the Ministry of Marine of a plan to copy a French "Lorraine" for the Greeks and, in what may have been a hint, spoke of the French yards scarcely daring to speak of a scheme which would yield to the Greeks a completed French dreadnought such as the *Paris,* which would be replaced by new construction, thereby giving the French navy a more modern ship in exchange.[127]

The Greeks obviously needed a dreadnought in a hurry, but if they obtained one outside of France they offered immediately to order a 5400-ton scout cruiser in France. This, however, gave the appearance of being a form of compensation which neither Doumergue nor the consortium would accept.[128] The director of Greek naval construction, Léondopoulos, was in Paris in early February to discuss with Felix Godard, director general of the Chantier et Ateliers de St. Nazaire (Penhoët), the possibility of building a ship derived from the *Salamis.* Godard was able to seduce Léondopoulos with an attractive scheme. To avoid the delay which might result from reproducing the *Salamis,* he proposed that Penhoët provide an exact replica of the dreadnought *Lorraine* which it was building for the French navy.[129] Although Godard probably did not mention it to the Greek engineer, this would have the added advantage for the French of possibly preventing the American firms who were furnishing the cannon and armor plate for the *Salamis* from doing the same for the new dreadnought. Admiral Le Bris agreed to this proposal providing the construction of the cannon would not delay the delivery of those destined for future French warships, and provided the Greeks furnished their own plans for the projectiles.[130] The Greek government ordered Léondopoulos, who appears to have been rather francophile, to embark for the United States to purchase

125 Compte rendu d'une Conversation Franco-Héllenique, 19 Jan. 1914, *DDF3*, IX, no. 185, pp. 228–229.

126 Guillain to Doumergue, 22 and 28 Jan. 1914, MAE, Grèce, vol. NS-44.

127 Cabinet du Ministre, "Visite de M. Aubin," 22 Jan. 1914, AMF, carton Ea-116.

128 Deville to Minister of Foreign Affairs, 5 Feb. 1914, MAE, Grèce, vol. NS-44; Doumergue to Deville, 7 Feb. 1914, *ibid.;* Deville to Minister of Foreign Affairs, 8 Feb. 1914, *ibid.;* note from Assoc. des Chantiers de Construction Navale, 18 Feb. 1914, *ibid.*

129 Cabinet du Ministre [Marine], Minute of a telephone communication from Admiral Le Bris, 12 Feb. 1914, AMF, carton Ea-116.

130 *Ibid.;* director general, Penhoët, to Monis, 14 Feb. 1914, *ibid.;* note by Le Bris, 16 Feb. 1914, *ibid.*

one of the Argentine dreadnoughts but, before leaving France, the Greek engineer helped Godard draft a note which would enable Deville to support the project in Athens without uncovering him.[131]

Venizelos, desperate for a dreadnought, had a proposal of his own to make to the French whereby they would sell Greece one of the ships shortly to be delivered to their navy, and the Greeks would immediately order another dreadnought from French yards, taking advantage of the facilities offered by the consortium in the question of payments. The Greek Prime Minister spoke of a secret convention which would place the dreadnought sold to Greece at the disposition of France in case of need, even in a situation in which Greece was in conflict with Turkey. This convention would be valid until France could put into service a replacement for the ship sold to Greece. Venizelos added that an affirmative reply by the French on this would cause him to break off all talks with other powers on the subject.[132] This was hardly a feasible proposal in the light of France's naval position and weakness in dreadnoughts. Doumergue, who apparently assumed the French had gotten a firm promise from Venizelos when he visited Paris, sent back an indignant refusal in which he claimed it would make the worst impression in France if it became known. He also implied that Venizelos was breaking his promises, and concluded with the thinly veiled threat that these procrastinations would be exploited by the enemies of the Greek loan.[133]

In a lengthy dispatch that followed the cables concerning Venizelos' offer, Captain Didelot explained that he thought the Greek Prime Minister had been sincere in his proposal, and had been annoyed at its refusal. Didelot also learned that the Argentine government was apparently insisting on the simultaneous sale of both their dreadnoughts, and that the Greek government was hostile to this idea because of the cost involved. Venizelos was, according to the naval attaché, delaying a decision about an order in the French yards until the question of purchasing a completed ship had been settled one way or another.[134] The French knew from their ambassador and naval attaché in Washington that the Argentine dreadnoughts had experienced considerable difficulty with their turbines during trials, and that the turbines might have to be replaced at the cost of con-

---

[131] Note by Godard, 17 Feb. 1914, *ibid.;* Godard to Dumesnil, Assistant Chief, Cabinet du Ministre, 20 Feb. 1914, *ibid.*

[132] Deville to Doumergue, 19 Feb. 1914, *DDF3,* IX, no. 329, p. 422.

[133] Annotation of the minister, *ibid.;* Doumergue to Deville, 20 Feb. 1914, MAE, Grèce, vol. NS-44.

[134] Didelot to Minister of Marine, 20 Feb. 1914, *ibid.;* Deville to Minister of Foreign Affairs, 21 Feb. 1914, *ibid.*

siderable delay in completion of the ships. This information was transmitted to Athens so that Captain Didelot might discreetly profit by it in influencing the Greek decision.[135]

The Greek Minister of Marine was none too keen on the Argentine dreadnoughts, for he also knew of their difficulties. However, the pressing need for a completed ship led the Greeks to delay their decision even after Didelot had formally offered a replica of the *Lorraine*. Venizelos offhandedly spoke of France giving Greece four of her submarines so that these, together with the others shortly to be delivered, would give Greece a total of eight which, supported by a flotilla of twenty destroyers, might allow her to await the completion of her large units with sufficient security. Didelot had naturally implied to the Greek Prime Minister that this was not possible.[136] Doumergue held a strong card in the form of the Greek loan, and he was not reluctant to use it since he did not want negotiations to be prolonged indefinitely. Venizelos, under heavy pressure from Doumergue and the somewhat less aggressive French minister in Athens, could have had few doubts that the date of the loan would depend on the order for a dreadnought.[137] Finally, at the end of March, the Greeks consented to order a replica of the *Lorraine*, although they still intended to obtain the artillery from the Bethlehem Steel Company in the United States so as to preserve homogeneity with the *Salamis*. The *Lorraine* was a few knots slower than the 23-knot *Salamis*, but the Greeks were in a difficult position. They expressed a strong desire that construction not exceed two years.[138]

Captain Didelot proudly listed the results of what from his and the French point of view was a successful "winter campaign" in Athens. The Greeks had decided to adopt Belleville boilers for the three old coast defense ships, despite the preference of the British naval mission for Babcock and Wilcox; they had purchased two Schneider submarines, despite Admiral Kerr's recommendation for Vickers and the British "E" class; an order was given for 400 out of a projected 1500 mines to the French firm of

[135] Jusserand to Doumergue, 6 Feb. 1914, *ibid.*; Minister of Foreign Affairs to Deville and Minister of Marine, 27 Feb. 1914, *ibid.* Similar information from the French minister at Buenos Aires was also forwarded.

[136] Didelot to Minister of Marine, 28 Feb. 1914, *ibid.*; Doumergue to Deville, 5 Mar. 1914, *ibid.*; Didelot to Minister of Marine, 7 Mar. 1914, *ibid.*; Minister of Marine to Didelot, 27 Mar. 1914, *ibid.*

[137] Doumergue to Deville, 8 Mar. 1914, *DDF3*, IX, no. 142, p. 529; Deville to Doumergue, 9 Mar. 1914, MAE, Grèce, vol. NS-44; Doumergue to Deville, 10 Mar. 1914, *ibid.*; Deville to Doumergue, 11 Mar. 1914, *DDF3*, IX, no. 433, p. 556.

[138] Deville to Minister of Foreign Affairs, 30 Mar. 1914, MAE, Grèce, vol. NS-44; Didelot to Minister of Marine, 31 Mar. 1914, *ibid.*

Harlé, and it was almost certain that French firms would get the order for the remainder; and finally, the crowning achievement came with the order of a dreadnought from Penhoët.[139]

The Greeks were still dissatisfied with the building time of thirty months which the French yards quoted for the dreadnought, even though this would actually have been six months less than the *Lorraine* itself. The speed of the *Lorraine*, 20–20.5 knots, was another problem since the *Salamis* would have a speed of 23 knots. Moreover, the *Salamis* would have 14-inch cannon while the *Lorraine* had the 13.4-inch (34 cm) caliber.[140] For a brief time there was a danger that the deal might fall through over the question of speed and building time, but Penhoët was able to promise that the progress in turbines and boilers since the *Lorraine* had been laid down was such that the speed would be over 22 knots and probably close to 23. If the Greeks signed the contract immediately, Penhoët promised to cut the building time to twenty-seven months without artillery.[141] The Greeks finally decided to take the 13.4-inch French cannon for both the economy in cost this meant, and the fact that modifications necessary for the larger caliber would entail delay. However, the question of the secondary armament, which the Greeks planned to order in England, remained open, along with that of munitions. Here the Greeks wanted the French to supply the plans for the projectiles, a request the French refused on grounds of security.[142]

The preliminary contract for the ship was signed at the Greek legation in Paris on April 22. The price was set at 59.3 million francs, including the primary armament.[143] Disputes between the Greeks and the French continued over the plans and the prices for the projectiles.[144] Schneider at-

[139] Didelot to Minister of Marine, 31 Mar. 1914, *ibid.* The Foreign Office informed a representative of an unsuccessful British shipbuilding consortium they were unable to intervene. Minute by Crowe, et al., 29 Mar. 1914, FO 371, vol. 1998, Greece, file 14453.

[140] Minister of Marine to Minister of Foreign Affairs, 2 Apr. 1914, MAE, Grèce, vol. NS-44; Deville to Minister of Foreign Affairs, 3 Apr. 1914, *ibid.*

[141] *Ibid.*; Minister of Marine to Minister of Foreign Affairs, 3 Apr. 1914, *ibid.*; Doumergue to Deville, 4 Apr. 1914, *ibid.*, vol. NS-45; Deville to Doumergue, 5 and 6 Apr. 1914, *ibid.*; Minister of Marine to Minister of Foreign Affairs, 6 and 7 Apr. 1914, *ibid.*

[142] Deville to Minister of Foreign Affairs, 11 Apr. 1914, *ibid.*; Minister of Marine to Minister of Foreign Affairs, 15 Apr. 1914, *ibid.*; Deville to Minister of Foreign Affairs, 18 Apr. 1914, *ibid.*

[143] "Contrat pour la fourniture à la Marine Royale Héllenique d'un Cuirassé d'Escadre de 23,550 tonneaux," 22 Apr. 1914, *ibid.* In 1914 the franc was worth approximately 19 cents (U.S.).

[144] Minister of Marine to Minister of Foreign Affairs, 4 May 1914, *ibid.*; Didelot to Minister of Marine, 8 May 1914, *ibid.*; Deville to Minister of Foreign Affairs, 14 May 1914, *ibid.*; Minister of Marine to Minister of Foreign Affairs, 16 May 1914, *ibid.*

tempted to get the order for the secondary armament of the ship, and the Greeks tried unsuccessfully to have the French navy's aiming and fire control devices installed.[145] Despite the difficulties, the final contract was signed early in June and the ship laid down on June 9. On August 3 work ceased because of the French mobilization and was not resumed. The entire affair had never been a very happy one for the Greeks and by the beginning of 1915, faced with a long delay in the completion of the ship and the experiences of the war which showed the vulnerability of large units to mines and submarines, they indicated a desire to break the contract. In March 1916 they ordered Penhoët to stop all work and orders for material, and in October of that year asked the Quai d'Orsay to mediate in the difficult question of assessing penalties and reaching a settlement with the yard.[146]

The dreadnought Venizelos had been pressured into ordering in France did not solve Greece's immediate peril, for it would not be finished before almost two and one-half years. Moreover the news, which became known toward the end of April 1914, that Turkey had ordered another dreadnought in England created a strong impression in Greece, where Venizelos was exposed to criticism over the artillery, speed, and building time of the dreadnought ordered in France. A committee was formed under the presidency of Admiral Condouriotis to raise funds through public subscription in order to offer the government a flagship.[147]

Naval preparations were also the object of great public enthusiasm in Turkey where a popular subscription to help pay for the dreadnoughts met with wide support.[148] Despite some doubts on the part of foreign observers, the Turks were confident they would be able to supply the necessary officers and specialists to man the huge ships, and that foreigners could be engaged to fill any gaps.[149] Admiral Limpus appears to have

---

[145] Schneider & Cie. to Minister of Marine, 6 May 1914, *ibid.;* Minister of Foreign Affairs to Deville, 13 May 1914, *ibid.;* Greek legation to Minister of Foreign Affairs, 24 July 1914, *ibid*, vol. NS-46; Minister of Marine to Minister of Foreign Affairs, 16 Aug. 1914, *ibid.*

[146] Note by De Margerie, Director of Political Affairs, 19 Jan. 1915, *ibid.;* Greek Minister to Minister of Foreign Affairs, Viviani, 24 Oct. 1915, *ibid.* The Greek government was also to become involved in lengthy litigation with Vulkan after the war over the unfinished hull of the *Salamis;* the case eventually went to the Hague Court; *The Naval Annual, 1929*, p. 44.

[147] Didelot to Minister of Marine, 1 May 1914, MAE, Grèce, vol. NS-45.

[148] Mallet to Grey, 14 Jan. 1914, FO 371, vol. 2114, Turkey, file 2465, and 16 Jan. 1914, file 2681; Henry Morgenthau, *Ambassador Morgenthau's Story* (New York, 1918), pp. 51–52, 76.

[149] Statement by Turkish Minister of Marine to Austrian military attaché, report by military attaché, 7 Jan. 1914, copy in OK/MS-X-4/1, 1914.

shared this optimistic view.[150] Moreover, the Ottoman government continued its naval development with orders for two light cruisers in England, six destroyers from the French yard of Augustin Normand, and two submarines from Schneider.[151] With complete impartiality the French consortium had been almost as active in Constantinople as it had been in Athens, and in June Djemal Pasha, Ottoman Minister of Marine since February 1914, promised the French he would order an additional six destroyers.[152] During the spring the Turkish navy also received eight small gunboats ordered in France whose completion and delivery had been delayed by the Libyan and Balkan wars.

The unresolved question of the Aegean islands served as a dangerous background to the Balkan naval race. The great powers were afraid that the Greeks might succumb to the temptation of a preventive blow before the dreadnoughts could be delivered to the Turks. King Constantine and Venizelos had alluded to this possibility in conversations with the German and British ambassadors in the spring of 1914.[153] Another danger was that the Greek navy, with or without the approval of the Greek government, might attack the *Reschadieh* and *Sultan Osman* on their passage to the Dardanelles. In assessing Greco-Turk relations, Sir Louis Mallet, now ambassador at Constantinople, thought that "the ground is prepared for an explosion." [154] The Russians were naturally worried about the progress of the Turkish navy, as well as a report the dreadnoughts might be brought to Constantinople under the protection of the British merchant flag. They hinted they might have to raise the question of the Straits to offset the disadvantage of having to rely solely on their own yards in the Black Sea.[155] Grey assured the Russians that if Britain thought the Ottoman navy signified a danger for Russia, British officers would not have been

[150] Mallet to Grey, 4 Jan. 1914, FO 371, vol. 2114, file 342. In May Captain Boyle visited Turkish naval schools and reported the Turkish navy had made "considerable progress," but that time alone would show if true efficiency would be reached. Report by Boyle enclosed in Mallet to Grey, 31 May 1914, *ibid.*, file 25448.

[151] Djemal Pasha, *Memories*, pp. 94–95. The contract for the destroyers was signed May 3. Aubin to Ponsot, official in the Direction des Affaires Politiques at the Quai d'Orsay, 17 July 1914, MAE, Turquie-Marine, vol. III. The two submarines were not to be delivered until 1916; Bompard to Minister of Foreign Affairs, 30 Apr. 1914, *ibid.*

[152] Bompard to Minister of Foreign Affairs, 4 June 1914, *ibid.*

[153] Graf Quadt, German ambassador, Athens, to Auswärtige Amt, 27 Apr. 1914, *GP*, XXXVI (pt. 2), no. 14574, p. 767; Elliot to Grey, 28 May 1914, *BD*, X (pt. 1), no. 274, p. 253.

[154] Mallet to Grey, 17 May 1914, Grey MSS, FO 800, vol. 79. See also Analysis of the report of French military attaché, Constantinople, 9 May 1914, *DDF3*, X, no. 218, pp. 345–346.

[155] Sazonov to Benckendorff, 8 May 1914, *Int. Bez.*, 1st series, II, no. 384, pp. 381–382, 382 n.l; memorandum by Benckendorff, 21 May 1914, FO 371, vol. 2114, file 23121.

permitted to enter Turkish service. Grey added he had no legal means to oppose the ordering and sale of warships in England.[156]

In their desperate search for ships the Greeks ranged far and wide. They even asked the Japanese government if it would sell the magnificent battle cruiser *Kongo* which Vickers had completed the previous year. Not surprisingly the Japanese declined.[157] The Greeks had more success with the Chinese government which agreed to sell the small 2600-ton cruiser *Fei Hung* then completing at the New York Shipbuilding Company. Renamed the *Helli,* the ship was ready to sail for the Aegean before the end of June, but could hardly be considered a match for the Turkish dreadnoughts.[158]

An excellent opportunity for the Greeks arose at the end of May when the United States Navy decided to sell the 13,000-ton battleships *Mississippi* and *Idaho* and use the proceeds to build an additional dreadnought to those authorized in the naval appropriations. The two pre-dreadnoughts had been launched in 1905 and completed in 1908. They were considered too slow at 17 knots, and too small with a low freeboard making their rear turrets unusable in a heavy sea. The U.S. Navy was therefore anxious to replace them.[159] Congress did not approve the sale of the ships to Greece until the end of June. The Turkish ambassador to the United States did his utmost to stop it, claiming it would result in Greece's declaration of war on Turkey because of the advantage that country would momentarily have over Ottoman naval power. On the other hand, he argued, the ships were no match for the new Turkish dreadnoughts, and would not therefore affect the naval balance of power once the dreadnoughts were ready.[160] Djemal Pasha pleaded with Henry Morgenthau, American ambassador to Turkey, to help forestall the sale, and offered to pay more than the Greeks.[161] On the Greek side, Venizelos was reported to have cabled President Wilson that the acquisition of the ships by Greece would promote

[156] Benckendorff to Sazonov, 12 June 1914, *Int. Bez.,* 1st series, III, no. 224, p. 207; memorandum by Grey, 9 June 1914, *ibid.,* no. 253, pp. 225–226.

[157] Russian Ambassador, Tokyo, to Sazonov, 1 July 1914, *ibid.,* IV, no. 54, p. 61.

[158] *Le Yacht,* 25 Apr. 1914, p. 261; Jusserand to Minister of Foreign Affairs, 15 and 21 June 1914, MAE, Grèce, vol. NS-45.

[159] Jusserand to Minister of Foreign Affairs, 1 June 1914, *DDF3,* X, no. 314, p. 468, and 28 June 1914, MAE, Grèce, vol. NS-45.

[160] Jusserand to Minister of Foreign Affairs, 20 June 1914, *ibid.; Washington Post,* 23 June 1914, enclosed with *ibid.;* Bachmetjew to Sazonov, 28 June 1914, *Int. Bez.,* 1st series, IV, no. 7, p. 10.

[161] Morgenthau, *Ambassador Morgenthau's Story,* pp. 52–53; Wangenheim to Auswärtige Amt, 14 June 1914, *GP,* XXXVI (pt. 2), no. 14608, pp. 808–809. The Turks also sought assurances from the Italians that the old battleships *Sardegna* and *Sicilia,* which they themselves had rejected, would not be sold to the Greeks. Report by Captain of the *Archimede* (Italian stationnaire, Constantinople) to Minister of Marine, 28 June 1914, USM, cartella 318/2.

peace since they would enable her to await a Turkish assault without fear.[162] The Greeks also asked if Grey could help influence the U.S. government to sell the ships, but the British felt they could not intervene.[163] It is easy to understand how the Greeks, with their own large units many months from completion and two Turkish dreadnoughts about to arrive in the Aegean, had the more cogent argument for the necessity of acquiring the two battleships to preserve the balance of power. The transfer was facilitated by the presence of the *Idaho* in the Mediterranean on a training cruise; a Greek crew embarked for Newport News to take over the *Mississippi*. In Greek service the *Mississippi* and *Idaho* were renamed *Lemnos* and *Kilkis* respectively.[164]

Admiral Kerr, head of the British naval mission, was highly critical of the transaction and characterized Venizelos as "penny-wise and pound-foolish." He described the battleships as old with worn-out guns and engines, "entirely useless for war," whose price (approximately $12.5 million) was about equal to that which would be paid for a new ship. Kerr claimed that the deal had been kept from him until it was concluded, and that it ruined the progress of the Greek navy for the rest of the time he was there.[165] These obsolescent ships, however, had a psychological value quite apart from their material strength. Venizelos was convinced that with them peace was more firmly secured, and that the Turks when they had their new dreadnought would not risk it outside of the Dardanelles.[166] The Greek Prime Minister believed that even after the delivery of the second Turkish dreadnought his country would have naval superiority.[167] This transaction between the United States and Greece on the eve of the war seemed mutually beneficial. The Greeks were happy to acquire badly needed ships, and the Americans had exchanged a pair of 13,000-ton obsolete pre-dreadnoughts with only four 12-inch cannon for money with which to buy a 30,000-ton dreadnought with 14-inch cannon. The French ambassador in Washington wryly observed that everyone was satisfied with the single exception, no doubt, of the Grand Seigneur.[168]

The Balkan naval race showed few signs of abating during the fateful

[162] Russian chargé, Athens, to Sazonov, 1 July 1914, *Int. Bez.*, 1st series, IV, no. 49, p. 58; Morgenthau, *Ambassador Morgenthau's Story*, p. 55.

[163] Erskine to Grey, 19 June 1914, FO 371, vol. 1998, file 27740.

[164] Jusserand to Minister of Foreign Affairs, 28 June 1914, MAE, Grèce, vol. NS-45; "The Greek Navy," *The Army and Navy Gazette*, 25 July 1914, pp. 682–683.

[165] Kerr, *Land, Sea and Air*, pp. 195–196.

[166] Urossow, chargé, Athens, to Sazonov, 24 June 1914, *Int. Bez.*, 1st series, III, no. 352, p. 307.

[167] Erskine, chargé, Athens, to Grey, 26 June 1914, *BD*, X (pt. 1), no. 291, p. 266.

[168] Jusserand to Viviani, 28 June 1914, MAE, Grèce, vol. NS-45.

month of July 1914. Djemal Pasha, apparently flirting with the French, intimated in June that he would like to attend the French annual naval maneuvers in July, and also requested French technical assistance in the inspection of the submarines ordered from Schneider as well as the training of their crews.[169] The Turks did not limit their attentions to France, for they were also interested in the Italian armored cruiser *San Marco* and destroyers built by Orlando.[170] The Italians, in turn, were alarmed that the syndicate for the reform of the Ottoman dockyards might create a naval base in the Bay of Giova or Marmaritza which lay in the zone of Anatolia they desired for their own interests. San Giuliano realized that he could not act directly in this question. But Vickers and Armstrong, the two British firms in the syndicate, received through their subsidiaries important naval orders from the Italian government; San Giuliano thought these orders might be subordinated to an agreement concerning work at Giova and Marmaritza.[171] The Turks had also ordered eight 12-inch (30.5 cm) coastal howitzers from Krupp, and to advise on their emplacement a retired German naval officer, Vice Admiral Wilhelm Schack, who had a reputation as an expert in coastal fortifications, was brought out to Constantinople. Since the presence of a German naval officer would have risked a British protest, and with memories of the delicate Liman von Sanders affair still fresh, Admiral Schack remained incognito.[172]

The French were naturally only too happy to invite Djemal Pasha to their naval maneuvers. Maurice Bompard, ambassador at Constantinople, advised the Quai d'Orsay on the personal flatteries upon which the Turkish Minister of Marine was supposed to place great importance. He also hinted that the Turks might order more submarines to compensate for reports the Greeks were planning to add an additional four from Germany.[173] While the French fêted their Turkish guest, the shipbuilding consortium was engaged in a fierce struggle to win the Greek submarine order.[174]

[169] Bompard to Minister of Foreign Affairs, 4 and 8 June 1914, MAE, Turquie-Marine, vol. III.

[170] Report of captain of *Archimede*, 28 June 1914, USM, cartella 318/2.

[171] San Giuliano to Millo, 1 June 1914, *ibid.*, cartella 2390/12.

[172] Report by Austrian military attaché, Constantinople, 27 May 1914, copy in OK/MS-X-4/1, 1914.

[173] Minister of Foreign Affairs to Bompard, 25 June 1914, MAE, Turquie-Marine, vol. III; Bompard to Minister of Foreign Affairs, 1 July 1914, *ibid.*; Djemal Pasha, *Memories,* pp. 103–104.

[174] Deville to Minister of Foreign Affairs, 8 June 1914, MAE, Grèce, vol. NS-45; Minister of Foreign Affairs to Deville, 11 June 1914, *ibid.*; Deville to Minister of Foreign Affairs, 13 June 1914, *ibid.*, and 1 July 1914, vol. NS-46; unsigned memorandum of a visit by a representative of Schneider, 23 July 1914, *ibid.*; Halgouët to Minister of Foreign Affairs, 28 July 1914, *ibid.*

Krupp was reported to be ready to sell the Greeks four submarines close to completion, but apparently tried to link the sale to an order of four destroyers from Schichau, while Admiral Kerr, at least according to Schneider's representative in Athens, was pressing for Vickers.[175] The World War appears to have broken out before a Greek decision about the submarines could be reached.

When war broke out most of the warships building for foreign powers in British or continental yards were appropriated by the respective governments for their own navies. A Turkish crew had actually arrived in England to bring out the dreadnoughts, but at the last moment the ships were requisitioned by the Admiralty to the "mental anguish" of Djemal Pasha and the great relief of the Russians.[176] This precaution was even wiser than the Admiralty might have imagined for the Turkish government had actually proposed to send the *Sultan Osman* to a German port and the Germans accepted the offer.[177] The news of the British action must have been even more welcome to the Greeks, although it will always remain doubtful how useful the ships might actually have been to the Turks in the restricted waters of the Aegean, and with the great lack of trained personnel in the Ottoman navy.

Thus the Balkan naval race became merged into the great European conflict. The numbers of ships involved in this rivalry were never large, but the race tended to make up in heat whatever it may have lacked in scope.

[175] Deville to Minister of Foreign Affairs, 13 June 1914, *ibid.*, vol. NS-45; note from Schneider, 30 June 1914, *ibid.*

[176] Churchill, *The World Crisis*, I, 209; Djemal Pasha, *Memories*, p. 117; Scott, *Vickers—A History*, pp. 110–111; Sazonov to Benckendorff, 30 July 1914, *Int. Bez.*, 1st series, V, no. 281, p. 195; Benckendorff to Sazonov, 1 Aug. 1914, *ibid.*, no. 399, p. 254.

[177] Ulrich Trumpener, *Germany and the Ottoman Empire 1914–1918* (Princeton, 1968), p. 24.

XII

The Anticlimax of War

The growth of the K.u.K. Kriegsmarine with its powerful dreadnoughts was one of the most unsettling factors in the Mediterranean in the decade preceding the outbreak of the First World War. This was particularly true from the British point of view, and the Admiralty realized in 1912 that the old pre-dreadnoughts based on Malta would no longer suffice. By July 1914 three of the first four Austrian dreadnoughts were in service. In May of that year, warships of the British Mediterranean Fleet visited Austro-Hungarian ports, and shortly afterwards an Austrian squadron visited Malta. The triple-gunned turrets of the Austrian dreadnoughts, as well as their cleanliness, particularly impressed the British officers, although the Austrians were generally regarded as still somewhat inexperienced.[1] Surprisingly, this exchange of courtesies between men shortly to become enemies has been little noticed, when compared, say, to a similar meeting between German and British forces at Kiel which occurred a short time later. In both cases the men and ships were to be put to the stern test of war far earlier than many supposed in those quieter days.

For the K.u.K. Kriegsmarine the outbreak of war proved almost anticlimactic. The anticipated advance southward to Sicilian waters and union with the Italian fleet for a decisive naval battle with the British and French naval forces in the Mediterranean never occurred. With the Italian decision to remain neutral the elaborate preparations which grew out of the Triple Alliance naval convention collapsed like a house of cards. At the same time Admiral Haus lost his opportunity to rank in naval history as another Nelson or Tegetthoff, or perhaps a Villeneuve. Instead of forming part of a combined fleet which equaled the combined British and French, the Austrian fleet was faced by an overwhelming force. In the hectic days

[1] Conversation with Vice Admiral R. D. Oliver, 26 Sept. 1963.

following the Austrian declaration of war on Serbia, during which the conflict expanded to include the other powers, a plan was put forward to send the Austrian fleet to Constantinople where, instead of being overwhelmed or bottled-up in the Adriatic, it might yet do useful work in the Black Sea. The scheme appears to have originated with Rear Admiral Erwin Raisp Edler von Caliga who was attached to the army high command as naval representative, and who made his proposal on August 4. The Dual Monarchy was not yet at war with either France or England, and Conrad told Graf Alexander Hoyos of the Foreign Ministry that such a declaration of war ought to be dependent on the fleet's reaching the Straits. He was anxious to avoid a state of war with France as long as possible.[2]

Haus, however, threw cold water on the plan from the very beginning. He did not think it could be executed without the guarantee of a base and coal stocks; the fleet had to be assured that it would not be attacked by overwhelming strength en route to the Straits; and if a large fleet train had to accompany it speed would be greatly reduced. Moreover, the state of the navy's mobilization on August 5 did not permit such an expedition. This was very disappointing news for Berchtold, who thought the appearance of the Austrian fleet in the Black Sea would have a decided effect on the attitude of Rumania and Bulgaria during the crisis.[3]

The German Admiralstab were anxious for Austrian support for the *Goeben* and *Breslau* which were in a precarious position in the Mediterranean. Again, Haus declined to take the Austrian fleet to Messina where the Mittelmeerdivision was reported blockaded, on the grounds that the German ships were faster than both their opponents and the Austrian fleet, and that Messina was closer to the French fleet than it was to Pola. On the evening of August 6 the Germans reported that the Mittelmeerdivision would attempt to break out and requested that the Austrian fleet be sent south to support the maneuver. The reluctant Haus was directly ordered to comply. The Marinekommandant with the first division and cruiser flotilla advanced to meet the Germans in Austria's southernmost territorial waters, but on receipt of information that the *Goeben* and her consort were heading for the Straits instead of the Adriatic, the Austrian force returned to Pola.[4]

---

[2] Conrad, *Aus meiner Dienstzeit*, IV, 174, 178, 181–182. Austria declared war on Serbia July 28, and on Russia August 6. Germany declared war on Russia August 1 and on France August 3. Italy's declaration of neutrality was on August 2. Although Great Britain declared war on Germany August 4, the British and French did not declare war on Austria until August 12.

[3] Conrad, *Aus meiner Dienstzeit*, IV, 178–179.

[4] *Ibid.*, pp. 180, 184, 190.

The Germans requested on August 7 that the Austrian fleet join the *Goeben* in steaming for the Dardanelles, and in the days that followed Kaiser Wilhelm, the representatives of the Admiralstab in Vienna, and Berchtold along with the Austrian Foreign Ministry energetically argued in favor of the plan, which Haus insisted was not feasible.[5] Haus also declined a German compromise suggestion which would have involved sending to Constantinople a few second-line Austrian ships or perhaps merely a pair of cruisers.[6] As a layman in marine matters Conrad was obliged to follow Haus. Moreover, he realized that behind the Marinekommandant's technical objections lay what was probably the strongest of the reasons for not sending the Austrian fleet out of the Adriatic. This was of course an intense suspicion in regard to the future attitude of Italy.[7] In a private letter to Kailer, his representative in Vienna, Haus admitted early in September that as long as the possibility existed Italy would declare against them, he held it to be his first obligation to keep the Austrian fleet intact for the decisive battle against this their most dangerous enemy.[8]

It will always remain debatable if when the idea of sending the fleet to Constantinople first came up on August 4–5 the operation could actually have been carried out. With reasonable luck and promptness the Austrians might well have been able to do it. The British Mediterranean Fleet was preoccupied with the *Goeben* and *Breslau*, and with only three battle cruisers it was weaker than the Austrian fleet with its first-line strength of three "Viribus Unitis" class dreadnoughts and three semi-dreadnought "Radetzkys." Moreover the British Mediterranean Commander-in-Chief had been ordered to avoid being brought to action against superior forces in the early stages of a war except in a general engagement in which the French were taking part, and his first task was to assist the French in their transport.[9] Lapeyrère with the much larger French fleet was primarily concerned with securing the North African convoys from the menace of the *Goeben* and *Breslau* until August 8, and did not concentrate French forces at Malta until August 13. The combined Anglo-French forces did not enter the Adriatic to break the Austrian blockade of Montenegro until August

[5] *Ibid.*, pp. 186, 189–190, 195, 205–206; Fregattenkapitän von Freyberg, "Aufzeichnungen des Marineattachés in Wien in der Zeit vom 5–15 August 1914," 17 Oct. 1914, GFM 26, reel 94, frames 184, 188–190.

[6] *Ibid.*, frame 190; Conrad, *Aus meiner Dienstzeit*, IV, 206.

[7] *Ibid.*, p. 205; Freyberg, "Aufzeichnungen des Marineattachés in Wien," GFM 26, reel 94, frame 190.

[8] Haus to Kailer, 6 Sept. 1914, Kriegsarchiv, Nachlass Kailer, B/242. See also Haus, "Promemoria über die Kriegslage in der Adria," 24 Oct. 1914, reproduced in Conrad, *Aus meiner Dienstzeit*, V, 304–305.

[9] Corbett, *Naval Operations*, I, 34; Sir A. Berkeley Milne, *The Flight of the 'Goeben' and the 'Breslau'* (London, n.d. [1921]), pp. 38–40.

15.[10] Much would naturally have depended on the speed and efficiency of the Austrian mobilization, and undoubtedly the technical problems involved in maintaining the fleet at Constantinople would have been great. One can never know what effect vigorous maritime action against Russia by powerful Austrian, German, and Turkish naval forces in the Black Sea would have had on the conduct of the war, although the possibility of the Austrian fleet passing the Dardanelles had obviously worried the Russian Admiralty staff before the war. A month after the outbreak of the war the Russians were still afraid of such an Austrian action, although Churchill considered their fears "baseless." [11]

The Germans tended to be rather bitter, or at their most charitable merely sarcastic, over the Austrian attitude in naval affairs.[12] Haus, in turn, considered the Germans completely blind to the Austrian situation, and spoke of the requests to send the fleet or part of it to Constantinople as incredible, frankly absurd, or nonsense.[13] Of course Haus's concern about Italy was justified. The Italian dreadnoughts, pre-dreadnoughts, cruisers, and destroyers did not even have to raise steam. The mere fact of their presence at Taranto or La Spezia closed the Mediterranean to the K.u.K. Kriegsmarine and confined it to the Adriatic. Only with the active support of the Italians could the Austro-Hungarian fleet think of challenging the British and French at sea. Italian neutrality was not enough, even if a fortuitous chain of events gave the Austrians a momentary advantage in the eastern Mediterranean. Austro-Italian relations being what they were, the K.u.K. Kriegsmarine had always to remain compact and ready to sail against its former ally.

The Italian fleet in 1914 was also the major Mediterranean uncertainty for the British and French navies, particularly the French with their primary interest in this sea. The other Mediterranean sea powers were minor in comparison. Spanish naval strength was apt to remain limited for many years although Spanish bases could be a valuable support. Greece and Turkey, however noisy and explosive their naval race, were likely to remain more a nuisance than a threat for the major fleets, and at any rate might tend to counterbalance each other in any line-up of the major powers. The distance of Germany from the Mediterranean and the geographi-

---

[10] Corbett, *Naval Operations*, I, 84–85; Thomazi, *La Guerre navale dans l'Adriatique*, pp. 37–38.

[11] Note by Russian ambassador, 5 Sept. 1914; Minute by Churchill, 13 Sept. 1914, Adm 137, vol. 880.

[12] Souchon, "La Percée de S.M.S. 'Goeben' et 'Breslau'," p. 42; Tirpitz, *My Memoirs*, I, 236, II, 82, 299.

[13] Haus to Kailer, 22 Oct. 1914, Nachlass Kailer, B/242.

cal position of Great Britain athwart her line of communications severely limited any activity by a major portion of the German fleet in this area even in a situation where the British remained neutral. The role of the Russian fleet in the Mediterranean was potentially much larger but not likely to be of any importance for many years, and even then surrounded by numerous qualifications. But the Italian navy, with three dreadnoughts in service by July 1914, another three under construction, the powerful quartet of "Caracciolos" to follow, and its older pre-dreadnoughts and numerous smaller units, was definitely a force to be reckoned with. By itself it was clearly overshadowed by the French fleet. Joined to the Austrian fleet the situation was completely changed, and command of the sea in the Mediterranean was an open question.[14] Moreover the "Caracciolos" along with the Austrian "Ersatz Monarchs" were more powerful, at least on paper, than the oldest or first-generation dreadnoughts which the Admiralty hoped to be able to spare for the Mediterranean starting in 1915.

The French were of course fully prepared to face the Italian navy as an enemy. This was the contingency toward which Lapeyrère had worked so hard in preparation, and even an Austro-Italian combination seemed to hold no terrors for this vigorous partisan of the offensive. The French navy believed itself to have an advantage in training and material over the Italians. (However, both the Austrians and Italians tended to believe the same of their own forces in regard to the French.) In their war plans both France and England seemed to concentrate on Italy as the weakest link in the Triple Alliance, a strategy which had its reflection in World War II. Yet there can be little doubt that Italy's entry into the war on the side of Germany and Austria in August 1914 would have enormously complicated the situation for the Entente. The French considered that their fleet with its unity of command would have an inherent advantage over the potential enemy fleet composed of disparate elements. There is much truth in this, but the French, on the other hand, were divided and hesitating in their own strategy because of the unresolved question of the North African convoys. The resulting delay and fumbling would probably have permitted the Austrians and Italians to join their forces as planned. The plans for Anglo-French cooperation were equally hazy. By British design, the commanders of each nation's Mediterranean naval forces had not been in contact before the outbreak of the war. Milne's difficulty in establishing

[14] Not surprisingly, the importance of the Italian navy in the summer of 1914 has been stressed by both the Austrian and Italian official historians. See Ufficio Storico, *La Marina italiana*, I, 181f; H. Sokol, "Einige nachträgliche Betrachtungen über Italiens Bedeutung für den Dreibund in Seekriege," *Marine Rundschau*, Jan. 1928, pp. 1–12.

radio contact with the French on Great Britain's entry into the war and the circumstances surrounding the escape of the *Goeben* and the *Breslau* to the Dardanelles do little to inspire confidence in the effectiveness of the planned cooperation.[15]

Had Italy entered the war on the Austro-German side one thing is fairly certain. A great naval battle would have occurred in the Mediterranean, probably in the Tyrrhenian. Both sides planned for it, and there would have been no great disparity between the opposing forces to mitigate against it as was the case in the North Sea. The forces would have been fairly evenly balanced although far more heterogeneous than those which later fought at Jutland because of the larger proportion of pre-dreadnoughts which each side would have used.[16] Some of the dreadnoughts would also have been recently commissioned ships. Consequently their crews would not have had time to work up to full efficiency, especially in gunnery. A Mediterranean encounter might have been relatively more decisive than Jutland, for at this stage of the war the opposing commanders might not have been as obsessed with previously prepared minefields or submarine ambushes, at least in the open sea, as they later were, and might therefore have pressed more recklessly for a decision. The smaller size of the fleets and the difference in climatic conditions between the North Sea and the Mediterranean might also have enhanced control by each Commander-in-Chief. The effect of a naval victory by either side in a Mediterranean Jutland is a question which must always remain unanswered.

The fact that the Triple Alliance naval convention proved meaningless in the final crisis does not alter the very considerable influence both the Italian and Austro-Hungarian fleets had by their very existence on the British and French naval staffs. In the late nineteenth century the Royal Navy had as its standard the combined fleets of France and Russia, while garrisons in the Mediterranean were small since the real safety of British possessions obviously rested on command of the sea. After the turn of the century the situation changed drastically. Of paramount importance was the growth of the German navy and Anglo-German rivalry. This led to a steady reduction both in quantity and quality of the British force in the Mediterranean, but the evolution of British and French relations from

[15] Corbett, *Naval Operations*, I, 35f; Milne, *Flight of the 'Goeben,'* pp. 48, 58.

[16] Lapeyrère's forces would probably have lacked the dreadnoughts *France* and *Paris*. The French would therefore have had only the *Jean Bart* and *Courbet* to oppose three Austrian and three Italian dreadnoughts, plus the *Goeben*. Under these circumstances the big guns of the three British battle cruisers would have furnished badly needed support. Thomazi, *La Guerre navale dans l'Adriatique*, p. 15.

rivalry to friendship made this acceptable. Initially the navies of Germany's Mediterranean allies were hardly considered. By 1912 this was no longer possible. But the failure of the Haldane mission and the pending German *novelle* meant no dreadnoughts could be spared from the North Sea. Churchill was led to the brutally logical step of withdrawing all major capital ships from the Mediterranean. This was, however, far too drastic for both the Foreign Office and the War Office, and the powerful opposition of influential parties in England forced the First Lord to back down somewhat and agree to the maintenance of a one-power standard (excluding France) in the Mediterranean, provided a reasonable margin of superiority over Germany could be maintained in home waters. But what the Admiralty promised and what the Admiralty were actually able to accomplish were different matters, for by the end of 1912 it was becoming difficult to match even the Austrian fleet in the Mediterranean. However reluctant they were to admit it, naval building on the part of Austria and Italy was almost forcing the British to rely on the French in the Mediterranean.

The French navy felt the challenge of Italy and Austria as keenly as Britain did that of Germany. Traditionally the world's second naval power, the French saw themselves pushed down the scale by the building programs of new rivals. By the turn of the century the French navy could think of an offensive against the Germans in the north or against Italy in the south, but not both at the same time. Within a few years the rapid growth of the German navy forced the French into a Mediterranean concentration. In 1907 the French naval staff favored this even in the event of a war against Germany alone lest an isolated squadron in the north be forced by public opinion to steam out to an unequal struggle; by 1912 there was no thought of steaming north even after a concentration. The North Sea was not vital to France; the Mediterranean was, if only to assure the transport of badly needed troops from North Africa in the event of mobilization. Above all lay a deep and fundamental mistrust of Italy, a colonial rival of France since the 1880's and an ally of Germany. In the early years of the twentieth century the French navy continued to suffer from the vicissitudes of politics and then, just when it seemed on the road to recovery with a clear program, it was shaken once again by the nightmarish problem of unstable powder. At the same time Austrian and Italian naval construction threatened that very control of the Mediterranean which the French had deemed so essential. The celebrated decision in 1912 to transfer the third squadron from Brest to Toulon was therefore dictated by logic, not by prior agreement with the British as so many assumed. The same was of course true of Churchill's actions. Moreover, since France's newest battleships were based on Toulon as soon as they entered service, a de facto Mediterranean concentration had been achieved the year before.

The French navy's problem was complicated by the appearance of the small but powerful German Mittelmeerdivision at the end of 1912. Nor was the problem simplified by the very nature of the Anglo-French Entente, as opposed to a formal alliance, and the desire of the Admiralty to deliberately keep Mediterranean plans vague and based on strategic instead of tactical cooperation with the French. The British refused to specify any permanent fixed Mediterranean standard, although they promised to try and maintain a force able to deal with the Austrian fleet if it emerged from the Adriatic. However the Admiralty did not hesitate to admit they regarded the north as the decisive theater and reserved the right to withdraw from the Mediterranean whatever was necessary to assure superiority here. This was only logical but obviously it bothered the French. Moreover any competent naval officer could see that the British force in the Mediterranean in 1914 was not equal to even a one-power standard, and Churchill admitted there would not be any capital ships available to reinforce it until the autumn of 1915. It is hardly surprising that by the outbreak of the war the French had accelerated their naval program and that the EMG were seeking an increase in capital ships in order to meet the challenge. Lapeyrère's plans in 1914 were mainly concerned with destroying the Italian fleet rather than the Austrian, but this was to be accomplished if possible before a union between the two had been achieved. There was, however, a fundamental disagreement between the French army and navy over the relative priority of a naval offensive and transport of the troops from North Africa. At the same time the big guns and relatively high speed of the *Goeben* were a major source of concern.

Obviously the growth of the Austrian and Italian fleets was a disturbing development. This was perhaps less true of the Italian navy, for Italy had ever since her unification maintained a relatively powerful naval force. Italy was a major rival of the French, but a traditional rival and one over which the French could with a reasonable effort maintain a comfortable margin of superiority. The really disturbing element in the Mediterranean balance of power was the Austro-Hungarian fleet. This was a completely new factor for the British and the French and had not entered their calculations in the past; at the most the K.u.K. Kriegsmarine had been considered solely a matter of concern for Italy in the Adriatic. Austro-Hungarian naval activity was therefore one of the most interesting naval developments of the twentieth century.

Initially the Austrian objectives were defensive: protection of the Habsburg Empire's Adriatic coast, with Italy as the most likely aggressor. To achieve this the advance of naval technology necessitated bigger and better warships: small coast defense ships could be pounded to pieces by faster and distant dreadnoughts. Admiral Montecuccoli's goal had been sixteen modern battleships or dreadnoughts by 1920. The internal situation of the Dual Monarchy—its financial problems and above all the recalcitrance of the Hungarians—would probably have prevented realization of this program, but by 1918 the fleet would probably have had eleven in service. This was more than enough to worry the Italians whose naval staff had recommended a 2:1 superiority over Austria as late as 1908. Such superiority became completely out of the question, especially after problems in the delivery of armor plate and heavy cannon caused enough delay in the Italian building program by 1913 to give the Austrians a slight lead in dreadnoughts. Italy would have caught up and moved ahead in 1915, but Admiral Thaon di Revel set a more realistic margin of superiority in 1913. The Italian fleet was to be four-thirds that of Austria and equal to 60 percent of the French fleet. Italy's objective was to remain the second Mediterranean power.

Both the Austrian and Italian fleets were initially aimed primarily against each other. Naval construction by one inevitably led to naval construction by the other. But as their fleets grew both sides eventually saw the same prospect. Alone neither was a match for France; together they might hope to win control of the Mediterranean. The prospect was naturally more attractive to the Italians who were rivals of the French, and who would be far more exposed at sea in the event of war, a vulnerability that only increased with the acquisition of Libya in 1911–12. To achieve Austrian naval support the Italians were even willing to agree, at least temporarily, to an Austrian Commander-in-Chief for combined operations. As long as Italy remained a member of the Triple Alliance such thinking and planning was only prudent. The resulting combination made the Mediterranean balance of power a close one as long as England's major concern was the North Sea. However, the nature of Austro-Italian relations made it a very unstable one too. The close balance also enhanced the importance of other factors: the Greek-Turkish naval race; the renascent Spanish fleet; the potential of Russia; and even the fate of the South American battleships building in England or the United States, whose appearance in the Mediterranean might suffice to tip the delicate balance.

All the Mediterranean naval powers prepared for contingencies that never presented themselves. They could not wisely have acted in any other way. For the French and British there was the possibility that Italy would be an opponent. If she was their naval supremacy would have been jeopardized; if she remained neutral or became an ally it would have been assured. But the Anglo-French situation was relatively simpler than that of the Austrians and the Italians. At least Milne and Lapeyrère could be certain they were not likely to be fighting each other in the near future. Haus and Revel had no such assurance and had to plan at the same time for cooperation with or war against each other. The Austrians were in the less advantageous position for their fleet was smaller than, but not hopelessly inferior to, the Italians. If Italy remained neutral they were far weaker than the French, and if Italy joined France and Great Britain in a war against Austria the K.u.K. Kriegsmarine was doomed to remain secure in its Adriatic bases except for hit and run raids. The development of the submarine helped to improve the situation somewhat for the Austrians by making the Adriatic unsafe for the large units of their enemies. Ironically, this weapon appears to have received far less attention in Austria before the war than it did in France, Great Britain, and Italy. Only an alliance with Italy gave the K.u.K. Kriegsmarine any hope of a significant role outside the Adriatic. The Italian fleet had at least some hope of naval victory whatever side the Italian government chose, although Italy's naval peril would naturally have been much greater if she chose to side with Austria and Germany. The Mediterranean naval situation before the First World War was therefore extremely unstable, and there were numerous unresolved questions when the war broke out. The Italian declaration of neutrality on August 2 resolved one of the largest.

The actual naval war in the Mediterranean was far different from the struggle that had been anticipated. The French found themselves in a somewhat similar position to the British in the North Sea, that is, faced by an enemy they could not reach. A naval convention was signed in London August 6 giving the French general direction of the war in the Mediterranean, although after the hoped-for destruction of the *Goeben* and *Breslau* the British battle cruisers might be withdrawn and the British force left under French orders reduced to one or two armored cruisers, four light cruisers, and eighteen destroyers.[17] The escape of the German ships necessitated detaching a pair of battle cruisers and a light cruiser to mask the Dardanelles. Once hostilities between the Entente and Austria-Hun-

---

[17] *Ibid.*, pp. 35–36; Laurens, *Le Commandement naval en Méditerranée*, pp. 48–51.

gary formally opened Lapeyrère responded with a characteristic offensive sweep into the Adriatic to raise the Austrian blockade of the Montenegrin coast and catch some of the Austrian fleet. In this Lapeyrère was to be disappointed, for all he and the British division which accompanied him succeeded in snaring was the small cruiser *Zenta* which was overwhelmed on August 16. Operations in the Adriatic became a French affair after the British division left for the Dardanelles. Their blockade of the Straits of Otranto was hampered by the 300-mile distance of Malta, the nearest available base. In September the French considered an expedition to capture Cattaro and in October they actually sent two siege batteries to assist the Montenegrins on Mount Lovčen. However, less than a week after the guns opened fire they were forced to evacuate their positions, largely by the counterfire of the Austrian battleship *Radetzky* which outranged them. The French also could not spare the 20,000 men considered necessary for an expedition. So Cattaro was left to become an important submarine base for the Austrians and Germans later in the war.[18]

Despite the large French naval superiority Lapeyrère found it difficult to protect the port of Antivari, Montenegro's outlet to the sea, from Austrian raids. Cattaro was only 35 miles away from Antivari; it was 200 miles from Antivari to the Ionian islands and 450 miles to Malta. Moreover the small number of Austrian submarines began to make the Adriatic highly dangerous for the large French armored cruisers which they attacked, unsuccessfully, in October and November. French submarines were to find few targets and had little luck. Eventually the Austrians scored when the *U-12* torpedoed the French flagship *Jean Bart* on December 21. Lapeyrère had been covering supply ships bound for Antivari. The *Jean Bart* managed to reach Malta for repairs, but major French warships were no longer risked in the Adriatic. Even the distant blockade of the Straits of Otranto became dangerous for large ships and on the night of April 26–27, 1915, the armored cruiser *Léon Gambetta* was sunk with heavy loss of life by the submarine *U-5*.

Italy's entry into the war on the Allied side failed significantly to improve Lapeyrère's position. The British had become preoccupied with the Gallipoli campaign early in the year. And the threat of submarines and mines meant that the overwhelming Allied naval superiority in capital ships could not prudently be risked in the relatively narrow waters of the Adriatic where the Austrian surface ships remained safely in port save for hit and run raids. By April of 1915 a form of stalemate existed, for if the

[18] Sokol, *Österreich-Ungarns Seekrieg*, pp. 90–96; Thomazi, *La Guerre navale dans l'Adriatique*, pp. 52–53, 57.

French could not operate in the Adriatic, the Austrian fleet was not likely to come out in force. Italy as an active participant in the war instead of a neutral actually complicated matters for the British and French for they immediately became involved in the problem of defending her exposed Adriatic coast. Before the war Italian naval planning had been dominated by what the Italians considered the great disadvantage geography had imposed on them compared to the Austrians. Their side of the Adriatic was open and exposed, the Austrian side highly irregular and partially sheltered by a screen of islands. The British and French found themselves obligated to provide reinforcements for the Italians whose margin of superiority over the Austrians still left something to be desired.[19]

At first Lapeyrère welcomed the prospect of the use of Italian bases for his light craft.[20] Once again, however, the actual results were somewhat disappointing, for the negotiations which took place in Paris for the naval convention of May 10, which complemented the Treaty of London, proved to be extremely difficult.[21] The Italians, perhaps understandably, insisted on command in the Adriatic. This was something which the French absolutely refused to concede, not surprisingly, since Lapeyrère was senior to his Italian counterpart and had the larger fleet. Both the British and French also disagreed with the Italian plan of operations. The fact that both sides had only recently planned to fight each other did not help matters. In the end four old British battleships and four light cruisers, drawn from the Dardanelles where they were to be replaced by corresponding French ships, as well as twelve French destroyers were placed under the orders of the Italian Commander-in-Chief. In the absence of agreement between the French and Italians, provision for joint operations by the main battle fleets should the Austrians ever come out in force remained ambiguous on the question of command.[22] The main French dreadnoughts and semi-dreadnoughts at Malta, unlike the older battleships which did gallant work at the Dardanelles, became a reserve force, absorbing precious destroyers for their defense, but basically without immediate prospects of serious employment. The same came to be true for the Italian dreadnoughts at Taranto.

---

[19] Memorandum by Churchill, 14 Apr. 1915, Adm 137, vol. 1088, p. 252; fourth section, EMG, "Considerations sur les conséquences de la cooperation Italienne dans les Operations Maritimes en Méditerranée," n.d. [13 Apr. 1915], AMF, carton Es-9.

[20] Lapeyrère to Minister of Marine, 23 Apr. 1915, *ibid.*

[21] See my "The Anglo-French-Italian Naval Convention of 1915," *The Historical Journal,* 13.1 (Mar. 1970): 106–129. The Italian side of the negotiations is covered in great detail by Mariano Gabriele, "La Convenzione navale italo-franco-britannica del 10 maggio 1915," *Nuova Antologia,* 493–494. 1972–1973 (April–May 1965).

[22] Thomazi, *La Guerre navale dans l'Adriatique,* pp. 82f; Corbett, *Naval Operations,* II, 395–396; Marder, *Dreadnought to Scapa Flow,* II, 329f.

A thorough analysis of the advantages and disadvantages of Italy's participation in the war on the Allied side is impossible here and must natually take into account the effects on land operations, but it is hard to escape the conclusion that from a strictly naval point of view August 1914 rather than May 1915 was really the decisive month. It was Italy's decision to remain neutral in 1914 that actually assured Anglo-French naval superiority in the Mediterranean; her entry into the war in 1915 merely reinforced a superiority that already existed.

Appendix

Bibliography

Index

Warships of the Mediterranean Powers

Dagger (†) indicates battle cruiser; asterisk (*) indicates armored cruiser (or French armored cruiser normally assigned to the Mediterranean).

	Laid down	Completed [a]	Displacement (tons)	Designed speed (knots)	Main armament		Maximum armor (belt)	Maximum armor (turrets)
Austria-Hungary								
"Ersatz Monarchs" (4) [b]			24,560	21	10	13.8"	12.2"	11"
					14	5.9"		
Viribus Unitis	July 1910	Oct. 1912	20,000	20.5	12	12"	11"	11"
Tegetthoff	Sept. 1910	July 1913			12	5.9"		
Prinz Eugen	Jan. 1912	July 1914						
Szent Istvan	Jan. 1912	Nov. 1915						
Radetzky	Nov. 1907	Jan. 1911	14,500	20.5	4	12"	9"	9.8"
Erz. Franz Ferdinand	Sept. 1907	June 1910			8	9.4"		
Zrinyi	Jan. 1909	Sept. 1911			20	3.9"		
Erzherzog Karl	July 1902	June 1906	10,600	20.5	4	9.4"	8.3"	9.4"
Erzherzog Friedrich	Oct. 1902	Jan. 1907			12	7.5"		
Erz. Ferdinand Max	Mar. 1904	Dec. 1907						
Habsburg	Mar. 1899	Dec. 1902	8,300	20	3	9.4"	8.7"	8.3"
Arpad	June 1899	June 1903			12	5.9"		
Babenberg	Jan. 1901	May 1904						

Ship								
Monarch	July 1893	May 1898	5,600	17	4	9.4″	10.7″	9.8″
Wien	Feb. 1893	May 1897			6	5.9″		
Budapest	Feb. 1893	May 1898						
* *Sankt Georg*	Mar. 1901	July 1905	7,400	21	2	9.4″	6.5″	5″
					5	7.5″		
* *Kaiser Karl VI*	July 1896	May 1900	6,265	20	2	9.4″	8.5″	8″
					8	5.9″		
France								
Lyon	Jan. 1915ᵉ		29,600	21	16	13.4″	at least that of	
Lille	Jan. 1915ᵉ				24	5.5″	the *Normandie*	
Tourville	Apr. 1915ᵉ							
Duquesne	Apr. 1915ᵉ							
Normandie	Apr. 1913	Mar. 1916ᵈ	25,230	21	12	13.4″	11.8″	13.4″
Languedoc	Apr. 1913	Mar. 1916ᵈ			24	5.5″		
Gascogne	Oct. 1913	June 1917ᵈ						
Flandre	Oct. 1913	June 1917ᵈ						
Béarn	Jan. 1914	June 1917ᵈ						
Bretagne	July 1912	Sept. 1915	23,540	20.5	10	13.4″	10.7″	13.4″
Provence	June 1912	June 1915			22	5.5″		
Lorraine	Nov. 1912	July 1916						
Courbet	Sept. 1910	June 1913	23,470	20.5	12	12″	10.7″	13.4″
Jean Bart	Nov. 1910	Aug. 1913			22	5.5″		
France	Nov. 1911	Aug. 1914						
Paris	Nov. 1911	Aug. 1914						

	Laid down	Completed	Displacement (tons)	Designed speed (knots)	Main armament	Maximum armor (belt)	Maximum armor (turrets)
Danton	Feb. 1908	Mar. 1911	18,027	19.25	4 12″	10.7″	11.8″
Mirabeau	May 1908	June 1911			12 9.4″		
Voltaire	July 1907	May 1911					
Diderot	Oct. 1907	Apr. 1911					
Condorcet	Aug. 1907	June 1911					
Vergniaud	July 1908	Sept. 1911					
Démocratie	Jan. 1903	July 1908	14,865	18	4 12″	11″	12.6″
Justice	May 1902	Dec. 1907			10 7.6″		
Vérité	May 1902	July 1908					
Liberté [e]	May 1902	Feb. 1908					
République	Feb. 1901	Apr. 1907	14,865	18	4 12″	11″	12.6″
Patrie	Dec. 1901	June 1907			18 6.4″		
Suffren	Jan. 1898	1903	12,750	18	4 12″	11.8″	11.8″
					10 6.4″		
					8 3.9″		
Iéna [f]	June 1897	1901	12,052		4 12″	12.6″	11.8″
					8 6.4″		
					8 3.9″		
Gaulois	Jan. 1894	1899	11,260	18	4 12″	15.75″	10.7″
Charlemagne	July 1894	1899			10 5.5″		
St. Louis	Mar. 1895	1900			8 3.9″		

Ship								
Henri IV[g]	July 1897	1903	9,000	17.5	2 7	10.8" 5.5"	11"	9.8"
Jauréguiberry	Nov. 1891	1897	11,882	18	2 2 8	12" 10.8" 5.5"	17.7"	14.6"
Charles Martel *Carnot*	1891 Aug. 1891	1897 1896	11,900 12,150	18	2 2 8	12" 10.8" 5.5"	17.7"	14.6"
Masséna *Bouvet*	1892 Jan. 1893	1898 1898	11,900 12,200	18	2 2 8 8	12" 10.8" 5.5" 3.9"	17.7" 15.75"	14.6" 14.6"
* *Edgar Quinet* * *Waldeck Rousseau*	Nov. 1905 June 1906	1910 1910	14,000	23	14	7.6"	6.7"	5.9"
* *Ernest Renan*	Oct. 1903	1908	13,644	23	4 12	7.6" 6.4"	6.7"	7.9"
* *Jules Michelet*	June 1904	1907	12,600	23	4 12	7.6" 6.4"	6.7"	7.9"
* *Léon Gambetta* * *Jules Ferry* * *Victor Hugo*	Jan. 1901 Oct. 1901 Apr. 1903	1903 1906 1906	12,550	22	4 16	7.6" 6.4"	6.7"	7.9"
Germany (Mittelmeerdivision)								
†*Goeben*	July 1909	July 1912	25,400	28	10 10	11" 5.9"	10.7"	9.05"
Breslau[h]	Apr. 1910	May 1912	5,587	27.5	2 10	5.9" 4.1"	2.4"	2"

	Laid down	Completed	Displacement (tons)	Designed speed (knots)	Main armament		Maximum armor (belt)	Maximum armor (turrets)
Great Britain [1]								
King Edward VII	Mar. 1902	Feb. 1905	16,350	18.5	4	12"	9"	12"
Zealandia	Feb. 1903	June 1905			4	9.2"		
Hibernia	Jan. 1904	Jan. 1907			10	6"		
Dominion	May 1902	July 1905						
Commonwealth	June 1902	Mar. 1905						
Britannia	Feb. 1904	Sept. 1906						
Africa	Jan. 1904	Nov. 1906						
Hindustan	Oct. 1902	July 1905						
Swiftsure	Feb. 1902	June 1904	11,800	19	4	10"	7"	10"
Triumph	Feb. 1902	June 1904			14	7.5"		
Duncan	July 1899	Oct. 1903	14,000	19	4	12"	7"	10"
Cornwallis	July 1899	1904			12	6"		
Exmouth	Aug. 1899	May 1903						
Russell	Mar. 1899	1903						
† Indefatigable	Feb. 1909	Feb. 1911	18,800	25	8	12"	6"	7"
					16	4"		
† Indomitable	Mar. 1906	June 1908	17,250	25	8	12"	6"	7"
† Inflexible	Feb. 1906	Oct. 1908			16	4"		
† Invincible	Apr. 1906	Mar. 1908						
* Defence	Feb. 1905	Apr. 1908	14,600	23	4	9.2"	6"	8"
					10	7.5"		

* *Warrior*	Nov. 1903	1907	13,350	23	6 9.2"; 4 7.5"	6"	7½"
* *Duke of Edinburgh*	Feb. 1903	Mar. 1906	12,590	22.8	6 9.2"; 10 6"	6"	7½"
* *Black Prince*	June 1903	Jan. 1906		23.65			7½"
* *Hampshire*	Sept. 1902	1905	10,850	22¼	4 7.5"; 6 6"	6"	5"
* *Lancaster*	Mar. 1901	1904	9,800		14 6"	4"	5"
* *Suffolk*	Mar. 1902	1904					5"
* *Good Hope*	Sept. 1899	1902	14,100	23	2 9.2"; 16 6"	6"	5"

Greece

"Lorraine class"[j]	June 1914	June 1914	23,540	22	10 13.4"; 22 5.5"	10.7"	13.4"
† *Salamis*[j]	1913		19,500	23	8 14"; 12 6"	10"	12"
Kilkis (ex *Idaho*)	May 1904	Mar. 1908	13,000	17	4 12"; 8 8"; 8 7"	9"	12"
Lemnos (ex *Mississippi*)	May 1904	Jan. 1908					12"
* *Averoff*	1907	1911	10,118	22.5	4 9.2"; 8 7.5"	8"	6½"
Psara	1888	1892 (1897)	5,000	17	3 10.8"; 5 5.9"	12"	13.7"
Spetsai	1887	1891 (1899)					
Hydra	1887	1891 (1900)					

375

Italy

	Laid down	Completed	Displacement (tons)	Designed speed (knots)	Main armament		Maximum armor (belt)	Maximum armor (turrets)
Caracciolo [k]	Oct. 1914		34,000	28	8	15"	11.8"	15.7"
Colombo [k]	1915				16	6"		
Colonna [k]	1915							
Morosini [k]	1915							
Andrea Doria	Mar. 1912	Mar. 1916	22,964	21.5	13	12"	9.8"	11"
Caio Duilio	Feb. 1912	May 1915			16	6"		
Conte di Cavour	Aug. 1910	Apr. 1915	23,088	21.5	13	12"	9.8"	11"
Leonardo da Vinci	July 1910	May 1914			18	4.7"		
Giulio Cesare	June 1910	May 1914						
Dante Alighieri	June 1909	Jan. 1913	19,500	23	12	12"	9.8"	9.8"
					20	4.7"		
Regina Elena	Mar. 1901	Sept. 1907	12,691	21	2	12"	9.8"	9.8"
Vittorio Emanuele	Sept. 1901	Aug. 1908	13,035	21	12	8"		
Roma	Sept. 1903	Dec. 1908	12,791	22				
Napoli	Oct. 1903	Dec. 1908	12,833	22				
Regina Margherita	Nov. 1898	Apr. 1904	13,427	20	4	12"	5.9"	7.9"
Benedetto Brin	Jan. 1899	Sept. 1905			4	8"		
					12	5.9"		

Emanuele Filiberto	Oct. 1893	Sept. 1901	9,800	18	4 8 8	10" 5.9" 4.7"	9.8"	9.8"
Ammiraglio di St. Bon	July 1894	Feb. 1901						
* San Giorgio	July 1905	July 1910	10,167	23.2	4 8	10" 7.5"	7.9"	7.1"
* San Marco	Jan. 1907	Feb. 1911	10,700	23.7				
* Pisa	Feb. 1905	Sept. 1909	9,832	23	4 8	10" 7.5"	7.9"	6.3"
* Amalfi	July 1905	Sept. 1909						
* Garibaldi	June 1898	Apr. 1901	7,350	19.7	1 2 14	10" 8" 6"	5.9"	5.9"
* Varese	Apr. 1898	Apr. 1901		20				
* Ferruccio	Sept. 1899	Sept. 1905		19.3				
Russia (Black Sea Fleet)								
Ekaterina II	Sept. 1912?	Oct. 1915	22,500	21	12 20	12" 5"	12"	12"
Imperatritsa Maria	July 1912	July 1915						
Imperator Alexander III	July 1912	1917						
Imperator Nikolai I [1]	Feb. 1914							
Evstafi	June 1903	1910	12,800	16	4 4 12	12" 8" 6"	9"	10"
Ivan Zlatoust	Nov. 1903	1910						
Panteleimon (ex Potemkin)	1898	1903	12,582	17	4 16	12" 6"	9"	10"
Rostislav	1893	1898	9,000	16	4 8	10" 6"	15"	12"
Tri Sviatitelia	1891	1898	12,540	18	4 10	12" 6"	16"	16"

	Laid down	Completed	Displacement (tons)	Designed speed (knots)	Main armament		Maximum armor (belt)	Maximum armor (turrets)
Georgi Pobiedonosets	1889	1896	10,250	16.5	6	12"	16"	12"
					7	6"		
Spain								
España	Dec. 1909	1913	15,700	19.5	8	12"	8"	8"
Alfonso XIII	Feb. 1910	1915			20	4"		
Jaime I	Feb. 1912	1921						
Pelayo		1890 (1897)	9,950	16	2	12.6"	16"	16"
					2	11"		
					9	5.5"		
* *Princesa de Asturias*		1902	7,000	18	2	9.4"	12"	
* *Cataluña*		1908			8	5.5"		
Turkey								
Reschadieh[m]	Aug. 1911	Aug. 1914	23,000	21	10	13.5"	12"	11"
Mehemed Fetieh ordered July 1914	ordered July 1914				16	6"		
Sultan Osman I[n]	Sept 1911	Aug. 1914	27,500	22	14	12"	9"	12"
(*ex Rio de Janiero*)					20	6"		

378

Heireddin Barbarossa (ex *Kurfürst Fried. Wilhelm*)	1890	1894	10,067	16	6	11"	15.7"	11.8"
					6	4.1"		
Torgud Reiss (ex *Weissenburg*)	1890	1894		16.5				
Messudiyeh		1876 (1902)	10,000	16	2	9.2"	12"	12"
					12	6"		

South American Dreadnoughts in Which the Mediterranean Powers Were Interested

Argentina								
Rivadavia	1910	1914	28,000	22.5	12	12"	12"	12"
Moreno	1910	1914			12	6"		
Brazil								
Minas Geraes	1907	Jan. 1910	19,281	21	12	12"	9"	12"
São Paulo	1907	July 1910			22	4.7"		
Chile								
Almirante Cochrane [c]	1913	Sept. 1915	28,000	22.75	10	14"	9"	10"
Almirante Latorre [d]	Dec. 1911				16	6"		

[a] Completion dates for Austrian ships refer to commissioning.
[b] Construction suspended because of the war.
[c] Scheduled date. Actual construction was abandoned during the war.
[d] Scheduled completion date. Construction suspended during the war and ultimately all abandoned except the *Béarn* which was completed as an aircraft carrier in 1927.

e *Liberté* destroyed by internal explosion Sept. 1911.

f *Iéna* destroyed by internal explosion Mar. 1907.

g *Henri IV* classified as coast defense battleship (*garde-côte cuirassé*).

h Scout cruiser. Her sister ship *Strassburg* and the older and smaller *Dresden* (3,600 tons) were also in the Mediterranean in 1913.

i List indicates ships employed in the Mediterranean 1912–14 rather than the Mediterranean Fleet at any particular moment.

j Work suspended during the war.

k Work suspended during the war.

l Never completed.

m *Reschadieh* completed as H.M.S. *Erin*.

n *Sultan Osman I* completed as H.M.S. *Agincourt*.

o *Almirante Cochrane* ultimately finished as aircraft carrier H.M.S. *Eagle*.

p *Almirante Latorre* completed as H.M.S. *Canada*. Returned to Chile after the war.

Sources: Data compiled primarily from Fred T. Jane, ed., *Fighting Ships, 1914* (London, 1914, reprinted 1968), supplemented by Viscount Hythe, ed., *The Naval Annual, 1912* (Portsmouth, 1912); Commandant de Balincourt, ed., *Les Flottes de combat en 1915* (Paris, 1915); B. Weyer, ed., *Taschenbuch der Kriegsflotten 1914* (Munich, 1914, reprinted 1967); Erich Gröner, *Die deutschen Kriegsschiffe, 1815–1945* (2 vols, Munich, 1966–1968); and Karl Gogg, *Österreichs Kriegsmarine, 1848–1918* (Salzburg, 1967). Most British information is based on Oscar Parkes, *British Battleships* (London, 1956), and most Italian data is based on Giorgerini and Nani, *Le Navi di linea italiane* (Rome, 1962), and *Gli incrociatori italiani* (Rome, 1964). The Kriegsarchiv, Vienna, have supplied the dates cited for Austrian ships, and Henri Le Masson provided the data on French ships.

Selected Bibliography

I. Unpublished Sources

The bulk of this study has been based on material found in the archives of Great Britain, France, Italy, and Austria. This includes staff studies; reports and memoranda by various service chiefs; the minutes, when available, of conferences between allies and the deliberations of higher councils; war plans; and the correspondence and directives of ministers and commanders. Reports by naval attachés are another important source. These might often reflect the opinion and perhaps prejudices of a single individual, but the attaché was generally an expert primarily interested in naval affairs, and frequently in a position to gather and record valuable information difficult or impossible to obtain elsewhere. In certain cases the attachés played a leading role in the drafting of the secret prewar conventions. They can also provide a healthy corrective to the dry statistics of official reports or the noncritical platitudes of certain popular naval journalists. Diplomatic dispatches form a useful supplement to the naval records, especially since this was an epoch when naval affairs were widely discussed and attracted much attention. Moreover, the diplomatic files often contain interesting reports that were not deemed of sufficient general interest to be included in the published documentary collections.

AUSTRIA-HUNGARY

The Kriegsarchiv, Vienna, is extremely rich in material on the K.u.K. Kriegsmarine for the prewar period. Most is contained in the records of the Operationskanzlei and Präsidialkanzlei of the Kriegsministeriums/Marinesektion. Here the majority of the files consulted were classified under Kriegsfalle (OK/MS-VIII), Mobilisierung (OK/MS-IX; PK/MS-II), and Fremde Macht (OK/MS-X; PK/MS-XII). Because of the great interest the heir apparent had in the navy, there are many interesting reports in the files of the Militärkanzlei des Thronfolgers Erzherzog Franz Ferdinand. Significantly there is somewhat less material on the navy in the files of the Emperor's military cabinet, the Militärkanzlei Seiner Majestät des Kaisers und Königs. Valuable supplementary information, particularly on Italy, is in the army records of the Operationsbureau des Generalstabes. There are a few interesting letters from Haus in the Nachlass Kailer (B/242), and some from Kailer in the Nachlass Haus (B/241). Unfortunately neither collection is very large.

The Haus-, Hof-, und Staatsarchiv, Vienna, contain the Protokolle, Ministerrates für gemeinsame Angelegenheiten. Those for the period 1911–1915 contain much of interest on naval affairs which was not included in the excerpts dealing with foreign policy published with the Austrian documents. In the Politische Archiv, Ministerium des Äussern, the Geheime Akten and the Berichte, Italienische Staaten, 1911–1914, contain some supplementary material but the most important documents appear to have been published. The Nachlass Franz Ferdinand, in contrast to the files of his Militärkanzlei, has little of interest about the navy.

FRANCE

The Archives Centrales de la Marine, Paris, contain a mass of material on the French navy in the prewar period. In fact, it looks as if the French never discarded a single piece of paper, for there are often several copies of the same document. Relevant material is scattered through the series BB2 (Correspondence générale, lettres envoyées), BB3 (Correspondence générale, lettres reçues), and BB4 (campagnes). Attaché and intelligence reports are in the series BB7 (marines étrangères), and the minutes of the Conseil Supérieur de la Marine are in the series BB8. There are also many important documents in the series SS (Guerre 1914–1918) including the invaluable files of the secretariat of the EMG which cover the prewar Anglo-French agreements (Carton Es-10), Franco-Russian agreements (Carton Es-11), and scattered minutes of the Conseil Supérieur de la Défense Nationale 1911–1915 (Carton Es-23). The file of minutes of the Conseil Supérieur, though incomplete, is particularly important, since—I was told at the Section Historique of the French army—the records of this important body are no longer extant for the prewar years. Lapeyrère left a few personal papers (Carton GG2-59) but unfortunately almost nothing of interest for this period. The papers of Vice Admiral Germinet (Cartons GG2-69, 69 bis) contain mostly technical material for the period when he was Mediterranean Commander-in-Chief, 1907–1908. The Bibliothèque Historique de la Marine has a number of valuable unpublished studies by student officers of the Ecole de Guerre Navale as well as some printed courses given at the school.

The Archives des Affaires Etrangères at the Ministère des Affaires Etrangères, Paris, contained valuable supplementary material in the Correspondence politique for Austria-Hungary, Germany, Great Britain, Greece, Italy, Russia, Spain, and Turkey. The most important material on the major powers has been printed in the *DDF*, but there are still many unpublished documents on the Balkan naval race. Unfortunately certain files on Franco-Spanish and Franco-Italian relations during the period 1908–1914 disappeared during World II and it has been possible only partially to reconstitute them. The Spanish files have been quite decimated, and one can be thankful that important documents were published before the war.

The Service Historique, Etat-Major de l'Armée, Château de Vincennes, holds the important minutes of the Conseil Supérieur de la Guerre, which are valuable to this study because of French mobilization plans and the transfer of the North African troops, as well as the problem of coast defense. The intelligence about Spain and attaché reports from Madrid, potentially important because of the Spanish railway question, are disappointing.

GERMANY

Copies of microfilms of captured German naval documents made at the Admiralty for Cambridge University and the University of Michigan were transferred in 1966 from the Public Record Office, London, to the Naval Historical Branch of the Ministry of Defence. Those consulted for this study (with PRO designation) are Admiralstab der Marine, Abteilung A: GFM 26, reel 68, and GFM 27, reel 19; Admiralstab der Marine, Abteilung B: GFM 26, reels 50, 51, 56, 61; and Reichsmarineamt: GFM 26, reels 90, 91, 93, and 94. GFM 26, reel 61, is particularly important for its material on the German side of the Triple Alliance naval convention. German naval plans against France for the period under consideration are in Cambridge University and University of Michigan Microfilming Project no. 2, reel 8.

GREAT BRITAIN

The Admiralty files at the Public Record Office are somewhat disappointing for the pre-1914 period. Records are often fragmentary and much of interest appears to have been weeded. Those consulted were Adm. I. (In letters), Adm. 116 (Secretary's Dept.), and Adm. 167 (Board Minutes). The logs in Adm. 53 were occasionally useful in checking movements, for example of the Admiralty yacht *Enchantress* in 1912. Admiralty Case 0091, invaluable on the question of Anglo-French cooperation, was still at the Admiralty when I consulted it, but has since been transferred to the Public Record Office as Adm. 116 Case 3109. The recently released Adm. 137 series dealing with World War I also contain useful material. The files of the Cabinet Office are extremely valuable for the material they contain relating to the Committee of Imperial Defence, particularly the series Cab. 2 which includes the CID Minutes. The files on Austria-Hungary, France, Germany, Greece, Italy, Russia, Spain, and Turkey in the Foreign Office, Political Correspondence (FO 371), are another rich source. There is much of interest on naval matters in them including a few copies of attaché reports, the originals of which were probably destroyed by the Admiralty as intelligence documents. The Public Record Office has a very useful collection of private papers in the FO 800 series, including those of Grey and Bertie.

The Bodleian Library, Oxford, has the Asquith MSS which are another important source on British policy for this period and also contain CID material. The National Maritime Museum, Greenwich, has the papers of Sir Howard Kelly as well as those of Sir Herbert Richmond and Sir Berkeley Milne. Included in the Kelly MSS is an unpublished journal for the period the admiral was naval attaché to France.

The Ufficio Storico della Marina Militare, Rome, contains the bulk and most important of Italian naval records since 1910. The cartella are not subdivided into any special series but are well indexed. The files hold much of value particularly on the Triple Alliance naval convention where in addition to the official reports, the private letters of the Italian delegate to the Capo di Stato Maggiore have been preserved. The most imporant files for this subject are in Cartella 286, 295, and 296.

At the Archivo Centrale dello Stato, Rome (EUR), the files of the Ministero della Marina, Gabinetto di S.E. il Ministro, Ufficio, Leggi e Decreti, are fairly routine. There is some material on the problem of Albania and the Corfu Channel in the 1913 records of the Presidenza del Consiglio dei Ministri. The Carte Giolitti yield very valuable supplementary material on foreign affairs particularly in the memoranda and in letters from San Giuliano. Only a small fraction of these have been published. The papers of General Ugo Brusati, aide-de-camp to King Victor Emmanuel, 1898–1917, contain some relevant material. The Archivo Storico, Ministero degli Affari Esteri, Rome, also contain a little of interest in the series Affari Politici, Serie "P," in the file for France and Great Britain.

II. Published Documents

AUSTRIA-HUNGARY

Österreich-Ungarns Aussenpolitik von der Bosnischen Krise 1908 bis zum Kriegsausbruch 1914. Diplomatische Aktenstucke des Österreichisch-Ungarischen Ministeriums des Äussern. Edited by Ludwig Bittner, Alfred Francis Pribram, Heinrich Srbik, and Hans Uebersberger. 9 vols. Vienna: Österreichischer Bundesverlag für Unterricht, Wissenschaft und Kunst, 1930.

Pribram, Alfred Francis (ed.), The Secret Treaties of Austria-Hungary 1879–1914. English edition by Archibald Cary Coolidge, 2 vols. Cambridge, Mass.: Harvard University Press, 1920–1921.

FRANCE

Ministère des affaires étrangères, Commission de publication des documents relatifs aux origines de la guerre de 1914, Documents diplomatiques français, 1871–1914. 38 vols. Paris: Imprimerie nationale, 1929–1959.

GERMANY

Die Grosse Politik der Europäischen Kabinette, 1871–1914. Edited by Johannes Lepsius, Albrecht Mendelssohn Bartholdy, and Friedrich Thimme. 40 vols. Berlin: Deutsche verlagsgesellschaft für politik und geschichte, m.b.H., 1922–1927.

GREAT BRITAIN

British Documents on the Origins of the War, 1898–1914, edited by G. P. Gooch and Harold Temperley. 11 vols. London: H.M.S.O., 1926–1938.
Parliamentary Debates (Commons), 5th Series. London: H.M.S.O.

ITALY

Ministero degli affari esteri, Commissione per la pubblicazione dei documenti diplomatici, *I documenti diplomatici italiani.* In progress. Rome: Libreria dello Stato, 1952–.
Pavone, Claudio (ed.), *dalle carte di Giovanni Giolitti. Quarant' anni di politica italiana.* 3 vols. Milan: Feltrinelli, 1962.

RUSSIA

Die Internationalen Beziehungen im Zeitalter des Imperialismus. Dokumente aus den Archiven der Zarischen und der Provisorischen Regierung. Translated and edited by Otto Hoetzsch. 11 vols. Berlin: R. Hobbing, 1931–1942.
Marchand, René (ed.), *Un livre noir: Diplomatie d'avant guerre d'après les documents des archives russes, novembre 1910–juillet, 1914.* 3 vols. in 6 parts. Paris: Librairie du Travail, 1922–1934.
Siebert, B. von (ed.), *Graf Benckendorffs Diplomatischer Schriftwechsel.* 3 vols. Berlin: W. de Gruyter and Co., 1928.
Stieve, Friedrich (ed.), *Der Diplomatische Schriftwechsel Iswolskis 1911–1914, Aus dem Geheimakten der Russischen Staatsarchiv.* 4 vols. Berlin: Deutsche verlagsgesellschaft für politik und geschichte, m.b.H., 1926.

III. Memoirs, Diaries, and Biographies

Arthur, Sir George, *Life of Lord Kitchener.* 3 vols. London: Macmillan, 1920.
Asquith, Herbert Henry, *The Genesis of the War.* New York: George H. Doran Co., 1923.
Asquith, the Earl of Oxford and, *Memories and Reflections, 1852–1927.* 2 vols. Boston: Little Brown and Co., 1928.
Auffenberg-Komarów, M. von, *Aus Österreich-Ungarns Teilnahme am Weltkriege.* Berlin: Ullstein and Co., 1920.
——— *Aus Österreichs Höhe und Niedergang.* Munich: Drei masken verlag, 1921.
Bacon, Admiral Sir Reginald H., *The Life of Lord Fisher of Kilverstone.* 2 vols. New York: Doubleday, Doran and Co., 1929.
Bardolff, Freiherr Carl von, *Soldat im Alten Österreich.* Jena: E. Diederichs, 1938.
Bayer von Bayersburg, Heinrich, *Österreichs Admirale und bedeutende Persönlichkeiten der k.u.k. Kriegsmarine 1867–1918.* Vienna: Bergland Verlag, 1962.

Béarn, Hector de, Souvenirs d'un marin. Geneva and Paris: La Palatine, 1960.

Bennett, Geoffrey, Charlie B: A Biography of Admiral Lord Beresford of Metemmeh and Curraghmore. London: Peter Dawnay Ltd., 1968.

Bertie of Thame, Lord, The Diary of Lord Bertie of Thame, 1914–1918. Lady Algernon Gordon Lennox, ed. 2 vols. New York: George H. Doran and Co., 1924.

Bonham Carter, Lady Violet, Winston Churchill: An Intimate Portrait. New York: Harcourt, Brace and World, 1965.

Bradford, Edward E., Life of Admiral of the Fleet Sir Arthur Knyvet Wilson. New York: J. Murray, 1923.

Brandl, Franz, Kaiser Politiker und Menschen: Erinnerungen eines Wiener Polizeipräsidenten. Leipzig and Vienna: J. Günther, 1936.

Brett, Maurice V., and Oliver, Viscount Esher, Journals and Letters of Reginald, Viscount Esher. 4 vols. London: Nicolson and Watson Ltd., 1934–1938.

Brière, Paul, Un Grand français: Le Vice-Amiral François Ernest Fournier. Mayenne: Imprimerie Floch, 1931.

Buchanan, Sir George W., My Mission to Russia and Other Diplomatic Memories. 2 vols. London: Cassell and Co., Ltd., 1923.

Bywater, Hector C., and H. C. Ferraby, Strange Intelligence: Memoirs of Naval Secret Service. London: Constable and Co., Ltd., 1931.

Cadorna, General Luigi, La Guerra alla fronte italiana. 2 vols. Milan: Fratelli Treves, 1921.

——— Altre pagine sulla grande guerra. Milan: A. Mondadori, 1925.

Callwell, Major-General Sir Charles Edward, Field-Marshal Sir Henry Wilson, bart. His Life and Diaries. 2 vols. London: Cassell and Co., Ltd., 1927

Cambon, Paul, Correspondance, 1870–1924. 3 vols. Paris: B. Grasset, 1940–1946.

Cataluccio, Francesco, Antonio di San Giuliano e la politica estera Italiana. Florence: Felice Le Monnier, 1935.

Cecil, Lamar, Albert Ballin: Business and Politics in Imperial Germany, 1888–1918. Princeton: Princeton University Press, 1967.

Chalmers, Rear-Admiral William S., The Life and Letters of David Earl Beatty. London: Hodder and Stoughton, Ltd., 1951.

Chamberlain, Sir Austin, Politics from Inside. New Haven: Yale University Press, 1937.

Charles-Roux, F., Souvenirs diplomatiques d'un âge révolu. Paris: A. Fayard, 1956.

Chatfield, Admiral of the Fleet, Lord, The Navy and Defence. 2 vols. London: William Heinemann, 1942.

Chlumecky, Leopold von, Erzherzog Franz Ferdinands Wirken und Wollen. Berlin: Verlag für kulturpolitik, 1929.

Churchill, Randolph, Winston S. Churchill. vol. II: Young Statesman, 1901–1914. Boston: Houghton Mifflin Co., 1967.

——— Winston S. Churchill: Companion Volume II. In 3 parts. Boston: Houghton Mifflin Co., 1969.

Churchill, Winston S., The World Crisis. 6 vols. London: Thornton, Butterworth, 1923–1931.

Collier, Basil, *Brasshat: A Biography of Field-Marshal Sir Henry Wilson.* London: Secker and Warburg, 1961.

Conrad, Feldmarschall [Franz Graf Conrad von Hötzendorf], *Aus meiner Dienstzeit 1908–1918.* 5 vols. Vienna: Rikola Verlag, 1921–1925.

Cork and Orrery, Admiral of the Fleet, The Earl of, *My Naval Life 1886–1941.* London: Hutchinson and Co., 1942.

Dartige du Fournet, Vice-Amiral L., *A travers les mers.* Paris: Plon-Nourrit et Cie., 1929.

Daveluy, Amiral, "Marine et marins d'hier—Souvenirs de carrère de l'Amiral Daveluy," in progress starting with *Revue Maritime* no. 188 (May 1962).

Decoux, Jean, *Adieu marine.* Paris: Plon, 1957.

Dewar, Vice-Admiral K. G. B., *The Navy from Within.* London: V. Gollancz, Ltd., 1939.

Djemal, Ahmad, *Memories of a Turkish Statesman, 1913–1919.* New York: George H. Doran Co., 1922.

Dugdale, Edgar T. S., *Maurice de Bunsen: Diplomat and Friend.* London: J. Murray, 1934.

Dumaine, Alfred, *La Dernière ambassade de France en Autriche.* Paris. Plon-Nourrit et Cie., 1921.

Dumesnil, Contre-Amiral C. H., *Souvenirs de guerre d'un vieux croiseur.* Paris: Plon-Nourrit et Cie., 1921.

Eisenmenger, Victor, *Erzherzog Franz Ferdinand.* Zurich and Vienna: Amalthea Verlag, 1929.

Epstein, Klaus, *Matthias Erzberger and the Dilemma of German Democracy.* Princeton: Princeton University Press, 1959.

Eubank, Keith, *Paul Cambon: Master Diplomatist.* Norman, Okla.: University of Oklahoma Press, 1960.

Faramond, Amiral de, *Souvenirs d'un attaché naval en Allemagne et en Autriche 1910–1914.* Paris: Plon, 1932.

Fisher, Admiral of the Fleet, Lord, *Memories and Records.* 2 vols. New York: George H. Doran Co., 1920.

Fitzroy, Sir Almeric, *Memoirs.* 3rd ed. 2 vols. London: Hutchinson and Co., 1925.

Funder, Friedrich, *Vom Gestern ins Heute.* Vienna: Herold Verlag, 1952.

Giolitti, Giovanni, *Memoirs of My Life.* Translated by Edward Storer. London: Chapman and Dodd, Ltd., 1923.

Görlitz, Walter (ed.), *The Kaiser and His Court: The Diaries, Note Books and Letters of Admiral Georg Alexander von Müller Chief of the Naval Cabinet, 1914–1918.* Translated by Mervyn Savill. London: MacDonald, 1961.

Gretton, Vice Admiral Sir Peter, *Former Naval Person: Winston Churchill and the Royal Navy.* London: Cassell, 1968.

Grey, Edward, Viscount Grey of Fallodon, *Twenty-Five Years, 1892–1916.* 2 vols. New York: Frederick A. Stokes Co., 1925.

Haldane, Richard Burdon, Viscount Haldane of Cloan, *Before the War.* London: Cassell and Co., 1920.

——— *An Autobiography.* London: Hodder and Stoughton, Ltd., 1929.

Hankey, Maurice P. A., *The Supreme Command*. 2 vols. London: Allen and Unwin, 1961.

Hantsch, Hugo, *Leopold Graf Berchtold*. 2 vols. Graz: Verlag Styria, 1963.

Hardinge, Sir Arthur, *A Diplomatist in Europe*. London: J. Cape, Ltd., n.d. [1927].

Hopman, Admiral A., *Das Logbuch eines deutschen Seeoffiziers*. Berlin: A. Scherl, gmbh, 1924.

Horthy, Admiral Nicholas, *Memoirs*. New York: R. Speller, 1957.

Huguet, General Charles J., *Britain and the War: A French Indictment*. Translated by Captain H. Cotton Minchin. London: Cassell and Co., Ltd., 1928.

James, Admiral Sir William, *A Great Seaman: The Life of Admiral of the Fleet Sir Henry F. Oliver*. London: W. F. and G. Witherby, 1956.

Jenkins, Roy, *Asquith*. London: Collins, 1964.

Joffre, J. J. C., *The Personal Memoirs of Joffre*. Translated by Colonel T. Bentley Mott. 2 vols. New York: Harper and Bros., 1932.

Kemp, Lieut.-Commander P. K. (ed.), *The Papers of Admiral Sir John Fisher*. Vol. I. Publications of the Navy Records Society, vol. 102. London, 1960.

———— *The Papers of Admiral Sir John Fisher*. Vol. II. Publications of the Navy Records Society, vol. 106. London, 1964.

Kerr, Admiral Mark, *Land, Sea, and Air*. London: Longmans, Green and Co., 1927.

———— *Prince Louis of Battenberg*. London: Longmans, Green and Co., 1934.

Keyes, Admiral of the Fleet Sir Roger, *Adventures Ashore and Afloat*. London: G. G. Harrap and Co., Ltd., 1939.

King-Hall, Commander Stephen, *My Naval Life, 1906–1929*. London: Faber and Faber, 1951.

Kiszling, Rudolph, *Erzherzog Franz Ferdinand von Österreich-Este: Leben, Pläne und Wirken am Schicksalsweg der Donaumonarchie*. Graz: H. Böhlaus Nachf., 1953.

Kopp, George, *Two Lone Ships*. Translated by Arthur Chambers. London: Hutchinson and Co., Ltd., 1931.

La Bolina, Jack [Vecchi], *Al servizio del mare italiano*. Turin: Paravia, 1928.

Laroche, Jules, *Quinze ans à Rome avec Camille Barrère, 1898–1913*. Paris: Plon, 1948.

———— *Au Quai d'Orsay avec Briand et Poincaré, 1913–1926*. Paris: Hachette, 1957.

Lowis, Commander Geoffrey L., *Fabulous Admirals and Some Naval Fragments*. London: Putnam, 1957.

Lumbroso, Alberto, *Cinque capi nella tormenta e dopo*. Milan: Casa Edit. Giacomo Agnelli, 1932.

Mäkelä, Matté, *Souchon der Goebenadmiral*. Braunschweig: Vieweg, 1936.

Marder, Arthur J., *Fear God and Dread Nought: the Correspondence of Admiral of the Fleet Lord Fisher of Kilverstone*. 3 vols. London: J. Cape, 1952–1959.

———— *Portrait of an Admiral: The Life and Letters of Sir Herbert Richmond*. Cambridge, Mass.: Harvard University Press, 1952.

Margutti, Lieut.-General Baron von, *The Emperor Francis Joseph and His Times*. London: Hutchinson and Co., 1921.

Martin, Paymaster Rear-Admiral William E. R., *The Adventures of a Naval Paymaster*. London: Herbert Jenkins, 1924.

Masson, Philippe, "Delcassé Ministre de la Marine," Thèse de Diplôme d'Etudes Supérieures d'Histoire, n.d. Unpublished study in the Bibliothèque Historique de la Marine, Paris.

Messimy, Général Adolphe-Marie, *Mes souvenirs*. Paris: Plon, 1937.

Milne, Admiral Sir A. Berkeley, *The Flight of the 'Goeben' and the 'Breslau'. An Episode in Naval History*. London: Eveleigh Nash Co., Ltd., 1921.

Miquel, Pierre, *Poincaré*. Paris: A. Fayard, 1961.

Moltke, Helmuth von, *Erinnerungen. Briefe. Dokumente 1877–1916*. Edited by Eliza von Moltke. Stuttgart: Der Kommende tag a.-g., 1922.

Montgomery-Cuninghame, Colonel Sir Thomas, *Dusty Measure: A Record of Troubled Times*. London: J. Murray, 1939.

Morgenthau, Henry, *Ambassador Morgenthau's Story*. New York: Doubleday, Page and Co., 1918.

Muret, Maurice, *L'Archiduc François Ferdinand*. Paris: B. Grasset, 1932.

Musulin, Freiherr von, *Das Haus am Ballplatz: Erinnerungen eines österreich-ungarischen Diplomaten*. Munich: Verlag für Kulturpolitik, 1924.

Nekludoff, A., *Diplomatic Reminiscences before and during the World War, 1911–1917*. Translated from the French by Alexandra Paget. London: J. Murray, 1920.

Neton, Alberic, *Delcassé*. Paris: Académie diplomatique internationale, 1952.

Nicolson, Harold, *Portrait of a Diplomatist*. New York: Harcourt Brace and Co., 1930.

Nikitisch-Boulles, Paul, *Vor dem Sturm: Erinnerungen an Erzherzog Thronfolger Franz Ferdinand*. Berlin: Verlag für Kulturpolitik, 1925.

Noël, Léon, *Camille Barrère. Ambassadeur de France*. Paris: Tardy, 1948.

Page, Thomas Nelson, *Italy and the World War*. New York: C. Scribner's Sons, 1920.

Paléologue, Maurice, *Au Quai d'Orsay à la veille de la tourment. Journal 1913–1914*. Paris: Plon, 1947.

Patterson, A. Temple, ed., *The Jellicoe Papers*, vol. I: *1893–1916*, Publications of the Navy Records Society, vol. 108. London, 1966.

Pelly, Admiral Sir Henry, *300,000 Sea Miles*. London: Chatto and Windus, 1938.

Petrie, Sir Charles, *King Alfonso XIII and His Age*. London: Chapman and Hall Ltd., 1963.

Po, Commandante Guido, *Il Grande Ammiraglio Paolo Thaon di Revel*. Turin: Lattes, 1936.

Pohl, Ella von (ed.), *Aus Aufzeichnungen und Briefen während der kriegszeit von Admiral Hugo von Pohl (Chef des Admiralstabes)*. Berlin: K. Siegismund, 1920.

Poincaré, Raymond, *Au service de la France. Neuf années de souvenirs*. 10 vols. Paris: Plon-Nourrit et Cie., 1926–1933.

Pomiankowski, Joseph, *Der Zusammenbruch des Ottomanischen Reiches. Erin-*

nerungen an die Türkei aus der Zeit des Weltkrieges. Zurich and Vienna: Amalthea Verlag, 1928.

Porter, Charles W., The Career of Théophile Delcassé. Philadelphia: University of Pennsylvania Press, 1936.

Redlich, Joseph, Emperor Francis Joseph of Austria. New York: Macmillan Co., 1929.

———— Schicksalsjahre Österreichs, 1908–1919: Das Politische Tagebuch Josef Redlichs. Fritz Fellner (ed.). 2 vols. Graz: H. Bohlaus Nachf., 1953–1954.

Regele, Oskar, Feldmarschall Conrad. Auftrag und Erfüllung, 1906–1918. Vienna: Verlag Herold, 1955.

Rennell Rodd, Sir James, Social and Diplomatic Memories 1884–1919. 3 vols. London: E. Arnold and Co., 1922–1925.

Révillon, Tony, Camille Pelletan, 1846–1915. Quarante-cinq années de lutte pour la République. Paris: M. Rivière, 1930.

Rheinbaben, Werner, Freiherr von, Viermal Deutschland 1895–1954. Berlin: Argon Verlag, 1954.

Ronge, Generalmajor Max, Kriegs und Industrie Spionage: Zwölf Jahre Kundschaftsdienst. Zurich and Vienna: Amalthea Verlag, 1930.

Rutter, Owen, Regent of Hungary: The Authorized Life of Admiral Nicholas Horthy. London: Rich and Cowan, Ltd., n.d. [1939].

Salandra, Antonio, Italy and the Great War. Translated by Z. K. Pyne. London: E. Arnold and Co., 1932.

Savinsky, A. A., Recollections of a Russian Diplomat. London: Hutchinson and Co., 1927.

Sazonov, Serge, Fateful Years, 1909–1916. London: J. Cape, 1928.

Scheer, Admiral Reinhard, Germany's High Sea Fleet in the World War. London: Cassell and Co., Ltd., 1920.

Schoultz, Commodore Gustav von, With the British Battle Fleet: War Recollections of a Russian Naval Officer. Translated by Arthur Chambers. London: Hutchinson and Co., n.d. [1925].

Sforza, Count Carlo, Makers of Modern Europe. Indianapolis: Bobbs-Merrill Co., 1928.

Sieghart, Rudolf, Die Letzten Jahrzehnte Einer Grossmacht. Berlin: Ullstein, 1932.

Sillani, Tommaso, Luigi di Savoia. Rome: Libr. del Littorio, 1929.

Sommer, Dudley, Haldane of Cloan: His Life and Times, 1856–1928. London: G. Allen and Unwin, 1960.

Souchon, Admiral W., "La Percée de S.M.S. 'Goeben' et 'Breslau' de Messine aux Dardanelles," Vice-Admiral E. von Mantey (ed.), Les marins allemands au combat. Translated by R. Jouan and Y. du Jonchay. Paris: Payot, 1930.

Sosnosky, Theodor von, Franz Ferdinand Der Erzherzog-Thronfolger. Ein Lebensbild. Munich and Berlin: R. Oldenbourg, 1929.

Steed, Henry Wickham, Through Thirty Years, 1892–1922. 2 vols. New York: Doubleday Page and Co., 1924.

Stieve, Friedrich, Isvolsky and the World War. Translated by E. W. Dickes. London: G. Allen and Unwin, Ltd., 1926.

Sydenham of Combe, Lord, My Working Life. London: J. Murray, 1927.

Szilassy, Baron Julius von, *Der Untergang der Donau-Monarchie Diplomatische Erinnerungen.* Berlin: Verlag Neues vaterland, E. Berger and Co., 1921.

Tirpitz, Alfred von, *My Memoirs.* 2 vols. New York: Dodd, Mead and Co., 1919.

———— *Politische Dokumente.* 2 vols. Berlin: Cotta, 1924–1926.

Tisza, Graf Stefan, *Briefe, 1914–1918.* Berlin: R. Hobbing, 1928.

Tittoni, Senator Tommaso, *Italy's Foreign and Colonial Policy.* Translated by Baron Bernardo Quaranta di San Severino. London: Smith, Elder and Co., 1914.

Trevelyan, George Macaulay, *Grey of Fallodon.* Boston: Houghton, Mifflin Co., 1937.

Trotha, Vizeadmiral Adolf von, *Grossadmiral von Tirpitz. Flottenbau und Reichsgedanke.* Breslau: Wilh. Gottl. Korn, 1933.

Urbanski von Ostrymiecz, Feldmarschalleutnant August, *Conrad von Hötzendorf: Soldat und Mensch.* Graz-Leipzig-Vienna: Ulrich Mosers Verlag, 1938.

Varillon, Pierre, *Joffre.* Paris: A. Fayard, 1956.

Walker, Sir Charles, *36 Years at the Admiralty.* London: L. W. Williams, Ltd., n.d.

Weldon, Captain L. B., *'Hard Lying': Eastern Mediterranean 1914–1919.* London: H. Jenkins, Ltd., 1925.

Wemyss, Lady Wester, *The Life and Letters of Lord Wester Wemyss.* London: Eyre and Spottiswoode, 1935.

Widenmann, Wilhelm, *Marine-Attaché an der kaiserlich-deutschen Botschaft in London 1907–1912.* Göttingen: Musterschmidt, 1952.

Young, Kenneth, *Arthur James Balfour.* London: G. Bell, 1963.

Zara, Ammiraglio Alberto da, *Pelle d' Ammiraglio.* Milan: Mondadori, 1949.

IV. Monographs, Articles, and General Studies

Abeille, Léonce, *Marine française et marines étrangères.* Paris: A. Colin, 1906.

Acton, Alfredo, "La Marina de guerra, 1900–1925," *Rassegna Italiana,* 16.91 (Dec. 1925): 740–758.

Adams, Charles F., "Der Wiederaufstieg der russischen Kriegsmarine in den Jahren 1905–1917," *Marine Rundschau,* 61.1 (Feb. 1964): 12–21.

Alberti, Colonello Adriano, *L'Opera di S.E. il Generale Pollio e l'esercito.* Rome: Stab. polig. Amministrazione guerra, 1923.

———— *Testamonianze Straniere sulla Guerra Italiana.* Rome: Edito a cura del giornale *Le Forze armate,* 1933.

Albertini, Luigi, *Venti anni di vita politica, 1898–1918.* 5 vols. Bologna: N. Zanichelli, 1950–1952.

———— *The Origins of the War of 1914.* Translated by Isabella M. Massey. 3 vols. London: Oxford University Press, 1952–1957.

Askew, William C., *Europe and Italy's Acquisition of Libya, 1911–1912.* Durham, N. C.: Duke University Press, 1942.

———— "The Austro-Italian Antagonism, 1896–1914," Lillian P. Wallace and William C. Askew (eds.), *Power, Public Opinion and Diplomacy: Essays in Honor of Eber Malcolm Carroll by His former Students.* Durham, N. C.: Duke University Press, 1959.

Auphan, Amiral, *La Marine dans l'histoire de France*. Paris: Plon, 1955.

Avarna di Gualtieri, Carlo, *L'Ultimo Rinnovamento della Triplice*. Milan: Alpes, 1924.

Avice, Capitaine de corvette J., *La Défense des frontières maritimes*. Paris: Challamel, 1922.

Barnaud, Lieutenant de vaisseau, "La poursuite des croiseurs Allemands en 1914 (Goeben, Breslau)," Ecole de Guerre Navale, Promotion 1922. Unpublished study in the Bibliothèque Historique de la Marine, Paris.

Bayer von Bayersburg, Heinrich, *Unter der k.u.k. Kriegsflagge*. Vienna: Bergland Verlag, 1959.

Belot, Contre-Amiral R. de, *La Méditerranée et le destin de l'Europe*. Paris: Payot, 1961.

———— and André Reussner, *La Puissance navale dans l'histoire*. vol. III: *De 1914 à 1958*. Paris: Editions maritimes d'outre-mer, 1960.

Bienaimé, Vice-Amiral, *La Guerre navale, 1914–1915. Fautes et responsabilities*. Paris: J. Tallandier, 1920.

Bonnefous, Georges, and Edouard Bonnefous, *Histoire politique de la troisième république*. 5 vols. Paris: Presses Universitaires de France. 1956–. In progress.

Bravetta, Ettore, *La Grande guerra sul mare*. 2 vols. Milan: A. Mondadori, 1925.

Brodie, Bernard, *Sea Power in the Machine Age*. 2nd ed. Princeton: Princeton University Press, 1943.

Cairns, John C., "International Politics and the Military Mind: The Case of the French Republic, 1911–1914," *Journal of Modern History*, 25.3 (Sept. 1953): 273–285.

Caprin, Giulio (ed.), *I Trattati segreti della Triplice Alleanza*. Bologna: Zanichelli, 1922.

Carroll, E. Malcolm, *French Public Opinion and Foreign Affairs 1870–1914*. New York: The Century Co., 1931.

Castex, Amiral R., *Théories stratégiques*. 5 vols. Paris: Société d'éditions maritimes, géographiques et coloniales, 1929–1935.

Cellier, Capitaine de frégate, "Les Idées stratégiques en France de 1870 à 1914 —'La Jeune Ecole,'" Centre des Hautes Etudes Navales, 1928. Unpublished study in the Bibliothèque Historique de la Marine, Paris.

Chastenet, Jacques, *Histoire de la troisième république*. 7 vols. Paris: Hachette, 1952–1963.

Clough, Shepard B., *The Economic History of Modern Italy*. New York: Columbia University Press, 1964.

Contamine, Henry, *La Revanche, 1871–1914*. Paris: Berger-Levrault, 1957.

Corbett, Sir Julian S., and H. Newbolt, *Naval Operations*. 5 vols. London: Longmans, Green and Co., 1920–1931.

Cormier, Charles (Captain Sorb, pseud.), *Quittons la Méditerranée et la Mer de Chine*. Paris: Chapelot, 1905.

———— *La Doctrine de la défense nationale*. Paris: Berger-Levrault, 1912.

Craig, Gordon, "The World War I Alliance of the Central Powers in Retrospect: The Military Cohesion of the Alliance," *Journal of Modern History*, 37.3 (Sept. 1965): 336–344.

Czedik, Alois Freiherr von, *Zur Geschichte der K.-K. österreichischen Ministerien, 1861–1916.* 4 vols. Vienna: K. Prochaska, 1917–1920.

Darrieus, Gabriel, *La Guerre sur mer.* Paris: A. Challamel, 1907.

Daveluy, René, *L'Esprit de la guerre navale.* 3 vols. Paris: Berger-Levrault, 1909.

——— *L'Action maritime pendant la guerre anti-germanique.* 2 vols. Paris: A. Challamel, 1920.

Dietrich, R., *Die Tripolis-Krise, 1911–1912, und die Erneuerung des Dreibundes 1912.* Würzburg, 1933.

Dollé, G., *Frégates et croiseurs.* Paris: Horizons de France, 1947.

Ducci, Ammiraglio G., "Accordi e Convenzioni durante la Triplice Alleanza," *Rivista Marittima,* 68.3 (Mar. 1935): 265–287.

Duffour, Général, *Joffre et la guerre de mouvement, 1914. Histoire de la guerre mondiale,* vol. I. Paris: Payot, 1937.

Durand-Viel, Capitaine de vaisseau G., "Delcassé et la marine," *Revue Maritime,* n.s. no. 41 (May 1923), pp. 577–605.

Duruy, Kapitän, *Österreich-Ungarn und Italien.* Vienna: L. W. Seidel and Sohn, 1910.

Egorief, V., and E. Schvede, "La Convention navale de 1912 et les relations navales franco-russes au cours de la guerre mondiale," Anders Zaiontchkovsky et al., *Les Alliés contre la Russie avant, pendant et après la guerre mondiale (Faits et documents).* Paris: A. Delpeuch, n.d. [1926].

Ehrman, John, *Cabinet Government and War 1890–1940.* Cambridge: Cambridge University Press, 1958.

Eisenmann, Louis, *Le Compromis austro-hongrois,* Paris: Société nouvelle de librairie et d'édition (G. Bellais), 1904.

Farrère, Claude, *Histoire de la marine française.* New ed. Paris: Flammarion, 1962.

Fay, Sidney B., *The Origins of the World War.* 2nd ed. rev. 2 vols. New York: Macmillan, 1930.

Feis, Herbert, *Europe the World's Banker 1870–1914.* New Haven: Yale University Press, 1930.

Fellner, Fritz, *Der Dreibund: Europaische Diplomatie vor dem ersten weltkrieg.* Munich: R. Oldenbourg, 1960.

Fioravanzo, Giuseppe, *Basi navale nel mondo.* Milan: Istituto per gli studi di politica internazionale, 1936.

——— "La Marina nell'occupazione di Scutari d'Albania," *Rivista Marittima,* May 1963, pp. 1–20.

——— P. M. Pollina, G. Riccardi et al., *I Cacciatorpediniere italiani, 1900–1966.* Rome: Ufficio storico della Marina Militare, 1966.

Fischer, Fritz, *Germany's Aims in the First World War.* New York: W. W. Norton and Co., 1967.

Foerster, Wolfgang, "Die deutsch-italienische Militärkonvention," *Die Kriegsschuldfrage,* 5.5 (May 1927): 395–416.

——— "Strategische Erwägungen des italienischen Generalstabs aus der Vorkriegszeit," *Berliner Monatshefte,* 11.5 (May 1933): 1247–1255.

Gabriele, Mariano, "La Politica navale italiana alla vigilia del primo conflitto mondiale," *Rivista Marittima,* 98.5 (May 1965): 15–32.

———— "Origini della convenzione navale italo-austro-germanica del 1913," in 2 parts, *Rassegna Storica del Risorgimento*, fasc. III–IV (1965), pp. 325–344, 489–509.

———— "La Convenzione navale italo-franco-britannica del 10 maggio 1915," in 2 parts, *Nuova Antologia*, 403–404. 1972–1973 (Apr.–May 1965): 483–502, 69–84.

Giglio, Vittorio, and Angelo Ravenni, *Le Guerre coloniali d'Italia*. 11th ed. Milan: Casa editrice dott. Francesco Vallardi, 1942.

Giorgerini, Georgio, and Augusto Nani, *Le Navi di linea italiane 1861–1961*. Rome: Ufficio Storico della Marina Militare, 1962.

———— *Gli incrociatori italiani, 1861–1964*. Rome: Ufficio Storico della Marina Militare, 1964.

Gogg, Karl. *Österreichs Kriegsmarine, 1848–1918*. Salzburg: Verlag das Bergland-Buch, 1967.

Gooch, G. P., *Before the War: Studies in Diplomacy*. 2 vols. London: Longmans, Green and Co., 1936–1938.

Gordon, Donald C., "The Admiralty and Dominion Navies, 1902–1914," *Journal of Modern History*, 33.4 (Dec. 1961): 407–422.

———— *The Dominion Partnership in Imperial Defense, 1870–1914*. Baltimore: The Johns Hopkins Press, 1965.

Gottlieb, W. W., *Studies in Secret Diplomacy during the First World War*. London: George Allen and Unwin, 1957.

Graf, H., *The Russian Navy in War and Revolution*. Translated from the Russian. Munich: R. Oldenbourg, 1923.

Grant, Robert M., *U-Boats Destroyed: The Effect of Anti-Submarine Warfare, 1914–1918*. London: Putnam, 1964.

Guéchoff, J. E., *La Genèse de la guerre mondiale*. Berne: P. Haupt, 1919.

Guglielmotti, Umberto, *Storia della marina italiana*. Naples: V. Bianco, 1959.

Hale, Oron J., *Publicity and Diplomacy with Special Reference to England and Germany, 1890–1914*. New York: The University of Virginia Institute for Research in the Social Sciences, 1940.

Halévy, Elie, *The Rule of Democracy 1905–1914*. Translated by E. I. Watkin. *A History of the English People in the Nineteenth Century*, vol. VI. London, 1932. Paperback edition, London: Ernest Benn, Ltd., 1961.

Halpern, Paul G., "The Anglo-French-Italian Naval Convention of 1915," *The Historical Journal*, 13.1 (Mar. 1970): 106–129.

Hantsch, Hugo, *Die Geschichte Österreichs*. 2 vols. Graz: Steirische Verlagsanstalt, 1951–1953.

Hasenclever, Adolf, "Zur Geschichte der spanisch-französischen Beziehungen vor Ausbruch des Weltkrieges," *Berliner Monatshefte*, 14.9 (Sept. 1936): 713–734.

Helbing, Gunther, "Die deutsche Marinepolitik 1908–1912 im Spiegel der österreichisch-ungarischen Diplomatie," *Marine Rundschau*, beiheft 6 (Oct. 1961): 32–70.

Helmreich, Ernest C., *The Diplomacy of the Balkan Wars, 1912–1913*. Cambridge, Mass.: Harvard University Press, 1938.

Herre, Paul, *Die Kleinen Staaten Europas und die entstehung des Weltkrieges.* Munich: C. H. Beck'sche verlagsbuchhandlung, 1937.

Hislam, Percival A., *The Admiralty of the Atlantic.* London: Longmans, Green and Co., 1908.

Hough, Richard, *Dreadnought: A History of the Modern Battleship.* London: Michael Joseph, 1965.

———— *The Great Dreadnought. The Strange Story of H.M.S. Agincourt, The Mightiest Battleship of World War I.* New York: Harper and Row, 1967.

Hovgaard, William, *Modern History of Warships.* London: E. & F. N. Spon, Ltd., 1920.

Howard, Harry N., *The Partition of Turkey. A Diplomatic History 1913–1923.* Norman, Okla.: University of Oklahoma Press, 1931.

Hoyos, Alexander, *Der deutsch-englische Gegensatz und sein Einfluss auf die Balkanpolitik Österreich-Ungarns.* Berlin and Leipzig: Vereinigung wissenschaftlicher verleger, 1922.

Hubatsch, Walther, *Die Ära Tirpitz: Studien zur deutschen Marinepolitik 1890– 1918.* Göttingen: Musterschmidt Verlag, 1955.

———— *Die Admiralstab und die Obersten Marinebehörden in Deutschland 1884 bis 1945.* Frankfurt am Main: Verlag für Wehrwesen Bernhard und Graefe, 1958.

———— "Die russische Marine im deutschen Urteil 1890–1914," *Das deutsche Bild der russischen und sowjetischen Marine.* Beiheft 7/8 der *Marine Rundschau.* Frankfurt am Main: E. S. Mittler, 1962, pp. 19–35.

Hurd, Archibald, *Italian Sea Power in the Great War.* London: Constable and Co., Ltd., 1918.

———— and Henry Castle, *German Sea-Power.* London: J. Murray, 1913.

Italy, Office of the Chief of Staff of the Royal Italian Navy (Historical Section), *The Italian Navy in the World War 1915–1918. Facts and Figures.* Rome: Ufficio Storico, 1927.

Jane, Fred T., *The British Battle Fleet.* London: S. W. Partridge and Co., Ltd., 1912.

Jászi, Oscar, *The Dissolution of the Habsburg Monarchy.* Chicago: University of Chicago Press, 1929.

Jedina-Palombini, Vizeadmiral Leopold Freiherr von, *Für Österreich-Ungarns Seegeltung.* Vienna: L. W. Seidel and Sohn, 1912.

Johnson, Franklyn Arthur, *Defence by Committee.* London: Oxford University Press, 1960.

Jouan, René, *Histoire de la marine française.* 2 vols. Paris: Payot, 1932.

Joubert, Vice-amiral H., *La Marine française.* Paris: Editions Alsatia, 1946.

Kalbskopf, W., *Die Aussenpolitik der Mittelmächte im Tripoliskrieg und die letzte Dreibunderneuerung, 1911–1912.* n.p., 1932.

Kann, Robert A., "Emperor William II and Archduke Francis Ferdinand in Their Correspondence," *American Historical Review,* 57.2 (Jan. 1952): 323–351.

Khuepach, Kontreadmiral Arthur von, "Endschicksal der österreich-ungarischen Flotteneinheiten," in 3 parts, *Marine Rundschau,* Oct.–Dec. 1938, pp. 750– 766, 830–841, 920–933.

Kiszling, Rudolf, "Die Entwicklung der österreich-ungarischen Wehrmacht seit den Annexionskrise 1908," *Berliner Monatshefte,* 12.9 (Sept. 1934): 735–749.

Kraus, Leutnant zur see Theodor, *Die Fahrten der 'Goeben' im Mittelmeer.* Berlin: Ullstein, 1917.

Krauss, General der Infanterie Alfred, *Die Ursachen unserer Niederlage.* 2nd ed. Munich: J. F. Lehmanns Verlag, 1921.

Lanessan, J.-L. de, *Le Bilan de notre marine.* Paris: F. Alcan, 1909.

———— *Notre défense maritime.* Paris: F. Alcan, 1914.

Langer, William L., "Tribulations of Empire: The Mediterranean Problem," *Foreign Affairs,* 15.4 (July 1937): 648–660.

Larcher, Commandant Maurice, *La Guerre turque dans la guerre mondiale.* Paris: E. Chiron, 1926.

Laurens, Capitaine de vaisseau Adolphe, *Précis d'histoire de la guerre navale 1914–1918.* Paris: Payot, 1929.

———— *Le Commandement naval en Méditerranée, 1914–1918.* Paris: Payot, 1931.

Laurin, Lieutenant de vaisseau, "Le Transport du 19me corps et des troupes coloniales en 1914," Ecole de Guerre Navale, Session 1930–1931. Unpublished study in the Bibliothèque Historique de la Marine, Paris.

Le Masson, Henri, *De la 'Gloire' au 'Richelieu'.* Paris: Horizons de France, 1946.

———— "La Difficile gestation du croiseur léger français 1910–1916," in 2 parts, *Revue Maritime,* no. 199–200 (May-June 1963), pp. 577–594, 747–763.

———— "Politique navale et construction de navires de ligne en France en 1914," *Revue Maritime,* no. 202 (Aug.-Sept. 1963), pp. 993–1008.

———— "Les Cuirassés à tourelles quadruples de la classe normandie," *Revue Maritime,* no. 203 (Oct. 1963), pp. 1172–1191.

———— "Des Cuirassés qui auraient pu être," *Revue Maritime,* no. 204 (Nov. 1963), pp. 1291–1309.

———— "Du Torpilleur d'escadre de 1500 t. etudié en 1914 au torpilleur d'escadre de 1500 t. de 1922," in 2 parts, *Revue Maritime,* no. 207–208 (Feb.-Mar. 1964), pp. 170–189, 327–340.

———— "Douze ministres, ou dix ans d'hésitations de la marine française," *Revue Maritime,* no. 233 (June 1966), pp. 710–733.

———— *Histoire du torpilleur en France.* Paris: Académie de Marine, n.d. [1966].

———— *Du Nautilus (1800) au Redoutable: Histoire critique du sous-marin dans la marine française.* Paris: Presses de la Cité, 1969.

Lewis, Michael, *The Navy of Britain,* London: G. Allen and Unwin, 1948.

Lorey, Hermann, *Der Krieg in den türkischen Gewässern.* Berlin: E. S. Mittler and Sohn, 1928.

Luigi, Giuseppe de, *Il Mediterraneo nella politica europea.* Naples: N. Jovene, n.d. [1926].

Macintyre, Captain Donald, *The Thunder of the Guns: A Century of Battleships.* New York: W. W. Norton, 1960.

Mack Smith, Denis, *Italy: A Modern History.* Ann Arbor: University of Michigan Press, 1959.

Madariaga, Salvador de, *Spain: A Modern History.* New York: Praeger, 1958.

Malaguzzi, Daria Banfi, *Marina d'Italia.* Milan: Treves, 1929.

Manfroni, Camillo, *Storia della marina italiana durante la guerra mondiale, 1914–1918.* 2nd ed. Bologna: N. Zanichelli, 1925.

——— *Guerra italo-turca.* Vol. II: *Dal decreto di sovranità sulla Libia alla conclusione della pace.* Rome: Stab. Poligr. Edit. Romano, 1926.

Mantegazza, Vico, *Il Mediterraneo e il suo equilibrio.* Milan: Fratelli Treves, 1914.

Marchand, A., *Plans de concentration (de 1871 à 1914).* Paris: Berger-Levrault, 1926.

Marchat, Henry, "Un Projet de pacte Méditerranéen avant la première guerre mondiale," *Revue Maritime,* no. 139 (Dec. 1957), pp. 1515–1532.

Marder, Arthur J., *The Anatomy of British Sea Power. A History of British Naval Policy in the Pre-Dreadnought Era, 1880–1905.* New York: Alfred Knopf, 1940.

——— *From the Dreadnought to Scapa Flow. The Royal Navy in the Fisher Era, 1904–1919.* Vol. I: *The Road to War, 1904–1914.* London: Oxford University Press, 1961. Vol. II: *The War Years. To the Eve of Jutland, 1914–1916.* London: Oxford University Press, 1965.

Masson, P., "La Politique navale française de 1890 à 1914," *Revue Maritime,* no. 251 (Feb. 1968), pp. 183–203.

May, Arthur J., *The Hapsburg Monarchy, 1867–1914.* 2nd printing. Cambridge, Mass.: Harvard University Press, 1960.

Melli, B., *La Guerra italo-turca.* Rome: E. Voghere, 1914.

Michelsen, Andreas, *La Guerre sous-marine (1914–1918).* Translated by R. Jouan. Paris: Payot, 1928.

Mirtl, Kontreadmiral Franz, *Unsere Flotte sinkt! Ein Mahnwort in letzter Stunde.* Vienna: K. Harbauer, 1912.

——— "Der Thronfolger und die Marine," *Erzherzog Franz Ferdinand unser Thronfolger. Zum 50. Geburtstag.* Illustriertes Sonderheft der *Österreichische Rundschau.* Vienna, 18 Dec. 1913, pp. 41–54.

Missoffe, Capitaine de frégate, "La Stratégie Maritime Alliée en Méditerranée de 1914 à 1918," Centre des Hautes Etudes Navales, Session 1936–1937. Unpublished study in the Bibliothèque Historique de la Marine, Paris.

Mitchell, Marin, *The Maritime History of Russia, 848–1948.* London: Sidgwick and Jackson, 1949.

Monasterev, N., *Vom Untergang der Zarenfotte.* Translated by M. Zimmerman. Berlin: E. S. Mittler and Sohn, 1930.

——— and Lieutenant Serge Terestchenko, *Histoire de la marine russe.* Translated by Lieut. Jean Perceau. Paris: Payot, 1932.

Monger, George, *The End of Isolation: British Foreign Policy 1900–1907.* London: T. Nelson, 1963.

Monk, W. F., *Britain in the Western Mediterranean.* London: Hutchinson's University Library, 1953.

Mousset, Albert, *L'Espagne dans la politique mondiale.* Paris: Bossard, 1923.

Mühlmann, Carl, *Deutschland und die Türkei.* Berlin: W. Rothschild, 1929.

———— Oberste Heersleitung und Balkan im Weltkrieg 1914/1918. Berlin: W. Limpert, 1942.

Nicolas, Louis, Histoire de la marine française. 2nd ed. Paris: Presses Universitaires de France, 1961.

Ogg, Frederic Austin, The Governments of Europe. New York: The Macmillan Co., 1913.

Parkes, Oscar, British Battleships: Warrior 1860 to Vanguard 1950: A History of Design, Construction and Armament. London: Seeley Service and Co., Ltd., 1956.

Pingaud, Albert, "Alphonse XIII et la France en 1914," Revue des Deux Mondes, 101 (1 May 1931): 194–202.

———— Histoire diplomatique de la France pendant la grande guerre. 3 vols. Paris: Editions Alsatia, 1935–1945.

Pinon, René, L'Empire de la Méditerranée. Paris: Perrin et Cie., 1912.

Pollina, Contrammiraglio Paolo M., I Sommergibili italiani, 1895–1962. Rome: Ufficio Storico della Marina Militare, 1963.

———— Le Torpediniere italiane, 1881–1964. Rome: Ufficio Storico della Marina Militare, 1964.

Ponteil, Félix, La Méditerranée et les puissances: Depuis l'overture jusqu' à la nationalisation du Canal de Suez. Paris: Payot, 1964.

Pribram, Alfred F., Austria-Hungary and Great Britain, 1980–1914. Translated by Ian F. D. Morrow. London: Oxford University Press, 1951.

Redlich, Joseph, Austrian War Government. Carnegie Endowment for International Peace, Economic and Social History of the World War. New Haven: Yale University Press, 1929.

Renouvin, Pierre, Les Questions méditerranéennes de 1904 à 1914. Université de Paris, Institut d'études politiques, Année 1953–1954. Paris: Centre de documentation universitaire et S.E.D.E.S. réunis, 1958.

———— Histoire des relations internationales. Vol. VI: Le XIXe siècle-II. De 1871 à 1914. L'apogée de l'Europe. Paris: Hachette, 1955.

Reussner, André, and L. Nicolas, La Puissance navale dans l'histoire, Vol. II: De 1815 à 1914. Paris: Editions maritimes d'outre-mer, 1963.

Richmond, Admiral Sir Herbert, Statesmen and Sea Power. Rev. ed. Oxford: Oxford University Press, 1947.

Ritter, Gerhard, Staatskunst und Kriegshandwerk: Das Problem des "Militarismus" in Deutschland. Vol. II: Die Hauptmächte Europas und das wilhelminische Reich (1890–1914). Munich: R. Oldenbourg, 1960.

Rochat, Giorgio, "L'Esercito italiano nell'estate 1914," Nuova Rivista Storica, 45.2 (May–Aug. 1961): 295–348.

Rollin, Henry, Marine de guerre et défense nationale. Paris: E. Giulmoto, 1911.

Roncagli, Capitano di fregata, Guerra italo-turca. Vol. I: Dalle origini al decreto di sovranità su la Libia. Milan: U. Hoepli, 1918.

Ropp, Theodore, "The Development of a Modern Navy: French Naval Policy, 1871–1904," unpub. diss. Harvard University, 1937.

———— "Continental Doctrines of Sea Power," Edward Meade Earle (ed.), Makers of Modern Strategy: Military Thought from Machiavelli to Hitler. Princeton: Princeton University Press, 1941, pp. 446–456.

———— *War in the Modern World.* Durham, N.C.: Duke University Press, 1959.

Rosinski, Herbert, "Strategy and Propaganda in German Naval Thought," Rear Admiral H. G. Thursfield (ed.), *Brassey's Naval Annual, 1945.* New York: Macmillan, 1945, pp. 120–150.

Roskill, Captain Stephen W., *The Strategy of Sea Power: Its Development and Application.* London: Collins, 1962.

Salaun, Henri, *La Marine française.* Paris: Les éditions de France, 1934.

Salamone, A. William, *Italy in the Giolittian Era.* 2nd rev. ed. Philadelphia: University of Pennsylvania Press, 1960.

Salvatorelli, Luigi, *La Triplice alleanza.* Milan: Istituto per gli studi di politica internazionale, 1939.

Salvemini, Gaetano, *La Politica estera dell'Italia (1871–1914)* Florence: G. Barbera, 1944.

Schloss, Max, *Der Jammer unser Seemacht. Die Politischen, militärischen und wirtschaftlichen Grundlagen des langfristigen Flottengesetzes.* Vienna: St. Norbertus, 1914.

Schmitt, Bernadotte, *The Coming of War, 1914.* 2 vols. New York: C. Scribner's Sons, 1930.

Schurman, Donald M., *The Education of a Navy: The Development of British Naval Strategic Thought, 1867–1914.* Chicago: University of Chicago Press, 1965.

Scott, J. D. *Vickers: A History.* London: Wiedenfeld and Nicolson, 1962.

Serra, Enrico, *L'Intesa Mediterranea del 1902: Una fase risolutiva nei rapporti italo-inglesi.* Milan: Guiffrè, 1957.

Silva, Pietro, *Il Mediterraneo dall' Unita di Roma all' Impero Italiano.* 2 vols. Milan: Istituto per gli studi di politica internazionale, 1941.

Smith, Gaddis, *Britain's Clandestine Submarines, 1914–1915.* New Haven: Yale University Press, 1964.

Sokol, Anthony, *The Imperial and Royal Austro-Hungarian Navy.* Annapolis: United States Naval Institute, 1968.

Sokol, Hans Hugo, "Einige nachtragliche Betrachtungen über Italiens Bedeutung für den Dreibund im Seekriege," *Marine Rundschau,* Jan. 1928, pp. 1–12.

———— *Österreich-Ungarns Seekrieg 1914–1918.* Zurich, Leipzig, and Vienna: Amalthea Verlag, 1930.

Sorb, Capitaine. See Cormier, Charles.

Stadelmann, Rudolf, "Die Epoche der deutsch-englischen Flottenrivalität," *Deutschland und Westeuropa.* Schloss Lauphcim, Württemburg: U. Steiner, 1948, pp. 85–146.

Stebbins, Richard P., "Italian Policy in the Eastern Mediterranean, 1911–1914," unpub. diss. Harvard University, 1939.

Steed, Henry Wickham, *The Hapsburg Monarchy.* 4th ed. London: Constable and Co., Ltd., 1919.

Steinberg, Jonathan, *Yesterday's Deterrent: Tirpitz and the Birth of the German Battle Fleet.* London: Macdonald, 1965.

Stone, Norman, "Army and Society in the Habsburg Monarchy, 1900–1914." *Past and Present,* no. 33 (Apr. 1966), pp. 95–111.

——— "Moltke-Conrad: Relations between the Austro-Hungarian and German General Staffs, 1909–1914," *Historical Journal*, 9.2 (1966): 201–228.

Teleki, Count Paul, *The Evolution of Hungary and its Place in European History*. New York: The Macmillan Co., 1923.

Temperley, H., and L. M. Penson, *Foundations of British Foreign Policy from Pitt to Salisbury*. Cambridge: The University Press, 1938.

Thaden, Edward C., *Russia and the Balkan Alliance of 1912*. University Park, Pa.: Pennsylvania State University Press, 1965.

Thayer, John A., *Italy and the Great War. Politics and Culture, 1870–1915*. Madison and Milwaukee: University of Wisconsin Press, 1964.

Thomazi, A., *La Guerre navale dans la zone des armées du Nord*. Paris: Payot, 1925.

——— *La Guerre navale dans l'Adriatique*. Paris: Payot, 1927.

——— *La Guerre navale dans la méditerranée*. Paris: Payot, 1929.

Tonnelé, Jean, "La Catastrophe de la 'Liberté'," *Neptunia*, no. LXVIII, Autumn 1962, pp. 24–29.

Torre, Augusto, *La Politica estera dell'Italia dal 1896 al 1914*. Bologna: Casa Editrice Prof. Riccardo Patron, 1960.

Toscano, Mario, *Il Patto di Londra. Storia diplomatica dell' intervento italiano, 1914–1915*. Bologna: N. Zanichelli, 1934.

——— *Pagine di storia diplomatica contemporanea*. 2 vols. Milan: Giuffrè, 1963.

——— "Rivelazioni e nuovi documenti sul negoziato di Londra per l'ingresso dell'Italia nella prima guerra mondiale," in 4 parts, *Nuova Antologia*, 404–405. 1976–1979 (Aug.–Nov. 1965): 433–457, 15–37, 151–165, 295–312.

Tramond, Joannès, and André Reussner, *Elements d'histoire maritime et coloniale contemporaine, 1815–1914*. Paris: Société d'éditions géographiques, maritimes et coloniales, 1924.

Trumpener, Ulrich, "German Military Aid to Turkey in 1914: An Historical Re-Evaluation," *Journal of Modern History*, 32.2 (June 1960): 145–149.

——— "Turkey's Entry into World War I: An Assessment of Responsibilities," *Journal of Modern History*, 34.4 (Dec. 1962): 369–380.

——— *Germany and the Ottoman Empire, 1914–1918*. Princeton: Princeton University Press, 1968.

Tyler, John E., *The British Army and the Continent, 1904–1914*. London: E. Arnold and Co., 1938.

Uhlig, Frank, "The Battlecruiser Era," *U.S. Naval Institute Proceedings*, 83.10 (Oct. 1957): 1106–1116.

Ufficio storico della R. Marina [now Marina Militare] (Capitano di vascello G. Almagià and Capitano di corvetta A. Zoli), *La Marina italiana nella Grande Guerra*. Vol. I: *Vigilia d'armi sul mare*. Florence: Vallecchi, 1935.

——— [Ammiraglio di Squadra (r.n.) Giuseppe Fioravanzo] *La Marina militare nel suo primo secolo di vita. 1861–1961*. Rome: Ufficio Storico della Marina Militare, 1961.

Vellay, Charles, *Le problème méditerranéen*. Paris: Berger-Levrault, 1913.

Vigezzi, Brunello, *L'Italia di Fronte alla Prima Guerra Mondiale*. Vol. I: *L'Italia Neutrale*. Milan and Naples: Riccardo Ricciardi, 1966.

Volpe, G., *L'Italia nella Triplice Alleanza 1882–1915.* Milan: Istituto per gli studi di politica internazionale, 1939.

Wagner, Walter, *Die Obersten Behörden der k.u.k. Kriegsmarine 1856–1918.* Mitteilungen des Österreichischen Staatsarchivs, Ergänzungsband VI. Vienna: Druck und Verlag Ferdinand Berger, 1961.

Waldersee, Graf, "Von Deutschlands militärpolitischen Beziehungen zu Italien," *Berliner Monatshefte,* 7.7 (July 1929): 636–664.

———— "Über die Beziehungen des deutschen zum österreich-ungarischen Generalstabe vor dem Weltkriege," *Berliner Monatshefte,* 8.2 (Feb. 1930): 103–142.

Wallisch, Friederich, *Die Flagge Rot-Weiss-Rot. Männer und Taten der Österreichischen Marine in vier Jahrhunderten.* Graz: Verlag Styria, 1956.

Webster, Richard A., "Autarky, Expansion, and the Underlying Continuity of the Italian State," paper read at the American Historical Association National Convention, Washington, 30 Dec., 1964.

Wedel, Oswald H., *Austro-German Diplomatic Relations 1908–1914.* Stanford: Stanford University Press, 1932.

Williamson, Samuel R., *The Politics of Grand Strategy: Britain and France Prepare for War, 1904–1914.* Cambridge, Mass.: Harvard University Press, 1969.

Wilson, Herbert W., *Battleships in Action,* 2 vols. London: Sampson, Low and Co., n.d. [1926].

Woodward, David, *The Russians at Sea.* London: William Kimber, 1965.

Woodward, E. L., *Great Britain and the German Navy.* Oxford: Oxford University Press, 1935.

Zöllner, Erich, *Geschichte Österreichs.* Vienna: Verlag für Geschichte und Politik, 1961.

V. Annuals, Periodicals, and Newspapers

Army and Navy Gazette: Journal of the Reserve and Territorial Forces.

Balincourt, Commandant de, *Les Flottes de combat en 1915.* Paris: Challamel, 1915.

Brassey, The First Earl, Viscount Hythe, and John Leyland (ed.), *The Naval Annual.* Title varies after 1914. Portsmouth: J. Griffin and Co., ————1913; London: W. Clowes, 1914–.

Die Flagge: Zeitschrift für seewesen und seeverkehr. Organ des Österreichischen Flottenverein.

Guihéneuc Collection, "Extraits de journaux marine, 1882–1918," 63 vols. Harvard College Library.

Jane, Fred T., *Jane's Fighting Ships.* London: S. Low, Marston and Co., Ltd., 1897–.

Journal of the Royal United Service Institute.

Marine Rundschau.

Moniteur de la Flotte.

Nauticus: Jahrbuch für Deutschlands Seeinteressen. Berlin: E. S. Mittler and Sohn.

Navy and Military Record (and Royal Dockyards Gazette).

Navy League Annual. A. H. Burgoyne (ed.), London: J. Murray.

Revue Maritime.

Rivista Marittima.

The Times (London).

United Service Magazine.

Weyer, Bruno (ed.), *Taschenbuch des Kriegsflotten 1914.* Munich: J. F. Lehmanns Verlag, reprinted 1968.

Le Yacht: Journal de la Marine.

Index

Harvard Historical Studies

OUT OF PRINT TITLES ARE OMITTED

33. *Lewis George Vander Velde*. The Presbyterian Churches and the Federal Union, 1861–1869. 1932.

35. *Donald C. McKay*. The National Workshops: A Study in the French Revolution of 1848. 1933.

38. *Dwight Erwin Lee*. Great Britain and the Cyprus Convention Policy of 1878. 1934.

48. *Jack H. Hexter*. The Reign of King Pym. 1941.

58. *Charles C. Gillispie*. Genesis and Geology: A Study in the Relations of Scientific Thought, Natural Theology, and Social Opinion in Great Britain, 1790–1850. 1951.

62, 63. *John King Fairbank*. Trade and Diplomacy on the China Coast: The Opening of the Treaty Ports, 1842–1854. One-volume edition. 1953.

64. *Franklin L. Ford*. Robe and Sword: The Regrouping of the French Aristocracy after Louis XIV. 1953.

66. *Wallace Evan Davies*. Patriotism on Parade: The Story of Veterans' and Hereditary Organizations in America, 1783–1900. 1955.

67. *Harold Schwartz*. Samuel Gridley Howe: Social Reformer, 1801–1876. 1956.

69. *Stanley J. Stein*. Vassouras: A Brazilian Coffee County, 1850–1900. 1957.

71. *Ernest R. May*. The World War and American Isolation, 1914–1917. 1959.

72. *John B. Blake*. Public Health in the Town of Boston, 1630–1822. 1959.

73. *Benjamin W. Labaree*. Patriots and Partisans: The Merchants of Newburyport, 1764–1815. 1962.

74. *Alexander Sedgwick*. The Ralliement in French Politics, 1890–1898. 1965.

75. *E. Ann Pottinger*. Napoleon III and the German Crisis, 1865–1866. 1966.

76. *Walter Goffart*. The Le Mans Forgeries: A Chapter from the History of Church Property in the Ninth Century. 1966.

77. *Daniel P. Resnick*. The White Terror and the Political Reaction after Waterloo. 1966.

78. *Giles Constable*. The Letters of Peter the Venerable. 1967.

79. *Lloyd E. Eastman*. Throne and Mandarins: China's Search for a Policy during the Sino-French Controversy, 1880–1885. 1967.

80. *Allen J. Matusow*. Farm Policies and Politics in the Truman Years. 1967.

81. *Philip Charles Farwell Bankwitz.* Maxime Weygand and Civil-Military Relations in Modern France. 1967.

82. *Donald J. Wilcox.* The Development of Florentine Humanist Historiography in the Fifteenth Century. 1969.

83. *John W. Padberg, S.J.* Colleges in Controversy: The Jesuit Schools in France from Revival to Suppression, 1813–1880. 1969.

84. *Marvin Arthur Breslow.* A Mirror of England: English Puritan Views of Foreign Nations, 1618–1640. 1970.

85. *Patrice L.-R. Higonnet.* Pont-de-Montvert: Social Structure and Politics in a French Village, 1700–1914. 1971.

86. *Paul G. Halpern.* The Mediterranean Naval Situation, 1908–1914. 1971.